Se Dio ti lasci,
lettor, prender frutto
di tua lezione

The Agnes Irwin School

Eleanor W. and Curtin Winsor

GEORGE C. MARSHALL

✳

STATESMAN

1945–1959

GEORGE C. MARSHALL:

STATESMAN

1 9 4 5
–
1 9 5 9

By FORREST C. POGUE

Foreword by Drew Middleton

VIKING

VIKING
Viking Penguin Inc., 40 West 23rd Street,
New York, New York 10010, U.S.A.
Penguin Books Ltd, Harmondsworth,
Middlesex, England
Penguin Books Australia Ltd, Ringwood,
Victoria, Australia
Penguin Books Canada Limited, 2801 John Street,
Markham, Ontario, Canada L3R 1B4
Penguin Books (N.Z.) Ltd, 182–190 Wairau Road,
Auckland 10, New Zealand

First published in 1987 by Viking Penguin Inc.
Published simultaneously in Canada

Grateful acknowledgment is made for permission to reprint
the following material:
Excerpt from *Present at the Creation*, by Dean Acheson, published by
W. W. Norton & Company, Inc., 1969. By permission.
Excerpt from diary entry "September 14, 1950," from *Off the Record:
The Private Papers of Harry S. Truman*, edited by Robert H. Ferrell.
Copyright © 1980 by Robert H. Ferrell.
By permission of Harper & Row, Publishers, Inc.

LIBRARY OF CONGRESS CATALOGING IN PUBLICATION DATA
(Revised for volume 4)
Pogue, Forrest C.
George C. Marshall.
Includes bibliographies and index.
Contents: [1] Education of a general, 1880–1939.
2. Ordeal and hope, 1939–1942.   —[4] Statesman,
1945–1959.
1. Marshall, George C. (George Catlett), 1880–1959.
2. Generals—United States—Biography.   3. United States
Army—Biography.   4. Statesman—United States—Biography.
I. Title.
E745.M37P6   973.918′092′4 [B]   63–18373
ISBN 0–670–81042–8

Printed in the United States of America by
The Book Press, Brattleboro, Vermont
Set in Baskerville, Weiss, and Trajanus

Contents

Contents

Illustrations follow page 236.

Foreword

BY DREW MIDDLETON

NOT long ago three Britons, an editor, a Cabinet member and an historian, and two Americans, a diplomat and a foreign correspondent, sat in a London club discussing the great men of the century. Great, that is, in strength of character, foresight, achievement and nobility of purpose. The five agreed on only two men; Winston Churchill and George C. Marshall.

Those who read Forrest C. Pogue's "George C. Marshall: Statesman 1945–1959" will understand the unanimity of the five on Marshall. For a generation that recognizes Marshall only as having been Army Chief of Staff in World War II, here is the man in his other dimensions as a statesman, humanitarian and peacemaker; the man whose vision saved Europe from economic collapse and political turmoil; the man who, well before his peers, understood the vast and challenging responsibilities laid upon the United States by the rearrangement of the global power structure as a result of the victories of 1945.

That year was the apex of George Marshall's military career. He had directed the organization and training of the American armies then everywhere victorious in Europe and the Pacific. With a few exceptions, the men who led those armies were Marshall's selections, drawn from the little black book he had kept since the prewar years at Fort Benning. Had he died in the moment of victory, he would be remembered as America's greatest military organizer and administrator.

Fortunately for the Republic and for millions around the world who never knew his name, Marshall went on to years of solid achievement. It is of those years that Mr. Pogue writes: Marshall's long struggle to bring peace to China, his support and leadership in the evolution of a foreign policy tailored to meet America's new responsibilities, his duels with Vyacheslav Molotov, the Soviet Foreign Minister, over the future of Germany and, above all, his leadership in formulating and selling the Marshall Plan first to Europeans and then to his countrymen.

Many wondered why Marshall took on these complex and

weighty challenges after years of military accomplishment, which should have earned him tranquil retirement. The answer lies in his character.

The Duke of Wellington, on being reproached for accepting a relatively minor position, explained "I am *nimmukwallah* as we say in the East; that is, I have ate of the King's salt and therefore, I conceive it to be my duty to serve with unhesitating zeal and cheerfulness, when or wherever the King or his government may think proper to employ me."

Marshall and the Duke had much in common. They were both plainspoken, untheatrical characters in eras that abounded with the bombastic oratory of military and political prima donnas. More important, they held similar convictions about duty to their country. Marshall considered himself a retained servant of the Republic. He saw it as his obligation to the United States to serve the country as envoy extraordinary to China, Secretary of State or Secretary of Defense, whatever the emotional or physical cost.

When World War II ended, Marshall prepared to leave the Pentagon and retire. Few Americans of those days fully realized how the national war effort and the victory had changed the position of the United States. Marshall saw the change more clearly and earlier than most. In a farewell speech in the Pentagon on November 26, 1945, he defined the position to his fellow Americans, most of whom were clamoring to "get the boys home" or trying to learn when the first post-war cars would appear.

> Most of you know how different, how fortunate is America compared with the rest of the world. . . The world of suffering people looks to us for such leadership. Their thoughts, however, are not concentrated alone on this problem. They have the more immediate and terribly pressing concerns—where the mouthful of food will come from, where they will find shelter tonight and where they will find warmth from the cold of winter. Along with the great problem of maintaining the peace we must solve the problem of the pittance of food, of clothing and coal and homes. Neither of these problems can be solved alone. They are directly related, one to the other.

When he said this, Marshall had not experienced his first great adventure in international diplomacy. This was his mission to a China driven by the growing rivalry between Chiang Kai Shek's Nationalists, supported by the United States, and Mao Tse Tung's Communists, favored by the Soviet Union. Marshall was unsuccessful in composing their quarrel or in bringing some order out of the increasing enmity between Nationalists and Communists. Mr.

Pogue seems to have expected too much from the General. My opinion is that anyone dealing with Chiang and Mao, plus characters like General Joseph Stilwell and former Secretary of War Patrick Hurley, had the cards stacked against him. Talleyrand, Metternich and Castlereagh could not have pulled it off.

When the Chinese civil war reached its inevitable conclusion with Mao in power and Chiang on Taiwan, Marshall was assaulted by the radical right led by Senator Joseph McCarthy. Charles P. Bohlen, a distinguished diplomat and an advisor to Marshall, told me once that, as Secretary of State, Marshall did not take these attacks too seriously. He understood, as few Americans did, that McCarthy and the "China lobby" were suffering from unrequited love. Here was the China for which the lobby, at least, had done so much, turning against the United States, a benefactor and friend.

George Marshall's greatest achievements as Secretary of State were his strong support for the Truman Doctrine, which meant military and economic aid to Greece and Turkey when Britain found its declining economy could no longer bear the burden, and the initiation and unswerving support of the Marshall Plan. In each he was faithful to those ideas he had expressed so vigorously to the Pentagon.

Most contemporary Americans have forgotten the Europe of the early post-war years. Cities, industries, communications ruined. The fabric of society destroyed in Germany and Austria. Millions living under the shadow of starvation. Communism prepared to pounce. Those stationed there saw it.

Only a few, a very few in the United States, understood the danger. Marshall was one. Dean Acheson another. Will Clayton, the Under Secretary of State, upon returning from a tour, tried to impress his colleagues and Congress of the dire consequences of inaction. In all their minds was the basic concept that the idea of American help must originate in Europe and that such help must be offered not only to Western Europe, but to the Soviet Union and the states of Eastern Europe now occupied by the Red Army; states whose economies were in even worse condition than those of France, Italy, the Netherlands or Belgium.

Marshall's speech on a national broadcast in April 1947 was the first blow. He had recently returned from the meeting of the Council of Foreign Ministers in Moscow where he found Molotov and Joseph Stalin, the Russian dictator, fully prepared to allow Western Europe to self-destruct with International Communism picking up the pieces. That slow, grave voice informed listeners of the results of American inaction and, possibly for the first time, told Americans that the Soviet Union, at the end of the war an esteemed ally of the United States, was set on a course hostile to American hopes and beliefs.

As Mr. Pogue demonstrates, many sought credit for the Marshall Plan. George F. Kennan, in particular, believed that his staff at the State Department had contributed three major elements to the plan. These were that Europeans should assume responsibility for initiating the program, the offer should include all Europe and the reconstruction of the German economy should be the key target. Bohlen, on the other hand, believes that Marshall's interview with Stalin at the end of the Foreign Minister's Council meeting inspired the Secretary of State to turn his department's resources to formulating the plan.

The reader will note that even in the speech that announced the Marshall Plan, it was not then called that. On June 5, 1947, the Secretary of State avoided oratorical flourishes. He talked to the audience and to his countrymen calmly and forcefully, laying the problem before them and proposing a solution. Above all, in a time when sabre rattling was all too common in the world, Marshall avoided emotion and passion.

Marshall's speech that day must be accounted the high point of American diplomacy since World War II. It led the way to the economic revival of Western Europe from which much flowed. Within two years many of those countries, with the assistance and support of the United States, were strong enough, politically and militarily, to defy Russian threats and join in forming the North Atlantic Treaty Organization. In time, NATO was followed by the European Economic Community or the Common Market. All these strides forward were possible largely because of the impetus given by George C. Marshall and his plan.

As the reader will see, the Marshall Plan, or as it was formally known, the European Recovery Program, may have been George Marshall's greatest contribution to history, but it was not to be his last. In fact, it may have been the unassailability of his character, the evident honesty of his motives, that helped the Plan gain Congressional approval. After all, the right said darkly, the Plan would help a British Labor government, which in turn might nationalize industries in the British zone of occupation in Germany. Marshall overcame these arguments.

These and other problems, major and minor, bedeviled the movement toward European acceptance. The Russians, caught off guard, did their best to interfere. Molotov charged that the United States was trying to divide Europe into two groups. Ernest Bevin, the doughty British Foreign Secretary, replied that, on the contrary, such a division was the Soviet Union's objective. The Russians, by one means or another, succeeded in preventing any of their satellites from accepting the Plan. In that sense the Marshall Plan may be said to have formalized the already existing division of Europe.

Those who worked in Europe in those years, as did this writer, will recall that although the thrust of American policy was basically toward the economic recovery of Western Europe, the period was replete with political dangers. Political turbulence in France raised the spectre of a totalitarian government under Charles De Gaulle. The Communists in Italy were gaining strength. The three western zones of occupation in Germany were making only meagre steps towards restoration of normal economic activity.

One of the strengths of this book is that, although the author never loses sight of the paramount economic issues, he is able to relate these to the political malaise that infected the continent from 1945 until 1950. Marshall, of course, saw it clearly. If the European situation continued to deteriorate, he warned Congress, America must expect the rise of "police states."

What a worker the man was! Remember that the Marshall Plan was only part of the job. While it was being fought through Congress, the Secretary of State attended another meeting of the Council of Foreign Ministers in London dealing with the future of Germany. Again Marshall saw that the only Germany the Soviet Union would accept would be one subservient to Moscow. On this Bevin agreed. Out of their mutual anxiety over Soviet ambitions came the first moves toward the establishment of NATO.

So, although the council had been a failure, the west began to see the Russians more clearly. In that respect the meeting had been a success.

Marshall and the western allies were soon to be tested severely. In April 1948, the Soviet Union began the series of steps that led to the blockade of the three western sectors of Berlin. Once again, Mr. Pogue demonstrates how Marshall's flinty calm in a crisis served his country well. The Secretary of State and Under Secretary of State Robert Lovett made it clear that the United States intended to remain in Berlin and would meet "force with force."

Although their personal and working habits differed widely, Marshall and Winston Churchill had something in common. Neither was diverted from work he considered important by physical ailments. Shortly before the total ground blockade of Berlin was imposed, Marshall entered Walter Reed Hospital. A kidney condition was diagnosed. To Marshall, this was a minor problem compared to those hanging over Europe. He stayed in the hospital for a few days and then returned to work.

A century hence, scholars may regard histories and biographies of our time as placing too much emphasis on the individual: Churchill in Britain, Roosevelt in the war years, Marshall in the turbulent post-war decade.

Theoretically, those scholars may be right. Actually, they will be wrong. For example, Marshall's character, his foresight and his stability rallied American sentiment over the Berlin blockade. And those same traits, when applied to the formation of NATO, induced his countrymen to support that organization at a time when even some of its original European sponsors were worried about Soviet reaction and their own military unpreparedness.

Here, it must be conceded, the former Chief of Staff was running what generals call "a calculated risk." No one knew better than the Secretary of State how far American military strength had declined since the rapturous hours of victory in 1945. The United States had the atom bomb and the Russians did not. But, would the bomb save the people of West Berlin or Paris or Brussels if the Kremlin decided to eliminate NATO, before it was formed, by massive invasion?

Marshall took this risk. The reader following the diplomatic meetings and exchanges faithfully reported by Mr. Pogue should keep this in mind. With Stalin in the Kremlin, the risk was very great. The Republic was fortunate to have Marshall as its Secretary of State and Harry Truman as President.

There was no end to the problems. The United Nations, Palestine and the foundation of the State of Israel was an issue in which Marshall played a major role. In these complicated, heated discussions, he drew the grudging compliment from a Republican politician, "He's like Al Smith, all he can see is the point."

Finally the tour of duty came to an end as Truman's inauguration approached. But his work as a servant of the nation was far from over. The President saw to it that Marshall was named president of the American Red Cross. He was 68 and not fully recovered from a recent operation. But he took the job. As was his habit, he devoted himself to his new tasks. He travelled constantly, reinvigorated the organization, and eliminated dissension. The Red Cross job did not last long.

In June of 1950 North Korea attacked South Korea. The war went badly for the South Koreans and their American allies. In August Marshall was summoned back to the service of the Republic as Secretary of Defense. Mr. Pogue relates in detail the fierce fight over his confirmation and the personal attacks, which today seem incredible, made by radical senators. Marshall answered them with calm logic, as he had answered all such charges, throughout a long public life.

So he assumed his last duty, one he was confident he could carry out. He knew all of his senior generals and their records; indeed he had picked most of them for promotion. The exception was Douglas MacArthur.

The removal of MacArthur as the United Nations commander in chief in Korea was the great dramatic event of that war. The author faithfully records the defeats and few triumphs of the Americans and their allies, the bold and decisive stroke by MacArthur at Inchon, and then leads the reader into the real drama. One is able to keep events in Korea and Washington in mind as the tragedy unfolds.

After the Chinese Communists attacked, the allied situation worsened rapidly. There were calls for withdrawal. Once again, Marshall's character illuminated the situation. He did not think the United States could "in all good conscience" abandon the South Koreans. In meetings with the British and other worried allies, he spoke with conviction based on his long military experience; for example, it would be folly to give up Formosa (Taiwan) to the Communists.

MacArthur's recommendations from the field read then, and do today, as those of a man eager to start a war with China and, if necessary, with the Soviet Union. As the military situation improved slightly, the general began to play a political game with a letter to Joseph Martin, Republican leader in the House of Representatives, supporting a move to allow Chiang Kai Shek's armies on Formosa to enter the battle.

Truman and his closest advisors were now thoroughly alarmed by the thought of an expanded war that could include the Soviet Union. If China were attacked by the Americans, the Russians, under the terms of the Sino-Soviet pact, were bound to go to China's aid. Then there was the political element: MacArthur was stimulating the Administration's bitterest enemies and alarming America's closest allies.

Marshall presided over a meeting of the Chiefs of Staff at which they decided that MacArthur should be relieved. He, like his colleagues, accepted fully the constitutional principle that the President had the duty to relieve a military commander who opposed his policy.

On September 1, 1951, Marshall resigned as Secretary of Defense after 50 years of duty as a servant of the government. Reflecting on his career and his towering achievements, one is likely to ask where shall we find his like again.

Anthony Eden once said that it was the particular genius of the American and British peoples to find great leaders in a time of crisis instancing Churchill in his country and Marshall and Eisenhower in the United States. Let us hope our luck holds.

In this book Mr. Pogue has done more than record the final successes of George C. Marshall's career. He has restored the man to us in all his great dimensions. In war and in peace he made a generation proud to be Americans.

Preface

WITH this book, the fourth volume of the biography of George C. Marshall, I complete a project that I began nearly thirty years ago in mid–August 1956, when I became director of the George C. Marshall Research Center. My job was to collect the General's papers, interview him and his associates, and write a multi-volume biography. Elsewhere I have recounted the grants of money and other means of support supplied by friends of the Marshall Foundation.

This final volume has presented problems which may disturb some readers. Two chapters on Stilwell and Wedemeyer in China were written as a part of Volume III. Shortly before that book went to press, a decision was made to have a complete volume on China. Much of the Stilwell chapter was removed as well as all of the Wedemeyer material. Several years later, a decision was made to combine condensed China pages with Volume IV, and I was presented with the problem of inserting these fundamental chapters even though I had described the end of the war in the Far East in a previous volume.

Some readers may regret the lack of discussion of the workings of the European Recovery Program and its benefits. From the standpoint of a life of Marshall, the background of the Harvard speech, the drawing up of a shopping list by Western Europe, and the enactment of the necessary legislation are the important aspects. The Marshall Foundation is sponsoring a multi-authored book, financed by German sources, on the Marshall Plan in Germany, which stresses the way the Plan unfolded.

A third difficulty arose in connection with the period when Marshall was Secretary of Defense, which I have chosen to end with the beginning of negotiations for a cease-fire in the spring of 1951. A number of proposals in which Marshall was interested and which he helped advance are not discussed. It must be remembered, as Mr. Lovett said, that what was needed in September 1950 was a presence in the Pentagon: someone of stature sufficient to restore cooperation between the State and Defense departments; return the armed forces to wartime standards; promote unity between the various services; obtain the support of Congress; and clarify the relationships of the Far East Commander with Washington and the United Nations. By the spring of 1951, Marshall had accomplished much of that program. He had promised to come back to public life for six months, and the time lengthened to a year. Marshall had asked Truman to appoint Lovett as his deputy in the belief that Lovett would succeed him and carry his policies to fruition. In his last months in office, the General handed many current projects over to Lovett.

In addition to the many formal interviews, listed elsewhere, that helped make this book possible, I benefitted from numerous contacts with officials while doing research in the Public Record Office during five or six trips to London, and from serving as a member of an American delegation, led by Paul Hoffman and Robert Murphy, to Bonn in 1967 celebrating the twentieth anniversary of the Harvard speech. At a meeting in Brussels organized by Paul-Henri Spaak, I gained much from a panel discussion led by Averell Harriman and Paul Hoffman with speeches by representatives of Marshall Plan countries. For nearly two decades I have been fortunate to participate in symposia held at the Truman Library, dealing with such topics as the Marshall Plan, the economic problems of the Truman administration, the Korean War, and the foreign policy of the Truman years. I added to the interviews which I had earlier held with many of the participants and got new information from former Truman advisers such as Ambassador J. J. Muccio, Secretary John Snyder, Richard Bissell, Philip Jessup, Clark Clifford, and Paul Porter.

As an official or trustee of the Marshall Foundation for thirty years, I was able at meetings, held once or twice a year, to gather answers to specific questions on Marshall from such board members as General Lucius Clay, General Lauris Norstad, General Lyman Lemnitzer, George McGhee, William McChesney Martin, William C. Foster, Howard Petersen, Ellsworth Bunker, John Kenney, Paul Nitze, General Charles Saltzman, James Bruce, and F. Warren Pershing, none of whom had been interviewed on tape.

When I began this project, Frank McCarthy told me that Douglas Freeman often talked of living for twenty years with Robert E. Lee. I think I can look back over at least thirty years spent with General Marshall. Longer, if I reflect on my consciousness of Marshall's presence in 1943 when I first began to write Army history as a combat historian in Europe, during the writing of the *Supreme Com-*

mand, and while at Headquarters, USAREUR, in Heidelberg for two years. Whether for thirty or for forty-five years, my "life" with the General increased my admiration and respect for this giant of the twentieth century.

Arlington, Virginia
Forrest C. Pogue

PROLOGUE

Response to Duty

ON November 26, 1945, General of the Army George Catlett Marshall, who had headed the Army and the Army Air Forces since September 1, 1939, received his only American military decoration of the war—a second Oak Leaf Cluster to the Distinguished Service Medal he had been awarded in 1919. He had refused all United States decorations during the war, as he had most of those offered by foreign countries. He said it was not proper for him to accept such honors while men were dying, or while he was still Chief of Staff of the Army. But the situation had changed. On November 19 he had submitted his resignation and Truman had announced reluctant acceptance on the next day. Dwight D. Eisenhower was the new head of the Army. At twelve-thirty on the 26th, in the courtyard of the Pentagon, President Truman, who had recently reiterated, "I have said that he is the greatest military man that this country has ever produced," read out the citation for the second Oak Leaf Cluster. It had been written by other hands, trained in the customary phrasing for such decorations, but the words came alive with the utter conviction of the President:

> In a war unparalleled in magnitude and in horror, millions of Americans gave their country outstanding service. General of the Army George C. Marshall gave it victory.

> Statesman and soldier, he had courage, fortitude and vision, and best of all a rare self-effacement. He has been a tower of strength as counsellor of two Commanders in Chief. His standards of character, conduct and efficiency inspired the entire Army, the nations and

the world. To him, as much as any individual, the United States owes
its future. He takes his place at the head of the great commanders
of history.[1]

The Army band played "Hail to the Chief," "The Star-Spangled
Banner," and, after a bit, "The Spirit of V.M.I." because Marshall
had been graduated from Virginia Military Institute in 1901.

Marshall's few remarks were brief, read without apparent emotion in a tone of honest common sense. He thanked the President
for his support in making certain that during the final stages of the
war not a moment was lost in bringing a swift conclusion to the
conflict. To those who had served with him in the War Department
he said simply: "You were the greatest protective force this nation
has ever known. . . . No one knows better than you that you did not
do it alone." Then, as he invoked all who had served in the armed
forces, his voice roughened with feeling:

> But of all these efforts yours was by far the greatest. You faced
> death and swallowed fear, endured the agonies of battle and of
> hearts torn by loneliness and homesickness and starvation for the
> normal life you loved. Yet you took it—all there was to take on
> the battlefronts of the world. And you had the strength and will
> to give it back, give back much more than your enemies could
> take. . . .[2]

In this hour of congratulations, he was also aware of problems
yet to be faced. There was still a peacetime task for those who had
served so well at war. In words that had a glint of ideas he would
proclaim in his 1947 speech at Harvard, he reminded those who
had served so faithfully that there was much left to do:

> Most of you know how different, how fortunate is America com-
> pared with the rest of the world. That is something those at home
> cannot fully appreciate. Today this nation with good faith and sin-
> cerity, I am certain, desires to take the lead in the measures neces-
> sary to avoid another world catastrophe, such as you have just
> endured. And the world of suffering people looks to us for such
> leadership. *Their thoughts, however, are not concentrated alone on this
> problem. They have the more immediate and terribly pressing concerns—
> where the mouthful of food will come from, where they will find shelter to-
> night and where they will find warmth from the cold of winter. Along with
> the great problem of maintaining the peace we must solve the problem of the*

pittance of food, of clothing and coal and homes. Neither of these problems can be solved alone. They are directly related, one to the other. [Emphasis supplied.]

Arms were stacked but the soldier's task was not ended.

It is to you men of this great citizen-army to victory that we must look for leadership in the critical years ahead. You are young and vigorous and your services as informed citizens will be necessary to the peace and prosperity of the world. [Emphasis supplied.][3]

This was no appeal to warring ideologies but to humanitarian concerns, and his words outlined no role for himself. The new leaders would be young. After forty-three years of service, the daily readings of the toll of battle for the last six years, his desire was for rest and quiet. He had set no final plans for travel, he had refused offers for writing, he wished for a season of inactivity. So George Washington must have felt when he bade farewell to his officers at Newburgh.

There was no packing to do. A few days earlier the Marshalls had quietly moved out of Quarters One to an apartment in the Officers' Club at Fort Myer so that arrangements could be made for the new Chief of Staff and his family. Some personal goodbyes remained to be said, and they were off next morning for the house at Leesburg, Virginia. In her memoir, Mrs. Marshall recalled that they turned in at the gate of Dodona Manor hearing a jukebox somewhere blaring out a chorus, and she joined in humming the words "Hallelujah! Hallelujah!" as they came home from the wars.

All the quiet years ahead fell like a blessing into her thoughts as they went through the house. She heard the telephone. The General answered it quickly, abruptly. He said nothing more, and Mrs. Marshall went up for a nap. When she came back downstairs she heard the radio announcing that President Truman had just appointed General Marshall as his Special Ambassador to China— "He will leave immediately." To his transfixed wife the General explained that the telephone call he had answered so briefly had been from the President. "I could not bear to tell you until you had had your rest."[4]

Her response was bitter. It would be a long time before she forgot her hurt and resentment. Her husband had again been called to duty. He had told his former troops that they had a duty to make the peace lasting. He had said the task was for the young, but suddenly he had been reminded that he too still had responsibilities to those who had survived. He could not do less than he expected of others. He had no thought of refusal when Truman asked him to undertake to make peace in China, although he knew well the terrible problems involved and the likely culmination in failure.

Between the end of the war in Europe and his assumption of a new effort in the world struggle, the General had helped to shape the strategy of the war in the Pacific and the Far East, and he had a role in the final days of the conflict—decisions involving the direction of the last battles on the road to Tokyo, the bringing in of the Russians, the dropping of the bombs on Japan, and surrender in the Far East. All of these directly or indirectly shaped the contours of the problem he had been set to solve in China and the conditions under which he would have to work.

Final Battles

V-E Day, Victory in Europe, May 8, 1945, meant momentary pause after six years of war in the West. But in the Pacific and in the Far East the Japanese fought on, and some Allied leaders feared that defeat of Japan would require the bloodiest fighting of the war. Marshall drew breath long enough to order the execution of elaborate plans already made to bring back, for victory parades in the cities of America, those who had led armies in Europe and North Africa, including younger officers and enlisted men who had earned the highest war decorations. At the same time, thousands of Americans had to be brought home from the battlefields of Europe to be refitted and sent off to the Far East to join those already there fighting the Japanese.[1]

Marshall's views of the war in the Pacific often differed from those of his colleague on the Joint Chiefs of Staff, Fleet Admiral Ernest J. King. The Chief of Naval Operations had been gruffly loyal in support of Marshall's European strategy but his heart had never left Pacific operations. With his control of supply lines supporting the conflict throughout the Pacific, and with command of all ships and landing craft necessary for amphibious operations, King dealt with the Army from a position of strength.

King and his chief Pacific commander, Fleet Admiral Chester Nimitz, were convinced that the Navy should play the major role in this theater of war. In the Southwest Pacific, General MacArthur complained of the Navy's Pacific activities, but he depended heavily on elements of the Pacific Fleet and divisions of United States Marines.

Looking at the Pacific area map from Australia and western New Guinea, MacArthur saw the logical path of advance as westward across the north coast of New Guinea and adjoining islands to the

5

west, then northward into the Philippines by way of Mindanao, then Leyte and Luzon. From his Pearl Harbor headquarters, Nimitz easily sold King his idea of an approach to Japan north of MacArthur's area, bypassing the Philippines and establishing air and naval bases nearer the Japanese home islands.

Marshall was made constantly aware—by official messages from the Army commander in the Pacific, by protests members of his staff sent back to the War Department, and by statements given to visiting members of Congress and the press—that MacArthur disagreed with the strategic views of the Joint Chiefs of Staff in general and with the strategic judgment of the Navy commanders in particular.

The Army chief also knew that King was prickly and protective of his subordinates and that he distrusted some of MacArthur's strategic plans. But Marshall had high regard for Nimitz, which was reciprocated, and he agreed with him that Navy commanders should have Army units under their command for their island operations.

Marshall listened carefully to the Navy's views as well as to MacArthur's demands, and he saw strategic advantages in the Navy's spring 1944 plan to bypass the Philippines from the Southwest Pacific and to advance westward from Pacific held islands to Formosa on the way to Japan. In response to MacArthur's impassioned pleas that he had a moral obligation to return to the Philippines, the Army Chief of Staff argued that advance by the Philippines was the slow way. Attacking against the southern tip of Japan might yield better results in the end than going by way of the Philippines. Here, as with Eisenhower's actions in Italy, Marshall supported the bolder approach. He recognized an obligation to the Islands, but held that their reconquest could follow, in a less costly manner, the attack on Japan proper. He knew that MacArthur wanted to keep his promise to return, but warned, "We must be careful not to allow personal feelings and Philippine political considerations to override our great objective, which is the early conclusion of the war with Japan." He has been accused of expressing anti-MacArthur bias in these ideas, yet this was the same argument he had long pursued with the British as to a cross-Channel versus a Mediterranean approach. The long way home worried him. He did not believe that a democracy could be indefinitely keyed up to fight a foreign war, especially if the way be strewn with dead and wounded.

The President apparently preferred MacArthur's plan when he met with MacArthur and Nimitz at Pearl Harbor, and in the end the rapid progress of the Navy's attack toward the Philippines favored the General. Admiral William Halsey's great success with carrier strikes in mid-September sparked a recommendation that an early attack be made against the Islands. From Quebec, Marshall and the other Chiefs of Staff queried MacArthur for his views. In his absence his Chief of Staff agreed that MacArthur could move up his date for an attack on the Islands.

One factor in Marshall's thinking was MacArthur's estimate that all organized resistance in Luzon would be crushed in six weeks. He might have reacted differently had he known that, although Manila would be cleared of resistance in early March, there would still be pockets of Japanese in Luzon when fighting ended in the Pacific in August 1945.

Admiral King disagreed vigorously with Marshall's arguments, and the Army agreed to postpone action on the directive until the next meeting of the Joint Chiefs of Staff. Their planners, meanwhile, helped kill the Formosa First strategy by reminding the Chiefs that if MacArthur cleared Luzon by February and gained bases for an invasion of Formosa, it might be unnecessary to invade it. In any event, the Formosa operation could be made only if troops could be withdrawn from the European Theater by November 1. Luzon would need no such support.

On October 3, when MacArthur was preparing a return to Leyte, the Joint Chiefs of Staff directed him to invade the northern island of Luzon on December 20, 1944, to establish bases there to support advances farther northward, and to give support to Admiral Nimitz's later attack on the Ryukyus. The Chiefs directed Nimitz to support MacArthur's invasion of Luzon, to occupy two or more sites in the Bonin Islands and Iwo Jima as of January 20, 1945, and to occupy one or more of the Ryukyu Islands with the target date of March 1, 1945.[2]

The Navy secured the entrances to Leyte Gulf on October 18 and landings began less than a week later. MacArthur's dramatic return to the Philippines and the victories of ground troops that followed burgeoned in the American imagination, but it was the Navy that won the tremendous victories. The battles of Sibuyan Sea and Sarigao Strait, those off Samar and Cape Engaño, and the fighting around Leyte Gulf should, as Admiral Morison later wrote, "be an imperishable part of our national heritage."[3]

As transports and ships pushed from the Southwest Pacific in support of the Luzon fighting and in preparation for Nimitz's later campaigns, the Japanese began to use kamikaze tactics—suicidal efforts to destroy naval forces. It became increasingly clear that as the Americans came closer to the home islands the Japanese would resist foot by foot on land as well as fight to the last by sea and air.

While MacArthur's Sixth (Walter Krueger) and Eighth (Robert Eichelberger) Armies fought to clear Luzon, Nimitz readied his attack against Iwo Jima and Okinawa. A Marine corps, with strong naval support, attacked in the Bonins on February 19 to get bases that could later be used for air action against Japan. In an action described by the Marine commander, General Holland Smith, as "the most savage and costly battle in the history of the Marine Corps," the Marines suffered some 23,000 casualties and the Navy 2,800. Twenty thousand Japanese were killed or sealed in caves and 218 taken prisoner.[4]

At last came the battle for the Ryukyus, for which Nimitz had been preparing. On Easter Sunday, April 1, 1945, began what military columnist Hanson Baldwin called "the greatest sea-air battle in history."[5] Forty carriers, eighteen battleships, twenty destroyers, and thousands of ships transporting 180,000 assault troops attacked Okinawa. Lieutenant General Simon Bolivar Buckner's Tenth U.S. Army and the III Marine Amphibious Corps had relatively light losses in getting ashore, but then they faced murderous resistance. Before the end of the fighting in June the Americans had 75,000 casualties. Of the Japanese defenders, 110,000 were dead and 7,400 surrendered. General Buckner was killed in the fighting. He was succeeded briefly by Marine General G. R. S. Geiger, then by Lieutenant General Joseph W. Stilwell, summoned by Marshall to the final fight against the Japanese. The Japanese showed grim intention to fight to their deaths; their air force redoubled its kamikaze attacks, and the largest ship afloat, their *Yamato,* sailed to its destruction without air cover.

While these battles were being fought, U.S. Air Forces used their bases in the Marianas, and the newly gained bases in Luzon, the Bonins, and the Ryukyus, for relentless bombing of the home islands. The U.S. Navy swept the Japanese Navy from the seas, but there was no indication of Japanese surrender. Rather, increased attritional warfare and brutal land fighting appeared certain.

The problem of attacking the Japanese home islands had occupied the minds of Joint Staff planners as early as the fall of 1944. A target date of November 1, 1945, was set for attack on the island of Kyushu (OLYMPIC) and the spring of 1946 for Honshu (CORONET). In the spring of 1945, the Pentagon directed MacArthur and Nimitz to outline plans for these two attacks.[6] Emphasis was on conventional weapons rather than the possible use of a secret weapon then being prepared, because of the extreme secrecy surrounding every aspect of that weapon.

The heavy losses as American forces came nearer the Japanese home islands grimly influenced the thinking of President Truman and General Marshall. Marshall had read the daily mortality lists in World War II, had seen the anguished letters of relatives, and knew that the bloodiest battles of an invasion of Japan would fall on the infantry. New to his responsibilities of Commander in Chief at the beginning of these Pacific onslaughts, the President was appalled by the growing slaughter that could be expected even from a beaten enemy willing to fight to the death.

In June, as preparations for landings in Japan proper had to be considered seriously, Truman asked for careful estimates of recent losses and possible casualties to come. The Joint Chiefs of Staff discussed the invasion with him on June 18. Marshall said that U.S. forces could be ready for the Kyushu landing on November 1, 1945, adding that by that time air operations should have destroyed virtually every industrial target and large parts of Japan's major cities. He thought that the Japanese Navy would likely be powerless by then.[7]

Even with this favorable scenario, Marshall believed Japan would have to be invaded. Air power, however great its destruction, would not break the Japanese people's resistance, especially since they would be scattered through mountainous country, making the problem far more difficult than it had been in Germany. He felt that an overwhelming invasion offered the only way the Japanese could be forced into a feeling of utter helplessness.

There was a possible way out of the bloodbath eventuality. Increasingly worried about the shortage of ground-force replacements, Secretary of War Stimson had asked Marshall in May if the United States could not hold off "from heavy involvement in casualties" in the Pacific until the secret atomic weapon now in preparation could be tested. The Chief of Staff thought they could probably get a trial of the "S-1," as it was called, "before the locking of arms came and much bloodshed."[8]

Marshall and Stimson were alluding to a tremendous secret that they had been told about two months before Pearl Harbor. President Roosevelt had been alerted by American and European scientists a few weeks before war began in Europe that, after years of investigation and experimentation, there was a possibility of developing a powerful source of energy by splitting the atom. These scientists believed that German scientists were searching for means of harnessing this energy to a destructive weapon that might make

Hitler invincible. The scientists wanted the President's aid for their investigations. Roosevelt was interested, but not until October 1941 did he appoint a Top Policy Committee to expedite the work that led to the atomic bomb.[9] The group included Vice President Henry A. Wallace; Vannevar Bush, head of the Office of Scientific Research and Development; James B. Conant, head of the National Defense Research Committee; Secretary Stimson; and General Marshall. The entry of the United States into the war two months later speeded up this work. In late December, Bush proposed that when "full-scale construction started, the Army should take over." Roosevelt's acceptance of Bush's recommendations in early March 1942 for expediting work on developing an atomic bomb brought the Army fully into the act.[10]

In handing over actual control of construction to the Army, Bush ran into bottlenecks caused by the heavy demands for conventional weapons and war supplies and the requirements of U.S. allies overseas. Looking back at this troubled period, when so much had to be done with so little, the official historians of the atomic effort marveled at the smoothness of the transfer of authority. "It was a tribute to Bush's administrative skill and to Marshall's forbearance that this delicate transfusion of authority from OSRD to the Army was accomplished without the slip of one heartbeat."[11]

To coordinate work on atomic plants, a headquarters was set up under the name of Manhattan Engineer District. For an aggressive officer to ride herd on the Army side of the project, Colonel Leslie R. Groves, then involved in pushing completion of the Pentagon Building, was recommended by General Marshall.[12]

Son of an Army chaplain, Groves was born in 1896 in Albany, New York. His training included a year at the University of Washington, two years at the Massachusetts Institute of Technology, and enrollment in the speeded-up wartime course at the U.S. Military Academy. After a commission in the Engineers, he served tours of duty in Nicaragua, Hawaii, and Europe, and had additional training in the chief Army service schools. It was his work as Deputy Chief of Construction in the Office of the Quartermaster General that brought him the task of driving the construction of the Pentagon Building to rapid conclusion. Concerning the Manhattan Project, General Marshall later recalled, "We had to construct these huge plants down in the South and out on the Pacific Coast and still try to do it in secrecy. Well, that was my job. I picked the General [Groves] that I put in charge of it. . . ."[13]

In the initial stages, Marshall struggled to keep abreast of the project, at a time when the fight for Guadalcanal was going badly and when plans for landing in North Africa were well under way. Because of his usual interest in a new field of knowledge and his belief that he must be familiar with matters on which he had to make decisions, he tried to acquire at least a basic acquaintance with this new development that seemed likely to revolutionize warfare.

"I was rather amused at myself," he confessed later, "because as time wore on [and] the long statements that would come . . . filled with complicated procedures . . . I would spend so much time with the *Encyclopedia Britannica* and the dictionary trying to interpret . . . that I finally just gave it up, deciding that I never would quite understand. What I must understand was all the procedure concerned with getting this done. I obtained the first money by taking twenty percent of the appropriations concerning such matters as the development of bombs, artillery, and kindred matters—which was legal. You could direct twenty percent away from an appropriation to a somewhat similar matter—one connected with defense, for example—and this bomb was certainly connected with defense."[14]

General Marshall had followed his normal procedure of picking a responsible man and leaving him great freedom to carry out his assignment. Groves—brusque, self-assured, accustomed to pushing ahead at full steam—found this arrangement to his liking, although he later said that, had his and Marshall's roles been reversed, he would have demanded monthly reports instead of the very few that he actually submitted.

Knowing that Groves was disinterested in War Department politics, Marshall talked freely before him about some of his own problems. Finding that the officer did not unnecessarily ask for personal interviews and that he kept his part of the conversation short, Marshall never refused to see him. (Groves recalled that the only time he ever had to wait was on an occasion when the King of Norway was in Marshall's office.) The routine of the interviews was always the same. The Chief of Staff would motion Groves to a chair while reading the latter's memorandum—usually less than a page in length. As he read through his copy, he would stop to pose a question or ask the meaning of some new word. (This was in contrast to meetings with Admiral King, who asked no questions. If a word was unfamiliar, King would turn to a reference book. Groves was amused on one occasion when the Chief of Naval Operations, after looking in vain for a term, turned around in solemn frustration: his dictionary gave no definition for "nuclear fission.")[15]

General Groves found that he could usually get action without calling for aid. When he did ask, it was forthcoming in the form of a short note from Marshall or Stimson, usually in longhand. "I was much disappointed you were not given proper support" sufficed to end one log jam.

When high-level decisions were required, Marshall effectively intervened. In 1943, he gave his full backing to efforts—first by Norwegian guerrillas and then by Allied bombers—to delay or destroy plants in Norway engaged in making heavy water, which might be of value to the Germans in atomic experiments. Recognizing the importance of foreign developments in this field, he asked Groves if there was any reason why he could not "take over all foreign intelligence in our area of interest." He informed the Army chief of intelligence of the decision, and Groves accepted the responsibility of notifying the Office of Naval Information and the Office of Strategic Services of the arrangement.[16]

This new task, as Groves saw it, was "to learn as soon as we could what the Germans might be able to do if they exerted every possible effort to produce an atomic weapon." Already under consideration was a plan for sending scientists and military personnel into Italy with the Allied forces as they marched northward—to interview Italian scientists who might be found in liberated areas. This proposal—outlined in September 1943 by the Army chief of intelligence, General Strong, at Groves's request—won the Chief of Staff's assent. It was understood that Bush, with Groves's approval, would select the scientific members of the small mission and that the military personnel would be selected by the Army G-2. This group in turn would form the nucleus of similar missions that would accompany Allied troops going elsewhere into Europe.

Through 1942 and 1943, the Army found the money for the Manhattan Project from funds not specifically allocated for atomic development. But as the expenditures moved up toward the half-billion mark in 1943 and it became clear that outgo the following year might reach $100 million a month, the funds could no longer be smuggled into the budget "for expediting production."

Stimson and Bush discussed the problem with the President over lunch at the White House on February 15, 1944. Roosevelt proposed that Stimson, Bush, and Marshall go to Capitol Hill and outline the problem to the Speaker of the House and the leaders of both parties. He suggested that they wait until later to take the matter up with the Senate, where more difficulty was expected.

Three days later, Stimson, Marshall, and Bush met with Speaker Sam Rayburn, Majority Leader John W. McCormack, and Minority

Leader Joseph W. Martin, Jr. More than a decade later, Rayburn recalled the meeting: "They said they had been working on an atomic bomb and had been getting the money out of Army funds but now they had to have some appropriated and they had to have it kept secret. I had invited in McCormack and Martin and it startled Stimson and Marshall and Bush when they saw them there. I thought it was a good idea, but later thought perhaps I made a mistake. Anyway, I said I would undertake to get the money."[17]

"We went up on the Hill," Marshall declared, ". . . and Mr. Stimson made the [first] talk. [He said] they would have to take his word for it and my word for it that it was of vital importance that we got this additional money and that it was of equally vital importance that not a word be breathed of what the thing really was." Bush followed with a statement of the scientific nature of the bomb, and Marshall emphasized its military importance.[18]

The House leaders readily agreed to what was required and suggested that if Marshall would present a list of the itemized sums needed, the leaders would see that the Committee on Appropriations did not ask to discuss the matter. Rayburn recalled that the members of the committee were to be assured that the requested sum was "for an important cause and it was something which would help us win the war, but that we couldn't afford to let anything get out about it." The Speaker soon feared that this would be the hardest part of the bargain to keep. "Sometimes afterwards," he later said, "I saw one of the two men who had been with me (they are both good men, of course) talking with a newspaper man and he looked funny when I saw him. I talked to the newspaper man later and said, 'You are a good American, aren't you; you love your country?' He said, 'Of course,' I said, 'Then don't print anything about what he just told you.' He didn't and it was all right."[19]

Some members of Congress were highly displeased by the demand for secrecy. Hearing of a mysterious construction project at Oak Ridge, Tennessee, a number of people began to make inquiries. Three weeks after the meeting in Rayburn's office, Senator Harry S. Truman asked the War Department to permit members of his investigating committee staff to look into charges of waste in another mysterious plant at Hanford, Washington. When Stimson asked him to wait, noting the secrecy involved, the Missouri Senator asked that two members of his staff then in uniform, Brigadier General Frank Lowe and Brigadier General Harry Vaughan, at least be allowed to look into the cost of housing and roads not connected with any secret process. When Stimson said that it could not be done, the peppery senator—in the Secretary's words—"threatened

me with dire consequences." Stimson retorted that "I had to accept
responsibility for these consequences because I had been directed
by the President to do just what I had to do." Truman ended by
withdrawing his demand. Not until a few minutes after he became
President, more than a year later, did he learn the full secret of
Hanford and Oak Ridge from the formerly obdurate Secretary of
War.[20]

Soon afterward, Stimson was informed by Republican Representative Albert J. Engel of Michigan, a member of the Subcommittee on Military Appropriations, that unless the War Department
furnished a detailed justification of its request and permitted him
to visit the plants, he would demand a thorough investigation. He
even suggested that he might strike the items from the deficiency
appropriation bill. If he hoped to provoke action from the War
Department, he was successful. Not only Stimson but also Marshall
favored him with personal attention.[21]

Stimson's account, written down shortly after the incident, identified Engel and was later corroborated by General Groves. Hearing of Engel's threat while Rayburn was away, Stimson approached
Representative John Taber, ranking Republican on the Military
Appropriations Subcommittee, and asked him to bring Engel to see
the Secretary and Groves. Taber, who would later stoutly oppose
Truman Administration expenditures as Chairman of the House
Appropriations Committee, proved to be friendly to the War Department. Without revealing the nature of the atomic project, Stimson managed to reveal that a delicate matter was involved and by
appealing to his "loyalty and decency" put him in a more favorable
state of mind. According to Stimson, he left agreeing not to object
to the Army's bill and not to reveal this conversation.[22]

Twelve years later, in telling of problems with atomic-energy
development, General Marshall gave a somewhat different version
of difficulties with an unnamed representative whose description
fits Engel. The vigor with which Marshall said that he acted was in
character. Illustrating the decisiveness with which he was prepared
to act in an emergency, the story is set down as he told it years after
the event:

> When the time came, I was told that one member . . . had brought
> up in the committee this matter of the Manhattan Project and the
> $600 million and stated that it had to be explained and he was going
> to insist on it . . . (he was a real busy bee in all this business and
> particularly resentful of the fact that he had driven out in his car and
> hadn't been allowed to go through the plants). Well, the Chairman

called me up and told me they couldn't do anything with him.
. . . They had gone into their final mark-up session, which was the
closing out of the whole affair, and they still hadn't handled this
man. So as nearly as I can remember . . . I went up to this meeting
at which I had no right to be present. . . . I just opened the door and
walked in and sat down. Well, they were all very polite to me. They
were all my friends. I sat down and then I addressed myself to this
man and, as nearly as I can recall, I told him that I had just learned
this. I just wanted to say to him that if he forced this thing into the
open—if he forced a discussion—which would be a public discussion
of something that Mr. Stimson, the honorable Secretary of War, and
myself had assured these people mustn't be discussed (they must
trust us on this as they did the hundreds of thousands of lives of our
soldiers) . . ., I was going to go [on] the . . . radio . . . make him
ashamed of himself the rest of his life. Then I got up and left the
room and he shut up and didn't make any more demands. I don't
recall exactly the English I used but that was the sense of it. And the
rest of [the committee] accepted my apology for barging in on them
and we got by that last stumbling block in the effort to get the $600
million.[23]

This and other flare-ups in Congress convinced the War Department that secrecy would have to be lifted for at least a few more
members of Congress. Groves soon proposed to Stimson and Marshall that the Speaker and certain key committee members be invited to inspect the plants at Oak Ridge and Hanford. Mr. Rayburn
declined the invitation, saying that all he would see would be a
bunch of test tubes and laboratories that would mean nothing to
him and that he was prepared to leave the work to the men then
in charge. The members of the Military Appropriations Subcommittee—Chairman Cannon, Snyder, Mahon, Taber, and Engel—
went to Oak Ridge. As they were leaving, Taber said he wanted to
ask Groves a question. Expecting a criticism, Groves was astonished when the Representative said, "Are you sure you are spending enough money at Oak Ridge?"[24]

From the earliest consideration of the invasion of the Japanese
home islands, Marshall believed that Soviet assistance would be
needed to reduce Allied casualties. The other Chiefs of Staff shared
his view as they discussed final planning for operations in north-
western Europe. In the fall of 1943, when Secretary of State Cordell
Hull was in Moscow to meet with Eden and Molotov in preparation
for the coming conference between Churchill, Roosevelt, and Sta-

lin, Hull raised the question with the Russian leader as to how soon after the defeat of Germany the Soviet Union would enter the war against Japan. The point was again discussed several weeks later during the Allied conference at Tehran. Marshall was pleased to hear that within ninety days after the end of the fighting in Europe, Soviet forces would enter the conflict against Japan.[25]

In later years Admiral Leahy, senior member of the Joint Chiefs of Staff, was to insist that Soviet assistance against the Japanese was unnecessary, but as late as September 1944 his views were similar to Marshall's. The shortening of the war and the reduction of U.S. casualties depended on Soviet action against Japan. In briefing Truman on June 18, 1945, for the meeting of the British, Russians, and Americans a few weeks later at Potsdam to determine the strategy for ending the war and the handling of postwar problems, Marshall mentioned the need for Russian aid in an invasion of Japan. MacArthur had already twice insisted to representatives of Marshall that Russian aid would be needed. Admiral King agreed that the "cost of defeating Japan without the aid of the Soviet Union would be greater." Admiral Leahy, reporting 35 percent casualties in recent returns from Okinawa operations, asked Truman if the final decision on the invasion of Japan did not depend on what the Russians agreed to do. Stimson and Marshall concluded in one of their last meetings before leaving for Potsdam that the force of the warning they wanted to present to Japan would be increased by the entry of the Russians into the war. That would certainly "coordinate all the threats possible on Japan," agreed the Secretary of War.

The question of the Soviet entry into the war also raised the more problematical question of avoiding an invasion of Japan and of hastening the end of the war if the atomic bomb then being developed were ready for use by the end of the summer. That hypothetical use had been considered in the fall of 1944, when Churchill met Roosevelt at Hyde Park and signed an *aide-mémoire* that after mature consideration the atomic bomb might be used against the Japanese, who would be warned that the bombing would be continued until they surrendered. They also agreed that their two governments would continue full collaboration in developing atomic energy for commercial and military purposes after the defeat of Japan or the termination of the agreement.[26]

Near the close of 1944, Groves had reported to Marshall that a gun-type bomb would be ready for use by August 1, 1945, and a second, an implosion-type, would be ready by the end of the year. Others of the second type would appear at shorter intervals thereafter. Stimson showed the report to President Roosevelt soon after-ward.[27]

Concerned about the need for international control of atomic energy, Stimson discussed that subject with the President on March 15, 1945—the last talk he had with Roosevelt before the latter's death less than a month later. It fell to the Secretary to brief the new President on the bomb shortly after he entered the White House. An agreement was soon made that the gun-type bomb did not have to be tested before it was used, but that a test of the implosion-type would be needed before its effectiveness could be evaluated.[28] In effect, any use of the first bomb would depend on the test of the second.

Growing problems with the use and control of atomic power led Stimson to propose to Truman the creation of another committee. After discussing alternatives with Marshall, Stimson suggested an advisory committee headed by himself, to include the scientists James Conant, Vannevar Bush, and Karl Compton, along with Navy Under Secretary Ralph Bard, Assistant Secretary of State Will L. Clayton, and a special representative of the President (after a short wait James Byrnes, who had recently resigned as War Mobilization Administrator, was named to fill this spot). This "Interim Commit-tee" was named by the President on May 2.[29]

As time neared for testing the bomb and deciding on the invasion of Japan, there were innumerable meetings of various coordinating committees on the best use of the bomb when it was ready. Mar-shall and Stimson were concerned no longer with whether the bomb should be used, but with how to end the war quickly.

On May 29, Marshall discussed ways of giving Japan prior warn-ing with Secretary Stimson and Assistant Secretary of War John J. McCloy. He thought the first target should be a military objective, such as a large naval installation. If that attack did not impress the Japanese, then they would select a number of manufacturing cen-ters and warn the enemy to advise the civilian population to leave these areas before a certain time. "We must offset by such warning methods the opprobrium which might follow from an ill considered employment of such force."[30]

Marshall suggested that they also consider other means of coping with "the last ditch tactics of the suicidal Japanese." He wanted to avoid the attrition Allied forces were now suffering "from such fanatical and hopeless defense methods." He spoke of a limited use of gas, "say on the outlying islands where operations were now going on or were about to take place." He said he was not speaking of our newest and most potent gas, which he did not identify, "but something to drench them and sicken them so that the fight would be taken out of them." He asked officers to see what could be used quickly. Recognizing the possibility of public disapproval of the use of gas, he declared that the "character of the weapon was no less humane than phosphorus and flame throwers and need not be used against dense populations or civilians—merely against those last pockets of resistance which had to be wiped out but had no other military significance." He was having studies prepared and would soon make recommendations.[31]

Two days later, the Interim Committee met with Marshall and Groves; two civilian advisers of Secretary Stimson, Arthur Page and Harvey Bundy; and the panel of scientists. They concluded that they could not give Japan prior warning of bombing. The argument was that the bomb might prove to be a dud, that the Japanese might move Allied prisoners to the threatened area or otherwise neutralize the effect of the bombing. A week later Stimson informed the President that the existence of the atomic bomb should not be revealed to the Soviets until after it had been used against Japan. If they had a query at Potsdam, he could say that the experiment was not yet ready.[32]

In preparation for a final briefing of the President before he left for Potsdam, the Joint Chiefs of Staff concluded that they should try to bring Russia into the war against Japan and an invasion of Kyushu should be mounted. On June 18, at the White House, Marshall outlined the Joint Chiefs' proposal—an invasion of Kyushu on November 1. Using statistics that did not reflect losses on Okinawa, he said that in the first month ashore the U.S. forces should not suffer more than the 31,000 they sustained in Luzon. He believed that the entry of the Soviet Union might end the war at once or shortly after the invasion. He did not believe that conventional air power alone could end the war. He was supported in his arguments by Admiral King. As the meeting was ending, the President noticed that Mr. McCloy had not spoken and called on him for an opinion. McCloy asked, "Why not use the bomb?" Mr. Truman then called everyone back to discuss that point.[33]

Meanwhile, targets for an atomic bomb had been considered by a committee under General Groves and his deputy, General Thomas F. Farrell. They began a search for targets with military installations that were still sufficiently intact to show the devastating effect of a bomb, were located in areas where hills or other restricting features would maximize the effect of the blast, where the extent of the damage would be quickly apparent to a large part of the population. The committee listed Kyoto, Hiroshima, and

Niigata as suitable for this purpose. Stimson immediately protested in dismay over the listing of Kyoto. He described the beauty and cultural importance of this former capital of Japan and directed that it be removed from the list. A later effort by the committee to change his mind had no effect, and at Potsdam in July he indignantly informed Truman of what the committee had proposed, adding that Japan's help against Russia might be needed in the future but that if Americans destroyed this cultural shrine they would never be forgiven. The President agreed and Kyoto was spared. By that time Kokura and Nagasaki had been added to the list.[34]

At the mid-June meeting, the bomb was considered as a weapon that would shock the Japanese into surrendering. If it was to be dropped before invasion time in November, there would be only two bombs completed, and the possibility of using the second, the "implosion-type" bomb, still waited on a late-July test. Marshall later explained why he considered a shock effect of great importance:

> We had just gone through a bitter experience at Okinawa. [This had been preceded] by a number of similar experiences in other Pacific islands, down north of Australia. The Japanese had demonstrated in each case they would not surrender and they would fight to the death. And even their civilians would commit suicide rather than to be taken under the control of American forces. With this knowledge, particularly of Okinawa, I think, where we killed 120,000 Japanese without a surrender (I think there were several badly wounded that we picked up but literally not a surrender), it was to be expected that the resistance in Japan, with their home ties, would be even more severe. We had the terrific [conventional] bombing. We had 100,000 people killed in Tokyo in one night [by] bombs and it had had seemingly no effect whatsoever. It destroyed the Japanese cities, yes, but their morale was affected, as far as we could tell, not at all. So it seemed quite necessary, if we could, to shock them into action. . . .[35]

On July 4, 1945, Stimson met with members of the Combined Policy Committee concerning British and American policy toward use of the atomic bomb. This committee, established in 1943 to provide for collaboration between British and Americans on atomic matters, formally agreed that the bomb would be used against Japan.[36]

The final Allied conference of World War II was set for July at

Potsdam. President Truman, accompanied by new Secretary of State Byrnes, Admiral Leahy, and the political members of the United States delegation, went by ship to Antwerp and on to Berlin by car and plane. Secretary of War Stimson, although not a member of the official delegation, had been invited by the President to attend because of his key role in the development of the atomic weapon. The three service chiefs flew from Washington by separate planes and reached Berlin about the same time as the presidential party.[37]

Stalin's delayed arrival on the 16th gave the U.S. delegation additional opportunity to work on issues for discussion. Stimson and Marshall were aware that time was approaching for the test of the "implosion-type" bomb, the one thereafter to be put into production, at Los Alamos, New Mexico. At seven-thirty in the evening a cryptic message from Washington arrived at Potsdam, indicating that it had been successfully exploded. Stimson informed the President and Byrnes. After lunch the next day he told Churchill of the results.[38]

On July 21, a courier arrived with a complete report on the test from General Groves, emphasizing that the destructive power of the bomb exceeded all expectations. Stimson gave the report to Marshall to read before presenting it to Mr. Truman. Stirred by an increasing feeling of confidence, the President followed a flinty line with the Soviets in discussions that day. When Mr. Churchill read the complete report the next day, he remarked that he knew something had given Truman extra force on the 21st because he was a changed man in the way he stood up to Stalin.[39]

The news from Washington came as the Russians appeared intent on increasing their claims. Averell Harriman, U.S. Ambassador to the Soviet Union, reported on July 23 that they seemed to be reaching out in all directions. Not only were they expanding their influence in Poland, Austria, Rumania, and Bulgaria, but they were also demanding bases in Turkey and former Italian colonies on the Mediterranean and elsewhere. Stalin insisted on a trusteeship for Korea, and Stimson thought that he might ask for sole control of that country.

Later in the morning Stimson found the President standing firm and apparently relying on possession of the bomb. Believing that many of the Russian claims were bluff, he told Stimson that he was "anxious" to know if Marshall still thought we needed the Russians "or whether we could get along without them."[40]

Stimson relayed Truman's question to Marshall on the 23rd. The Chief of Staff did not give a direct answer. He explained that he had believed Soviet help was needed to counter Japanese forces in Manchuria, a purpose that had now been served by the massing of Russian troops along the border. "But he pointed out that even if we went ahead in the war without the Russians, and compelled the Japanese to surrender to our terms, that would not prevent the Russians from marching into Manchuria anyhow . . . to get virtually what they wanted in the surrender terms."[41]

Stimson told Truman the next day that he inferred from Marshall's remarks that the Russians would not be needed to defeat Japan. He also showed Truman reports from Washington that the first bomb would be ready between August 1 and 3. Truman replied that this would fit in with an ultimatum on his desk ready to send the Japanese.[42]

Already in train was the preparation of a directive for the dropping of one or more atomic bombs. After discussing the matter with Stimson and others at Potsdam, Marshall directed General Handy, then acting as Army Chief of Staff in Washington, to send over a draft directive for approval. This document, largely prepared by Groves, arrived on the evening of July 24 and was sent back within six hours by Marshall. The draft itself had carried the statement that it had been approved by Stimson and Marshall. Truman made clear in his memoirs that it was done on his responsibility. "I had made the decision. I also instructed Stimson that the order would stand unless I notified him that the Japanese reply to our ultimatum [scheduled for release on July 26, demanding unconditional surrender or prompt and utter destruction of Japan] was acceptable."[43]

The final directive, signed by Handy, went to General Carl Spaatz, commander of the Strategic Air Forces. The 509th Composite Group was to deliver the first special bomb as soon after August 3 as weather conditions would permit visual bombing, on one of these targets: Hiroshima, Kokura, Niigata, or Nagasaki. Additional bombs were to be delivered as soon as they were available. Information on the bombings would be issued by the President and the Secretary of War. Copies of the directive were to be delivered by Spaatz to MacArthur and Nimitz. As Stimson wrote later, this order thus set into motion the machinery for the first use of the atomic bomb against a military target. Unless the Japanese accepted the ultimatum that was to be issued on the 26th or unless the President gave a direct order to desist, the attacks would proceed.

The ultimatum to Japan went out as scheduled, from the President of the United States, the President of China, and the Prime

Minister of Great Britain. After discussions in Tokyo, the Cabinet —influenced by the lack of assurance that the position of the Emperor would be preserved—on July 29 announced the government's intention to carry on the war to a successful conclusion. The Japanese Foreign Minister, however, instructed his representative in Moscow to seek Soviet assistance in negotiating a settlement. Stalin told President Truman, who already knew of the approach through the broken Japanese code, that he had given a negative reply.[44]

Stimson returned to his New York home on the evening of Saturday, July 28, and was back in the Pentagon on Monday. He asked the President to approve the announcement of the coming attack so that it would be ready for release on August 1. Still abroad, Truman approved but asked that the release not be sent out before August 2. When Marshall returned to his office on July 31, he found that plans had been made for a drop on Friday, August 3. Unfavorable weather led to a postponement, so Stimson, suffering from the Washington heat, went to Long Island for the weekend. He was there on Monday morning, August 6, when Marshall telephoned him that the bomb had been dropped on Hiroshima some twelve hours earlier. Soon afterward came the President's statement that the weapon was an atomic bomb and more would follow until the Japanese surrendered.[45]

When the Japanese response proved unsatisfactory, the plan for the second drop continued. Late on August 8, the Japanese Ambassador sought the aid of Soviet Commissar of Foreign Affairs Molotov for mediation. He was told that on the following day the Soviet Union would consider itself at war with Japan.

August 9 brought announcement of the drop of the second bomb, on Nagasaki.

In Tokyo, the Cabinet still argued over whether or not to surrender, until the issue was at last submitted to the Emperor. He replied that the war should be ended.[46]

As Secretary Stimson was about to go to the airport to begin a brief vacation on the morning of August 10, Colonel Frank McCarthy of General Marshall's staff called to say that the Japanese government had accepted the list of terms, provided the Emperor could retain his position as a sovereign ruler. Stimson led the fight at the White House and at the War Department for a formula that would meet the Japanese request. The arrangement stipulated that the Emperor and Japanese government would be subject to the authority of the Supreme Commander of the Allied Powers, a position Marshall had helped to secure for General MacArthur. Ultimately the new government would be chosen by the Japanese people. This formula strengthened the Emperor in his insistence on peace against the fanatical military leaders who wanted to continue the fight. On August 14, the Japanese government reported its acceptance of Allied terms.[47]

Marshall was willing to adjust the surrender offer to make it more palatable to the Japanese, but he had no doubt that the shock effect of the two bombs had hastened the coming of peace. The Japanese had been warned from Potsdam of the great destruction that awaited them, but they did not believe in its scope. Later, he recalled:

> Now it had happened and they got the full word of what had happened at Hiroshima. And very shortly afterward it occurred again at Nagasaki. The fact that we had no more [bombs] completed at the time was unknown to the Japanese and they could imagine Tokyo being wiped out next. And they were, I think, shocked into immediate action which otherwise we could not have gotten out of them. And we would have had a terribly bitter and frightfully expensive [fight] in lives and treasure, etc., if we had to proceed with a landing in Japan. . . .

> I regarded the dropping of the bomb as of great importance and felt that it would end the war possibly better than anything else, which it did, and I think that all the claims about the bombings and afterward were rather silly. . . . I think it was quite necessary to drop the bomb to shorten the war.

> In retrospect, I feel the same way about it. There were hundreds of thousands of American lives involved in these things as well as billions of money. They had been perfectly ruthless. We had notified them of the bomb. They didn't choose to believe that. After that what they needed was shock action. And they got it. I think it was very wise to use it.[48]

Following Stimson's meeting with the President and his chief advisers on the morning of August 10, the Secretary talked with Byrnes about the general form of the surrender, noting that Marshall wanted as one of the conditions that the Japanese surrender of American prisoners be accessible to sites where planes could land to take them out. When he learned a few days later that General Wainwright was being flown from his prison, he told MacArthur that it would produce a good effect in the United States if this commander, who had been forced to surrender the last regular Army units in the Philippines to the Japanese, were brought to the *Missouri* to witness the final ceremonies of the Japanese surrender on September 2. His presence would be a fitting symbol of victory in the Pacific.

Controversy is still noisy over the necessity for dropping the bomb and the reasons for dropping it. Marshall strongly doubted that Japan could be defeated without an invasion of the home islands. His view was reinforced by the virulence of the kamikaze attacks and by the suicidal resistance of the Japanese at Iwo Jima and Okinawa. He was unpersuaded by Air Force and Navy arguments that Japan could be quickly strangled to death by the bombing of its cities and attacks on its shipping. He thought these tactics might prolong the war for at least a year and that the bulk of mop-up fighting would still fall heaviest on the Army, and that public opinion would not accept the continuing casualties, which would begin to seem endless. So he resumed his urging that the Soviet Union be brought into the war to place maximum pressure on Japan, and he wanted to use the atomic bomb, if a test proved it effective, to shock the enemy into surrender without resorting to an invasion that could only be bloody.

The United States had taken up the business of splitting the atom to forestall Germany's getting a weapon from it first. Now the main idea was to shorten the war. As far as Marshall was concerned, he went to Potsdam with his mind set on using the bomb to reduce casualties. So, in fact, did Truman, although he, like Stimson, was increasingly willing to get psychological advantage in any way to bolster the U.S. position at the Potsdam Conference. Stimson's *Diary* spells out his own growing concern as to how to persuade the Soviets to listen to reason about Manchuria and Eastern Europe. Truman was also worried about the growing truculence of the Russians. He may have delayed the opening of the conference to make certain that he could have the bomb as a ploy in his negotiations with the Soviets.

Completely aside from any political implications of the bomb vis-à-vis the Russians, the meeting on June 18, 1945, set the United States on the course of using whatever bombs were available in August to shorten the war, if the tests of the implosion bomb proved successful. For the President and the Army, the whole procedure depended on success in the July test. The news from New Mexico merely assured continuance of the countdown.

Close scrutiny of Marshall's role in the development of the bomb shows that he saw it as a weapon to wind up the war swiftly and thus effect enormous reduction in casualties. He continued to depend on conventional plans for invasion until the very day of the announcement of a successful test. There is no evidence that at any time his thinking or plans were influenced by any possible political effect use of the bomb might have on the Russians. Testing and planning proceeded almost automatically from the moment a decision was made that the bomb be used to end the war. Once it was proved that the bomb would work with terrifying potency, the next step was to set a date after which it would be launched. This was approved with no fanfare, and then the matter lay in the hands of General Spaatz, who had been given the duty of executing it. After August 2, only a definite order could stop the process. The process had been set in motion for military reasons and the bombing approved for military reasons.

Marshall and Stimson and the officers and civilians who had worked with President Roosevelt long before the meeting at Potsdam had then recommended the use of the bomb to a new President almost before he knew of its existence or potential. Truman was delighted to find a six-gun on his hip as he talked to the Russians; but, failing a Japanese offer to surrender before the Potsdam meeting ended, the military factors that determined the drop had been set moving long before the chief actors left Washington.

Not by Still Waters

FROM Tokyo on November 22, General MacArthur sent farewell good wishes to the retiring Chief of Staff. He cabled: "The entire command sends sincere greetings and hopes you will find full contentment in green pastures and by still waters." A Marshall aide, scanning the message after Marshall had accepted the Chinese mission, underlined the last seven words and drew an arrow towards a word he had added: "CHINA!!!" Laconically, Marshall replied to MacArthur, "Thanks for your message. My retirement was of rather short duration and the outlook does not indicate still waters."[1]

Fortunately, Marshall had some moments in which to savor words of appreciation for his war services before his official retirement. In addition to Churchill's laudation near the end of the war in Europe and Eisenhower's warm praise after V-E Day, Secretary Stimson had called a small group to his office on V-E Day to hear him say to Marshall:

> I want to acknowledge my great personal debt to you in common with the whole country. No one who is thinking of himself can rise to true heights. You have never thought of yourself. Seldom can a man put aside such a thing as being a commanding general of the greatest field army of our history. The decision was made by you for wholly unselfish reasons. But you have made your position as Chief of Staff a greater one. I have never seen a task of such magnitude performed by man.
>
> It is rare in late life to make new friends; at my age it is a slow process but there is no one for whom I have such deep respect and I think greater affection.

I have seen a great many soldiers in my lifetime and you, sir, are the finest soldier I have ever known."[2]

As Washington awaited Japan's reaction to the atomic bomb, Stimson suggested to Truman that with the closing of the war he must resign his position. One of his final acts before leaving Washington was to propose in mid-September that the President suggest that a medal be struck to express the thanks of Congress to Marshall for his wartime service. Stimson summarized high points of the Chief of Staff's contributions to a President who totally agreed with those words, and at his last press conference, on September 19, the Secretary added other tributes. The two occasions constitute a splendid valedictory for work well done.

Of Marshall he wrote to Truman:

His mind has guided the grand strategy of our campaigns. . . . It was his mind and character that carried through the trans-Channel campaign against Germany. . . . Similarly his views have controlled the Pacific campaign although he has been most modest, and careful in recognizing the role of the Navy. His views guided Mr. Roosevelt throughout.

The construction of the American Army has been entirely the fruit of his initiative and supervision. Likewise its training. As a result we have an army unparalleled in our history with a high command of supreme and uniform excellence. . . . With this Army we have won a most difficult dual war with practically no serious setbacks and astonishingly "according to plans." . . .

Show me any war in history which has produced a general with such a surprisingly perfect record as his in this greatest and most difficult of wars of all history.[3]

At his final press conference, Stimson continued:

From the very beginning, he insisted on unity between the services and among our allies. He realized that only by this means could our combined resources be employed to the fullest advantage against the enemy. To achieve wholehearted cooperation, he was always willing to sacrifice his own personal prestige. To him agreement was more important than any consideration of where credit belonged. His firm belief that unity could be preserved in the face of divergent opinions was a decisive factor in planning throughout the war.

General Marshall's leadership takes its authority directly from his great strength of character. I have never known a man who seemed so surely to breathe the democratic American spirit. He is a soldier, and yet he has a profound distaste for anything that smacks of militarism. He believes that every able-bodied citizen has a personal responsibility for the nation's security and should be ready to accept that responsibility whenever an emergency arises. But he is opposed to a large standing army as un-American.

His trust in his commanders is almost legendary. During the critical period of the Ardennes breakthrough no messages went from the War Department to General Eisenhower which would require his personal decision and reply. This is standard practice with General Marshall. When one of his commanders is in a tight spot, he does everything possible to back him up. But he leaves the man free to accomplish his purpose unhampered.

He is likewise the most generous of men, keeping himself in the background so that his subordinates may receive all credit for duties well done.

His courtesy and consideration for his associates, of whatever rank, are remarked by all who know him. His devotion to the nation he serves is a vital quality which infuses everything he does. During the course of a long lifetime, much of it spent in a position of public trust, General Marshall has given me a new gauge of what such service should be. The destiny of America at the most critical time of its national existence has been in the hands of a great and good citizen. Let no man forget it.[4]

From many of his wartime staff, who had worked long hours with and for him, there were letters of gratitude and respect. Tough old soldier Bedell Smith, usually short on sentiment, wrote on December 3:

I am forced to put in a letter what I had hoped to tell you in person. It leaves all of us with a sort of "lost feeling" to realize that you have retired from active service. I doubt if you ever could realize the deep and sincere affection you inspired, particularly in those of us who had the good fortune to serve directly under you. Aside from any personal gratitude, and in my own case, there is so much of this that there is no use trying to put it in a letter, we all feel a personal loyalty and admiration for you which couldn't possibly change or diminish. I wish that I could be like you. I never can, of course, because I have a bad temper, and get irritable over small things, but I have tried very hard to be, and will continue to do so, as long as I live.

I dare say you will think this is sloppy, but it had to come out. Probably better in a letter, after all. At any rate, please be assured of my continued affection and devotion.[5]

Soon the deluge of good wishes for years of quiet retirement was replaced by mixtures of regret and praise that he had been called again to duty. Colonel Isaac Newell, his first commander in China in 1924, said that he had assumed that Marshall would soon be at Pinehurst as master of hounds. Instead, "You have jumped back into harness and have been given a problem almost as difficult as the one you have just solved. I have confidence that you will be able to pour oil on the troubled waters. As much as I admire the Chinese, I fear it will be years before China can be made a modern nation. Here is wishing you all success."[6]

For Katherine Marshall, who had counted the days until they could have hours of lazy peace, it was a devastating development. To Colonel Frank McCarthy, whose long service to Marshall as military secretary and later, as Secretary, General Staff, had won him the status of a trusted member of the family, Mrs. Marshall poured out her bitter grief at the year's end. Mindful that McCarthy was still recuperating from a near physical breakdown which had led him to resign an Assistant Secretary of State position he had received at the end of the war, she wrote:

Your yellow roses really made this Christmas more like my past ones than anything that happened. How sweet and thoughtful of you, for my heart was truly sad. This assignment to China was a bitter blow. If General Marshall could have had even a few weeks rest and have had you and Sergeant Powder with him, I would not have had such fears about his going. I know that you were more than ready to make the sacrifice but it was one he could not run the risk of accepting. You have always been perfectly selfless in your loyalty to him and therefore someone else had to think of your good. It would have been madness for you to face that trip and a Chinese winter.

When I saw his plane take off without anyone to be close to him whom he had known and depended on, I felt I could not stand it. A new secretary, new orderly, new cook. I know just how he felt too, but neither of us could speak of it for it was too close to our hearts.

I give a sickly smile when people say how the country loves and admires my husband. That last week testifying from nine to five every day, with the luncheon hours spent with the President and Secretary Byrnes, trying to get some idea of what might be done on this mission, then dumped into his lap to write the whole policy after he got home at night. I shall never forget that week and I shall never forget how this country showed its love and admiration.

This sounds bitter. Well, I am bitter. The President should never have asked this of him and in such a way that he could not refuse.

This is a long way from yellow roses, but I have kept silent so long I had to get it out to someone and it will be safe with you. His trip was fairly comfortable and now my daily prayer is that he can bring some sort of unity out of chaos somehow.[7]

Too Many Hats—Too Many Hates

MARSHALL'S first encounter with China came in 1914. On leave from his regiment in the Philippines, he spent almost a month visiting Manchurian battlefields of the Russo-Japanese War. Later, from the summer of 1924 until late spring in 1927, he was in Tientsin as executive officer of the 15th Infantry Regiment stationed there. His regiment, like military units of Japan and a number of European powers, was kept in Tientsin under terms of the treaty ending the Boxer Uprising of 1900, to keep communications open from Peking to the sea. In Tientsin, Marshall learned enough Chinese to deal with court-martial cases in which Chinese citizens were involved, and gained more than a passing knowledge of Chinese culture.

From reading and from talking with officers on China duty, he picked up knowledge of the weaknesses of the Manchu Dynasty in the late nineteenth century, which had opened the country to demands for special concessions by Japan and the major nations of Europe. He knew of the growing antagonism to the existing regime of many Chinese which had led to the Revolution of 1911 and the establishment of a republic at the beginning of 1912 under Dr. Sun Yat-sen. But factional quarrels and divisions developed, so that more than a decade later national unity had not been achieved in a China of quarreling parties and feuding warlords.

In 1923, about a year before Marshall was assigned to Tientsin, Dr. Sun came home to Canton in Kwangtung Province to establish a base from which he could begin anew. He was not abandoning his hope for a republic, but had decided that the overthrow of the old government must be followed by an intermediate period of political tutelage to prepare the public for democratic responsibilities. In 1912 he had established a one-party government, the Kuomintang, made up of representatives of various interests and parties. In 1924 he called the first National Congress to strengthen the Kuomintang by centering its power in the Central Executive Committee.

By the time Marshall came to Tientsin, Dr. Sun was using Soviet assistance and advice in building a base from which he could work for national unity and curb foreign powers still posting their troops in China. Believing that a strong military was essential for his purposes, he established Whampoa Military Academy on an island near Canton in 1924, choosing as its head Chiang Kai-shek, one of his young supporters who had been trained in military schools in both China and Japan. In his relatively short tenure as commandant, Chiang trained many of the officers who helped him fight his early campaigns, and they became a powerful clique in the Kuomintang to back his policies. When Sun died in 1925 while trying to get help from northern warlords, a struggle for leadership ensued at Canton in which Chiang's rise to power was aided by the Chinese Communists and other left-wing elements in the Kuomintang. Before many months, his growing unease about Communist power led him to begin curtailing their influence in the government.

Chiang nevertheless accepted further Russian assistance as he prepared to carry on the Northern Expedition that Sun Yat-sen had planned. This campaign was aimed at breaking the power of three coalitions that centered in cities in Hunan, Hupeh, and Kiangsi provinces, and in Shanghai, Nanking, and Peking. In July 1926, after he was named Supreme Commander of the Armies from the South, Chiang Kai-shek launched the Northern Expedition. By the end of the year he controlled the south-central cities; his attacks in Chekiang Province in January opened the way to the East; Shanghai fell on March 22, and Nanking two days later.

When Marshall left for the United States in May 1927, Chiang appeared ready to unify China, but he was increasingly at odds with the Chinese Communists. Within a few months he forced Soviet advisers to leave the country and instigated widespread arrests of Communist leaders. Marshall had followed developments in 1926 and 1927 through reports of U.S. observers with units in the field. After his return to the United States, he profited from in-depth reports on the contesting leaders by Colonel Joseph W. Stilwell, who had been one of his battalion commanders at Tientsin.

A temporary military setback in the summer of 1927 led Chiang to retire from his post for several months. At the year's end he took as second wife Soong Mei-ling, thus acquiring as in-laws various members of the remarkable Soong family, several of whom were already his financial and political backers, such as T. V. Soong and H. H. Kung (married to a Soong), and the widow of Sun Yat-sen (also a Soong).

Chiang returned to the Northern Expedition at the beginning of 1928; in June, National forces captured Peking (shortly afterward renamed Peiping). Chiang Kai-shek, now the Generalissimo in power as well as in name, established the new capital at Nanking in October 1928.

As the Communists lost power in the cities, under the leadership of Mao Tse-tung they began developing support among the peasants. Beginning in the winter of 1934, Chiang sent five expeditions against the Communists. Late in 1934, he forced Mao to evacuate the south-central province of Kiangsi. In October, Mao and his supporters, numbering an estimated 100,000, began the Long March on foot that was to wind over 6,000 miles until they ended at Yenan in Shensi Province a year later. One historian thinks that as few as 6,000 of the original group made the trip all the way. But the Long March became a legend that strengthened the Chinese Communists and added to the suspicion and hatred between Nationalists and Communists, which never disappeared.

The Japanese, with certain rights in Manchuria won in the Russo-Japanese War, decided they could profit from turmoil in the North to extend their power there. An incident in September 1931 in Mukden was used to justify the ultimate overrunning of Manchuria by the Japanese and the establishment of the puppet state of Manchukuo in 1932. Marshall later in Chicago heard the details of these developments from his neighbor Major General Frank McCoy, who was named to the League of Nations commission under Lord Lytton that was sent late in 1931 to investigate the Manchurian situation.

Obsessed with the Communists, Chiang seemed more interested in fighting them than the encroaching Japanese. This issue came to a head in December 1936, while Chiang was on a visit to Sian. He was seized by one of his supporters, the former ruler in Manchuria, Chang Hsueh-liang, who made common cause with Communist leaders to insist that Chiang turn his full energies against Japan. An uneasy truce was worked out and Chiang was released.

Before plans for united resistance could be implemented, an incident near Peiping in July 1937 between Chinese and Japanese soldiers led to out-and-out war between Japan and China. The Japanese poured in from Manchuria and by the end of the year had captured the Chinese capital at Nanking. The Japanese advanced into central areas of the country, forcing Chiang to withdraw to the

West and establish his government at Chungking. The Chinese Communists held out southwest of Peiping at their headquarters in Yenan.

In 1938, National China began to seek credits for the purchase of arms and munitions from the United States. Chiang placed a retired American Air Corps officer, Claire Chennault, in charge of the Chinese Air Force, and made vigorous efforts to expand the ground forces.

From 1939 onward, Marshall was intimately aware of Chinese problems and Chinese needs. With the entry of the United States into the war, the Generalissimo pressed for expanded financial aid and for the appointment of a high-ranking American officer to advise on the organization and training of Chinese forces and to act as his American Chief of Staff. Marshall and Stimson selected Major General Joseph W. Stilwell to head the mission.

Stubborn, brash, profane, inclined to coarse, plain speaking, Stilwell had first visited China in 1911, while stationed in the Philippines. At the end of World War I, he was sent to Peking as a language officer, serving from 1920 until 1923. In 1926–29 he returned as a battalion commander of the 15th Infantry Regiment at Tientsin, where he served under George Marshall and impressed him with his reports on Chinese commanders. Stilwell returned to the United States in 1929 to be assigned the Tactical Section at the Infantry School at Fort Benning under Marshall. In 1935 he returned to China as Military Attaché and was there until 1939, becoming familiar with Chinese leadership, military problems, and difficulties in fighting the Japanese. On his way back to the States he learned that his old friend Acting Chief of Staff Marshall had proposed his promotion to brigadier general, one of the first two officers to be thus advanced.[1]

On the basis of his knowledge of China, its language, and its problems, and some ten years of service there, Stilwell appeared the best choice for the job. He was well prepared for a fighting assignment, but he was totally the wrong man to handle the smooth approach necessary for an adviser to the proud, highly sensitive Chiang Kai-shek, who held to ancient views of China's greatness and resented any suggestion of encroachment on his powers. Had Stilwell possessed infinite guile and subtlety along with his other qualities, he might have been able to work with Chiang, but his delight was in coarse, crude frankness. The defeat of British and Chinese forces in Burma shortly after his arrival in China set the stage for disagreement.

Stilwell's various command roles made him even more difficult for Chiang to control. U.S. Chief of Staff to Chiang Kai-shek, later U.S. Commander of the China-Burma-India (CBI) Theater, in general control of Lend-Lease aid to China, acting deputy to Lord Louis Mountbatten, commander of the Southeast Asia command after that headquarters was established in 1943, Stilwell wore many hats, which he switched from time to time as it suited his purposes. Chiang fought back through his brother-in-law T. V. Soong, sometimes special representative to the United States and sometimes Prime Minister of China, who had strong and special ties to anti-Stilwell Americans with entrée to the White House. Several representatives of the President who went out to see what was needed returned with anti-Stilwell reports. Twice the President asked Marshall if he should not be recalled, but the Chief of Staff and the Secretary of War held firm for their selection.

Two basic problems, other than those of conflicting personalities, persisted. The Generalissimo was determined to break his adviser's control over Lend-Lease to China, and he was violently opposed to Stilwell's insistence that China needed the services of every Chinese able to fight—even if that meant using the forces of the Chinese Communists. Stilwell's advocacy of the dispatch of a special group, the Dixie mission, to Yenan to get special intelligence on the Japanese from the Communists, intensified Chiang's opposition. Stilwell responded with a running indictment of National stupidity, incapacity to lead, bungling, and corruption. Marshall saw and deplored the irascibility of "Vinegar Joe" but at the same time was uneasily acquiring from him a growing impression of the untrustworthiness of the National regime.

The fight over Stilwell moved toward a showdown in the spring of 1944. Marshall sympathized with Stilwell's problems but also felt that obvious disdain for Chiang Kai-shek and a self-righteous tactlessness were responsible for many of them. "At Cairo, in late 1943, I suggested that he go elsewhere. He said he wanted to stay. 'Then stop your talking.' He said he hadn't called Chiang 'Peanut.' I said, 'You have never lied. Don't now.' He mumbled something. I said, 'Stop talking to your staff about these people.' "[2]

> The trouble was that with all his ability, he dissipated [it] by his open criticism of the Generalissimo and allowing his staff to do the same thing—which is the worst thing you can do. . . . Of course, staff cliques and staff talk . . . play a great part in these things. But if you permit them and feed them grist for their mill, why, you've got an awful mess on your hands. And that was the greatest mistake Stilwell [made] aside from his open criticism of the Generalissimo.[3]

Marshall also soon realized that Stilwell's dislike of the British equaled his distaste for Chiang Kai-shek. Chiang himself hated the British because he felt they treated him with indifferent contempt, but the two men were never able to create any sort of bond out of this common aversion. In later years Marshall complained that Stilwell "didn't even try to get along with Mountbatten. . . . I wrote Stilwell how to [deal with] him. He made cute remarks about Mountbatten. [He developed] bad relations with the British."[4]

It was surprising that Marshall had continued to back Stilwell as Mountbatten's deputy or hoped that the American could serve as a commander under Chiang Kai-shek, but he had a conviction that Stilwell was

> a splendid fighting man. Give Stilwell a fine corps and, I think, a fine army, but certainly a fine corps, and he would have put up a magnificent performance. He knew the game, he was courageous to the limit, and he was adventurous, and yet he was calculating. It was too bad that he had to be laboring with this kind of semidiplomatic situation and being played off by a superb performer at the game, Chennault.[5]

On another occasion he said, "When they characterize Stilwell, they fail to mention the big thing—that he was a fighter. It was like Lincoln finding Grant."[6]

Marshall thought that Stilwell was the one man who could get good results out of the Chinese armed forces. He was impressed by the fact that Stilwell was interested not in ideology but in the fighting qualities of his troops. For that reason he was willing to use Communist troops.

Stilwell saw the battle against the Japanese in Burma and China as a war to be settled by ground forces. In pushing all-out ground operations, he ran into Chiang's desire to save his best-trained and -equipped troops for the postwar period to strengthen his position against possible enemies. Stilwell also confronted General Chennault's belief that a well-equipped and -supplied air force could win the battle with little ground help. It was an idea that appealed to the Generalissimo and to President Roosevelt, who shared Marshall's opposition to committing large numbers of ground troops to Asia.

Stilwell was sure that Chennault was continually undermining his position. The airman's hand was strengthened because he could work through his civilian assistant (and later military aide) Joseph Alsop, a relative of the Roosevelts.

Alsop's position also disturbed Marshall. In 1943, Chennault had asked Stilwell to give an Army commission to his civilian assistant. Seeing Alsop as a dangerous opponent, Stilwell opposed the commission and Marshall agreed. Near the end of the year, Chennault approached General Arnold about the matter, indicating that Stilwell had withdrawn his objections.[7]

Meanwhile, Marshall had been handed copies of Alsop's correspondence with T. V. Soong, which showed how Alsop was undercutting Stilwell. In a protest to Roosevelt in February 1944, Marshall enclosed an Alsop letter that Soong was circulating in an effort to get Stilwell removed. In this letter Alsop called himself Soong's man and indicated that he would clear his letters to Harry Hopkins in the White House through the Chinese official. He bitterly criticized Stilwell and his staff, characterizing some of the officers as second-rate and one chief assistant as virtually half-witted. Alsop admitted disliking Stilwell so much that he almost mistrusted his own judgment in regard to him. He expressed anger at indications that the War Department intended to break most of its promises to the Generalissimo.[8]

Marshall warned of the ill effects Alsop's commission would have in the CBI Theater, but his warning was not effective. Roosevelt replied that he had carefully read the enclosures and said he wanted the commission issued. Some of Marshall's staff were incensed and drafted a reply for the General's signature, strongly challenging the President. But the Chief of Staff bowed to his Commander in Chief, directing Stilwell in mid-February 1944 to issue the commission in accordance with the request of Chennault, on the understanding that Stilwell's previous objections were withdrawn.

Within a short time, Marshall concluded that his suspicions about Alsop were correct. Vice President Henry Wallace landed in Chungking on June 20 on a fact-finding mission for the President. Chennault assigned Lieutenant Alsop as his escort. In his report to the President, Wallace agreed with some of Stilwell's ideas, but he proposed that the commander be recalled and that Major General Albert C. Wedemeyer, now deputy to Mountbatten, replace him.

Marshall would have preferred a better time for grappling with the problem, but on July 1 he told Stilwell that the situation in China made it necessary "for me to trouble you in the midst of your terrific struggles with jungle, Japanese, logistics and scrub typhus complications which beset you to a degree I do not believe any other commander of modern time has experienced." He reviewed points of the controversy and then asked if Stilwell thought there was still a job for him to do there.[9]

Marshall had offered Stilwell a way out. He was less than three years younger than the Chief of Staff, unwell, harassed at every turn. Obsessed with the desire to repay the Japanese for the humiliation in Burma, he believed that the Chinese soldier, decently equipped and properly led, would fight, and he was convinced that the Chinese Communists in the North would welcome a chance to battle the Japanese. He was equally confident that he was the person who could provide a bridge between the Nationalists and the Communists. So was he tempted.

His price for staying was high. There must be no more arguments with Chiang Kai-shek and no more battles with the Generalissimo's chief advisers, who countermanded Stilwell's orders or reneged on their commitments. The Generalissimo must be impressed with the need for a change. "If the President were to send him a very stiff message, emphasizing our investment and interest in China, and also the serious pass to which China had come due to mismanagement and neglect of the Army, and insisting that desperate ills require desperate remedies, the Generalissimo might be forced to give me a command job." But he had to have complete control. Action "must be quick and radical and the Generalissimo must give one commander full power."[10]

Despite forebodings about the situation in Chungking, General Marshall decided to make a last effort. With Stimson's aid, he determined to get the President's support. He persuaded the Joint Chiefs of Staff to back his appeal.

On July 4, they painted for Roosevelt a picture of approaching collapse. Chennault's air force could do "little more than slightly delay the Japanese advance." Only a unified effort by Chinese forces under one effective leader could succeed. For this job there was only one man: "That man is Stilwell." They recognized that if he did this he would have to lay aside his other duties and he must be named by Chiang as commander of all Chinese forces. To give him the requisite prestige for the assignment, they proposed four-star rank for "Vinegar Joe"—a rank at that time held by only four men on active duty, Marshall, MacArthur, Arnold, and Eisenhower. There would then be no chance for the Generalissimo to miss the point.[11]

The deteriorating situation in China helped sway the President. On July 6, he took the stand that Stilwell had long urged. The message, which Marshall helped prepare, asked that Stilwell command all forces in China. "I know of no other man who has the ability, the force, and the determination to offset the disaster which

now threatens China and our all-out struggle for the conquest of
Japan."[12]

Marshall coached Stilwell in his future role. Kindly but firmly, he
chided Stilwell for failing to work easily with those about him, for
attracting antagonism instead of good will. "The difficulty," in
Marshall's opinion, "has been the offense you have given, usually
in small affairs, both to the Generalissimo and to the President."
He must do everything possible to minimize troubles. Saying in
effect that he was putting Stilwell into the game when his side was
still ahead, he begged him not to lose his advantage. "I ask you
please this time to make a conscientious effort to avoid wrecking
yours and our plans because of inconsequential matters or disregard of conventional courtesies." Further, he stressed the importance of the gracious gesture: "Win over to your side anyone who
can help in the battle that will result from the violent hostility of
those Chinese who will lose face by your appointment."[13]

The Generalissimo was not prepared for this development. He
was fully aware of Stilwell's strong views, but hitherto he had enjoyed the President's support. Clinging to the power he had once
won in battle, he was weakened by military leaders who had neither
his ability nor his love for China. Beset by the Japanese and by
economic and political unrest, he could only brood over his trials
and hope that some leader from abroad—Chennault, or Roosevelt,
or even a reformed Stilwell—might bring him victory. The perfect
victory for him would mean not only the defeat of Japan but also
triumph over the Chinese Communists and other factions, both
liberal and reactionary, that opposed his rule. His troops armed by
the United States would be needed to assure his position.

In China, as in some other countries it would support, the United
States faced a thorny problem. How far should it back governments
whose paramount interests were in gaining domestic political
power rather than in helping American forces defeat a common
enemy?

The Generalissimo was stunned but not finished. He accepted
Roosevelt's proposal in principle but asked for a period in which
to prepare the way for Stilwell's assumption of command. To reduce friction with the American, he suggested that the President
send a representative with "far sighted political vision and ability"
to ameliorate relations between him and Stilwell.[14]

The reply reached Roosevelt just before he left the United States
for a meeting with MacArthur and Nimitz in Hawaii. Recently
renominated by the Democratic Convention to run for an unprece-

dented fourth term, the President wanted to tie up all the loose
ends, such as cooperation with China, before he began his fall
campaign. Noting that there was "a great deal in what the Generalissimo says," the President agreed to send a political representative to work with the Chinese leader.[15]

The Generalissimo now used his skill in delay to the fullest.
Roosevelt had asked that he act promptly, but Chiang Kai-shek
insisted that political arrangements must precede settlement of the
military command. If Chinese Communist troops were to be used,
he wanted a firm commitment by their leaders to obey the orders
of the National Government. Second, there must be a careful definition of Stilwell's powers. And, at last, the basic stipulation: the
distribution of all Lend-Lease supplies must be under the control
of the National Government. The issues on which Stilwell's hopes
would be destroyed had been forcefully stated.[16]

The Generalissimo had demanded what any sovereign ruler
would have exacted from an ally in return for cooperation. He
would not risk an infusion into his armed forces of troops that
obeyed the orders of another leader. He would limit the boundaries
of Stilwell's authority. He would ensure that his American subordinate could not get concessions by threatening to withhold American supplies. The problem, of course, was that Chiang Kai-shek's
sovereignty now rested completely on American support.

While Roosevelt was away, Marshall and Stimson looked for
someone they could recommend to the President as his representative to China. They finally settled on Major General Patrick Hurley,
whom Marshall had used earlier in Australia in an unsuccessful
effort to get supplies to MacArthur in the Philippines. Marshall had
pushed him for Middle East Command but Roosevelt did not act
on the suggestion. Near the end of July 1944, Hurley called on
Stimson and asked for a job. When Stimson mentioned this to
Marshall, the latter agreed that they should get Hurley into a position where he could use his energy and vigor.

A few days later, Marshall proposed that the President appoint
Hurley as Ambassador to China. He was the only man, wrote Stimson, "that Marshall and I can think of who can revolutionize the
backbiting and recrimination and stalemate surrounding poor Stilwell." There was a possibility that he could offset Stilwell's "acid-
ness." Stimson feared only that Hurley, "a fast traveler," might also
make the mistake of "trying to hustle the East."[17] Marshall was
equally wrong in his appraisal of the new Ambassador when he told
Stilwell, "I am inclined to think that he could pour more oil on the

troubled waters out there to your advantage than any other individual that may be selected."[18]

Acting for the President, General Marshall asked the Generalissimo on August 9 if the United States could send Hurley as political representative. The Chinese leader accepted with pleasure.

Awaiting the President on his return to Washington in mid-August were Chiang Kai-shek's various messages and a proposed reply, drafted in the War Department with the aid of Marshall and initialed by Marshall and Stimson. The President softened the language somewhat and sent it out on August 23. In view of the sharp controversy that arose over a later presidential message, in September, it is useful to examine the determined tone of this earlier statement. Urging that the Generalissimo place Stilwell in command of the Chinese forces at the earliest possible date, the President declared that extended deliberations "may well have fateful consequences in the light of the gravity of the military situation." Although he understood that there were problems, he urged the appointment "because I feel that with further delay, it may be too late to avert a military catastrophe tragic both to China and to our allied plans for the overthrow of Japan." As to the control of Communist troops, he added: "I do not think the forces to come under General Stilwell's command should be limited except by their availability to defend China and fight the Japanese. When the enemy is pressing us toward possible disaster, it appears unsound to refuse the aid of anyone who will kill Japanese."[19]

In preparation for the next stage in China, Marshall moved to rearrange the command structure in the CBI Theater. Telling Stilwell that it was important that he be relieved of responsibility for Burma and India, he suggested General Daniel Sultan as commander in the India-Burma area and General Wedemeyer as deputy for Mountbatten. He also proposed changes in the handling of Lend-Lease that would give the Chinese a place on a special committee in Chungking.[20]

Marshall assured Stilwell that the changes would make it possible for him to function as effectively as possible. At first the theater commander sharply questioned limitations placed on American control of supplies, since without it he would "report with an empty satchel" to Chiang Kai-shek, but after some hesitation he decided to accept Marshall's suggestions.

Clearly Stilwell's doubts persisted. He continued to write of corruption and chaos in China. In this he was not alone. His old enemy Chennault also voiced criticism of the National Government in

1944. He declared that relationships between the War Ministry and commanders in the field in East China had "deteriorated to the point where supplies were slow in arriving, and Chungking took to second guessing the field commanders via long-distance telephone and telegraph, only adding to the confusion and demoralization."[21]

In Stilwell's eyes, the cure for China's troubles lay in the removal of Chiang Kai-shek from power.

> The only thing that keeps the country split is his fear of losing control. He hates the Reds and will not take any chance on giving them a toehold in the government. . . . If this condition persists, China will have civil war immediately after Japan is out. If Russia enters the war before a united front is found in China, the Reds, being immediately accessible, will naturally gravitate to Russia's influence and control. The condition will directly affect the relations between Russia and China, and therefore indirectly those between Russia and the United States.[22]

Chiang's dilemma was succinctly stated in a conversation that John P. Davies, Stilwell's political adviser, had with Harry Hopkins in Washington in early September. The two men agreed that civil war in postwar China was inevitable and that "if the Generalissimo did not suppress the Communists, the Chinese Communists would remove him." Under these circumstances, it is difficult to see how anyone could imagine that the Generalissimo would give full powers to Stilwell if the Chinese Communists would thereby gain a larger role in military affairs.[23]

No ground existed for compromise between the views of the Generalissimo and of Stilwell. Someone had to give way. Strongly backed by Marshall and Stimson, Stilwell's chief interest was to get the Chinese moving against the Japanese. He wanted to save China but not necessarily Chiang's position. He was willing to use Chinese Communist troops if they would help defeat the Japanese. The Generalissimo's position was equally tenacious. He wanted to save China but also retain power. To avoid a crushing defeat from the Japanese, he was willing to use Communist divisions, but only on his own terms. If they were truly interested in defeating Japan, he argued, the Reds should be willing to surrender their autonomy in political and military affairs.

The Communists were also intent on gaining advantage. With Stilwell as their commander, perhaps they could get arms and prestige. The question was, what was Chiang Kai-shek willing to do to be saved?

It is doubtful if Hurley was aware of all these angles when he arrived in Chungking. He knew that there were difficulties but he seems not to have been completely briefed. The official historians say that he was unaware that Stilwell's campaign in North Burma had been in accord with Combined Chiefs of Staff directives. As to the Chinese Communists, his preliminary information seems to have come principally from the Soviet Commissar of Foreign Affairs, with whom he talked in Moscow on the way to China. The Russian had assured him that the Chinese Reds were not true Communists, a statement Hurley apparently accepted and repeated to Washington.

Supremely confident of his ability to settle all differences, Hurley outlined a ten-point program on September 12, stressing that the permanent objective of Sino-American collaboration was "the unification of all military forces for the immediate defeat of Japan and the liberation of China." While the Generalissimo considered the proposals, the Japanese were increasing their pressure on Chinese forces.[24]

Joining Hurley at Chungking, Stilwell found Chiang Kai-shek alarmed principally by recent enemy advances near the Salween River on the western Chinese border. He told Stilwell that if he did not attack within the week from North Burma, he would pull the forces west of the Salween back across the river to protect Kunming. In his diary, Stilwell exploded with fury against the Generalissimo. To Marshall he wrote: "The jig is up in South China. We are getting out of Kweilin now, and will have to get out of Liuchow as soon as the Japs appear there. The disaster south of the Yangtze is largely due to lack of proper command and the usual back-seat driving from Chungking." Stilwell said he was convinced that the Generalissimo "regards the South China catastrophe as of little moment, believing that the Japs will not bother him further in that area, and that he imagines he can get behind the Salween and there wait in safety for the U.S. to finish the war."[25]

Determined to force a showdown, Stilwell asked Hurley for authority to reward and punish commanders, to move troops, to activate new units, to change the army organization. There must be major changes in the high command, including a new War Minister and a Chinese Chief of Staff. The Generalissimo must refrain from interference in operations. In his zeal, Stilwell spared no feelings. He was set on a "damn the torpedoes" course, and his determination on plain talk seemed to affect even Hurley. When T. V. Soong asked that Lend-Lease control pass to Chiang Kai-shek, Hurley exploded. It was our property and we could handle it as we pleased.

When Soong reminded him of the dignity of a great nation, Hurley retorted that the dignity of 130 million Americans was involved. "Hooray for Pat!" wrote Stilwell.[26]

Although Stilwell reserved his most pungent observations for his diary, the burden of his complaints reached General Marshall. Reports that the Generalissimo was threatening to withdraw across the Salween reached the Chief of Staff at the Quebec Conference, where the British and United States military and political leaders were discussing Pacific and Far Eastern strategy.

A team of planners from the War Department Operations Division now undertook to spell out for the Generalissimo what they deemed necessary to defeat Japan in China. Revised by General Marshall, the message was laid before the President. After moderating some of the language, he directed that it be sent to Chiang Kai-shek. No American message to China during the war was to cause stronger reactions.

For a proud head of state, even one facing defeat, the tone was severe. But it was not demeaning. It did not justify General Chennault's remark that "one of the two or three Americans who have ever seen a copy of the message told me it sounded like a communication from Adolf Hitler to the puppet head of a conquered satellite state. . . . There were strong suspicions that Stilwell had actually written the message himself."[27]

The opening statements were straightforward and in no way humiliating. The President said:

> The men of your Y forces crossing the Salween have fought with great courage and rendered invaluable assistance to the campaign in North Burma. But we feel that unless they are reinforced and supported with your every capacity you can not expect to reap any fruits from their sacrifices, which will be valueless unless you are to assist in opening the Burma Road. Furthermore, any pause in your attack across the Salween or suggestions of a withdrawal is exactly what the Jap has been striving to cause you to do by his operations in eastern China. . . . [If you do not aid these efforts] we will lose all chance of opening land communications [from India] with China and immediately jeopardize the air route over the Hump.

The stinger came next: "For this you must yourself be prepared to accept the consequences and assume personal responsibility." The message made clear what the developments might be:

The advance of our forces across the Pacific is swift. But this advance
will be too late for China unless you act now and vigorously. . . .
Otherwise political and military considerations alike are going to be
swallowed up by military disaster.

The tone became somewhat harsher as the President recalled earlier efforts to support China.

I have urged time and again in recent months that you take drastic
action to resist the disaster which has been moving closer to China
and to you. Now, when you have not yet placed General Stilwell in
command of all forces in China, we are faced with the loss of a
critical area in east China with possible catastrophic results. . . .

Roosevelt informed the Generalissimo of steps then being taken at
Quebec on the assumption that Chiang Kai-shek would continue
vigorous efforts.

The action I am asking you to take will fortify us in our decision and
increase our aid to you. . . .

There was a hint that aid might be withheld if the Chinese leader
did not act decisively. But Mr. Roosevelt personally tried to soften
the blow. He concluded:

I trust that your far-sighted vision, which has guided and inspired
your people in this war, will realize the necessity for immediate
action. In this message, I have expressed my thoughts with complete
frankness because it appears plainly evident to all of us that all of
your and our efforts to save China will be lost by further delays.[28]

Strong messages had been exchanged earlier between Chungking and Washington without creating a crisis. This one assumed
serious proportions because Stilwell's decision to present it personally gave the Generalissimo an excuse for demanding his recall.
Even more, it gave him a chance to postpone actions relating to the
Chinese Communists that he did not propose to take whether the
pressure came from Stilwell or Roosevelt.

Two messages from the President reached Stilwell on September
19. One from Roosevelt and Churchill, describing their recent
decisions at Quebec, was to be handed to the United States and
British ambassadors for delivery to Chiang Kai-shek. The other,

from the President for the Generalissmo, did not specify the method of delivery. To guide Stilwell there was a directive of May 1944 from the President that his messages, with a translation, were to be delivered personally to Chiang Kai-shek.[29] General Handy wrote Stilwell on May 7: "The President is telling Gauss [American Ambassador to China] that all messages for Gmo must be delivered personally by the CG or Ambassador accompanied with a complete Chinese translation and all messages are to relate to the WD [War Department] the time of delivery."

There is no official evidence that Stilwell was instructed to present this particular message. However, it is evident that some members of the Operations Division assumed he would do so and speculated whether he would have time to read it before it was delivered. Apparently no one saw in the language the basis for an international incident.

Stilwell seems to have carried out his mission with zest. He reached the Generalissimo's residence at 5:30 P.M., when Chiang Kai-shek was talking with Hurley, Soong, and members of the National Military Council. He entered the conference room, accepted a ritual cup of tea, and after a proper wait announced that he had a message to deliver. He handed it to the interpreter, General Hu Chi-mung. Before General Hu could begin reading, Hurley intervened. Learning from Stilwell that there was a translation, he asked for it and handed it to the Generalissimo.[30]

If Stilwell had any misgivings about whether to present the message, he showed none in recording his glee in his diary: "Mark this day in red on the calendar of life. At long, at very long last, F.D.R. has finally spoken in plain words, and plenty of them, with a firecracker in every sentence." Months of frustration and bitter resentment prompted his next lines, which did him no credit: "I handed this bundle of paprika to the Peanut and then sank back with a sigh. The harpoon hit the little bugger right in the solar plexus and went right through him." Stilwell admitted that the Generalissimo took it gamely. "Beyond turning green and losing the power of speech he did not bat an eye. He said, 'I understand,' and put the cover on the teacup upside down to indicate that the conversation was at an end."[31]

Stilwell did not sense that more was ended than a meeting. He had miscalculated badly. It would be difficult for his friends in Washington to save him again. His diary entries, admittedly written only for the delight of his family and close friends, reveal not only the depths of his injured feelings but also an amazing insensitivity, which later made it almost impossible for his supporters to mount

an effective defense of his actions. Joyously he set down the mock-
ing lines: "After two and a half years the Big Boys have finally seen
the light and when it dawned, I played the avenging angel."[32]

Neither Hurley nor Stilwell helped matters with their failure to
alert Washington as to the effect of the delivery of the message.
Hurley's biographer states that the Oklahoman dined with Chiang
Kai-shek on the evening of the incident and was told that the time
had come to break with Stilwell and that there could be no further
discussion while he remained in China. Yet four days later Hurley's
report to the President failed to make this plain. Instead he spoke
of indications leading "toward harmony with the so-called Communist troops." He added that he had informed the Generalissimo

> that the so-called Communist troops in China are not considered
> real Communists by Molotov; Russia's attitude toward China is
> friendly and that Russia is not attempting to use the Communists
> troops to prevent military unification of China. Russia desires closer
> and more harmonious relations with China.[33]

Hurley said that he was advising the Generalissimo to make a response to Roosevelt's message of the 19th that would not create a
deadlock.

In view of the warning signals that he got from Chiang Kai-shek,
it is remarkable to follow the report Hurley initially wrote to Washington. In a message to Roosevelt that Marshall saw in brief and
which could not have been without telling impact, Hurley said:

> The nature of General Stilwell's mission, the obstruction he had
> met due to jealousy and concern for face of the Chinese Chief of
> Staff and others, the inherent dislike for any foreign control on the
> part of the Chinese and in particular of the Generalissimo, the
> necessity for safeguarding American interests have put General Stil-
> well frequently in a position where he had to differ with the Genera-
> lissimo and stand alone in telling the truth. . . . I believe in spite of
> the differences in their viewpoints the situation will now iron itself
> out. . . .

This was amazing enough, but the following lines were even more
baffling:

> The extent to which General Stilwell has agreed to a reasonable
> allotment of authority and the fact that his chief concern is to avoid
> having responsibility without adequate authority and the fact that

the Generalissimo has said he will give General Stilwell field command of Ground and Air Forces and with it his complete confidence should indicate to you that while the situation is difficult harmonious solution is possible. General Stilwell has read and approved this report.[34]

Not until several weeks later did Hurley tell the President that a more accurate draft had been softened because Stilwell complained that it would be equivalent to a request for his relief. For Hurley had written initially that the Generalissimo and Stilwell appeared to be "personally and fundamentally incompatible."[35]

Stilwell also failed to alert the War Department. His first report to General Marshall was optimistic:

> We are maintaining our stand on the vital questions of a united front and a united command, both are feasible and necessary; and when the shock of the President's communication wears off, there is a good prospect for solving them, but any releasing of pressure will only confirm CKS in his belief that he can continue his policy of delay with ultimate success.[36]

Shortly after sending this message, Stilwell began to have second thoughts. From Ho Ying-chin, Chief of Staff of the Chinese Army, Stilwell gathered that the Generalissimo was sulking principally over his failure to gain control of Lend-Lease operations in China. It was a serious matter of face with him that Stalin and the British could handle U.S. supplies and he could not. In a reasonable mood that might have been helpful earlier, Stilwell suggested arrangements by which friction and difficulties between the Nationalists and Communists could be carefully reduced and by which Chiang Kai-shek could attain substantial control over Lend-Lease materials.[37]

Like so many last-minute proposals, this one came at least one step too late in negotiations. On the 24th, Hurley found the Generalissimo set more firmly than ever on his decision to have nothing further to do with Stilwell. The next day, Chiang Kai-shek handed Hurley an *aide-mémoire* explaining why he could not appoint the American officer as field commander. "General Stilwell is unfitted for the vast, complex, and delicate duties which the new command will entail," he declared, concluding that to appoint him would cause widespread dissension in the Chinese forces. He asked that Stilwell be immediately replaced. Hurley implied that these points had been in the Generalissimo's mind earlier by explaining that he was still undecided when Stilwell handed him the President's message on September 19, a statement at odds with Hurley's later testimony that Chiang Kai-shek had been about to sign the commission when Hurley appeared with the message. In retrospect it is evident that the Generalissimo had never veered from his earlier distrust of Stilwell.[38]

Chiang had yielded to presidential pressure in the spring of 1944 and ordered his troops to cross the Salween as Stilwell had wanted, but he delayed as long as possible. He balked when Stilwell asked him to commit the Yunnan forces against the Japanese. It is difficult to believe that he ever intended that Stilwell be given overall command in China. After the July message arrived, he temporized. He was still seeking restrictions on the matter when the President's message of September 19 came. Thereafter his actions suggest that, rather than acting in a fit of anger, he had at last found the perfect pretext for ridding himself of a long-unwelcome commander. The argument was one that President Roosevelt was most likely to accept and Marshall least able to counter.

Stilwell got the bad news late on September 25. According to his diary for that day: "At 9:30[P.M.] the 'aide memoire' came in. 'Throw out General Stilwell. He is a non cooperative s.o.b. He has broken his promises. General Stilwell has more power in China than I have.' Etc., etc."

In his rebuttal to Marshall the following day, Stilwell reiterated his old complaints that Chiang had no intention of putting into effect any democratic reforms or of establishing a united front with the Communists. Perhaps uneasy over old sins he told Marshall that "the Gissimo might have the notion that I am trying to array the Communists against him," or that perhaps Chiang assumed that Stilwell was responsible for the September 19 letter. In an effort to calm Chiang's fears, Stilwell had recently informed the top Chinese generals that the use of Communist troops could be dropped, adding that he was not insisting on the use of Communist troops as a condition for the agreement.[39]

During this time General Marshall was working on possible replies for Roosevelt to send the Generalissimo. Uncertain of the President's reaction, he outlined messages both accepting and denying Chiang Kai-shek's request for Stilwell's recall. While these messages were being drafted, Harry Hopkins was allegedly feeding information on the President's intentions to representatives of Chiang. It seems evident that T. V. Soong sought Hopkins's assistance after Chiang's receipt of the China message. What is not clear is what Hopkins said to Soong. On October 1, Soong informed

Hurley that his brother-in-law Dr. H. H. Kung had been assured by Hopkins that the President would accede to a request for recall. Both Hopkins and Kung later denied the statement, but the damage had been done. On the assumption that he had the President in his corner, the Generalissimo told the Central Executive Committee of the Kuomintang on October 2 that he would not accept Stilwell as commander but would take another American.[40]

Hurley broke the bad news to Stilwell. The tired old soldier recorded that Roosevelt had cut his throat and thrown him out. He was badly hurt. Whether or not it was any consolation, he still had the backing of the War Department. Marshall said to Stimson "that if we had to remove Stilwell he would not allow another American general to be put in the position of Chief of Staff and commander of the Chinese armies for it was evident that no American would be loyally supported."[41]

At this point Stimson asked the Chief of Staff to seek a presidential letter urging Chiang Kai-shek to reconsider his decision. The President obliged with a message intended to make the Generalissimo think carefully before taking final action. Roosevelt declared: "The ground situation has so deteriorated since my original proposal that I now am inclined to feel that the United States Government should not assume the responsibility involved in placing an American officer in command of your ground forces in China." He suggested that Stilwell could be retained only as commander of Chinese troops in Yunnan and Burma, while relieved of his responsibilities as Chief of Staff for Chiang and controller of Lend-Lease in China. He hinted at difficulties that might arise if Chiang removed Stilwell from Burma "because I feel that . . . the results would be far more serious than you apparently realize." Stimson thought this letter made the best of a difficult situation. Even Stilwell considered the letter fairly strong and "far better than I expected." According to Hopkins, Kung promised to cable the Generalissimo at once and urge that he make an affirmative reply.[42]

Hurley delivered Roosevelt's message on October 6. That weekend the Generalissimo said again that he would not retain Stilwell in any capacity. In a note for the President and in a longer *aide-mémoire,* he was bitter in his criticism of Stilwell. He was certain that if the President would send in his place a qualified American officer, they could reverse the present trend "and achieve a vital contribution to the final victory."[43]

Hurley was now won over completely to the Generalissimo's point of view. He said in an accompanying message that the choice lay clearly between Stilwell and Chiang Kai-shek. If this one point were settled, no other issues would be involved. Stilwell totally disagreed. He radioed Marshall, "It is not a choice between throwing me out or losing CKS and possibly China. It is a case of losing China's potential effort if CKS is allowed to make the ground rules now."[44]

The President ended the unhappy affair by recalling Stilwell. But in Stilwell's defense he added an explanation—a note written by Marshall, who had made numerous changes in the first draft—that the decisions for an attack on North Burma, cited by the Generalissimo as an example of Stilwell's bad judgment, had been made by the Combined Chiefs of Staff and approved by the Prime Minister of Great Britain and the President of the United States.[45]

It is difficult to believe that the Generalissimo did not know that he was using Stilwell's dismissal as a means of getting back at the distasteful decisions of the Combined Chiefs of Staff. He had a victory over Stilwell, but it was not complete. Marshall had helped see to that. Roosevelt reflected the Chief of Staff's views when he said that no American should assume responsibility in a command post for the operations of Chinese forces in China. He did agree, nevertheless, that the War Department would furnish an American officer to act as American Chief of Staff for Chiang Kai-shek. The Generalissimo had anticipated this offer and had already suggested to Hurley the names of Eisenhower, Patch, Krueger, and Wedemeyer.

Heavily engaged in current campaigns in Europe or in the Pacific, the first three were obviously unavailable. Near at hand was Lieutenant General Albert Wedemeyer, Deputy Chief of Staff in Mountbatten's headquarters, conversant with plans for China and Burma, a former member of Marshall's Operations Division. At the War Department's suggestion, Roosevelt offered to name Wedemeyer commanding general in China, and he was accepted.

Thus ended a sad chapter. General Marshall felt it keenly and his views were echoed by Secretary Stimson's lament that it was a "terribly sad ending of the most courageous and finally successful piece of work that any of our generals have done, and poor Stilwell is the sacrifice." The fault lay, Stimson thought, in the incapacity and wrongheadedness of Chiang Kai-shek and in the President's practice of sending special envoys who, with the exception of Hurley, had filled his head with poison.

After the war, Stilwell's American critics, such as General Chennault, charged that Stilwell was so obsessed with Burma that he used his control over U.S. supplies to bar effective aid to Chiang Kai-shek, that his policies tended to strengthen the Chinese Communists, and that he spent lives and money on the opening of the Burma Road, which was "without military value except for pipeline paralleling it. . . ." British writers questioned the value of Stilwell's Burma campaign, the necessity of the road, and the General's ability to rise above division or corps level.[46]

As noted earlier, these critics were attacking the decisions of the U.S. Chiefs of Staff. The British were lukewarm to American suggestions for winning back Burma. China desperately wanted help but not at the risk of losing additional battles to the Japanese, or of losing men and material painfully amassed. Chennault, convinced that only air power could win, bitterly resented any diversion for ground operations.

In his mission to China, Marshall drew on Stilwell's intimate day-by-day reporting on conditions in that country and the views and vagaries of the Generalissimo. A partial analysis of what Marshall had gained from developments in China during the Stilwell mission appears in the Chief of Staff's final report on the last two years of the war:

> The mission that the Joint Chiefs of Staff had given General Stilwell in Asia was one of the most difficult of the war. He was out at the end of the thinnest supply line of all; the demands of the war in Europe and the Pacific campaign, which clearly were the most vital to final victory, exceeded our resources in many items of material and equipment and all but absorbed everything else that we had. General Stilwell could have only what was left and that was exceedingly thin. He had a most difficult program of great distances, almost impassable terrain, widespread disease and unfavorable climate, he faced an extremely difficult political problem, and his purely military program of opposing large numbers of the enemy with few resources was unmatched in any theater.
>
> Nevertheless General Stilwell sought with amazing vigor to carry out his mission exactly as it had been stated. His great efforts brought a natural conflict of personalities. He stood, as it were, the middleman between two great governments other than his own, with slender resources and problems somewhat overwhelming in their complexity. As a consequence it was deemed necessary in the fall of 1944 to relieve General Stilwell of the burden of his heavy responsibilities in Asia and give him a respite from attempting the impossible.[47]

Stilwell did not live to see all of Marshall's frustrations during the China mission. He might have reflected that the wartime Chief of

Staff saw confirmation of his charges of corruption and incapacity.

In later years, General Marshall insisted that he went to China at the end of 1945 uninfluenced by the treatment Stilwell had received in China. But it would have been too much for this man of long memory to divest his thoughts of the protracted struggle between Stilwell and the Generalissimo and to forget the continuous flow of charges from "Vinegar Joe" that Chiang Kai-shek had refused to dismiss dishonest, incompetent, time-serving subordinates. Marshall made no effort to avenge Stilwell, but neither could he forget what the Chinese had inflicted on the acidulous old fighter. Chiang Kai-shek, living out his years in Taiwan, looking across to the vast Chinese mainland, had many long and bitter days to think of Stilwell. He and Chennault, who justified their actions by recriminations against Stilwell, seemingly never wondered what might have been the course of their history had they accepted the Roosevelt-Marshall proposal in the fall of 1944 to give Stilwell effective control of the Chinese forces, with power to institute reforms.

IV

Problems Multiply in China

WEDEMEYER'S initial reports on China after succeeding Stilwell in October 1944 were favorable. He profited from Chiang Kai-shek's delight at being rid of Stilwell, his own clear knowledge of China's problems, and his accommodating nature.

General Hurley had predicted that if Stilwell were removed all would be well; General Wedemeyer discovered that it was not so simple as that. Within a month, he was reporting to Washington his own problems with the Chinese armed forces. Marshall found the complaints familiar: (1) the Chinese lacked unity of command; (2) Chiang's attempt to command all forces from Chungking eliminated any flexibility; (3) no coordination of operational plans existed; (4) leadership at the divisional level and above was mediocre; (5) equipment and food for troops were insufficient.[1]

The early reports mirrored Stilwell's fears of the deteriorating Chinese position in the face of Japanese advances. Wedemeyer reported the Chinese apathetic and the Generalissimo and his staff "impotent and confounded." The Chinese were "not organized, equipped and trained for modern war." Political intrigue, false pride, and mistrust of the motives and honesty of their leaders complicated the situation further. Chiang's generals hesitated to make accurate reports because they were afraid they would expose their stupidity and inefficiency and they were incompetent to plan operations, issue directives, or execute orders.[2]

"Vacillating" was Wedemeyer's term for Chiang's policy. He feared a successful Japanese advance against Chungking and Kunming but hoped for the best. The American believed that he had gained the Generalissimo's trust through his friendly, decent, and firm approach, but deplored "the influence and chicanery of his advisers, who have selfish, mercurial motives and who persuade him when I am not present to take action that conflicts with agreed plans." But Wedemeyer was continuing his efforts to "massage his ego and to place myself in an advisory position so that he will not lose face or feel that I am trying to coerce him in action not in consonance with sound military plans." The new commander had learned much from observing Stilwell's fate.

General Wedemeyer may have been much more tactful with Chiang Kai-shek than his predecessor, but his indictments to Marshall were equally severe. He described to his American chief Chinese generals who sought permission to visit Europe or the United States at a time when they were desperately needed to counter Japanese advances. He listed his efforts to improve the diet of Chinese soldiers, who had been reduced to starvation because of "graft" and a "terrifyingly inefficient" service of supply. The Generalissimo's acceptance of Wedemeyer's insistence that he refrain from commanding troops long-distance was violated almost at once. Chiang had failed to give him his best general for an important assignment and had held on to General Ho Ying-chin, a man loathed by Stilwell, who in Wedemeyer's words was a "suave, self-seeking individual, very rich and dissolute."[3]

In later years, General Wedemeyer was to criticize Marshall for his failure to back Chiang Kai-shek during the days of the China mission. But in 1944–45 he contributed decisively to convincing Marshall that Stilwell's portrayal of the Generalissimo and China's weaknesses was accurate.

General Wedemeyer also had reservations about Chennault and Hurley. Aware of General Marshall's disapproval of Alsop, he hastily parried Chennault's suggestion that he make that officer his aide. He wrote the Chief of Staff: "Knowing how you felt toward Alsop I told Chennault that I would think about it." (What he really told Chennault was that he could not accept Alsop because of the attitudes of certain people in Washington.) Knowing Marshall's reservations about Chennault, Wedemeyer added, "I believe that he is an outstanding fighter pilot, but it is my conviction that he is not a man of fine character."[4]

In January 1945, Wedemeyer reviewed for Marshall and the other Chiefs of Staff the strategic situation in his theater. He reported a view, long held by Marshall, that "it would be unsound for the United States to undertake extensive land campaigns on the Asiatic continent." Limited communications and unfavorable terrain made impracticable "the large-scale employment of modern land armies . . . in the interior of China." It was a conviction Marshall would repeat in 1946.[5]

As the war in the Far East neared its end, General Wedemeyer suggested to Marshall that there should be an American military mission to China, or, as the Generalissimo preferred, a U.S. Military Advisory Group. Such a headquarters would have Army, Navy, and Air Force groups with instructors, advisers, and technicians for the Chinese forces and a logistics group to ensure an efficient Chinese establishment for supply and the movement of military forces. The objective would be to organize modern military forces "capable of coping with any situation that may confront China." The Generalissimo wanted such a group to remain in China for at least five years.[6]

Wedemeyer had been mentioned for the post of chief of the mission but he preferred not to be considered, noting reluctance to be away from his elderly mother for an extended period, his health (sinusitis), the jealousy some of the Chinese felt about his control over the Generalissimo, and the fact that he would be drawn into the Chinese political confusion.

He feared the spread of Communism in the Far East. In passing, he noted that the British were merely paying lip service to the ideas of democracy and unification in China. He was not optimistic about China's gains from the recently concluded thirty-year pact between the Soviet Union and China. Stalin, while avoiding force in dealing with China, had created conditions favorable for "peaceful" or "surreptitious" penetration of communistic ideologies. "The Sino-Soviet pact will not militate against his plan for extension of Communism in the Far East."

He noted that throughout the war the United States had favored the National Government of China and that recent instructions had indicated such backing would continue. Mao Tse-tung, currently in Chungking, had remonstrated with Wedemeyer on this continued support of the Nationalists, charging that U.S. forces and materiel "are being employed to facilitate Central Government plans against Chinese Communist forces." Wedemeyer and his advisers worried that the redistribution of Nationalist forces, designed to prepare for orderly repatriation and deportation of 10 million enemy troops, would precipitate civil war.

Dismayed at the tangled situation confronting him, Wedemeyer asked Marshall for a clear and concise statement on American policy in the Far East so that at the end of the conflict he could avoid the confusion that existed in Europe in the closing days of the war there.

The Joint Chiefs of Staff complied with Wedemeyer's request for a new directive on August 10, 1945, the day the Japanese asked for terms. Retained were parts of the earlier directive of October 24, 1944, which said that his mission was to aid Chinese air and ground forces by training, operations, and logistical support, and to assist operations against the Japanese. He was not to use United States resources to suppress civil strife except where necessary to protect American life and property. Previous provisions of the first directive were to apply "only in so far as action in accordance therewith does not prejudice the basic U.S. principle that the United States will not support the Central Government of China in a fratricidal war." U.S. ground forces were not to be involved in a major land campaign in any part of the China Theater.

If the Japanese continued to fight, he was to aid the Chinese in their efforts to disarm them. If they capitulated, he was to assist the Chinese Nationalists to reoccupy areas in the China Theater now held by the Japanese and place Chinese occupation forces in Japan, Formosa, and Korea. Areas liberated by American forces were to be turned over to the National Government. He was to aid the National Government in the rapid transport of its forces to key areas in China.[7]

Wedemeyer felt that the directive did not clarify his problems. He warned Marshall that since many areas in North China had been marked by the Chinese Communists for takeover, any effort by U.S. forces to occupy these areas and turn them over to the Nationalists would be interpreted as blocking Chinese Communist operations.

He saw his fears turned into realities when U.S. Marines were ordered into North China to expedite evacuation of the Japanese from the area. They were soon in control of Peiping, Tientsin, Chinwangtao, and Tsingtao, controlling the railroads from Peiping to the sea. The Chinese Communists who wanted to get the arms of the Japanese in the North protested vigorously against the Marine presence. While Marshall was asking Wedemeyer about the situation, he received from the State Department a report by Walter Robertson, U.S. Chargé in China, that the Communists were trying to prevent National troop trains from reaching North China or Manchuria. Robertson commented, "Obviously for Communists to desist from exploiting their advantages of position would be military suicide." He added, "Because of increasing reluctance of either party to compromise its military position by making concessions in any area, it appears at present almost hopeless that any permanent satisfactory solution can be reached."[8]

Trying to push any advantage he might have, Chiang Kai-shek

urged General Wedemeyer to expand his activities. He also asked
that U.S. forces land Chinese troops at Tangku (near the Communists) rather than at remoter Tsingtao to the east. In notifying
Marshall of Chiang's requests, Wedemeyer recalled that he had
recommended withdrawal of the Marines from China by mid-
November because the Nationalists would be in a position to take
over. Any additional Nationalist forces would undoubtedly be used
against the Communists, which would be contrary to his directive.[9]
Wanting to make his statement a matter of record, Wedemeyer
asked that his message be acknowledged and his decision
confirmed. In discussion on the following day by representatives of
the State, War, and Navy departments, Byrnes was cautious about
further committal of U.S. troops, but Assistant Secretary of War
McCloy feared that the chaos that might follow American departure
would be used by the Soviets as an excuse for keeping troops in
China.[10]

Their discussion of the situation led members of the War Department Operations Division to pass on to Wedemeyer their view that,
whereas their initial intent was merely to disarm the Japanese and
send them out of China, their new purpose was to ensure the
National Government's control of the areas in the North. The Joint
Chiefs of Staff instructed Wedemeyer on November 9 not to deactivate his theater until the U.S. Advisory Group took over, and not
to remove the Marines pending a State Department final decision.[11]

This shift in his favor was not enough to satisfy Chiang Kai-shek.
He assumed that the United States was completely committed to his
cause and asked Wedemeyer to use U.S. planes and personnel to
move Chinese troops into Manchuria. When he told Marshall of
this request, Wedemeyer said that he understood the reoccupation
of Manchuria was a matter to be decided by China and the Soviet
Union according to agreements reached earlier by T. V. Soong and
Stalin. The Russians had indicated that they would be out of that
area by the end of November 1945. He asked that his policy of
refusing U.S. troops for this purpose be confirmed.[12]

Wedemeyer radioed Marshall on November 14 that Communist
strategy was intended to arouse Chinese and American public opinion against retaining U.S. armed forces in China. Unfortunately,
Nationalist actions were playing into their hands. "Inept and corrupt administration of Kuomintang officials newly arrived in North
China is gaining support for the Communists." The Russians were
now creating favorable conditions for the Communists to take over
key areas in North China and blocking the Nationalists from recovering the area. Unstated but heavily latent in his message was the

theme that had been quietly visible in earlier messages for several weeks: U.S. forces should intervene decisively on the side of the National Government in North China.[13]

The likelihood of U.S. intervention increased as Chiang Kai-shek's position weakened. Chinese Communist strength joined with Russian support reduced the National Government's ability to clear North China and Manchuria. The U.S. military, committed only to clearance of the area and repatriation of the Japanese, now faced broader responsibilities. The Joint Chiefs of Staff planners concluded that the limited directive of August 10 was no longer broad enough. They believed that the Japanese-occupied areas should be secured by Nationalist forces and not "usurped" by the Chinese Communists. As a result, the Pentagon asked Secretary Byrnes to review the matter from a political standpoint before they issued a final directive.

The Joint Chiefs feared that if civil strife had not ended in North China and Manchuria by the time the U.S. forces withdrew, outside forces, obviously the Soviets, would intervene. The recent Sino-Soviet treaty had recognized the special interests of the Soviet Union in Manchuria, and the Russians might decide they must restore order. If not, the National Government might use Japanese forces still in China to oppose Communists. In either of these events, the Joint Chiefs believed that the United States would be failing to capitalize upon the advantages gained in China during the war, at the expense of huge amounts of American money, resources, and manpower.

Alarmed by recent developments, such as sending a large U.S. Advisory Group to China, John Carter Vincent, chief of the Far Eastern Division of the State Department, asked "whether we are not moving toward the establishment of a relationship with China which has some characteristics of a *de facto* protectorate with a semi-colonial Chinese Army under our direction?" A decision to send an advisory group should depend on whether it would increase the security of the United States. There should also be a reasonable assurance that such a group would encourage a unified and democratic China rather than a development along military lines. Congress should be informed of these suggestions, since it would have to provide authorization once emergency powers lapsed.[14]

Vincent's warning emphasized the divergence between old China hands of the State Department and many of the military leaders involved with Far Eastern affairs. Chiang and his supporters in Washington had already criticized Foreign Service personnel unfriendly to the National Government. Lieutenant General Stanley D. Embick—Marshall's representative on the long-range strategy committee of the Pentagon, and father-in-law of General Wedemeyer—reflected the latter point of view in November when he warned War Department planners working on the new directive that "that Communist" Vincent was causing trouble in China.[15]

General Hurley was also growing critical of State Department experts on China. In November, while in Washington for conferences with the President and the Secretary of State, he told Byrnes that his efforts to carry out President Roosevelt's directive to aid Chiang had been undercut by Foreign Service personnel in China. Some of these officers had been recalled at his demand but were now in important positions in the Far Eastern Division or assigned to key positions at MacArthur's headquarters in Tokyo. Byrnes declared the charges untrue.[16]

Whether Hurley was stirred to anger by Byrnes's dismissal of his complaints, whether he was prompted by Washington supporters of Chiang to make a dramatic protest, or whether long-suppressed anger suddenly boiled, he announced his resignation on November 27 to a group of newspapermen after castigating the State Department and the administration. Truman, who had concluded what he thought was an amiable conversation with Hurley two hours earlier, received the news at his weekly luncheon with the Cabinet. Secretary of Agriculture Clinton Anderson, former representative from New Mexico, suggested that Truman head off political criticism by naming Marshall to head a mission to China. It was Anderson's proposal that led Truman to telephone Marshall at Leesburg the same afternoon, recalling the General to active duty.[17]

Before Hurley's resignation the secretaries of War and the Navy had notified Byrnes that they would outline the Pentagon views on the Chinese problem. Not long afterward, some Operations Division members, including General John E. Hull, Colonel G. A. Lincoln, and Colonel Trevor Dupuy, informed Wedemeyer that a new directive was being prepared. This draft was amended by Marshall after his China mission appointment and sent off at the month's end. Marshall had placed the word "probably" in the statement that Wedemeyer would *probably* be responsible for making necessary arrangements to repatriate the Japanese from the China Theater, with the United States giving assistance in the form of military supplies and advice to the Chinese. The United States Marines would *probably* remain in North China for the moment to aid in repatriating Japanese nationals. Marshall also added a sentence that the Marines would be more or less restricted to holding ports and beachheads.

Even as this draft went out, officials at the White House, the State Department, and the Pentagon worked on a broader directive for General Marshall as head of the China mission. An extended role for Wedemeyer was also outlined.[18]

The later directive reflected sharp exchanges between the State Department and the Pentagon on questions raised by General Wedemeyer. His proposals for future relations with China led the Joint Chiefs of Staff planners to suggest a U.S. Advisory Group and a United States assistance program for China. This proposal was under consideration when General Wedemeyer announced that it would be possible to commence withdrawal of U.S. Marines from China by mid-November and to deactivate the China Theater on January 1, 1946, by which time all U.S. forces could be withdrawn. His later statements show that he did not favor this action. The Joint Chiefs of Staff reflected that he must have spoken thus because of the restrictions of the old directive, under which he was then working: an insistence on following that directive to the letter was undoubtedly the best way to get it changed.

Responding to Washington queries, Wedemeyer analyzed the situation in China as he saw it then. He believed Chiang Kai-shek sincere in his desire to bring stability, initiate democratic procedures, unify China, and implement sweeping social reforms. But he balanced this judgment with qualifications about Chiang's leadership that had been voiced earlier by Stilwell and other observers of the China scene:

> Considering his background, training, and experience as warlord, politician, and his oriental philosophy, his approach to problems presented would probably be inefficient, incomprehensible and unethical by American standards. . . . He lacks not only the organization but also competent advisers and assistants. The Generalissimo is selfless in his approach to the problem presented, however, he is surrounded by unscrupulous men who are interested primarily in their self-aggrandizement. The Generalissimo is extremely loyal to those warlords and officials who have supported him in the past. Consequently, even though they are unscrupulous and/or incompetent, he appoints them to responsible positions in the Government. They exploit the opportunities presented. Further they appoint worthless subordinates to lesser positions. Many are members of the same families or have connived at chicanery in the past.[19]

Still, he thought Chiang could stabilize the situation in South China if he accepted the aid of foreign administrators, inaugurated wide reforms, and used honest and competent officials. To stabilize North China would require an agreement with the Chinese Communists. The Manchurian question could not be settled without agreement with the Chinese Communists and the Russians.

Wedemeyer followed this analysis with a reply to the new Chief of Staff, General Eisenhower, who had written him on November 20 asking for more information about the China Theater. Wedemeyer restated the dilemma facing the United States: American aid was necessary to clear the Japanese from the northern area, but continued U.S. presence would involve us in civil war. He was at last ready to state exactly what he thought was needed. The State Department "must in my opinion assume full responsibility for the acts of the armed forces faithfully employed in the implementation of United States policies. . . ." More important:

> If the unification of China and Manchuria under Chinese National Forces is to be a United States policy, involvement in fratricidal warfare and possibly in war with the Soviet Union must be accepted and would definitely require additional United States forces far beyond those presently available in the theater to implement the policy. [20] [Emphasis supplied.]

This was the tough course that a close observer of the China situation believed essential. It would have required U.S. assumption of the chief responsibility for the Nationalist cause and a preparation to enforce a military solution, based on American interests, even if it meant the United States would be back at war. It was clearcut, although difficult if not impossible to implement at that time. However divided policymakers were as to what to do about China, there was little inclination in Washington to take so bold a line. Marshall, with his long opposition to involving United States forces in Asian land warfare, was never willing to accept it.

Secretary of War Robert Patterson and Secretary of the Navy James Forrestal reacted forcefully to the various statements. They said that Wedemeyer's estimate that Nationalist China's control of North China and Manchuria was remote "should not be accepted as a basis for United States action without the most serious considerations and further exploration. . . ." This was particularly true given that wartime U.S. policy had favored a unified China, including Manchuria, and the return of Japanese-held areas to the Chinese. Wedemeyer's earlier statement, they suggested, had been affected by the limitations of his directive, and his reactions might have been different with more definite policy guidance.[21]

The two secretaries believed that only the National Government had a chance of unifying China, including Manchuria, in the near future. But they thought this solution depended on political rather than military factors. "Soviet policy, as far as known, does not appear to oppose at this time this unification." From a short-range view, U.S. objectives in the Far East had been largely achieved. From a long-range view, "the most important military element in the Far East favorable to the United States is a unified China, including Manchuria, friendly to the United States. This is the best assurance against turmoil and outbreak of war in the Far East. . . ."

They concluded that the Joint Chiefs of Staff should amend Wedemeyer's directive to continue his forces in North China and to aid the Chinese in repatriation of the Japanese there, with the knowledge that such action "will probably involve at least incidental aid to the National Government in the controversy with the Communists." They suggested that the State Department provide a definitive policy that would cover the next five years in China. After consulting with the Chinese, the United States should seriously consider approaching the other great powers, especially the U.S.S.R., with a view toward handling problems such as that of Manchuria by political means, rather than depending on U.S. unilateral military action.[22]

The changed directive requested by General Wedemeyer was intended to strengthen the hand of the military commander in the China Theater. Before it was completed, its framers at the State Department, the Pentagon, and the White House had to consider a somewhat different directive for Marshall's mission. In some cases these directives represented two points of view; in others they overlapped. But they contained two different aims and show the contradictions that made the success of the mission ultimately impossible. In a sense they pointed up the dichotomy in the Truman Administration's approach to the China problem. In late November General Wedemeyer had reached a "fish or cut bait" stage in proposing expanded aid to Chiang Kai-shek, even if that meant clashes with the Communists and possible trouble with the Soviet Union or total withdrawal of U.S. troops. The State Department wanted a diplomatic approach with a negotiated truce under American pressure between the Generalissimo and the Chinese Communists. Professor Tang Tsou in his able study of this period recalls that the United States, with all its good will for China, had never favored armed confrontation in the Far East to defend China.

Thus the Hoover and Roosevelt administrations were willing to join the League of Nations in objecting to Japan's encroachments on China in the 1930s, but not to intervene militarily. After the Japanese attack on Pearl Harbor, the United States would provide credits and technical advice, but not commit major ground forces to fight in China.

Discussing policy with representatives of the War and Navy departments, Byrnes stressed the point that was to be crucial in the directive for the Marshall mission. He said, "Perhaps the wise course would be to try to force the Chinese Government and the Chinese Communists to get together on a compromise basis, perhaps telling Generalissimo Chiang Kai-shek that we will stop the aid to his government unless he goes along with this." It might be well, he thought, to tell the Russians of these views in an effort to line them up with this policy. Patterson felt it would clearly be in American interests to see China united under Chiang Kai-shek.[23]

As the State, War, and Navy departments set about drafting a course of action for General Marshall, they agreed that a unified China—and, more, a stable China—was essential to the best interests of the United States. But there was no agreement about a greatly increased military effort to achieve these aims under the National Government. The political approach included possible appeals to the Soviet Union or the United Nations, but this approach seemed to focus on an American effort to pressure the warring factions to make peace.[24] This was the method, already suggested by Byrnes, that gained ground as the terms of Marshall's directive were set down. Hovering over these efforts was the past history of the National Government and the doubt that the Generalissimo's ramshackle apparatus, with some United States aid, could unify China. The United States armed forces were rapidly demobilizing and the country was ready to resume peacetime production and return to normal business. There was no American mind-set, no disposition, to take the major responsibility for furnishing all the guidance and control and supplies and additional troops that would be necessary to bring into existence the precise type of stable China that the United States wanted.

Near the end of November, Secretary Byrnes read to General Marshall the draft of a directive that the General concluded Byrnes was seeing for the first time. Marshall thought it not sufficiently plain to be understood by the public and "susceptible of serious misunderstanding." An old hand at editing papers, he asked Byrnes if he could try his hand at a redraft. But his heavy duties in testifying at great length before the Joint Congressional Pearl Har-

bor Inquiry claimed most of his time before his departure for
China. He turned to his wartime aides in the War Department, and
they worked to ensure that the "Old Man" was protected when he
set off on what they feared was a losing cause.[25]

Generals Handy, Hull, and Craig, Colonel Lincoln, and others
who had long served Marshall when he was Chief of Staff tried a
stint of drafting. "We did not have much confidence in the possibility of the success of the Mission," General Hull later recalled, "and
wanted to make sure that the General's instructions were plainly
stated."[26]

Describing their work to Admiral Leahy, Marshall said they had
tried not only to make the language plain, but to make it state
clearly to Chiang Kai-shek what the United States would make
available and "at the same time be couched in such manner that we
could hold him to action in other matters more purely political."[27]

Speaking of Wedemeyer's problems, Marshall said that he did
not think that the United States Marines should be scattered
around China, "but on the other hand, I feel we must hold them
in certain ports to protect our beachheads." This arrangement
would allow the Generalissimo to release Chinese troops guarding
the ports and use them to protect the railroads.

Marshall at this stage was not sanguine about Chinese Communist cooperation. He assumed that "the Communist group will
block all progress in negotiations as far as they can, as the delay is
to their advantage." He was also doubtful whether the drafters of
directives could boil down all the conflicting views about China into
a plain statement of American views. He feared they would find
themselves on the horns of a dilemma—"on the one side the reluctance of the Government or the State Department to make so plain
and bold a statement; and on the other side, the necessity of saying
what we mean so that people at home and the people in China, and
the Russians also, will clearly understand our intentions."[28]

Byrnes, who had already tried his hand with the Senate Foreign
Relations Committee, outlined to Marshall on December 9 the view
that it was necessary to bring the Chinese Communists, other dissident groups, and the Nationalists into a unified government. If not,
the Russians would likely take over North China and Manchuria.
Byrnes thought that Marshall should go to China "with sufficient
weapons in his hands to induce the Central Government and the
Communist Government to get together."

At this point Marshall sought clarification. What if the National
Government refused to give ground after the Communists had
agreed to concessions that would appear acceptable? In that case,

said Byrnes, the National Government should be informed "that the assistance which we could otherwise give to China would not be given, such as loans, supplies, military and civilian, establishment of military advisory groups, etc., that we would be forced to deal directly with the Communists in so far as the evacuation of the Japanese from North China was concerned." When Marshall asked what if the Communists failed to make concessions, he was told that "in such case our full support would be given the National Government and we would move its armies into North China as required."[29]

On the afternoon of December 11, Marshall reviewed United States policy toward China with the President, Secretary Byrnes, and Admiral Leahy. Mr. Truman emphasized his desire for a complete understanding of the basis on which Marshall was to operate in China. Byrnes disclosed that the Army and Navy were empowered to move Chiang Kai-shek's armies to Manchuria and support them and to evacuate the Japanese troops from China. In secret, the services were authorized to arrange shipping for the movement of troops to North China. Secrecy on these points, noted Byrnes, was intended to enable Marshall to use pressure on both sides to come to agreement. President Truman gave his full backing to Marshall, declaring he would support his efforts "whatever they might be to bring about the desired results."[30]

Summarizing what he had been told, Marshall said that he understood that "he would do his best to influence the Generalissimo to make reasonable concessions in his negotiations with the democratic and communist leaders, holding in abeyance the information that this Government was actually preparing shipping to assist the Generalissimo in moving his troops into North China for the purpose of releasing the Japanese in that region and, incidentally, taking over control of the railroads." He understood that he was to use the same vagueness "to bring the Communist leaders to the point of making reasonable concessions in order to bring about desirable political unification."[31]

Thus was outlined a Machiavellian approach to both sides, calculated to bring pressure on the two main groups—a recognition that otherwise there would be no agreement. It was quite clear that the General was going not merely as an honest broker but as a tough persuader who could promise the carrot or the stick to the negotiating parties. This position gave the General great power but also meant the likelihood of great failure.

Marshall then asked the hard question: if the Generalissimo failed to make reasonable concessions and brought on a breakdown of negotiations leading to a divided China and possible Russian control in Manchuria, should Marshall still help Chiang Kai-shek in sending troops to North China? "This would mean," he noted, "that this Government would have to swallow its pride and much of its policy in doing so."

Despite their earlier suggestion that Marshall would be left all weapons needed to force agreement, the President and the Secretary decided that under the circumstances mentioned the United States would have to aid the Generalissimo to the extent of moving government troops to North China to evacuate the Japanese from that area. This reaction, which historian Tang Tsou declares the Generalissimo continued to bank on, treating Marshall's veiled suggestions merely as ploys, was to strengthen Chiang Kai-shek's recalcitrance. Truman and Byrnes seemed in accord with General Wedemeyer's recommendations and earlier Army-Navy views but they made clear to Marshall that no United States divisions would be sent to China.

Marshall was now aware that his instructions would include a letter from the President stating U.S. policy toward China, Secretary Byrnes's memorandum to the War Department on the Army's role, and a public statement by the President. The main outlines were those of the State Department, with fewer concessions to Chiang Kai-shek than the War Department was willing to make. In that sense, Marshall was right in saying later that he had not written his directive. Although there are some editorial changes in his handwriting in the War Department draft and indications that his Army staff advisers had revised some of the State Department views, the tone of the directives—"inducing" the Generalissimo to cooperate—was a concept of State's that had been accepted by Truman and Byrnes. General Hull recalled that Marshall did not press the views of the military advisers on the State Department.[32]

Marshall displayed in this instance his shift from a purely military view to the soldier-statesman position he was to maintain in his later talks. As Army Chief of Staff he upheld Pentagon views. Once committed to a new role, in which he represented the President and had his directive through the Secretary of State, he listened to both sides. But as to risking major military involvement in China to uphold Chiang Kai-shek against all odds, neither he nor Byrnes nor the President was prepared, a few months after a long war's end. Demobilization was rapidly proceeding under congressional and public pressure for an even faster return home of "our boys." To adopt the proposal, which was backed by a number of officers in the Pentagon and by some State Department officials, was likely to mean U.S. participation in widespread conflict in the Far East.

Marshall met with President Truman and Under Secretary of State Dean Acheson on Friday, December 14, and the President handed him his letter of instruction, asking if it was satisfactory. "I replied in the affirmative," wrote Marshall. "The President stated that if I desired a directive from him in any other form for me to prepare it and he would sign it, [and] that he wished to back me in every way possible." Marshall added that he understood one point latent in the directive: that if he could not secure action by the Generalissimo "which I thought reasonable and desirable, it would still be necessary for the U.S. Government, through me, to back the National Government of the Republic of China—through the Generalissimo—within the terms of the announced policy of the U.S. Government."[33]

Enclosed with the letter Truman gave Marshall on December 14, dated the following day, were the guidelines for his mission. The U.S. government judged it essential that

a cessation of hostilities be arranged between the armies of the National Government and the Chinese Communists and other dissident Chinese armed forces for the purpose of completing the return of all China to effective Chinese control, including the immediate evacuation of the Japanese forces.

It asked that a conference of all "major political elements be arranged to develop an early solution to the present internal strife which will bring about the unification of China."[34]

The United States, the directive continued, had recognized the National Government as the only legal government in China. The Cairo Declaration of 1943, the Potsdam Declaration, in which the Soviet Union joined in July 1945, and the Sino-Soviet agreement of August 1945 were all committed to the liberation of China and the return of Manchuria to China.

To remove Japanese forces remaining in China, the United States had assumed an obligation to disarm and evacuate Japanese troops. As a result, the United States was assisting and would continue to assist the Nationalists in carrying out this objective. The United States would also continue transport of Chinese troops so that the National Government could regain control of the liberated portions of China, including Manchuria. Deliberately omitted from press releases was the statement to which the War Department had objected: that the Nationalist troops would not be transported to areas such as North China if that would prejudice the truce and political negotiations.

The United States would continue to recognize the National Government and cooperate with it—specifically in removing Japanese influences. But the United States was convinced that everything was subject to prompt cessation of hostilities. The United States would not extend its support to "military intervention to influence the course of any Chinese internal strife."

The United States was aware that the current government was one-party in nature but thought that "peace, unity and democratic reform" would be furthered by a broadened base of the National Government. The existence of autonomous armies, the warning ran, made political unity impossible. "With the institution of a broadly representative government, autonomous armies should be eliminated as such and all armed forces in China integrated effectively into the Chinese National Army."

The United States wanted China to work out its own national unity but felt it had a clear responsibility "to the other United Nations to eliminate armed conflict within its territory. . . ." For this purpose the United States was willing to participate and to invite the United Kingdom and the U.S.S.R. to aid in bringing pledges to assure prompt cessation of hostilities. Held out as a carrot was a vision of "economic and financial aid and advisers for the military."[35]

Marshall asked that Under Secretary Acheson be charged with handling contacts with his mission. He also required a uniformed liaison officer with the War Department to handle Pentagon communications for transmitting messages. Acheson selected Colonel James C. Davis for this assignment. Davis was an attorney in civilian life and headed the Supply and Economic Branch, Civil Affairs Division, War Department, under Major General John H. Hilldring. Acheson had to explain to Marshall that Hilldring did not want to lose his assistant. Marshall knew Hilldring, who had served under him as director of personnel and then as head of civil affairs. Acheson recalled the resulting telephone conversation as somewhat like this: " 'Hilldring? General Marshall speaking. Do you have a Colonel James Davis? Very well. Have him detached and assigned to duty with Acheson at the State Department.' A dull crackling came from the receiver. 'Did you say something, Hilldring? Tomorrow morning will do.' "[36]

Davis had been previously told by Hilldring that he could leave the Army in August 1945, but he had stayed on to finish certain projects on which he was working. When he complained to Marshall that he had spent nearly five years in the service and needed to get back to his family and his law practice, Marshall smiled and replied, "You know, Colonel, I had rather a difficult war too." Then he agreed that if Davis would organize the rear echelon in Washington, staff it, and stay three months to select and train a suitable successor, he would release him. To Davis's question when he proposed to leave, Marshall said at nine the following morning. When Davis then asked, "General, can you tell me just what it is you want me to do in maintaining governmental coordination?" Marshall answered, "Colonel, if you don't know, I've got the wrong man."[37]

The next day General Hull of the Operations Division described to Colonel Davis Marshall's methods of operation:

His system . . . whenever there is something that is tough and difficult is to put some chap directly on that thing and ride herd on it, that is the way he functions and that is what he has in mind. . . . Whether you understand it or not . . . throughout the War Department at different times there have been things somewhat smelled up. He has picked some man to straighten it out. He has always used that man to cut across command channels or anything else. Of course he always works along with the machinery, utilizing the machinery in existence but he rides herd on it. And that is what he has in mind I think so far as you are concerned. You act as sort of a [coordinator] and iron out all these things and you know from your own experience in the War Department that we have the machinery to implement anything that is our business.[38]

A few days later (Truman's letter is dated December 18), Colonel Davis had as one of his first tasks the distribution of Truman's presidential statement that spelled out Marshall's broad powers.

In order that General Marshall's Mission may not be prejudiced in any way, I desire that all conversations with Chinese officials regarding extension of American economic or financial aid to China, in which officers of your organization may be participating, be suspended, and that for the time being no member of your staff engage in conversations with Chinese officials, which might encourage the Chinese to hope that this Government is contemplating the extension of any type of assistance to China, except in accordance with the recommendations of General Marshall.[39]

Impressed by the letter and by Mr. Truman's earlier statements to Marshall on this point, Colonel Davis notified staff advisers of Secretary of the Treasury Fred Vinson that a loan of $500 million that Vinson wanted to offer Nationalist China could not be made at that time. Vinson promptly called the young lawyer to his office and said that the loan was going to be made and there was nothing Davis could do to stop it. Davis said that he was acting in accordance with Mr. Truman's advice to Marshall that all such matters had to be cleared through him and that if he (Vinson) insisted, Davis's instructions were to take the matter to the President for decision. When Vinson asked why the loan was improper, he replied, "The General does not approve it."[40]

The only trouble, Davis said later, was that Marshall did not know anything about it. However, in accordance with daily practice, Davis told Marshall what he had done. No comment came from China. On Marshall's return to Washington in the spring of 1946, Vinson asked to see him. The General took Davis with him to the Treasury, where Vinson had with him Under Secretary of State Acheson, Secretary of Commerce Henry Wallace, and others. When Vinson asked Marshall's views on the loan, the General replied, "Colonel Davis will give you my views." Vinson indicated that he had had enough of Davis's views, but Marshall insisted that Davis speak for him. At the conclusion, Vinson asked if these were Marshall's views and the latter agreed. This terminated the discussion. On his way back to their office, Marshall said, "Well, Colonel, I guess that ought to settle the matter with Secretary Vinson." Davis expressed concern over this and other matters on which he had acted without orders. Laconically, Marshall replied, "I never complained, did I?" That ended the conversation. "I learned," wrote Davis later, "the extent to which General Marshall was willing to go to support his subordinates in the exercise of responsibility which he assigned to them."[41]

As Military Attaché, Marshall chose Colonel Henry Byroade, a native of Indiana and a West Pointer, with a master's degree in engineering from Cornell, who had served forty months in China before coming to the Operations Division in the Pentagon. He had been a member of a special mission to the Far East shortly after Pearl Harbor, when it was thought that a future attack on Japan would be made from the south. The group ended up ultimately in Karachi, where General Lewis Brereton took from them their sorely needed bombers but told them to start working on an air lift to China. Byroade was instructed to prepare airfields for the operation. He became head of supply for the eastern third of China and got acquainted with both Stilwell and Chennault, learning at first hand many of China's problems and facets of the "China Tangle."[42]

When Marshall asked Byroade if he would like to return to China, Byroade said he hoped it would not be for too long a time; Marshall replied that it would not, and that seemed to settle matters. Byroade later recalled:

> And he told me . . . to get him to China, with the best possible instructions from the President. I was a litle stunned by this—it was all so unexpected. I went down to my desk and made a list of about forty questions which I thought I should ask him. I remember the first thing on the list was, did he want to go East or West? . . . Well, I asked him that question and he said, "Which way should I go?" and I said, "West," and I asked him the next couple of questions and he said, "What to you think I should do?" and with that I just stopped my list. He had given me a job to do and there wasn't any point in worrying him about the details.[43]

China Passage

P A R T of Marshall's time on the long flight to China was spent in reviewing a summary of the Chinese political situation as prepared by James Shepley from material furnished by the State Department and the Pentagon. Captain James Shepley, formerly a *Time* correspondent in the CBI, Southwest Pacific, and European theaters, had so impressed Marshall with his coverage of the Ardennes fighting that Marshall had him commissioned in early 1945. At the end of the war Shepley was assigned to write much of the Chief of Staff's final report to the Secretary of War. Marshall asked special permission from *Time* publisher Henry Luce to take Shepley with him on the early part of his China Mission and used him not only as a press secretary but as a staff member to prepare briefing notes for the mission.[1] Of particular interest to the General were details pertinent to efforts at bringing the warring Communist and Nationalist factions into agreement.

When almost all Chinese factions determined that defeat of the Japanese was of prime necessity after the kidnapping of Chiang Kai-shek in 1936, logical strategy indicated gathering all non-Kuomintang groups into some kind of coalition with the National Government. The existing Kuomintang had little interest in sharing its power and few changes were made. On the last day of 1944, however, Chiang Kai-shek proposed to call a National Assembly meeting to discuss changes in the following year. A week later a Kuomintang committee proposed a special conference on May 6, 1945, to discuss the establishment of constitutional government in China. Ambassador Patrick J. Hurley, anxiously trying to carry out President Roosevelt's directive to bring together the warring factions, persuaded Mao Tse-tung, chairman of the Chinese Communist Party, to send his deputy, Chou En-lai, to Chungking to discuss plans for a coalition government. This effort failed when the Kuomintang made clear in March that it would not give up its power to rule until a National Assembly was convened to draw up a constitution.

After the Japanese defeat in August 1945, the Generalissimo invited Mao Tse-tung to Chungking to discuss the changed situation. The Communist leader made no reply, but his military commander, Chu Teh, demanded that the Communists be authorized to accept the surrender of the Japanese forces in North China. In refusing this request, Chiang repeated his invitation to Mao. Upon reflection, the Communist Chairman agreed to send Chou En-lai for a meeting and then, under Hurley's pressure, agreed to come himself. Meanwhile, the Democratic League demanded the election of representatives to the National Assembly after existing election laws were changed to give proportional representation to all factions. A week later, the Communists submitted a package of requirements that asked for a coalition government, their right to accept Japanese surrender in North China, and new elections for the National Assembly.

Mao Tse-tung's decision to come to Chungking may have been influenced by the announcement of the Sino-Soviet Treaty in mid-August 1945, in which Stalin appeared to favor the Nationalists over the Chinese Communists. His decision was a fine gesture but his desire to benefit from the vacuum left by the Japanese defeat made any meaningful cooperation doubtful.

Chiang was already complaining of Communist General Chu Teh's efforts to prevent the Nationalist forces from taking over the northeastern provinces of China from the Japanese. He charged him with ordering the capture or destruction of rail lines in North and South China and the coordination of his forces with those of the Soviet Army "in order to be able to carry on war in both China and south Korea."[2]

All of this seemed to spell trouble for the Marshall mission. Most disturbing was the possibility that the new constitution would be written by the Kuomintang. "The constitution proposed," wrote Shepley, "provided nothing more than what charitably could be called a constitutional dictatorship."

From the summary, it is clear that the first move toward a coalition had been taken long before Marshall was named to his mission. Hurley favored it and had persuaded Mao to come to Chungking for discussions. In directing Marshall to press for a coalition, Truman and Byrnes were not imposing a foreign concept on the Chinese, but supporting a policy set in motion by Chiang Kai-shek at the end of 1944.

With his small staff, Marshall arrived in Shanghai on December 20, after brief stops in California and Hawaii and refueling stops across the rest of the Pacific. The Generalissimo arranged for an honor guard to join General Wedemeyer, commanding general of the China Theater, and Walter Robertson, Chargé of the U.S. Embassy in China, in meeting his plane.

General Wedemeyer, whose book *Wedemeyer Reports!* contains one of the strongest indictments of the failure of the Marshall mission, declares that on the first day and evening Marshall started off on the wrong foot. Possibly tired from the burdens of the war and even more so from his trip, the General refused to accept Wedemeyer's statements that there was no possibility of bringing about a coalition between the Nationalists and the Chinese Communists. Wedemeyer suggests that Marshall's wartime position of power made him positive that he could achieve success in his mission and that he thundered that Wedemeyer must assist him in fulfilling his mission.[3]

A somewhat different impression was recorded by Walter Robertson, who sat in on the evening discussions. He recalled that Wedemeyer briefed Marshall on the military situation, then Robertson on the political scene. They both said that there was no basis for a coalition between the factions—the Nationalists wanted to stay in power and the Communists wanted to get in. He added:

> ... my own impression of that interview [was that] Marshall listened very carefully to what we had to say. How he evaluated it, he didn't say. He asked questions. We discussed it. I had the very distinct impression that he had been given a directive ... which at least the policymakers in Washington thought was possible of achievement. Neither Wedemeyer nor I thought it was possible of achievement.[4]

Marshall's normal practice when beginning a new job did not include a rough confrontation. Whatever the nature of this discussion, he was grateful to Wedemeyer for suggesting personnel to aid him and he was intent on keeping Robertson at the Embassy.

Robertson, a courtly Virginian, was an investment banker in Richmond at the beginning of World War II, and had served as head of the U.S. Lend-Lease mission to Australia in 1943–44. On returning to Washington for a time in 1945 as economic adviser to the State Department, he was asked by the new Secretary of State,

Edward Stettinius, Jr., to go next to one of the embassies. He was
groomed for the Hague, but when Ambassador Hurley asked Stettinius for someone to be Minister or Counselor of Economic Affairs
at the Embassy in China, Robertson was selected. In September
1945, when Hurley returned to Washington, Robertson became
Chargé d'Affaires and was at the Embassy when Marshall arrived.

The Virginian had not met Marshall before. The war was now
over and he wanted to return home. He told Marshall that he had
resigned twice before he knew the General was coming and was
using all the influence he had to return to his home and family.
"And he looked at me," recalled Robertson, "and he said, 'I want
to go home too.' And he told me how at the end of six years as Chief
of Staff, he had been asked to go to China. He smiled, handed [a
message] to an orderly, and continued to talk about the mission,
and that's the way I happened to be in China until late 1946 after
I had resigned in September 1945."[5]

On December 21, Marshall flew to Nanking for his official reception by the head of the Chinese government. In the late evening he
talked with the Generalissimo, Madame Chiang, Foreign Minister
Dr. Wang Shih-chieh, Wedemeyer, and Robertson. The meeting,
reported Wedemeyer in his notes, was remarkable for the defer-
ence Marshall showed Chiang Kai-shek.

Marshall spoke of America's warm feeling for China and its reluctance to interfere in the local affairs of another country. But the
U.S. government would hesitate to keep American troops and ships
and planes in the Far East unless there was a definite move toward
peace. The President's power to aid in China's reconstruction
would be favorably affected by genuine mutual concessions offered
by the National Government and the Communists. The solution
apparently lay in the handling of the Communist Army, which did
not want to surrender its autonomy. Unless the Chinese Communists contributed a solution, "they would lose very quickly any
vestige of sympathy in the United States."[6]

Marshall added that American public opinion would react quickly
and favorably to the termination of hostilities. The United States
wanted to end the commitment of its troops in the area. The President also insisted on the prompt evacuation of Japanese troops.
Marshall concluded:

> I come to China as the President's personal envoy to the Genera-
> lissimo and to his Government. That defines my position. I will
> listen to such statements as the various groups may make but any

statement of my views and my suggestions will be confined strictly to the Generalissimo. It is not my purpose to make known such views to anyone else, even in general to the American group. . . .[7]

In reply to Marshall's initial comments, which had put no pressure on the Generalissimo, Chiang Kai-shek declared that an autonomous Communist Army made unity impossible. As a soldier, Marshall conceded that point but asked what could be expected of the Chinese Communists.

They would not act spontaneously, Chiang replied. They would first determine what the Soviet line was, since in all matters of broad policy they relied on them. From the end of October until the middle of November, they had been active and had scored considerable success, with Russian help, in taking over areas evacuated by the Japanese. More recently, they had suffered heavy losses in local clashes, and now wanted to gain time by seeking a political settlement. In view of the tense situation in Manchuria, the Soviets had agreed to leave occupation forces until February 1.[8]

Recognizing the lack of trust between the Nationalists and the Soviets, Marshall underscored to the Generalissimo the differences between dealing with a head of state and diplomatic representatives. He said, "I found in my personal dealings with Stalin that he inspired me with confidence in contrast to his Foreign Office. I felt this [same situation] in my contacts with the British Office. I dealt all right with the Prime Minister. Our own State Department might be considered in a similar manner—they use mysterious language."[9]

After this meeting, Marshall discussed personnel matters with Robertson and decided to set up temporary headquarters in Chungking, still the capital of Nationalist China. In 1941, Chungking had nearly two million people. It was on a promontory above the confluence of the Yangtze and Kialing rivers, and journalists execrated its climate as one of the worst in the world, with temperatures usually over 100 degrees in summer.[10]

Two days after his conversation with Chiang at Nanking, Marshall talked with Chou En-lai and members of his staff at Chungking. Chou outlined his platform, which he would still be upholding at the end of the year. The Kuomintang, he said, professed support for a National Assembly that would write a new constitution, but all delegates to that assembly had been selected by the Kuomintang ten years earlier. This was unacceptable to the Communists, who wanted a true coalition government. With such a government the armies could be unified. In such a coalition they expected the Generalissimo to remain as head and the Kuomintang to be first in importance in the government. But the government would have a different makeup, a different balance between forces.[11]

His arguments were sweetly reasonable, but the deep hatred and fanatical feuding between the two major groups led Marshall to search for a third force which might help him in his negotiations. Near the end of the year he investigated the Democratic League as a possibility. The League, established in 1941 by a combination of six minority parties, claimed to be "the largest political group representing the middle classes in China" and with the aim of ending one-party-rule dictatorship in China. The League demanded cessation of hostilities, a representative National Assembly, and a coalition government. Marshall briefly considered that Carsun Chang (Chang Chia-sen), one of the League's founders and an early champion of parliamentary government for China, might supply leadership strong enough to unite the government, but soon realized that Carsun Chang could not even control the League.[12]

When Marshall sounded out T. V. Soong, Chiang Kai-shek's brother-in-law, for opinions on the League, Soong was impatiently scornful. The parties making up the League were of little consequence, he said. One, the Youth Party, was started with the aid of the Kuomintang but had broken away and was now in the hands of a militant warlord. Another element of the League was the National Socialist Party, established by a student who had come to admire the Nazis while in Germany. Not totally discouraged, Marshall continued to poke and pry among various minority groups until the last days of his Mission.

Over all the discussions of government reform and coalition hung the question of Soviet activity in Manchuria. Knowing that Soong had discussed with Stalin the Yalta and Potsdam arrangements relating to China, Marshall asked whether the Russians were handling property as war booty in Manchuria as they had done in Germany. Soong replied that they were claiming everything that could be used aggressively against them. The General noted that this followed the pattern of Soviet action in the West, where they had "completely wrecked the economy of Germany.... When they went in and claimed war booty they cleaned the place out. They left the place completely out of balance.... Evidently they are doing the same thing in Manchuria."[13]

He continued in this vein at the Generalissimo's cottage near Chungking, where the Chiangs took Marshall, Robertson, and Foreign Minister Wang Shih-chieh for a talk after Christmas dinner in the city. Chiang said that Stalin had invited him to send a representative to Moscow and he thought he might send his son. The Russians had also invited him to send troops into Changchun, capital of Manchuria, and he had directed that a division be flown in. Despite these friendly actions, the Generalissimo was disturbed by inimical behavior in parts of Manchuria where the Soviets were collaborating with the Chinese Communists and excluding the Nationalists from some important areas. Aware that the Nationalists had hoped to get supplies left by the disarmed Japanese in Manchuria, Marshall tried to encourage Chiang by telling him that he was looking into stores of winter equipment in Alaska that might be made available to China and that there was some $50 million worth of supplies in Burma that might be used for the rehabilitation of China.[14]

Reporting to Truman on his observations thus far in December, Marshall said he thought he had made the Generalissimo realize that many of the difficulties in Manchuria were "not peculiar to that problem but common to Russian procedure everywhere. . . ." Marshall's week had been full of long talks with all parties: "Communists, Democratic League, Youth Movement, T. V. Soong, various National Government officials, specialists from our Embassy, Americans in the employ of the Chinese Government."[15] For the moment he was playing the role of the honest broker, searching out the views of everyone and quietly leaving the impression that there must be changes if the United States was to continue or increase its assistance. From his talks thus far he had gathered that there was general agreement on the need for continued leadership by Chiang Kai-shek, for a more democratic government, a coalition, and a nationalized army. But methods for achieving a working agreement had not been found.

On the next-to-last day of the year, James Shepley summarized for Marshall contrasting ideas for ending the fighting in China. The Nationalist list went: (1) a cease-fire; (2) withdrawal of the Communists ten kilometers from railroads and from railway police posts that would be set to guard the area; (3) government willingness to consult the Communists on any moves into North China except along the Peiping-Mukden railway. The Communists agreed on a cease-fire but proposed negotiations of all detailed arrangements and the creation of a commission to investigate the area of conflict. The U.S. approach included some of both viewpoints: (1) a cease-fire; (2) withdrawal of both sides ten kilometers from railroads; (3) creation of a committee consisting of one Communist representative, one government representative, and one American, to proceed to North China and make recommendations on the reception of Japanese surrenders and the movement of troops.[16]

These suggestions were helpful but there was another interested party to be considered. In Moscow, during the meeting of foreign ministers in December, Secretary Byrnes pressed the Soviet Union on its delays in evacuating the Japanese from Manchuria. Aware that this was a prelude to a request for setting the date for Russian withdrawal from the area, Stalin asked Byrnes when the United States planned to pull out its troops. Byrnes replied that the United States would like to withdraw at once but that the Marines were there to help disarm the Japanese in the area surrounded by Communist troops. He reminded Stalin that at Potsdam the Russian had said that Chiang Kai-shek's government was the only possible one in China.

Byrnes added that Marshall was going to attempt a prompt disarming of Japanese troops. Stalin said that he was confident that "if any man could settle the situation it would be General Marshall whom he regarded as one of the few military men who was both statesman as well as soldier."[17]

Marshall began to move more purposefully on December 30, the day before his sixty-fifth birthday. Meeting with three Nationalist leaders, including Foreign Minister Wang Shih-chieh, and finding them grimly bent on maintaining every facet of the *status quo,* he spelled out some necessary concessions which he repeated to the Generalissimo on the following Monday. As a result of his lecture, Wang told Marshall that his government had decided to submit proposals to the Communists that afternoon for (1) an immediate cease-fire; (2) the appointment by the government and the Communists of representatives to discuss with Marshall means of enforcing a cease-fire and disarming the Japanese; and (3) the appointment by the Political Consultative Conference of a commission to visit the disputed areas and make recommendations.[18]

To avoid a leak of details before a final agreement had been made, Marshall suggested that the negotiators delay public announcement of their discussions. "This is not a political consultations [sic] which you murder with the press sometimes if you can. This is a military matter for the good of China. . . ." When Chou En-lai remarked that it was unfortunate that the government had immediately published its proposal so that the Communists were forced to answer, Marshall replied, "I hope that is water over the dam because I have a new dam."[19]

On January 5, Marshall was again troubled by leaks to newspapers. He declared, "I feel that I have a right, if the Communist Party and the Central Government use me, I have a right to insist that they do not make my position impossible, and the premature announcement can easily be fatal to negotiations."[20]

By mid-January, Marshall felt that he had some knowledge of the chief figures in China's political life, whose views and actions would determine his success or failure. He had met Madame Chiang Kai-shek and her brother, T. V. Soong, early in the war, and was at Cairo in 1943 with the Generalissimo, accompanied by Madame. Stilwell and Wedemeyer had seen to it that he knew a great deal about the virtues and faults of the remarkable Soong family and their political and financial connections. He also came to like and trust Chang Chun, who often represented the Generalissimo in discussion with the Communists and Marshall, and Wang Shih-chieh, the Foreign Minister.

Slightly younger than Chiang Kai-shek, Chang Chun had met the future Generalissimo as a fellow cadet in North China and later was one of forty cadets sent (with Chiang) to military school in Japan. Chang was a loyal supporter of Chiang Kai-shek from the beginning of his fight to power; in 1939 he became Secretary General of the Supreme National Defense Council, and a year later was governor of Szechuan, a post he held until 1945. In August of that year he was one of the Nationalist representatives to deal with the Communists in trying to settle differences. With the calling of the Political Consultative Conference, Chang was selected as one of the Kuomintang members. It was natural for Chiang to choose him to represent the Nationalists on the new Committee of Three, which also included Marshall and Chou En-lai, for, besides having been proved loyal to the Generalissimo, Chang Chun was a skilled negotiator, a quality evident in his dealings with Marshall. The General's later opinion was that Chang Chun was one of the Chinese leaders capable of saving China from civil war.[21]

In all discussions involving Chinese foreign policy, Marshall depended strongly on Wang Shih-chieh, a true scholar among the Chinese Nationalists. Born in 1891 in Hupeh Province, he was graduated from Peiyang University in Tientsin before taking a degree in economics and political science from the London School of Economics in 1917, and the *docteur en droit* degree in Paris in 1920. He spent several years as a teacher of constitutional law and later as dean of the Law School at Peking University before taking a position in the National Government near the end of 1927—a rare member of the inner political circle who had not shared military service with the Generalissimo. Wang served the government in a

number of educational and political positions, sometimes occupying more than one post at a time. In 1943 he headed a good-will
mission to Great Britain; he visited the United States with one of
the mission groups on his way back to China. At the end of July
1945, he succeeded T. V. Soong as China's Foreign Minister; in
that capacity he signed the Sino-Soviet Treaty, which Soong had
negotiated just before his resignation.

As a student of constitutional law, Wang was a leader in the fight
within the Kuomintang for greater democratization of the regime.
He emphasized that Sun Yat-sen had believed that the one-party
system must ultimately be succeeded by a broadly based republican
government.[22]

Under the pressure of Japanese invasion, a provisional constitution was drafted and an advisory People's Political Council formed,
with which Wang became closely connected in 1938. He urged
broadening of participation in government and assisted in negotiations with the Communists in the later summer and fall of 1945.

Wang welcomed Marshall's selection by President Truman to
head the mediation effort in China and was his strongest advocate
among the Nationalists. Marshall recognized Wang's contributions
when he wrote in a 1945 memorandum:

> I should state here, and most confidentially, that Dr. Wang in
> China was my principal supporter and privately and frequently
> strongly advocated the continuance of my efforts along the lines I
> was then following. He was not at all in accord with the political
> advice and military advice the Generalissimo was receiving from his
> officials, but was very reassuring to me. . . .[23]

Marshall increasingly felt that the chief antagonist to all his
efforts in China was a man of whom he often heard but whom he
almost never saw—Chen Li-fu, who, with his older brother, headed
the ultra-right "CC Clique," which was powerful in the Kuomintang.

Nephews of an early adherent of Sun Yat-sen, the two Chen
brothers were among the first dedicated followers of Chiang Kai-
shek. Chen Kou-fu, eight years the elder, helped organize Chiang's
financial resources and encouraged his early break with the Communists. He became chairman of the Kuomintang's Central Finance Committee.

Better known to Americans was Chen Li-fu, born in 1900, sent
by his brother after World War I to the University of Pittsburgh to
get a B.S. degree and then an M.S. in mining engineering. He

capped this training with a stint in the Pennsylvania coalfields, which was cut short by a strike called by John L. Lewis. In later years, Chen Li-fu liked to say that it was there he learned of the dangers of Communism and it was this strike that sent him back to China to be a leader in the fight against Communism.[24]

In addition to helping his brother develop the Chinese economy, Chen Li-fu spent seven years training Chinese youth, as Minister of Education. More crucial to Chiang's party control was the period 1928–38, in which Chen's task was "the identifying and the removing from the Kuomintang Communists or persons suspected of Communist sympathies or connections." In this he was aided by Tai Li, a graduate of the Whampoa Military Academy who had become the head of Chiang's intelligence service and of an organization described as China's secret-police force. Because Tai Li's organization could give important weather information and intelligence on Japanese movements, Secretary of the Navy Frank Knox and T. V. Soong entered an agreement in 1943 in Washington for the formation of the Sino-American Cooperative Organization, to establish weather stations and plan guerrilla operations. The United States furnished some military personnel as well as considerable equipment and general intelligence. U.S. Navy cooperation with Tai Li was under the direction of an energetic Navy officer, Captain Milton E. Miles, who had come to the Far East the previous year to work with the Chinese. His activities led to complaints from the OSS as well as from the commanders in the China Theater, Stilwell and Wedemeyer.

Chen Li-fu headed the organizational division of the Kuomintang in 1932–36, 1938–39, and 1944–48. He likened his role to that of the director of a Chinese FBI and later claimed the he had been personally responsible for converting 20,000 Chinese from Communism. Through financial agencies, control of important newspapers, and the selection of party members and leaders, he and his brother and close adherents not only furnished a power base for Chiang Kai-shek, but were also in a position to control any move the Generalissimo might make to come to terms with dissident elements in China. Seeing any weakening of the Kuomintang as an ultimate aid to Communism, he could only view the Marshall mission as unfriendly and dangerous, a source of weakness, with proposals of compromise and conciliation that must be resisted.

Chen Li-fu made no pretense about his attitude. When Foreign Minister Wang Shih-chieh applauded Marshall's appointment to head the mission to China, Chen Li-fu begged the Generalissimo to prevent the General's coming. His argument, he later explained, was that since Marshall had been the leader in the great victory over the Axis, he would not consider failure in a later mission, and this boded ill for China. When his efforts to get agreement between the parties failed, he would turn his face against the National Government. This time Wang Shih-chieh's influence prevailed, and Chiang Kai-shek approved the Mission.

Chen Li-fu held tenaciously to his goal of making sure that Chiang did not carry his offers of cooperation too far. Years later, in Taipei, he admitted that he might have been mistaken, that perhaps he and Marshall could have worked out a more satisfactory program. But, as events were to show, the Kuomintang allowed Chiang Kai-shek to make offers or suggestions of compromise only when such offers could do no damage to the power of the Kuomintang.

Opposing the Kuomintang was Chou En-lai, the brilliant, dangerously charming representative of Chairman Mao Tse-tung. From a schoolboy admiration of Sun Yat-sen and his Revolution, Chou had gone on to Marxism as a university student, and in the early 1920s went with a group of young Chinese to Europe, where he became successful in spreading left-wing sentiment among Chinese students in France, Germany, and Belgium. At that time the Chinese Communists had not broken with the Kuomintang, and Chou En-lai became one of the executive committee when the Kuomintang established a Paris headquarters. In meetings of various factions, he was an effective speaker for the Communists.

Returning to China in 1924, Chou became secretary of a provincial branch of the Chinese Communist Party, then deputy director of the political department of the Whampoa Military Academy, headed by Chiang Kai-shek. He sometimes served as secretary to General Vasili Bluecher, Russian adviser to the future Generalissimo. When the Kuomintang formed a national revolutionary army in 1925, Chiang became head of its First Army. Under it came the First Division, composed of Whampoa Academy cadets, and Chou En-lai was made head of the political department of that division.

During the period when Chiang Kai-shek and the Communists were cooperating, Chou continued to advance in political power, keeping a foot in each camp. In 1927, when Chiang moved against the Communists, Chou barely escaped capture by Kuomintang agents. Driven into opposition, he became a member of the Central Committee of the Communist Party in 1927 and later that year helped organize the Nanchang uprising against the National Government, an event associated with the beginning of the Chinese Red Army. In 1931, he was a delegate to the Sixth National Congress of Soviets when Mao Tse-tung was elected Chairman of the New Chinese Soviet Government. Chou became a member of its Central Executive Committee.

Chou became an active organizer of Communist groups in South China and in 1932 was named political adviser of the First Front Army, commanded by Chu Teh. In 1934, when Chiang Kai-shek forced the Communists out of Kiangsi Province, Chou played a key role in organizing the Long March northward and served ably as deputy to Mao Tse-tung during its progress.

The Japanese invasion made the Chinese Communists decide to support the National Government. Chou En-lai was given a leading role in the political department of the Military Defense Commission of China. He spent the latter part of 1939 and early 1940 in Moscow, then returned to Chungking in 1940 as a member of the Supreme Military Defense Council. In this position, he worked against Japan, but he was also adroit at winning Chinese scholars and intellectuals away from the Kuomintang. His opponents charged that he had a major role in creating the Democratic League and in a propaganda campaign to win support from the Western press.

Chou's activities during this period of cooperation aroused Chiang Kai-shek's old suspicions of his motives, and at times the loose coalition threatened to fall apart. Chou En-lai remained away from Chungking from the summer of 1943 until the fall of 1944, returning at last to insist on the formation of a coalition government. It was to deal with this issue that General Hurley, in 1944, urged Mao Tse-tung and Chou En-lai to meet Chiang at Chungking.[25]

Among the Communist leaders that Marshall would meet, Chou En-lai was the ablest negotiator. Plausible in his approach and often completely open in his conversation, he seemed capable of reaching a workable arrangement with the Nationalists. But his past record in organizing and building the Communist organization and in fighting the conservative leadership of the Kuomintang was heavily against him in the Nationalists' estimation. It was unlikely that his former colleagues would enter fully into any arrangement that he strongly recommended.

The ideal climate for a cease-fire agreement had not been created. General Wedemeyer, closely following developments from Shanghai, observed that both sides were full of suspicion. Though usually favorable to the Generalissimo, Wedemeyer admitted that Chiang's initiative in calling a meeting of the National Assembly for May 5, 1946, without prior elections, meant that he intended "to insure that the National Assembly is overwhelmingly packed with old party line members of the Kuomintang." Wedemeyer thought there should be village, district, and provincial elections, even if it meant delaying the National Assembly. The National Government, he added, was suppressing free speech and assembly. Tai Li and his secret police blocked all views critical of the government and a Kuomintang group used violence against any students who voiced criticism.[26] Wedemeyer's words reinforced Marshall's growing belief that the National Government had no desire for a true cease-fire.

At the beginning the Communists seemed the more willing of the two parties to work for peace. Walter Robertson, Chargé in Chungking, reported to Washington at the end of the first week of January that the Communists appeared not to be interfering with Nationalist occupation of Manchuria: "Communists are not on the offensive in any important sector."[27]

Marshall's early meetings with the Nationalists and the Communists were filled with the issue of limiting troop movements to Jehol and Chahar in North China. Governor Chang Chun referred repeatedly to the open dealings of the Chinese Communists with Soviet forces that had taken over certain areas from the Japanese. Chou En-lai could not understand why there should be any Nationalist troops in North China, since this area had been taken over by the Communist Eighth Route Army. Despite these differences, the two chief Chinese representatives made a point of keeping their sense of humor as General Marshall tried to steer a careful passage.[28]

Over all the negotiations hung the suspicion that the views Chou En-lai advanced so blandly were shaped to fit Soviet desires. On January 10, George Kennan, who was U.S. Chargé d'Affaires in the Soviet Union and had a long experience in Moscow, sent the State Department a summary of his views on the designs of the Russians. In this summary, which was reported to the U.S. Embassy in Chungking, Kennan declared that the U.S.S.R. sought a predominant influence in China. So far, the Soviets were cautious, avoiding a direct confrontation with the United States or a posture that would be unfavorably regarded by Far Eastern countries. So they favored coalition rather than division in China. In Manchuria the U.S.S.R. outwardly played up to the Nationalist Chinese, and made no demands for Chinese Communist control of the area. The current relationship of Moscow with Chinese Communist headquarters at Yenan was unclear, and it could not be proved that the Chinese Communists were acting on the Kremlin's orders.

Kennan believed that since the Soviet Union had plucked the plums of Manchuria, the Chinese Communists had little reason to feel grateful to Moscow. The Chinese had their own, mature Communist Party with its own brand of Marxism. The Yenan Communist Party was no fugitive group. For years it had its own *de facto* regime, developing its own vested interests. As a result, this Yenan regime had absorbed a nationalistic coloration, with its own type of external propaganda. The rapid expansion of the armed forces had been based on Yenan's form of Chinese nationalism.[29]

There is nothing to indicate how much these views influenced Marshall. He had met Kennan in 1944 and had been favorably impressed. Perhaps Kennan's memorandum was one reason the General kept asking Chou En-lai how he could uphold the Soviets when he knew what they had done in Manchuria.

Marshall had felt there was almost a point of agreement on January 7, but the National Government insisted on continuing its troop movements into the provinces of Jehol and Chahar to take over key rail centers that the Communists claimed they already held. At ten o'clock on the evening of January 9, Marshall appealed to the Generalissimo to break the deadlock. Chiang agreed to leave this point to be settled by political negotiation. Marshall suggested that he announce the cessation of hostilities at the opening of the Political Consultative Conference the next morning, to be followed by press statements issued by the National Government and the Communists.

On January 10, the Committee of Three submitted to Chiang Kai-shek and Mao Tse-tung a proposal for an immediate cease-fire, the cessation of all troop movements (with certain exceptions), and an end to interference with all lines of communication. To supervise the implementation of the agreements, there was to be established at once in Peiping an Executive Headquarters, including representatives of the United States, the National Government, and the Communists. Walter Robertson was to be the American commissioner of the headquarters, and Colonel Byroade, soon to be promoted to Brigadier General, was to head the operations section. The United States was to furnish twenty-five officers, sixty-five enlisted men, and thirty-five civilians. The Nationalist and Communist sections were each to have forty officers, ninety enlisted men, and forty civilians.[30]

Marshall hoped that his mission was off to a good start with apparent agreement on the mechanics of getting a cease-fire, but he could not shake the Nationalists' fear that every move by the Chinese Communists was dictated from Moscow. However gratified he was by the quick agreement on this first step of his mission, he knew, as he told Truman, that his success had come only because the Generalissimo had wanted to make the negotiations work.[31] Almost at once, in a characteristic shift, Chiang veered into a counterreaction. In March he was still delaying permission for the Nationalist team to go to Manchuria.

Uneasier still were the negotiations for a coalition government. The war and factional disputes had delayed the closer government cooperation envisaged in 1937. In 1938 the Kuomintang had set up the People's Political Council as a "compromise measure between the proposal for a European-type united front government, based on popular elections to a national convention, and a continuation of the Kuomintang monopoly of government hitherto prevalent." Representatives were selected from four different groups: the provinces, Mongolia and Tibet, the overseas Chinese, and political leaders in China. The last group contained some liberals, but the final decision on selections was made by the Central Executive Committee of the Kuomintang.[32]

In the fall of 1945, after discussions with the Communists, Chiang Kai-shek agreed to call a Political Consultative Conference in the new year to discuss terms of a new constitution, and promised to convene a National Assembly to approve such a document. Of the thirty-eight delegates to the conference, eight were to be from the Kuomintang, seven from the Communist Party, nine from the Democratic League, five from the Youth Party, and nine independents.

Control of the conference obviously lay in the orientation of groups and members outside the Nationalist and Communist parties. Chiang Kai-shek asked Marshall to intervene when the Communists and the Democratic League threatened to challenge Kuomintang dominance on December 21. Chiang wanted to upgrade the power of the existing Council of State, which in wartime merely transmitted orders of the National Defense Council to the chief decisionmaking body of the government. Half of its members would be taken from the Kuomintang. This solution was less acceptable to the non-Nationalist groups than the arrangement proposed for the forthcoming Political Consultative Conference.

Marshall replied that he could act informally but that he was confused by the debates and by the fact that neither side had any written proposals to advance. He suggested an interim coalition government giving the Generalissimo power as President of all of China, rather than as head of the Kuomintang, with a Bill of Rights and a provision for drafting a new constitution for submission to the National Assembly in May. Marshall said that his proposal did not change the basic governmental structure save at the highest level but did provide for a Bill of Rights. To the amusement of the Generalissimo, he called this "a dose of American medicine."[33] It was medicine the Nationalists had no intention of swallowing.

Marshall declined to be an official mediator between the Generalissimo and his opponents in a political struggle, but agreed to act unofficially. He urged the Generalissimo to reach an agreement soon on a unified government and army. China, he believed, was vulnerable to low-level Russian infiltration and to the strengthening of the Communist regime, while the National Government's position in North China and Manchuria was gradually weakening. The United States could not keep its military and naval forces much longer in China.[34]

At the request of both sides, Marshall proceeded, as he described it, "to draft a complete reorganization of Chinese military forces with prohibitions and stipulations familiar with our democratic system, adapted to China and to the menace of Chinese warlords and the uncertainties of provincial officials." After several meetings with the Nationalists, he got their approval to discuss the plan with Chou En-lai. Chou then flew to Yenan for consultation and returned to report that Mao Tse-tung was ready to cooperate with the Nationalists in the interim period and under the constitution. Though his party was socialist, he added that it recognized that socialism was at present impractical and that for the moment they should follow a political system patterned after that of the United States. He insisted that by this he meant "that prosperity and peace of China could only be promoted by the introduction of the American political system, science, and industrialization, and of agrarian reform in a program of free individual enterprise." Mao was convinced of Marshall's fairness, according to Chou, and was willing to cooperate with the American program. When asked about reports that Mao was to visit Russia, he laughed and said that "on the contrary he would like very much to go [to] the United States where he believed he would be able to learn much."

The Americans were wary. "Whether or not he was implying that his party would cooperate with the United States rather than Russia was differently interpreted by my staff who listened to the conference," reported Marshall. Nor is it certain that Marshall was aware that almost exactly a year earlier Mao and Chou had supposedly offered to come to the United States to confer with President Roosevelt and explain the current situation and problems of China. These proposals, received in Chungking January 10, 1945, were not forwarded by Ambassador Hurley, a decision with which General Wedemeyer concurred.[35]

Chou's statements were encouraging, but there were indications that reactionary elements of the Kuomintang might balk at accepting the agreement. Even some Kuomintang moderates feared Communist domination under the reformed regime.

On February 15, 1946, the counselor of the American Embassy reported that reactionary elements of the Kuomintang had attacked meetings of liberals. The violence stemmed, he believed, from followers of the CC Clique, the ultra-conservative group formed by the Chen brothers, and from officers from the Whampoa Military Academy, which Chiang Kai-shek once had headed; these elements feared loss of influence and perquisites in any reorganization of the government or the armed forces.

Counselor Smyth was dubious about reports in mid-March that the Kuomintang's Central Executive Committee had ratified the Political Consultative Conference agreements. Though he believed that the Generalissimo was acting in good faith, he feared that right-wing intransigency and Communist reaction to it might very well end negotiations.[36]

Marshall understood that under American pressure the Generalissimo might agree for a season. But as old friends and advisers, influential members of the Kuomintang, and old colleagues from the Whampoa Academy sensed any loss of control, they magnified Communist threats and intrigue. Such interaction of opposing elements threatened every precarious agreement and washed away Marshall's repeated efforts to patch up a cease-fire. His response was to persevere, to begin again.

Integration of the armed forces occupied Marshall's mind as much as the cease-fire and reorganization of the government. He had asked Wedemeyer for proposals in the middle of January. Long at work on the matter, Wedemeyer's headquarters replied with a plan on the same day. Any settlement, said the staff, should require that the two groups (Nationalists and Communists) be brought under a single, governmental authority. Neither side was to keep a secret, independent military force. Integration must begin at the higher army group level rather than with divisions or armies. Three days later, Wedemeyer suggested a timetable for progressive reduction of army units. He felt that the large number of existing divisions was "a cancerous sore that must be eliminated."[37]

Both Nationalist and Communist leaders urged Marshall to act as adviser to the Subcommittee on Integration of Armed Forces.

After meeting several times with General Chang Chih-chung, the Generalissimo's representative on the subcommittee, Marshall decided they must consider four points: (1) organization of a "real" national army under the National Government; (2) developments whereby the Communists would give up inherent power in their organization; (3) creation of an army that would not bankrupt China but would be sufficient for national security and national defense; and (4) insurance that the army would not become a political instrument of any National leader.[38]

With no relief from continual disagreements between the two sides, on the following day Marshall laid out specific requirements for a proper reorganization: (1) the army should not be in politics; (2) military commanders should not hold political positions; (3) there should be approximately twenty armies directly responsible to the Generalissimo; and (4) service forces with no connection to command forces should handle supply. He suggested six months to deal with these problems. In retrospect, it is clear that Marshall, the Communists, and the Nationalists were all speaking in different tongues.[39]

As early as December 31, 1945, Chiang Kai-shek, after reading Marshall's suggestions, indicated his willingness to change the proposed ratio of ninety Nationalist to fifteen Communist divisions to ninety-twenty, in order not to embarrass General Marshall with the Chinese Communists. Marshall was pleased. He said that if the Nationalists wanted him to say twenty, he would do so, but that the Communists had accepted six to one. He added that the National Government should accept the Western idea of a nonpolitical armed force. Chiang's representative, General Chang Chih-chung, hoped that the Generalissimo would become the Washington of China by emulating Western ideas.[40]

Marshall lectured Chou En-lai about Western views on armed forces on February 1. It was important, he said, to establish a democratic army. From the reign of Charles I to that of George III he traced the safeguards established by the British Parliament on which the modern U.S. Army rested. He emphasized over and over that commanders should have no position in civil government and no authority except for the troops under their command. After thought and discussion, Chou promised to seek extended conferences with General Chang Chih-chung.[41]

Three days later, Chou reported that he and his advisers had carefully examined the proposals, and a sanguine Marshall informed President Truman that prospects for an agreement seemed favorable.[42]

Soon thereafter, Marshall outlined a plan for the orderly reduction of the number of Nationalist and Communist units. He pro-
posed to bring a small group of U.S. officers to Chungking to assist
in the process. After plans were approved, he would have a small
group from Executive Headquarters help carry out the agreements.
Chang Chih-chung was sure that he and Chou En-lai would agree.[43]
After talking with the two on February 11, Marshall arranged with
General Wedemeyer for several officers under Brigadier General
Paul Caraway to work out details "with high Chinese officials in
Chungking." Beginning on February 12, this group worked out a
draft plan that sought to incorporate the special interests of both
sides.[44]

As usual, Marshall suggested possible steps without pressing
them. Often one or another of the Chinese representatives asked
for compromise solutions. Chang Chih-chung occasionally lightened tensions by saying that school was in session and they were
interested in what the professor had to say. In his meeting with
General Chang on February 15, Marshall noted that in the next
general conference Chou En-lai would ask for more than the four
army commanders provided in the plan and suggested that Chang
Chih-chung be prepared to make concessions on this point. On the
other hand, Marshall added, he had drawn out the discussion on
the number of Communist divisions in the first phase. This might
be a bargaining point that Chang Chih-Chung could use.[45]

That afternoon Marshall began with Chang and Chou a step-by-
step examination of the draft plan for reorganizing the Chinese
armies. In many instances there was quick agreement; in others
Marshall had to find a formula that both parties could accept; in still
others he said firmly that he did not agree with the arguments of
either side. Throughout the whole discussion, he made clear that
the Committee of Three had no power to issue orders, but must
wait for agreement of the Generalissimo and Mao Tse-tung.[46]

Disagreement developed over the date for the beginning of the
integration of ground forces. At first Marshall had favored beginning at the end of six months—a position backed by the National
Government. Chou argued that they should wait until after twelve
months of demobilization, with complete integration at the end of
eighteen months. He evidently felt that the Communists would
benefit from a process that began after the Nationalists had demobilized a substantial portion of their troops. Chang Chih-chung
held to the six-month suggestion but insisted that he did not want
to hold up discussions. He asked for General Marshall's views.[47]

Chou En-lai reminded Chang that the two armies had been hostile for eighteen years and would need additional time to integrate. He thought that it would be an extraordinary accomplishment to achieve integration within eighteen months. Marshall was impressed by Chou's points, remarking that he had a better understanding of the problems of integration than he had held two months earlier.[48]

The meeting on February 18 centered on the number of military police and their control over civilians. Chou En-lai held that they should be restricted to control of military personnel. "Only in this way may we set up a proper democratic system for China."[49]

Through all the lengthy discussion, which Marshall presided over with great patience and good humor, he tried to keep matters on a harmonious level. Amused when told by a member of his staff that a translator had omitted Chang's remark that if the contending parties arrived at a compromise Marshall would be temporarily out of a job, the General said that if he could find such a compromise it would be welcome. Later, he remarked, "Tell General Chang that they ruin his jokes in translation. I hope they don't ruin this one."[50]

At the conclusion of the meeting, Marshall asked Chou to remain behind, then spoke of an offer to aid the Communists in the training of selected officers and noncommissioned officers prior to integration. Chou welcomed the suggestion and said he would pass it on to Mao. They next considered integrated staffs for integrated army groups. Chou affirmed that he was backing Marshall's proposals for integration so that China could quickly rid itself of the warlord system and arrange for a unified democratic army. Perhaps encouraged by the response, Marshall told Chou confidentially that in four weeks he would return to the United States to get a loan for China. He also noted that he believed he could arrange for General Wedemeyer to be Ambassador to China.[51]

It was a happy Marshall who wrote of great progress to President Truman on February 19. Four formal conferences on practically all the central issues relative to the armed forces had ended in agreement. He spoke of the fine work of the special staff of American officers from Shanghai and Chungking that was working on detailed plans for implementing the agreement. He planned to transfer these elements to the Executive Headquarters at Nanking. This headquarters, initially mistrusted by the two factions, had demonstrated that it was the only practical means for terminating the fighting. Once combined policy had been agreed upon, Marshall intended for Executive Headquarters to send twenty-one teams of three men each, representing the United States, Nationalists, and

Communists, into the field to make plans effective. The American officers already assigned to some of the teams had been received with tremendous acclaim and overwhelming gratitude. The Chinese seemed to think that the Americans "represent their one hope for the return of peace and security."[52]

To hasten final agreement on unification of the armies, Marshall proposed to send Chou En-lai to Yenan by American plane to confer with Mao Tse-tung, while Chiang Kai-shek was trying to get his generals lined up behind the agreement. "[The Generalissimo] is in an extremely difficult position," Marshall acknowledged, "struggling with the ultraconservatives and determined wing of each group, many if not most of whom will lose position and income all or in part by the changes proposed." He hinted at action if these efforts did not succeed: "I hope for the successful outcome of his efforts and especially hope that I will not be compelled to move in more or less in the open to intervene in this phase of the matter. The conservative political and military are naturally rather bitter against me. I have avoided public statements in order not to give them an opening."[53]

Marshall balanced his talk with Chou En-lai with a discussion with Chang Chih-chung on February 20, telling him of the American offer to train Communist officers and men. He asked Chang what should be done if Chou came back from Yenan with proposals to delay still further. The Nationalist representative replied that he "would respect General Marshall's decision in this regard." Marshall recalled that Chou En-lai wanted the Committee of Three to go into Manchuria on its trip to North China. Marshall said he "would have to hold this for later decision, since he did not want to give the Russians a new opportunity for conjecture and possible propaganda lines that might be injurious to his present mission." He might favor going to Mukden if the Russians had withdrawn.[54]

Chou's report on his return from Yenan on February 20 was hopeful. He told Marshall the next morning that Mao accepted in principle the American proposal to integrate in two stages, and had been enthusiastic about the American offer to train Communist military personnel. Later the same day, in the Military Subcommittee, Chou asked for a somewhat different timetable for integration, adding two months to the proposed schedule. Chang Chih-chung replied that he would abide by Marshall's decision.[55]

The title of the agreement was debated at length on the 22nd and finally settled by acceptance of Marshall's version. He believed that inasmuch as this was an agreement between the two Chinese groups, he should not sign. Under pressure from both sides, he finally signed as "Advisor," saying as he wrote, "If we are going to be hung, I will hang with you."[56]

Shortly before the hour for signing, the Generalissimo returned from a ten-day trip and told Marshall that the plan had been approved for demobilization, reorganization, and integration of the armies. At 4:00 P.M. on February 25, in the office of the aide to the Generalissimo, the three representatives met to sign the agreement.

After the ceremony, General Chang Chih-chung commented that their action had ended eighteen years of struggle between the Communists and the government.

> The so-called Communist problem or civil war problem in this country in the struggle . . . has cost the lives of millions of people, the delay in the reconstruction of this country for a very considerable period of time. . . . Henceforth, we are entering into a new period of peaceful reconstruction of the country and we will give up the military force as an instrument for political supremacy.

For the success of the enterprise he gave credit to General Marshall.

The people of the country, he continued in graceful tribute, had created several titles for General Marshall.

> Certain people call [him] the midwife of unification and peaceful reconstruction of China. Certain people call General Marshall the great Ambassador of Peace sent by the American Government and the American people to China. I am of the opinion that no matter which you like best, one will suit General Marshall completely. Now the materializing of the unification and the reconstruction of the country will be in sight and we must say that we owe so very much to the greatest friend of China, General Marshall. . . . I, representing the Government, would like to express my sincere thanks and appreciation to General Marshall.[57]

Chou En-lai also hailed the agreement and pledged to carry out its provisions, and ended his speech by praising Marshall's assistance and efforts. Marshall concluded the ceremony by observing:

> This agreement, I think, represents the great hope of China. I can only trust that its pages will not be soiled by a small group of irreconcilables who for a separate purpose would defeat the Chinese people in their overwhelming desire for peace and prosperity.[58]

Second Secretary of the U.S. Embassy John Melby, who was present at the ceremony, wrote in his diary: "Marshall is convinced that unless this one works the rest is pure delusion, the cease fire will be meaningless and the PCC only a dull debating society. The two-sentence speech that he gave at the signing was a real shock to all present."[59]

The signing was to be the high point of the Marshall mission. It seemed then that in only two months he had brought a truce and a hope for agreement to a land apparently doomed to years more of war and chaos. It was not a true peace. Some of the parties could never be reconciled. On each side were those who believed that an unyielding stance was merely the exercise of one's highest duty. For them the peace and prosperity of China depended on the dominance of their philosophy. Fair words for Marshall under such conditions meant nothing. Before many weeks he was to realize how little he had achieved with the signing.

Seeking a Cease-fire

POLITICAL settlement and integration had gone hand in hand with negotiations for cease-fire, but the interplay of conflicting interests magnified the problems facing Executive Headquarters and charged the atmosphere in which Marshall had to work. In January, before the plane carrying the representatives of the Committee of Three could get airborne from Chungking to set up Executive Headquarters in Peiping, Chou En-lai charged the Nationalists with violating agreements by advancing in the North, in Jehol and East Hopei. Governor Chang Chun retorted that the Communists had already erred by attempting to occupy Northern Honan. The Committee of Three ordered investigations of the violations.[1]

As each side piled up data, Marshall tried soothing tactics. He reminded Chou that many of his complaints could be handled by Executive Headquarters and told Chang Chun that the Generalissimo would be placed in an untenable position if his troops did not observe the cease-fire.[2]

Marshall soon realized that he had too few field-team members to deal with growing complaints, and he asked for more staff. Executive Headquarters observed that neither side wanted teams sent to areas where they were winning. Marshall's reports of progress by the teams drew from Truman an expression that confidence "in your judgment and ability" had been amply justified. Robertson reported to the State Department near the end of the month that he thought the problems in Jehol had been solved.[3]

No sooner had field problems in North China subsided than Nationalist Foreign Minister Wang Shih-chieh reported political problems in Manchuria. He had recently spoken to the Soviet Ambassador in China about the Russian failure to withdraw forces from the area by February 1, as promised in the Sino-Soviet Treaty. Wang concluded that the rate of withdrawal would depend on Chinese concessions as to what the Soviets could claim as war booty. The Russians wanted 50 percent ownership or participation in coal and hydroelectric systems, future air-transport systems, and virtually every phase of the Manchurian economy. Their demands were far in excess of any legitimate claims.[4]

Marshall reminded Wang that the current situation in Manchuria emphasized the need for rapid unification of Chinese factions, to lessen their vulnerability to Soviet demands. He recommended that Wang make no commitment to the Soviets as to war booty unless a settlement of limited nature were possible on the basis of the Sino-Soviet Treaty.

Although Marshall believed that time was running against the Soviets as long as their troops remained in Manchuria contrary to their promises, he was disturbed by the situation. Not only did it involve him in matters far beyond his mission, "but it is perhaps more dangerous to world accord than any other present issue." He believed that the survival of the most recent arrangements in China depended "to an important degree on the disposition of the festering situation in Manchuria. I also believe that our Government must shortly do more for China in this matter than give advice."[5]

Marshall was not certain what steps could be taken with reasonable hope of success, but he suggested to President Truman that unification in China should be expedited, that Headquarters, China Theater of Operations, be changed to a Military Advisory Group, and that the Marines be removed as soon as possible. To strengthen their position, the Nationalists should announce their intention of sending troops to Japan and should be prepared to carry the Manchurian question to the Far Eastern Commission. Their case would be strengthened by unification, the removal of American forces from China, and the presence of Chinese troops in the occupation forces of Japan. Truman expressed interest in the first two points but doubted whether the Far Eastern Commission should go beyond matters of surrender, disarmament, and control of Japan, which could include disposition of Japanese external assets in Manchuria.[6]

Despite promising results in the field, disquieting incidents continued. Walter Robertson asked Marshall to intervene with Chiang Kai-shek to get proper instructions issued to National commanders who wanted to deal with Communist forces as guerrillas. Soon afterward, 500 National protesters invaded Executive Headquarters in Peiping to demonstrate against the Communists. Protests were made to the Generalissimo, but other demonstrations, possibly incited by his supporters, sprang up elsewhere. On the 23rd, 10,000 university students paraded in Chungking, demanding the return of Manchuria and the evacuation of Soviet forces. Later, a small group there attacked news offices of the Communists and of the Democratic League, and stormed into headquarters of the Communist delegation. Counselor Smyth of the U.S. Embassy suggested these incidents were instigated by the CC Clique in order to disrupt implementation of the Political Consultative Conference.[7]

When Chou En-lai complained two days later, Marshall reminded him that the guilt was not all on one side, since a recent Yenan press release had raised new questions about the situation in Manchuria. Chou shrugged off the difficulties, declaring that the Communists were willing to demobilize large forces in Manchuria and had not objected to five Nationalist armies in the area.[8]

In spite of such continual troubles, Marshall decided as early as February 21 that negotiations were progressing well enough for him to make a mid-March trip to Washington. On the 22nd, in a chatty letter to his wartime aide Frank McCarthy, he wrote:

> . . . most confidentially, I have plans to make a quick trip home to be gone about four or five weeks in all. In Washington, I will work on loans, surplus property, shipping, etc. I hope to bring Mrs. M. back with me for the remaining months of my stay—until about August or September. I am going to try and have Wedemeyer made Ambassador to take my place. . . .
> I have forced so many compromises on both sides that I am in the awkward position of being obligated by pressure from both sides to stay on and maintain a balance between the mistrusts of the two parties in their attempt to make a coalition government work.[9]

Near the end of February, Marshall radioed the President that he wished to return to Washington about March 12 to discuss such matters as the transfer of surplus property, shipping, and the arrangement of loans. He thought he could be back in China in time "to balance the differences that are yet to rise over the major adjustments there that will be getting under way, political as well as military."[10]

He had much to do before he could leave. He faced a strenuous trip to the North, where he, Chang Chih-chung, and Chou En-lai, as the Committee of Three, would be briefed by members of Executive Headquarters on developments in various cities. Then they would try to clear up local problems interfering with a cease-fire. The omens were not very favorable, but at least his staff at Chungking noted a slight lessening of tension in the office as he left the city.[11]

In the afternoon the Committee of Three was briefed by Robertson at Executive Headquarters in Peiping; then Marshall spoke to the staff in a nearby auditorium. He praised the headquarters as unique in world history, stressing the way in which the agency reached into remote regions to promote peace. He added: "Many individuals will be called upon to make what may seem to them at this time to be a great personal sacrifice. Some must sacrifice but I think that the majority will profit greatly. The prosperity of China is directly dependent upon your execution of this new mission. . . ."[12]

A day later, Marshall pleaded strongly for agreement.

I think the important thing here is that we are not interested in the past now, but we are interested in the future, and until conditions have been restored to normal, personal feelings will have to be buried. The general objective we are working for is far too great and far too important to be stopped by small disagreements, no matter how large they may appear on the ground.[13]

At Tsinan on March 2, Marshall praised the work of the field teams, which had labored under great difficulties. He knew that local groups might resent their interference in local affairs, which the teams and headquarters might not understand. But sometimes there had to be an arbiter. He cited the example of American baseball. Although the umpire was unpopular, both sides recognized that there must be such an authority: ". . . . the game can't go on without him. It becomes a riot. We have not the authority of an umpire, but we endeavor to interpret the rules and agreements that have been arrived at in Chungking. And baseball goes along with American democracy."[14]

This peripatetic evangelism was a new style of diplomacy for both Marshall and the Chinese, but he was hopeful. At Taiyuan, the Committee of Three listened patiently while complaints were registered of delays in turning over areas or railroads or arms seized from the Japanese, of disputes over removal of obstructions along the railroads, and of the challenges to efforts by the field teams to hasten the cease-fire. Marshall was encouraged by Chang Chihchung's proposal that they stop arguing over who was at fault and abide by the decision of Executive Headquarters, to which Chou En-lai at once agreed.[15]

Yenan was the big stop on the trip, for there Marshall at last met Mao Tse-tung. Since late December, Marshall had heard almost every day something about the Chairman of the Chinese Communist Party. No matter what agreement Marshall won from Chou En-lai, the final decision had to be made at Communist Headquarters in Yenan. Pudding-shaped Mao at first seemed far less impressive than the handsome, trim Chou En-lai. As usual, Mao's clothes were "rumpled and plain as if picked up from a pile of hundreds."[16]

Marshall hoped to bring Mao and Chiang closer together. A Soviet-Nationalist agreement of November 27, 1945, by which the Soviet Union had agreed to withdraw from Mukden and Changchun and permit Nationalist forces to be flown in, and had promised to leave Manchuria in January 1946, had put a damper on Chinese Communist efforts to bar Nationalist forces from the area. Reluctantly, Yenan dropped its criticism of the United States and its demands for the withdrawal of U.S. forces from the North, thus making possible some of Marshall's success.

But the situation soon began to change again, and there was evidence of greater Communist dissatisfaction with anything going on in Manchuria that favored the Nationalists or the Americans. Whatever intentions Chou En-lai might have to engage in further negotiation counted less and less with Mao and his advisers. His military commanders, who had earlier wanted to take over cities in the North as the Soviet forces withdrew, were reluctant to stand by while the Nationalists strengthened their positions. Increased criticism of the American position and flurries of attacks on the reactionary policies of Chiang Kai-shek reflected a growing impatience with all that Marshall hoped to accomplish.

Marshall did not know the degree of Soviet control of Chinese Communist policy, but he sensed that Mao was the key to settlement of problems in the North. Ross Terrill, in his biography of Mao Tse-tung, says that Mao expected little from the negotiations and seemed detached, moving automatically through the discussions during Marshall's visit. But he felt impelled by Marshall's presence to toast the "durable cooperation between America and China and between Nationalists and Communists."[17]

Mao promised to abide by the terms of the various agreements. Marshall praised Chou En-lai for his friendliness and cooperation during the long negotiations at Chungking. Declaring that he had no desire to interfere in China's affairs, the American emphasized the need for a cease-fire. Then he stated to Mao directly the point that he had already made to Chiang Kai-shek: the United States could not continue to give aid unless there was unification of the country. (Despite the implication that unification would bring U.S. assistance to both Communists and Nationalists, Mao was not inclined to rely on such aid.)

As the talks progressed, Mao said he hoped that the agreements for a cease-fire would extend to Manchuria and that field teams would be sent there. Recalling that Yenan had shown little enthusiasm for measures likely to limit Communist gains in Manchuria, Marshall decided on plain speaking. He wrote President Truman that he had been frank "to an extreme" and that Mao had not shown resentment. It had been his understanding, Marshall said, that the agreements did extend to Manchuria, but the Communists had thrown doubt on that by making premature announcements of their special claims there. Chiang Kai-shek was reluctant to send field teams to Manchuria, lest the American presence on the teams lead to international complications. (The Generalissimo had said more bluntly that he feared the Soviets would demand representation on the teams.)

Leaving his role of stern uncle, Marshall shifted to honored visitor. That evening he caught cold "watching an elaborate performance of drum dancers and folk singers in an icy auditorium."[18]

Of the farewell as Marshall left the next day, Terrill wrote:

> Marshall was sincerely proceeding, in deep fog, down a straight road. Ready to depart at the Yenan airport, he asked Mao when he would be prepared to go and talk to Chiang again. "I shall go whenever Chiang asks me," Mao replied, as distant as a mountain. He could find a way of agreeing with Marshall's emotional declaration: "I can tell that an unprecedented era of progress awaits China."[19]

In common with many a touring leader, Marshall was momentarily blinded by the friendly reception and did not fully see the realities of the situation. With considerable pride he reported to Truman that he had completed a 3,000-mile trip with the Committee of Three to all the principal field commanders and "there was every indication that affairs would clear up quickly and communications be reopened and normal life for the poor civilians actually gotten under way. . . . My reception everywhere was enthusiastic and in cities tumultuous." He might tire enormously of the arguments among the leaders, but he never forgot the ordinary Chinese. Members of his staff recalled his saying, again and again, "I want to do something for these poor people."

But China was vast and its problems overwhelming. He mentioned to the President the shortage of U.S. officers for the field teams.

> The presence of an American in such circumstances will be mandatory for some time to come. . . . A single American with a Communist and Government representative of his committee and with communications almost non-existent will have to dominate a region larger than Pennsylvania and bring factions who have been at war for 18 years to a peaceful understanding and communications restored. . . . Our men have been splendid and are performing a great service for China and for American prestige.

He had enough hope so that he dared to go ahead with his plan to return home soon to prepare for loans to reward the factions for keeping peace. Marshall completed his report to the President by asking that he be called home for consultation. Truman was glad to agree, noting that Churchill was in the country and would like to see Marshall, but that this would require his return to Washington before March 12.[20]

As Marshall was writing Truman, James Shepley of his staff, who had just returned to the United States in accordance with earlier agreements, was explaining the General's thinking on China to the President. The President said that Marshall's visit would be helpful with regard to Congress and the general public, and that he personally understood the great need for liberal assistance to China. If the country had more men like Marshall, Truman added, "It could lick this period of crises every hour on the hour." He understood Marshall's desire to wind up his mission and would do what he could to help.[21]

The fragility of recent peace initiatives was soon evident. On March 9, Raymond Ludden of the U.S. Embassy at Chungking alerted Marshall to veering Communist views on cooperation. Recent Yenan broadcasts were playing down American contributions to victory over Japan and Germany. The Yenan radio had adopted the Soviet use of "fascist" to describe any policy they opposed. The editor of the Central Committee paper in Yenan had been bitter over American sea and air transport of Nationalist troops northward, and over American presence in Iran and North China. The Communists also professed to know nothing of the Soviet stripping of industries in Manchuria or of Russian demands for a share in

Sino-Soviet development companies there. Ludden thought it time for the Chinese Communists to make clear whether they were Chinese-Nationalist reformers following Marxist ideology or a satellite of the Soviet Union. Whether or not Ludden's memorandum at this particular time influenced Marshall, something angered him about Manchuria that morning. John Melby of the Embassy staff wrote in his diary: "We had a rough session on Manchuria with Marshall this morning. He is furious about the Russian looting, and he is irritated that the Communists, although not defending the Russian actions, remain silent about them."[22]

Marshall's last days before leaving for six weeks in the United States were filled with efforts to get field teams into Manchuria. Hoping to hasten an agreement, he proposed: (1) that field teams accompany Nationalist troops; (2) that they should bring fighting to an end and arrange to prevent further incidents; (3) that government troops could occupy places necessary for the establishment of national sovereignty and hold a strip thirty kilometers wide on either side of the two railroads mentioned in the Sino-Soviet Treaty.[23]

It was not likely that the Communists would ever agree (1) to the evacuation of any place they held that the Nationalists needed for the establishment of national sovereignty, or (2) to the prevention of Communist forces from occupying places evacuated by Soviet troops. When Soviets troops seemed about to leave Manchuria, Yenan abandoned its policy of working with Marshall for a course of self-help.

While Chou En-lai was insisting that the field teams should be empowered to deal with military and political matters, Marshall announced that he had to leave for the United States and that Lieutenant General Alvan C. Gillem would represent him in his absence. Gillem, an able corps commander in Europe during the war, was one of the senior officers proffered by Marshall to MacArthur, who accepted him for command in case of an invasion of Japan. After the war in the Pacific ended, he was shifted to China. Events would show that he could not hold the warring factions to their agreements.

On his way home, Marshall radioed Truman about the problems he had met in his last day's discussions. Gilding the situation's flaws, he said he thought he had won agreement from the two opponents. But arguments from Chiang and Chou on the day before his departure left little basis for optimism.

The Generalissimo had bluntly stated that he was convinced that the Communist Party of China was loyal to the Soviet Union and that its interest in entering the National Government was to be able to play the Soviet hand. He felt that the Chinese Communists looked upon Marshall as their protector and had accepted his proposals "largely for the purpose of obtaining well-trained, organized, and equipped 18 divisions." Chiang was concerned because the U.S. President had announced that loans to the National Government were predicated on certain political changes. He believed that this had "defeated the entire effect of the message except in so far as it was of great advantage to the Communist Party. He hoped that any loan which might be granted to China would have no conditions attached to it. At least there would be no public announcement of such conditions."[24]

On the same day, Chou En-lai had declared to Marshall that his party shared no blame for the political situation in China. The Communists had never interfered with negotiations between the Nationalists and Soviet Russia and they had never rejected consultation. He said that a Communist representative had assured the Nationalists that they could move to Mukden without opposition. The Communists, he averred, had kept their word on this and acted only when the Nationalist forces struck westward toward Jehol.[25]

Chou explained the recent increase of Communist forces in Manchuria by saying that the withdrawal of Soviet forces along the railways left a kind of vacuum into which the Nationalists poured troops without notifying Executive Headquarters. Dispatch of field teams had been delayed a month. The result was that "we were left in such a situation that somehow we have to clarify our position in Manchuria ourselves."

He laid chief blame on the CC Clique. It had not only provoked great disturbances against the Communists but also opposed those Political Consultative Conference delegates who did not belong to their clique. He accused the reactionaries of trying to torpedo the conference proposals.

The next day, Chou En-lai insisted that political and military matters must be considered together in Manchuria by the Committee of Three. He begged Marshall to keep in touch with the situation from the United States and said that if the matter of Manchurian supervision could not be solved before Marshall left, "I hope you will still render a great help to it from afar, after your leaving. The coming month is indeed the critical period, as you have said."[26]

Chiang Kai-shek also stressed Marshall's key position in the negotiations. In thanking President Truman for sending Marshall, who he felt had fulfilled "your expectations," he added that he

hoped the General would return to China at once on the completion of his immediate mission, ". . . to my mind, not only is General
Marshall's speedy return to China of urgent necessity, but his continued presence here for the next three years will play an important
part in the stabilization of the Far East."[27]

These testimonials to his crucial importance to the success of
negotiations were affirmed on March 11 by General Wedemeyer's
message to General Eisenhower concerning the former Chief of
Staff. Although he would later bitterly attack Marshall's policies in
China, Wedemeyer then wrote:

> He [Marshall] has done a fine job, quickly winning the respect and
> admiration of all with whom he came in contact. His approach to the
> problems presented has been logical, first accomplishing cessation
> of hostilities, and now he is well on the way toward the successful
> implementation of a plan that will integrate military forces of the
> Central Government and the Communists. All of this has been
> accomplished in the background of intrigue, mistrust, selfish per-
> sonalities, and oriental cunning. Really a stupendous accomplish-
> ment, and I doubt seriously whether any other person in the world
> could have done as much in so short a time. The permanence of his
> accomplishments however is in my mind contingent upon his physi-
> cal presence. If he were to be eliminated from the picture for the
> next several months, I feel that the opposing factions would soon be
> at each other's throats and the situation that existed last October
> would again prevail. General Marshall's international prestige and
> the very stature of the man have dominated the field and brought
> about conciliatory action on the part of the Communists and Central
> Government representatives.[28]

Marshall knew nothing of this estimate, but he did draw comfort
from a March 18 message from the Generalissimo saying that the
Plenary Session of the Nationalist Central Committee would soon
close. He was pleased that the members of that group had en-
trusted him with full power to handle Manchuria—a welcome
change from their earlier attitude of wanting to overturn the arrangements made regarding that area. "You need not worry,"
Chiang Kai-shek concluded, "about the anxieties I expressed to
you before you left Chungking."[29] Unfortunately, there would be
other seriously disquieting messages to speed his return.

Disastrous Interlude

GENERAL Marshall's return to Washington had full coverage in *Time*, which spoke of him as "the tall man, with a weathered homely face, in which there was the visible touch of greatness," and described his work as "the most significant mission undertaken by a U.S. citizen since the end of World War II." Marshall's picture was on the front cover of that issue of the magazine over the caption "We must not waste the victory." *Time*'s publisher, Henry Luce, China-born son of an American missionary, was one of the most fervent supporters of Chiang Kai-shek. His magazine declared of Marshall:

> For the first time in a major postwar issue, the power, prestige and principles of U.S. democracy have been brought to bear in constructive, positive fashion. . . . The great citizen-soldier who, in a totalitarian war, had assembled and directed an army without deviating an inch in the direction of totalitarian practice, had become a leader and spokesman of the drive for a nontotalitarian peace.[1]

On the day after his return, Marshall told reporters at his press conference, "If the world wants peace, China's effort must succeed and that success will depend largely on other nations." He continued:

> The United States at the present time is best able to render national assistance to China, but I am not quite as certain . . . of the understanding of their political leaders of the vital importance to the United States of the success of the present Chinese efforts toward unity and economic stability if we are to have [the] continued peace we hope for in the Pacific.[2]

Anticipating Marshall's probable questions about the Army's plans for China, Pentagon officers were busy preparing answers at the time of his arrival. High on their list was inactivation of the China Theater by May 1, 1946. Marshall and Wedemeyer had suggested that date, but the U.S. Navy believed it too precipitate. The Army's plan would leave in China the Military Advisory Group and Executive Headquarters in Peiping. By July 1, the Army expected to have in China 2,250 officers and men, with 750 in the Military Advisory Group. Remaining activities would be divided between the Navy, the Military Advisory Group, and the Executive Headquarters.[3]

Marshall became aware that Admiral C. M. Cooke, remembered as a peppery and able wartime Navy planner, was the strongest opponent of a reduction of American forces in China. Many naval officers stationed in China were admirers of Chiang Kai-shek and sharply criticized the few admirals who were dubious about his qualities of leadership. Cooke was a passionate adherent of the Generalissimo's cause, and after he retired from the Navy he worked for a time for the National Government. In later years his feeling about Marshall's role in China wheezed out in hoarse rasps at the mention of Marshall's name: "Feet of clay! Feet of clay!"[4]

At the time Cooke argued that premature deactivation of the U.S. Theater in China would damage U.S. interests there. Marshall declared that early withdrawal of U.S. forces would increase pressure on the Russians to get out of Manchuria, but Averell Harriman, former Ambassador to the Soviet Union, supported Cooke when he said that nothing had been gained anywhere in the world by trying to shame the Soviets into good behavior.[5]

Marshall had scarcely begun work on his aid program for China when his cease-fire efforts began to fall apart. Gillem reported delays in agreeing on final instructions to field teams in Manchuria. Alarmed, Marshall radioed Gillem to go to that area at once. Further delay might be fatal to the truce.[6]

To bolster Gillem in his talks with Chiang, Marshall revealed that he had discussed China's economic problems with the President, the Secretary of State, the president of the Export-Import Bank, and other important officials. He hoped that additional economic assistance would soon come.[7]

Gillem replied that he and Byroade thought it unwise for Gillem to go to Mukden before the field teams. They feared that the Committee of Three would be unproductive and lose prestige. An impatient Marshall insisted that Gillem would have to force agreement.

Remember, I worded these stipulations, hurriedly dictating them after a conversation with the Generalissimo. It seems to me you could get a concession from each side sufficient to permit entry of teams. You will have to force the issue. We cannot delay any longer. If there is to be further delay over the teams I feel you yourself must go to Mukden. I am not in agreement with the opinion of Byroade and you that the Committee of Three loses face in this matter. Face will be lost if the fighting develops more seriously in Manchuria and spreads south into Jehol. That will be serious consideration, not face.[8]

Gillem was embarrassed. Chou En-lai had gone to Yenan for further instructions and had not returned, having complained that he was being blamed at home for making concessions to the Nationals in the North while they were attacking Communist forces in the south.[9] Two days later, Chou warned Marshall that National China lacked the stability necessary to qualify for financial aid.

Appalled by the crumbling of all his work, Marshall again prodded Gillem on April 6. It was fatal, he said, to delay his appearance in Manchuria. "The teams are there and the trouble is there and we cannot just sit back and let affairs stew. . . . I am inclined to think that Byroade cannot further negotiate effectively on this matter without the presence of your rank and prestige."[10]

Marshall's dismay was natural, but Gillem felt that there was much to be said on his side. Disposed in later years to be defensive about the deterioration of the situation while Marshall was away, Gillem argued that Marshall had not completed the final agreement for the field teams to go to Manchuria before leaving for Washington, and that delays might have been avoided if Marshall had been there. Gillem favored the Nationals, but he conceded that the Generalissimo could be difficult. Normally, he explained, Chiang tried to be understanding, but when Gillem urged him to come to terms with the Communists still in the South, the leader was unwilling to lose an opportunity to destroy the group. When Gillem explained that he was trying to arrange the release of a National group bottled up in Central China in exchange for release of a Communist group in the South, Chiang flew into a rage and declared he would not let Communists escape.[11]

Despite severe disappointment, Marshall continued to work for economic aid to China. He made the rounds of various agencies, seeking money, appearing before Senate and House committees and conferences with the press. "All in all, I think I have sold China," he told Wedemeyer on March 29.[12]

An impressed Wedemeyer wrote to Hurley:

It is my conviction that were it not for the international prestige and the stature of General Marshall, the negotiations between the Chinese Communists and the Central Government representatives would break down. In other words, if we removed Marshall in the next year or two, I can foresee no permanence in what he has accomplished so far, for both sides will be at each other's throats again.[13]

Perhaps the breakdown would have occurred if Marshall had not left China in March, but it is certain that his absence was critical. New crises developed in the North by the time he was ready to leave Washington in mid-April. For several weeks pressure built up for his immediate return. Madame Chiang Kai-shek was one of the most persistent suppliants. Marshall had met her early in the war and had seen her infrequently at meetings since then. He knew she had been helpful as a go-between for Stilwell and her husband, and he also knew that Stilwell did not trust either her or her relatives. In 1946 she sat in as translator on some of Marshall's conferences with Chiang. On April 2 she wrote Marshall that, though Gillem had done his best, the situation was critical, and that "I feel that I should tell you frankly that your presence is vital if further deliberations take place. I hate to say 'I told you so' but even the short time you have been absent proves what I have repeatedly said to you— that China needs you. . . . And so hurry back to us and bring Mrs. Marshall."[14]

The General did bring Mrs. Marshall when he flew back from Washington to Peiping soon afterward. On the day they arrived, Chinese Communist forces entered Changchun, an important rail junction in Manchuria, which the Japanese had made the capital of Manchoukuo when they set up the puppet state in 1932.

The Marshalls next went to Chungking, but only for a short time, for at the beginning of May the government and the diplomatic delegations accredited to it made the long-awaited move to Nanking. Here the Marshalls lived in a compound that had living quarters for them and members of the mission staff as well as offices. A large second-floor room served as a meeting place for the staff. It could also be transformed into a recreation room where motion pictures were often shown in the evenings.[15]

Marshall found the days of late spring and early summer "hot and swampy even beyond Washington" and worried about the effect on Mrs. Marshall's health. From mid-July on, she was the guest of Generalissimo and Madame Chiang at their summer place in the mountains at Kuling, some 250 miles west of Nanking. Mrs. Marshall was given a large, comfortable cottage with servants, a small swimming pool, and trees. Madame Chiang seemed "quite devoted to her in admiration and affection," Marshall wrote a friend, describing a close relationship that would continue long after his death.[16] When Marshall came there for discussions, the Generalissimo joined the group.

Getting to Kuling from Nanking was not easy, but Marshall made the effort frequently during the summer negotiations. The trip required a little less than two hours by plane, then a forty-five-minute ride on a captured Japanese gunboat down and across the Yangtze, followed by a thirty-minute automobile ride, and, last, two and a quarter hours in a sedan chair borne by bearers up steps cut out of the mountainside.[17]

This relatively pleasant side of Marshall's stay in China contrasted sharply with the clashes he faced almost daily with Chiang and the Communists. The General had returned to China more in sorrow than in fury, disheartened by the collapse of so much of his earlier efforts. Hours spent in comfortable, even charming, surroundings could not cancel his feeling of futility. But this domestic friendliness may have been responsible for the Generalissimo's discounting of Marshall's stern warnings.

When Marshall was in Washington trying to get loans for the National Government, indiscreet statements issued by top National officials constantly bedeviled the General, making his task even more difficult. He suggested that Chiang Kai-shek get an American public-relations adviser who could brief him on American ideas and outlook. Asked by the Generalissimo to suggest such a person, Marshall came up with the name of John Robertson Beal, a newsman in Washington for the last ten years, of which the last two had been with the Time-Life Bureau. Very aware that Beal's boss, Henry Luce, had contributed perhaps more than any other American to the legend of the Generalissimo as the savior of China, Marshall told the publisher that he needed someone "to keep the Chinese out of trouble with the United States." Luce gave Beal leave of absence and he departed for China to arrive at the time of Marshall's return.[18]

In China, Marshall found he must constantly urge the need for calm while negotiations were in progress. To General Yu Ta-wei, Minister of Communications, he deplored the Generalissimo's re-

cent attacks on the good faith of the Chinese Communists, which
had "murdered" his efforts in the United States. "Things like that
can ruin the public opinion in the United States and it is a terrible
price to pay."[19]

Because patience had become ingrained into Marshall's character, he had not entirely abandoned hope of securing peace in
China. He searched again for a basis for agreement. On April 23
he handed Chou a proposed cease-fire accord and sent a copy to
the National negotiator. On the 27th and the 28th he had further
talks with Chou, giving him National proposals.[20] Hearing Marshall
talk at a press conference on May 1, John Melby of the U.S. Embassy staff thought he sounded depressed and worried. But on the
4th he was back negotiating, suggesting to the Communists that
they evacuate Changchun in favor of a group to be sent in by
Executive Headquarters.[21]

The news from China that got back to Washington made General
Wedemeyer, undergoing treatment there for sinus complications,
feel that Marshall was more indispensable than ever. Whether or
not he had heard that the President might be replacing Byrnes as
Secretary of State, he extolled Marshall's critical importance to the
nation in a letter to the General:

My experience in Washington, political and military, would indicate definitely and more strongly than ever that you should take the
post of Secretary of State, and when the time comes for the nomination of a presidential candidate, you should accept same. We need
leadership of the calibre you and you alone are capable of giving
during this critical period in our country's history. Your abject hu-
mility in approaching problems disarms the opposition and your
experience in coping with problems both national and international
would do something constructive toward bringing about clear-cut
solutions of problems. You are still young and vigorous mentally
and I do hope that conditions will be created whereby your talents
will be exploited. General, I am not a damn flatterer when I state
sincerely that we need now a man of your character to serve as a
bulwark in defending the principles of democracy as well as decency
in human relationships.[22]

Marshall's own judgment of his effectiveness was somewhat
lower. He wrote President Truman on May 6 that "the outlook is
not promising." He must have felt even less hope the next evening,
when he was met coldly by Chiang Kai-shek at a reception. When
Marshall talked with General Yu Ta-wei of an attempt to get the

Communists to evacuate Changchun, Yu said that Chiang did not think the time was ripe for Marshall to re-enter mediation activities. Sensing that Chiang wanted time to move against the Communists, Marshall warned General Yu that an attack on Changchun would "preclude further negotiation for peace."[23]

It was at this juncture that General Eisenhower, on an inspection tour of U.S. Army posts in the Far East, came to Nanking. After lunching with the Generalissimo and Madame Chiang, he delivered to Marshall President Truman's invitation for the General to succeed Byrnes as Secretary of State around July 1946. It was expected that Byrnes would have to resign then because of a heart ailment.[24]

Marshall told Eisenhower that his answer was "yes," but that "to be fair" he could not leave before September, by which time he hoped that the Nationals and Communists might have reached agreement. He and Eisenhower agreed on several code words so that the President's response could be sent to Marshall by radio without risking a leak. After seeing the President in Washington on May 28, Eisenhower sent a personal letter to Marshall to say that the President was pleased with his response and had said, "This gives me a wonderful ace in the hole." The timing and delayed sequence suggested by Marshall could be easily arranged. In June, Eisenhower followed his letter with a message to Marshall using the established code words. Under Secretary Acheson was so puzzled by the message that he asked the President if he required clarification of its meaning. Truman explained what was afoot.

Throughout early May, Marshall was uneasy over the Generalissimo's insistence on further Communist concessions. When he proposed some measures to defuse the Manchurian situation on May 12, Chiang agreed provided the Communists promised not to take Harbin.[25]

The Generalissimo took an even firmer stand a week later, when Nationalist forces defeated the Communists at Szepingkai, seventy miles southwest of Changchun. Marshall called this battle the turning point in the negotiations, since it convinced the Nationalist generals that they could settle the Manchurian problem by force.[26]

Finding their position seriously threatened, the Communists tried to bargain with Marshall: if they withdrew from Changchun, they must be allowed five divisions in Manchuria. His reminder that the original agreement specified only one was waved aside.[27]

While talks went on between Marshall and Chou, Nationalist troops under General Tu Yu-ming continued to move northward. According to Chiang Kai-shek's later account of this period, "Gov-

ernment troops were ordered to push on along the Chinese Changchun Railway with Harbin as their target, and met with practically
no opposition."[28]

Chiang informed Marshall on the 22nd that he had not heard
from his generals for three days and that he feared they were
moving on Changchun. He proposed going to Mukden to get the
situation under control. Marshall offered the use of his own plane.
The Generalissimo accepted and set out the following day.
Strangely optimistic over this action, Marshall told Chou that perhaps a solution was "within grasp." He later realized that Chiang's
actions started "a chain of events which were almost completely
disastrous in their effects on the situation. . . ."[29]

National troops entered Changchun on May 22, following Communist withdrawal. Marshall heard nothing from the Generalissimo
and continued to talk to Chou of the need for a cease-fire. These
discussions were disrupted when, in Chiang's absence, National
officials in Nanking closed a Communist daily newspaper and the
Communist news agency. Deciding that Chiang's continued absence from Nanking might be a signal for offensive action by the
Nationals, Marshall radioed the Generalissimo on the 29th:

> The continued advances of the Government troops in Manchuria
> in the absence of any caution by you to terminate the fighting other
> than on the terms you dictated via Madame Chiang's letter of May
> 24th are making my services as possible negotiator extremely diffi-
> cult and will soon make them virtually impossible.[30]

Receiving no reply from Chiang but many angry protests from
the Communists, Marshall radioed him that the continued movement of National troops meant that "the integrity of my position
is open to serious question." It was one of his earliest allusions to
the problem that would make him the object of virulent Communist
attack.

The National leaders never understood Marshall's determination to hold the scales in China even. They expected him to protest,
but found it absurd for him to insist that they refrain from finishing
the Communist forces if they could. Instead of worrying over his
integrity as a negotiator, they rejoiced that breaking off negotiations would leave them free to control events in Manchuria.

Not until June 3 did the Generalissimo return to Chungking. On
that day Chou En-lai bitterly attacked the Kuomintang's recent
moves against the Communist press. In a frank exchange with
Marshall, he flung at him the charge that the National generals now

"had the bit in their teeth and the United States was following a double policy."[31]

Resigned to dropping his mediation efforts, Marshall was surprised and relieved when the Generalissimo agreed to establish an advance section of Executive Headquarters at Changchun and accepted a ten-day truce during which he would stop the advance of his forces. Marshall promptly notified Chou En-lai of this concession. After a Communist counterdemand for a month's truce, Marshall won an agreement for an additional five days. Such eternal unraveling of understandings and the emotional cost of beginning again and again over familiar ground at last affected the General. A member of the Embassy staff noted that "Marshall, whose patience seems infinite at times, is really getting short-tempered."[32]

Chou En-lai scored points with Marshall when he chose this moment to say that the Communists still had faith in the General, and were willing to continue efforts to achieve an understanding. Marshall wrote his liaison officer, Colonel Carter, that although the Communists were convinced that he favored the Nationals (Chiang had gone to Mukden in his plane), they still seemed to respect his integrity. "This is a hell of a problem," he declared, "but we will lick it yet, pessimists to the contrary notwithstanding." Actually, he had bounced back; he did not intend that a subordinate thousands of miles away in Washington would catch him with his guard down.[33]

He was sensitive to coming troubles. Chen Li-fu, leader of the most conservative forces in the Kuomintang, bluntly warned a member of the U.S. Embassy staff in mid-June that he had fought the Communists for nineteen years and would fight them that much longer if necessary. In what Marshall felt to be a serious effort to change U.S. policy, Chen stated that if negotiations were to be based on good faith and integrity, talks with the Communists were futile. He did not think that failure of these discussions would end in civil war, for the Communists were bluffing "and can be destroyed with little difficulty."[34]

A day later, Marshall got an unfriendly reaction from the Russians. Eugene Vinogradov of the Russian Embassy in China declared that (1) Marshall's mission was a failure, (2) American activities in China, Japan, Korea, and the Pacific islands were aimed offensively at the Soviet Union, and (3) thus far Soviet Russia had kept hands off but "it may become necessary to intervene in China if the present unsatisfactory situation continues."[35]

As early as the 17th, Marshall reported to President Truman that the parties had reached an impasse.

The situation is extremely critical and has not been helped throughout by the belief, freely expressed, by some of the National Government's military officials and some politicians that only a policy of force will satisfy the situation and the Communists can be speedily crushed. I consider the last view a gross understatement of the possibilities, as a long and terrible conflict would be inevitable, I am sure. Also, the Soviet Government would probably intervene openly or undercover. All of my views have been stated to the Generalissimo. . . .[36]

Marshall saw hope in only one particular. He had recently sent Byroade to Changchun to open the Advance Section, Executive Headquarters. By June 15 there were eight truce teams in the area, and by the end of the month the truce in Manchuria was being observed fairly by both sides. Marshall took advantage of this state of affairs to get the truce extended briefly.[37]

Marshall had another flicker of hope on June 24, when he won an oral agreement in the Committee of Three for a permanent cease-fire in Manchuria, for a reopening of communications there, and for the resolution of differences over field teams and Executive Headquarters. The Generalissimo destroyed that hope by refusing to sign the agreement unless the February accord on military reorganization and demobilization was revised.[38] At the end of the month, Marshall told Truman that he saw little prospect of success in his efforts in the face of the "strong desire of Government military leaders to settle matters by force for which the plans of the Government are completely well known to the Communists."[39]

He had already tried to warn the Nationals that they would get no U.S. aid in the policy they were pursuing. When General Yu Ta-wei, now chief representative of Chiang in the Committee of Three, wanted to limit the renewal of the truce to one day, Marshall flashed a warning light. He said that the government could not count on U.S. support for a civil war in China. When the Chinese general wanted to know what would happen to the Marines, the Seventh Fleet, and American support, Marshall replied that the first two would probably be withdrawn and the aid stopped. Yu Ta-wei and other Nationals believed differently. They knew that many U.S. officers were strongly pro-National and they thought they could depend on their support, while anti-administration congressmen gave them noisy encouragement. It was to offset such ideas that Marshall sought an interview with Chiang in Nanking on June 30.[40]

Beginning at 9:30 A.M. and continuing through lunch until 3:00 P.M., Marshall outlined the dangers of existing government policy.

He referred to obvious signs that the National military group intended to dominate the situation. He alluded to recent "remarkable statements" that Chen Li-fu had made. To Marshall it seemed "that the Government was washing its hands of any democratic procedure and was pursuing a dictatorial policy of military force." He warned that there would be an "inevitable comparison of this procedure with that of the prewar army dictatorship in Japan which led to the destruction of that nation." In later years, Marshall recalled telling Chiang that at present his people looked on him as their George Washington but one day they might change their opinions. The Chinese leader had said nothing in response to Marshall's statement, but the latter had learned to watch the movement of the Generalissimo's foot as a gauge of his reaction. It shook with impatience.[41]

Marshall's words were bitter medicine for the Generalissimo, just when everything seemed to be moving in his favor. Disclaiming responsibility for any statements of his generals, he issued orders that no action should be taken except by way of defense. Marshall reported to Beal that Chiang almost wept as they talked.[42]

VIII

Picking Up the Pieces

M A R S H A L L had concluded before he returned to Washington in March that he needed a full-time ambassador in China. Robertson had done outstanding work as Chargé but was now fully occupied with Executive Headquarters duties. Byroade was in charge of the field teams. Colonel George "Bud" Underwood, who had taken Byroade's place, and Colonel John H. Caughey were working overtime with other mission business, so an ambassador was more essential than ever. Marshall had less assistance than at any time since he had become Chief of Staff in 1939. His China files are full of reports and correspondence drafted entirely in his own hand.

Marshall had mentioned the possibility of Wedemeyer's appointment before he returned to Washington for medical treatment of his sinuses, not long before Marshall came back in March. Wedemeyer appeared ideal for the ambassadorship when Marshall thought that the Nationals and Communists were on the verge of concluding several basic agreements.[1] But as the negotiations were drawn out, Marshall asked Secretary Byrnes to delay action on the appointment. Wedemeyer, who had expected to return shortly to China, kept up a stream of correspondence to Marshall, noting his observations on conditions at home and indicating all he had been doing to strengthen Marshall's hand. He reminded Marshall that the Generalissimo had expected him back and worried that his prolonged absence might lessen his influence in that quarter. Marshall replied that if Wedemeyer were announced as Ambassador at this state of the negotiations, the action would be construed as an indication that Marshall was leaving and his negotiating power would be reduced. After the General returned to China,

Wedemeyer continued his letters, making clear that he was defending Marshall's policies, especially to Representative Walter Judd, one-time medical missionary to China and a strong partisan of Chiang Kai-shek's cause. Wedemeyer said he thought he had convinced Judd "that he must continue full support of [Marshall's] plans to eliminate private armies in China."[2]

Aware of Marshall's problem, Eisenhower told his former chief that if Wedemeyer's return to China would be embarrassing, he could assign him to another post in the United States. As quarrels and countercharges increased in China, Marshall concluded that it would be unwise just then to name Wedemeyer, because of his close connections with the Generalissimo. At the time, Wedemeyer said he understood the reasoning. Referring to himself in the third person, he wrote General Thomas T. Handy, Eisenhower's deputy, "It is only natural that the Communists will not accept Wedemeyer as a mediator or in any indispensable role in China for they recall that he served two years as the Generalissimo's Chief of Staff." In *Wedemeyer Reports!*, the General expressed deep disappointment that Marshall would allow the Communists to dictate which American representative they would take.[3]

In early July, Marshall found his Ambassador in the person of an old China hand, John Leighton Stuart, who had spent more years in China than in the United States. Stuart's great-grandfather, a Presbyterian minister, had come to eastern Kentucky from Virginia before Kentucky was a state, at almost the same time that Marshall's great-great-grandfather, a Baptist preacher, was moving there from Virginia. The elder Stuart's wife, a Todd, was an aunt of Mrs. Lincoln. Stuart's father, born in Kentucky in 1840, also became a Presbyterian preacher, and then a missionary to China. The future Ambassador was born in Hangchow in 1876. He did not see the United States until he was eleven, when he was sent back to his mother's home in Mobile, Alabama, to go to school. He went to a preparatory school in Charlottesville, Virginia, was graduated from Hampden-Sydney College four years before George Marshall entered Virginia Military Institute, studied at Union Theological Seminary at Richmond, and was ordained as a minister of the Southern Presbyterian Church.[4]

After nearly eighteen years in the United States, Stuart went back to China as a missionary. Three years later, he began teaching at Nanking Theological Seminary, where he remained until 1919. In that year he was invited to become president of the newly formed Yenching University, established just outside Peking as the result of the merger of two small colleges, one Methodist, the other Presbyterian. His vice president was Harry Luce, father of the later head of Time-Life.[5]

A few hours after the Pearl Harbor attack, Stuart was arrested by the Japanese and, with two friends, was kept under house arrest in Peking for the rest of the war. When he was released in 1945, he went briefly to Chungking for a victory celebration, was received by the Generalissimo, and met Ambassador Hurley, Mao Tse-tung, and Chou En-lai. He went back to the United States for several months, then returned to China about the same time that Marshall came back from his March trip to Washington. While he was visiting in Nanking, Chiang urged him to talk with General Marshall. Marshall talked with him at length, was impressed by his knowledge of the Chinese situation and of China, and asked for his help and advice. Stuart promised to come back to Nanking when needed.

Their next meeting came at Stuart's initiative. During an education conference in Shanghai, Chen Li-fu twice discussed Chinese problems with the college president. Although Marshall thought of Chen Li-fu as "the leader of the reactionary forces which were blocking his efforts," Stuart was of two minds about the Chen brothers. He later wrote of them that they

> were very intelligent, free from any suspicion of venality, but fervent believers in the Kuomintang and its leaders as well as the necessity of eradicating communism from China. The so-called CC Clique, named after them, was not so much a clique as the members of the Kuomintang organization which they had built up and controlled in all of its ramifications. This and the patronage that went on gave them enormous influence. Their minions exploited this for blackmail and other selfish ends, but they themselves worked with singlehearted loyalty to build up their leader against all rivals within the party and to suppress all outside opposition.

Stuart wrote Marshall of Chen Li-fu's visits and asked if he would like a summary of what Chen had said.[6]

Marshall already knew in some detail what Chen Li-fu believed. The General must also have seen *Time*'s issue of May 27, 1946, which carried a portrait of Chen on its cover. Discussing China's problems in terms of Chen's career and philosophy, *Time* said:

> If Americans are going to know China they will have to know the grave, gray man with the face of an aristocratic saint, who sometimes wears a rumpled business suit and sometimes a blue mandarin

gown, who sometimes plots little intrigues and sometimes dreams great dreams.

After listing many solid virtues, including freedom from corruption, the *Time* story said that so great was his anti-Communist obsession that he had in fact made new Communists. "So heavy is Chen's hand on all unorthodoxy that many youths who might have taken a middle course choose communism's extreme instead of Chen's." In his years as Minister of Education, he had emphasized practical courses and cut down on history, philosophy, and economics.

Time caught the implacable antagonism between the Nationalists and the Communists in reporting an icy exchange some months earlier between Chou En-lai and Chen Li-fu. Chou had said, "In those years when you were working against the Communist Party and I was underground, I once escaped five minutes before your men arrived. Let me compliment you on your skill." Chen replied with deliberate, measured emphasis, "Let *me* compliment *you* on your skill in escaping." These were not pleasantries. As the writer remarked, "Men who thus accept the fact that they hunt each other to death are not expected to bury the hatchet except in each other's neck."[7]

Certainly Marshall was interested in anything Stuart had to add concerning Chen Li-fu. He sent a plane almost at once, and Stuart arrived in Nanking as the temporary truce in Manchuria was about to expire. Stuart was kept so busy he never got around to Chen's conversations. As he made ready to return to Peiping, Marshall pressed him to remain for the Fourth of July celebration at the U.S. Embassy. There, Marshall asked him if he would accept the post of Ambassador.

Protesting that he had passed his seventieth birthday and that he had submitted his resignation to Yenching University, Stuart at last reluctantly agreed to accept. Marshall moved quickly. In less than a week, Truman had sent the nomination to the Senate, which at once approved the choice.[8]

In common with many American missionaries who had lived long in China, Stuart deplored Nationalists who were corrupt or repressive, but he still saw Chiang Kai-shek as China's most feasible hope against Chinese Communism. He shared Marshall's idea that compromise solutions could be worked out and that perhaps liberal leaders associated with neither extreme might be found.

Marshall needed help so desperately that he made much of the fact that Chiang's secretary was a former student of Stuart's and might be of assistance for that reason. The General flew with Stuart on July 18 to see the Generalissimo, warning him as grimly as he had Chou that current fighting might well spread into uncontrollable civil war.[9]

Marshall was especially distrustful because of the recent assassination in Kunming of two professors who had leading positions in the Democratic League, by persons allegedly connected with the Kuomintang's secret police. He was stern with Chiang Kai-shek about the alienation of American public opinion. The attacks were on the best-educated group in China, Marshall pointed out, many of them graduates of U.S. universities. Americans were likely to compare their records with the less educated military leaders who "were participating, in his opinion, in a civil war."[10]

Chou En-lai hoped to use the assassination of the Democratic League leaders to force a reorganization of the National Government, but any advantage he may have gained with Marshall was lost when Communist guerrillas ambushed a Marine convoy near Anping, between Harbin and Tientsin, killing an officer and two enlisted men. Chou's denial of the official American report did not convince Marshall.[11]

In the new muddle, Marshall seized on Stuart's proposal that he head a five-man committee that would proceed with plans to reorganize the government. Although weakened by dysentery, Stuart summoned the strength to win a temporary agreement from both sides. Trouble soon developed when Chiang Kai-shek insisted that the committee's formation must await the Communist withdrawal from five positions in North China and Manchuria.[12]

New leverage was applied on both parties in mid-August. A Truman letter, based on a Marshall-Stuart draft, warned Chiang Kai-shek that if real moves toward peace were not made soon, the United States would have to redefine its position. Soon thereafter, Marshall, who had warned Chou against obstructing a proper investigation into the Anping incident, furnished the Communist leader with evidence supplied by Robertson showing that the Kuomintang and the Marines had not been involved. There was a violent attack on the American General in the *Yenan Emancipation Daily* on August 14, the first press assault Marshall had suffered in China. The next day, he warned Chou that it was increasingly difficult for him to negotiate under such circumstances.[13]

Chiang was determined to attack in the North, and Marshall warned in mid-August that Chiang's plan of attack would be catastrophic because his extended lines of communication and the mountainous terrain favored Communist guerrilla tactics. Insisting that the Communists were violating cease-fire agreements, Chiang brushed aside the arguments. Marshall reported to Truman that Chiang had become more demanding in his approach than ever before.[14]

The Chinese Communists responded to National movements by mobilizing troops to hold their defense areas, and the U.S. Embassy alerted Washington to a virtual declaration of civil war in China. Again Marshall prepared to fly to Kuling to appeal to the Generalissimo, but before his trip took place, events in Washington forced the Nationalists to stop and think.

On the morning of August 30, General Yu Ta-wei arrived from Nationalist headquarters to protest that the U.S. State Department had disapproved export licenses that would permit Chinese purchases of certain types of small-arms ammunition from the United States. When Yu remonstrated, Marshall reminded him that he had been warning of such possible action for some time, though this move had been made without reference to him.[15] Marshall was honest in saying that he had not been responsible for this particular ruling, but it had followed logically from his use of powers under his presidential directive to pressure the Nationalist leader.

More than a month earlier, the State Department had told Marshall that the China Aid bill that had been introduced in the current special session of Congress would likely not pass before adjournment unless he issued a strong personal appeal. Marshall replied that, in the present state of affairs, he did not want to push the legislation. At the same time, he did not want it withdrawn. He thought it best for the State Department to put it forward and the Congress not to act upon it. Secretary Byrnes concurred in this view, as did Representative Sol Bloom, Chairman of the House Committee on Foreign Affairs. Not aware of Marshall's message, Bloom declared that, unless the rules were suspended, the bill could not be considered that session, and that an effort to force passage would be defeated. He proposed to let it die on the vine. Marshall accepted this view.[16]

On July 23, the China Supply Commission in Washington had asked for an export license for the delivery of small-arms ammunition from American commercial firms and the War Assets Administration. Colonel Carter asked that Marshall verify his assumption "that until the situation clears, shipment of military end-use items to China obtained from any source should continue to be deferred." Marshall replied on the 26th, "There is no objection that I see for the Chinese to purchase equipment and ammunition in the United States providing it is stipulated that delivery on undelivered items, whether paid for or not, can be withheld by the United States should that course appear to be in the best interests of the United States. . . ." He added that he had recently instructed General Gillem in the same vein.[17]

It was not until late September that Marshall made the embargo explicit in orders issued to General Gillem. At this point Colonel Carter interpreted Marshall's action as "another implement in his negotiations and not a retraction of the over-all United States commitment to equip Chinese peacetime forces." In October, in giving additional instructions about the embargo, Marshall said he still considered it "preferable, under the circumstances, that my name be kept out of the transaction." Marshall later explained in his official report:

> As it became apparent during my mission in China that the continuation, at that time, of some phases of these (military aid) programs [was] not conducive to peace and unity in China nor in the best interests of the United States, action was taken to suspend certain portions of the programs which might have a bearing on the prosecution of hostilities and the internal situation in China.[18]

American efforts in early September to find a basis for settling immediate problems between the warring parties bogged down over the mixture of military and political demands. The Communists wanted a cease-fire before they were willing to join in a five-man group effort to get agreements on the representation of various parties in the reorganized State Council and the National Assembly. Here the core of the argument lay in the Communist effort to get enough votes to prevent the Nationalists from making changes in the new government once it was started. They wanted a cease-fire in fighting before agreeing to negotiate politically but the Nationalists did not want to stop their winning forces without Communist concessions on political arrangements. Chou En-lai tried to draw from the Americans their guarantee of a cease-fire if he agreed to make political concessions. This they declined to make.[19]

In reporting developments to Truman, Marshall stressed that his problems arose from the National drive on Kalgan, a rail center in Chahar province, called the "Gate to Mongolia." He noted, "As the Government campaign in Jehol continues to develop to its advantage, the Government's stand regarding the Communists has become the more implacable regarding the conditions for the termination of hostilities."[20]

Immediately after his talk with Chou, Marshall flew to Kuling to talk with Chiang. Afterward the General reported to the President that the Generalissimo had agreed to some concessions, then nullified their effect by imposing new restrictions on the naming of Communist delegates to the National Assembly, a demand that Chou En-lai rejected totally.[21]

The Communists blamed Marshall. A Yenan broadcast on September 14 attacked him for not opposing the "aggravation of China's civil war" and declared that his mediation had failed. The broadcast added that Marshall's prestige had reached its lowest ebb; even his integrity was in question.[22]

Chou kept up a flow of memoranda, demanding a meeting of the Committee of Three and threatening to publish minutes of earlier meetings if the committee was not convened. Stung by the Communist attacks on his integrity and honesty of purpose, Marshall saw no reason to mediate. If the Communists so distrusted him, there was nothing for him to do. He would withdraw if that was what they wanted.[23]

Angry as he was, Marshall doubted that the Communists wanted him to quit. Perhaps they yet "can pull this chestnut out of the crossfire which rages about it," he cabled the President. If his spirit had needed a vote of approval from Washington, he got it. Truman replied: "I have the utmost confidence in you. I know you can 'pull the chestnut out of the crossfire,' if it can be done at all."[24]

Thus encouraged, Marshall urged Chou to return to Nanking. However, he failed to take recent military events into consideration. The reason was clear in Stuart's report to the State Department a short time later: "The loss of Jehol province was a severe blow to the Communists, as it resulted in the cutting of their line of communications between Kalgan and Manchuria." Government forces were moving on Kalgan, "the largest and most important city in the hands of the Communists south of the Great Wall."[25]

Marshall worked at keeping the furious Chou in line by lecturing to him on their mistakes. They had erred, he pointed out, by (1) their failure to submit troop lists after the February 25 agreement, thus playing into the hands of Kuomintang extremists; (2) their attack on Changchun, which gave the Nationals a precedent; and (3) their June offensive in Shantung, which wrecked Marshall's efforts to get a truce then.[26]

The next day, Chou En-lai counterattacked. Ignoring the list of errors, he said that if the government did not immediately halt its advance against Kalgan and vicinity, "the Chinese Communist Party feels itself forced to presume that the Government is thereby

giving public announcement of a total national split, and it has
ultimately abandoned its pronounced policy of peaceful settlement. . . ."[27]

Chiang Kai-shek appeared to confirm this view when he returned
to Nanking and demanded that the completion of military and
other agreements must precede a cease-fire. Marshall felt this made
nonsense of his previous proposal and said that under the circumstances he would be unable to continue mediating. He told Stuart
that he thought the Nationals were using him as cover while continuing to advance against the Communists.[28] That day Marshall
wrote the Generalissimo that unless a basis was found for ending
the fighting, he would recommend to the President that he be
recalled and U.S. efforts to mediate terminated.[29]

Ambassador Stuart underscored the increasingly strained relations on October 3 when he reported that Chou En-lai, in a recent
press conference, had accused the United States of aiding civil war
by supplying war materiel to Chiang Kai-shek. Chou had mentioned current negotiations by which the Nationals would get $200
million in munitions from the United States. The United States had
given the Nationals warships, extended Lend-Lease, made a surplus-property agreement, supplied bombs, fuel, and spare parts for
the Chinese Air Force. Fifty-seven U.S.-equipped divisions had
been thrown against the Communists, and U.S. forces had moved
400,000 National troops into North China. If the United States
would cease aiding the Nationalists, they would have to give serious
consideration to ending the war. The argument that American
troops were needed to bar Soviet forces from China was an insult
to China, since the Chinese had no intention of becoming a colony
of any power. There were areas of China, he noted, free of United
States troops where no other foreign troops had entered. Chou had
no desire to oppose United States aid once the National Government had been reformed, but if Marshall's mission was to be successful, "American forces must be withdrawn immediately and
material aid stopped."[30]

The Generalissimo called a conference at Nanking with Marshall
and Stuart on October 4. He was distressed at Marshall's suggestion that he be recalled. "He stated," reported Marshall,

> that he had searched his mind for any action that might have been
> construed as lack of integrity in action on his part without result.
> Such an action by him was unthinkable—that, aside from his posi-
> tion as head of the Government of China, his own conscience as a
> Christian would forbid.[31]

But Chiang wanted to keep Kalgan, for Communist possession of that city threatened Peiping. Once National forces occupied Kalgan, in about ten days, he would be ready to cease hostilities.

Marshall recalled that in June the Generalissimo had said that the Communists might have Kalgan but must give up Chengteh, northeast of Peiping. Now, with Chengteh in his hands, Chiang must have Kalgan as well. Marshall did not question the importance of Kalgan, but he could not escape the conclusion that while the Communists were calling for a cessation of hostilities, the government "was actually pursuing a policy of force." Negotiations would be time-consuming as military operations continued, and talks would be at the "point of a gun." Under these conditions Marshall said he could not continue as a mediator.

> I based my discussion on the grounds that there must be no question regarding the integrity of my position or actions, that I could not place the United States Government in a position where the integrity of its actions as represented by me could be successfully questioned.

Chiang clearly felt that Marshall was bluffing. His advisers, Marshall believed, thought that "because of Soviet considerations, we would be forced to [go] along with protracted negotiations while the campaign progressed as they desired." Under the circumstances, Marshall thought that despite the current

> vicious Communist propaganda of misrepresentation and bitter attacks, and their stupid failure to agree to the proposal of Doctor Stuart and me for the five man group to settle the State Council issue . . . the United States Government can not afford before the world to have me continue as a mediator and should confidentially notify the Generalissimo accordingly.[32]

Marshall believed that his recall was the only way "to dispel the evident belief of the Government generals that they can drag us along while they carry through an actual campaign of force." If it took as long as a week to decide on a course of action and then wait for a reply, the government troops would probably have Kalgan. What effect this would have on future cooperation with the Communists could only be guessed. Still, Marshall wanted the matter handled confidentially. As long as there was still time for the Generalissimo to reverse himself, "I think it of the greatest importance that no intimation of this action leak into the press where it could do irreparable injury to the Chinese Government in favor of the Communists." The Communists, he added, probably would not want to see him leave.

Before the message could be delivered to Truman, there were new developments in China. General Peter Pee, aide to the Generalissimo, while visiting Ambassador Stuart on the evening of October 4, learned that Marshall was suggesting his recall. He hurried back to see Chiang and called a half-hour later to ask that Stuart visit the Generalissimo at once. On Stuart's arrival, Chiang said he would suggest a short truce in the advance to Kalgan. This led Marshall to ask Colonel Carter in Washington to delay delivery of his message to President Truman.[33]

Two days later, Marshall reported that Chiang was now ready to consider a ten-day truce during which the five-man group under Stuart would select members for the State Council and establish the basis for a Communist delegation to take part in the National Assembly. Under Marshall the Committee of Three would arrange for the immediate implementation of the program for the reorganization of the Army, the location of Chinese divisions, and the schedule of movements thereunto. The Generalissimo wanted this put forward as a proposal by Marshall and Stuart, who would also make the announcements on the truce.[34]

For a moment it seemed that something could be worked out. But Chou En-lai was not impressed, seeing the whole procedure as a National effort to gain time. Marshall found his own position now reversed, since the government had offered a temporary cease-fire and the Communists declined.[35]

He decided to fly to Shanghai in an effort to persuade Chou to come to Nanking for further discussions. Knowing that Gillem had a house in Shanghai, Marshall asked him to bring Chou there. "I've got to see Chou En-lai once more. I've got to make one final move more. . . ." Marshall was at Gillem's house on the 9th, when Gillem ushered in Chou. As they entered, Marshall stepped from behind a screen. Chou had had no inkling that Marshall was to be there and "damn near died," Gillem recalled, but he stayed for an afternoon's talk.[36]

Simmering with rage over the attack on Kalgan, Chou declared that only an absolute cease-fire would now be acceptable. He charged Marshall and Stuart with trying to sell a bogus plan for peace and demanded that National troops return to the positions they had held on January 13 in China proper and on June 7 in Manchuria. Marshall recalled to Chou that earlier he had said, "If you don't trust me, say so. You have now said so. I am leaving immediately for Nanking."[37]

Displeased as he was, Marshall could recognize the dangers Chou had faced in coming to see him in Shanghai. Gillem said later, "I had a very grave time with Chou En-lai. When the Nationals found he was in there, some of the gunmen and so on took to positions across the street from my house, and I had to get the secret police and so on. For a couple of days we had quite an episode there. . . ."[38]

The fall of Kalgan came on October 10, at the same time that the National Government announced that the National Assembly would meet a month later. The Communists declined to take part unless they and their allies got sufficient seats in a projected State Council to block measures they did not like. Ambassador Stuart believed that the Generalissimo was now prepared to go through with the writing of a constitution, with or without the Communists.[39]

Struggling to keep negotiations alive, Marshall and Stuart drafted a statement that they hoped the Generalissimo would make in an effort to get a peaceful settlement. It proposed an immediate meeting of the Committee of Five under Stuart to discuss the reorganization of the National Government and a meeting of the Committee of Three under Marshall to discuss settlement of other remaining problems. Key points among the nine set forth for the two committees included: (1) National troops in North Central China were to remain where they were until the Committee of Three agreed on relocation of forces; and (2) "whatever understanding is reached by the Five Man Committee headed by Doctor Stuart . . . is to be confirmed by the Steering Committee of the PCC without delay."[40]

Madame Chiang Kai-shek brought a revised version of the proposed statement to General Marshall on the evening of the 15th. Finding the new version "jumbled in thought and provocative in nature," Marshall struck out a considerable part of the new material. Relating to Stuart details of the development next morning, Marshall said that (1) there must be a clear understanding as to the meaning of the cease-fire; (2) there would be a problem in getting agreement on the location of divisions; and (3) the Communists would oppose Chiang's exclusion of Manchuria from the settlement of local administrative problems. Marshall added that, in view of the vicious personal attacks on him by Communists, he could not handle negotiations until after the Committee of Three was convened.[41]

Marshall analyzed for Truman the recent developments, pointing to the efforts of third-party groups to get Chou back to negotiating and noting the unfortunate effect Chiang's unilateral convening of the National Assembly had exerted on peace efforts. He mentioned current Communist attacks on U.S. policy and the fact that Stuart was now being included in the propaganda attacks. Although it would be months before nonmilitary products of the surplus-property transaction would become available to the government, the Communists believed these items would affect current operations. "They are of course unaware of the restrictions that have been placed on the National Government in the shipment of ammunition, airplanes and similar items." The fact that the surplus equipment went back to a 1943 agreement did not enter into their reasoning. "Their argument, in effect, is that the National Government should be disarmed, which would be the case if denied the use of American munitions which are the basis of their Army organization. I elaborate on this point of view not at all as an argument but merely to assist you in evaluating psychological reactions at the present time."[42]

A modicum of hope appeared on October 21 when some liberal third-party leaders persuaded Chou En-lai to return to Nanking by agreeing to support the Communists in refusing to name delegates to the National Assembly before the government was reorganized as had been agreed by the Political Consultative Conference. At Marshall's urging, the Generalissimo delayed a trip to Formosa to speak briefly with Chou and third-party representatives. However, Chiang left later that day, a step which the Yenan government promptly branded as an affront. Irked by the Generalissimo's action, Marshall told government officials that a prolonged absence would appear to outsiders as an attempt to avoid negotiations.[43] He soothed Chou's hurt feelings by saying that the trip had been planned in advance of any knowledge of Chou's intention to come to Nanking. To Truman, Marshall had explained that Yenan had recalled Chou on hearing of Chiang's departure but that Chou had asked to be allowed to continue negotiations. The General added, "The important point of the interview today was the fact that Chou called on me. . . ."[44]

The Nationals captured Antung on October 25, during the Generalissimo's absence. Marshall told Chiang, on the latter's return, that recent government advances and the Generalissimo's absence had seriously affected prospective negotiations. He warned that "the Communists had lost cities but not armies." They have "no intention of making a stand or of fighting to a finish at any place."[45]

As if the fall of Antung was the signal he had been waiting for, Chiang announced that the time had come to stop the fighting. For Marshall, the situation had become ludicrous. Talking to John Melby, Second Secretary of the U.S. Embassy, about the recent operations which abrogated the June agreement, Marshall said that it had taken three weeks to negotiate that one and it would take longer for the next. "And I can't go through it again. I am just too old and too tired for that."[46]

He did not stop trying. Beginning on November 5, he had a series of meetings with Chiang, attempting to draft an acceptable statement for a cease-fire. When it was finally completed on November 8, Marshall was disappointed because of certain qualifications the Generalissimo had made. He reported his distress to President Truman, saying that Chiang Kai-shek had missed a great opportunity by threatening to renew battle and by his unfortunate approach to the convocation of a National Assembly.[47]

Not only did the announcement fail to go far enough; Chiang's advisers opposed even its few concessions. Still, Marshall put a good face on matters when he spoke to Chou En-lai on November 10 to ask that the Communists make a favorable reply. Chou, conscious of borrowed time, said that if Marshall thought there was still another chance for agreement, he would continue his efforts for a little while longer. If the General thought not, he must go back to Yenan. When Marshall requested that he meet again with the Committee of Three, Chou stated, "I will make another try."

At an informal meeting of the Committee of Three on the morning of the 11th, General Chen Chang presented Chiang's cease-fire proposal. Chou agreed to send it to Yenan but warned that if Chiang convened the National Assembly unilaterally, there would be a political split. Doggedly, Marshall asked that the Communists accept the cease-fire despite political differences.[48]

In another last-minute effort to prevent a break, Chiang agreed with a nonparty delegation's request to delay the meeting of the National Assembly until November 15. Marshall met again with Chou but failed to shake his demand for a complete halt in calling for the meeting. The Generalissimo replied by convening the National Assembly on November 15 with no Communists present. Of the opponents of the Kuomintang, only members of the Youth Party and a few nonparty delegates attended the sessions.[49]

The door to negotiations "has now been slammed," Chou announced in his official statement on the 16th. He visited Marshall to say that negotiations had failed despite the General's efforts and that he was now going back to Yenan. "But I feel that I still have high respect for you personally," he told the American General. "The Chinese problem is too complicated and the changes are tremendous." Chou said that he was leaving a representative in Nanking, but warned that if the government were readying an attack on Yenan, as he suspected, all negotiations would be at an end. Summarizing these developments for Truman, Marshall said that if the government did launch an attack on Yenan, "I would feel that it terminated my Mission."[50]

The President promptly regretted these developments but assured the General that this "in no way detracts from the high estimate we place upon the quality and utility of what you have done." Marshall's presence had prevented many adverse developments, and benefits would follow. "You have my constant gratitude and confidence."[51]

The words sounded like a valedictory. Marshall was in need of encouragement. He spoke frankly of his disappointments to staff members after Chou had left for Yenan. "I know," Melby wrote, "Marshall now believes he made a mistake in ever thinking coalition was desirable or useful or possible."[52] Marshall complained bitterly to Beal about the actions of Chiang's generals, who on several occasions had torpedoed negotiations with their attacks on the Communists. Noting that the National Government was pressing him for loans, he asked Beal to convey his word to the "militarists": "The army is draining 80 to 90 per cent of the budget and if you think the American taxpayer is going to step into the vacuum this creates, you can go to hell."[53]

Apparently now convinced that he had about reached the end of effective negotiations, Marshall left Nanking for Tientsin on November 23 to discuss the immediate reduction of the garrison there, and then went on to Peiping to determine the future of Executive Headquarters.[54] Briefly, the visit to Tientsin cheered him up, for it revived pleasant memories of his 1924–27 stay there. He showed his pleasure by writing to old military colleagues who would treasure his description of changes and vestiges of an older life that still remained.

He was soon drawn back to realities. On the first day of December, Marshall and Stuart spent three hours with Chiang Kai-shek, with Madame as interpreter, a grueling experience that Melby remarked would qualify both men for the Order of Saint Simeon Stylites.[55] Marshall commented that the Communists were too large a military and civil force to be ignored and an effort should be made to bring them into the government. In a flow of words lasting more than an hour, Chiang said that the Communists had no intention of cooperating with the Nationals, that they were under the influence of the Soviet government, and that their purpose was to disrupt the government and influence foreign policy. Marshall reported: "The Generalissimo stated that he felt that it was necessary to destroy the Communist military forces. If that were done there would be no great difficulty in handling the Communist question. . . . He was confident that the Communist forces could be eliminated in 8 to 12 months." Since the Communists had shown no desire to cooperate, Chiang thought the United States should redefine its mission, emphasizing the need for stability in the government and throughout the Far East. "It should no longer be considered practical to consider the Communists as a working part of the Government." Marshall reiterated his conviction that the government could not ignore such a large group and that it was impossible for the government to complete its program of eliminating Communism before the country would be faced with complete economic collapse. Marshall's frankness displeased Chiang. As Marshall reported to John Beal, "His old foot went round and round and round and almost hit the ceiling."[56]

There was a touch of finality about the report. But since he was not completely sure, President Truman left the ending of the mission up to Marshall. "Pat" Carter passed on the heart of the message:

> He stated that at such time as you felt the situation called for your return, all you had to do was to notify him how you wanted the matter handled and it would be done that way. He admonished that I should not in any way give you the impression that he or anybody else in a responsible position was attempting to influence you or to urge you to withdraw. On the contrary his only desire is to impress upon you that the matter is yours and yours alone to determine. . . .[57]

The course of events waited now on the Communist reaction to Marshall's earlier query whether or not they wanted him to continue to mediate. The reply was soon forthcoming. On the 5th, he received Chou En-lai's statement of the previous day. Charging that a basis for agreement had been destroyed by the Nationalist manipulation of the National Assembly, the Communist leaders declared that further discussions depended on the dissolution of the "illegal" National Assembly and the restoration of troop positions as of January 13. When Marshall asked Ambassador Stuart for his reaction, the diplomat called the message unrealistic and added that Chou had still not indicated whether he wanted the Americans to continue their mediation. Marshall saw the Communist challenge as playing into the hands of the reactionaries of the National regime. Believing that he could destroy the Communist forces in the field, Chiang Kai-shek saw no reason to make any concessions to Yenan. Stuart was still hopeful. He believed that Chiang could be separated from the reactionary forces of the Kuomintang and sold on a policy of strengthening China. Marshall was much less certain. He wanted more indication of agreement before he would recommend a new American effort.[58]

End of the Mission

I N the next two weeks a stream of Chinese individuals and delegations came to sound Marshall out. In addition to Nationals and Communists, representatives of various minority groups tried to convince him that they might be able to help reach an agreement. This had been Marshall's hope from the beginning, as he had discussed with Stuart the likelihood that moderates and liberals could get together. No one splinter group seemed capable of furnishing adequate leadership, so Marshall insisted that all minority groups form an alliance. He put greater trust in the possibility that government figures such as Governor Chang Chun of Szechuan Province, or Foreign Minister Wang Shih-chieh, or even the ubiquitous T. V. Soong—men not part of the CC Clique or the Whampoa Academy group—would be able to win reforms and cooperation in the government that would provide a basis for peace.

Marshall was frank about China's urgencies. To the former Ambassador to the United States, Dr. Wei Tao-ming, he summarized on December 9 some of the government's difficulties. The official recorder wrote:

> General Marshall stated that democracy probably could be made to work in China if there existed a free press and an active, unrestricted opposition party. He referred to the deplorable economic situation confronting China. He commented on the vicious inflation which, combined with the low salary of public officials, caused widespread corruption to the detriment of the Government, both as a servant of the people and in the eyes of the world. He stated that economic recovery was blocked by the military stalemate along the railroads of north China. He was sure that the Communist Party was aware of the economic perils of the Government and was planning

accordingly. Although the National Government felt that economic collapse was at least two years away, he considered it a definite possibility in a matter of months. . . .[1]

Marshall warned against false hopes based on a pro-National publicity campaign then being launched by Henry Luce of *Time-Life* and Roy Howard of Scripps-Howard. He believed that a countercharge against the Nationals, of reaction and corruption, would follow from other sources. He hoped that the reactionaries would not cripple the government by weakening the proposed constitution.

On December 6, recalling that it would soon be a year since the mission to China was launched, Dean Acheson suggested to Marshall that it was about time for the President to report to the country on the General's problems and accomplishments. Marshall agreed on the value of such a statement but insisted that the timing was all-important. Acheson thought that the proper time had been reached, since the administration was being charged with failure to support the Generalissimo or to take a strong line with the Communists. He proposed to draft a statement for Truman's use very soon. This could be followed by a complete report from Marshall later. The General agreed and, with a few minor changes, approved Acheson's draft.[2]

Beal listed in his diary as early as December 4 indications that Marshall intended to return home. He soon had a clearer sign. Chiang Kai-shek had recently purchased in the United States a new C-54 plane for his use and had invited Mrs. Marshall's daughter and her children to fly on the plane as far as China, where they could take a commercial flight to India to join her husband. Chiang suggested that after the plane arrived it could take Mrs. Marshall eastward as far as Guam, where she could catch a Navy transport to Hawaii. Here she could escape the winter's cold, which was aggravating a sinus problem. "If I go back," Marshall remarked to Beal, "I could pick her up there. Pinehurst at the end of January would be just about right." But to inquisitive Chinese who wondered about his plans he made no comment.[3]

Those closest to Marshall could sense that he wanted to go home, but he stayed on to watch the creation of a new constitution. A Chinese moderate later told Marshall that his presence had made it possible to frame a good constitution. The Generalissimo had scolded Chen Li-fu and had made the ultra-rightists get in line. Marshall agreed that Chen Li-fu had changed tactics enough to help put through the constitution, but he was not certain that the

CC Clique was through maneuvering, and he proposed to watch carefully the organization of the State Council to see if the rightists tried to prevent liberals and Communists from coming in.

The year limped to a close. On Christmas Eve, the Generalissimo gave a party in Nanking, inviting Chinese and U.S. officials. At Chiang's home they found a lighted Christmas tree and Christmas music issuing from a phonograph, with the host impressive in black mandarin gown and Madame charming in black silk trimmed with green-and-gold brocade. While the Generalissimo sought to draw out the Americans on recent developments, Madame mixed old-fashioneds and martinis. It was late when Marshall arrived with Colonel Underwood and Colonel Caughey. The General was not in a Christmas mood. He had a bad cold and longed for his bed.[4] Earlier in the evening, when he was in bed, Underwood had reported that demonstrators were headed for the Marshall house. A Chinese girl had charged two Marines with rape, and the demonstrators wanted to demand proper justice from Marshall. He told Underwood to get an interpreter. Since most of the Chinese-speaking Americans happened to have gone to Shanghai for some athletic event, Underwood settled for an officer proffered by a Navy representative. He turned out to be a Marine. When Marshall saw him in his uniform, he summoned Underwood to his room. As Underwood recalled years later:

> I got up there, and this was a fearsome sight. I was standing rigidly at attention at the foot of the bed. "What are you thinking about, getting a Marine up here to be an interpreter for an anti-Marine demonstration?" His lower jaw was out about a foot. I tried to answer but it didn't have any effect. I really couldn't get the floor and I certainly got the message. I told Mrs. Marshall about this later and when I said his jaw protruded about a foot . . . she said, "Oh, my goodness, he certainly was angry!"[5]

Ultimately, the demonstration was handled without incident, and Marshall cooled down outwardly, but Beal said he returned to "real fury" whenever he remembered the Marine interpreter.

Chiang's Western-style dinner probably helped to calm Marshall as he and the other guests were served roast turkey, raisin pie, fruitcake, and ice cream. Later, a huge Chinese officer, J. L. Huang, who headed the equivalent of a military YMCA, arrived dressed as Santa Claus to distribute presents. Marshall was given a stand for reading in bed. A present was no comfort for Underwood, who felt he was not fully forgiven for many days.

On Christmas Day—the day marking, Marshall observed, the
tenth anniversary of Chiang's kidnapping at Sian—the National
Assembly acted favorably on the new constitution. The Communists were unhappy. Chou En-lai had again asked for the selection
of a new assembly, for a restoration of the January 13 line, and the
re-establishment of the military positions of that period; he rejected completely the new constitution. Marshall notified Truman
that the constitution was a good one but that he had told the
Generalissimo it was necessary to reorganize the government and
create a liberal party out of minority groups.

Despite Chiang's success with the new charter, he was visibly
uneasy. The economic situation continued to worsen, and he kept
trying to discover whether or when Marshall was returning home.
On December 28, the two men met for more than two hours. At
Chiang's request, Marshall went into a lengthy analysis of the situation. He doubted that the Communists would make any agreement
at that time, because they believed that the Nationals were trying
to destroy them. Marshall must have thought so too, for he declared that Chiang's military commanders were in error if they
believed they could bring the Communists to terms within a few
months. He urged that the military not be allowed to destroy the
possibility of further negotiations. He also asked that Chiang see
to it that moderate and liberal members of the Kuomintang be
brought into key posts in the government. If the Communists declined to take part at the moment, he should still leave places for
them in the new framework. All that he had won by forcing through
the constitution would be lost if it appeared that he was continuing
one-party rule. If he took the lead, he could move into the position
of being the father of his country and not the leader of a one-party
government.

Marshall again emphasized that he could not accept the position
of adviser to Chiang Kai-shek. So much anti-American feeling had
developed among the Communists that his future position would
be seriously jeopardized. Further, the opposition to him of reactionaries in the National Government was such that he would be
limited as an adviser. Privately, Marshall said in his report to Truman, he felt that the government's idea in keeping him there was
to increase the chance of getting American support to strengthen
the position of the existing Kuomintang regime.

It now seemed to Marshall that the Communists would refuse to
reopen negotiations and the government would resort to military
action to reopen the railroads. Under these circumstances, the staff
of Executive Headquarters should be reduced to a mere cadre and

U.S. participation in mediation should cease. This would at once facilitate withdrawal of the Marines from Tientsin and Peiping.

In addition, Marshall declared, "I think I should be recalled." He felt he could help defeat the reactionaries in the National Government and increase the possibility of bringing in liberal groups by making his views known back home. At the same time, he could denounce the vicious propaganda that the Communists had recently been issuing against the United States.[6]

No specific word had leaked out that Marshall was going home, but the likelihood was in many minds. Chiang Kai-shek arranged for a stag birthday party in the General's honor on New Year's Eve. Some fifty people had been invited, including Chen Li-fu of the CC Clique and some representatives of minority groups. Madame Chiang helped her husband receive the guests but retired before dinner. The meal was similar to the one served on Christmas, accompanied by a birthday cake. With T. V. Soong translating, Chiang offered a toast to Marshall, thanking him for the year he had been there and his efforts toward peace. "Marshall replied with a toast to the Gimo, put seriously with an air of holding emotion in check lest he speak too encouragingly." It was all very proper but lacked the spontaneity of the Christmas celebration.[7]

With more genuine friendliness the Generalissimo paid his respects personally the next day. Ambassador Stuart had stopped to see him on New Year's afternoon. When Chiang learned that Stuart was on his way to see Marshall, whose heavy cold kept him in bed, he insisted on accompanying the Ambassador. John Beal was impressed because he thought it was the only time the head of the Chinese government had called on the General.[8]

Washington was already moving to end the mission early in January. The State Department radioed on January 3 that the President wanted Marshall to return "for consultation on China and other matters." A short time later, Colonel Carter said the President would like to have him back by January 10. For various reasons, Truman had decided on an early acceptance of the resignation that Byrnes had put at his disposal months before. Marshall was surprised at Truman's haste to get him back: he had hoped to be more leisurely in his return. To meet that deadline would mean making a wearing flight and losing the short rest he had hoped to get in Hawaii on the way back. He knew what lay ahead and was not anxious to rush to his new assignment: "I think I fully understand the question to be discussed. My answer is in affirmative if that continues to be his desire. My personal reaction is something else."[9]

The President said that the return should be arranged to fit Marshall's convenience. He believed that he must make the announcement of his appointment as Secretary of State on January 10 because he feared there would be a leak, but he was quite content for the General to have his rest in Hawaii if the White House could make the announcement on or before the 10th. Actually, the date had to be moved up. Speculation in some of the American press on Byrnes's resignation was surfacing, and Truman considered it important to act quickly. Marshall proposed that the announcement be made in Washington on January 6 and that the statement he was preparing on the failure of his mission be released the following morning. It was understood that a January 6 announcement would reach Nanking on the 7th.

On January 6, Marshall went with Stuart to tell Chiang of his departure for consultation, without mentioning the coming announcement of his nomination as Secretary of State. He struck sparks when he remarked that two American senators, Murray and Flanders, had suggested that an American, British, French, and Russian group attempt "to provide a stabilizing influence for China." Although Marshall said plainly that there was no possibility of the United States' adopting this suggestion, Chiang Kai-shek made it the subject of the rest of his conversation. He described his shock at the Yalta agreements relating to China. Under the circumstances the Generalissimo had accepted these arrangements, although they were contrary to the United States' traditional stand toward China and would create great resentment. Action of the Moscow Conference of the Council of Foreign Ministers regarding China, in late 1945, had also been offensive to Chiang. He would go no further toward accepting such treatment.

> The Generalissimo asked me to tell the President that under no circumstance, while he was at the head of the Chinese Government, would he accept any action regarding the internal affairs of China which involve the Soviet Union or the British Government, and if such action were taken and forced on China, he would step aside as President because such procedure would be intolerable and an insult to the Chinese Government and people. . . .

Thereafter Marshall had no illusions about Chiang's willingness to accept anything resembling a three- or four-power trusteeship for China. He would remember this much later when such an idea was again proposed.[10]

On January 7, Marshall met with the Chinese Foreign Minister, who outlined a message that the Generalissimo was sending to President Truman, accepting many of the reforms that had been requested. Later he talked with Prime Minister Soong, who was soon to resign. Marshall warned him that soon he was going to speak out concerning the faults of both sides in China, and it would not be pleasant. He added that the military leaders clouded issues when they talked to Chiang. For that reason, Marshall said, he had always spoken frankly with Chiang, and Chiang had accepted that frankness. Soong replied that few knew it but Chiang had greater need of Marshall than Marshall had of him. He had permitted the General to speak frankly "because he truly believed that although General Marshall did not understand the whole situation, he was speaking honestly for the good of . . . the Generalissimo and the good of China as he saw it."[11]

In the course of the afternoon, Marshall and Stuart talked again with the Generalissimo and with Madame Chiang. Chiang once more pressed the General to return as his special adviser, offering to give him all the power he possessed and promising to work with him to make China all that the Chinese and the Americans desired. Marshall promised to consider with care what Chiang had to say. But his mind was made up. After dinner that evening, he asked Stuart to explain carefully to Chiang next day why he could not accept the offer.[12]

The next morning, January 8, a large gathering, including the Generalissimo and Madame and one or more Communist representatives, gathered at the airfield to see the General leave for Honolulu, where he would have a short vacation with Mrs. Marshall before going on to Washington.

Announcement in Washington of Marshall's appointment as Secretary of State had been timed to coincide with his departure from China. Marshall had also arranged, as a second shock the following morning, for his farewell message to be announced when he was flying to Hawaii.

His statement on the failure of his mission reviewed the situation that had existed before he came to China, and which still existed. The great obstacle to peace had been the mutual suspicion between the National Government and the Communists.

> On the one hand the leaders of the Government are strongly opposed to a communistic form of government. On the other, the Communists frankly state that they are Marxists and intend to work

toward establishing a communistic form of government in China,
though first advancing through the medium of a democratic form of
a government of the American or British type.

Each side had exaggerated the clashes and violations of agreements. Marshall paid tribute "to the superb courage of the officers
of our Army and Marines in struggling against insurmountable,
maddening obstacles to bring some measure of peace to China."[13]
It had been difficult to work with the government: the Kuomintang was dominated by reactionaries who had rendered all Marshall's efforts to work for a coalition impossible. On the Communist
side, the older element, wanting to bring down the National Government, was content to stop the working of China's communications system in order to produce economic chaos. Yet Marshall
believed that there was a younger element of Chinese who had
joined the Communist Party in their disgust at the corruption of the
local governments, and who seemed willing to put the interests of
China above ruthless measures to establish Communist ideology.
Marshall was particularly caustic about the deliberate misre-
presentations and violent propaganda of the Communists, intended to mislead the Chinese and the world into "a bitter hatred
of the Americans." Irreconcilable elements in the Kuomintang
wanted to keep their feudal privileges and had no intention of
making a new system work. "Though I speak as a soldier, I must
here deplore the dominating influence of the military." Yet he
recognized that the Communist Party was not a small group but a
growing power, with more than a million men under arms. The
reactionaries seemed to count on the Americans to support them
in their actions, while the Communists seemed to count on economic collapse, accelerated by guerrilla attacks against the railroads, regardless of the long-term effect on the Chinese people.
Hope rested on the assumption of leadership by liberal elements
and minority groups, particularly if they worked under the leadership of Chiang Kai-shek for a better China. A move had been made
in the right direction by the recent National Assembly and the new
constitution. It was important to reorganize the State Council and
the executive branch to bring in independent and minority groups,
and to leave the door open to Communists to join.
His pronouncement has been termed a "plague on both your
houses," as if he had washed his hands of China. Although he had
spoken with brutal candor about the problems, he still mentioned
the elements of the situation that could be mobilized to bring

peace. For those Chinese who had faith in his leadership, there was still hope that he would be able, in his new position, to influence their future. For those who had looked at the prospect of his retirement with equanimity, there was the chilling realization that he was now a key figure in the making of future U.S. foreign policy.

In a Civilian Setting

T HE Marshalls came to Washington by train from Chicago on
the cold morning of January 21, 1947. Two weeks earlier, the
General had ended his mission to China and had flown to Hawaii
to relax with Mrs. Marshall and to work on his final report. Tanned
and rested, the Marshalls and his aide, Colonel Caughey, flew to
Los Angeles on the 18th, to be greeted at the airport next morning
by Frank McCarthy, wartime Secretary General Staff, now a mo-
tion-picture producer. The Marshalls then flew on to Chicago,
hoping to reach Washington in time for swearing in on January 20,
but the weather became frigid and severe icing on the plane forced
them to change to a train and arrive a day later. Under a shed at
Washington's Union Station, scoured by "bitter gales," a group of
shivering reporters awaited the new Secretary of State. The newsmen later wrote that the General looked "ruddy and fit" and that
he was wearing the camel's-hair coat trimmed with beaver that he
had worn to Yalta.[1]

As Marshall was getting off the train, Colonel Carter, his liaison
officer with the State Department and the Pentagon, handed him
a note. James Shepley, now back with *Time-Life,* had alerted Carter
that Republican Senator Arthur Vandenberg, Chairman of the Senate Foreign Relations Committee, saw in the new Secretary of State
a possible future presidential candidate.[2] Two weeks earlier, when
Truman had submitted the nomination, Vandenberg had put it
through his committee without a hearing and without opposition.
By asking for a suspension of rules, he had run the appointment
through Senate approval on the same day. Still, Shepley had
warned, Vandenberg was very watchful. The note prompted Marshall to clear the air immediately.

He reminded the reporters that this was his second postponement of retirement, and refused to speculate on foreign policy beyond saying that he would continue the course of his predecessor, James Byrnes. He then asked for questions, and when none came about his political future, he said he would like to make an announcement on that subject.

> I think this is as good a time as any to terminate speculation about me in a political way.
>
> I am assuming that the office of Secretary of State, at least under present conditions, is non-political and I am going to govern myself accordingly. I will never become involved in political matters and therefore I cannot be considered a candidate for any political office.
>
> The popular conception that no matter what a man says, he can be drafted as a candidate for some political office would be without any force with regard to me. I could never be drafted for any political office.
>
> I am being explicit and emphatic in order to terminate once and for all any discussion of my name with regard to political office.[3]

Politicians and pundits reacted favorably. James Reston saw Marshall's decision as a wise act that solved a dilemma for the Republicans, who would now be able to back the new Secretary's policies without fear that they were helping to build him up for the presidential contest. It also killed any possibility of a conflict with Mr. Truman for the 1948 nomination. Columnist David Lawrence, publisher of *U.S. News & World Report,* added that although the announcement would disappoint some "because he is just the kind of man who ought to be President—he is one of the great statesmen of our time," his words had at once "surrounded him with a prestige both inside and outside this country which no man in public office, not even President Truman, can command." Lawrence continued:

> First, he has been an Army officer all his life, and has learned to keep out of politics, but, second, he knows better than any man in government that the best way to keep faith with the boys who made the supreme sacrifice under his wartime command is to forge an enduring peace. . . . America and the world have gained by reason of a simple act of selfless conduct by a great man.[4]

Marshall was sworn in by Chief Justice Fred Vinson in the presence of President Truman, Secretary Byrnes and others at the White House. He had lunch with the two, and then a long talk with

Byrnes. For a few weeks he again worked in the elephantine old
State, War, and Navy Building at 17th and Pennsylvania, where he
had reported in 1902 as a young VMI graduate with a brand new
Army commission and a new wife. He had worked there as aide to
General Pershing from 1919 to 1923 and had returned there for a
time in 1938, before moving with the Army to the Munitions Building on Constitution Avenue, next to Main Navy. In 1941 the new
building being erected for the Army at 21st Street and Virginia
Avenue proved too small for its purpose, and so began the massive
sprawl of the Pentagon across the Potomac. Among Marshall's first
acts as Secretary of State was to approve moving the department
into the 1941 building, which the Army had outgrown before it was
completed. One change necessary to convert the building from the
uses of war to those of diplomacy was to cover with wall hangings
a huge mural in the lobby, depicting an amphibious landing.[5]

Marshall had never liked to make wholesale staff changes when
he took over a new position, and he asked the chief members of
Byrnes's staff to remain. Acheson, anxious to return to private law
practice, agreed to stay until mid-year of 1947 as Under Secretary.
Will Clayton, Under Secretary for Economic Affairs, promised to
remain through the conferences then being held in Geneva. Both
men were thus in a position to continue administration policy and
to influence the thinking of the new Secretary.

Acheson's father had come from England to Canada as a young
man. After brief military service, he studied for the Anglican ministry. Soon after taking holy orders, he moved to the United States
and eventually became the Episcopalian bishop of Connecticut.
There, in Middletown, Dean Gooderham Acheson was born in
1893. From Yale University and then Harvard Law School he came
to Washington after World War I, as law clerk to Justice Louis D.
Brandeis, and stayed on as a member of one of the great law firms
of the city. Early in Roosevelt's first term, Acheson was named
Under Secretary of the Treasury. Before the end of the year, he
resigned in disapproval of the President's gold policy, and remained outside the administration until February 1941, when he
returned to government service as Assistant Secretary of State for
Economic Affairs.

In politics he did not always appeal to those he met for the first
time. A certain aloofness suggested arrogance, and his impatience
with fools infuriated many with whom he had to deal and made
them long for the comeuppance of this intolerable "smarty-
pants."[6]

Amazingly, he won and kept the respect, support, even affection, of Marshall and Truman, both so different from him in personality. Acheson did not hesitate to question Marshall's handling of a policy matter, and he was capable, particularly after the President retired, of chiding Truman gently for mistaken ideas. Acheson's special grace came from his wry sense of humor and lightning quickness with a phrase. These qualities rescued him from many a storm.

From the beginning of their acquaintance, Acheson had admired and liked Marshall, and the General reciprocated the feeling. This mutual respect and enjoyment resulted in a give-and-take that was like that earlier reciprocity between Marshall and Stimson; it became fruitful in the first six months of Marshall's secretaryship.

Acheson recalled that his first real contact with Marshall came in October 1944 at a dinner of the Business Advisory Council at Hot Springs, Virginia. Before the General rose to speak that evening, he was handed a message. He read it without comment, then spoke at length without indicating in any manner that he had just learned of the death of Field Marshal Sir John Dill, one of his closest friends. Acheson was impressed by this display of self-control and poise.[7]

In a thoughtful appraisal of Marshall that Acheson recorded on tape in 1957, the Under Secretary described their first talks and the type of organization Marshall wanted in the State Department. The General made clear that in the running of affairs, he was not the one to be considered. Acheson said:

He was the commanding officer, and he would take the responsibility, but people were not to do things to please him, and try to find out what he wanted and then take that action. They were to do the very best they could. He was quite merciless on people that were self-seeking, on people that were trying to suck up to him or get approval, but he was infinitely patient with people who were doing their best.

. . . He said to me that I was to be the chief of staff and that I was to run the Department and that all matters between the Department and the Secretary would come to the Secretary through me with my recommendation, whatever it might be, attached to the action proposed. This we did. I think for the first time in the history of the State Department, there was a line of command. Instead of having every officer in the Department run to the Secretary, as we did under General Marshall's predecessor, each one getting his authority, leaving the Under Secretary bewildered, and not knowing whether he had the authority or what he was supposed to do. The thing was put into a direct line of authority.

This had its drawbacks and on several occasions, I spoke to the General about the tendency to rely too much on me as Under Secretary to bring him a more or less completed product for his approval, disapproval, or modification, and told him I thought, as distinct from the military services, the Department of State required at all stages of the development of an idea the imprint of the Secretary's wishes, because these views would reflect the opinion of the Administration, of which the Secretary and the Under Secretary were a part. I said to him on many occasions that it was not enough, in regard to relations with Israel or whatever the difficulty might be, to have a recommendation which would really mean that at some stage the Under Secretary would make a series of decisions, would rule out certain ideas and these would never reach the Secretary. Therefore, what would be presented to him would be alternatives. I thought while he should leave to me the development of the whole matter, he should from time to time sit with those who were working on it so that they would always have the guidance of an attitude which would come from his relations with the President. He understood this and agreed with it and during my period there attempted very hard to do it, but you could see it was distasteful to him. I remember his saying at one time, when various section chiefs got into an argument, "Gentlemen, don't fight the problem, decide it." The point is that if this ought to work for some period of time, you have to fight the problem. These problems are not susceptible to an answer, they are susceptible to an action which is less disagreeable than some other action and probably no action is altogether good. The General, I think, came to this conclusion slowly, and he did not like the methods by which it was done, but he came to it finally and he carried it out very strongly after that.

As a commander in charge of the department . . . he was most unmilitary in regard to his attitude of approach. His approach was [that] of a man who was not seeing things as a soldier, [although he had] spent most of his life in the government in a soldier's role, but [of] a man who understood forms of public leadership and forces of international friction, very far indeed from what we call a purely military point of view. The military point of view, to me, seemed to be reserved for organization and responsible action, but in the field of ideas, there hardly was a less military mind than his. Indeed, it has seemed to me the best military minds were not military at all. General Bradley was in the same class as General Marshall. . . .[8]

When Acheson needed quick decisions in several matters, he readily accepted Marshall's invitation to list priority items. The decision to move to new quarters has been noted. A second decision involved a noisy debate that had raged for several weeks between two senior members of the Department. Spruille Braden, former Ambassador to Argentina, now Assistant Secretary for Latin American Affairs, was at odds with his successor in Buenos Aires, George Messersmith, as to policy toward that country. On Acheson's presentation of the problem, Marshall moved both men from their current assignments.[9]

In making Acheson his chief of staff and directing that recommendations come through him, Marshall was repeating his 1942 actions to make the War Department a better command post. He also asked for a State Department Secretariat to direct the flow of communications in a system resembling that which he had known in the War Department. Carlisle Humelsine, who as a colonel had organized communications at several of the overseas conferences during the war, took over the job of arranging the flow of correspondence and checking on directives, under general direction of Colonel Marshall Carter, who now became Marshall's personal assistant. This arrangement gave both the Secretary and the Under Secretary a firmer control of the department.

To make transition easier for his successor as Under Secretary in mid-year, Acheson in April suggested that Robert A. Lovett of New York, former Assistant Secretary of War for Air, come to Washington as an assistant to Will Clayton. Lovett showed little interest in the assignment until Marshall told him that much more was involved than the job under discussion: he wanted Lovett for Under Secretary. Immediately Lovett accepted the offer and came down early to become familiar with current problems several weeks before Acheson's resignation. Having come to the War Department in 1940, he knew the Washington scene and was completely at home with George Marshall.

Lovett's father, a lawyer from Texas, had come to New York early in the century and became executive officer of the Union Pacific Railroad. His son got his first degree at Yale and then his law degree at Harvard. He became a member of Brown Brothers, Harriman, in time succeeding his father as executive officer of the railroad. While at Yale during World War I, Lovett became a member of a flying unit organized there and was commissioned as a flier in the Navy. His interest in planes made him a concerned observer of European military air development before World War II. When Henry Stimson became Secretary of War, he asked Lovett to be his Assistant Secretary for Air. With Patterson and McCloy, Lovett was

one of the brilliantly effective civilian team in the department.
Through his close connection with General Arnold, Lovett came to
know and value Marshall. They had worked well together in the
development of the Army Air Forces.

Urbane and genial, of such physical spareness as to suggest
frailty, Lovett projected an aristocratic version of the Wall Street
banker. His tongue, like Acheson's, could cut with suavity, but he
had no condescension in dealing with politicians, and he handled
those on the Hill more easily than did Acheson. Though he had
Truman's confidence, he never developed the easy relationship
with the President that Acheson had quickly gained.

With Marshall, Lovett's rapport was remarkable. Both men were
reserved and low-keyed in public action. Although Marshall worked
extremely well with Acheson in the months they served together at
State, he achieved a closeness to Lovett similar to the mental processes of identical twins. "I was," Lovett said later, "his alter ego.
We worked together almost as brothers." They did not need to
have long talks about policy because they normally reacted the
same way to issues and problems. In his State Department post, as
in his later assignment as Under Secretary of Defense, Lovett
worked so harmoniously with Marshall that it is difficult to separate
their thinking and their actions.[10]

Marshall was always proud of his early decision to establish a
Policy Planning Staff. Soon after he became Chief of Staff of the
Army, he had concluded that the Army spent too much effort in
reacting to immediate crises. There should be, he thought, several
people who could put up their feet and think hard about policy for
the future. He had helped set up such an organization in the War
Department. He told Acheson that he wanted this type of staff at
State. Within a few days after Marshall's return from China, Acheson was talking to the man who would ultimately head the staff,
George F. Kennan. Kennan was already known as an expert on
Soviet and Eastern European affairs. In the Foreign Service since
the late 1920s, he was fluent in several languages, including Russian, had spent a number of tours in Russia and Central Europe,
and thought, spoke, and wrote with informed intelligence and lu-
cidity.[11]

The new approach was not always popular in the State Depart-
ment. It was too military, and murmurs were heard that the new
Secretary was filling the Department with military men. The pres-
ence of Colonel Marshall S. Carter, Colonel Charles H. Bonesteel,
Jr., General John Hilldring, Colonel Carlisle Humelsine, Brigadier
General Charles Saltzman, Colonel Dean Rusk, and Brigadier Gen-

eral Henry Byroade seemed to prove the point. Actually, with the exception of Byroade, who was soon to give up his Army rank for a career in the Foreign Service, all these officers had been brought in by Marshall's predecessor.

Once Marshall left the department, his successors never went back to the older administrative ways. In 1970, when the State Department did a self-study, a panel decided that Marshall had done more than any secretary since the war to strengthen the department's administrative organization. The wording of the evaluation was specific as to his contribution:

Essential challenges and opportunities have always been important and in some cases the major spurs to creativity. It seems no coincidence, however, that the Department's most creative contributions to foreign policy occurred under the Secretary of State with the strongest managerial background. According to key people who worked under him, George Marshall was an orderly man, a master of administration and, as a result of his enormous responsibilities during the Second World War, an effective manager of staff. More important than simply using his staff resources well, he carried out the recommendations of his subordinates. Instead of relying on the clearance system, one of the great barriers to creative thinking, Marshall would assign primary responsibility to one office for a given issue, instructing it to consult with all other interested parties, clearly setting out problems and options. He would then hold that office accountable for its recommendations, and come down hard and quickly if the office did its work poorly or failed to consult fully.

Under Marshall's management the Policy Planning Staff was created and became the focus of creative thinking in the Department during a vital period. It was in this office that the Marshall Plan and other bold innovative responses to the foreign policy challenges of the late forties were originated and developed. Marshall took the advice of his planning staff and respected it as an institution.[12]

The first challenge of Marshall's tenure as Secretary of State would be the Moscow Conference of the Council of Foreign Ministers in March. Taking up where Byrnes had left off after meetings in Moscow, London, Paris, and New York, Marshall was to seek agreements with representatives of Britain, France, and the Soviet Union on the German and Austrian treaties and the political and economic problems that accompanied them. Not completely briefed on the situation in Washington, Marshall told reporters in Union Station in January that he proposed to follow the policies of his predecessor. The statement has been brushed aside by some revisionist historians who charge that Marshall was chosen deliberately to institute a hard line in dealing with the Soviet Union. Byrnes was often called "a fixer," but to suggest that he was an appeaser of Communists ignores his strong conservatism and the numerous evidences of his anti-Soviet views. Henry Wallace did record at the end of 1945 that Harry Dexter White of the Treasury opposed Marshall for the China mission because the General favored a hard line against the Soviet Union. It is also on record that Marshall was attacked by many hard-liners as not being sufficiently anti-Communist.

Because he was against any type of authoritarianism in civilian rule, Marshall disliked Stalinist autocracy, but neither did he judge the worth of wartime allies by the degrees of their anti-Communism. He had been, along with most Westerners, shocked by the Nazi-Soviet pact, but he welcomed the aid of the Soviets after they were attacked by Hitler, and he believed it important to prevent their defeat by the Nazis. After meeting Stalin at Tehran and Yalta, he concluded that the Russian leader would keep his word if he had positively and unequivocally given it. At the fateful meeting of Truman with his advisers on April 23, 1945, Marshall joined Stimson in opposing a belligerent approach toward the Soviets. Averell Harriman was later to say that Marshall was the last of the great Allied leaders to give up hope of working with the Russians. That shift, Harriman believed, followed the meeting at Moscow in 1947.

During the closing days of the war, Marshall grew disturbed by the deterioration of relations with the Soviet Union, and he deplored the postwar Soviet plundering of East Germany and Manchuria, but he was far from embarking on a crusade against Communism in his new assignment. His realistic awareness of widespread reductions of U.S. forces around the world made it all too evident that he could not rely on heavy battalions to back up his negotiations with the Soviets. Nor was he prepared to flaunt the atomic bomb.

The foreign policy of the United States had certainly hardened toward the Soviet Union since the war. While he was yet Chief of Staff, Marshall had seen rancor develop in Poland, Greece, Turkey, Iran, and Korea. Byrnes's hopes for compromises had been dissipated by smoldering disagreements in the various conferences of late 1945 and 1946. He had remained as Secretary of State long enough to get treaties with Italy, Rumania, Bulgaria, Hungary, and Finland, but the more difficult treaties with Germany and Austria were still in the future, and major problems remained in occupied

Germany. While in China, Marshall had not been kept fully aware of the widening rift between President Truman and Secretary Byrnes. Byrnes's independence of action and confidence born of long service as "assistant President" to Roosevelt increased the Secretary's natural tendency at conferences to seek some agreement for home consumption, and led him to take actions that had been magnified into charges that he was "babying the Russians."

Taking over from Byrnes almost on the eve of the Moscow Conference, Marshall had to spend much of his time from January until his departure for Europe in early March in finding out what had been done and what still must be agreed on in his first major trip abroad as Secretary of State.

In contrast to Marshall's briefing before he went to China in late 1945, when there was a new approach in policy and a specific course laid down, now the President entered little into the conferences and briefings; there were no special new directives, guidelines, or public announcements. Instead, the staff that had served Byrnes explained to Marshall what had happened and the policy that had been developed.

When Marshall was on his China mission, his mind was wholly occupied by his problems there, and he sensed only fragmentary currents of what was happening elsewhere in American foreign policy. He received information copies of important dispatches on Europe, but in the hectic day-to-day negotiations of Nanking, copies of cables gave no body of information to build a background of what had been done in European conferences. It was difficult, in the six weeks that he had before Moscow, for him to assimilate and digest the chunks of information fed him by his staff about previous actions of Secretary Byrnes or General Lucius Clay.

Many records exist of briefing books and of papers that technically went to the Secretary, but in no case is it likely that he received the carefully molded body of knowledge acquired by a professor reading a lengthy position paper or a carefully carpentered foreign-policy view prepared in a quiet study several decades after the event. Marshall's views, like those of many men suddenly handed a new and difficult job, were a meld of what he recalled of his experiences as Chief of Staff with fugitive impressions he had gained from cursory reading of information cables from Europe, of conversations he had had in Washington in March and April 1946, and from short talks with the President and Secretary Byrnes after his return in January. The detailed briefings were perhaps mainly helpful in showing him the change that had taken place the past year in Washington's thinking about the Soviets and Central Europe.

In Nanking, Marshall had seen a copy of the long telegram of
George Kennan, Chargé d'Affaires at the U.S. Embassy in Moscow
in February 1946, but the General had likely paid close attention
only to Kennan's suggestions that Russia was not at present dominating Chinese Communist policy. Marshall had met Kennan briefly
on two occasions during the war, once when Kennan had come from
Portugal to get clarification on the Army's views about the Azores,
and another time to get instructions on occupation zones in Germany. Because of Kennan's long telegram and its enormous influence at various levels of the administration, and because he would
become a prime mover in policy planning in Marshall's tour as Secretary of State, his background as a Foreign Service officer becomes
essential in understanding developments in 1947–49.

Born in Milwaukee in 1904, Kennan was a distant cousin of
another, earlier George Kennan who had written on the Russia of
the tsars. Kennan had gone to Princeton. Two years after his gradu-
ation in 1925, he entered the Foreign Service. He held minor
assignments in Germany, Finland, and Latvia and was then invited,
with several other young officers, to specialize in the language and
culture of a particular country. He and Charles Bohlen, who also
became important in Marshall's administration, were among six
young diplomats who elected to study the Russian language, history, and literature. Kennan chose to do his study in Berlin, while
Bohlen went to Paris. Both men spent vacations in areas bordering
the Soviet Union where they could practice the language and get
some understanding of the people. Kennan, in particular, studied
and talked with Russians who had fled from the Communists. Russian literature interested him at first more than Communist ideology, and he considered writing on Chekhov.

On a trip back to Washington in 1933, Kennan met William C.
Bullitt, who had just been named by the President to be the first
American Ambassador to Russia after Roosevelt's recent decision
to recognize the Soviet state. Bullitt asked Kennan to go with him
to Moscow on a brief inspection tour. As a result, Kennan helped
pick the Embassy's quarters and organize the first staff, while Bullitt
went back to Washington to complete his arrangements for opening the new Embassy.

Bullitt's high hopes soon vanished in Moscow as he found little
cooperation. Kennan and other staff members adopted his views.
Their growing anti-Russian feeling was fed by the beginning of the
purge trials in 1935, which horrified them and produced a violent
anti-Communist reaction among the members of the State Department, as well as a wave of anti-Stalinism in much of Europe.

In Moscow and on temporary assignments in Austria and Czechoslovakia, Kennan found his anti-Boshevist antipathy growing. He was outraged by the Nazi-Soviet pact and by Russia's destruction of Poland and takeover of the Baltic countries. When Hitler attacked Russia in the summer of 1941, Kennan felt that Russia was not a fit partner for the United States and Britain.

Assigned to Berlin before Pearl Harbor, Kennan was briefly interned when war was declared by Germany. His next assignments were in Lisbon and London, and he returned to the Soviet Union in 1945 and was acting as Chargé d'Affaires during Ambassador Harriman's absence in the United States when the war ended in Europe. He was there in the spring of 1946 when State Department requests for an analysis of Soviet views led him to send the famous message that was to shape thinking in many parts of the administration. Secretary of the Navy James Forrestal, who led all Cabinet members in warning of the dangers of Soviet expansion around the world, gave the Kennan telegram wide circulation. In the State Department, out-and-out opponents of the existence of Soviet Russia were strengthened in their positions. Shortly afterward, President Truman asked his naval aide, Clark Clifford, to draft a statement showing the number of agreements with the United States that the Soviet Union had failed to keep. Clifford and his assistant, George Elsey, picked up elements of the Kennan telegram along with other dire warnings about the Soviets from the State, War, and Navy departments.

Kennan's basic point was that the leaders of the Soviet Union saw themselves living in a state of constant "capitalist encirclement" with which they could not have peaceful coexistence. This insecurity, built on older fears from the time of the tsars, had led to a belief that the Soviet Union must have ever-increased national security and build larger and larger armed forces.

Never losing their distrust of capitalism, the Soviets would cooperate in international organizations only to gain advantage or to inhibit the work of such groups. The Soviet Union would develop ties to countries opposed to the Western powers and discourage efforts at economic collaboration. In summation, Kennan declared, the Soviet Union is "committed fanatically to the belief that there can be no permanent modus vivendi—that our traditional way of life must be destroyed, the international authority of our state be broken if Soviet power is to be secure."[13]

This frightening statement left its mark on subsequent thinking at the Capitol, the White House, the Pentagon, and the State Department. Kennan later softened his pessimism by suggesting that there might be a policy of containment, but such a policy should not include thinning U.S. resources by opposing the Soviets everywhere in the world. In his memoirs, Kennan characterized his early outpourings as too sweeping and similar to primers issued by patriotic organizations on the subversive activities of the Soviet Union. But the harsh rhetoric of these initial statements left a sort of tidal stain, and some of what he had said found its way into the briefings of new Secretary of State George Marshall.[14]

Added to Kennan's views was a memorandum sent from Moscow by Walter Bedell Smith, former assistant to Marshall at Fort Benning and in the office of Chief of Staff, now U.S. Ambassador to the Soviet Union. His Embassy staff had sketched various warnings for the guidance of Secretary Byrnes in early January 1947.

This memorandum arrived on the day Marshall's appointment to succeed Byrnes was announced. It recalled that Lenin had considered Germany to be the European country best suited for the development of Communism. Stalin took Lenin's view, and the current line was that "the proletariat of Germany carried the key to the proletarian revolution of all Europe." The current political and economic conditions in Germany seemed to make Germany even more favorable for Communist expansion. Aside from ideological gains, the Soviets were determined to prevent Germany from becoming too strong. They were on their way to controlling East Germany and they wanted to spread their influence to the Western zones.[15]

Smith believed that the Russians wanted a central administration in Germany rather than the development of federalism, which they could not control. They would push de-Nazification in the West, but in their zone would attempt also to get rid of democratic groups opposed to Communism. Reparations would be demanded, not only because of Russia's economic needs but in order to delay economic growth in West Germany. They would oppose the economic unification of Germany while charging the West with splitting the country. The West must be prepared to agree to further separation rather than accepting "hollow" unification. The Western powers must favor democratic and progressive forces in their zones while opposing infiltration and subversion. In a cautionary note, Smith predicted that the forthcoming conference would likely be a long one and that the United States delegation should be prepared to wait out the Russians. Smith's tone was pessimistic without blustering. While intended for Byrnes, his memorandum would have a strong effect on Marshall.

Added to Smith's cautions were detailed statements about points on which the Secretary would be expected to take a stand. James Riddleberger, chief of Central European Affairs, outlined in detail General Lucius Clay's positions on economic unity and reparations, while Benjamin Cohen, legal counselor of the State Department, who had worked closely with Byrnes in the same capacity, stressed the guidelines the United States delegation should follow. Since he did the main briefings for Marshall's delegation each day, his press conferences indicate what Marshall had been told.

Basically, the United States and Britain had no disposition to be soft on Germany. Byrnes had already opposed a revival of German military might and did not want that country to "become a pawn or a partner in a struggle for power between the East and West." Cohen emphasized that German economic recovery was essential to that of Europe. The occupying forces should not use their military power to gain special privileges for themselves, and their troops should be limited to special constabulary forces needed to protect Allied military governmental functions in Germany. The Americans should try to carry out their principles in conjunction with the other Allies, but if this became impossible, the Americans should observe these concepts in their zone and cooperate with those Allies willing to follow agreements.

The military Marshall was all too aware of the rapid reduction of American armed forces at a time when the State Department would need power to back its arguments in world conferences. He could remember the helter-skelter demobilization of U.S. forces at the end of World War I, and that memory led him to want a better plan at the end of World War II. As early as 1943, he had set up a small section in the War Department to work out a system that would satisfy the public's natural desire to reduce the expense of armed forces and to return to normal conditions of living. But the suddenness with which the war ended disrupted all planning.

Troops abroad began to demand discharges. Some of them remembered the Depression years and the large-scale unemployment and wanted to get out of uniform and back into civilian jobs before such jobs vanished. Pressure built up in Congress and in the press for rapid demobilization. Military leaders, so recently adulated for victory, were attacked for trying to keep large forces under arms in order to retain large budgets. In October 1945, Marshall, addressing the demand for the immediate return of troops home, spoke of an emotional crisis in the country. An immediate return, he felt, would lead to "both a disintegration of the Army" and the ending of all conception "of world responsibility."[16] Marshall's presentiments were accurate, and he was to feel the effect of a rapid loss in military efficiency in dealing with political problems in the Far East. The problem was acute when he took the position of Secretary of State.

When War Department officials stated that the rate of demobilization might have to be reduced, near the end of 1945 and early in the new year, protests from troops to Congress mounted rapidly. During the first week of January, in Guam, in the Philippines, in a camp near Le Havre, and in an airfield near Washington, groups of soldiers asked for a congressional investigation. Troops in the Philippines called for the resignation of Secretary of War Robert Patterson, then en route from Washington to Tokyo. When he reached Yokohama, a demonstration against him by American troops had to be broken up by U.S. military police. In Germany on the same day, January 9, a group of soldiers marched on the Army Theater headquarters in the I. G. Farben building in Frankfurt. Even the Marines, it was reported, had staged at least one demonstration in the Far East. General MacArthur responded by reducing the number of points that troops in his theater needed to return home. Promises of prompt congressional action seemed to still the soldiers' uproar, but relatives and friends continued to protest. General Eisenhower, on Capitol Hill for a hearing, was cornered by groups of indignant relatives demanding the release of troops abroad.[17]

Much of the demobilization problem came from lack of any clear-cut foreign policy to cover the postwar period. Without a statement that the United States would have a different role to play in the postwar world, the services found it difficult to sell soldiers and taxpayers on the need for a large occupation force or on a much larger armed force than the nation had possessed between the wars. In 1944, American strategy consisted of ending the war in Europe by the spring of 1945 and ending the war in the Pacific as soon thereafter as possible. Plans for early occupation of conquered portions of Germany were just being completed as U.S. forces moved to the Rhine. Changes in the postwar directive for Germany were still being made at the war's end.

Here and there, thoughtful staff members speculated on the role of the United States after the war was over. The reduced power of Britain and France was recognized, and the last year of fighting had made it chillingly clear that Soviet forces were prepared to fill the vacuum left by the defeat of Germany and Japan. Still, even military leaders assumed that the tremendous losses in manpower, the widespread material destruction, and the necessity for vast reconstruction, would make the Russians incapable of following an aggressive policy for five or ten years to come.

As Chief of Staff, General Marshall had personally called for a Joint Chiefs of Staff study outlining the size, composition, and development of a force competent to deal with postwar world problems. His call was reinforced by the budget director's request for a detailed statement by the military chiefs as to the needs of the armed forces.

Within less than a week after the end of the war with Japan, Marshall had tried to inject an element of realism into plans for demobilization. Recognizing the expected demands for fast action to reduce the size of the army and the staggering military costs, he called for his staff to demobilize the army with the greatest rapidity consistent with national commitments for occupation forces in defeated countries.[18]

In his final report to the Secretary of War, issued shortly before he resigned as Chief of Staff, Marshall suggested the heavier commitments that the United States had tacitly assumed. He spoke of the changed nature of war and the shift in the balance of power: "For probably the last time in the history of warfare those former ocean distances were a vital factor in our defense." Relating that he had been asked in 1940 to analyze dangers against which the country should prepare, he said that he had listed areas of the world where American troops had been in action since 1898, but he had not considered the jungles of Burma or the far-flung islands of the Pacific and the "garrisoning of areas across the entire land and water masses of the earth." From the conflict just ended, he concluded "that the nation must be prepared to defend its interest against any nation or combination of nations which sometimes feel powerful enough to attempt the settlement of political arguments or gain resources of territory by force of arms." His statement reflected the change of viewpoint imposed by the years of fighting but did not specify guidelines for future military policy, which must be decided only after future foreign policy was defined.[19]

The maintenance of hemispheric security was no longer sufficient for the protection of the United States, he declared. "We are now concerned with the peace of the entire world. And the peace can only be maintained by the strong." But this was a rhetorical statement rather than a careful listing of the reaches of future policy, although it was plain that the time had passed for a retreat to the concept of Fortress America.

In the closing months of 1945, the services agreed on a basis for the formulation of military policy and on strategic concepts and plans for the development of the armed forces. Many of the proposals—such as the maintenance of national policies set by civilian authorities and the taking of action abroad to maintain American security—were restatements of what had been done in the conflict just concluded. Marshall's report stressed that the American armed forces had to maintain world peace "under conditions which insure the security, well-being, and advancement of our country."

Despite these suggestions of a bolder peacetime stance, the Chiefs of Staff were not certain whether the country was prepared to sustain a large force. There were strong indications that the Congress and the President wanted a sharp cut in military expenses. Although Secretary Byrnes said in a speech at Stuttgart on September 4, 1946, that U.S. forces would remain in Germany as long as the forces of other powers remained there, on February 1, 1947, the United States had 202,000 troops in Europe as compared with 247,000 for Britain, 80,000 for France, and 1,110,000 for the Soviet Union. The War Department thought the Russians likely to make reductions by mid-year but noted that Soviet numbers must be considered with caution because of their practice of using demobilized troops in quasi-military positions. The department proposed that the United States and Britain each retain 140,000 troops, France 70,000, and the Russians 200,000. The Russians would also keep 20,000 in Poland, 5,000 in Hungary, and 5,000 in Rumania to protect communications. The United States, Britain, and Russia would each keep 10,000 men in Austria until independence was restored.[20]

Secretary of War Patterson asked Marshall in February 1947 about proposals to reduce air personnel in Germany to 37,000 by mid-May. He said that Secretary Byrnes had always asked for a good-sized force to be kept on while the earlier conferences were in session, and wanted Marshall's advice as to what number should be retained during the Moscow Conference. Patterson added that current pressures for economy in men and money, the unsatisfactory status of air units in Europe, and difficulty in maintaining the units in proper operational condition all made desirable, from a military standpoint, the reduction of air units in Europe. On the point of leaving for Moscow, Marshall replied that General Carl Spaatz, commanding the Army Air Forces, thought that having 8,000 to 12,000 airmen would adequately maintain flexibility, and suggested they proceed along that line. Marshall would go to the meeting of the Council of Foreign Ministers with no illusions as to having great military leverage.[21]

The Truman Doctrine

MARSHALL assumed that his troubles in the new office would begin with his trip to Moscow in early March, but they came on February 21 with a call from the British Embassy to the State Department. Early that morning, Marshall and General Eisenhower had gone to New York by train to accept, in common with other World War II leaders, honorary degrees from Columbia University. Mrs. Marshall met him in New York and they continued on to Princeton for his first address as Secretary of State at a special convocation on February 22, marking Princeton's bicentennial.[1] Thus he was not in his State Department office on the afternoon of February 21 when someone from the British Embassy phoned that the Ambassador, Lord Inverchapel, had an important *aide-mémoire* to present personally to the Secretary. Under Secretary Acheson suggested that the message be conveyed unofficially to him, so that he would be prepared for discussion with Marshall on his return from Princeton.

The news was unpleasant but not wholly unexpected. After six years of war, the liquidation of much of Britain's financial investments abroad, the loosening of imperial ties, the loss of markets in former colonies and elsewhere, and the steady drain on remaining funds for food and raw materials, Great Britain found its financial pressures intolerable. The situation was made worse by President Truman's abrupt suspension of Lend-Lease supplies at the close of the war in Europe, although it was eased when a British loan was authorized in 1946. But British attempts to continue imperial commitments strained the country's economy to such an extent that drastic remedies were necessary in 1947.

Not long before Marshall became Secretary of State, there were intimations that the British could not continue to bolster the governments in Greece and Turkey, but the immediacy of the crisis was not seen until the Embassy's call on that Friday afternoon. When Acheson was told that the messages dealt with the British need to abandon their role in Greece and Turkey, and with suggestions that the United States pick up the burdens, the Under Secretary immediately alerted Loy W. Henderson, Director of the Office of Near East and African Affairs, and other staff members. During the day, Acheson prepared a summary of messages coming in from Athens, to show Marshall. In retrospect he thought, incorrectly, that he had then discussed the problems of a possible crisis in Greece and Turkey with Marshall, who had instructed him to begin studies of the situation.[2]

The specific crisis did not figure in Marshall's February 22 speech, his first public address as Secretary of State. The speechwriter who had drafted a proposed address was unacquainted with Marshall's style and had written a speech full of scholarly allusions, which the writer had deemed appropriate for a leading university. Marshall made numerous excisions and changes, until the speech was almost completely rewritten, and sent the result over to Acheson as something "I scrabbled together." He wanted to know the Under Secretary's reaction.[3]

Speaking again at Princeton a year later, Marshall referred to his earlier speech there as "the first statement leading up to the subject in a speech at Harvard the following June." He was not outlining a plan for economic rehabilitation or a doctrine to assume responsibility for ensuring the strength of democratic government. He was repeating a thought mentioned in his farewell speech at the Pentagon on November 26, 1945, that Americans should learn of their past, of their relations with other powers, and of the new position of the United States in the world. His idea was a plea for the United States to assume the responsibilities of a world power. He declared:

> You should fully understand the special position that the United States occupies in the world geographically, financially, militarily, and scientifically, and the implications involved. The development of a sense of responsibility for world order and security, the development of a sense of overwhelming importance of the country's acts, and failures to act in relation to world order and security— these, in my opinion, are great "musts" for your generation.[4]

When Marshall came into his office on Monday, Acheson had a summary of reports from Athens and memoranda prepared by the State Department staff for him to read before the British Ambassador formally delivered his messages from London. Inverchapel brought two notes from Foreign Secretary Bevin explaining that, because of the serious economic situation in Great Britain, his country could no longer support the Greek and Turkish governments with economic and military aid. Greece would cost a quarter of a billion dollars for the remainder of 1947 and a smaller but equally important sum would be required for Turkey. Without help, Greek and Turkish independence would not last and all the Middle East would come under Russian control. The British asked whether the United States would be willing to assume the bulk of these burdens.[5]

Marshall asked that his State Department staff make a more detailed study of the situation as soon as possible. Acheson's summary of messages from U.S. representatives in Greece had detailed consequences of a failure to support Greece and Turkey. The representatives recommended (1) unification of all Greek parties with the exception of the extreme right and the Communists, (2) domestic reforms in government and tax programs, (3) economic and financial aid, and (4) military aid. These were alarming reminders to Marshall of problems left behind recently in China.

Later that day, Henderson, as chief of the desk concerned with the Near East, presided over a group of State Department representatives, including Bohlen and Kennan. Most of them felt that the United States must assume the British responsibility; first accept it, then determine how to do it. The main dissenter was General James K. Crain, Deputy Chairman of the Policy Committee on Arms and Armaments, who declared that the United States would be compounding Britain's mistaken approach. The United States should withhold aid, while saving our arms for a strategic showdown with the Soviets. We should let the Russians know we would use force, if necessary, to prevent their takeover of Greece and Turkey.[6]

Henderson summarized the various views in a paper that he gave Acheson on February 25. Acheson approved the recommendations and took the paper to Marshall the next day. Later that morning, the two men discussed the situation and what they believed should be done with Secretary of War Patterson and Secretary of the Navy Forrestal, and in the afternoon Marshall and Acheson took all the recommendations to President Truman. Acheson made the presentation, summing up the general recommendation as urging "immediate action to extend all possible aid to Greece and, on a lesser scale, to Turkey." The President accepted in principle the proposal for immediate aid.[7]

The secretaries had agreed that Congress must be fully advised of the problem, the American people apprised of the situation, and all concerned made to realize the global issues involved. The next morning, President Truman invited to his office the majority and minority leaders of the Senate, H. Styles Bridges and Alben Barkley; the ranking majority and minority members of the Senate Foreign Relations Committee, Arthur Vandenberg and Thomas Connolly; Speaker of the House, Joseph Martin; House Minority Leader Sam Rayburn; and Charles Eaton and Sol Bloom, ranking majority and minority leaders of the House Committee on Foreign Affairs. Marshall opened the meeting by reading the recommendations of his department.

Fourteen years later, Acheson said that Marshall had failed to put his case across, and Joseph Jones had indicated much the same in 1955. Acheson felt that his chief, "most unusually and unhappily, flubbed his opening statement."[8] Perhaps the Secretary read too calmly, but the words he read were frightening: "A crisis of the utmost importance and urgency has arisen in Greece and to some extent in Turkey. This crisis has a direct and intimate relation to the security of the United States." He read the growing warnings from our representatives in Greece of the danger of that country's collapse and possible loss of independence.

Contrary to Jones's belief that "he conveyed the over-all impression that aid should be extended to Greece on the grounds of loyalty and humanitarianism, and to Turkey to strengthen Britain's position in the Middle East," Marshall declared, "Our interest in Greece is by no means restricted to humanitarian or friendly impulses." He warned:

> If Greece should dissolve into civil war it is altogether probable that it would emerge as a communist state under Soviet control. Turkey would be surrounded and the Turkish situation . . . would in turn become still more critical. Soviet domination might thus extend over the entire Middle East to the borders of India. The effect of this upon Hungary, Austria, Italy and France cannot be overestimated. It is not alarmist to say that *we are faced with the first crisis of a series which might extend Soviet domination to Europe, the Middle East and Asia.* [Emphasis supplied.]

He knew no power other than the United States that could prevent this crisis. There was no assurance that even this aid would save this situation, but "the choice is between acting with energy or losing by default." A war of nerves by Russia had kept Turkey in a state of crisis and imposed a heavy strain on her economy. The maintenance of the integrity of Turkey "is essential to the entire independent structure of the eastern Mediterranean and the Middle East." They could not permit inaction or delay.

We are at the point of decision. We cannot enter upon the first steps of policy without the assurance and determination to carry it through. To do this requires the support of the Congress and certain legislation. I hope this legislation may be obtained with bipartisan support and without protracted controversy. Internal division and delay might gravely imperil the success of the program we are proposing.[8]

His statement seems to have made an impression. Truman quoted from it in his memoirs and made no mention of remarks by Acheson; and the editor of the *Vandenberg Papers* speaks only of Marshall's statements. Senator Vandenberg's files show no diary entry regarding the February meeting but include two copies of the Marshall statement. However, in later years, Dean Acheson recalled that Marshall's poor efforts spurred him to ask if it was a private fight or if anyone could get in. Marshall asked the group to hear the Under Secretary. Acheson recalls a dramatic scene: "Never have I spoken under such a pressing sense that the issue was up to me alone." His brief summary was in the tone of a lawyer working to sway a skeptical jury. His closing sentence was followed by a short silence, then by a shocked Vandenberg saying to the President that the problem must be presented to the American people as it had been presented that day.[9] The facts presented by Marshall and Acheson had not been different, but, in the words of an old story, about an energetic pulpit pounder, advocate Acheson had supplied "the rousements." Marshall always shied away from rhetoric, yet, some years earlier, his congressional appearances had been just as magnetic. He was now several years older and aware of different factors. Later, after the heat of battle for the Marshall Plan, Marshall apologized for strong anti-Communist blasts, remarking that it was easy to get too shrill. He did not believe at that time that the United States had the armed forces to back excessive rhetoric. When you don't have the strength, he often said, you don't hit a man across the face and call him names.

But the matter had become a strongly political one, since the assumption of a responsibility previously borne by the British in an area not regarded as within the U.S. sphere marked a clear shift in policy. The White House advisers were now concerned with the President's role and the way he announced the new "doctrine."

A preliminary draft of a presidential statement presented by Loy Henderson to the White House seemed too mild to the President's special counsel, Clark Clifford. Clifford was an able St. Louis attorney who had served in the Navy during the war and had been brought into the White House in 1946 by Truman's naval aide, John Vardaman, as his assistant. When Vardaman received a higher position during the same year, Clifford became naval aide and soon began to help write presidential speeches. By 1947 he was Special Counsel to the President. He saw early the need to improve Truman's image as a decisive leader, and the time seemed ready for a strong stand in favor of countries menaced by the U.S.S.R.

Clifford had watched the growing distrust of the Soviet Union in the United States. In 1946, Truman had asked him to prepare a study on the number of unfulfilled Russian agreements. This report, drafted largely by his assistant, George Elsey, helped strengthen Clifford's conviction that the country should take a harder line with the Communists. In the problem of Greek-Turkish aid, he saw an opportunity for Truman to be spokesman for the free world. Elsey shared Clifford's wish to promote a strong presidential image and felt the need to draw a line in the international debate with Moscow, but he questioned whether this was the proper issue for an all-out challenge to the Russians. Clifford replied that this was the opening gun in a campaign to make the public realize that the war was not yet over. Some thirty years later, at a Truman Library symposium on Truman's foreign policy, Clifford admitted to former colleagues and a number of diplomatic historians that perhaps the rhetoric had been overheated. He observed that he had been accused of intensifying the cold war.

To give aid to countries threatened by Soviet Russia was not a new idea. No one in authority doubted that the United States should assume the burdens that Great Britain could no longer bear in Greece and Turkey. After Bevin's note of February 21 was given to Acheson, all State Department studies accepted the need for congressional action, as did Marshall, the service secretaries, and Truman. But it was the special decision to create from this situation a new doctrine challenging Communism, to invite all countries threatened by Russia to call on the United States for aid, and the sharpness of the rhetoric that led later critics to charge the White House with recklessness.[10]

After several revisions of Henderson's original draft in the State Department by Acheson, Joseph Jones, and others, Clifford modified the language to make some passages more forceful. Other points were deleted at Acheson's request. Marshall, busy with final arrangements for the Moscow meeting, played no part in the drafting of the text.

The final text of the President's speech announcing what was called the "Truman Doctrine" was completed after Marshall left for Europe. Bohlen, who was with his chief, says they received the copy in Paris and that he and the Secretary indicated that the rhetoric was too strong and that they protested. When the answer to their protest was that they could not get action without a strong statement to Congress, they did not insist.[11]

Truman's speech on March 12 stressed the danger of failure to aid Greece and Turkey and the importance of helping free people to work out their destinies in their own way. In a passage borrowed from a statement by the State-War-Navy Coordinating Committee (to become one of the most controversial parts of the address), he declared, "I believe it must be the policy of the United States to support free peoples who are resisting attempted subjugation by armed minorities or by outside pressures." This statement had gone into the State Department draft that went to the White House, although George Kennan, then at the National War College, thought that it was too broad and that it invited almost every country with problems to turn to the United States for support. But it frightened Congress and gained bipartisan majorities in both houses. The Senate passed the bill to aid Greece and Turkey 67–23 on April 12; the House, 287–107 on May 8. Truman signed the bill on May 22.[12]

Before leaving for Moscow in early March, Marshall told Acheson to work on the Greek-Turkish aid program without consideration for the success of his negotiations with the Russians. A courageous act, thought Acheson, as if a commander had called down fire on his forward position to defeat the enemy.[13] But Marshall left for Moscow expecting a measure of success despite the effects of the President's words. At best the negotiations were a calculated risk. The message of the President would make the risk incalculable.

Meeting at Moscow

EARLY in the morning of March 5, 1947, Marshall and his personal staff left Washington by plane for Paris. After refueling stops in Bermuda and the Azores, the plane touched down at Orly just after noon on the following day. The group was met by the U.S. Ambassador to France, Jefferson Caffery, who had invited the Secretary to stay at the official residence, along with Colonel Marshall Carter, Charles Bohlen, and orderly Richard Wing, on his last trip with Marshall before leaving the Army.[1]

Others of the United States delegation were en route by other planes to Moscow. The delegation included: Benjamin Cohen, counselor of the State Department, who would have the daily task of coordinating American views for each meeting, and H. Freeman Matthews, director of the Office of European Affairs. Not long before leaving for Europe, Marshall had added a man of whom he had heard much but whom he had not previously met. Senator Vandenberg had declined Marshall's invitation to go with the delegation to Moscow because of the pressure of his duties at the time. When Marshall asked if he would like to suggest someone else to represent him, Vandenberg said it was not necessary to appoint anyone to represent the Republican majority in the Senate, but if the Secretary thought it proper, John Foster Dulles of New York would be a good man. Marshall talked with Dulles at the State Department and suggested he fly ahead to Paris and Berlin.[2]

Dulles was well equipped to represent his party and his country. Grandson of President Benjamin Harrison's Secretary of State, John W. Foster, and nephew of Wilson's Secretary of State, Robert Lansing, Dulles had been counsel to the American Commission to the Paris Peace Conference in 1919 and a member of the Reparations Commission. Later, he attended the 1933 conference that dealt with the German war debt. In 1945, he was a member of the U.S. delegation at the San Francisco meeting that established the United Nations organization. He was an adviser to Secretary Byrnes at the Conference of the Council of Foreign Ministers in London after the war and served as U.S. representative to the General Assembly of the United Nations as early as 1946. Son of a Presbyterian minister, he had strong convictions on right and wrong which led him to favor a high moral tone in foreign policy.[3]

Particularly important to Marshall at Moscow and at later conferences was Charles Bohlen. Born in New York State in 1904, Bohlen was a grandson of James B. Eustis, one-time Senator from Louisiana and the first Ambassador to France after the post had been elevated from a ministry to an ambassadorship. Bohlen had decided on a career in the Foreign Service three years after completing his A.B. at Harvard, in 1927. After two years in Prague as vice consul, Bohlen went to Paris to study Russian for two and a half years. Once the United States had recognized the Soviet Union, U.S. Ambassador William Bullitt selected Bohlen as an Embassy staff member. He served at the Embassy in Moscow under First Secretary Loy Henderson, along with two other third secretaries, George Kennan and Ertel Kuniholm.

After fifteen months in Moscow, Bohlen returned to Washington and was assigned to the Eastern European section of the State Department until 1938, when he was sent back to Moscow as Second Secretary. He was there during the final round of purge trials, in which many former Soviet leaders were led to confess crimes against the state and executed. He followed the maneuvers that led to the signing of the Nazi-Soviet pact in 1939; was there when the Soviets helped Germany crush Poland, when Russia invaded Finland, and when the Soviet Union took over Lithuania, Latvia, Estonia, and Bessarabia.

Transferred to Tokyo near the end of 1940 to advise on Russo-Japanese relations, he was in the Japanese capital at the time of Pearl Harbor and was interned with the Ambassador and others of the Embassy staff. Returning to Washington on diplomatic exchange in 1942, Bohlen became assistant chief of the Russian section of the State Department, serving under Loy Henderson, whom he succeeded in the summer of 1943.

He went with Secretary Hull to Moscow in the fall of 1943 to help prepare for the conference near the end of that year between Churchill, Roosevelt, and Stalin at Tehran, and was then assigned temporarily to Roosevelt's party for the Tehran meeting. After he came back to Washington, he was tapped repeatedly by Harry Hop-

kins for information on the Soviets. Near the end of 1944, the new
Secretary of State, Edward R. Stettinius, Jr., named Bohlen as special liaison officer with the White House. In January 1945, he accompanied Hopkins on a tour of European capitals in preparation
for the Yalta Conference the following month. At that conference
he served as Roosevelt's interpreter and kept notes of high-level
talks between the President and Stalin.

Although he had not met Truman before he became President,
Bohlen was at the White House conference on April 23 when Truman said he would take a firm line with the Russians, and Bohlen
subsequently interpreted for the President in his early talks with
Foreign Minister Molotov. He served as the President's interpreter
at Potsdam, and as Byrnes's special assistant he went with him to
Moscow later in the year to discuss reparations problems not fully
settled at Potsdam. He was present with Byrnes at the Council of
Foreign Ministers in Paris in the latter part of the same year.

When Marshall succeeded Byrnes in January, 1947, he kept
Bohlen as special assistant and listened carefully to his advice because of his familiarity with high-level discussions carried on with
Soviet leaders since 1943. Critics of State Department hard-line
advisers often put Bohlen in that group, but concede that he
showed some evidence of Roosevelt's Yalta orientation. A careful
examination of his memoranda to Marshall indicates that Bohlen
did not follow any rigid ideological bias in his advice to the Secretary.[4]

Marshall was invited to dinner by the President of France on his
first evening in Paris. He arranged to talk with President Vincent
Auriol and Prime Minister Paul Ramadier before the meal. Although the French Foreign Minister, Georges Bidault, had already
left for Moscow, Marshall thought it both politic and important to
get a better understanding of France's problems before the conference in Moscow.

The French question was of particular concern to the United
States and Great Britain. Division in France created by the German
occupation and quarrels between the Gaullists and remnants of
prewar parties had given to the Communist Party considerable
power in the postwar government. Now opposed to the Gaullists,
their allies during the Resistance days, the Communists were
nevertheless prepared to join with them again to bring down the
government if it failed to demand strong measures against the
defeated enemy.

The French dread that Germany would be reconstructed more
rapidly than France or other victims of German aggression sparked

friction between the French and British and American occupation chiefs in the German occupation zones. President Auriol voiced the fear that the Germans would be allowed a centralized army and that the Ruhr would be left in control of German industrial magnates. This fear often caused the French to line up with the Russians in debates in the Allied Control Council in Berlin, to the fury of General Lucius Clay, who declared he had more trouble with the French than with the Russians.

Marshall was reluctant to go into detail as to the American position until he had talked with Bevin. He fell back on expressing his warm personal feelings about France's problems, which he had acquired from cooperating with the French in two world wars. Recalling his two and a half years in France in 1917–18 and his visits to France in 1944, the Secretary felt without boasting that he knew as much of the sufferings of that country as any non-Frenchman could understand. But he added that he had a responsibility for the plight of defeated peoples as well as that of liberated countries. There must be a balance between the import needs of Germany and those of France. He was reiterating the arguments of British and American occupation commanders, who said that their forces should not have to keep on and on contributing to the welfare of the occupied zones, that the zones must be helped to stand on their own.

Marshall ended his talk at the meeting with Auriol and Ramadier with a theme he had mentioned earlier to Ramadier: the importance of a system of security to keep the peace of Europe. Byrnes had proposed a twenty-five-year disarmament treaty, and Marshall meant to work for it. Seeking to convince Auriol that this was not a maneuver to gain greater concessions, Marshall declared: "I am not a diplomat. I mean exactly what I say and there is no use trying to read between the lines because there is nothing to read there."[5]

After the usual wreath-laying at the Arc de Triomphe the next day, Marshall left for Berlin. Colonel Carter, his liaison officer, noted that before leaving Washington Marshall had seemed optimistic that the conference could be made to work. But on the way to Berlin, Carter wrote his wife:

Still no sign of how long it will last but there is not too much optimism of our really getting complete results, as it may be cut shorter than we originally expected. I have not talked to General Marshall about it, but from watching him operate in the past, he will not, in my opinion, hang around without results.[6]

Marshall was going to Moscow as he had to China. He knew that the odds were against him, but he must try. He had admitted to members of the Senate Foreign Relations Committee that there was little possibility of getting a final treaty with Germany at this conference, but he hoped to get an acceptance "of the principles that would guide the representatives in drafting such a treaty." He thought that they might get a treaty with Austria, and he would try to persuade the other powers to place that on the agenda. He assured his staff that he was not giving up in advance, but some State Department experts were pessimistic, saying that the conference would last five or six weeks without doing more than clarifying and reducing issues.[7]

From Paris, Marshall flew on to Berlin for two days, to talk with General Clay, who was soon to take command of U.S. troops in the European Theater and to discuss with Dulles (who joined him there) what he had found out in France and Germany. He went on to Moscow on the 9th, arriving at the General Airport at 3:30 P.M, where he was met by Ambassador Bedell Smith, Deputy Foreign Minister Vishinski, and representatives of major diplomatic delegations.[8]

Smith found that his former boss was unimpressed by the "bowler hat" he had recently picked up in Paris. For the Ambassador it was a reunion with a revered chief. Reminiscing about Marshall in a book he later wrote on his Moscow days, Smith said that some of the foreign diplomats had wondered how Marshall would fare in his dealings with "a group of tough, Middle Eastern bazaar traders." He had no misgivings.

> I had seen General Marshall under all conditions of stress and strain, and I had never seen him fail eventually to dominate every gathering by sheer force of his integrity, honesty, and dignified simplicity. Moreover, his whole service had been a preparatory course for high-level negotiations. I knew that he would say little until he had the situation and all the facts well in hand and that he would make no mistakes. . . .[9]

Although he had been away from service with Marshall for a number of months, Smith soon felt at home. He recalled that the General began to say, " 'I want you to do this and this,' and I said, 'Yes, sir,' and thought, 'Here we go again.' "

The Ambassador's residence, Spaso House, where Marshall and his small personal staff were to stay, had been built before World

War I by a wealthy Russian dealer in sugar and had become the U.S. Embassy residence after the United States recognized the Soviet Union. Rooms were at a premium in the city, so the ballroom housed the stenographic pool and mimeograph machines. Halls, the billiard room, and parlors became offices, and the dining room became a cafeteria ready to serve meals at any hour. Morning briefings and discussions were held in this building. Marshall was given the Ambassador's bedroom and adjoining reception room, and here he carried on most of his work. Others of the delegation were assigned to the Hotel Moscow, the best hotel in the city, just across the square from the Chancery, which had been refurbished for the conference. The meetings of the Council of Foreign Ministers were held in the Aviation Industry House near the hotel.[10]

Bohlen and Carter shared a bedroom next to Marshall. Although Marshall's reception room had an electric heater, it was chilly enough that he often worked in a floor-length blue lounging robe, high-necked and quilted, which Carter said made him look like Chiang Kai-shek. On a typical day, the Secretary first considered messages that Carter relayed to him between nine and eleven-thirty each morning. At ten-thirty he moved to the main reception room, where he met with members of the delegation and tried to work out the line to be followed in the afternoon deliberations. After lunch, Marshall and Carter tried to get some exercise, but they found their walks included a crowd of Russian security men. When they left Spaso House, a Russian car with six men would swing out in front of the car carrying the Secretary, and another car with six men would fall in behind. Marshall and Carter often drove to the park area; a favorite spot there was at the edge of the city, where Napoleon supposedly had his first look at Moscow. As they left the car and walked along, they were always conscious that their escorts had left *their* cars and were walking along at a visible distance.

At three-thirty each afternoon, Marshall and members of the delegation went by automobile to the conference site. Here again was a set routine. As their car left Spaso House, the Russians sent ahead a signal. By the time Marshall's car reached the main street, all traffic was cleared and no one was allowed to cross the street. Sessions began at 4:00 P.M., continuing until seven or eight. Then the advisers had a quick meal and went back to rework papers or draw up new ones to put before Marshall the next morning. Ben Cohen had to reconcile opposing views, or, if he could not, to put all sides of various opinions before his chief. The ideas of delegation members were not all that was involved; there were proposals from the Ambassador and Embassy staff, from General Mark Clark and his advisers from Vienna, and from General Clay and his staff from Berlin.[11]

About to take over full control of the U.S. command in Germany from General Joseph McNarney, Clay would have liked to skip the Moscow meeting. However able he was as an administrator, Clay had been ground down into touchiness from constant, abrasive crises brought on by the French and the Russians. He was ill at ease with Marshall, in contrast to the easy rapport he had with Byrnes, and he delayed response to the invitation to Moscow until Marshall had to insist. In Moscow, Clay had troubles from the first with John Foster Dulles, who was inclined to lecture others on their duties. Clay decided Dulles was pro-French and their early relations were not pleasant. Dulles also rubbed Mark Clark the wrong way by attempting to speak for Austria, which Clark considered his own bailiwick.[12]

Dulles's main problems at the conference flowed from his wish to internationalize the Ruhr, in order to aid European recovery and provide a guard against a Germany that might again menace Europe. The U.S. delegation wondered if this approach would encourage the French to act more closely with the Soviets. Ronald K. Pruessen's analysis of Dulles's role at Moscow shows that Dulles's colleagues were not impressed by his views on the Ruhr. Despite Dulles's early-March insistence on a firm stand on the Ruhr, Marshall did not bring up the issue until April 10, and then defined it so broadly that it ended the discussion. However keen his disappointment, Dulles "never offered sharp criticism and never allowed incomplete success on the one matter to cancel out his overall support for American policy on Germany. He had retained some qualms about what Truman administration policy makers were doing, but he shared enough of their beliefs to give them loyal support, especially in public."[13]

Dulles was at the meeting to represent the Chairman of the Senate Foreign Relations Committee (Vandenberg), but he sometimes acted as though he were in charge of the delegation.

The Moscow conference opened on March 10 at the Aviation Industry House, in a huge, ornate room that had a table seating twenty delegates. British Foreign Secretary Ernest Bevin, Soviet Foreign Minister Molotov, French Foreign Minister Georges Bidault, and Marshall were placed across from one another, one to each side and at the ends of the table. Four delegation members sat by each chief. Behind each delegation head were other small tables where other advisers sat with supporting papers and incidental information that might be wanted. Marshall did not like to be whispered to during meetings, so his advisers were aware they must have memoranda to pass to him when needed.[14]

There was a certain amount of shuffling about in each delegation as members were summoned to give information on subjects pertaining to their special assignments. The ability to sit through long harangues became highly prized. "Old iron bottom" Molotov gave every indication that he could sit out the debates if they took all summer.

Each talk was translated at least twice, and those delegates not interested in listening used the time this took for personal correspondence or for jotting down arguments. During one of the meetings, Colonel Carter described the chief delegates for his wife:

> Molotov is in his usual pose. Hand covering chin, elbow on table, slowly nodding his head. Completely poker-faced. Bevin looking like a cross between Santa Claus and a Welsh coalman, tortoise shell glasses, cigarette hanging loosely from his mouth, glancing with raised brows through papers and books. Bidault trying to look bigger than he is, smoothy type, trying to give the impression that he is bored and thinking above the lot.[15]

Marshall was to work more closely with Bevin than with any of the other delegates. This British leader was in no way the American image of the tall, lean Oxbridge Foreign Secretary so perfectly realized in Anthony Eden. He was "fat and unwieldy," according to one observer, and his mannerisms and speech failed to mitigate this impression. As a young man he had driven a horse-drawn delivery wagon in Bristol. Later, he was caught up in the rough-and-tumble of labor unions. He never went to a public school, yet his workingman's accent could be formidable in debate. He became a lay preacher whose gruff eloquence always impressed opponents and moved crowds. He could never remember how to pronounce foreign names—his pronunciation of Bidault as "Bidet" was completely innocent, as was "Biddle," which was not so much noticed. He was perceptive and stubborn in considering issues before the conference. He was indeed overweight, and he had a heart problem, and his choler rose easily, even with friends, if he felt they were slighting the British or engaged in under-the-table activity. His temper subsided as quickly as it rose.[16]

The Americans had assumed that Bevin would follow a strong Labour Party line, with considerable sympathy for some Soviet views. They discovered that he, like trade-unionists elsewhere, was wary of Russian attempts to control labor movements in other countries. They also found out that he would not bargain away British Empire positions. Marshall consulted him frequently throughout the conference, and each often supported the other in attempts to get action on certain measures during delays by Molotov and Bidault.

Marshall pitied Bidault. Harassed by Gaullists and Communists in the National Assembly who constantly threatened to bring down the government, he was always trying to assure Marshall and Bevin that he was on their side, but he dared not seem to follow an Anglo-American line. Though Marshall was sympathetic with his problems, he at length tired of Bidault's continual pleas not to be pressed too hard to take a firm stand. Bidault had been an effective Resistance leader during the war and had once been close to de Gaulle. Later he accused de Gaulle of throwing him over. His memoirs do not make pleasant reading, although he gives his highest praise to Marshall.[17]

Marshall had dealt with Molotov as early as 1942, when the Russian Foreign Minister was in Washington trying to secure the opening of a second front. He did not like Molotov's doctrinaire pronouncements, or his tendency to insist that Rooseveltian suggestions of possible intent were solid promises. Molotov had succeeded Foreign Minister Maxim Litvinov in the spring of 1939 and represented his country in negotiating the Nazi-Soviet pact of that year. Second to Stalin in power during the war, he continually badgered the Allies for a second front and for increased military aid. To Marshall and others who dealt with him, he was a negotiator who never gave up. Agreeing to compromises one day, he returned the next day to argue precisely the same points. Marshall had respect for his adroitness in discussions, but decided that he was afraid to reach any agreement on his own; the only solution was to take arguments to Stalin.

As host to the conference, Molotov took the chair at the opening meeting. The delegates soon agreed that the post of chairman would rotate daily, but other procedural questions ran into trouble. From the beginning, Marshall and Bevin let it be understood that they would raise difficult questions to counter those brought up by Molotov. The Russian soon proved that he intended to use the conference as a sounding board to demand greater speed in de-Nazification and disarmament of Germany, greater control over the economy of Germany, plus a demand for compliance with the $10 billion in reparations that the Soviets insisted had been agreed on at Potsdam and which the Allies felt to have been merely mentioned as a figure to be discussed but not to be specifically determined until later. These matters had been debated through several meetings since Potsdam, by many of the same officials, but since Marshall was now sitting in for Byrnes they had to hear them again.

Having sat through every major Allied conference in World War II from 1942 to 1945, Marshall knew well the need for patience in negotiation. A year of postwar discussions with the Nationalists and the Communists in China had prepared him for sessions that went on and on. In the forty-three meetings with the foreign ministers of Britain, France, and the Soviet Union from March 10 until near the end of April, he found the routine drearily familiar. Particularly trying, he told Truman, was the tendency of delegations, especially the Russian and the French, to use the discussions solely as chances to create propaganda for the people at home. In retaliation, he and Bevin made increasing use of their publicity opportunities.

In China, Marshall had had no allied delegations to support him, but neither did he have to persuade other allies to agree. In Moscow, he and Bevin usually agreed closely, but repeatedly he found France intransigently supporting Soviet demands on Germany. Early in the conference he determined to settle a number of questions that Bidault brought up, and to give him moral support to stiffen his spine.

He had heard some of the French arguments during his stopover in Paris on his way to Moscow. On March 13, he got them in great detail from Bidault. In bringing up control of the Ruhr, the French Minister suggested that French and American technicians be placed in operating positions there. Marshall disagreed. He was willing to have British, French, and Americans supervise German managers at the top but said that actual operations should be left in German hands. When Marshall added that France could ease her problem of getting German coal by cooperating with British and American bizonal arrangements, Bidault smilingly referred to his "special problems," which Marshall translated to mean "Communist participation in the French Government and their reluctance to permit the French to join in bizonal arrangements." Marshall remarked that it was sometimes difficult to see the forest for the trees. Bidault, aware of the Gaullists' anti-American stance on Germany, said that he had once worked for de Gaulle and that the General could only see the forest and this was equally bad.

During the wartime conferences, Marshall often spoke for the Army and Air Force and sometimes for the Navy. His words usually had the support of the President and, particularly in later conferences, had behind them the power that could supply men and munitions for victory. In those conferences, he had always tried to use tact and reasonableness, but he could force the issue. Now he found it necessary to change his approach in negotiations. In dealing with the Russians, he decided to be very firm, to match Soviet obstructionism and delays with his own brand of the same. With the British, he sought frequent discussions to smooth out disagreements. France required something more. It was necessary to convince Bidault that he was a friend of France, that he understood the special problems of France, and that it would not help France to divide the Western Allies.

In his meeting with Bidault on March 13, Marshall chose to be the blunt old soldier. As a newcomer to diplomacy, he said he was having trouble in adapting to the practices of the Council of Foreign Ministers. As a soldier, he had found that conducting a war was a simple profession, "because one understands clearly the objective to be attained." Making peace seemed much more complicated. "It is my experience that I form certain opinions when, suddenly, a new element is introduced which is misleading. It is difficult for me to decide on the best methods to adopt." He expressed admiration for the way in which Bidault had recently presented the problem of demilitarization so "as to avoid giving a too provocative aspect to your proposals." Bidault did not eagerly accept this blandishment. He said he had been disappointed that his effort to separate demilitarization from other issues had not been better received.[18]

Marshall recalled that he had twice fought the Germans, but had no fear that Germany would again become powerful if the four victors could remain united. The danger was that the conquered country would ally itself with one of its former enemies. Twice in the past the Germans had evaded obligations imposed by conquerors. "If we are not careful, they will start all over again. And we should recall that her motto is: 'Divide in order to rule.' "

Alluding to the earlier proposal of Secretary Byrnes for a Four Power Pact, Marshall thought such an agreement the best guarantee for peace. As Chief of Staff during the war, he had concluded that the war could have been avoided if the United States had made a prewar commitment to the Allies, and if "American military preparation had been more advanced."

Sensing the latent thrust of Marshall's remarks, Bidault admitted that he had disappointed Byrnes with his lack of enthusiasm for the proposal. He had never doubted the importance of an American presence in Europe, especially in Germany, but he feared that the proposed treaty would be considered a substitute for other guarantees. ". . . we firmly believe that a whole series of measures are indispensable to guarantee peace: demilitarization, control, Four Power Pact and alliances, occupation." France remembered the treaty of 1919. "In a troubled world where the United States and the Soviet Union can affront each other, it seems necessary to us to superimpose on the treaties guarantees of a territorial and industrial character."

Bidault spoke of the need for global solutions. Marshall agreed that everything possible should be done to enhance the prestige of the United Nations, but that body was still young, without tradition, and untested. At the moment, the Four Power Pact was essential. He reminded the Foreign Minister that such a treaty would demonstrate to Europe and especially to France that the United States intended to accept responsibilities in Europe, and would forcibly remind Americans of their promises. It would, in fact, require the country to be prepared to carry out its responsibilities. With his obligations defined in advance by treaty, a future President would not face the difficulties Roosevelt had to deal with in combating isolationists in Congress. It was because France did not seem to realize that, in offering such a treaty, the United States was making a "revolutionary" change in its policy that Byrnes "may have seemed disappointed."

Only a little persuaded, Bidault demanded that "the French economy not be destroyed by the German economy." Marshall agreed and said they could soon proceed to talk about coal. Sensing some progress, Marshall went on to recall that after the first war he had heard Foch and Weygand discuss the Ruhr. Foch had said that force was the only solution. Did not Bidault agree that there was force in a Four Power Pact, and an element of continuity? Marshall said that the problem was not so much what was going to happen the next four or five years in Germany, but "the situation in which we will find ourselves within 10 years."

His arguments did not fully satisfy Bidault but at least they indicated that he was sympathetic to French problems. The importance of seeking French support was soon evident when Molotov, on the 13th, attacked the Western powers for failing to disarm German forces and non-German nationals. The Russian wanted to order the Allied Control Council to speed up the process. Marshall countered with a request that the council be asked to report on present progress and to continue along similar lines. Bevin strongly defended the council. He and Molotov clashed on several issues; the British Foreign Secretary insisted that the Soviets report on the destruction of captured German capital ships and declared that Britain could not agree on much more destruction of war-potential plants in Germany unless there were agreement on a unified German economy.[19]

By March 14 the pattern of conflict had become more pronounced and the debates, which had been mostly between Bevin and Molotov, had become more general. In a challenge to Soviet practices, Marshall emphasized the need for uniform regulations on human rights for postwar Germany. He thought it essential to have effective and uniform guarantees of (1) civil rights, (2) rights of free trade unions, (3) rights of political parties, (4) freedom of press and radio, (5) freedom of movement for persons and goods. Molotov retorted that the Soviets were not concerned with "the generalities of democracy, but only those facts which bore on Allied responsibilities in Germany." Freedom of press and radio did not include the right to propagandize for the restoration of a Hitlerian regime. Freedom of trade unions and land reforms were rights requiring prompt decision by the Council of Foreign Ministers.

Seeing small chance for a meeting of minds on the guarantees that he sought, Marshall decided to use the meeting as a sounding board for a public statement of what democracy meant to his country. Ambassador Bedell Smith declared Marshall's words "constituted what was probably the most forthright statement of the rights of man ever made in Russia." The Secretary said that the American people understood that there were certain inalienable rights that could not be taken or given away. These included "the right of every individual to develop his own soul in the ways of his choice, free of fear or coercion—only that he does not interfere with the rights of others."

He probably had no hope of reaching the Russian people, but perhaps the thought of former followers or victims of Hitler impelled him to say:

> To us, society is most democratic if men who respect the rights of their fellow men are free to express their own beliefs and convictions without fear that they may be snatched away from their homes and family. To us a society is not free if law-abiding citizens live in fear of being denied the right to work or of being deprived of life, liberty, and pursuit of happiness.[20]

The issue of German economic unity, more controversial since the creation of Bizonia by Britain and the United States in 1946, again came up for debate on March 17. Molotov fiercely objected to the arrangement as a violation of early quadripartite control of occupation laws. In an argument later repeated in a number of accounts by revisionist historians, he castigated the arrangement as an "opportunity for British and American industrialists to penetrate the area and establish economic empires. . . ." He deplored the "cock-sureness" of monopolistic industrialists in the British-American zones, and their attempts to revive cartels, trusts, and other forms of capitalistic monopoly.

Marshall calmly denied Molotov's assertions, observing that charges and countercharges only complicated the problems the foreign ministers were trying to solve. The American people were mindful of Russian losses in the war, but they believed German economic unity essential to a successful occupation and the peace of the world. With an eye on Molotov's ideas about economic unity, he emphasized the point that he and Bevin never ceased to reiterate: "We cannot accept a unified Germany under a procedure which in effect would mean that [our own] people would pay reparations to an ally." He defended the bizonal merger of the British and Americans and invited the Russians and the French to join on the same terms.

Marshall read his remarks from a lengthy paper. Earlier, he had tried to get an agreement that such papers be distributed before the meetings as a means of shortening the sessions. When that failed, he grimly determined to try a reverse approach. He wrote Truman:

> Reading last and struggling through two laborious translations, I held the meeting until even Molotov was restless. I then took occasion to apologize for my time-consuming procedure and referred to the failure of the Council to accept my previous recommendation. . . .[21]

Marshall got what satisfaction he could from anticipating Molotov's attacks and being prepared with irrefutable rebuttals. On the 18th, after a wearisome debate on reparations, Molotov charged that Britain and the United States had waived payments because they had already received more than $10 billion in assets by seizing all gold found in their zones, all German assets except those in the eastern zone, the German commercial fleet, and German patents, plus reparations from current production such as coal and lumber.

Bevin laughed at this litany of British-American sins and said it was based solely on Russian press reports, that his government was prepared to reveal what it had received in reparations and hoped that others would do the same. Molotov then walked into the trap by declaring that J. C. Green, Executive Secretary of the Bureau of

Publications, U.S. Department of Commerce, had recently commented on the immense value to the United States of seized German patents. To Marshall's amused satisfaction, one of his staff had prepared for this question and handed him a memorandum from Green, asking if General Marshall could inquire whether the Russians had taken scientific and technical information out of their zone, and if the United States could have "access to it on similar terms to which they are acquiring the mass of material released by this office." Marshall added that AMTORG, the Soviet purchasing agency in the United States, had been "the largest single purchaser of pamphlets concerning information on patents and processes."[22]

Molotov's deputy, Vishinski, guffawed loudly, but became abruptly silent as Molotov gave him a baleful glare. Marshall then explained that the gold was not being kept by the United States but was held for disposition by the Reparations Agency. Not only had the United States taken no money from exports from its zone, plowing back all receipts, but it had actually contributed large sums from appropriated funds for German relief.

Again they were back to the problem of reparations. This issue was tied to the economic unity of Germany, payments from current production, and industry levels to be permitted in Germany. The overall economic problem worried Bevin, who reminded Molotov that Britain could not give priority for reparations over payment for imports in the British zone because of the necessity of reducing the cost of occupation to the Allies. Marshall strongly supported this stand.

Molotov grew a bit milder, promising that the Soviet Union would account for every kopek's worth of assets it had taken from its zone. He favored setting the level of industry for Germany high enough so that country could meet internal needs and pay for imports and reparations.

Marshall saw Molotov's last remark as illustrative of the danger of planning to pay reparations out of current production. After World War I, the Allies had insisted on increased production to pay for reparations and for foreign loans, resulting in a German economy geared for future war. Marshall did not want to repeat this mistake. "At the same time," he insisted, "under no conditions should we set her economy so low that a democratic way of life could not hope to survive in Germany."[23]

Molotov's slightly softer approach seemed to spark a tougher French line. Bidault asked for an international agency to control the use of all German coal, and he opposed an increase in the German level of industry. He talked of special control of the Ruhr.

France would not accept an increase in the German level of industry until French views on security had been honored. He declined to accept any of the points being urged by the Western Allies until France's coal requirements were met. Steel production for Germany should be limited to 7,500,000 tons annually, one-fourth less the figure suggested by the United States and Britain.[24]

This cold shower of French obduracy chilled both Marshall and Bevin as they compared notes during lunch on March 22. Bevin recalled that twice before the current meeting French representatives had asked that exports of coal from the British zone continue because of the "critical French election situation." Bevin finally had to tell Bidault that massive repairs were needed to increase coal production. When the Frenchman replied that he could not support Britain on other points unless he got what he wanted on coal, Bevin declared that he would not submit to such a procedure, a statement intended for Molotov's ears as much as for those of Bidault.[25]

Near the end of March, Marshall led an effort to concentrate on the Austrian and German peace treaties, which Senators Vandenberg and Connolly wanted signed before the conference adjourned. The inability of the various representatives to agree as to who should be involved in the treaties added to the delays. The three Western powers urged that China be brought in on the German treaty, but the Soviets were opposed. Bevin suggested that the Dominions be involved. Marshall thought Canada's contributions to the war were important and insisted that Mexico and other Latin American countries should also be consulted.[26]

The points of disagreement about Germany were so overwhelming that the Western powers suggested a focus on Austria, but they immediately disagreed over which Austrian assets were to be considered. The three Western countries were not willing to list as assets subject to reparations claims properties that had been seized after 1938 by the German-controlled government in Austria from victims of aggression. Marshall's proposal for the arbitration of Austrian claims was strongly opposed by the Soviet Foreign Minister.

Months before, during the war, Marshall had learned that Molotov was unyielding in asserting Russian claims and views. He saw Molotov as a tough old negotiator who always chose to rehash previous arguments rather than seek any compromise. After the shift from working toward a German settlement to getting an Austrian treaty, Marshall concluded there was no Soviet enthusiasm for either. Since continual chaos in occupied countries was likely to play into Soviet hands, Molotov had no incentive to be gracious. To salvage something from the conference, Marshall decided to return to the problem of Germany. This required that he and Bevin pay further attention to France.

In his perceptive *The Origins of the Marshall Plan,* John Gimbel shows the difficulties Marshall and Bevin faced. Alert to opponents from right and left in the French Assembly, Bidault expounded on the export of German coal and the control of the Saar as the German problems France wanted settled first. Payment of reparations from current production had to be decided on the basis of its possible effect on German coal for export, German war potential, and the German balance of payments.[27]

Bevin's reply to Molotov and Bidault reflected Marshall's views. He said that full economic unity of Germany depended on: freedom of movement throughout the occupation zones of Germany of persons, ideas, and trade; the priority was to be given the payment of imports cost from proceeds gained from German exports from current production and stocks; the sharing of four-power occupation costs; and the establishment of a central German administration with German executive powers. To Molotov's earlier objections he said that payment of reparations out of current production was not possible at the moment, a four-power agency for the Ruhr could not be established as long as a unified economic German system was lacking, and the bizonal U.S.-British system, which arose from delays in implementing the Potsdam decision on economic unity, would be changed when economic unity for Germany was a fact.

Bevin would support French claims as to the Saar, provided agreement was reached on the area to be included and the readjustment in reparations after the transfer. He hoped that the French would not block the settlement of major German problems because of the demand for coal and suggested that the United States and Britain try to help France in this respect. He insisted that the level of industry be raised to improve the German standard of living, asked for imposition of a time limit, and stressed the need to arrive at a simpler plan for evaluating and allocating plants to be removed. He reiterated the basic questions of the conference—the level to be set for German industry and the amount and distribution should be settled at the Moscow meeting so that the Germans would know what to expect.

Molotov replied that he thought he could facilitate the Allied problems in Germany. He believed that increase of food supply there could be accomplished by land reforms such as those carried out in the Soviet zone. No German territory now controlled by Poland could be included in economic plans, however. He was willing to raise the German level of industry but insisted that the destruction of Germany's war potential be hastened.

Discussion then turned from economic to political settlements. In considering a possible German constitution on April 2, the delegates soon revealed how they viewed the role of a revived Germany. Molotov proposed that a provisional political organization be set up first. Bidault suggested that representatives of the *Länder* (state) governments prepare a provisional constitution and that this be approved by the Allied Control Council and then submitted to the German people. Marshall thought that the Council of Foreign Ministers should establish a provisional government representing the *Länder,* initiate the framing of a permanent constitution, and recommend a pattern for permanent territorial organization. He said that the council should ensure basic human rights, guarantee the autonomy of state and local governments, and define relationships between the council and the provisional government and between zone commanders and the provisional government.

Molotov objected to Marshall's plan as one that would federalize Germany. He wanted a democratic Germany resting on free elections with an executive of limited powers. He asked that central administrative departments be instituted on the basis of the Potsdam agreement as a first step toward a provisional government. At this point, Bevin suggested a series of steps to achieve a provisional government leading to a permanent constitution. Marshall agreed in part, adding that a provisional government might not prove necessary. He thought that the Allied Control Council could issue a charter to the German people that would permit the Germans to consider a permanent constitution.[28]

The issue was still under discussion near the end of the day when Molotov added that any advisory council should include representatives of democratic parties, trade unions, and other anti-Nazi organizations. Fearing that such loosely defined groups could be a means of packing the council, Marshall and Bevin objected, though agreeing that such organizations could be consulted.

Searching for ways to get action from the conference, Marshall and Bevin mapped plans over lunch three days later. Bevin proposed that 10 million tons of steel be considered for German production. He admitted that this figure would require a reexamination of transfers of plants and compensation for plants allocated but not transferred. He thought that the Soviets might be willing to consider this approach because some of the plants had not been profitable and in other cases it had been necessary to build sites for which they lacked money and were out of pocket for transportation costs. There were reports of plants on railway cars sitting in open yards. Marshall was willing for the British and the Americans to work out recommendations, but he warned Bevin that at the moment the United States was not prepared to discuss a fixed figure. He also doubted that they should put forth a program for a German political organization, because this would give the Russians an opportunity to charge that the British and the Americans were seeking a definite partition of Germany. Both men tacitly agreed that although they would prefer a united Germany they were resigned, at least temporarily, to a division if unity meant Soviet influence in all zones. State Department discussions before the delegation left for Moscow had indicated a growing belief that keeping the zones united meant strengthening the Soviet presence in the whole of Germany.

The earlier arguments over central versus limited government for Germany filled the meeting on April 7, until Marshall finally proposed that they go on to the next question. When Molotov opposed this motion, Bevin fulminated that they had been in Moscow for four weeks and had done nothing and he "didn't care what the Council discussed next."[29]

On April 8, Marshall and Bevin again huddled over strategy during lunch. Marshall proposed that they hold comments to a minimum in later meetings and pass over matters on which they could not agree. Some comments, of course, should be made on all issues, to help the delegates in their further studies. He later informed Truman that it was "very important to reach some understanding which would permit the prompt reduction of military forces, otherwise, these expenditures would dwarf the obligations for direct appropriations to meet the deficiency in the standard of living of the German people." No matter what arguments the Truman Doctrine advanced for American toughness in Europe, Marshall seemed set on reducing armed forces in Germany.[30]

The negotiators found few areas of agreement at the conference. Marshall wanted a special boundary commission to decide on Poland's boundaries. Bevin preferred a study of boundary questions as a whole. Bidault believed that the provisional agreements at Potsdam had been accepted as permanent. Molotov, according to Marshall, proved to his own satisfaction that the existing western boundary of Poland had been agreed upon. Marshall cited quotations from the Potsdam minutes indicating that boundaries were provisional. Molotov found Stalinist statements proving the opposite. Bidault said it was unfortunate that the French had not been invited to Potsdam so that "a disinterested, unbiased, and correct interpretation [would be] available."[31]

Shades of post–World War I settlements were evoked by Bidault's next demand, that the Rhineland should be separated from Germany and troops should be stationed permanently on the left bank of the river, and that the Ruhr should be internationalized and its basic industries transferred to the Allied countries. These proposals concerning an area mostly in the British occupation zone led Bevin to insist that, until economic unity of Germany was a fact, there be no special arrangement for the Ruhr. He favored giving the Saar to France but not the separation of the Rhineland from Germany.[31]

Marshall pointed out that the United States was interested in preventing German military use of Ruhr resources but wanted to ensure that they be made available for European states, including Germany. As a country that had twice been forced to send troops to Europe, the United States wanted a settlement that the people of Europe would maintain willingly. He hoped that claims to permanency of frontiers would be based on more than force. Molotov agreed with the American view that the Ruhr and the Rhineland should not be separated from Germany, and that the Ruhr resources should be open to all, but disagreed with the American notion that quadripartite control was not necessary. He lectured Britain and the United States for improperly severing western Germany from the rest of the former Reich and for taking control of the Ruhr without the agreement of Soviet Russia and France.

Bevin and Marshall promptly retorted that failure to restore economic unity had blocked quadripartite control; Bizonia had been necessary because of the lack of economic unity. If such unity were attained, there would be four-power control of the Ruhr.

Both Marshall and Bevin again attacked Molotov's arguments on April 15. To Bevin's complaint that five weeks had gone by with nothing accomplished, Marshall added that the Soviet desire to bring all committee disagreements into the council for debate had resulted in no action on the Four Power Pact. "If we cannot agree on this basic first step of keeping Germany disarmed and unable to wage war," he said, "we have indicated to the world a complete lack of unity of purpose in our approach to the German settlement." Most of the delay and disagreements came from Soviet insistence that reparations should be drawn from current production. After Molotov insisted that his amendments were intended to meet the Western Allies halfway, he then launched into what Marshall called "a long perversion of our draft treaty which nullified his previous remark." Terming Molotov's amendments largely a redraft of previous disagreements, Marshall concluded that, since they could not agree on the Four Power Pact, they should move on to other matters. Thus was abandoned one of the two hoped-for results of the conference.[32]

In later years, Marshall said that he had decided that Molotov's only policy was delay and propaganda, so he determined to go to the source of power in the Soviet Union—Stalin himself.

At Tehran, Yalta, and Potsdam, Marshall had sized up Stalin as a tough customer, a bank robber for the Soviet cause before the Revolution, who should be spoken to—as Marshall wrote Eisenhower—in tough Abilene language. The important thing, he believed, was to make certain that the Russian leader had agreed to a certain course of action. He recalled that Stalin had said that three months after V-E Day he would enter the war against Japan, and had kept his promise to the day. In a message to Roosevelt in the spring of 1945, Stalin had implied that Marshall had given him incorrect information based on intercepts. Marshall had drafted the sharp reply that Roosevelt had sent shortly before he died. Later, Stalin had asked Eisenhower to express his regrets to Marshall and to emphasize that he had great respect for him. Still later, he told Byrnes that if anyone could solve the Chinese stalemate it was Marshall. Perhaps these words were mere flattery, but they made Marshall believe that he had more chance to wrest some degree of accord from Stalin than from Molotov, who he felt lacked the authority to make decisions.

Unlike the other heads of delegations, Marshall had postponed his courtesy call on the Russian leader until he had "real subjects to discuss." He now set up a meeting at the Kremlin for April 15, through Bedell Smith. With Stalin were Molotov, Ambassador Kirill V. Novikov, and interpreter V. N. Pavlov. Smith and Bohlen accompanied Marshall.

The Secretary decided to use the direct approach that he had found effective with the Chinese. He described his depression and concern over the misunderstandings and disagreements that had arisen. At the end of the recent war, no country "had enjoyed such public esteem and even admiration in the United States as the Soviet Union." This sentiment had later deteriorated because of Soviet actions or failure to act, which had created unfortunate impressions. The difficulty of getting answers to correspondence had led to other difficulties. The Soviet Union was the only country to make no effort to reach a settlement on nonmilitary material furnished under Lend-Lease.[33]

Marshall reviewed his differences with Molotov. The United States had not opposed economic unity for Germany, but it did oppose a centralized government that might become dangerous. Britain and the United States had not broken the Potsdam agreement by establishing Bizonia but had been forced to act because of the lack of economic unity. He had concluded that there was no Soviet desire for a Four Power Pact and would so inform the President. Perhaps to ease the effects of the President's Truman Doctrine speech, Marshall said that the United States and the Soviet Union had two different forms of government and the United States had no desire to convert the Soviet people to American democracy.

Marshall mentioned larger issues, questions obscured by the innumerable details of plans, drafts, and resolutions in which the Moscow talks were mired. "The Government of the United States," he declared, "was frankly determined to do what we can to assist those countries which are suffering from economic deterioration which, if unchecked, might lead to economic collapse and the consequent elimination of any chance of democratic survival." He said that it was the American intention to help, as much as possible, to reform the economy of such countries. "The United States had no intention of dominating or trying to dominate any country in the world."

He concluded by saying that he desired to restore the cooperation that had existed during the war and that he had come to Stalin with the hope that some of the suspicion could be cleared away as a first step toward regaining the former spirit of understanding.

Stalin sat doodling during the talk, receiving the plain words calmly and affably. When he spoke, it was to suggest, disarmingly, that the Soviet delay was due to sloppiness or to great losses suffered by his country during the war. Then he recalled that a Russian request for additional Lend-Lease had remained unanswered for two years and suggested that perhaps there was sloppiness in American procedures. When Ambassador Smith passed to the Russians a written reminder that he had presented a reply to this request when he had reported the previous year, Stalin nodded, but said that even a year's delay seemed a little excessive.

As for Germany, the Soviet Union did not want a strong central administration, but it was not right that the *Länder* be above the central government. He did not love Germans, but he opposed dismemberment. He wanted to avoid Napoleon's mistake. The Emperor had gained a temporary advantage by setting up a number of small German states, but ultimately he had come to the idea of a united Germany. Stalin argued that if the Allies could not agree on this point, the German people should settle it by a plebiscite. He favored economic unity as much as the Americans and British, but there could be no economic arrangement without political unity first.

He had been leading up to reparations and his words were blunt. If reparations were to be limited to what had been removed from Germany, then the Russians were being deprived of payments. What had been removed from Germany by the Russians was only $2 billion, an insignificant sum. In a statement that was later to be heatedly debated, he insisted that at Yalta Roosevelt and his advisers had said that $10 billion was very little. Now the Americans had changed their minds.

> The United States and England might be willing to give up reparations; the Soviet Union could not. Ten billions in reparations might not be popular in Britain and the United States; ten billions were very popular in the Soviet Union.

Marshall had expected this argument, and it was something that could be negotiated, but Stalin's next statement dismayed him. Just when he was hoping that by appealing directly to Stalin he could get action, he heard Stalin say "he did not think the situation was so tragic, and he was more optimistic than Mr. Marshall." Apparently unconcerned that the conference was at the point of breaking up with nothing accomplished, he showed no worry and no evidence of a wish to hurry. Bohlen, Marshall's translator and the author of the official record of the conversation, conveyed to Marshall the chilling impression that Stalin was quite content to allow the eternal rehashing of arguments to continue. Instead of the contrariness of Molotov, Marshall was dealing with the deliberate policy of Stalin. His report to Truman on the conversation shows an unctuous Stalin:

> "After all," Stalin said, "these were only the first skirmishes and brushes of reconnaissance forces on the question. Differences had existed before on other questions, and as a rule after people had exhausted themselves in dispute they recognized the necessity of compromise. It is possible that no great success could be achieved at this session, but they should not cause anyone to be desperate."

He thought that compromises were possible on all main questions
including demilitarization, political structure of Germany, reparations and economic unity. It was necessary to have patience and not
become depressed. . . .

The appeal to Stalin had no effect on Soviet tactics at the conference. In the council meeting on April 16, efforts to win agreement
on the production and allocation of coal in the Ruhr led to the usual
deadlock. When the draft treaty for Austria was taken up, Molotov
insisted the the preamble should note Austria's war responsibility.
Marshall pointed out that Austria had been annexed by Germany
before the war began and could not be responsible as a separate
state. "War guilt clauses," he said, "are easy to write, but, as history
shows, they poison the atmosphere." Bevin agreed about Austria
but Molotov did not, and the matter was left in suspense.[34]

Marshall did not give up. Reporting to Truman on April 17 as
to the number of items postponed, he thought it might still be
possible to get an Austrian settlement, unless the Russians were
determined to block it. He thought that action on German assets
in the Soviet zone would show decisively what the outcome was
going to be. He initially hoped that the Soviets would compromise
sufficiently to allow a Four Power Pact, but concluded they did not
want one and had tried to kill it with amendments. He believed,
however, in spite of Bohlen's opinions, that they were seeing some
favorable results of his conference with Stalin. Therefore he insisted that there be no leak of his report in Washington, since
publication of his frank statements might "stiffen his [Stalin's]
backbone in resentment. Later on we might find it desirable to
release his statement, but I doubt it." As in China, Marshall's hope
that something might be salvaged was so great that it obscured
realism. His miscalculation was in continuing his stubborn belief
that Stalin was more reasonable than Molotov. In a day or so he
concluded that Molotov's policy of delay was ordered by Stalin.

Any hope Marshall had for any agreement had faded by April 22.
Trying to save something that afternoon, he proposed that the
council meet in restricted session. They were still debating German
assets in Austria. Molotov had asked for a delay on two issues but
now said he was not ready to discuss them. Marshall radioed Truman: "In our opinion, he is merely prolonging the meeting in an
effort either to force us to a compromise or to put us in a position
of initiating the conclusion of the conference." He had avoided any
statement that would enable Molotov to claim that the United
States had terminated the conference, "because it had been alleged

in Soviet propaganda that I am determined the conference shall not succeed." He did propose to stand firm on positions that had been taken on the Austrian treaty, even if that meant the end of the meeting. He wanted to make one more effort to bring up the Four Power Pact, but the Soviets would probably block this agreement, because they did not want to bring the United States "officially or formally into the military picture of Europe in such a manner."[35]

At the forty-second meeting, on April 23, it was obvious that the conference was near its end. The Foreign Ministers decided to refer all agreed or unaccepted points on the future political organization of Germany to the Allied Control Council for information.

Marshall was disturbed and discouraged by the Soviet Union's virtual rejection of the Four Power Pact. Still dilatory, Molotov insisted that the Soviet Union agreed with the aim of the treaty but found the draft unsatisfactory. Marshall's refusal to discuss Soviet amendments barred a discussion of the substance of the treaty.

Carefully stating that the main problem on the Austrian pact was handing over German assets in Austria, Marshall asked the council to decide if any action could be taken on the treaty. Britain, France, and the United States had basically agreed on the terms, and they could not accept the Soviet position. Unless the Soviet delegation could make clear that non-German assets in Austria could be restored to non-Germans, they had to accept the fact that no treaty could be reached at the conference. If this were the case, they should refer it to the General Assembly of the United Nations for recommendations. The council agreed to consider the matter the following day. At Marshall's request, they also agreed to discuss his proposal for the reduction of occupation forces.[36]

The forty-third and final meeting, on the 24th, was mostly a matter of referring disagreements to various bodies for further study or reports and discussing the next meeting of the council, which was set for London in November 1947. Molotov used the last meeting to attack the United States' position on the Four Power Pact, declaring the United States had tried to force its will on the council by refusing to discuss Soviet amendments. He argued that the American definition of German assets would deny the Soviet Union reparations promised at Potsdam. He rejected Marshall's proposal to refer the matter to the General Assembly, because the United Nations had no jurisdiction over the treaty. The council thus ended with its main accomplishment the firm establishment in the minds of Marshall and Bevin that the Soviets had no desire for an early restoration of order in Germany.[37]

Marshall now found little to reassure him in the attitude of the head of the Soviet Union. Despite the lack of accomplishment and all the squabbling and ugly language, manners required a final dinner by Stalin. Ambassador Smith described the banquet in the great hall of Catherine the Great in the Kremlin. Members of the various delegations gathered in an anteroom outside the hall. Marshall, Cohen, Bohlen, Dulles, and Smith made up the American group. The guests were met in the anteroom by the entire Politburo, except Stalin and Molotov, the chief dignitaries of the Foreign Office, and several Soviet marshals. After the group was complete, Stalin and Molotov entered and went up and down the line shaking hands; then Stalin led the way to the dining area. Contrary to tales of lavish banquets, Smith found the dinner excellent but not pretentious. The atmosphere seemed friendly, with Stalin drinking toasts to Truman and Attlee, and Molotov drinking to Bevin and Marshall. Smith thought the omission of Bidault in the first round was deliberate, but the French Minister was added as if by afterthought. Smith believed Bidault was furious but too cautious to show offense.[38]

After completion of the toasts at the end of the meal, the group went downstairs, where they were shown a recently released color movie, *The Snow Flower,* based on a Russian folk story, which had recently won prizes in Europe for excellence. At the end, Smith had a sober thought: "Many present, I am sure, wondered if this would not be the last conference of Foreign Ministers."

Some critics of American policy accept the argument made by the Soviets that the Western powers went to Moscow with the intention of getting all they wanted or nothing. Even a less critical writer has suggested that German resources could have paid the $10 billion in reparations that Stalin wanted and believed Roosevelt had promised. If granting this sum would have avoided the future costs of troops and armaments and air lifts, the concession would not have been excessive even if the United States itself ultimately had to pay the German contribution. But Marshall and Bevin had had enough. They recognized that Byrnes's earlier attempts to compromise with Stalin had not been fruitful and had led to criticisms by President Truman.[39]

Marshall had been briefed repeatedly on the need for firmness at Moscow, but memories of a more reasonable Stalin at earlier meetings gave him hope that, despite the weeks of numbing discussion with Molotov, if he could just reach Stalin there might be a chance. He left Moscow with little reassurance about the attitude of the Russian leader.

As the impossibility of reaching any agreement with the Soviets became clear, Marshall sought final talks with the French and British leaders before he returned home. Both France and Britain were desperate for economic assistance from the United States. Even if Marshall had seen no reports on Europe's economic condition and had not received careful studies on the state of Europe, he got the dire picture from Bidault and Bevin at Moscow.

Recognizing that the failure of the conference had left many serious matters in the air, Bevin wanted to settle certain key points with the United States. He suggested that the level of the steel industry for the bizonal area be set at 10 million tons, and Marshall hoped that the final total would be around that amount. They agreed that plants still available for reparations should be allocated on a quadripartite basis and made available to the U.S.S.R. and Allied countries with claims against Germany. To avoid a Russian charge that by proposing a bizonal arrangement on reparations, Britain and the United States had been insincere in their demands for economic unity, Marshall urged that the announcement concerning reparations be postponed for six weeks. He also suggested that any statement on bizonal government be worded so as to try to avoid the implication that the two countries were trying to set up a provisional government for western Germany.[40]

Bidault talked to Marshall on April 20, emphasizing how completely France was pressed against the wall. France had very limited means to pay for construction, for wheat, coal, or other necessities. The country had applied for $500 millions from the World Bank, but the bank had reduced this figure by half and placed conditions on the loan that a sovereign country could not accept. France was trying to replace German prisoners of war with German volunteer workers but lacked dollars to pay these men, who needed money to send their families. Though France wanted to behave properly toward the German workers, it could not find dollars to pay them. He hoped that the commander of the American zone could be given liberal instructions on handling these payments.[41]

Bidault said some Americans wondered if they could depend on France. They could, of course, but France had "to have time and avoid a civil war." He was also worried about the Saar. The French Communists were annoyed. It was necessary that positions be taken soon concerning Saar frontiers. He expressed appreciation for Marshall's understanding.

Marshall was sympathetic. He was not familiar with the World Bank loan policy but would speak personally to John J. McCloy, head of the bank, on his return. Though he was not aware of all the problems concerned with financial transactions involving the

American zone, he was disposed to do his best to relieve the French of any harsh demands from American zonal control. He would talk to Clay on his way home. "I wanted him to know that there is every disposition by the United States to help the French Government in its present dilemmas. . . . I am impelled and motivated by a desire to help the French Government. . . . I said that I had a general comprehension of the delicate political situation in France and take it into account in my reactions to the problems which arise." He added that he was aware of the urgency of the Saar situation.

Having proved his understanding, Marshall noted that there was a great difference in the way Americans looked upon Europe and the way the French or the Russians, who had suffered terribly, looked at matters. But he was fearful of the effect of these horrible experiences, which might lead the Allies to solutions that appealed for the moment but might "be fatal for the future. The struggle in my mind on the conference issues," he added, "concerned the danger that we may now make commitments under the impact of present feelings which would not be logical for an enduring peace."

Bidault interrupted to say that he understood, "but that France needs time." It would take a little time before Germany could be integrated into Western Europe, but, he concluded, "there is no question that Germany is a part of Europe."

The French Foreign Minister was deeply impressed with the genuineness of Marshall's friendship. Eight years later, he wrote in his memoirs that of all the Americans he ever met,

> I put General Marshall in a category all by himself. . . . No other man since 1945 approaches him in uprightness and stature. Compared to Truman's Foreign Secretary, the most brilliant reputations seem shabby. He was not vain; he spoke with great simplicity and humor about his career. . . . He was unaffected and did not pretend to be infallible. He would ask others for advice and could be unsure, even hesitant. But once he made up his mind, nothing could have made him change it. . . . He was quite cautious and sure enough of himself not to strike up rash poses or to speak off the cuff in public.[42]

The great significance of the meeting at Moscow was that it signaled the stifling of one more hope for cooperation between the West and the Soviets. Writing of this period, Robert Murphy, Clay's State Department adviser, said that he and others had left Moscow with very somber thoughts. They had not expected a final treaty for Germany, but neither had they imagined such total lack of agreement. They felt certain that henceforth their economic plans for Germany would meet relentless opposition. "It was the Moscow conference, I believe, that really rang down the Iron Curtain."[43]

Marshall confirmed that view in 1956:

> We recognized that the Russians had a formidable setup. We thought they could be negotiated with. Harriman came back and said they could not be. I decided finally at Moscow, after the war, that they could not be. I always thought we had to make a try to negotiate with them, and I think the American people thought that.[44]

Flying back to Washington with Marshall, Bohlen found the Secretary still focused on the long and almost fruitless stay in Moscow. Writing in 1973, Marshall's adviser and translator thought back to the Secretary's reaction:

> Stalin's seeming indifference to what was happening in Germany made a deep impression on Marshall. He came to the conclusion that Stalin, looking over Europe, saw the best way to advance Soviet interests was to let matters drift. Economic conditions were bad. Europe was recovering slowly from the war. Little had been done to rebuild damaged highways, railroads, and canals. Business alliances severed by years of hostilities were still shattered. Unemployment was widespread. Millions of people were on short rations. There was a danger of epidemics. This was the kind of crisis that Communism thrived on. All the way back to Washington, Marshall talked of the importance of finding some initiative to prevent the complete breakdown of Western Europe.[45]

XIII

The Harvard Speech

BEFORE Marshall left Moscow, he had decided to follow Byrnes's practice on returning from conferences to give a national report on radio soon after he got back. His advisers and members of the Embassy staff who had been following the conference debates must have supplied material. Bohlen and Carter, who were with him on his return flight, during which he stopped at Berlin to talk with Clay and Robertson, remembered that he was mulling over his statement. Carter recalled that Marshall had handed him a mass of material, full of repetitions, to reduce to manageable coherence.[1]

After reaching Washington at mid-morning on Saturday, April 26, Marshall was pleased with a White House suggestion that he take a short break while arrangements were made for the broadcast. He left immediately for Pinehurst, where Mrs. Marshall had stayed during his absence. They had to return to Washington early Sunday evening, because he was to meet then with congressional leaders.

Marshall's report was broadcast over a national hookup at eight-thirty Monday evening, April 28. What he was to say a short time later at Harvard would have more impact in Europe, but a much larger American audience heard this earlier speech.

Despite his frustration and disappointment, Marshall did not call for a break with the Soviet Union. Not only was this a matter for the President rather than the Secretary of State, but Marshall still wanted to avoid a rupture, although he was not very optimistic. He said that a specific attempt at international understanding had failed and that the possibility of curing Europe's current ills by cooperative action was slight. The speech was not electrifying. It defined the problem and, in measured tones, placed the blame where Marshall believed it belonged. In a brief review, he outlined the hopes and the failures of the Moscow Conference.

He underlined the importance of Germany and Austria to European revival. He had hoped to conclude treaties with both of them, but general talk and vague formulas—what Lincoln had called "pernicious abstractions"—were not enough to solve problems "which bear directly on the future of our civilization." Europe had to have concrete solutions for definite and complicated questions "which have to do with boundaries, with power to prevent military aggression, with people who have bitter memories, with the production and control of things which are essential to the lives of millions of people."

He had believed in the possibility of completing in Moscow a peace treaty for Austria and a Four Power Pact guaranteeing the demilitarization of Germany. Conclusion of a treaty with Germany had seemed less likely, but he had hoped for agreement that would permit deputies of the four secretaries to prepare for the subsequent conference.

Next he took up economic problems. Coal was needed for factories, utilities, railroads, homes. Damaged mines must be reopened, and that in turn required steel, and steel depended on even more coal. Less coal meant less production. The coal shortage had become critical to France, to Britain, and to the Soviet Union. They all needed increased German production in their zones to produce goods to pay for needed imports, and yet he knew that with any buildup of heavy industry in Germany would rise fears of future aggression.

His careful balancing of factors was prosaic and effective. The negotiations over Germany "involved not only the security of Europe and the world, but the prosperity of all of Europe." In considering long-term goals, he was mindful of immediate issues —and here he was groping toward the Harvard speech—such as fuel, food, and the necessities of life. There was the bitterness of those who had suffered at the hands of the Germans. And there was the fact that the occupying powers could not keep on pouring out millions of dollars to keep Germany alive because immediate measures were not being taken to solve its ills.

The Soviet Union wanted a strong central government, the French wanted a powerless government, and the British and the Americans wanted a government of limited power that could not be seized by a Hitlerian-type regime. Economic unity was needed at once for Germany, along with rehabilitation of the country so that it could become self-supporting. Though the occupying powers had agreed on such unity, the Soviet Union had acted independently in its zone. It had given little or no information on its zone, shown little evidence of reciprocity, and refused to report on available foodstuffs or the amount of goods taken from the zone as reparations.

To improve the economic situation, Britain and the United States had combined their zones economically and invited France and the Soviet Union to join. The Russians bitterly attacked "dismemberment" and refused to join, and Bizonia was the result.

The problem of reparations was all-pervasive at the meeting. Recalling the lessons of the Versailles Treaty, at Potsdam the United States and Britain had tried to soften the impact of reparations payments on the German economy. The Americans and the British insisted that no agreement had been reached at Potsdam on taking reparations out of current production, but the Russians held to the opposite view.

Truman had declared at Potsdam that the delimitation of any new frontier would depend on a final peace settlement, but the Russians held that the Potsdam arrangements were final. Marshall agreed that the Poles should be compensated with bits of German territory for their eastern lands, which had been swallowed by the Soviet Union, but urged that new boundaries not lead to future troubles.

Marshall explained his efforts toward a Four Power Pact as assurance that the United States would not withdraw from Europe, a proposal expected to calm European fears of a rearmed Germany. But the Russians had brought forth amendments indicating that they either did not want such a pact or wished to delay it as long as possible.

His hopes for an Austrian treaty had also been defeated. The Soviets demanded reparations from Austria and cession of Carinthia to the Yugoslavs. More important, they not only insisted on cession of German assets in Austria to Russia, but also wanted assets that had been Austrian or non-German before Austria was seized by Hitler.

From this laying out of different points of view, Marshall moved to the stronger statement that the Western Allies had attempted to get a workable central government for Germany, the establishment of economic unity, the setting of boundaries that made sense, and the guarantee of continued Allied security against Germany by a Four Power Pact, with Austria to be treated as a liberated power. But the Soviet Union wanted "a centralized government, adapted to the seizure of absolute control of a country which would be doomed economically through inadequate area and excessive population, and would be mortgaged to turn over a large part of its production as reparations, principally to the Soviet Union"; the same yoke would be imposed on Austria in a slightly different form.

Still he had not abandoned hope. An effort had been made to blunt the sharpness of differences. The United States could not compromise on great principles merely to get a form of agreement, but it could try to understand those who held differing views.

He turned to his meeting with Stalin and said that the Marshal had held out hope of future understanding. The Secretary feared that understanding might be too long delayed. He declared, ". . . we cannot ignore the factor of the time involved. Disintegrating forces are becoming evident. *The patient is sinking while the doctors deliberate.* So I believe that action can not await compromise through exhaustion. . . ."

To get action without delay, he asked for bipartisan unity in the United States. Citing the support of Vandenberg and Connolly during the crisis, he said: "The state of the world today and the position of the United States make mandatory in my opinion, a unity of action on the part of the American people. It is for that reason that I have gone into such lengthy detail in reporting my views on the conference."[2]

The way to the Harvard speech was open, but much had to be done in the next five weeks. While Marshall was yet in Moscow, studies were under way in Washington on what different countries needed in assistance from the United States. Initiated for other purposes, the studies provided background for the Marshall Plan speech, for government budget makers, and for military-assistance plans.

From talks with military leaders about Greek-Turkish aid, Under Secretary Acheson realized the need for a careful study of broader financial requirements. Army Chief of Staff Eisenhower wanted a full-scale survey of global requirements. On March 29, he wrote General Clay that it would be a great relief to him to have time for a couple of long talks with Marshall about the situation throughout the world. He believed it necessary to agree on a general plan and the areas "in which we can concentrate most advantageously. Beyond this it is equally important that the plan be so simple and on so high a moral plane that our people as a whole will understand its essentials and will earnestly and unitedly support it."[3]

Not only Eisenhower, but Secretary of the Army Patterson spoke to Acheson along similar lines. Acheson responded by asking Assistant Secretary of State John Hilldring, in his capacity as Chairman of the State-War-Navy Coordinating Committee, to begin a study of possible requests that might be addressed to the United States "for substantial economic, financial, or technical assistance, or for military equipment." This study was to be made ready for General Marshall as soon as possible.[4]

The emphasis of this particular study was on aiding American national security rather than on the economic reconstruction of Europe. It stressed military requirements. A preliminary report was issued on April 21, shortly before Marshall came back from Moscow, and the final report was finished that fall. Circulated on October 3, the report was related only indirectly to development of the Harvard speech. It did focus attention on the broadening of foreign aid. It provided some data for immediate planning for Marshall Plan purposes but would have a greater impact on the later military-assistance program.[5]

In early March, as Marshall was leaving for Moscow, Will Clayton, Under Secretary of State for Economic Affairs, warned the department against forces that threatened to create chaos in countries vital to American national security. He stressed the type of experience that Marshall was to describe publicly a month later, how hunger and misery undermined stability in democratic countries. Clayton foresaw that the United States would have to provide large emergency funds to support Europe. The general idea that had been sketched by Marshall in November 1945 at the Pentagon, concerning America's role in making peace, and which he had noted at Princeton in February 1947, was again emphasized. It helped planners prepare a statement of what Europe needed for recovery.

A political dilemma for Truman gave Under Secretary Acheson the opportunity to make a statement about aid to Europe. Every year a group of Mississippi businessmen and civic leaders, the Delta Council, met to discuss economic problems. Truman had promised to speak to the organization at Delta State Teachers' College in Cleveland, Mississippi, then decided it was politically unwise for him to appear there. He asked Acheson to speak in his place. Truman later called the result "the prologue to the Marshall Plan," and Acheson felt it may have been the sound of reveille for the country. He described the alarming financial problems of Europe. He noted, as Marshall had done ten days previously, that Western Europe must have economic help, and went beyond the observation to list the grants and loans that might be required to make up the difference between exports from the United States needed by Europe and whatever goods these countries had to pay for them.[6]

In addresses throughout the country, Harold Stassen, Henry Wallace, and Benjamin Cohen stressed the necessity for European revival despite the cost to the United States. Senator Vandenberg, no longer the supreme isolationist, was nevertheless aware of great concern about costs on his side of the Senate. He revealed his anxieties to Marshall, who arranged to meet with Vandenberg and Acheson at Blair House, just across Pennsylvania Avenue from the White House. It was the first of many discussions with the Republican Senator.

In his volume *Present at the Creation,* Acheson has given an account of Marshall's methods with Vandenberg. The Senator would voice shock that a moderate Democrat such as Senator Barkley was talking of giving away billions to support countries all over the world: it was impossible for the United States to support such a program. Quietly listening until the flood of Vandenberg's outpourings subsided, Marshall then carefully explained that there was no proposal for great appropriations in the present session of Congress, that perhaps a small sum might be necessary to carry over the administration's programs until next year. He used no harsh rhetoric about the Soviet menace, but spoke of the need for careful study, of information the administration would share with congressional leaders, of a great bipartisan effort to carry out an essential global program in a presidential-election year. Acheson suggests that Marshall deliberately played on Vandenberg's vanity:

> Who would carry on an agreed policy no one was bold enough to predict—Vandenberg still had hopes that he might be that man. The security of the country was the great consideration. At the end of the meeting conversion had been accomplished and a search for a Vandenberg brand had begun. It was to turn up about a month later.

Marshall had nailed down vital support for the program he would soon enunciate.[7]

Marshall had told Acheson in one of his first meetings, in January, that the State Department needed a long-range planning staff. He had met Kennan twice during the war, when the young diplomat visited the Pentagon in connection with problems in the Azores and occupation zones in Europe, and was impressed by his analysis of the Soviets and China.

Acheson talked to Kennan in January. He also asked Kennan in February to work on the Greece-Turkey problem. On his return from Moscow, Marshall insisted that the Policy Planning Staff be activated. He hesitated to ask at once for Kennan's transfer to the

State Department before he had served out his tour as a deputy commandant of the National War College. Also, Kennan was reluctant to leave before his tour expired at the end of June. The solution was an arrangement by which he could work on plans for European aid without leaving the War College prematurely. The staff of the Policy Planning Staff was activated on May 5, 1947, in the office of Under Secretary of State Acheson.

Kennan realized that he had to assemble a preliminary report for Marshall within a few weeks and that it was therefore necessary to draw heavily on ideas already floating around in the department. He had been lecturing on aid to Europe at the War College, and on April 24, before he became director of the Planning Staff, he had asked various experts for statements on current economic trends in the United Kingdom, France, Italy, and the western zones of Germany and Austria, and what they would need to to sustain life in case nothing more was done to make the countries self-supporting.

Ronald Steel in his *Walter Lippmann and the American Century* has suggested considerable contribution by Lippmann. He says that Lippmann in March, 1947, talked to Acheson, Forrestal, and Will Clayton about the need for a massive infusion of dollars into the European economy, and, later, talked to Kennan at the Army War College about such a program.[8]

In his staff meeting on May 15, the various experts agreed on the need to bring American resources to the aid of Europe's shattered economy. They thought that

> the greatest and most crucial problem is in western Europe; that the areas most urgently concerned are France, Italy, the occupied zones of Germany and Austria, and Great Britain; that the problem is both political and economic, and not military (except insofar as maintenance of U.S. military effectiveness is concerned); that the approach to the political problem for a while must be economic; that it will not be possible to evolve in a short space of time any program to meet the long-term problem, but that some sort of immediate action is necessary for psychological reasons; and that since coal is so vitally important in western Europe, we should examine the problems to see what the United States can do immediately to bolster production in Europe.[9]

Kennan reported these conclusions the next day. He stressed that "the most important and urgent element in foreign policy planning is the question of restoration of hope and confidence in

Western Europe and the early rehabilitation of the economics of that region." Critics of the Marshall Plan who were to call it a scheme to control the economy of Europe missed this point. Marshall remembered that, in 1917, French leaders had begged for even one American division to display to the people of France—to show that help would be coming.

Tentative principles the Planning Staff considered were: (1) American aid should supplement a program "of intramural economic collaboration among western European countries, which should, if possible, be initiated by one of those countries, and cleared through the United Nations Economic Commission for Europe"; and (2) the schedule of aid should be part of a master plan that would look four or five years ahead, when Europe would not have to rely on outside aid. To avoid Communist interference, the memorandum suggested that U.S. assistance depend on guarantees from those European countries seeking aid that any assistance would not be misused or sabotaged by Communists. The planners urged encouragement of some form of "regional political association of western European states" and suggested that policies for the western zones of Germany and Austria should be framed so that these areas would contribute to the economic reconstruction of Western Europe. Significantly, no effort was made to exclude Eastern Europe from these plans. The Planning Staff believed that the way should be kept open for Czechoslovakia and other states under Russian influence to come in, as long as their participation was constructive.

In forwarding his first report to Under Secretary Acheson, on May 23, Kennan stressed the difficulty of making a firm recommendation after so little study. He proposed a hasty short-term effort to be followed by a long-term plan of European initiative, with the United States prepared to give aid on European request. Kennan underlined the importance of secret talks with the British.

In words seemingly at variance with some of his earlier statements, Kennan said that the staff did not see "Communist activities as the root of the difficulties of Western Europe." Instead, the disruptive effect of the war on the social, economic, and political structure of Europe and the exhaustion of physical plants and spiritual vigor were the causes of Europe's helplessness. The division of Europe into East and West made the task of economic reconstruction more difficult. Although the Communists were exploiting the economic crisis and further Communist successes would endanger United States security, "American effort in aid of Europe should be directed not to the combating of communism as such but the restoration of the economic health and vigor of European society." Europe's economic maladjustment made it vulnerable to all totalitarian movements, and it was to combat this trend that a recovery plan should be directed.

In language almost identical to a paragraph in the Marshall Plan speech, Kennan wrote:

> The formal initiative must come from Europe, the program must be evolved in Europe; and the Europeans must bear the basic responsibility for it. The role of this country should consist of friendly aid in the drafting of a European program and of the later support of such a program, by financial and other means, at European requests.

European cooperation was essential, and it should be given in such a form that the Russian satellites either excluded themselves by declining to accept the proposed conditions "or agreed to abandon the exclusive orientation of their economies."

Kennan had been unable to influence the tone and implications of the Truman Doctrine speech, but he resolved to rule out its application to the current problems of Western Europe. He urged that the Doctrine be clarified so that it would not appear that the United States was merely reacting to Communist pressure and that our aid would be given only in response to a Communist threat. "The notion should be dispelled that the Truman Doctrine was a blank check to be used for economic and military aid anywhere in the world where the Communists show signs of being successful."

On reception of the Kennan report, Marshall called a May 24 meeting of his advisers, including Acheson, Cohen, and Bohlen. The Secretary went around the circle asking for reactions. Kennan later recalled that there were misgivings about Europe's ability to draw up an effective program and also about the wisdom of offering aid to Europe as a whole. What if the Russians accepted? Kennan defended his proposal, insisting that Europe could unite on a program. If not, there was nothing that could be done to help. As for the Russians—the United States should play it straight. We could test their good faith by asking that they contribute to the program as well as derive profit from it. If they refused to do this, they excluded themselves. But the United States should not take the responsibility for dividing Europe. Marshall made no final comments, merely asked that they guard against leaks.[10]

Four days after Kennan's report was completed, Under Secretary of State Will Clayton, back in the United States from a recent economic conference in Geneva, brought to Acheson a memorandum on the economic crisis in Europe. Even before he went to Geneva, he had decided that some form of economic aid was necessary, and may well have passed his views along to some of his departmental staff. But the statement he now gave Acheson was stronger than anything he had said before, depicting so vividly the seriousness of European economic chaos that, more than anything else, it speeded up the date of the Marshall Plan speech.[11]

Clayton declared bluntly that the United States had "grossly underestimated" the destruction of Europe's economy by war. "Europe is steadily deteriorating. The political position reflects the economic. . . . Millions of people in cities are slowly starving." He said that the deficit in the current balance of payments to the United States by Britain, France, Italy, and the U.S.-British zones of Germany was at least $5 billion. The deficit could not be reduced at present, because the standard of living was at absolute minimum. "If it should be lowered," he predicted grimly, "then there will be revolution." French and British gold reserves, drastically low from war costs, would be exhausted at the end of the year, and Italy's would not even last that long.

Before the war, Europe had been self-sufficient in coal and had to import little grain. It was necessary to restore this self-sufficiency and to help the maritime nations restore their merchant marines. "If there was no aid, economic, social, and political disintegration would follow."

European and American critics later deprecated America's lack of true concern about Europe's travail, except as a possible breeding ground for Communism. Clayton saw the disastrous effect European economic collapse would have on the United States. He would have known that in the 1929–31 years the United States had belatedly moved to help economically floundering Europe. The aid had been insufficient and too late. A bank failure in Austria toppled the fragile financial structure of Germany. The bankruptcies that followed brought increased tariffs, blocked currencies, disrupted markets, and ruthless efforts at economic autarky. Out of this wreckage came the confusion and misery that started Hitler on his way to power and paralyzed the West in the face of threats from Central Europe. Clayton did not spell out all of this—it was too well known to need repeating. But the warning signs were there again and he believed that this time a strong United States could make a difference. Europe needed a three-year grant of aid. The President must appeal to the American people to make some sacrifice and pull in their belts a little "in order to save Europe from starvation and chaos (*not* from the Russians) and, at the same time, to preserve for ourselves and our children the glorious heritage of a free America." (Emphasis supplied.)

Like Kennan, Clayton felt that there should be a European plan that the principal European countries should draw up. This plan would be based on an economic federation such as the Benelux countries had recently worked out. He thought that countries with surplus food and raw materials, such as Canada, Argentina, Brazil, Australia, New Zealand, and the Union of South Africa, could help. At the same time, he was opposed to another UNRRA (United Nations Relief and Rehabilitation Administration) in which the United States provided much of the money and other countries ran the organization. Clayton believed that *"the United States must run the show."* This was one main aspect of the Clayton memorandum that Marshall did not buy.

Acheson was impressed by the memorandum and at once arranged for a meeting with Marshall and his chief advisers. Though Clayton had written powerful words, he spoke with even greater effectiveness, using simple illustrations to provide more impact. However, with Marshall as his audience he was preaching to the previously converted. After his return from Moscow, Marshall had described some of the suffering he had seen and heard about. Acheson and others had produced additional evidence, but the acceleration of Europe's disintegration and its precise effect on the American economy were frighteningly emphasized by Clayton's report.

Marshall asked Acheson on the morning of May 28 how the intensity of Europe's problems could best be presented to the American public. He obviously wanted no "scare the hell out of the people" tactics such as had been effective in the Truman Doctrine speech but were now being questioned.[12]

Before Acheson replied to Marshall's question, he had lunch on the Hill with Les Biffle, staff director of the Minority Policy Committee of the Senate, and a dozen Democratic senators. Having been caught unaware by the President's Truman Doctrine speech, several wanted to be forewarned about the administration's plans. Senator Brien McMahon of Connecticut, usually an administration backer, said that if the Senate was to be presented with a *fait accompli* he would vote against it.

Acheson then urged Marshall to talk at once to Senator Vandenberg and to prepare to speak to the public in the next two or three weeks. His speech should not propose a solution but state the problem, not as "an ideological one, but a material one." This

could be followed by speeches by Benjamin Cohen, Clayton, and
Acheson, "still dealing with the problem and not the solution."
Later, after full discussion on the Hill, in the government, and with
the President, Marshall and other Cabinet officers might begin to
outline solutions.

Harvard was nowhere mentioned as the place for the proposed
address. Less than a week after it was made there, incorrect stories
multiplied that, only a short time before commencement, Marshall
had asked the university to renew the offer of a degree that had
been proffered earlier. Harvard had, in fact, repeated in 1946 and
1947 the offer of an honorary degree that it had first suggested in
1945, when President James B. Conant of Harvard wrote Marshall
that the Governing Board of the university had voted to give him
an honorary doctorate-of-laws degree and invited him to receive it
at commencement. The first offer was declined in accord with Marshall's view "that it would not be advisable for me to accept any
honorary degrees as long as the war continued."[13]

On March 8, 1946, Conant notified Marshall that the Governing
Board was again offering the degree. Marshall replied that he
would be in China at the time of commencement and would again
have to decline, since Harvard did not give degrees *in absentia.*

A week after Marshall became Secretary of State, Conant once
more proffered the degree, this time for June 5, 1947. Marshall said
that at the moment he did not know his plans for that time, but was
willing to hold his reply in suspense if the delay did not embarrass
Conant. The matter was left for later decision.

Aware that the degree had been offered, the president of the
Harvard Alumni Association, Laird Bell of Chicago, wrote Marshall
on April 12 that it was customary at Harvard for degrees to be given
at a morning ceremony, followed by a Chief Marshal's luncheon for
the recipients. Another luncheon was given at the same time for
alumni, the graduating class, and friends. Speeches to the latter
group would then follow, in Harvard Yard. The alumni president
invited Marshall to speak at that time—not at the formal commencement exercise. He told Marshall that it was not an onerous
task, for there would be other speakers. Nonetheless, Marshall
decided he would have to postpone acceptance.

Angling for a more specific reply, Conant invited the Secretary
and Mrs. Marshall on May 5 to spend the evening before the address with the Conants at Harvard. He referred to Bell's invitation
and hoped that Marshall would accept. Still uncertain of world
events, Marshall replied that it would be several days before he
could give a definite answer. "I am quite certain," he added, "that

it will not be convenient for me to make a formal address, and I must ask you to let me off with expression of appreciation and a little more." Again he asked if his delay would cause embarrassment. Conant said that everyone was aware of the tremendous strain under which he was working and assured him that he could wait longer on making a definite reply.

On May 23, General Carter told Marshall that General Bradley, who was also receiving a degree, was flying up with Mrs. Bradley and wanted to know if the Marshalls would like to accompany them. Then Marshall said that Carter might tell Bradley's aide that he and Mrs. Marshall would attend the commencement and the alumni meeting. Much later, in 1957, he recalled his reasoning:

> ... there was so much feeling about further opposition in the United States to aid Europe that we knew the whole problem was how to meet the opposition. And I first decided to talk at Madison [invited for May 24] and I thought that was out in Bert McCormick's area and they were favorable to me at the university. . . . And then we decided it was too soon and switched over to Amherst [whose commencement was near mid-June]. Then things changed so much in Europe that it appeared that was too late.[14]

By May 28, he informed Conant of the decision he had made nearly a week earlier. He could come, he said, but would not promise a formal address. However, he would be pleased to make a few remarks and perhaps "a little more" at the alumni meeting. The "little more" was to have global reverberations.

By May 30, Marshall had determined to make a formal address. He wrote Carter that day to have a draft prepared for a speech of less than ten minutes' duration to be delivered to the alumni group at Harvard. He was precise in his short summary of the material he wanted the speech to cover:

May 30, 1947   MEMORANDUM FOR GENERAL CARTER

Please have someone consider the various suggestions as to talks that I might make and prepare a draft for a less than ten-minute talk by me at Harvard to the Alumni. I will supply the polite references to the occasion. The substance of the talk might be reference to the extremely critical period through which we are passing, the volume of public and political suggestions and the absolute necessity for a very calm and careful consideration of the proper policy to be followed. Irritation and passion should have no part in the matter. It

is of tremendous importance that our people understand the situation in Europe, the plight of the people, their very natural reactions,
and particularly the dominant character of the economic factors, as
accentuated by the complete breakdown of the business structure—
the fact that since 1938 there had been practically no development
of peaceful business. All machinery was obsolete or obsolescent.
Nationalization had disrupted the business structure. Firms had lost
contact of years standing with each other, particularly across borders, or had gone out of business entirely. Currency offered more
of difficulty than substance to the resumption of trade. We have
possibly been too prone to estimate the collapse of business on the
basis of visible destruction, but it now appears that the conditions
I have referred to above are more serious than the actual demolish-
ing of plants and rupture of communications.

G.C.M.[15]

General Carter, who had been on the plane with Marshall and
Bohlen when they returned from Moscow in April, knew that Mar-
shall liked Bohlen's views and his style. Apparently for that reason,
Carter selected Bohlen to do the drafting. Bohlen recalled that the
Secretary sent him Kennan's study and Clayton's memorandum
"and asked me to draw up a speech for Harvard."

Kennan has claimed that his staff contributed three elements of
the speech: (1) Europeans should assume responsibility for initiating the program, (2) the offer should be made to all Europe, and
(3) a decisive element should be the rehabilitation of the German
economy. The dramatic statement of the economic plight of
Europe was from Clayton's memorandum.

Bohlen was to insist later that the Marshall speech was born in
the Kremlin—that it came after Marshall's interview with Stalin,
following the frustrating negotiations with Molotov. Stalin's bland
assurance that things would work themselves out indicated to Marshall that he wanted to delay settlements until Western Europe
collapsed. In later years, Marshall disclaimed any major part in
writing the Marshall Plan speech. He agreed with Acheson that
many people were worrying aloud about Europe, that American aid
to European reconstruction was in the air. Marshall felt his own
main contribution was his insistence that the program come from
Europe and that it be opened to all European states willing to abide
by the rules.[16]

Once he had decided to make the speech, Marshall wanted to
avoid a premature announcement as to its subject. He apparently

did not show the draft to the President, and Kennan did not see it
until after it was delivered. The text was available to newsmen at
the State Department on June 4.

On June 4, the Marshalls and the Bradleys flew to Boston and
motored to Cambridge, where they dined and spent the night with
the Conants.

Commencement Day, June 5, the eve of the third anniversary of
D-Day, "dawned with pleasant warmth." Toward mid-morning, the
crowd began to fill the open area between Widener Library and
Memorial Chapel. The university's Marshal and the sheriff of Middlesex County led the procession. Next came President Conant and
Provost Paul H. Buck, the Governing Board of Harvard, and the
governor of Massachusetts. Then followed the deans and the
twelve men chosen to receive honorary degrees. In addition to
Marshall and Bradley there were J. Robert Oppenheimer, the
atomic physicist; Professor I. A. Richards, proponent of Basic En-
glish; the poet T. S. Eliot; Marshall's old friend former Senator
James J. Wadsworth of New York; newspaper publisher Hodding
Carter, Jr.; typographical designer William Dwiggins; head of Deer-
field Academy Frank Boyden; former dean of the university George
Henry Chase; naval architect William Gibbs; and President Ernest
Colwell of the University of Chicago.[17]

An ovation began as members of the audience of 7,000 saw
Marshall, in civilian dress, at the head of the honorary recipients,
and continued until members of the procession reached their
places. When the group was seated, the sheriff of Middlesex County
rapped for order three times with his sword and Harvard's 286th
commencement began. More than 2,000 degrees were awarded,
one of them being the 100,000th conferred in the history of the
institution.

As was commencement custom, speeches were given by members of the graduating classes. James B. Peabody gave the traditional Latin oration, drawing laughter with his reference to the
"little roses of Radcliffe." He became solemn in asking "whether
blessed by peace we shall live with laws, or whether vexed by
torments we shall perish under atomic bodies; whether we shall
choose peace and the good life or chaos and a monstrous doom."
The next speaker, Douglass Cater, future newsman, political adviser, and educator, attacked the suppression of dissent in "A Challenge to Free Men": "If we are to keep tolerance or a continuing
tradition in America, we must call a halt to the terrifying paralysis
which has gripped us. Then we can turn and begin to show, by our

positive acts, that democracy is . . . an affirmative belief. . . ." Robert
V. Hansberger called for better educational standards to prepare
citizens to take their places in a democracy.

Then President Conant awarded the honorary degrees. Marshall
was called forward to hear the citation accompanying the doctor-of-
laws degree, written in Latin and read both in Latin and English.
"An American to whom Freedom owes an enduring debt of gratitude, a soldier and statesman whose ability and character brook
only one comparison [George Washington] in the history of the
nation."

After commencement, the honorees and special guests went to
the Fogg Museum for the Chief Marshal's traditional luncheon,
while nearby on the lawn the alumni, graduates, and friends ate a
lunch provided by the university. At 2:00 P.M., the "largest group
of older alumni ever in Cambridge for many years" was called to
order by Alumni President Bell, class of 1904. In his brief remarks
he suggested that a standard be set for the times, asking, "How far
does any activity contribute to freedom of mind and spirit, to tolerance, to the improvement of our troubled world?"

Governor Bradford expanded on the theme. "If we can make
democracy work, the world can accept democracy. But if we run
away from our responsibilities, we fail not only here, but everywhere. And with our failures ends the best, perhaps the last, great
hope of mankind. . . ."

General Bradley continued in the same vein. Outlining the work
of the Veterans Administration, which he then headed, he explained its vast program of continuing education for those who had
fought in the war. He declared that "the most dangerous enemies
of democracy are not underground plotters, but unemployment,
hunger, and housing—the deadly cycles of boom and bust—that
can make DP's [displaced persons] of the American people." Read
later, these various sentiments sound like common, unmemorable
commencement oratory. Read against the perspective of the times,
they form a splendid backdrop, a perfect prologue for what Marshall was about to say.

Francis Williams, Bevin's first biographer, has claimed that Marshall was surprised at the effect of his speech, that he did not expect
so much reaction to it. If so, he was surprised only at the speed of
European reaction. The speech made the point that Marshall had
designed it to make, and which Bohlen, knowing Marshall's intent,
had fashioned it to say. More than a simple statement of Europe's
plight, it contained the essence of Clayton's warnings but also
included something more, although it was not a well-articulated

blueprint for action. No master plan was suggested—deliberately
—even as the tone was deliberately calm. On seeing the basic text,
Acheson accepted the aptness of the quieter voice, in contrast to
his own, emotional tone in March. This was Marshall at his most
typical—calm, intent on avoiding violent confrontations in Europe.
He pointed a finger at the problem, made clear that Western
Europe was in a state of economic chaos, announced the need for
outside help for three or four years.

The question whether the speech was addressed to all of Europe
could be viewed as both open and limited: "Our policy is directed
not against any country or doctrine but against hunger, poverty,
despotism, and chaos. Its purpose shall be the revival of a working
economy in the world so as to permit the emergence of political and
social conditions in which free institutions can exist."[18]

He held open the door to all European countries that would
cooperate. This clause had been his wish as well as Kennan's suggestion. He specified: "Any country that is willing to assist in the
task of recovery will find full cooperation, I am sure, on the part of
the United States Government." He also warned that "governments," political parties or groups which seek to perpetuate human
misery in order to profit therefrom politically or otherwise will
encounter the opposition of the United States." Then he took up
the European initiative that Kennan had urged so strongly. It would
not be fitting for the United States to draw up unilaterally a program to put Europe on its feet economically.

> The initiative, I think, must come from Europe. The role of this
> country should consist of friendly aid in the drafting of a European
> program and of later support of such a program as far as it may be
> practical for us to do so. The program should be a joint one, agreed
> to by a number of if not all European nations.

At the last he made clear the role of the American people. There
must be an understanding by Americans of the character of the
problem and the remedies to be provided. "Political passions and
prejudice should have no part. With foresight and a willingness on
the part of our people to face up to that responsibility which history
has clearly placed upon our country, the difficulties I have outlined
can and will be overcome."

He was not finished: although he had reached the logical perora-
tion, he wanted to sum it up forcefully and, apparently on the plane,
had added a few more sentences. In what was, for him, an oratorical
finale, he concluded:

But to my mind it is of vast importance to our people to reach some general understanding rather than to react to the passions and prejudices of the moment. We are too remote from all these countries to grasp at all the real significance of the situation. It is virtually impossible, merely by reading or looking at photographs, to grasp the real significance, and yet the whole world's future hangs on a proper judgment, hangs on the realization by the American people of what can best be done, of what must be done.

Rhetorically, perhaps, the speech was not a success. The General did not read a speech well, though in extempore summaries he sometimes mesmerized cold-blooded reporters and practical politicians. This important speech, unaided by a teleprompter and obviously read, was not dramatic. A new graduate in the audience, speaking from later eminence as outstanding diplomatic historian at the University of Michigan, Bradford Perkins, has said that he tells his students of the way in which participants in great events are often unaware of it: the speech was not stirring and he was not moved. Acheson was surely right about commencement speeches going unheard, but the Secretary had won some attention. He had been greeted by applause as he approached the table, and during his speech he was interrupted several times by applause, particularly when he said that those who opposed the effort to end economic chaos would get no aid. How much of the ovation was for the Secretary of State and how much for his Plan is not clear.

The address was on the front page of *The New York Times,* and a follow-up noted Europe's initial favorable response. Slightly overshadowing the speech story was President Truman's blast against a Communist coup in Hungary. Charging the Soviet government with another breach of the Yalta agreement, Truman asked for an investigation by participants in the conference.[19]

The interesting question now would be the reaction of Europe to the speech. Marshall had considered tipping off Ernest Bevin but decided that to do so would offend the French and other Europeans.

He had not wanted to talk of costs to the United States or to promise great sums to Europe before he could talk with possible opponents of his Plan in Congress. The fact that commencement speeches were seldom played up suited his purpose.

Under Secretary Acheson had made an effort to send some signals to the British. Sir John Balfour, Chargé at the British Embassy then, recalls arranging a luncheon at the Metropolitan Club with Acheson and Gerald Barry of the London *News-Chronicle* on May 22.

In a discussion of his earlier Delta Council speech, Acheson indicated that Marshall might speak along similar lines soon. He then gave them the gist of State Department thinking at that time. He was aware of points that Kennan was considering in his study, but that document was not sent to him until the following day. Balfour was sufficiently impressed to tell Ambassador Inverchapel of what was in store. On the eve of departure for a trip, the Ambassador called in several staff members and asked for a study of the prospective speech. Believing himself throughly briefed on definitive Washington plans, Balfour prepared a lengthy summary and sent it off to London. As a result, when his Embassy press officer received the actual text of Marshall's speech, on June 4, he sent it by surface mail rather than by cable.[20]

In his talk with Balfour and Barry, Acheson revealed that Marshall might soon make a speech on European recovery. Balfour understood that Marshall was organizing a Policy Planning Staff and that the administration had faced the fact that it had to produce a more positive program if it wanted Congress to act, since members of both houses were increasingly critical of piecemeal programs that furnished only temporary solutions.

Although Acheson gave helpful hints, it is clear that Balfour received even more current information about State Department thinking from someone to whom he referred as a high government source. Later, Balfour confirmed that the source had been George Kennan, who talked to the British diplomat about contemplated developments before Acheson had even seen Kennan's final study. Kennan underscored his idea that the initiative must come from Europe. He said that a forthcoming Marshall speech would contradict Communist charges that the United States was trying to impose something on Europe. He suggested that the British government might want to bring forth proposals to deal with its dollar problems while Belgium, Holland, and France might outline economic rehabilitation.

Kennan thought that the plan should include as many countries of Europe as possible and should be framed in such a manner as to exercise what he called a "squeeze play" on governments behind the Iron Curtain, with the object of persuading them to participate in it.[21]

But Kennan had no precise plan to propose, a specific sometimes overlooked in discussions of the Marshall Plan speech. Neither he nor Acheson nor Clayton nor Marshall had or proposed to have a specific plan for Europe to accept: that was to be worked out. Kennan told Balfour that, once Britain and countries on the Continent had elaborated their various plans in collaboration with the Americans, "the moment would have arrived to confront Congress and the people of this country with concrete proposals for American aid."

Balfour recognized that Kennan was feeling his way and recorded that some of his remarks "took the form of post-prandial musings without method." The diplomat took advantage of this fluidity of Kennan's concepts to suggest that one root of the problem was America's unwillingness to "enable the rest of the world to pay its way in trade with her," concluding at the same time that most American leaders were generous in their views. Balfour pointed out that "such disparate personalities as Hoover, Acheson, Stassen, and Wallace have urged aid on a scale which may make any eventual Administration proposals seem moderate and business-like by comparison."

Acheson does not refer to his talk with Balfour in his memoirs, and he likely was unaware of Kennan's meeting with the British diplomat. He does mention a conversation he had on June 2 with Leonard Miall of the BBC, Malcolm Muggeridge of the *Daily Telegraph,* and René MacColl of the *Daily Express.* Miall has several times recorded a detailed account in which he says that the three men, believing that they should get to know Acheson better, invited him to lunch at the United Nations Club, near the State Department. Miall recalled that, contrary to his memoirs, Acheson made no allusion to the forthcoming Harvard speech. He talked of his Delta Council address and of administration ideas on aid to Europe. Acheson too emphasized that initiative on American aid must come from Europe. He and others in the administration had been to the Hill too often. UNRRA, the British loan, the Truman Doctrine had all been supposed to bring peace and prosperity, but the problems were still there. With a strong Republican majority in the Senate and the House, initiative had to come from Europe.[22]

By accident, Miall was in a position two days later to give early notice to London of the importance of the Marshall speech. The "American Commentary," a regular BBC feature, was usually broadcast from Washington by American newsman Joseph C. Harsch, but he had been invited to tour European defense establishments and was unavailable to give the commentary at this time. Miall, selected to handle the assignment, decided to use some of what Acheson had said. And on June 4, Philip Jordan, British Embassy press officer, showed him the text of the Marshall speech for the next day, just released by the State Department.

There was nothing in the release to indicate the exact hour of the speech. Miall found that Acheson's hints had not given the full implications of the talk, and notified the BBC London manager that he had more information on the background of the speech and what Marshall was going to say.

Discovering that he would have to tape his remarks well ahead of the delivery of the speech, and aware that some emergency could lead to its cancellation, Miall decided to record something for the nine o'clock news, which could always be dropped, and then to do a commentary that would be heard in London at 10:30 P.M. He was later told that Bevin actually heard this broadcast on the evening of June 5 and thought he was hearing parts of Marshall's "live" speech.

Bevin was galvanized into action, demanding the full text from the Foreign Office. Since that full text was being sent to the Foreign Office by surface mail, he had for the moment to rely on Miall's report, which spoke of an "exceptionally important speech" in which Marshall "had propounded a totally new continental approach to the problem of Europe's economic crisis, an approach which for some, recalls the grandeur of the original concept of Lend-Lease."

Balfour's May 29 memorandum, enclosing a May 23 summary of his talk with Acheson on May 22, was registered in the Foreign Office for delivery to Nevile Butler, a member of the European section, the day after Marshall's speech. Because it was addressed to Butler, it was not immediately placed on Bevin's desk. Butler wrote Balfour on June 10, "Many thanks for your admirable letter . . . about United States foreign economic policy. In his talk to you of the 23d May Acheson seems really to have spilled the beans as regards the Harvard speech."[23]

Without the full text, Sir William Strang, of the Foreign Office, wanted to ask Washington for clarification. But, as Bevin later told an appreciative National Press audience in Washington, he concluded they should assume that Marshall meant what he said: "I grabbed the offer with both hands." On the morning of June 6, he got in touch with Georges Bidault and arranged for a meeting. They decided to call a conference in Paris of representatives of interested European countries to discuss what they would do to meet Marshall's suggestions. The main question on their minds was, what would the Soviets and their satellites do?

XIV

Preliminaries for ERP

MARSHALL promptly began to gather information on the economic situation in Europe. On June 3, as the Harvard speech was being completed, he approved the Policy Planning Staff's recommendation that major U.S. diplomatic missions survey conditions in the specific countries to which they were assigned. On June 12 they were asked to report on: (1) the current economic situation and the immediate help needed; (2) the seriousness of the economic situation for the coming year; (3) whether matters would improve with the exchanges of goods with other countries of Western and Central Europe; (4) obstacles to overcome; (5) the extent of contribution each country could make to general European rehabilitation; and (6) the degree of Soviet or Communist pressure likely to inhibit the country's initiative and cooperation in a recovery program.[1]

The extent and form of such a program would depend on the answers to these questions. If there were real prospects for the cooperation of all European countries, the U.N. Economic Commission for Europe could be used. If the Soviets were going to be obstructionist, the Western European countries might have to establish a regional program.

Early responses were most favorable. A dispatch from London in *The New York Times* of June 7 declared that the British government "warmly welcomed" the proposal and was urgently willing to follow up the invitation. The article stated that the British would probably take the lead in calling a conference of interested countries and that at least two satellite countries, Poland and Czechoslovakia, might join. The British government hoped to avoid building a Western bloc against the Soviet Union.[2]

Bevin considered Marshall's address of the greatest historic significance. It was proper to hold Europe responsible for the next move and to have a plan. Shrewdly, he compared the position of the United States with that of Britain after the Napoleonic wars. Then Britain had 30 percent of the world's wealth. Now the United States had 50 percent. After the Napoleonic wars, the British had practically given away their exports for eighteen years, but there had been stability and a hundred years of peace.[3]

Bevin's enthusiasm stirred suspicions in Paris that he was maneuvering to cast himself as lead in the show. Jefferson Caffery, U.S. Ambassador to France, told Marshall that Bidault coveted such a role for himself, but was worried about Russian reactions. Bevin immediately informed Stalin that he was beginning talks with France and asked for Soviet comments on the American proposal. Bevin and Bidault suggested that the three powers take the initiative in answering Marshall and invited Molotov to meet them in Paris on June 23. Privately they told Caffery that they hoped the Russians would refuse to cooperate so they could get on with the plan.[4]

A week after the Harvard speech, French Ambassador Henri Bonnet came to the State Department to state his country's interest in Marshall's address. He suggested that European countries make an outline of their total resources and list their basic needs. They should stress those essential resources that Europe could not supply. These should be separated according to items needed to rebuild production and those needed for daily consumption.[5]

The Polish Ambassador in Washington, Josef Winiewicz, was the first representative of a Soviet satellite country to sound out the State Department. To State Department counselor Benjamin Cohen he said he thought that Marshall's address had indicated that Eastern Europe was included in the proposal, though press interpretations implied that only Western Europe was being considered. The counselor advised him to study what Marshall had said rather than what the newspapers said he meant. Emphasizing that he had no official instructions, Winiewicz said there was great public interest in the address. The only thing he had seen about the Soviet attitude was an article in *Pravda* that did not exclude Soviet participation or indicate Soviet opposition. Rather bluntly, Cohen replied that recent statements reported in Eastern Europe did not encourage a favorable mood in the United States toward countries in that area. He recalled that anti-American remarks made by Eastern European delegates to an earlier conference had interfered with possible American aid to Czechoslovakia.[6]

A glance at a copy of *Pravda, Ukraine* for June 11 would have left no doubt of Soviet reaction. Under the title "Marshall Doctrine," K. Morozov foreshadowed the line later taken by the Soviet Union and its satellites. Attacking the earlier Truman Doctrine as a policy of supporting antipopular regimes and grossly interfering in the affairs of other governments, the newspaper declared:

> The doctrine is spread in bloodstains on the slopes of the Thessalian Mountains where Greek Government troops, equipped by British and Americans, obliterate from the face of the earth insurgent villages; this doctrine has contributed to bitter economic conflicts in France and threatens French finances and the whole French economy with confusion. It has called into action black forces of reaction and oppression in Italy and other lands.

In Marshall's speech the author saw:

> . . . evidence of even wider plans of American reaction, of a new stage in Washington's campaign against forces of world democracy and progress. . . . Marshall proposes or rather demands quick formation of [a] notorious western bloc but under unconditional and absolute leadership of American imperialism. . . . From retail purchase of several European countries, Washington has conceived design of wholesale purchase of whole European continent.[7]

As other nations considered their reactions, Bevin and Bidault in Paris informed Caffery that they were ready to get on with planning even if the Soviets wanted no part of the proposal. They suggested that an agenda for talks should include: (1) supply of raw materials, foodstuffs, and animal feed; (2) supply of equipment and means of production; and (3) financial credits.[8]

By the middle of June, there was sufficient European response for a presidential statement. On June 22, President Truman combined world freedom and U.S. enlightened self-interest when he said:

> I believe we are generally agreed that the recovery of production abroad is essential both to a vigorous democracy and to a peace founded on democracy and freedom. It is essential also to a world trade in which our businessmen, farmers and workers may benefit from substantial exports and in which their customers may be able to pay for these goods.[9]

He announced the appointment of three committees that had been recommended by the State Department Policy Planning Staff to give guidance on an international assistance program. The first, headed by Under Secretary of Interior Julius Krug, would deal with the state of United States national resources; the second, under Edwin G. Nourse, Chairman, Council of Economic Advisers, would deal with the impact on the American economy of aid to other countries. Secretary of Commerce Averell Harriman was to head a nonpartisan committee "to determine the facts with respect to the character and quantities of United States resources available for economic assistance to foreign countries," and the limits within which the United States could plan to extend aid. The committee would include representatives of business, labor, agriculture, and educational and research institutions.

Kennan, head of State's Policy Planning Staff, followed up on the request for the appointment of these committees by asking Willard Thorp, Assistant Secretary of State for Economic Affairs, for brief background studies on the European economy, on such topics as coal, electric power, steel, agriculture, food, inland transport, and shipping and shipbuilding. Secretary Marshall, he noted, would need to know quickly the main elements of the problems of European reconstruction.

Aware of the importance of an early understanding of Britain's problems, the State Department sent Clayton from Geneva to London for five meetings with U.S. Ambassador Lewis Douglas, members of the British Cabinet, and other key officials. These meetings, which began on June 24, were summarized for Marshall. At the first meeting, Bevin urged an immediate interim financial arrangement so that Britain could begin its part in rebuilding Europe. He said he had approved Marshall's initiative at once and without questions, since his proposal was the quickest way to destroy the Iron Curtain. It would be difficult for the Soviets to hold their satellites against the attraction of the economic revival of Europe. Bevin explained that the earlier American loan to Britain was running out; he had been forced at Moscow to pull in his horns to a degree, and was not able to support Marshall to the extent that he desired. He thought that it would pay the United States and the world for the United States and Britain to have a financial partnership.

Clayton was watchful. Earlier in the year, Anglo-American talks on the dollar exchange had raised questions about British trade intentions. In March and April at Geneva, sharp arguments on a British and Australian wool agreement had resulted in congressional legislation to protect U.S. wool against that accord. This had been vetoed by President Truman at the urging of the State Department. Clayton did not remind the British of these points, but he was aware that they knew Bevin would understand his caution. He praised Bevin for his quick and favorable reaction to Marshall's speech, but he opposed any piecemeal action and insisted that Britain's problems could not be dealt with separately. He spelled out that he had talked with Secretary Marshall about the coal problem and that any other ideas he expressed were largely his own. But he said he could not visualize the administration going to Congress with a financial plan for only one country. Revisionist historians have in retrospect pictured this and other statements by Clayton as examples of economic bullying. But, viewed from a different angle, Clayton was reflecting political realities in Washington.

British Foreign Office memoranda make it clear that Ambassador Inverchapel and others of the Foreign Office were fully aware of the pressures facing President Truman in getting financial aid for the Marshall Plan, but they sought the best possible arrangement. Bevin held out for a special loan. With a million tons of grain, he said, he could break the back of the production problems of Germany. Chancellor of the Exchequer Hugh Dalton added that the main difference between Britain's position and that of other European countries lay in the expense of maintaining its zone of Germany.[10]

Clayton continued to insist on getting information needed by the United States before it could act: (1) why was European recovery proceeding so slowly; (2) what could Europe do to help itself; and (3) with minimum aid from the United States, how long would it take Europe to get back on its feet?

One of the sorest points Clayton raised was the congressional fear of British support for socialization of many German enterprises in their zone. He said there would be widespread opposition to American support for the export of Labour Party economic theories to Germany. Prime Minister Attlee, present when Clayton brought up this point, declared that the new socialist structures in Germany had been built as alternatives to the former Nazi syndicates. Bevin added that the troubles in Britain's German zone lay in the level of industry rather than in political arrangements.

Clayton's questions led Bevin to ask for a more precise statement of American requirements of Europe. After rephrasing his earlier statements, Clayton explained the difficulties of selling a recovery program for Europe to the people of the United States. Congress would want to know how soon they could expect Europeans to get on their feet, and would be interested in proposals for a more closely integrated European economy.[11]

Wary of the Russians, Bevin asked what the United States' position would be if the Soviet Union demanded priority in its request for credits and swept all other applicants aside. Clayton declined to speak categorically on this point but suggested that the Soviet Union would have to change its attitude on the recovery of Europe and other related matters "before the American people would approve the extension of financial assistance to Russia." Still wanting to nail down something definite, Bevin threw out the idea that the Russians would not play if they did not get into the short-term phase of the plan and wondered if, in this event, American support would be given Britain in going ahead with other countries. Clayton said, "Yes."[12]

Bevin's predictions as to Soviet attitudes were accurate. No sooner had Foreign Minister Molotov arrived on the 26th to talk to Bidault than he asked what the British and French had been doing behind his back. Bidault insisted that nothing had been done except to invite Molotov to join them. The French Foreign Minister relayed this conversation to Caffery, adding that he hoped the Soviets would cooperate, but, if not, France planned to go ahead with the existing arrangement. He admitted that he agreed with Bevin in hoping the Russians would stay out rather than be in a position to block any agreement between Western Europe and the United States.[13]

Molotov next proposed that Bevin and Bidault ask the United States how much money would be available and whether it was likely that the Congress would vote that sum. Bevin lectured Molotov on U.S. constitutional law, pointing out that in a democracy the executive could not make promises binding the legislative branch. Marshall had mentioned no specific sum. Also, recipients of aid could not lay down conditions.[14]

In relating this conversation to Caffery, Duff Cooper, British Ambassador to France, described Molotov as obviously feeling his way, and said that Bevin was determined not to let him get away with obstructionism. Cooper believed that Bidault would go along with Bevin but had a problem because of the strength of the Communist Party in France.

On June 29, Molotov argued that the United States should not require the European countries to list their resources, but that the countries should study their own resources and indicate what they needed. The total of all such lists would then be given to the United States. Maurice Couve de Murville of the French Foreign Office succinctly summed up the views of Bevin and Bidault when he said, "The Soviets want to put the United States in a position where it must either shell out dollars before there is a real plan or refuse outright to advance any credits." Bidault added to Caffery, "Molotov clearly does not wish this business to succeed but on the other hand his hungry satellites are smacking their lips in expectation of getting some of your money. He is obviously embarrassed." Bevin also was blunt: "Molotov is dragging his feet. However, Bidault and I gave him to understand yesterday that we are determined in one way or another to go ahead with this, with or without him."[15]

Desiring that Marshall be fully informed of Britain's views, Bevin asked Caffery to relay his account of the talks. On the evening of June 30, he said that Molotov had reiterated all his former arguments and showed no sign of changing his approach. Bevin thought the conference would break up the following day, a view confirmed by Couve de Murville. Bevin praised the courage that Bidault had shown in the matter, in view of the divisions in the Chamber of Deputies.[16]

The meeting of the three foreign ministers dragged on one day longer, because Molotov asked for an adjournment in order to consider a compromise proposal submitted by France. Couve de Murville had already told the American Ambassador that he knew Molotov would not accept it, but it would strengthen the French position domestically when Molotov rejected it.

On July 2, Molotov reacted as expected with charges that they were faced with Big Power domination of the smaller European states and interference with national sovereignty. He warned Bevin and Bidault that persistence in their course would divide Europe into two groups. Bidault declared that it was the Soviet Union that was dividing Europe, and Bevin added that he had come to Paris in an effort to see that Europe was not divided. Whatever Molotov did, Bevin intended to cooperate as closely as possible with the United Nations and to continue to work on what Bidault termed "the study called for by Marshall."[17]

Marshall had followed closely the various twists and turns of the discussions. On July 3, he sent the French and British secretaries a message that had been approved in draft by the President and the new Under Secretary of State, Robert Lovett. He wrote:

> I have followed with complete understanding the course of your patient efforts to find agreement with the Soviet Government on a broad and constructive approach to the problems of European recovery. We realize the gravity of the problem with which you have

been confronted and the difficulty of the decisions which you have been forced to make. At least the Soviet attitudes in these questions have been clarified at this stage and will not continue to represent an uncertainty in the working out of a recovery program for other countries.

We here are prepared to do all in our power to support any genuine and constructive efforts toward restoration of economic health and prosperity in the countries of Europe.[18]

On the afternoon of July 3, Couve de Murville and Hervé Alphand, Director of Economic Services of the Ministry of Foreign Affairs, showed Caffery the invitation agreed upon by Bevin and Bidault, addressed to twenty-two European countries, omitting Spain but including Turkey.

Their statement seemed as much to seek American reassurance as to warn of Soviet schemes. The two Frenchmen declared that Europe was now at the crossroads. The Russians scoffed at the idea that Europe could draw up an effective plan and doubted that the United States could provide the needed credits, because in the next eighteen months that country would be in a recession.

> . . . the Soviets are counting on this depression to put an end to the American aid for European reconstruction. This will mean that the European economies will disintegrate and economic, social and political chaos will follow. When this catastrophe occurs the Soviets hope to take over the Western European countries with their well-organized Communist parties.[19]

For various reasons, the two Frenchmen continued, they had not wanted to take the lead in dividing Europe, but the Soviets had forced the Western powers to form a bloc to save themselves. Now it was up to the European countries and the United States to see that the Western bloc succeeded. France intended to publish all of the papers relating to the present talks so that they would be read and understood by the American people and the American Congress and so that "Moscow's design to sabotage European reconstruction will be as clearly revealed as our determination to do everything in our power to save ourselves and to profit from the splendid initiative taken by Secretary Marshall."[20]

The Soviet attitude settled the question of using the U.N. Economic Commission for Europe to handle plans for aid. At the beginning there had been some backing within the State Department for working inside the United Nations. In the light of the

French statement, Marshall notified Clayton on July 3 that the Europeans should use whatever organization would ensure prompt and effective cooperation.[21]

Meanwhile, Bevin was pleading the cause of France with U.S. Ambassador Douglas in London. He said that if the United States failed to give France short-term financial assistance by early fall or winter, he feared that she and with her most of Europe would be lost. Bevin was frank about the chances of solid European support for the plan. He thought that Poland and Czechoslovakia would be kept out, and possibly Norway would not join. In Italy he saw strong Communist strength let loose on the government, and urged that all legitimate pressure be used by the West to influence the Italian government to participate.[22]

Bevin had immediate problems of his own, arising from his government's backing of socialization of the coal mines in the Ruhr. Germany would be lost to the Communists, he believed, unless commitments were made that the coal mines would ultimately be publicly owned. Douglas felt that Bevin wanted to ensure strong trade-union support at home, which he felt he could not do if he abandoned, even temporarily, a program for public ownership of the mines.[23]

In Paris, Caffery heard a different version from Bidault, who opposed British socialization of the Ruhr mines, noting that some of them were French-owned. Now he was faced with opposition from both Communists and Gaullists. Yet he did not expect immediate trouble from the French Communists, because he believed that the Soviets would concentrate elsewhere first.[24]

As for Czechoslovakia, the first reports from Prague concerning the Marshall proposals were favorable. U.S. Ambassador Laurence Steinhardt told Marshall that Foreign Minister Jan Masaryk had accepted the invitation to the Paris meeting and that the Czechoslovakians would attend unless forbidden by the Soviets. But, he noted, Masaryk, Prime Minister Klement Gottwald, and Minister of Foreign Trade Hubert Ripka were to go the next day to Moscow for instructions.[25]

Moscow acted quickly, leaving no doubt as to its intent to embarrass the Western effort. A Prague source furnished Steinhardt with Gottwald's telegram discussing with Stalin the meeting of the Czechoslovakian delegation and his command that the Cabinet meet and withdraw its acceptance of the invitation to Paris. Stalin was surprised that the Czechoslovakian government had at first reacted favorably. It was clear that the Marshall Plan was intended to isolate the Soviet Union by promising loans that either could not be made or that would be forthcoming only with severe limitations on the political and economic independence of the countries receiving aid. The Soviet Union would consider participation in the meeting a break in the front of Slavic states and an act against the Soviet Union. ". . . our participation at Paris would be proof to the people of the USSR of the fact that we have allowed ourselves to be used as an instrument against the USSR, something which neither the Soviet public nor the Soviet Government could tolerate."[26]

In talking to the Czechoslovakians, Stalin mentioned that Poland, Yugoslavia, and Rumania had refused to participate in the Paris meeting. The new U.S. Ambassador to Poland, Stanton Griffis, noted on July 10 the quick shift in Polish behavior. On his arrival a few days earlier, he had been received cordially and told that Poland would participate in the conference. On the 9th, he was notified that the government would make a decision later in the day. He could have little doubt of the decision: the Polish President stressed that Poland would have little part in decisions, since Britain and France would control the conference and had made their decisions in advance. The present American policy, he pointed out, was to aid aggressor nations instead of helping victims of aggression. Later on the 9th, Polish Foreign Minister Zygmunt Modzelewski summoned the U.S. Ambassador and announced, rehashing the same arguments stated by the Polish President, that Poland would not attend. Griffis reported that the Foreign Minister was apologetic and that he believed Modzelewski had been honest in his earlier statement that Poland would participate.[27]

Watching developments from Moscow, Ambassador Bedell Smith radioed Marshall that the Czechoslovakian reversal at Moscow's command was "a declaration of war by the Soviet Union on the immediate issue of the control of Europe." Smith thought that the Russians had decided that they could win by taking a firm stand. They were counting on the United States' not giving enough aid to get a workable plan, or on a "crisis" that would prevent the United States from making such a plan work. They had been startled by the Czechoslovakian acceptance without consultation, and their quick reaction in forcing the Czechoslovakian government to eat crow publicly signaled firm handling of satellites. Smith thought it was necessary to answer the challenge. Failure to do so would mean unfavorable repercussions on the control of Europe and affect the Middle and Far East and the colonial world.[28]

On July 21, George Kennan furnished Marshall with background notes to use in further discussions on the Marshall Plan. The United States, he recalled, had no specific plan for European recovery, and the Europeans must be prepared to take responsibility. "Our main object," he added, was "to render the principal European countries able to exist without outside charity." The enlightened self-interest of the United States was underlined in his reminder that it was necessary (1) to enable the Europeans to buy from us, and (2) to give them enough self-confidence "to withstand outside pressures."[29]

Kennan was convinced that recent events had imposed a strain on Communist parties in Europe by making them show their hands. Happenings of the past weeks constituted "the greatest blow to European Communism since the termination of hostilities." If the United States could continue along the same line, it could weaken the Soviet movement further.

The French, Kennan reminded Marshall, feared that the Marshall Plan would favor German reconstruction over theirs. But it was necessary to aid German recovery in order to reduce the costs of occupation to the American taxpayer and make certain that Germany contributed to general European recovery. At the same time, he recognized France's fear that the existing government would be sharply attacked by the Communists in France for leniency toward Germany.

Kennan saw Britain's financial situation as worse than anyone had realized. He thought it might be necessary to provide emergency aid to prevent Britain from pulling out of many commitments that would force the United States to assume greater costs than those envisaged by the Marshall Plan.

In Paris, under the chairmanship of Sir Oliver Franks, former Oxford don and member of the Finance Office in World War II, the newly formed Committee of Economic Cooperation was making progress on a study of economic problems by the third week of July. Franks combined scholarly detachment with a diplomatic perspective on world politics, and an economist's appreciation of technical financial problems. He could work with French experts, such as Hervé Alphand, who brought to the subject an understanding of British and American views as well as a knowledge of the special problems of continental countries. All the nations that had been invited to take part in considering the European Recovery Program were gathering information for the committee's use in answering Marshall's questions.

Will Clayton agreed with Franks that the German problem was closely linked to European recovery. Initially, however, he did not accept Franks's insistence on added American guidance in drafting a reply for Washington. Finally, he, Caffery, Ambassador Robert

Murphy (General Clay's political adviser in Germany), and Paul Nitze (Deputy Director of the Office of International Trade Policy of the State Department, who had been sent over in July to bring to the U.S. representatives in London and Paris the latest thinking in Washington) all concluded that U.S. views on certain key points might profitably be passed on informally to members of Franks' committee. To Secretary Marshall the group suggested that hints be dropped as to actions that might accelerate American aid, such as (1) increasing production of coal and food, (2) stabilizing national currencies, and (3) reducing or eliminating exchange controls and tariff barriers.[30]

Strong emphasis was placed on assistance to Germany, although Caffery warned that French officials feared that moving too rapidly would have an adverse effect on French opinion. Bidault recognized that Germany must be brought into the reorganization of Europe, but he did not relish being forced to this conclusion by the British. Murphy emphasized that the economic problems faced by the Germans were much worse than those of Britain and France. He pointed out that the political direction taken by 66 million Germans would have a decisive effect on the future of Europe.

With Marshall out of the country at a conference in South America, Under Secretary Lovett was reluctant to weaken the Secretary's insistence that all initiative must come from Europe. Lovett warned that nothing should be done that would lead Europeans to think that acceptance of suggestions made by American experts meant that the United States was automatically committed to give any aid requested. There would be a danger of adverse congressional reaction, and some Europeans would accuse the United States of dictating the terms under which aid could be given.[31]

Clayton agreed that assistance in drafting requests should be confined to a few broad policy suggestions but held that a clearcut decision was needed on giving such assistance. So there could be no mistake about American intentions, Lovett reiterated his fear that there was not enough stress on European self-help.

He restated earlier measures that should be taken to restore the exchange of goods and to end restrictions on finances and trade.

The program should provide for the greatest possible European self-help, should provide for action on the part of the participating countries which they will in fact be able to carry out, and should be such as to assure the maintenance of the European economy without continued support from the US."[32]

American representatives could indicate to Europeans what resources the United States might be able to supply. They could
informally go over a first draft with European delegations and help
put requests in a form that would be best understood in the United
States. But such help must not give any suggestion of a commitment binding on the United States.

While Lovett was warning Europe against expecting too much,
Kennan's group in the State Department feared that a delay in
starting an aid program before the end of the year could lead to
unfavorable "political and moral reactions in Europe." Special
emergency measures taken by European countries might adversely
affect American interests outside Europe and complicate the pattern of European recovery. The Policy Planning Staff proposed the
creation of a center in the State Department to expedite action and
conduct advance planning for implementing the program. The staff
emphasized that Britain, already financially stricken, would need
assistance by October 1947 and France and Austria would need
help early in 1948.[33]

Lovett pursued his admonitions about unrealistic European estimates of what they needed. In London, Ambassador Douglas suggested that the French be persuaded to drop their insistence that
the wide-ranging and expensive Monnet proposal for improvement
of French industry and agriculture had to be accepted without
change.[34]

Deciding that firmness was necessary to deal with such diverse
problems, Lovett sent an outline to Marshall in Brazil on August
24 concerning the need to insist that the Europeans should begin
to improve their industrial production to the point where they
could become self-supporting through the principle of self-help,
"rather than have them lean on us to rebuild, on a long-term capital
basis, their entire production machine." He suggested that Kennan
be sent to Europe to make sure that Clayton and Caffery understood recent thinking in the State Department. To bring other
government departments up to date, Lovett proposed that a secret
summary of recent suggestions be sent to the Secretaries of War,
Commerce, and the Treasury. Marshall promptly agreed, suggesting only that the Secretary of the Navy be added to the list.[35]

Even as Lovett was outlining his statement, Franks warned that
the four-year requirements for the sixteen European countries now
seeking aid would be higher than expected. He feared that they still
would not be self-supporting at the end of a specified period.[36]

Although U.S. insistence on self-help and short-term programs
may have been baffling to Europeans desperate for deliverance of

war-wrecked economies, the State Department had good reason for its concern. The New Deal welfare programs, Lend-Lease, and UNRRA had been regarded as short-term projects but later seemed to have a life of their own. The present Congress was in no mood to approve more large, self-perpetuating schemes.

On his return from Rio, Marshall was greeted with a report summarizing the most serious problems. Kennan found that differences over what should be done had produced a kind of paralysis. Some countries did not want their situations spotlighted. The Scandinavians were jumpy with fear of the Russians. There seemed no likelihood of "bold or original approaches to Europe's problems."[37]

Kennan was full of gloom. "As a body politic," he declared, "England is seriously sick." The tragedy of the Labour government lay in the fact that the party had waited for decades to put certain principles into effect and now found them inapplicable. If the United States treated Britain like a fully responsible adult, we might have to despair of it. If we treated the country like a sick man, it might be possible to achieve some results.

Kennan felt that part of the serious German problems had arisen because that country was shut off from the effective scope of the conference in Paris. Thus the participants had not been forced to take responsibility for the area. His report stressed the plight of England and France, whose economic conditions were deteriorating with "terrifying rapidity." Unless something was done in the next two or three months, "both faced hunger by winter, and other complications of unpredictable dimensions, with unforeseen effects in other areas of the world."

At the moment, the United States seemed to be facing the alternatives of giving no aid because of an unsatisfactory report from the countries, or of telling them what they had to do. He believed that many of them wanted exactly that—to be told.

Marshall saw his first task as the reassurance of the European countries that were participating in the planning. He alerted President Truman to the critical conditions in Europe, worsened by recent crop failures, and asked permission to release a statement on the situation. His statement was promptly approved and was released in Washington on September 10.

Marshall's words made his sympathy with Europe obvious.

> Bad droughts, following an unusually severe winter, increasing crop shortages and restrictive financial measures which certain European governments have already been obliged to take, have had

serious repercussions and have accelerated the need of some European countries for assistance in reducing hunger and cold this winter.[38]

The Secretary could not commit Congress, but he pointed out that various congressional committees would soon be home from fact-finding visits to Europe and that there would be working papers from the various European countries for Congress to consider. He emphasized that Washington was fully aware of current crises and that information would soon be at hand on which Congress could act. Although he touched slightly on a program that would prevent conditions favorable to totalitarianism, his main stress was on dealing with cold and hunger and on the restoration of the economy.

These assurances were accompanied by a degree of American pressure in Paris and London. Noting that none of the delegations in Paris included prominent members of the sixteen governments involved, Lovett suggested to U.S. embassies that they approach high officials in the home countries and ask them to make clear the importance of submitting proposals likely to obtain congressional approval. This, in turn, meant the need for greater guidance from the United States.

Efforts by Clayton, Douglas, and Caffery to get changes in proposals by the executive committee of the conference in Paris were met by Franks's warning that the committee's report should not be treated by the United States as merely provisional. As a compromise, he proposed that the executive committee go to Washington and go over the European proposals with American officials. It could be understood in advance that he, as chairman, would be authorized to reconvene the conference to discuss Washington's suggestions for revision.[39]

Since there was no time to recast the proposed committee report before it was to be reviewed by the foreign ministers on September 15, the conference members decided to call it a first report and recess the conference while the executive committee went to Washington. Foreign Secretary Bevin grumbled that the work would have to be done over under American pressure, but he accepted the decision.

The initial report was approved on September 12 by representatives of Austria, Belgium, Denmark, Ireland, France, Greece, Iceland, Italy, Luxembourg, the Netherlands, Norway, Portugal, Sweden, Switzerland, Turkey, and the United Kingdom. The report was given to Bevin, secretary of the conference, who relayed it to Marshall, who forwarded it to President Truman.[40]

The report outlined a four-year program to promote economic recovery in the sixteen participating countries and West Germany by: (1) strong efforts to restore agricultural production levels to prewar standards, and industrial production to somewhat higher totals than those established immediately before the outbreak of the war; (2) creating and maintaining stable internal economic conditions; (3) establishing and continuing an organization to promote and increase economic cooperation among the countries involved; and (4) undertaking to solve the dollar deficit in each country through expansion of exports. It had at first been assumed that the required sum would amount to $22 billion but this total had been scaled down to $17 billion before it was formally presented.[41]

Franks began informal talks with State Department officials soon after the mission arrived in Washington on October 9, mixing praise for the United States with a defense of the report. "Europeans," he said, "feel that the initiative taken by Mr. Marshall is, perhaps, the most important single step that any government has taken since the war." Europeans had made an honest effort to bring recovery, not temporary relief. If they achieved only the latter, Europe would soon be back on the doorstep of the United States. That prospect would mean that Europe had gone so far downhill that full recovery would not be possible, "and the social and political policies of Europe so altered and strained as to force other solutions than those for which we are both working and hoping. The forging of the recovery of Western Europe can only be done once and it has to be done now."[42]

Franks's words were followed by a more formal statement from the Committee of European Economic Cooperation (CEEC) delegation. They insisted that dollar deficits estimated for their countries in the next four years could not be reduced without risking damage to the program. Though aid might be in dollars or in goods, they would prefer dollars, since some of the items needed could not be found in the United States. They tactfully pointed to the criticism that would come if foes of the Marshall Plan in Europe could enumerate instances when the aid was used to encroach on the autonomy of the governments receiving it.[43]

The delegation to Washington had been kept small and was determined to avoid any suggestion that the report must be rewritten. Technical experts were to show how they had reached their conclusions, and explanations made that the meeting was necessary to decide how the arrangements affected Germany, and to discuss developments in the countries since the talks had started.

The discussions were carried on mainly by working-level members of the State Department, with occasional meetings with Under Secretary Lovett, acting for Marshall while the latter was attending United Nations sessions in New York or preparing for the Council of Foreign Ministers meeting scheduled for November and December in London. In his informative volume on these activities, Ernst van den Beugel shows that there were no true negotiations and few contacts with high-level officials. Rather, the group was part of a team trying to make "the Paris Report as attractive as possible for presentation to Congress."[44]

Van den Beugel wrote:

> There was an inclination on the part of the Administration to change accents, to color presentations, to minimize some problems and overemphasize others, to hide existing shortcomings and to applaud practically non-existing achievements, in its efforts to win Congressional approval. . . . The aim was Congressional approval for a program created solely for the benefit of the Europeans. . . .

Basically, the work of the group lay in providing data and compiling additional information from questionnaires that had been sent back to Europe. These activities were accompanied by discussions of problems such as "the production program, financial policy, trade policy, the organization of the European cooperation and, finally, policy questions arising from the technical discussions."[45]

In the final meeting, the Washington Advisory Steering Committee, led by Secretary of Commerce Harriman, Under Secretary Lovett, and Under Secretary of the Army William H. Draper, Jr., and their advisers, conferred with the full delegation led by Franks. Mr. Lovett distributed an *aide-mémoire* that he had given Franks earlier that day, describing the Paris Report as a "well reasoned analysis of the problem [that] presents fundamental lines of action for the achievement of genuine European recovery."[46]

Many problems remained to be settled concerning the amount of aid to be made available, the method of giving assistance, and the like. The delegates returned home, as one of them put it, having worked closely with the men who would have a part in the development of later plans, and with the knowledge that the Americans were totally involved in the program but that the Europeans would have to enlarge their contributions to ensure the program's success. Lovett emphasized Marshall's early statement that Europe must lay aside national approaches in favor of a joint effort toward recovery.[47]

Crucial for the moment were the immediate needs of desperate national economies. The State Department's Advisory Steering Committee prepared a memorandum for presidential guidance in late September, which urgently stressed the need for immediate emergency aid for several countries, warning specifically that the "collapse of France and Italy could initiate expanding economic depression and political repercussions throughout Europe and, potentially, over a wide part of the world." The Communist danger was played up. Although the Communists' political strength had declined somewhat in the spring and summer, allowing governments to be formed in France and Italy that excluded Communists from key positions, they would regain strength if food shortages and economic weakness in the coming winter were severe.

Current Soviet attacks on American "warmongers" were believed to be intended as a basis for militant Communist action. There was also a risk that extreme rightist groups in France might try to establish a regime under the leadership of General de Gaulle. If France became totalitarian, the United States would have difficulties in maintaining its position in Germany.

The establishment of a totalitarian Europe would require the United States to reorganize its foreign policy, sacrificing much of what it had fought for. It would be forced to adopt drastic domestic measures and expand national-security preparations on an enormous scale. "With a totalitarian Europe which would have no regard for individual freedom, our spiritual loss would be incalculable."[48]

Summarizing those arguments in mid-October, Lovett expounded on the need for interim aid. He proposed a special session of Congress in November and urged that appropriations be authorized to cover food and fuel requirements in France and Italy through June 1948. He wanted additional credits allocated for essential imports to Europe until Congress could act on the European Recovery Program.[49]

The President acted promptly. On October 23, he called Congress into a session to begin on November 17, asking that it start hearings at once. Secretary Marshall appeared before the joint meeting of the Senate Foreign Relations Committee and the House Foreign Affairs Committee to outline the reasons for interim aid as a part of the larger, long-range plan. He urged immediate action on the emergency measure. President Truman addressed the joint session of Congress on November 17, proposing short-term aid of $597 million to cover pressing needs until the end of March of the following year.

As Marshall left to attend the Council of Foreign Ministers in London in late November, he was hopeful that Congress would act quickly. However, Lovett reported to his chief on December 4 that, although the Senate committee had reported favorably on the full amount of aid proposed, the House committee had added $60 million for China, or a tenth of the amount asked for Italy, France, and Austria. Moreover, some members of the Senate Appropriations Committee had that morning handled State Department witnesses roughly in a session "devoted almost entirely to attacks on past Lend-Lease shipments to Russia, Communism, grain shortages, previous relief abuses, German plant dismantling and reparations deliveries, and the German currency system." Lovett concluded that, "while no direct attack had been made on sin, I judge that the Committee omitted that feeling that the State Department was an adequate substitute."[50]

In questions from Senator H. Styles Bridges that were attacks rather than requests, Lovett was buffeted concerning what the State Department would do in case an aid-receiving country fell under Communist control. Lovett answered that he could not speak for the Secretary of State but that in such a case, if he were acting in Marshall's absence, he would recommend to the President that the aid be stopped.

Finally, on December 15, the legislation was actually approved, and the President signed it two days later. An appropriation bill, passed on December 23, provided $522 million for Italy, France, and Austria, and $18 million for China.

The proposal for authorization of a European Recovery Program, held up at the State Department's request until the interim aid legislation was adopted, was sent to Congress by President Truman on December 19. In recognition of Marshall's leadership and his standing in the country, the President began to refer to the measure as the "Marshall Plan." Realistically, he told his supporters, "Can you imagine its chances of passage in an election year in a Republican congress if it is named for Truman and not Marshall?"[51]

President Truman congratulates General George C. Marshall after presenting him with an Oak Leaf Cluster to the Distinguished Service Medal in the Pentagon building courtyard, November 26, 1945. *(Harris and Ewing)*

As President Truman looks on, General George C. Marshall is congratulated by ex-Secretary of State James Byrnes after being sworn in as Secretary of State, Washington, D.C., January 21, 1947. (*International News Photo*)

Secretary of State George C. Marshall (*left*) with Lewis W. Douglas (*center*), new Ambassador-designate to Great Britain, and Under Secretary of State Dean Acheson, before the Moscow Foreign Ministers Conference, March 1947. (*Associated Press*)

Senators Vandenberg *(left)* and Connolly *(right)* with General George C. Marshall while he makes a report to the Senate Foreign Relations Committee, February 14, 1947. *(Associated Press)*

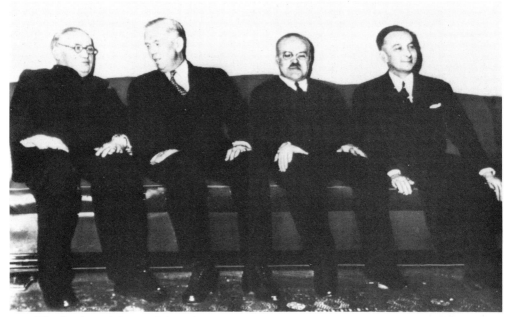

The foreign ministers of the Allied countries, Ernest Bevin of Great Britain, Vyacheslav Molotov of the Soviet Union, and Georges Bidault of France, with Marshall during a recess of the Moscow Conference, March 1947. *(Associated Press)*

Leaders who met with President Truman to hear Secretary of State George C. Marshall tell of the Moscow Conference. *Left to right:* Senator Arthur Vandenberg; Senator Alben Barkley; Representative Sam Rayburn; General Marshall; Under Secretary of State Dean Acheson; Representative Sol Bloom; Representative Charles Eaton; Representative Joseph W. Martin, Jr.; and Senator Tom Connolly. *(George C. Marshall Research Foundation)*

Honorary degree recipients at Harvard's commencement exercises, June 5, 1947. Front row, left to right: J. Robert Oppenheimer; President Ernest Colwell, University of Chicago; George C. Marshall; President James Bryant Conant; General Omar N. Bradley; T. S. Eliot; Senator James W. Wadsworth. Back row, left to right: W. A. Dwiggins; Professor George H. Chase; W. Hodding Carter; I. A. Richards; William F. Gibbs; Frank L. Boyden. *(George C. Marshall Research Foundation)*

Honorary degree recipients in the procession, June 5, 1947. *(George C. Marshall Research Foundation)*

Senator Arthur Vandenberg and Secretary of State George C. Marshall review their scripts the night of September 4, 1947, in Washington just before both gave a report to the nation on the Brazil Conference where the Inter-American Pact was drafted and signed. *(Associated Press)*

On November 11, 1947, Secretary of State George C. Marshall, flanked by Under Secretary of State Robert Lovett, appeared before a U.S. Congressional committee to explain the need for European aid. He said that nations in more fortunate circumstances should help those in need, provided that they are prepared, as well, to help themselves. *(George C. Marshall Research Foundation)*

George C. Marshall chatting with Ambassador of the United States to Great Britain Lewis Douglas and Foreign Minister of Great Britain Ernest Bevin at a luncheon at the American Embassy, London, December 2, 1947. *(Associated Press)*

Secretary of State George C. Marshall testifying before the House Foreign Affairs Committee on the China Aid Program, February 20, 1948. *(George C. Marshall Research Foundation)*

Secretary of State George C. Marshall testifying before the Senate Appropriations Committee regarding State Department appropriations for the fiscal year (starting July 1, 1948),
March 23, 1948. *(Associated Press)*

President Truman, Secretary of State George C. Marshall, ECA Administrator Paul Hoffman, and W. Averell Harriman, ECA's Special Representative in Europe, confer on the Marshall Plan at the White House, Washington, D.C., November 29, 1948. *(Harris and Ewing)*

President Truman congratulates General George C. Marshall on his assumption of duties as the President of the American Red Cross, October 1, 1949. *(Associated Press)*

Mrs. Anna H. Rosenberg takes the oath of office as Assistant Secretary of Defense, adminis-
tered by Felix Larkin, as Secretary of Defense George C. Marshall and Robert Lovett look
on at the Pentagon, Washington, D.C., November 15, 1950. *(Department of Defense)*

Secretary of Defense George C. Marshall and Secretary of State Dean Acheson meeting at the White House to discuss the Korean War situation, November 28, 1950. *(Associated Press)*

Secretary of Defense George C. Marshall and Mrs. Eisenhower bid goodbye to General Eisenhower as he leaves on a tour of North Atlantic pact countries, January 6, 1951. *(Harris and Ewing)*

Secretary of Defense George C. Marshall is greeted by Deputy Secretary of Defense Robert A. Lovett, after returning from an inspection trip in Japan and Korea. *(U.S. Army Photograph)*

George C. Marshall reading his mail at his home in Leesburg, Virginia, soon after his retirement as Secretary of Defense, September 15, 1951. *(Harris and Ewing)*

General Marshall receiving the Nobel Peace Prize from Committee President Gunnar Jahn at Oslo University, December 10, 1953. *(Associated Press)*

General and Mrs. Marshall with President Eisenhower at Blair House on the 10th anniversary of the Marshall Plan, June 1957. *(George C. Marshall Research Foundation)*

General and Mrs. Marshall at home in Leesburg, Virginia. *(George C. Marshall Research Foundation)*

XV

The Fight for ERP

"HOPE for those that need it" was the caption of the cover of *Time* for January 5, 1948. A dramatic portrait of George Marshall, his features subtly sharpened to resemble the head of the eagle poised behind him, bore the title "Man of the Year." For the second time in four years, the magazine had given that title and its cover to Marshall. In January 1944, it had declared:

> He had armed the Republic. In a general's uniform, he stood for the civilian substance of this democratic society. *Civis Americanus,* he had gained the world's undivided respect. In the name of the soldiers who had died, General George Catlett Marshall was entitled to accept his nation's own gratitude.[1]

In 1947, the world again needed leadership. "One man symbolized U.S. action. He was Secretary of State George Marshall." Marshall, *Time* said, was more a figure to his countrymen than a personality,

> a homely, reassuring man with compressed, unsmiling lips, a man who was curiously unimpassioned and unimpressive when heard on the radio. As Chief of Staff of the Army, he had established a reputation for brilliance. Congressmen and others who dealt with him in Washington also knew him as a man of stubborn, unswerving honesty—a good man. His countrymen generally knew him as admirable and let it go at that.[2]

On his return from the frustrating Council of Foreign Ministers meeting in London at the end of 1947, Marshall began to concentrate on the passage of European Recovery Program authorization. Detailed planning had been in progress through the latter half of 1947, but he had waited for interim aid appropriations before asking for additional assistance.

The individuals and committees who had provided suggestions and reports on the need for aid, and who had then worked in Washington and Europe to assist members of the CEEC to outline a report that would convince Congress, were soon at work drafting legislation and justifications to lay before Congress.[3]

Early in 1948, the State Department's bill was introduced into the House and brought before the House Committee on Foreign Affairs. Although not presented at that time in the Senate, it did become the subject of hearings before the Senate Committee on Foreign Relations.

In the debates that followed, the leadership of Senator Vandenberg, head of the Senate committee, and of Representative Charles A. Eaton, Chairman of the House committee, proved decisive. Born in Grand Rapids in 1884, Vandenberg was tall, rather heavy, bald, a bit inclined to public ponderosity. He had been a newspaper man before his congressional days and was a strong isolationist. He came to the Senate to fill an unexpired term in 1928 and had been regularly re-elected. He had been President *pro tempore* of the Senate since January 1947. In January 1945, he had renounced his isolationism. An early friend of Marshall's, he undertook to help him in the fight for ERP.

Eaton of New Jersey, born in Nova Scotia in 1868, would turn eighty during the ERP fight. He was a short, white-haired man who had been a Baptist minister for nearly twenty years and then an editor before election to the House of Representatives in 1926. He believed wholeheartedly in ERP and would do all that he could in its behalf.

Marshall led off for the administration before the Senate Foreign Relations Committee on January 8, 1948. He and Vandenberg were at home with each other. Eight years later Marshall said of the Senator:

> Vandenberg . . . was just the whole show when we got to the actual [working out] of the thing. I used to meet him at Blair House. I didn't go to his office and he didn't come to mine. We would meet over at Blair House and at that time [a writer in] *The New York Times* was attacking me for not having a bipartisan policy. . . . He was profound in his knowledge and he didn't know a damn thing. Vandenberg and I were just handling this business.[4]

Fairly certain that he would have heard about everything that the committee would have to offer, Marshall sat placid and collected, with his supporters beside and immediately behind him. James Reston found him "even more relaxed and self-possessed" than when he had returned from China a year earlier.[5]

As in 1940, he indicated that lack of time bothered him most. He assumed that the committee accepted the need for aid, explaining that various committees had made careful studies of Europe's needs and the existence of American resources to meet those demands. He would work to make the program efficient and effective, but he opposed placing requirements on recipients that would damage their sovereign rights.

The chief emphasis in the question period was on the type of organization that would run the American side of ERP. Involved were the natural desires of Congress to keep firm control of an agency making billions of dollars available to Europe, the tension between a Democratic President and a Republican Congress in a presidential election year, fears that the program was too expensive, dread of a possible waste of money, the danger of getting too closely tied to Europe, doubts about the capacity of the State Department to manage such an enterprise, and belief that large sums advanced might be used against American interests. Marshall also faced a Senate determined to assert its control. When he was perhaps overly persistent in urging larger appropriations, Senator Walter George reminded him that the Senate still made decisions. Vandenberg warned Ambassador Lewis Douglas, who had been brought back from London to help sell the program to Congress, that the State Department must get the confidence of the American people or the plan would be sunk without a trace.[6]

The State Department's call for a four-year commitment and a $17-billion figure startled many congressmen. Senator Vandenberg had suggested to Marshall that no precise sum be named and that they proceed one year at a time. Marshall felt it was better to speak of a four-year commitment and a sizable sum. He went into his second round of testimony aware that he could no longer take for granted the congressional enthusiasm that his words had evoked in the war years.[7]

Congressional suspicion of the State Department's ability to administer such a program was plain in a proposal to establish a special corporation to run the entire European Recovery Program and to appoint as administrator a businessman who would owe a special responsibility to Congress. Proposals for congressional oversight were common.

Four days later, Marshall explained many of the same points to the House Foreign Affairs Committee. In his opening statement, he spoke, as he had to the Senate panel, of the great sacrifices that might be required of the American people, of what would be necessary in order to "enjoy security and peace tomorrow." His requests were not based on "light or sentimental grounds but on the highest considerations of national interest which surely included an enduring peace and freedom for the individual." It was seven months since his June 5 address, but he knew he must intone the same warnings again and again: ". . . so long as hunger, poverty, desperation, and resulting chaos threaten the great concentrations of people in Western Europe—some 270 millions—there will surely develop social unease and political consequences on every side."[8]

He touched up lights and shadows on a frightening picture:

> Left to their own resources there will be, I believe, no escape from economic distress so intense, social discontents so violent, political confusion so widespread, and hope of the future so shattered that the historic base of Western civilization, of which we are by belief and inheritance an integral part, will take on a new form in the image of the tyranny we fought to destroy in Germany. The vacuum which the war created in Western Europe will be filled by the forces of which wars are made. . . . Durable peace requires the restoration of Western European vitality.

He praised Europe's initial postwar efforts at revival. But Europe needed dollars. Congress now had before it the reports of sixteen countries that for the first time in history had collectively outlined their economic contributions and facilities and described measures that would be of assistance to all. On our side, there had been careful studies ending in a program that would consist not of piecemeal dribbles but of sufficient sums to achieve genuine recovery.

He recalled how the ravages of the recent conflict had deformed the world situation. The war had destroyed the delicate mechanism by which Europeans made their living. It had ruined coal mines, wiped out steel mills, eliminated transportation lines and equipment, destroyed livestock, made fertilizer nonexistent, poisoned the soil. Merchant ships had been burned or sunk, and income from that source was gone. Foreign investments and earnings from them had evaporated. Working capital and inventories had disappeared. Business relationships were shattered; the flow of raw materials, the whole pulse of trade, was gone.

Although industrial output had been restored in some cases, it was not enough to meet new requirements, particularly with populations swollen by refugees from elsewhere. These problems would exist even if there were no ideological struggles to complicate them, but Soviet Russia and Communist regimes elsewhere in Europe were opposed to the recovery of Western Europe. Economic distress was to be exploited for political ends.

Many Americans, he added, accepted these needs, but why, they asked, should the United States have to do so much? Because we alone had the economic power and the productivity to start the task of reconstruction. Once that was assumed, the next step was to ask how much aid was needed and how it should be given. Aid must be adequate, prompt, and effectively applied.

Time mattered as much now as in those desperate days when he had tried to prepare the Army for war. Interim aid would tide countries over until April 1, but after that the situation would rapidly deteriorate.

To plan properly, he asked for acceptance of a four-and-a-half-year period. For the present, the participating countries would need enough money for fifteen months only, but the whole amount should be approved.

Of particular interest was the organization to be established to run the aid program. Marshall believed that there must be an executive agency under one man "fitted into the existing machinery of government." He told the House committee that he wanted a businesslike administration but did not believe they could change the method of handling government activities, or alter foreign governments to fit the case. The organization had to be related to the "foreign policy of the nation." This great project could not be carried out in a normal way "against the avowed determination of the Soviet Union and the Communist Party to oppose and sabotage it at every turn."

This did not mean that the Economic Cooperation Administration would be under the thumb of the Secretary of State. There were many details that could not be subordinated to the State Department. In political matters the President's responsibility was paramount; he could not have two secretaries of State.

When members of the House committee pressed him further on this subject, Marshall pointed out that unless the Administrator had sufficient autonomy for his actions, the President would be unable to attract a highly qualified person to the job. He admitted that Congress might feel that clearcut authority was lacking "except to the extent that when it comes to foreign policy, the Secretary of State has the say unless the President overrules him." He could not agree that any differences that arose between the Secretary of State and the Administrator should be referred to the President. It was possible that the President would be kept busy trying to settle conflicts. Other suggestions, such as a special court to hear disputes or a board of directors to represent various interests, including Congress, did not seem feasible. The solution seemed to lie in getting the right man to head the new administration.

Marshall's closing statement before the committee reflected his growing conviction that Congress would not act quickly unless alarmed by the specter of Communist aggression, which he had tried to avoid summoning in the speech at Harvard. If the United States refused to aid in the reconstruction of Europe, he now warned, "we must accept the consequences of the collapse into the dictatorship of police states."

Marshall's statement in the House was followed by a fascinating give-and-take with committee members that displayed his familiarity with national interests and his ability to handle hard questions on a variety of topics. The group of advisers with him—Lovett, Douglas, Bohlen—responded quickly to his calls on them, and he relied especially on his economic adviser, Willard Thorp, for detailed answers to queries about costs. Usually he depended on his own grasp of the question at issue.

Chairman Eaton touched a sensitive consideration when he asked whether the ideology behind the U.S. offer of aid would not result in accusations of American interference with the sovereignty of nations. Marshall replied that, if the United States were engaged in a conspiracy of economic imperialism, we would need to "have a basis of a more Machiavellian approach than is exhibited here with public hearings and public discussions on every side with regard to every issue."

One representative wanted to know whether Marshall had the current plan in mind when he made the Harvard speech. Claiming no such prescience, the Secretary said that (1) he was aware that the economic situation in Europe was becoming tragic and something had to be done, (2) under difficult circumstances, some states might adjust to threats of a police-state form of government, which otherwise they might not consider, and (3) we must make no commitments beyond our capacity and do nothing to interfere in the affairs of sovereign nations. He believed that the initiative must come from Europe. In this matter he had been surprised by the rapidity of European response, as constrasted with the slower reaction here.

Representative Mike Mansfield of Montana asked questions intended to let Marshall expand his views more fully, such as: What if Congress failed to pass this legislation? Marshall said that we would find the European situation in a process of disintegration "which would quickly permit the development of the police state regime." We would be confronted with barriers to our trade and required to spend much more on national security. Mansfield wondered to whom Europe would be lost in case of our default. Marshall made the desired point: "It is quite plain that the leadership in such procedure, which is antagonistic to all that we find moral and desirable, is dictated by the Soviet Union."

When Mansfield wanted to know whether plants would continue to be dismantled in Germany, the Secretary reminded him of one thorny aspect of that problem: France feared a reconstructed Germany. Though she agreed that Germany should be reconstructed, she had very real fears. "We may dispute the basis of the fears. But we cannot dispute the fact of the fears."

The most searching questions in the House committee came from Dr. Walter Judd, elected to Congress in 1943 from Minnesota. A medical missionary and hospital superintendent in China from 1925 to 1931 and 1934 to 1938, he had returned to the United States in 1938 to speak against Japanese expansion in the Far East. He was a strong supporter of Nationalist China and a severe critic of the administration's China policy, on which score he had opposed Marshall. At the same time, he supported the European Recovery Program. His questions concerned possible abuses.

He began by asking whether the State Department had taken European estimates without checking. The sums being asked for seemed too high. When Marshall asked his economic adviser to respond, Thorp made it clear that the State Department had also seen the estimates as too high and had asked for reductions. Marshall added that the sixteen European countries had then reduced their preliminary estimate from $29 billion to $22 billion. Then the State Department economists reworked the estimates, which went to other government departments, the Bureau of the Budget, and to Congress Committees for further revision.

Arguing for an administrator not too closely tied to the State Department, Judd insisted that during the war Marshall, as Chief of Staff, had been able to proceed with his war duties without being tied to the State Department. Marshall denied that he had been a free agent: he could not, as Chief of Staff, usurp functions of the State Department.

In thanking Marshall for his testimony, Eaton recalled Judd's desire for an administrator like the wartime Army Chief of Staff. "I can only say on behalf of the Committee and the entire House of

Representatives, I think, that if we can find in this country an
Administrator comparable to the Chief of Staff, and his ability and
success, the whole country will be immensely pleased."

Marshall eventually had to accept an administrator more independent of the State Department than he would have wished, but
he had reason to be pleased with his treatment at the hands of the
House committee. While trying to avoid heated rhetoric about the
Soviets, he had made the point that passage of the ERP appropriations would lessen the danger of Soviet expansion of influence in
Western Europe.[9]

With the administration's case solidly placed before Congress,
President Truman faced the problem of selling a program requiring billions of dollars to a public already demanding reductions in
expenditures. If he led the fight in a presidential election year, he
risked a political backlash in a Republican-controlled Congress.
Outstanding leaders of both parties were following Marshall to
Capitol Hill to give their blessings to the proposed legislation.
Members of Averell Harriman's committee, whose actions were
coordinated by Richard Bissell, its executive secretary, were hard
at work informing the public of the merits of the program over
the radio, in newspaper and magazine articles, and in leaflets by
mail.

Late in 1947, former Secretary of War Stimson had agreed to
head a national committee for the Marshall Plan. Former Secretary
of the Army Robert Patterson was chairman of its executive committee, with eminent members of both parties and various political
and economic interests participating. But it was necessary that a
national figure, respected by the public and the Congress and
above party, focus national attention on the central issues of the
plan, in appearances before highly publicized conferences in various parts of the country. Marshall, who had gained fame and admiration during the war, who had a knack for getting along with
Congress, who had the friendship of Senator Vandenberg, was in
a perfect position to take the lead in rallying the troops before a
vote on the recovery plan. He had scarcely finished his testimony
before he set out on the road to argue for the plan that bore his
name. Ten years later he recalled:

I worked on that as if I was running for the Senate or the presidency. That's what I am proud of, that part of it—because I had
foreigners, I had tobacco people, I had cotton people, New York,
Eastern industrialists, Pittsburgh people, some of them good
friends, but opposed to the idea, the whole West Coast, going in the

opposite direction, [and] up in the Northwest. It was just a struggle from start to finish and that's what I am proud of—that . . . we put it over.[10]

Backers of the plan tried to select conferences of various organizations to which Secretary Marshall might speak in order to mobilize specific groups behind the plan. As he later described this aspect of the campaign,

> The selection of the time and place [for speeches] was largely done on the basis of what the opposition would be, because [it seemed] that all America was opposed to appropriating anything else because of the way the first appropriation, right after the war [United Nations Relief and Rehabilitation Administration funds], had been wasted. We had Bert McCormick [of the *Chicago Tribune*] *leading the fight [against the bill] and putting up a very heavy barrage. I remember Vandenberg said to me, "You need to belittle [attacks like] this. You think they talk about you. I have to sit up and be called Benedict Arnold."* [Emphasis added.]

The first speaking opportunity came on January 15, when he was on the program for a meeting of the Pittsburgh Chamber of Commerce. This meeting gave him an opportunity to talk to businessmen in a congenial setting. Pittsburgh was near his boyhood home; he recalled trips to the city as a boy with his parents, both of whom were buried there. Yet he found strong opposition awaiting him.

The questions he had answered before the Senate and House committees proved an excellent rehearsal for the situations he had to deal with in his various appearances. At Pittsburgh, he tackled the problem of making additional spending palatable, of persuading a group of businessmen that money spent in taxes for the recovery program was money that would be recovered in revived trade, freer markets, and greater security. He spoke of Soviet intransigence, the dangers of a lack of Western European cooperation, especially if countries tried to recover by imposing greater restraints on trade, and the political consequences of economic collapse. The dilemma could be posed in business terms: whether to make a capital investment within our means that would bring long-term gains, or to spend abundant capital for immediate wants in the hope that the day of reckoning could be postponed.[11]

A week later, he was in Atlanta, before the National Cotton Council, trying to win the minds and support of cotton and tobacco farmers who felt that shipments to Europe would deprive them of fertilizer, farm machinery, and other items in short supply.[12]

Again he appealed to self-interest, to what they would gain by keeping Western Europe free of Communist influences and the restoration of trade. He dwelt on the importance of European trade to American prosperity. While granting that ravaged European farms competed for fertilizers and farm machinery with American farmers, he suggested that perhaps small amounts could be shared which would make the difference to European production. There was great need for clothing in Europe, and factories there required cotton. Although some called tobacco a luxury, it was an incentive to workers.

This was a classroom approach by the man the Chinese had called "the Professor": a simple demonstration of the interdependence of world economics, the importance of removing barriers on world trade. Marshall was hammering away at an old isolationism, a view of American self-sufficiency, a tendency to withdraw from any sense of responsibility for global problems. "We are a strong nation. But we can not live to ourselves and remain strong. . . . The cause of liberty cannot have too many defenders. And its defenders must stick closely together for their collective effort . . . will be required if the cause is to be effectively served." He found audiences reacting to him, and for the first time he caught a campaigner's fire.

In February he took his fight to the Middle West, where the *Chicago Tribune*'s editorial policies were given scriptural reverence by isolationists. In late January, some senators described by *Time* as "diehard inheritors of the old isolationist bloc" met at Stoneleigh Court, near the Mayflower Hotel in Washington, to discuss strategy. Majority Whip Kenneth Wherry of Nebraska was the leading spirit. Others were Clyde Reed of Kansas, John Bricker of Ohio, Weyland Brooks of Illinois, James Kem of Missouri, William Knowland of California—some twenty in all, who had grown restive under Vandenberg's bipartisan approach. They wanted to make certain that whatever was adopted was a Republican plan, one that kept the administration of aid in business hands, and appropriated only money that was absolutely necessary. Ghosts of the Irreconcilables, who had kept the United States out of the League of Nations, seemed to be materializing.[13]

Marshall had seen hope in Wilson's vision during the period after World War I. In recent months, he had seen hope in Vandenberg's new purpose, and was prepared to carry the fight to McCormick country. He chose as his first platform the meeting of the National Farm Institute at Des Moines, Iowa. A radio hookup was arranged.

The weather was threatening that morning as he set out from

North Carolina, and grew worse as he flew into Tennessee. He was forced down at Knoxville after a flight that he described in 1956 as the most dangerous of his career. Before he could get from the plane into the airport building, the storm struck with full force. It did an estimated $10 million damage to nearby Chattanooga. When it was evident that Marshall could not complete the flight in time for his speech, arrangements were made for a telephone broadcast from Knoxville; the address was given on time.

Just as Roosevelt had earlier warned the Middle West of the dangers of Fascism, Marshall now spoke of the threat of Communism. His emphasis was on the struggle between good and evil, and the question before the American people was "the greatest decision in our history—a decision which would affect the whole world." The success or failure of the ERP would "determine the survival of the kind of world in which democracy, individual liberty, economic stability, and peace can be maintained."[14]

Two incidents in the next few days lifted his spirits. One was the announcement by Senator Vandenberg that the Senate Foreign Relations Committee had given unanimous approval to the draft of the ERP legislation and had sent it to the floor for debate. The other, which may have pleased him even more, was a visit to his office by a group of Cub Scouts from Bethesda, Maryland, with an idea for a Junior Marshall Plan. He was so delighted that he arranged for photographs and a publicity release, and he told the story on several occasions in his campaign for the ERP.

The seven Cub Scouts, aged nine to eleven, of Troop 232, Bethesda, with sharply pressed uniforms, well-scrubbed faces, and slicked-down hair, called on him to present a plan by which they could raise money to feed eight European boys for a year. They proposed to secure the use of a movie theater in their community for one or more showings of a film that they would sponsor and for which they would get a share of the receipts. On learning of their mission, Marshall was touched and decided to make a production of it. He had the boys shown into his office and shook hands all around. He then asked to meet the chairman of the group, Robert Keith Linden, aged nine, who declared, "Mr. Secretary, we are proud and happy to have met you and want to do everything we can to help the children of Europe." "That is a fine speech," said Marshall. "You said it all in one sentence."[15]

But the Secretary was not quite so brief. Moved by the performance, he spoke of the gesture and of the changes in the world since his own boyhood. What they were proposing was a fine thing, which he did not believe would have been possible in his day. Boys in his era knew little of the world except through their school texts. "We learned something of Europe, something of Africa, something of Asia. We knew that they had kangaroos in Australia, and hot springs in New Zealand, but not much else."

Not until he was halfway through college did he know much of the world. "I remember the first time I was aware of Manila, of the Philippines, was when Admiral Dewey sailed from Hong Kong at the beginning of the Spanish-American War. That was in 1898. I knew all about Manila rope, but that was all I knew about the Philippines." Within a few years, though, he was serving in the Philippines, and was to spend much time abroad.

Between 1902 and the present, the world had changed and the role of the United States had become greater. What they had done was impressive, and he praised them and their organization for what they were setting out to do. "I wish that I could have something like that in my record as a boy. And I thank you very much." He then shook hands with them all again and gave each of them an autographed photograph.

Marshall's worries multiplied in late February and early March with the takeover by the Communist party of the Czech government with the evident backing of the Soviet Union. In the midst of this development, Marshall avoided violent rhetoric. He reflected on these events in an address in Washington to the Federal Council of Churches at the National Cathedral on March 11. To the assembled churchmen who filled the benches of the unfinished Gothic structure, with lights from its magnificent stained glass falling occasionally across anxious faces as they strained to hear his voice in the ascending space, he spoke of the crisis as "influenced by propaganda, misunderstanding, anger, and fear." Still, it was necessary to have cool judgment lest we "grow passionate or fearful, overzealous in our passions or failing in action because of our fears."[16]

The situation seemed fluid, rapidly changing, and Americans were angry, perplexed, and fearful, all at the same time. President Truman proposed resumption of the Selective Service System, adoption of Universal Military Training, and prompt enactment of the European Recovery Program. In discussing these measures with the White House staff, Truman had said that Marshall was cautious and feared that Truman might pull the trigger, but that he had decided to act.[17]

These announcements and the growing fear that Italy might go Communist in the mid-April elections elicited tougher language than usual from Marshall at the University of California at Berkeley on March 19, and at Los Angeles the next day. The Secretary alluded to the Czechoslovakian crisis and Truman's response. He was uncertain what he could add to convince the American people that "This is a world-wide struggle between freedom and tyranny, between the self-rule of the many as opposed to the dictatorship of the ruthless few." The United States must act rapidly, but it was important that troubles in every part of the world not prevent concentration on Western Europe. The country must act now on the ERP. It would soon be a year since he had sounded the alert at Harvard.[18]

He did not deplore the time that had been spent in discussion of the plan—that was in the nature of democracies—but no more time must be lost in implementing the concept.

His words now carried a hint of ruthlessness. He gave stern warning to the Italians, told by Communists that they could vote Red in the coming elections and still get American aid. If they voted Communist in face of opposition to the ERP by Moscow and its satellites, who were bent on making it fail, then the United States had to assume that they were voting not to be a part of the recovery program.[19]

He insisted that the United States would stand firm but would also "keep the door wide open for any conciliatory move" by the Communists and would do anything possible to terminate the existing dangerous situation. Meanwhile, it was our policy "to discourage and oppose further encroachment on the rights and lives of free people."

As he continued his swing, Marshall's conviction inevitably began to come through. Though he was never really a great or even a good speaker, the quality of his speeches came from their ideas and the sincerity with which he spoke. At the University of California at Los Angeles, his emphasis shifted slightly to the struggle between good and evil, and the special task imposed on the United States to lead the fight for good.

In past years, he recalled, the United States could depend on powerful friends abroad to bear the brunt of the struggle against totalitarianism. Such luxury no longer existed. Western European countries were showing determination to defend themselves, but they were exhausted and must have help. "We must assure them that they are firmly backed by a united, alert, and strong America." More pointedly than he had ever before spoken, he warned that the Soviet Union and its satellites would go to any length to prevent the revival of a strong democratic and independent Europe. But the United States and Western European nations were determined "that recovery shall be achieved, that tyranny of government shall be checked, and the people who wish to govern themselves shall remain free to do so." He pleaded for a united effort equal to that of the war, and asked that in this fight the country stand above divisions of the presidential campaign then getting under way to give Europe the backing that it needed.

In his speeches to various groups in the country, Marshall had been explaining the importance of winning the cooperation of Congress. In the upper house, Senator Vandenberg, with the support of the White House and the State Department, was grappling with powerful opponents in his own party who were trying to reduce the proposed appropriations or add crippling amendments. Senator Homer Capehart of Indiana proposed the establishment of a private loan agency to replace the U.S. government in giving aid. Marshall asked that he withdraw the amendment because it would lessen European confidence in American good faith, for it was evident that private organizations could not handle a loan of such magnitude. Senator George Malone of Nevada appealed to anti-British sentiment by saying that there would always be an England as long as the United States financed her. He said, incorrectly, that one British leader had declared that Britain could handle its own financial problems but could use American funds to develop its own special areas in Africa.

The big battle in the Senate centered on the claim that the amount being considered was too large and that the concession of cutting the total amount but also reducing the time from fifteen months to twelve did not represent a reduction. Opponents of the appropriations now demanded a slash from an authorization of $4.3 billion to $3.5 billion.

In the final phases of the fight, Senator Wherry, acting Majority Leader, and a few of his adherents pounded the measure because it would help Communist countries by encouraging East-West trade. Pro–Marshall Plan newspapers, such as *The New York Times, Washington Post,* and *Philadelphia Inquirer,* denounced various opposition maneuvers as pure obstructionism, and the State Department pointed out that East-West trade would help Western Europe far more than it would benefit Communist Europe.

The last big attack came near 5:00 P.M. on the next-to-last day of debate. Senator Taft, increasingly in the limelight as a candidate for the Republican nomination, took the floor to list defects of the measure for one and a half hours. Though he was willing to vote for aid, he wanted the bill cut to $4 billion. He was opposed to endorsing such aid for more than a year: Try it for a year and then see, he said. This was a dangerous move by a powerful senator. But

Vandenberg of Michigan, also a possible candidate at the coming Republican convention, was ready for the fight.[20]

Taft finished his list of objections. Vandenberg, who had been doodling as he listened, arose and said that if at the end of the year Europe was cooperating with the United States, as he believed it would be, he hoped that Taft would join him in voting to continue Marshall Plan aid. Taft said he might indeed do that. Vandenberg moved at once to call for a vote to kill the amendment, and it died 56–31.[21]

The next day, Vandenberg delivered a powerful defense of the European Recovery Program. He used the Soviet menace effectively, stressing the recent threatening developments in Czechoslovakia and current Russian pressure on Finland to bring the foreign policy more in line with that of the USSR. It was time for the United States to accept the responsibilities of leadership. He rallied Republican forces and, just past midnight the following evening, thirty-eight Democrats were joined by thirty-one Republicans to pass the Economic Cooperation Act 69–17, in much the form Vandenberg had favored.

The fight now shifted to the House, where the leadership seemed prepared to accept most of the Senate version. But at that point an attempt was made to add to the ERP measure additional funds for China, Greece, and Turkey. Fearing that delays might follow this amendment, Marshall made one of his rare visits to key members on the Hill. Just as he and Stimson had once gone to seek additional funds for the atomic bomb, so he, Lovett, and Douglas now went to see floor leaders of the two houses. They begged for action before the Italian elections in mid-April.

Representative Eaton promptly called the amendment wrong and proposed a fast vote, but the legislation struck a snag when CIA head Admiral Roscoe H. Hillenkoetter told the House committee that the bill with proposed amendments would have a good psychological effect abroad. As a result, the top Republican leaders reversed themselves and endorsed the so called omnibus bill. The door was opened to other tinkering. Representative Judd wanted an amendment pledging support for countries resisting subjugation by armed minorities or external forces. Ultimately this idea was dropped, and, on the day Marshall spoke at Berkeley, the House Committee on Foreign Affairs accepted much of the Senate bill and reported favorably a bill authorizing $5.3 billion ($4.3 billion in appropriations and $1 billion in flexible credit).

When the bill reached the floor, Representative Karl Mundt of South Dakota proposed an amendment to forbid ERP aid to coun-

tries that produced goods for sale to Communist countries. The
final factor in its defeat was a letter from former President Hoover,
who insisted that the Marshall Plan countries must be able to trade
with the Soviet satellites to regain economic viability.

Marshall continued to urge House acceptance of the Senate measure until he had to leave for the conference of Latin American
states at the end of March. Three days later, he was elated to hear
that by a vote of 329–74 the House had authorized economic aid
of $5.3 billion for Europe for a twelve-month period, plus $150
million in military aid and more than $400 million in economic aid
for China, and $275 million in military aid for Greece and Turkey.
Major newspapers of the United States hailed the move, but the
Chicago Tribune thundered that it should be called the "Marshall
slush fund." Differences in the Senate and House measures were
speedily worked out, however, and the House approved the compromise measure by 318–75; later the same day, the Senate approved it by voice vote. The President signed it the following day.

Foreign Secretary Bevin at once expressed his appreciation to
Marshall for his statesmanship and the display of American confidence in Europe. The London *Economist* paid tribute to the vision
and work of a small group of men—to Marshall and Acheson for
the "sweep and courage" of the initial project, and to Vandenberg
and Douglas among others for the skill, patience, and speed with
which the measure had been put through both houses.

The signal had flashed in time to reassure anti-Communists in
Italy, where behind-the-scenes assistance would bring an anti-
Communist victory on April 18. The European Cooperation Administration had been voted. The appropriation had been
authorized. But the actual provision of specific funds for the fiscal
year still had to be enacted. Once more, opponents tried to cut the
amount of the appropriation. Alarmed, Marshall decided to make
one final appeal—an address to the General Federation of
Women's Clubs at Portland, Oregon, on May 28. He later said that
some of his backers wondered why he had not found a platform
nearer the capital. During the war, he replied, he had discovered
that if he could get the understanding support of women voters, he
was halfway toward getting what he wanted.

He again sketched the confusion and fear that existed in Europe,
insisting that only the United States could play the leading role in
solving the current problems. But the United States must stand
firm. Europeans had the constant fear that the United States would
change its mind, that it would turn away from "a formally adopted

policy like the European Recovery Program without notice and without regard to the devastating effect of such vacillation."[22]

In earlier speeches he had begun to cite the threat of Communism, but in this address he raised a different point. The profound unrest of the world was based on something more than ideology: "The great mass of the ill-favored people of the world have come to realize all that they lack in comparison with the advantages enjoyed by others." The great developments of modern communications and radio had brought to these masses at least a partial understanding of the "unfairness of this situation." It was necessary to keep in mind this great surge of feeling, which was a ground-swell now but might become a tidal wave later, "when met by some desperate hope of improvement through the rehabilitation of the economy of the world, which is the purpose of our present program." He called for the help of the women of America in achieving this purpose.

Eight years later, Marshall remembered:

I talked to the representatives of a number of women's organizations about ERP. "You will put it over," I said, and then I went into it. My goodness, they went back home and they scared Congress to death in the next twenty-four hours. You never saw such rapid action in your life as I got out of that. I said, The men will agree with me but they won't do a damn thing. This [Federation] represented, I think, 10,000 subsidiary little clubs and the [leaders] went to those and everybody went after these [congressmen]. It was electric, what happened, just electric.[23]

Perhaps his memory overestimated their effectiveness, but he had called for help none too soon. John Taber, economy-minded Chairman of the House Appropriations Committee, was already preparing his strategy. In early June, he pushed through a proposal to provide that money authorized for twelve months would be spread over a fifteen-month interval, thus sharply cutting the money initially available. Outcries abroad brought alarmed reports from U.S. ambassadors in Western European countries. Angered by this shift in the House, Senator Vandenberg, in an unusual move, asked permission to address the Senate Appropriations Committee. Marshall was thankful for the close association with the Senator, which had grown over many months.

In language akin to that which Marshall had used at Portland, Vandenberg asked the committee members to oppose this House action. He declared that it undermined "that confidence and morale abroad upon which recovery, independent freedom, and peace so heavily lean, and that it serves the alien critics who plot to have these peace plans fail."[24] In mid-June, the Senate voted 60–9 to restore the original appropriation. The House Appropriations Committee held firm for a brief time but gave way in a conference of the two houses to accept the Senate version, with the exception that the total sum was to cover a fifteen-month period unless the President and the head of the European Cooperation Administration stipulated that the expenditure of the approved sum in twelve months was needed to accomplish the purpose of the act. The conference report was approved by both houses in mid-month and signed by the President before the end of June. In December 1948, he and the Administrator decided that the sum approved would be needed in the first twelve months, thus achieving the purpose of the Senate proposal.

Before the bill's passage, careful attention was given to the choice of an administrator for the new Economic Cooperation Administration. Before debate on the measure was seriously under way, rumors that Under Secretary of State Will Clayton was being considered for the post stirred trouble on the Hill. Vandenberg wrote at once to Secretary Marshall that he had sustained many unhappy repercussions in Congress. Though he and others had great respect and affection for Clayton and there would be widespread acceptance of him or of Ambassador Lewis Douglas, there was greater insistence on a man with an industrial background who had not come in through the State Department. Congress wanted a man with impressive business credentials without diplomacy. "I think it is seriously necessary—for the sake of E.R.P.—to keep that fact in mind."[25]

The Senator's message was obviously intended for the eye of the President, and Marshall so understood it. He promised Vandenberg that he would be consulted when Mr. Truman had "boiled down" the list to two or three names. The President kept Marshall's promise, but apparently without reading the fine print of Vandenberg's message. Calling the Republican leader to the White House, Truman said he had exactly the right man in mind and that his candidate had agreed to take it despite personal sacrifice. The man he had in mind was Dean Acheson, now back in private law practice.

According to Acheson, when the President approached him Acheson said that the Republicans would not accept him because he was too close to the administration, and this was election year.

He suggested that the President mention his name and then ask Senator Vandenberg's advice. If he agreed, Acheson would take the job, but it was more likely that Vandenberg would suggest Paul Hoffman. "In that case, the President should take him."[26]

Truman did propose Acheson. Vandenberg at once said that Acheson would do a fine job but that the Senate would not confirm him, but he did not then suggest Hoffman. *Time*, reporting the appointment in April, declared that Marshall was Hoffman's chief sponsor, but that Vandenberg was also involved. There can be no doubt that it was the Michigan Senator who was responsible for the appointment. He later said that he had checked with numerous businessmen and Hoffman's name was on half of the lists. Hoffman, outstanding businessman and Republican, prominent member of the Harriman committee, had appeared as a forceful supporter before Vandenberg's committee and had won his admiration.[27]

There is no indication of Marshall's role in the naming of the Administrator, but it is unlikely that the President would have acted without checking with the Secretary. Though Marshall was not in Washington at the time of the appointment, he had been aware since January that the Senate would probably not accept someone too close to the administration. He was aware of Hoffman's work as Chairman of the Committee on Economic Development, an advisory group he had headed from 1942 to 1948, and his work with the Harriman committee.

On April 5, 1948, Paul Hoffman accepted Truman's request to head the Economic Cooperation Administration. Born in Chicago, he had attended the university there for a year before going to Los Angeles, where he became a Studebaker car dealer and later a West Coast supervisor of sales. In 1925, he went to South Bend as vice president of the Studebaker Company; he became its president in 1935 and was in that position when appointed head of the ECA. Hoffman set about his task in a nonpolitical way. To a critic who later accused the ECA of playing politics, Vandenberg declared that Hoffman had said definitely that any effort to influence him politically would lead to his resignation. This attitude suited Marshall completely, since it was the approach he had always taken in government activities.

Once Hoffman was appointed, Marshall left the running of the ECA to him. Hoffman later commented:

> He never made a suggestion on appointing anyone, never made a suggestion on how to run the show. I kept him informed because he was Secretary of State, but I think his feeling was that as long as

it was going all right, that was it. . . . We never had any differences ourselves. . . .

I have never known anyone who in my opinion was as completely selfless as General Marshall was in the handling of any problem. I don't think he ever gave it any thought as to how this would affect General Marshall. His decision was always based on what he thought was the best decision for the country or the best decision for a good project. I never felt that I ever had that problem in discussing anything with him, where he would think "What will this do to me politically?" or "What will it do to me historically, what will it do to me?" because that was never in his thinking.[28]

To represent the United States with the various European countries involved in the recovery program, Congress had provided for a special representative in Europe. Hoffman proposed Harriman or Douglas to the President, who chose Marshall's fellow Cabinet member Averell Harriman. President Truman needed no recommendation for this selection, and it was welcome to Marshall, who had wanted Harriman as head of a military secretariat in Washington early in the war, and had favored him for Ambassador to the Soviet Union in 1943. His only concern, voiced to Lovett from Rio, was that Harriman was needed more in the Cabinet. Lovett urged the appointment, pointing out that Clayton was available as a substitute in the Commerce Department, and that Lewis Douglas, who had given such great service in getting the ECA bill through Congress, thought he could help most by returning to London as Ambassador. As deputy to Harriman, the President selected William C. Foster, Under Secretary of Commerce.

Many people had helped put the Marshall Plan through Congress. A detailed study in 1968 of various influences during enactment of the bill notes the careful work of the Truman Administration, the appointment of committees with standing, effective efforts in the State Department by Acheson and Lovett under Marshall's leadership, the support of various interest groups (many of which Marshall addressed), and the vital leadership of Senator Vandenberg. Along with the crucial role of White House and Democratic leadership in Congress and the highly important work of Vandenberg in bringing essential segments of his party in Congress into line, Marshall deserves special credit. He represented a nonpartisan stand and he managed to keep a warm and affectionate relationship with Vandenberg throughout the fight. He would have little part in the naming of various heads of missions, in the working out of the organization in various countries. Before many weeks, he was busy with the development of NATO, with sessions at the United Nations in New York, and with the Berlin crisis. In September, he went to the United Nations meeting in Paris. He was busily engaged there until almost 'he end of his active service in the State Department. The great story of the administration of the Marshall Plan belongs to another history. But Marshall could take special pride in a program that he had enunciated at Harvard, defended before congressional committees, and helped sell to various groups and regions of the country by appealing for American unity in a movement that served American interests by aiding Western Europe to survive. The Nobel Prize for Peace in 1953 would honor his achievement.

XVI

American Division Over China

O N assuming his post as Secretary of State, Marshall asked John Carter Vincent, Director of the Office of Far Eastern Affairs, for a summary of U.S. national policy on China. Vincent believed that it was not in American interest to build a China policy on sentiment, but that it was valuable to have there a unified and democratically inclined state. "We did not think that a Communist China could make such a contribution any more than a feudal-fascist state could do so. It was our policy to prevent China from becoming an irritant in our international relations, particularly with the Soviet Union."[1]

Certain decisions had to be made after careful study of several specific items: establishment of a Military Advisory Group at Nanking; transfer by the U.S. of certain naval vessels to China; completion of the 8 1/3 groups of an aviation program; transfer of arms and ammunition to the Chinese; and extension of credit through the Export-Import Bank for economic projects. Truman had stated that the U.S. would give aid when conditions improved. Marshall had emphasized that there must be an assumption of leadership by liberal groups, a genuine welcome for all political groups to share in the responsibility of a reorganized government, and a ceasing of financial support to the Kuomintang from the government. In determining improvement, the U.S. should count sincerity of purpose rather than actual length of steps taken. The projects should not be related to civil strife and should give priority to improvement of transportation and agriculture, and promotion of Chinese-American business activity.

It would not be realistic to withhold shipments of arms and munitions if such action reduced the government's ability to resist a successful Communist offensive; a problem that would involve careful monitoring. Vincent warned that many Chinese other than the Communists were opposed to military aid to the government, because of the danger that such aid would encourage the reactionary members of the Kuomintang and would likely lead to an inconclusive war that would destroy them. If the United States let down the bars and sent arms freely to the Nationalists, other countries would follow. Reactionaries would be strengthened and any possibility of reform would be lost. From the American standpoint it would be preferable to allow the opposing forces to reach a kind of equilibrium. Only if the Soviets appeared to be aiding the Communists should we reassess our policy.

Vincent was in favor of a larger Military Advisory Group, but as for a bill to send arms and munitions, he favored waiting to ask for legislation to allow the Secretary of State to have the final say about the "time, type, and quantity of disposals of military equipment to China." He recommended that the U.S. continue to withhold means for completing the 8 1/3 air groups, but that approval be given to the transfer of a proposed number of mercantile ships.

Marshall forwarded copies of Vincent's statement to Army Secretary Patterson and Navy Secretary Forrestal, and a meeting was arranged for discussion on February 12, during which Marshall said he believed that leaders of the Kuomintang overestimated their ability to solve the Communist problem. He had found it most difficult to convince the Generalissimo that only drastic reform would save China, and the only solution seemed to be to oust the reactionary cliques from the Kuomintang. Forrestal, increasingly leaning to a strong anti-Soviet position, did not accept Marshall's views. He believed that any withdrawal of military aid to the Nationalists was bound to help the Communists. He suggested sending an economic mission to China to outline proper measures. China, he believed, had to go through a wringer as Germany did in the early twenties. He then suggested that a visit by MacArthur to China might be helpful. Marshall answered that a member of the U.S. Government was then working with Chinese officials on economic problems, and it would be well to await his report before proceeding further.[2]

Both Forrestal and Patterson wanted to help Chiang Kai-shek. Patterson did not believe that a broadening of the base of the Chinese Government to include the Communists would aid the National Government. He did not share the State Department's views on insisting on political reforms. He thought that the improvement of China's economic position was so dependent on U.S. aid that any delay to get political reform might mean that the U.S.

would do nothing in the foreseeable future. To withhold aid lest it add to civil strife repeated the dilemma which Wedemeyer faced in his 1945 directive. The main issue was whether the United States should be willing to accept the collapse of the National Government.

Questions in Congress and in the press influenced the reactions of the service secretaries and the President. Uneasy over recent communications about China, Truman had asked Marshall in February whether or not the time had come to give ammunition to the Nationalists. Marshall replied that giving ammunition would open the United States to charges of aiding the civil war in China. Such action would encourage Government reactionaries to resist bringing in more liberal elements. He told the President that the situation of the government was rapidly deteriorating and that the United States must ultimately act, but at the moment any U.S. action would strengthen the most reactionary elements of the Kuomintang.

It was at this juncture that Marshall left for Moscow. Before his departure he indicated the great importance of "the rapid completion of the civilian end-use program of the 8 1/3 group Chinese Air Force program."[3]

Although Marshall's attention was focused on European problems for the next several weeks, Ambassador John Leighton Stuart did not let him forget China. Stuart's mid-March message on distressing developments in the Far East prompted Marshall to ask for a new assessment of the Chinese situation.[4]

The resulting roundup of information included an estimate from the military attaché, Brigadier General Robert Soule, aided by other observers. He reported that the Chinese Government had decided on an all-out effort against the Communists. At present, the Nationalists had superiority in arms and equipment and should be able to achieve success in the initial phases of a campaign, but other factors might work against them in the next three or four months. Ammunition stocks were at a critical level and might be exhausted in three months, although there was no estimate on the amount of captured Japanese ammunition still available. Various items of equipment were wearing out and repair was beyond Government capability. "Government forces are widely dispersed and dangerously over-extended, particularly in Manchuria." Poor pay and bad economic conditions were lowering troop morale. Furthermore, the civil war was generally unpopular and Government troops were listening to the slogan that "Chinese should not fight Chinese".[5] The Chinese Government's inability to handle necessary measures such as price control or rationing had led to repressive measures. Instead of attacking the evils, the Government was using force to quell unrest.

The report suggested a wait to assess the effect of the proposed reorganization of Government. At the moment the Government was engaged in a vigorous anti-Communist military effort, including the occupation of Yenan, which had caused the attrition of government forces as well as serious supply problems. It seemed clear that the Communists were not about to join any coalition except on their own terms. Many of the more liberal elements needed for the reorganized government seemed reluctant to enter it. The more extreme anti-Communists seemed encouraged by the Truman Doctrine speech to believe that all they had to do to get American aid was to make faces at Russia and continue to fight the Communists. The military appraisal added that the United States must be prepared to adopt at some stage an "affirmative policy of such conditional assistance as may be necessary to our national welfare and security in the light of broader world commitments, particularly in connection with American-Russian relations.

Many of the Nationalists took hope from the capture of Yenan, headquarters of the Chinese Communist Party. Ambassador Stuart cited the reaction as an example of the way plans developed in China. In February, T. V. Soong had agreed with the Generalissimo that Yenan should not be attacked. As it was attacked, Stuart concluded that the move had been made solely for purposes of prestige and the desire to discourage Russian moves into North China. He explained to Marshall that the Communists had made no plans to defend Yenan and that their handling of the situation was in keeping with their tactic of pulling the enemy into a pocket and then sapping his strength with guerrilla attacks. An American officer who had talked with Chinese Communist leaders said that he was told it would cost the Nationalists seventeen brigades to hold onto Yenan and the surrounding area. Both Wedemeyer and Marshall in 1946 had warned Chiang against over-extension of forces.[6]

At a time when Stuart was reporting that hope for the Nationalists lay in cessation of military operations and in radical reforms in government, the Chinese High Command was pleased with the current military situation. The Chief of Staff of the Nationalist Army said that two months should suffice to defeat and destroy the main Communist forces. Stuart became convinced that as military operations expanded, the role of the reactionaries became stronger in the National Government. He deplored the role of the Chen brothers. Chiang Kai-shek had attempted to curb their power but he was personally too attached to them to do this effectively. Yet, the Chens were not tainted by graft and were almost left-wing on some social issues, and Stuart hoped he might encourage the brothers to embarrass the Communists by proving that they could outdo them in dealing with agrarian problems.[7]

Even as evidence multiplied that the necessary changes in the National Government were being delayed, there were signs of a softening in the U.S. position. At the end of March, when General Gillem, who had been U.S. Commissioner of Executive Headquarters while Marshall was in China, called on the Generalissimo before returning home, Chiang took up the matter of ammunition shortages. Next day, Gillem talked with Yu Ta-wei, Minister of Communications, who also spoke of the shortages of small arms and mortar ammunition, which were hampering the Nationalists. He mentioned in particular 9.2 mm ammunition which was needed for arms already supplied by the U.S. Two days later in Washington, the chairman of the Chinese Supply Commission called on the Chief of the Division of Chinese Affairs, Arthur Ringwalt, and asked specifically about the release of this particular ammunition, which had been procured during the war by the U.S. Army for China under Lend-Lease arrangements, but never shipped. The ammunition was of no use to the U.S. Army and was deteriorating. On the same day, John Carter Vincent drafted a letter for Acheson to send Marshall, approving release of these stores. He told Acheson that the telegram was the result "of some wrestling I have been doing with my soul in recent weeks."[8]

An inquiry by a member of Marshall's party in Moscow for a justification of the changed China policy was followed by a report by Brigadier General Thomas Timberman, U.S. Embassy in China, who said that the quantity of U.S. types of ammunition, as reported by the Chinese, "is inadequate for protracted operations by the Chinese Army units equipped with U.S. weapons." This view and a favorable reaction by the State Department's Chief of the Division of Chinese Affairs may have influenced Secretary Marshall's directive on May 26th that "necessary steps be taken to remove the prohibition established on July 29, 1946, on issuance of export licenses covering the shipment of arms to China . . . [and] that the Chinese be given normal commercial access to the arms market in this country." He said also that in addition to civilian end-use of the 8 1/3 group program now being readied for shipment to China, authority was given to transfer transport planes and spare parts. He also directed that foreign nations that had been cooperating in the export embargo on shipments to China should be notified of our change of policy.[9]

In making this move, Marshall was aware that the National Government was far from improving the political situation in China. Stuart's messages continued to depict a sordid story. In late March he added new details to the government's handling of Formosa. The "maladministration" of the island in the eighteen months since the Nationalists had taken over "can scarcely be exaggerated," he said. At one time he suggested appointing T.V. Soong, recently ousted as prime minister of the mainland government by the CC Clique, as governor of Formosa. This proposal was received with silence. The only hope for China that Stuart could see was the appointment of able men to the reorganized State Council, although evidence indicated it was still strongly dominated by the Kuomintang reactionaries. He was disturbed by growing anti-Americanism in China, both from the Communists who blamed the United States for keeping in power a corrupt and ineffective regime, and the reactionary group among the Kuomintang, which felt that, had the United States left them free, they could have soon settled the Communist question by force. Stuart emphasized that the influential, anti-foreign group in the Kuomintang still believed that American assistance would be forthcoming. "There is little reason to believe," he concluded, "that their ideology will undergo any basic transformation as a result of American aid."[10]

In early May Stuart reported that the Communists were beginning to take advantage of overextended Nationlist forces in the North, yet Chiang still believed that his military objectives would be gained by September. His troops suffered from poor pay, physical drudgery for officers and troops, war weariness, Communist propaganda, and the lack of a motive to inspire them. The High Command was split on strategy. Defections to the Communists and disintegration of entire units were being reported. "The essence of the problem," he declared, "seems to be as to whether the financial structure of the country can endure until the military operations will have opened the way for a negotiated peace."[11]

Stuart's reports continued to add bad news. May had seen rice riots in some of the cities and student demonstrations and strikes in nearly every academic center. There were hints that the CC Clique had encouraged some of the student riots in an effort to prove that the reform government could not keep order and a more disciplined society was needed. The student protests, fused initially by economic concerns, at length focused on demands for an end to civil war in China.[12]

The next alarming news was that Communist troops were in the outskirts of Changchun, the city controlling communications to Manchuria, which had been hotly fought over while Marshall was in China.

The Government's response to student unrest was repression. When Stuart urged Chiang not to use violence, the Generalissimo insisted there must be a restoration of order. After numerous arrests and clashes with the police, in early June quiet had been restored for the moment, but Stuart doubted that the repressive policy would be long effective since the students were determined to be heard.

After the first week of June, Stuart's report was totally despairing. He deplored Chiang's attempt to explain the demonstrations as Communist-inspired. Dr. Hu Shih, Chancellor of Peking University, had already protested such terminology as untrue and unfair. Chiang and his supporters exaggerated the power of the Communists to influence the rest of the Chinese. Most of the people belonged to no political party and were interested only in their livelihood. The students and intellectuals were "radical" because of their "bodily distress and spiritual disillusionment. To attribute all this to Communist machinations, and to try to crush it out by brute force is to intensify the growing disaffection." For failure to persuade Chiang, Stuart blamed himself. "I feel myself pitifully impotent for having failed to help him apply in this concrete issue the idealist abstractions to which he has given his assent when the emergency was less apparent.[13]

In forwarding Stuart's and other reports to Marshall, Vincent said that recent action on completing most of the China Air Force program, the transfer of surplus ammunition, and the granting of licenses for shipment of munitions to China might bolster Chinese morale and fighting strength, but could not make up for poor leadership or abusive treatment of troops. There seemed to be no action that the United States could take soon to correct these problems except through more or less complete U.S. involvement in the civil war.[14]

In was in this climate that the Joint Chiefs of Staff on June 9 submitted its study of the military aspects of U.S. policy toward China that had been requested by the State Department. It was a stark revelation of the tremendous dichotomy of the administration's policy toward China. The study ignored or swept aside all efforts made by the presidential directive of December, 1945, to achieve an understanding between warring factions in China, to broaden the base of the National Government, and to promote political reform in China. The question that concerned the Joint Chiefs was: What policy shall we pursue to block Soviet expansion in Manchuria and North China?

The chief conclusions of the study were: (1) The United States must prevent the growth of any power or coalition to the point that it threatened the Western Hemisphere; (2) U.S. security demanded that China be free from Soviet domination; (3) it was to the interest of United States security that Eurasian nations oppose Soviet expansion; (4) Soviet expansionism is furthered by the Chinese Communists; (5) Soviet expansionism is incompatible with U.S. security; (6) with Japan disarmed, the only nation in Asia capable of resisting Soviet expansion is Nationalist China; (7) unless the National Government is given sufficient military help to resist Communist expansionism the government will collapse; (8) U.S. commitments to the United Nations, in which China is listed, at U.S. insistence, as one of the great powers, requires that we support National China in getting control of Manchuria; (9) chaos in China works to the advantage of Soviet Russia; unless immediate military aid is given, the National Government will collapse; (10) U.S. aid to nations on the periphery of Soviet-controlled areas in Eurasia should be given in accordance with an overall plan; the plan should take in account aid for the Nationalists to meet and ultimately eliminate all Communist armed opposition.[15]

In addition to these conclusions, the study dealt specifically with the points which Marshall had forwarded. On the two suggestions that the United States continue to encourage China to achieve democratic unity and the belief that certain conditions in China should improve before the United States gave economic aid, the Joint Chiefs judged that such were political matters for which they were not responsible. On the thorny issue of withholding aid that might encourage or help civil war, the Joint Chiefs declared that any aid to the Nationalists risked provoking civil war as long as there was opposition to the National Government. Withholding aid was inconsistent with other policies relating to blocking Soviet expansion. If there was to be no aid, there was no need of a military advisory group.

A State Department reaction to this report appeared in Vincent's Memorandum of June 27. Noting that the deterioration of the Nationalist military position brought up the question of further U.S. military assistance, he reviewed what had been done recently to help the forces of Chiang Kai-shek. Since the end of the war with Japan, the United States had given $700 million in Lend-Lease assistance, it had transported Nationalist forces and supplied them

with ammunition and equipment, munitions in Tientsin and Tsingtao had been abandoned to them, in recent weeks export permits
had again been permitted, small arms ammunition had been desig-
nated as surplus property so that it could be transferred, and transport planes were being supplied. Despite all this, it was
questionable, in the face of the incompetence of the Nationalist
High Command, whether any assistance would enable them to hold
their own against the Communists.[16]

Then Vincent put bluntly what Marshall had feared and what the
Joint Chiefs of Staff seemed prepared to accept: U.S. military assistance sufficient to insure the Nationalist defeat of the Communists
would be on such a large scale as to involve direct American participation, probably requiring that the United States take over direction of Chinese military operations and administration and remain
in China for an indefinite period. The Chiefs had made clear that
we could no longer avoid taking part in civil strife if we would save
the Nationalists, but they had stopped short of spelling out the
likely end. No one was yet prepared to face that.

Marshall and members of his staff met with Patterson and Forrestal on June 26. He concluded that the issues involved were of such
importance that it was necessary to consult the President. The
Secretary then directed Vincent to prepare a memorandum setting
the points before Truman. The resulting paper briefly noted the
issues previously set forth by the State Department, along with a
statement that the United States had an obligation to supply ammunition for weapons we had promised China.

Under Secretary Acheson reviewed the memorandum at Marshall's request. He underlined the point that supplying ammunition
would not insure elimination of the Chinese Communist threat.
That could be accomplished only with large-scale American participation in the civil war—neither practical nor desirable. In this conclusion, Acheson concurred with Vincent. There was also a moral
obligation for us to supply ammunition to those units which we had
agreed to arm.[17]

Marshall had before him two sets of recommendations: the proposal by the Joint Chiefs for all-out aid to the Nationalists; and
the more moderate course recommended by Vincent and Acheson. On July 3, he instructed Stuart to tell the Generalissimo that
the State Department had been closely watching developments in
China. It was keenly aware of Chiang's needs just as he in turn
was aware of Marshall's ideas. Marshall could not presume to give
advice on the current situation in Manchuria. But, he added, "I
must point out that he [Chiang] was forewarned of most of the

present serious difficulties and advised regarding preventative actions." The United States could not initiate and carry out a solution of problems but could assist only when there was some assurance that the aid given would have practical, beneficial results. "Please assure Gmo of my continued deep personal concern over events in China and of my earnest desire to find ways of being helpful.[18]

The language was cold. It was no different from the tone he had used in his last weeks in China, but it was clear from Stuart's reports that the idea still hung on in inner circles that the United States would bail out the Nationalists. Marshall wanted it made unmistakable that he must have some sign of change. Actually, he had already decided on another approach.

While Marshall mulled over means of dealing with the China problem, he received nothing from Ambassador Stuart but indications that the Generalissimo had "learned nothing and forgotten nothing." Chiang recognized the dangers of continuing the old arrangements, talked about reform, yet allowed the Kuomintang to dictate his actions. Despairingly, Marshall ventured on a new tack. General Wedemeyer, now commander of Second Army at nearby Fort Meade, had been Chief of Staff for the Generalissimo, and understood the weaknesses of Chiang's position. Why not send him on a fact-finding mission? He knew Chiang; knew what was needed. Looking at this action later, Wedemeyer suspected he had been set up as a scapegoat, but nothing in the exchange of documents or in Marshall's files suggests anything but a clear desire to try once more to see what could be done. Marshall had always worked patiently, picking up crumpled plans, when the objective seemed worth the effort.

Marshall called Wedemeyer into his office on July 1 and asked him to think over the proposed mission and to come back the next day. Pressed for time because he had to testify on Capitol Hill, Marshall asked Wedemeyer to dictate a memorandum giving his ideas of what should be in such a directive.[19]

Wedemeyer's proposed draft showed that he well understood what was in Marshall's mind. In words that went into his final directive, he said that the mission was to appraise political, economic, psychological and military situations. The mission, as he understood it, "would be to obtain factual information on which you and the President could base appropriate action." He thought that piecemeal assistance to China would not work. Whatever loan or assistance that we gave China should be based upon the premise "that appropriate safeguards are initiated and maintained to insure

that such assistance contributes to political and economic stabilization in the area."[20]

The final directive took note of points Marshall had mentioned
plus suggestions by Lovett and Vincent. Truman approved it on
July 9. According to the directive the United States would consider
assistance only if "the Chinese Government presents a satisfactory
evidence of effective measures looking towards Chinese recovery
and provided further that any aid which shall be made available
shall be subject to the supervision of representatives of the United
States Government." Wedemeyer was asked to proceed with detachment from any feeling of prior obligation to support any program of aid which did not conform to sound American policy with
regard to China. He was also asked to proceed to Korea and check
on the situation there. In China he was to estimate the "character,
extent, and probable consequences of assistance which you may
recommend," and the likely consequences if aid were not given.
Emphasis was laid on MacArthur's blessing on the trip to Korea,
but Wedemeyer was told to ask if he could proceed there by way
of Tokyo.[21]

The announcement of Wedemeyer's Mission on July 11 reached
Ambassador Stuart through a newspaper account before he received Marshall's personal message explaining the appointment.
Deeply hurt, Stuart wired Marshall that he was sure that the Secretary had his reasons for not notifying him ahead of time. He
thought the announcement could have been made in a way to spare
embarrassment to him and the staff in China. Marshall hastened to
explain that a leak had occurred and the announcement was made
to still Washington rumors. "I regret you were embarrassed but
know that you will ride out the storm as you so often have done
before." To stop speculation on Wedemeyer's future role, he
added that the Mission was a temporary expedient.[22]

The Chinese Nationalists viewed the mission most favorably
while the Communist press said that when Marshall wanted to
appear as a neutral mediator, he had sent Wedemeyer home. Now
the American imperialists, Marshall and Truman, saw the Nationalists tottering on the brink of collapse and were sending "this infa-
mous Wedemeyer back to China." The Americans were becoming
panicky and expected to intervene in China as they had in Greece,
but they would find that they had misjudged the Chinese people.

Arriving in Nanking on July 22, Wedemeyer made clear the nature of his Mission and indicated that he could not make statements
on U.S. policy since his purpose was to get information for the
President. He and members of his group were soon visiting various

parts of China, collating reports from the Embassy staff and military advisers, interviewing representatives of various factions. General Wedemeyer made a point of renewing former associations with governmental figures.

Embassy reports continued to list problems which Stuart had been stressing for weeks. Again the conclusion was that only Chiang Kai-shek could hold together all non-Communist groups and only American assistance could save Nationalist China.

Contrary to assertions later made in the United States that the U.S. Embassy was fooled by the Chinese Communists, some of those afterward attacked as leftists showed in their reports to Wedemeyer that they clearly understood the nature of the Chinese Communist regime. Such an Embassy report to the Wedemeyer Mission near the end of July declared:

> It is obvious that there exists in China an important and growing Communist problem. It is not necessary to establish proof that there is direct connection between the Chinese Communist Party and the Soviet Union. The ideological affinity between the Chinese Communists and their brethren of the Soviet Union is in itself sufficient to assure that in the event the Communists were to achieve majority control of a government in China, its basic orientation would be toward the Soviet Union rather than toward the United States.

The author of that report judged that the social structure and history of China were opposed to Marxist beliefs and Communist form of society, and would be anti-Communist if the social and economic burdens of Chinese life were lightened to any degree. However, as the current state of Chinese society offered fertile ground for the growth of Communism, it seemed improbable that Communism could be eliminated in China even with substantial outside assistance.[23]

Near the end of July, General Wedemeyer sent Marshall a summary of his first impressions. Militarily and economically, the situation in China had deteriorated since Marshall left it in January. From every side he gathered the impression that drastic reforms and important changes in government leadership were necessary "or the Generalissimo's position as President will become untenable, resulting unquestionably in its fall." He found the Chinese apathetic and bewildered. "Inflation, corruption, disregard and disrespect for constituted authority is witnessed on all sides." On the other hand, reports indicated excellent spirit, "almost a fanatical fervor" on the part of the Communists. He feared that the

Nationalists "were spiritually insolvent." They foresaw complete collapse and many in positions of responsibility were trying to get what they could before that collapse. There was a tendency to blame the Yalta agreements for the unfavorable position of the Nationalists in Manchuria and North China.[24]

Ten days later when he had returned from North China and Manchuria his report was much the same. He repeated charges of corruption, but noted that people in positions of lesser responsibility were forced by inflation to resort to dishonest measures in order to live. The new note he struck was that after the United States entered the war in 1941, the Chinese were content to let the Americans do the fighting. The United States must be alert to Chinese "machinations" and compel them to contribute to the current fight against Soviet aggression.[25]

A week later, after studying Shanghai, Canton, and Formosa, he made an equally caustic summary. In Formosa the former Governor sent by the Central Government had alienated the local population. Formosan problems could not be attributed to Communists or dissidents but to the failure to establish honest and efficient administration. The Governor and his henchmen had "ruthlessly, corruptly, and avariciously imposed their regime upon a happy and amenable population. The Army [acted] as a conqueror. Secret police operated freely to intimidate and to facilitate exploitation by Central Government officials." He found indications that the Formosans would favor governorship by the United States or trusteeship under the United Nations. "They fear that the Central Government contemplates bleeding their island to support the tottering and corrupt Nanking machine and I think their fears are well-founded."[26]

Coming from a proved friend of China and a supporter of Chiang Kai-shek, Wedemeyer's thunderous charges had a profound influence on Marshall. His short, personal messages were read more carefully by the Secretary than was the final, longer report which came just as he was leaving for meetings of the U.N. General Assembly in New York, and then going to London for the Foreign Ministers' Conference which would continue until near the end of the year.

What Wedemeyer heard and saw in July and August boiled up in remarks he made to the Joint Meeting of the State Council and the Ministers of Government on August 22. He later said he was encouraged to speak with complete frankness by the Generalissimo and by Ambassador Stuart. In his memoirs, he explained that he was aware that the United States was against giving necessary assistance to China because of Central Government weaknesses. Since he was going to recommend massive aid, it was necessary for the record to show that he had made the Nationalists aware of needed reforms. He obviously thought that his later recommendations of increased aid would blunt the sharpness of his remarks.

Much of what he had to say he had already said to Marshall. Chiang Kai-shek may have wanted some hard truths told, but in a country which valued "face" and where Chiang had urged Marshall to avoid public remarks that would hurt the prestige of the government, it must have been only the firm belief that desperate situations require frank talk that led Wedemeyer to deliver the home truths embedded in his speech.

He started with the topic of taxation, noting that corrupt officials taxed the peasants unfairly while businessmen and rich Chinese avoided paying proper taxes. A picture of unfair and corrupt officials using the government against the bulk of the people appeared in many of his other statements. He declared that in the first year after the war, it would have been possible to defeat or curb the advance of Communism had the Government concentrated on controlling industrial centers, main centers of production, important cities, and the lines of communication. This effort required the appointment of highly efficient and scrupulously honest men as provincial governors, mayors, magistrates, and such. Political and economic stability would have resulted and the people would not have been so receptive to Communist ideas.[27]

He stated grimly that he did not believe that Chinese Communism could be defeated by force. Nationalist China was being invaded by an idea that could be stopped only if the Central Government eliminated incompetence and corruption, and insured justice, equality, and the personal liberties of the people, especially of the peasants.

He must have startled many officers present by insisting that they should show interest in the welfare of their troops, provide care for their wounded, visit their men in hospitals, play basketball and soccer with their men, see that junior officers knew the names of men in their units, state the objectives of the government and encourage questions, and explain why they were fighting. These were views widely held in the American Army, but wholly alien to the men to whom he was speaking.

He followed this gospel of fairness and responsibility in his criticism of the way conscription was handled, so that the burden of service fell largely on the peasants while sons of the wealthy paid money to get out of military duty, or went abroad to school. He urged military men to be more cooperative with civilians. In Manchuria and in Formosa, Nationalist troops were described as arrogant, treating people as though conquered, looting their possessions. In the beginning the Communists had behaved the same way, but more recently they were perceptive enough to change. He urged that officers be promoted only on the basis of merit, noting that there were too many generals, and insisted that the military should stay out of politics, and that generals should never be used in positions of civilian responsibility, such as governors, mayors, magistrates.

He repeated the statement that he had made to Marshall that many men had turned to corruption in order to live, but he attacked the rich who used their position in government and business to further enrich themselves, the widespread practice of nepotism in politics, and the practice of placing relatives in firms where they made huge profits at the expense of the government and of the people.

Wedemeyer then turned his lecture toward self-help. China had resources, food, raw materials, and manpower. Honest, efficient administration and good organization would solve many of their problems. He mentioned that some ten million Chinese lived abroad and large sums of money were invested abroad by citizens in China. It had been estimated that Chinese living in the United States could provide at least one billion dollars for their country. China was not financially bankrupt, but was almost bankrupt in spiritual resources. He recounted strong-arm measures by the secret police in which people were seized and held without trials, in which citizens disappeared, in which students were arrested for attending a meeting. As a result people lost confidence in the government.

Realizing that he had been severe, he dwelt on the importance of constructive criticism and the willingness to accept it. He had spoken frankly in a spirit of helpfulness and he hoped that it was clear that he was willing to do anything he could to help China become a strong, happy, and prosperous nation.

The General's hopes were blighted. The Chinese leaders were already upset because they had expected his Mission to signal an immediate cornucopia of money and material. They were totally unprepared for his candor. It was true that some who heard him agreed that what he said was true, but they shuddered at the loss of face. To Wedemeyer's dismay, Ambassador Stuart's report to the State Department gave the impression that his speech had been a mistake. Wedemeyer wrote promptly to correct the impression,

reminding the Secretary that he had been urged by the Generalissimo to speak frankly and that Stuart had said he had performed
a valuable service.[28]

His final statement to the press two days later, before leaving
China, like Marshall's farewell in 1946, gave additional offense to
the Chinese leaders, for he now stated publicly the essence of what
he had said to the Council and ministers. He spoke in friendly
fashion, but was none the less disturbing. He again noted the
lethargy and apathy in so many quarters, said that instead of seeking remedies, the leaders blamed outside influences. He was dismayed by the abject defeatism of so many Chinese.

The Generalissimo apparently took personally Wedemeyer's
statement that "Recovery awaits inspirational leadership, and
moral and spiritual resurgence which can only come from within
China." Wedemeyer insisted that if the Communists were patriotic
Chinese, they would stop their use of force, but he also emphasized
that too many Nationalist officials were corrupt and incompetent.
Immediate drastic and far-reaching political and economic reforms
were necessary. Force alone could not defeat Communism.

Wedemeyer went from China to Korea and after approximately
a week there he went to Hawaii to prepare his report and recommendations. State Department staff members who had a preview of
the report convinced Marshall that the contents of Wedemeyer's
report should be kept secret until the Department could carefully
review U.S. policy in the light of its recommendations. Marshall
accepted their advice and recommended to President Truman that
he suggest a temporary policy of secrecy to Wedemeyer. Marshall
was personally uneasy over Wedemeyer's recommendation of a
five-power trusteeship for Manchuria. He asked if this recommendation could be removed from the report and its deletion concealed. Wedemeyer did not like this suggestion. Walton
Butterworth of the State Department then suggested that the deletion be made, with the notation that one suggestion of the report
had been removed by request of the Secretary of State. Marshall
feared this arrangement would still cause trouble. He said if the
suppressed part of the report should leak out it would be dangerously embarrassing to the U.S. delegation's position in the United
Nations.[29]

The report to the President, dated September 19, summarized
much of what Wedemeyer had been saying about problems in
China and recommended items of military and economic aid that
had already been proposed by the Joint Chiefs of Staff. Shortcom-
ings of the National Government were all set forth. The need for

political and economic reform was added. A lengthy and valuable statement followed on Chinese resources, assets, and financial needs. Despite his detailing of the faults of the National Government and criticism of the weaknesses of the Nationalist command, Wedemeyer proposed more military aid, including completion of the aviation program, extension of the advisory program, and immediate shipment of more ammunition. Although mention was made of the use of U.S. military personnel, he ruled out U.S. armed intervention as contrary to U.S. policy. There was nothing in these proposals, introduced by such sweeping criticism which had already been reported in the U.S. press, to indicate why the U.S. Government would feel it necessary to suppress this part of the report. There seems no reason to doubt Marshall's later testimony that he thought the proposal "that Manchuria be placed under a Five Power Guardianship or, failing that, under a Trusteeship, in accordance with the United Nations Charter," might cause trouble. In his first experience as head of the delegation to the United Nations, he wanted to be cautious in throwing questions of this kind into the United Nations General Assembly, and was especially reluctant to invite the Soviet Union to serve on a guardianship for Manchuria or elsewhere. He recalled repeatedly that Chiang Kai-shek had been vehement against bringing in British or Soviet control.[30]

For the moment, at least, a stop had been placed on all publicity about the report. Within the framework of earlier proposals by the Pentagon, numerous parts of the recommendations such as shipment of small arms ammunition, transfer of ships, and aid for the machine parts program, were already underway. In Congress a strong move by friends of China and by Republican critics of the Administration was being made to add funds for China to any appropriation for the European Recovery Program. An estimate for the use of the Central Intelligence Agency, made while Wedemeyer was writing his report, said that two billion dollars would be needed in the next three years to help economic stability in China, plus equipment and munitions for at least thirty divisions, merely to restore Nationalist control of China proper. Control of Manchuria would take 100 per cent more.

During the fall of 1947 support grew in Congress to add Nationalist China to the list of countries receiving assistance. Discussions began between representatives of both countries. Early in 1948, Marshall's former fellow negotiater, Chang Chun, now Premier of China, signaled the adoption of some of the reforms that Marshall had advocated and asked aid to stabilize his country. Congress incorporated $570 million dollars for China into an omnibus aid bill for fifteen months.

As Secretary of State, on February 20, 1948, Marshall made one of the main presentations concerning this bill before the congressional committees on Foreign Relations and Foreign Affairs. In view of the zealous fight he was then making for aid to Western Europe, determined advocates of more aid to China were to accuse the Truman administration of an attempt to still criticism rather than to meet the problem. Marshall favored help for the Chinese, but he built a powerful case against making it an item of first priority.

In Executive Session, he sketched a picture of the incompetence and corruption that various American leaders who had served in China had noted over the years. At the same time, he detailed his doubts about the Chinese Communists, who drew strength from the failure of the National Government to develop effective military leadership, or to attract support among the young. He thought that many bright and vigorous Chinese had joined the Communists not for ideological reasons but from disgust with the older government.

The National Government, he said, seemed incapable of taking steps toward reform of economic disorder that was sapping the country's economy; it had failed to rid its ranks of rampant corruption, and it had not ended one-party domination.

He believed it necessary to help China achieve some measure of stability, but drew the line at trying to insure Nationalist victory over the Communists. He made clear what had been done since 1942 to arm and equip the Chinese forces, the arms that had later been transferred, and the funds advanced for that purpose. But to guarantee success against the Communists demanded far more than he thought the American people would be willing to pay.

"There is a tendency to feel," he observed, "that wherever the Communist influence is brought to bear, we should immediately meet it, head on as it were." Such action gave the initiative to the Communists. They could "spread our forces so thin that they could be of no particular effectiveness at any one point." To reduce the Chinese Communists to a negligible force in China would require that the United States underwrite China's military effort and economy. "The U.S. would have to be prepared virtually to take over the Chinese government and administer its economic, military, and governmental affairs."

Such a course would likely make China an arena of international conflict. It could force the United States into an indefinite commitment of men and resources, playing into the hands of the Russians or leading to "another Spanish type of revolution or general hostilities."

From the standpoint of American interests it was worthwhile to contribute to an economic program that would help prevent further deterioration of the National Government. Underwriting a broader battle was something he could not recommend.[32]

The Marshall Plan, talk of NATO, and the Berlin Blockade reduced any likelihood of a larger United States role in China. Stuart and U.S. consuls in Northeast China continually reported Communist gains and Nationalist weakness. Even Stuart's late October plea for a reappraisal of United States policy and greater effort to help China lacked confidence. Lovett cabled Marshall that the Ambassador's message actually confirmed Nationalist inability to fight effectively. Lovett concluded, "There is just no will left in the Nationalist forces to change the situation."

Marshall reiterated that aid to China was never intended to underwrite a military campaign, and that effective resistance to the Communists in China would require the United States to take over the National Government and administer its economic, military, and governmental affairs. "It would be impossible to estimate final costs of a course of action of this magnitude."

A year after Marshall's statement, Nationalist control had dwindled to Taiwan.

The German Problem

S E C R E T A R Y Marshall arrived in London by plane on November 21 for the Conference of the Council of Foreign Ministers that had been tentatively arranged in Moscow in April. This time he had no great hopes and, after the weeks of frustrating sessions of the spring, he did not intend to go through such a routine again. He gave special instructions to John Hickerson, chief of the Office of European Affairs at the State Department, to pay careful attention to developments, and if there appeared absolutely no basis for negotiation, he planned to terminate the meeting. But if there was any evidence of a willingness to reach an agreement, he was prepared to spend all the time needed to achieve one, for he believed that Europe desperately needed peaceful solutions.[1]

Little had occurred in Europe since the April adjournment to encourage him about the Soviet Union's attitude. In accordance with Moscow Conference decisions, representatives of the four occupying powers met in Vienna from May 12 to October 11 to discuss terms of an Austrian treaty. After rehashing the points of the earlier conference, they adjourned without taking any final action. The head of the U.S. delegation, Joseph M. Dodge, reported to Marshall that "the heart of the problem is the matter of the amount and the nature of the Soviet claim on Austria." These claims "were unbearably excessive, far more than was agreed at Potsdam, and far more than a free Austria can afford."[2]

Also in accordance with recommendations at Moscow, a meeting of deputies was held November 6–22 to settle some of the disagreements that had been deferred by the Foreign Ministers in April. Here too little progress had been made before the London Conference began.

Not long before leaving for the session in London, Marshall had

made an effort to hasten the congressional approval of the European Recovery Program legislation, and to clarify the U.S. position
in Germany, with a major speech carried over a national radio
hookup before a meeting organized by the Chicago Council on
Foreign Relations and the Chicago Chamber of Commerce, at the
Palmer House on November 18. Again he declared the importance
of European security to that of the United States:

> The stabilizing influence which Europe as a concert of indepen-
> dent nations exercised on the remainder of the world was a basic
> factor in assuring the security of our own nation—a fact which we
> acknowledged by twice committing our total resources to the preser-
> vation of the integrity of the continental community, free of single-
> power domination.[3]

Two of the three great powers that had helped defeat Hitler
wished to restore the former Europe, while a third seemed willing
to allow chaos to continue. Though Marshall disagreed with such
a reaction, he was careful not to attack that power, for

> . . . we cannot expect the same conceptions to be held by all coun-
> tries. Different races, different traditions, different histories and
> rates of development lead to different results, but on fundamentals
> I think we find a general agreement among peoples the world
> around.

He denied that the United States was trying to thrust Europe into
a role of dependency. Since the war, the United States and Great
Britain had reduced their control throughout the world; meanwhile, the Soviet Union had consistently expanded its frontiers.
The United States was accused of wishing to dump its surplus
goods on Europe. This, he said, must have a strange sound to
"those Europeans now desperately seeking the very essentials of
life."
    As for good will toward the Soviet Union, he repeated what he
had said to Stalin the previous spring, that at the close of the war
the people of the United States had had as high a regard for the
Soviet people and their sacrifices and the Soviet Army and its
leaders as for any people in the world. Since that time, the Soviet
government had proceeded in such a way as to change that feeling.
In recent meetings of the United Nations, there had been a high
degree of vituperation and abuse, but he believed that it was helpful to have a forum for free debate.

At the forthcoming meeting in London, the critical problem would be Germany. He wanted to leave no doubt of the need to prevent a renewal of German militarism and to guard against giving Germany priority over any other part of Europe in economic recovery. But rehabilitation of the German economy was essential to European recovery; the occupying powers owed it to their own people to make Germany productive again, to reduce the direct costs of the occupation on taxpayers. And German stability required the restoration of a measure of self-government and the establishment of peace.

A summer of name-calling had further soured relations with the Soviets. In declining to meet with Western European countries to arrange European Recovery aid from the United States, the Soviet Union had not only accused the United States of bad faith, but had also excoriated the states of Western Europe for selling their souls.

The United States did not intend to watch the disintegration of the international community to which it belonged.

> But at the same time we are aware of our strength, and of the fact that there is great need in many countries for our help and our friendship, we can afford to discount the alarms and excursions intended to distract us, and to proceed with calm determination along the path which our traditions have defined.

Several changes had been made in the U.S. delegation since the spring meeting. Charles Bohlen had succeeded Benjamin Cohen as counselor; Carlisle Humelsine would handle the tasks of General Carter (left behind because of an emergency appendicitis operation). Lieutenant General Geoffrey Keyes, now High Commissioner of Austria, was replacing General Mark Clark. The delegations of the four countries still had the same heads: Marshall, Bevin, Molotov, and Bidault. Ambassador to Russia Smith, General Clay, and Robert Murphy were in their familiar roles, and John Foster Dulles was again on hand to represent the Chairman of the Senate Foreign Relations Committee. Ambassador to Britain Lewis Douglas, with whom Marshall would stay, was an important figure in the negotiations. Marshall had known and liked Douglas during World War II and had strongly recommended him to Truman for the ambassadorship to the United Kingdom when the President's first choice, Max Gardner, suddenly died. Marshall had admired his combination of firmness and smoothness in handling problems as a member of the board that coordinated shipping under Admiral Emory S. Land during the war.

Douglas told his guest how warmly the British were preparing to welcome him. The King wanted Marshall to come to lunch, the Society of Pilgrims hoped to get him for a speech, and Lord Halifax, chancellor of Oxford University, was inviting him to come to All Souls' College in early December to receive an honorary degree. Old friends from the war years were planning lunches and dinners for any free time he would have.

Problems in the London meeting promised to repeat those of the Moscow sessions, but the atmosphere would be distinctly friendlier. Although Marshall had stayed with a valued old friend in Moscow, he had not otherwise been at ease. The constant escort of Russian security guards, even during a walk in the park, stifled him, and he had been sure that the U.S. Embassy was bugged.

On the evening before the opening of the Council of Foreign Ministers, Marshall and Douglas dined with Bevin, Sir Edmund Hall-Patch (Deputy Under Secretary of State for Foreign Affairs), and Defense Minister A. V. Alexander to discuss the problems they expected to meet the next day. Bevin and Marshall stayed after the others had gone, to consider topics, outside the German question, that would dominate the meetings.

The foreign ministers' meeting opened formally at Lancaster House on November 25. A clash arose immediately when Molotov opposed Marshall's proposal to take up the Austrian treaty first. Since the ministers had seemed closer to agreement on that point than on anything else, the American thought that a positive decision would "reassure the people of the world." Molotov held up proceedings until the following day, when he agreed that the Austrian accord be taken up first but asked that it then be referred to their deputies with instructions to report back on December 5.[4]

In making this concession, the Soviet Minister accused the United States and Britain of delaying the German treaty in hopes of imposing an imperialist peace rather than the democratic one sought by the U.S.S.R. Marshall sternly demanded that he drop the propaganda and stick to business: the United States wanted the substance, not a shadow, of a German settlement.

Marshall settled resignedly into the pattern of operation that he had followed at Moscow. The delegation worked at 5 Grosvenor Square, near the U.S. Embassy, looking out on the wintry foliage of a square so well known to Americans stationed in London during the war; a memorial was being built there to Franklin Roosevelt. The Secretary met his advisers at his office each morning to analyze the discussions of the previous day. Briefings were easier than at Moscow, because they were now traveling over familiar ground and positions could be prepared well in advance. General Clay seemed much more in accord with Marshall's policy than at Moscow, and spoke highly of the Secretary during this period. He wrote:

> Marshall was in top form and measured his decisions and moves in the light of the speech which he had made in Chicago to define American policy. It was evident that he enjoyed developing any divergencies in viewpoint within the delegation so that they could be weighed in reaching his decisions. I found these meetings invigorating and helpful. It was interesting to note the technique used by Marshall, who held open staff meetings and listened to conflicting views, as compared to that of Byrnes, who had preferred to discuss special issues with the several experts before making up his mind.[5]

Marshall observed France was still making it difficult to present a solid Western front to the Soviets, so he began early to work on Georges Bidault. Knowing that France's insistence on Allied Control of the Ruhr gave Molotov an opportunity to advance a claim to share control, a move opposed by Britain and the United States, Marshall warned that temporary settlements, which might seem to satisfy the French public, might adversely affect U.S. public opinion on the European Recovery Program. France's insistence on a special regime for control of the Ruhr meant that the question of a Soviet demand for participation in that regime would be put forward.[6]

Bidault knew that opposition groups in the U.S. House of Representatives were proposing cuts in proposed interim aid to France, and he said that the French Communists were using this as an argument for refusing to trust the United States. Still, though such appeals were part and parcel of the current Communist drive for power, Bidault thought that the present French government would be able to handle the situation.

When the council met later that evening, Bevin proposed that a special commission be established to deal with all claims against Germany made by states bordering on that country. Bidault and Marshall agreed, but Molotov killed the proposal. When Bidault announced that the United States and Britain had agreed that the Saar should be economically integrated with France, Molotov made no comment.[7]

This Western cooperation led Molotov to ask if it was true that Bevin planned to establish a three-power government in western Germany. Bevin retorted that he had been trying for months to achieve a democratic government for Germany and that he was being pilloried at home for assuming that Four Power agreement could be reached. The British did not assume in advance that the conference would fail, but they must be expected to take action if the present council took none. Marshall interjected that U.S. backing of German unity was a matter of record and that the American offer of September 1946 to unite the American zone with other zones still held good. Molotov responded by making a motion asking that the meeting go on record against the formation of a government for any zone of Germany.

The London Conference held only seventeen sessions, compared with the forty-three in Moscow, but most of the old disputed issues were trotted out again. Hotly contested was the makeup of permanent committees to draw up provisions for a peace treaty with Germany. Marshall and Bevin insisted that all countries that had had a a crucial part in the war should have a hand in the peace. Molotov and Bidault held that those other than the Big Four should sit in only on those parts of treaties vital to them. Marshall also wanted the conference to include all those countries that had been at war with Germany and states that were neighbors of Germany. Molotov objected that this would mean fifty-five nations, instead of the twenty-five he envisaged. He specifically rejected Marshall's efforts to include China, and spoke disparagingly of including Latin American countries that had declared war on Germany. Marshall reminded him that some of these countries had provided ports and airfields through which supplies had been sent to the Soviet Union.[8]

The chances of an Austrian treaty appeared slight when Molotov charged that the United States had violated Austrian sovereignty in giving economic assistance and had intervened to prevent the Soviet Union from reaching an agreement with Austria. Well aware that the Austrian President feared Soviet intervention, Marshall branded the statement as untrue. He was getting tired of this delay, and held to his initial intention of pushing on to the next item on the agenda.[9]

After ten days of tedious quibbling, Marshall asked if it was possible to accept the British plan presented at Moscow as the basis for the principles of a new German government. Molotov challenged the proposal by stating that, even as Marshall pressed this motion, Mr. Harriman in Washington was calling for a new government in West Germany. The U.S. Secretary denied that there was any basic division in their views and asked if the Soviet Union was determined to delay any political and economic unity for Germany until Germany paid $10 billion in reparations. If that was his idea, how did he expect them to pay it?[10] He and Bevin agreed that if this sum were required, it would have to come out of German production in the British and American zones, and those two countries would ultimately have to pay the bill.

By December 4, sensing that time was running out with no actions taken, Marshall and Bevin had examined measures they might use to salvage anything from the stalemate. Bevin had been considering making some concession on the Austrian treaty, while Marshall thought of listing a number of possible actions and announcing that if the Soviets did not want to go along, the United States would proceed alone. Bevin assured him that in such a case he could rely on the British, who seemed prepared for a breakdown in negotiations. Marshall admitted, "Quite frankly, what would be popular in the United States would be that I should break off and tell the Russians to go to the devil. . . ." But, he reflected, this action would have only a temporary popularity, and later, when its implications were clear, a different view would prevail.[11]

Marshall was still not ready for a final break; even if the two nations ended up having to say they would go it alone, they should make it clear that they were not making a permanent break. They must choose their ground carefully and not let the Russians maneuver them into a position where it could seem that they were breaking up the conference over some inconsequential matter.

In the following session, Molotov piled up old issues, demanding $10 billion in reparations, the abandonment of Bizonia, and the establishment of a central administration. These demands were accompanied by a slashing attack on the European Recovery Program and a charge that the United States was planning to set up a separate government for western Germany. Lord Pakenham, representing an ailing Bevin, termed the statement a "shocking attack on the Western powers which was not conducive to an atmosphere in which agreement could be reached."[12]

President Truman must have concluded at this point that Marshall needed backing from Washington in case he had to make a final break. On December 11, Lovett passed along the President's assurance: "Your firm and constructive actions in London have my complete support. We are all with you. Warm regards. Harry S. Truman."[13]

Although Molotov had dropped some of his more offensive tactics after the attack by Pakenham, Marshall saw more difficult times ahead. He believed that Molotov might be preparing to take advantage of a British-Russian trade agreement, then in the making, which would make it difficult for the British to oppose a proposal

the Soviets might make concerning reparations. Marshall feared
that U.S. actions might be misunderstood both by the British and
the American publics if Molotov could possibly arrange it. He considered the situation so delicate that he asked Lovett to delay for
the moment the return of Ambassador Douglas to Washington to
aid in negotiations there on other questions, so that he would have
his aid with the British if needed.

Molotov resurrected well-known arguments from Moscow on
reparations, zonal control, and the like on December 12. Germany,
he insisted (and some able Western writers have supported his
argument), could pay the $10 billion from current production if the
country was allowed to produce without hindrance. His final blast
was a charge that the United States was trying to make Germany a
strategic base against the democratic states of Europe.

The Western leaders were prepared for this outburst; they all
made sharp rejoinders, and the meeting adjourned for the day.
General Clay, who observed the scene, recalled that Marshall's
advisers were busy passing him suggested replies. "He hardly gave
them a glance as with superb and quiet dignity he told Molotov that
it was evident his charges were designed for another audience and
another purpose, and that such procedures in the Council of Foreign Ministers made it rather difficult to inspire respect for the
dignity of the Soviet Government." As Clay recorded, "This was
the only time I ever saw Molotov wince perceptibly."[14]

In effect, the conference was ended, but there were a few final
scenes on Monday. In what the Westerners regarded as still another propaganda maneuver, Molotov asked that the council hear
delegates to the German People's Congress speak for the German
people on pending proposals. Believing that the delegation was
made up of hand-picked agents of the Soviet Union, the Westerners declined. Bidault and Bevin replied to some of the Russian's
earlier charges; then Marshall summed up the council's progress.
He showed how Molotov had blocked agreement on the Austrian
treaty and made acceptance of the German treaty dependent on
"terms which would enslave the German people and retard European recovery." He proposed that the council adjourn without
discussing the remaining items on the agenda, "since no real progress could be made because of Soviet obstructionism."[15]

Molotov attempted a rejoinder: he denied responsibility for the
impasse and charged Marshall with seeking an adjournment so that
the United States could have a free hand in Germany.

On that shrill note, the council adjourned, after referring the

Austrian treaty to the deputies for further study. No date was set for another meeting. Marshall and Bevin hoped that the next conference could be held in a better atmosphere; they did not voice their feeling that another meeting would not be held.[16]

At 6:00 P.M. on December 17, Marshall went to the Foreign Office to make a farewell call on Bevin. The Foreign Secretary appeared to be in a deep study. His advisers, such as Gladwyn Jebb, had been looking for possible answers to the questions Bevin had put to Marshall: What comes next? Where is the power to rest? Bevin thought that there now must be a Western democratic system, including the United States, Britain, France, Italy, and the British dominions. This would not be a formal alliance but "an understanding backed by power, money and resolute action." In a suggestive phrase, he added, "It would be a sort of spiritual federation of the West." He preferred that the understanding be informal but thought that if the consolidation of the Western powers could be achieved, the Soviet Union would see that it could go no further.[17]

The concept was not new. First Churchill, then the Labour government, had favored the idea of a Western community. In the United States, Clarence Streit had enlarged his wartime proposal of a Western union for defensive purposes. But Bevin raised the issue with Marshall at a crucial moment. Just as the American's perception of Soviet policy at the Moscow Conference had led him to the Marshall Plan, so did the Soviet performance in London impel him toward undertaking new American responsibilities in Europe.

Bevin was groping for the spirit that would spark the North Atlantic Treaty Organization. The result would not be so informal and unstructured as he suggested, but it followed his idea of a Western agreement to halt the advance of the Soviet Union toward the West. The British Foreign Secretary wanted the whole problem of Germany to be fully examined by the Western powers. In a consideration of the future political organization of Germany, the aim should be a united Germany. Bevin noted talk of a three-power treaty that was like the Four Power Pact sought by Byrnes. Now, he believed, the Benelux countries and Italy should be included. "The essential task was to create confidence in Western Europe that further communist inroads would be stopped. The issue must be defined and clear."

In this bold outlining of future steps, Bevin displayed an optimism that followed the powerful Trade Union Congress's recent endorsement of his foreign policy and pledge of support to the Marshall Plan; the congress had also "decided to oppose the communists resolutely if they attempted to start any trouble here."

Marshall believed that they must distinguish between the material and spiritual aspects of their programs. As he had said at the Society of Pilgrims dinner on December 13, he thought that if the powers concerned acted sensibly, "material regeneration should be the outcome of the European Recovery Program, the purpose of which was the rehabilitation of the European patient." But, in his opinion, what "was already being done on the material plane should now be given greater dignity." He agreed with Bevin that there did not have to be a written agreement, but there should be a clear understanding. "Indeed, there was no choice in the matter. They had to reach such an understanding. They must take events at the flood stream and produce a coordinated effort."

On the 18th, Bevin and Marshall met at Douglas's residence with the Ambassador, Robertson, Clay, Murphy, and Frank Roberts to discuss Germany. Marshall drew from Clay an outline of ways to deal with occupied Germany. Clay spoke first of proposed currency reforms, which he still wanted handled on a quadripartite basis. The Secretary agreed and said that Clay should make clear to the Soviets that we wanted their agreement and were not expecting to be turned down. He was anxious to "avoid 'a frozen front,' which was tragic to contemplate."[18]

A working political organization for West Germany was next examined. Clay proposed expanding the existing Economic Council, looking eventually "to the creation of an elected German government," at least in the British-American zones. Marshall believed that any arrangement agreed on by Clay and Robertson would be acceptable in London and Washington. It would make clear to the Soviets that at last they were up against a solid front. He hoped that the Russians would not be misled by "any wishy-washy" press articles in Britain or the United States.

Clay next focused on the continued presence of the Allies in Berlin. Despite the difficulties, he thought they should hold on as long as possible. If the task became too difficult, he and Robertson would so report to their government, but not until that became necessary. Foreseeing a possible Soviet challenge, Marshall asked about the Allied capacity to hold out. Clay replied confidently that they had "adequate resources on which to live in Berlin for some time." He did not foresee the serious nature of a future Soviet challenge. He still hoped that quadripartite action could be strengthened. There was to be no "unseemly haste" in working out plans for a political showdown in Bizonia and no attempt to force French participation in a trizonal agreement—the initiative was to come from the French.

Left unsettled was the matter of reparations. Bevin still clung to the belief that the Allies should deliver to the Soviets the "share of dismantled industrial equipment to which the Soviet Union would be entitled under the Postdam Protocol." Marshall did not argue the question but insisted that it be submitted to the President and Cabinet. Clay recalled his earlier proposal that, although dismantlings and allocations should be allowed to continue, the Soviet share should be placed in escrow "pending the development of the general situation in Germany."

The London meeting of the Council of Foreign Ministers proved a greater failure than the Moscow Conference, illuminating clearly the division of East and West that the Moscow meeting had foreshadowed. Before the American delegates left for home, they discussed with the British united action in Germany.

Marshall flew home from Northolt Airport at 4:00 P.M. on December 18 and arrived in Washington the following morning. After a brief stop in the capital, he went to Pinehurst to spend the holidays with Mrs. Marshall.

Not long after his return to his State Department office in the new year, Marshall was pleased to hear from Bevin that the British Cabinet wished to go ahead rapidly with "a stable, peaceful, and democratic Germany and to avoid the creation of a situation which could eventuate in the emergence of a Communist controlled Germany." Marshall agreed the trend should be in the direction of a West German government that "would be responsive to popular will," and that would perform clearly defined and limited government functions, although it should not be constituted as a government for West Germany. There should be an evolutionary development dependent on "which action is taken in the Soviet zone."

Marshall referred to the political principles presented by the Western Allies at Moscow. Within the requirement of security and the extension of the bizonal area to include the French, "emphasis should be given to the need of affording the Germans greater initiative and freedom of action commensurate with the extent of the responsibility which they are to assume, particularly in connection with food production, collection and distribution."[19]

Meanwhile, in Berlin, the British and American zonal commanders had begun to consider their late-December instructions. On

January 6, they went to Frankfurt, where they discussed measures for strengthening and extending bizonal organization. Caught by surprise at these moves, the French strongly protested to London and Washington. Bidault came back from a vacation on the Riviera dismayed by angry blasts from his political opponents. He implored Caffery to "endeavor to persuade your people to make it a little easier for us. What happened at Frankfurt is being exploited in such a fashion here as to make my position well-nigh impossible; and you know that I have burned my bridges behind me."[20]

Despite explanations made later, there is little doubt that General Clay, goaded by what he considered French intransigence, had plunged ahead. The associate chief of the Division of Western European Affairs, Woodruff Wallner, summed it up: "The British and ourselves have a different conception of how far and how quickly and with how little communication Clay and Robertson should proceed in bizonal reconstruction." However, both Washington and London were equally surprised at the scope of the Frankfurt decisions and the dramatic manner of their presentation to the world.[21]

Clay's habit of energetic action with more regard for military dispatch than diplomatic niceties had caused mutterings before. He had fared better with Secretary Byrnes than he did with Marshall, who was accustomed to granting his colleagues independence in military matters but not in those having political consequences.

Marshall assured the French that there was no intention at the moment of setting up a West German state, that Clay had been instructed to give them details, and that in any Anglo-American fusion in West Germany, the French would be welcome to participate. Bidault remained uneasy, however, troubled by rumors that representatives of the United States and Britain were holding secret meetings in Washington. These preliminary talks about some form of Western alliance had been held without the French because of the fear that there might be serious opposition in Paris. Marshall again spoke soothingly. The British had recently proposed a meeting to discuss mutual problems in Germany, but Marshall had insisted it be preceded by a meeting of the British and the French. He also downgraded newspaper trial balloons: "If I were affected by every press report it would be impossible for me to fight the very real battle which I was putting up. M. Bidault must realize the importance of this battle not only to France but to all of us. I must expect that he will help us."[22]

Seeking to force revelations of what was afoot in the Washington talks, the French Foreign Office asked why the United States was no longer pushing the Four Power Pact. State Department representatives hinted that something else was being considered: "The whole question of Western European security should be dealt with primarily by European initiative and . . . our representatives at the [forthcoming] London talks would be open-minded." In fact, two days before, Secretary Marshall had told President Truman that the Four Power Pact was "unworkable in the absence of four-power agreement and does not provide a basis for tripartite discussion. Although we maintain an active interest in the subject we do not contemplate further specific proposals at this time."[23] The United States and Britain were headed toward a Western union and NATO.

Privately, Marshall made clear to the U.S. ambassadors in London and Paris that the "French pre-occupation with Germany as major threat at this time seems to us outmoded and unrealistic." Germany had been disarmed and demilitarized. The Soviet Union was now reshaping eastern Germany into a totalitarian pattern with an economy that fitted into an Eastern European mold.

> Unless Western Germany during the coming year is effectively associated with Western European nations, first through economic arrangements, and ultimately perhaps in some political way there is a real danger that the whole of Germany will be drawn into Eastern orbit, with all obvious consequences that such an eventuality would entail.
>
> Solution of German problem, at least in so far as Western Germany is concerned, has a two-fold aspect:
>
> (a) economic and political reorientation of Germans, fostered by common policies of Western occupation powers; and
>
> (b) integration of Western Germany into Western European community.[24]

The United States and Britain had not given up on the eventual unity of Germany, but they were opposed to the establishment of unity under conditions that meant Soviet domination of all Germany. Though they did not rule out the chance of an agreement with the Soviet Union on this point in the future, they considered the possibility remote for the time being.

Such was the uncertain situation when the first part of the London Tripartite Conference met, February 23 to March 6. Organized at the ambassadorial level to seek Western agreement on unsettled questions left by the recent London Conference, Britain, France, and the United States were joined by representatives of the Benelux countries. Ambassador Douglas, General Clay, Ambassador Murphy, and Assistant Secretary of State Charles Saltzman represented the United States; Maurice Couve de Murville of the French Foreign Ministry and René Massigli, French Ambassador to London, sat in for France; and Sir William Strang, General Robertson, and Sir Edmund Hall-Patch, Deputy Under-Secretary of State, headed the group for Great Britain. The Benelux countries asked that hereafter they be represented in all conferences dealing with German questions. Marshall suggested that Italy be invited to present its views on economic questions.[25]

As the meeting opened, Bevin objected to stopping deliveries to the Soviets of resources from the Western zones. Earlier agreements had promised the Soviet Union a share of dismantled plants and other resources in the Western occupation areas, but, during the argument over economic arrangements, Clay and Robertson had stopped dismantlings and deliveries. The British repeated Bevin's earlier argument that deliveries of reparations had been promised at Potsdam and should be carried out regardless of Soviet violations of other agreements. Ambassador Douglas reported to Marshall that he believed Bevin's mind could be changed, however, since he had remarked that afternoon that he had never seen the House of Commons so "violently anti-Soviet."[26]

Douglas was proved wrong: Bevin dug in. Some of the British Cabinet believed that a question of good faith was involved and that it was unwise to goad the Soviets too far. Douglas, usually friendly to the British, warned Bevin that the Congress might impose drastic limitations on appropriations for the European Recovery Program if the deliveries were made. Bevin showed what was worrying him by asking whether, if the deliveries were not made, the Soviets would disrupt quadripartite control or would undertake "to drive us out." With unusual assurance, Douglas said that he doubted that the Russians would move, since that would be a hostile act. He thought that the Western powers should not be overly apprehensive about Soviet action. But Bevin held firm. Betraying no sign of being intimidated by reference to the stopping of aid, he hoped that his country "would not have to operate under a threat affecting the European Recovery Program and believed that this would react badly against the United States." Douglas recognized his earlier error. He sensed the growing anxiety of the British and the French and reported that he did not think he could influence Bevin to change his mind before he himself returned to Washington that Saturday.[27]

Finding that the question of security against the Germans ran through the fears of several of the countries, Douglas talked with Strang and Massigli on March 5, and later with these two and the Dutch representative, to indicate that the United States was prepared to provide for consultation in case of a German threat and would also consider setting up a military-security board as an adjunct to a military government. He also reflected developments at home by saying that it was unlikely that U.S. forces would be withdrawn from Europe until "the threat from the east had disappeared."[28]

The London Tripartite Conference recessed on March 6 with the idea of meeting again in April. Its communiqué held no surprises. Failure to get Four Power agreement in the council meeting forced the three powers to ensure the economic reconstruction of Western Europe and to arrange a basis on which the Germans could participate in the community of free peoples. The delegates had examined Germany's relationship to the European Recovery Program and concluded that a close association of the economic life of West Germany with Western Europe was essential to the economic and political well-being of all. Acceptance of the division of Germany was being more thoroughly nailed down.[29]

The delegates agreed that the resources of the Ruhr must never again be used to aid aggression and their access to these resources must be increased for extensive parts of Europe, including Germany. A federal form of government, adequately protecting the rights of the several states, was hailed as the best form for the restoration of German unity.[30]

For the next three weeks, the French, British, and U.S. military governors discussed questions relating to the greater fusion of their interests. Clay and Murphy wanted a provisional government or administration before the adoption of a constitution, while French Governor Pierre Koenig pressed for a constituent assembly first, fearing that the U.S. proposal would bring a Soviet propaganda attack. He was willing to consider the calling of a constituent assembly in the fall, and if such an assembly adopted a constitution that the three powers could approve, it might be possible to establish a West German government in 1949. Clay and Robertson urged greater speed. Robertson feared that the hammer and sickle might end up on the Rhine and Clay warned that delay might lose the support of 45 million Germans.[31]

Marshal Vasily D. Sokolovsky's walk out of the Allied Control Council during this period led the French to take a second look. Couve de Murville, of the Foreign Office, then vacationing on the Riviera, told Clay he would like to discuss the current situation.

Flown to Berlin in Clay's plane, the Frenchman said he had concluded that war might come with the Soviet Union in the next two
or three years or even in 1948. The French were prepared to
advance the date for a constituent assembly. Relieved, Clay said he
was willing to postpone the establishment of a provisional government if the French would agree to a constituent-assembly meeting
by September 1.[32]

With this meeting of minds, attention turned back to the London
Tripartite Conference, which resumed on April 20 and continued
until June 1. Remaining to be settled were the questions of control
of the Ruhr, the deliveries of reparations, and the French acceptance of the conclusions.

It seemed at first that a subsidiary quarrel would have to be
settled between the State Department and Douglas on the one
hand and Clay and Murphy on the other. Douglas kept referring to
Marshall's Chicago speech with its declaration that the resources of
the Ruhr should not be left under the exclusive control of any
future German government and should be used for the European
community as a whole. Determined to protect the interests of Germany and his own authority, Clay apparently saw a danger in Douglas's statements. His strong reactions led the Ambassador to ask
Washington if the government intended to follow Marshall's pronouncement. Apparently nettled by the positions taken by Clay and
Murphy, Marshall declared that the principle enunciated in Chicago "has never been challenged by any responsible authority here
and has served as the basis of all discussions I have had on the
subject of the Ruhr."[33]

Douglas asked for State Department intervention when Clay and
Murphy objected to a proposal for an international authority to
make allocations for coke, coal, and steel in accordance with the
OEEC program. Clay feared that control would pass from the governors to the Administrator for the Ruhr. Douglas argued that the
United States was merely being asked to do the same as the other
countries, which feared that Clay's demands would allow the Soviets to claim that the United States was dominating the Ruhr. Clay
"was violently opposed, particularly in regard to the OEEC," and
said he was advising the Department of the Army of his position.[34]

Secretary of the Army Kenneth Royall now took up the cudgels
for Clay, opposing putting control of the German economy under
the OEEC, subject to some degree to the approval of the ECA
Administrator. He suggested that Congress had been assured that
Clay would have the predominant voice in the control of German

foreign trade, and that any shifting of the control would meet with congressional disapproval.[35]

Lovett, acting for Marshall, was not upset by the reference to Congress. He said that arrangements in Germany should be coordinated with the recovery administration and noted that the government's position with respect to Germany must be understood in relation "to the subsequent and overriding policy of the President and Congress as expressed in the Economic Cooperation Act which covers the European economic problem as a whole."

Douglas worked more closely with Clay on reparations than on the control of the Ruhr. Although he still doubted that Bevin would budge on deliveries to the Soviet Union, Douglas had tackled him again on May 1. He argued that, since the Soviets had walked out of the Allied Control Council, their share of the reparations should be put on ice. The French, who had feared that their deliveries might be held up, agreed, and Clay added that deliveries to the Russians should be made only after they met all other conditions.[36]

After a week of talks, the British accepted a suggestion similar to one made earlier by the Americans. Seventy-five percent of the reparations would be delivered to countries sharing in reparations. Of the 25 percent being allotted to the Soviet Union, 15 percent would be exchanged for commodities and the other 10 percent held up until other conditions were met. Though Douglas accepted this, he doubted that the Soviets would agree.

With this problem at least temporarily out of the way, the next issue was the settlement of French uncertainties on the proposed constituent assembly. Apparently feeling that the United States was in no position to give vital aid in case of a showdown, the French wanted to delay provocative action. Marshall said that he sympathized with the French position but thought that their recent actions had "some appearance of a last-minute pressure campaign." Douglas and Strang argued that weakening on this point would be considered by the Soviets as a sign of weakness and would be damaging to German morale. The American delegation recommended that, if the French held to their position, Britain and the United States should go ahead with bizonal arrangements and leave security matters until France clarified her position. Marshall and Lovett accepted the recommended proposal. Marshall, of course, was influenced by his current cooperation with Bevin in studying the whole question of Western European security. In asking the French to cooperate, he emphasized that the United States intended to strengthen free nations in their resistance of aggression.[37]

Bidault was desperately unhappy. He told Ambassador Caffery that he wanted to go along with his allies, but pleaded that they not "make it too hard on me." His opponents would ask, he said, what the United States would do if the Soviets took aggressive action in Berlin. "In the long run if war comes, the victory on your side is certain but what will happen to us in the meantime." Three days later, he seemed to feel a little better; he said to Caffery, "Tell your Government I am on your side and in the long run I am sure we will work something satisfactory out, but at the same time I must think about our public opinion here." Marshall had not liked the haughtiness of General de Gaulle, but at times he must have longed for a firmer hand in France. Learning that the French Assembly's Foreign Relations Committee was about to have a debate on matters being decided in London, he warned that nothing was more likely to destroy the work of the London Conference. He wanted to send a strong official statement, but Caffery persuaded him to allow a more personal approach.[38] Ambassador Murphy pressed Washington for congressional approval of the London agreements before the French began their debates.

Douglas reported Bevin's promise to make strong representations to Paris. More hand-holding was necessary; from Paris, Caffery cabled that Bidault's nervousness increased as a showdown approached in the French Assembly. What would happen if the Russians tried to force the Allies out of Berlin? Would the Americans drop the bomb, or would they act speedily enough? "It would be easy for the Russian armies to overrun France and we shudder to think of what would happen to our beautiful country. We are defenseless, as you well know."[39]

Marshall suggested that Caffery speak to some of de Gaulle's advisers concerning the importance of approving the London agreements. He followed with a personal message to Bidault:

My Government has now decided to give definitive approval to the London agreements on Germany. . . . Unity of purpose and action shown at London by the three governments and Benelux also marks a further important step in our efforts to enhance our joint security against any aggressor. . . .[40]

In Brussels, U.S. Ambassador Alan Kirk was asked to appeal to Belgian Foreign Minister Paul-Henri Spaak to intervene with Bidault and see if he could get a socialist political leader to speak with

Léon Blum, former socialist Premier. When the French Council of
Ministers agreed on June 9 to submit the agreements for debate,
Caffery reported that there was strong Cabinet opposition, one
member angling for Bidault's job in case he fell from office, others
insisting that East and West Germany not be divided. Outside the
Assembly, de Gaulle made it clear he would not approve the Anglo-
American proposal. Marshall authorized our Ambassador to say it
was possible that modifications could be made later in some of the
agreements. Meanwhile, the other powers were ready to act. To
avoid any suggestions of pressure on Britain, Marshall waited for
Bevin to announce Britain's acceptance in the House of Commons.
When the Benelux countries followed shortly afterward, Marshall
proclaimed that the United States also approved.[41]

Marshall's actions and the intervention of Britain and Belgium
apparently decided the fight in the French Assembly. In a wild
session that saw both Communist and Gaullist motions to delay or
reject the recommendations, the Foreign Affairs Committee, by a
21–20 vote, submitted the agreements to the full Assembly. Once
the Communists and Gaullists had united, uncertain socialist members came to the support of the London Tripartite agreements.
Still, there was no reason for special celebration, because strong
reservations had been added and the French Government was
urged to impose a veto on any actions that went contrary to the
principles they set forth. Final French approval awaited the vote of
the full Assembly.[42]

At issue in France was the support of some of the Conservatives.
Caffery learned from Joseph Laniel and Paul Reynaud that there
was considerable opposition to the agreement among their supporters. Reynaud suggested that it might help if Washington made
clear to French leaders that, unless Paris agreed, the United States
would go along with Britain without the aid of France. He added
that overseas press criticism of de Gaulle might be of assistance.
Apparently on the assumption that Marshall's earlier statements
concerning American determination to go through with the agreements were sufficient, the Americans decided not to follow this
advice. Marshall was more worried about the proposed instruction
to the government to veto certain actions. This was defended as an
effort to calm some of the French Socialists, who insisted that the
quadripartite arrangement be continued. Douglas and Strang replied to Jean Chauvel of the French Foreign Office that he could
recall British and American efforts at the London Conference to
bring in the Soviets and indicate that both Marshall and Bevin were
still willing for them to join with the Westen powers.[43]

Having failed to effect any weakening on the recommendations, Chauvel asked what would happen if the French rejected them. Douglas and Strang replied that they would try to put the recommendations in effect on a bizonal basis, but that they did not know what could be done about French wishes on the Ruhr or the matter of French security. Apparently accepting this as the last word that he could report back to his government, Chauvel said it should dispel rumors that the United States and Britain might be willing to reopen negotiations, accept amendments of the Ruhr management, or postpone application of the plans.[44]

Firmness paid off. On June 17, the French Assembly approved an order of the day accepting the recommendations. The language of the final resolution was less restrictive than the earlier one, and the request for a veto was dropped. Caffery jubilantly reported to Marshall that the French government had done well and "shown real courage."[45]

The Western Allies had proclaimed a united stand. The question now was, how would the fourth power react?

XVIII

The Berlin Crisis

G EORGE Kennan had warned Marshall in November 1947, in a paper that Marshall had summarized for the President and the Cabinet, that once the European Recovery Program began to work, the Soviets would react in Central Europe. Their purpose would be not to make war but to stop any move of their satellites toward independent action. He had suggested that Czechoslovakia would be the first victim, but it soon appeared that Berlin would be the center of Soviet attention. Rumors of a move toward a West German government and tripartite meetings, along with proposed currency reforms and, perhaps, a trizonal economic accord, had been accompanied since January 1948 by fulminations of the military governor of the Russian zone of Germany, and by calculated insults by the commandant of Berlin's Russian zone.[1]

In late February, Sir William Strang, Permanent Undersecretary of Foreign Affairs, bluntly warned Foreign Secretary Bevin to prepare for trouble in Berlin. While urging that British troops remain in that city, he also pointed out that the Russians had the power to force the Allies out and to put intolerable pressure on the Berliners. Probable clashes would occur in April, when new currency was issued in Bizonia, and in the fall, when proposed elections were held in the Western zones. The Soviets might then withdraw from the Allied Control Council or demand that the Western Allies justify their continued stay in the city.[2]

The first ominous moves came, as Kennan had predicted, in Prague. Red Army forces had occupied Prague in the closing days of the war and had kept Allied representatives out of the area for a long period. In 1946, a coalition government had been formed in which the Communists were the strongest faction. Klement Gottwald, a Communist, became Prime Minister, and a Communist became Minister of the Interior, with control over the police. Jan Masaryk, son of the founder of the Czechoslovakian Republic, was Foreign Minister. He and twelve other Cabinet members were non-Communists. By February 1946, the Minister of the Interior was strengthening Communist membership in the police force and Gottwald insisted on greater control of the government. The twelve non-Communist members of the Cabinet resigned, apparently in the belief that their action would permit President Beneš to appoint a government more to his liking. Instead Gottwald persuaded the ailing Beneš to allow him to take control of the government, leaving Masaryk as the only non-Communist member with any power. Although this shift seemingly came from Czechoslovakian Communist pressure within the country, the hand of Moscow was apparent.

The unsettling effect of this February 25 action on Germans and other neighbors of the Soviet Union apparently was in the mind of General Clay when he wrote the chief of U.S. Army intelligence on March 5 or 6 that, whereas in the past he had not believed in the possibility of imminent action by Moscow, of late he had the feeling that action might come with "dramatic suddenness." (Historians still debate whether Clay had sudden insights or whether he was trying to accommodate an Army friend with a war scare to influence Congress in favor of larger army appropriations.)[3]

Throughout the early weeks of 1948, Clay made clear that the American forces would not be driven out of Berlin. The late February events in Czechoslovakia led General Robertson to report that the action in Prague reminded Germans of Hitler's moves against Czechoslovakia, which preceded the outbreak of World War II. Robertson advised a firm stand by the Allies. Ambassador Murphy told Marshall that the growing attacks on the Western representatives by Russian generals in Berlin followed an old Soviet pattern in which they accused opponents of actions they themselves were preparing to take.[4]

On March 10, the body of Jan Masaryk was found on the ground outside the window of his apartment in the Czechoslovakian Foreign Office. It was unclear whether he had been killed by the Communists or had committed suicide in despair over recent developments.

Reaction to the news from Berlin had influenced the efforts of Clark Clifford and George Elsey, White House staff members who were working on a Saint Patrick's Day address for Truman to give in New York City. On March 6, Clifford had come back from Key West, where he had talked to the President about a speech he should make to Congress on foreign policy. Elsey agreed and jotted down succinctly why such a talk was necessary: "Pres. *must* for his prestige, come up with strong foreign speech—to demonstrate his *leadership*—which country needs and wants. Pres's prestige in foreign matters now low (Palestine, China—Vandenberg and Marshall getting all credit on Marshall Plan)." Elsey suggested stressing relations with Russia. The decision was made that the President should make a speech to Congress on March 17, before giving the New York address.[5]

The White House had already sent word to MacArthur and Clay to review their plans for emergency action. In a meeting with Secretary of Defense Forrestal at Key West, the Joint Chiefs of Staff called for a revival of the draft and an increase in defense appropriations. Truman and his advisers were already working in that direction.

In his recent speeches urging passage of the European Recovery Program legislation, Marshall had called attention to Communist actions in Czechoslovakia, but at the same time he had controlled his rhetoric. He was shocked when he saw a draft of the speech prepared for Truman. Over the weekend he tried his hand. When he returned to Washington from Pinehurst, he sent the draft and his comments by way of Bohlen to a conference with Clifford and Elsey on March 15. Bohlen quoted Marshall as terming the language "too tough." What was needed was businesslike language, no ringing phrases, nothing warlike or belligerent. Clifford rejoined that the statement had to be blunt to justify the message. At another staff meeting, Elsey recorded that all present thought Marshall's draft "stank." These views were passed on to the President, who thought the Secretary was scared by the language of the earlier draft. He seldom treated Marshall's advice lightly, but on the 16th he commented to his staff that, though Marshall feared that the President would "pull the trigger," the President still had to warn the Congress and the people. On March 17, he told Congress that the United States must make its position clear. He asked for reenactment of the Selective Service Act, passage of legislation for Universal Military Training, and a rapid approval of funds for the European Recovery Program. At the dinner that evening in New York, he repeated his firm stand against the Soviets and attacked former Secretary of Commerce Henry Wallace, now a potential presidential candidate on the Progressive ticket, for defending Communist action in Czechoslovakia.

Without full access to Soviet military and diplomatic files, it is not possible to say whether American statements accelerated or merely accompanied the quick reaction in Berlin. When the military governors of the four occupation zones assembled for their regular meeting of the Allied Control Council on March 20, Marshal Sokolovsky, the Russian member, who was presiding that day, demanded a full report on the Tripartite Conference and asked the other military governors what directive they had received. Clay and Robertson, who had been told only to report to their governments what course they proposed to follow, replied that they had received no directives.[6]

As if their answer were the evasion he had expected, Sokolovsky read a formal statement to the effect that the Western powers were breaking the Four Power arrangement and the Allied Control Council no longer existed as an organ of government. Declaring the meeting adjourned, he and the other Soviet representatives marched out, leaving the Western representatives to condemn their withdrawal.

Further Soviet action came rapidly. On March 30, Lieutenant General M. I. Dratvin, Soviet deputy military governor, announced to his U.S. counterpart that, as of April 1, restrictions would be imposed on military rail and highway traffic from the West through the Soviet zone, which lay between West Germany and the Allied sectors of Berlin.

Murphy advised Marshall to be prepared for a Soviet demand that the Western Allies leave Berlin. If they did not withdraw, the Soviets might take "further action toward splitting the city, bearing down on non-Communist political parties in the Soviet sector, and the like." Recent Russian growls about the entry of "western bandits into Berlin" hinted at what might come. The Soviets knew that if they could force Allied withdrawal from the former capital, the psychological impact on the Berliners would be severe.[7]

In Washington and Western European capitals, searches were made for copies of agreements guaranteeing the Western powers access to Berlin. No such formal accords existed, but the agreement to form an Allied Council in Berlin and the establishment of four sectors within the city seemed to be sufficient base for right of entry.

Although Marshall and Bevin had discussed plans for handling German problems with the American and British military governors at London in late December, Clay's immediate bosses in Washington were Secretary of the Army Kenneth Royall and Army Chief of Staff Omar N. Bradley. Clay was charged with managing the military government in the American occupation zone, and it was to Army officials in Washington that he turned for directives and support. Murphy—his political adviser, with the rank of ambassador—kept the State Department abreast of Clay's actions and Clay aware of Marshall's reactions. As soon as the Russians announced their proposals, Clay arranged for trans-Atlantic conversations with Army officials at the Pentagon. He reported that he had issued orders for train commandants to furnish Russian guards with lists of passengers and manifests of freight on military trains. Highway traffic would be subject to the identification of passengers and freight. Train commandants were not to permit Soviet soldiers to enter cars but were not to shoot unless fired upon. Although Clay proposed that he be permitted to double the guards on trains, this request was disallowed and he was cautioned against militant reaction.

Marshall, who had landed at Bogotá on March 29 for the Ninth International Conference of American States, was immediately alerted to these actions by Acting Secretary of State Lovett. There was no immediate crisis, and Clay believed he could hold out indefinitely. He opposed the evacuation of dependents (some 3,000) or the offer of compromise proposals.[8] Aware that Lovett would keep a careful eye on developments and share his views on avoiding war, the Secretary of State took little direct part in the unfolding crisis in Berlin until after his return to Washington on April 24.

When U.S. troops refused to allow Soviet guards to enter U.S. military passenger trains, the Soviet authorities stopped military highway traffic toward Berlin; they did, however, permit civilian trains loaded with supplies to go through for a while. Clay continued to urge stronger American action to test Soviet intentions.

Once military action in the U.S. zone threatened to involve all of the occupying powers, diplomatic discussions became increasingly important. Clay and Murphy met with Strang and Douglas in London on April 27. Ambassador Douglas reported to Marshall, now back in Washington, that the British would fight if the Russians committed an act of war but were not prepared to "take the categorical position that under all circumstances and in all events they will fight to maintain a position in Berlin." To underscore the State Department's firm backing of Clay's actions, Marshall and Lovett stated publicly on April 30, "We intend to stay in Berlin and will meet force with force."[9]

Perhaps the announcement gave some assurance to the Germans; it did not appear to affect the Russians. In May, they tightened restrictions on military passengers and freight. June found increasing stoppages of civilian freight trains on the basis of technical details. Finally, on June 24, all rail and highway traffic between the West and Berlin was terminated.[10]

The Russians seemed to be bent on revenge for the U.S. and British announcement that they were introducing a new deutschmark in their zones on June 24—an action much discussed for nearly two years, since it had become clear that a new currency designed to deal with inflation, the black market, and loss of confidence in the old reichsmark required a new German mark backed by effective economic control. The Allied Control Council proposed the issuance of the new currency through the quadripartite machinery in Berlin, but the economic question was caught up in the growing issue of who controlled that city. By the spring of 1948, Clay and Robertson had made it clear that, unless they had a share in the financial control machinery, they would issue their own deutschmark in Bizonia, or, if France agreed, in the three zones. The Soviets countered with a plan to issue their own currency, the ostmark, which, they disclosed, would be the only one accepted in Berlin, and began issuing their currency on June 23. The Western powers followed with theirs the next day. Sokolovsky insisted that the closing of access to Berlin from the West was necessary to prevent the circulation in Berlin of a currency the Russians did not accept.

The imposition of the full blockade faced the Westerners with the problem of feeding and supplying 2,500,000 Germans in their sectors of Berlin from the reserve supplies in the city and what could be brought in by air. General Clay estimated that there was food for thirty-six days and coal for forty-five. He asked that plans be made to air-lift daily 4,000 tons for Germans and 500 tons for Allied forces. But this tonnage would not sustain a civilian economy, and, when winter came, it would not supply heat and light.[11]

During the earlier, partial interruptions of rail and highway traffic, Clay had used an air lift to supply his forces. He had available from Headquarters, U.S. Air Forces, Europe, 100 C-47s (the two-engine transport planes of World War II, which could carry two and a half tons). The British could furnish a much smaller number of planes, and the French had none. Clay now asked the U.S. Air Commanding General in Germany, Lieutenant General Curtis LeMay, for all available planes. The first planeload of supplies arrived in Berlin on June 25. These and the large C-54s made available later would steadily increase supplies to Berlin until September, 1949.

General Robertson decided that perhaps an agreement to accept

the ostmark for use in all of Berlin would end the crisis, and proposed that the Western commanders approach Sokolovsky. The
French representative, Lieutenant General Roger Noiret, agreed,
and Clay accepted reluctantly. When the three visited Sokolovsky's
headquarters near Potsdam on July 3, the Soviet commander raised
the price. He would end the blockade only when the Western
powers gave up the plan for a West German government.[12]

Officials in Bizonia, London, and Washington were not surprised. Although currency reform had triggered the first action, the
Soviet authorities became more concerned about preparations for
a constitutional convention in the Western zones. The reply to
Sokolovsky from the State Department was that if the blockade
continued, the Western powers would bring that issue before the
United Nations. The British and French were more conciliatory,
preferring to continue negotiations while the airlift went on, day
after day, with its dramatic and tremendously difficult task.

Shortly before the total ground blockade went into effect, Secretary Marshall entered Walter Reed Hospital for a complete physical
checkup. After a series of tests, the doctors found that his right
kidney was twice the size of the other and recommended an operation for removal of a renal tumor. They agreed that surgery could
be deferred because of Marshall's activities. Years later, one of the
senior physicians involved said that he had been convinced that
Marshall thought little of his health in comparison with the critical
problems hanging over Europe. The tests required that he stay
several days at the hospital, but he kept in touch with Berlin developments.[13] Always in tune with Marshall's thinking, Lovett could
speak for his chief in important June meetings.

After the Cabinet meeting on June 25, Defense Secretary Forrestal, Under Secretary of State Lovett, and Secretary of the Army
Royall met with the President to discuss U.S. legal rights to access
to Berlin. Royall reported that no documents had been found but
that Roosevelt supposedly had discussed this matter with Stalin
when quadripartite control of Berlin was discussed early in 1945,
and Eisenhower had supposedly discussed the matter with Russian
officials in the summer of 1945. Lovett remarked that the casual
handling at that time by all those involved had come from their
feeling that the Russians would give no difficulty.[14]

Two days later, top diplomatic and military leaders, with Lovett
representing Marshall, met at the Pentagon to discuss (1) the
effects on the U.S. position in Europe and on Western European
opinion of American withdrawal from Berlin; (2) problems arising
if U.S. forces remained in Berlin; and (3) risks attendant on supply-

ing Berlin by force. They also thrashed out whether to send two
B-29 squadrons to West Germany and the possibility of offering to
base two B-29 groups in Britain. They decided that State and Army
officials must prepare a paper for Clay to use in renewing talks with
the Russian military governor in Berlin on the currency problem.
Clay was to be asked what he thought about sending the B-29
squadrons, and Bevin was to be sounded out on basing these planes
in England.[15]

Forrestal, Royall, and Lovett saw the President the next day.
Lovett outlined the course of the Pentagon meeting. When he
mentioned the question of whether the U.S. forces would remain
in Berlin, Truman said there was no need to discuss the matter:
"We would stay period." After he added that he approved the move
of the bombers to Germany, Lovett casually mentioned that he
assumed the two bomber groups would also go to England.

In a Policy Planning paper submitted on June 23 by Kennan on
factors affecting U.S. defense arrangements and Soviet policy, the
authors argued that, although the Russians still relied on political
means to achieve their ends, they were likewise prepared to use
military intimidation, which could lead to miscalculation on their
part. This was not very probable but had to be considered as a
possibility in American military planning. Implying that the United
States must strengthen its weak military posture, the study pointed
out that Soviet aggressiveness was likely to continue for a long
time, and U.S. preparedness must reflect that.

It is unlikely that Marshall saw this study at the hospital, but
Lovett reported the gist of it to him, as well as a summary of the
Pentagon meetings, and, for the rest of the summer, Marshall followed the study's suggestion of taking a firm stand in Germany that
avoided provocative measures.[16]

The cautious tone of the study contrasted sharply with Kennan's
earlier pronouncements. In his study of the U.S. policy of containment, John Gaddis comments on how the diplomat began to limit
the scope of his original statements. From a firm stand against
Soviet expansion wherever it appeared, Kennan had shifted to a
selection of points at which resistance was reasonable. Kennan
spoke against overextending U.S. capabilities, especially in view of
limited military reserves.[17]

The tempered view can be seen in the words Marshall issued to
the press on June 30:

> We are in Berlin as a result of agreements between the Govern-
> ments on the areas of occupation in Germany, and we intend to stay.

The Soviet attempt to blockade the German civilian population of Berlin raises basic questions of serious import with which we expect to deal promptly.

Meanwhile, maximum use of air transport will be made to supply the civilian population. It has been found, after study, that the tonnage of foodstuffs and supplies that can be lifted by air is greater than had at first been assumed.[18]

On July 2, Marshall attended a crucial Cabinet meeting. He read a copy of the message that the State Department proposed to send Stalin on the right of the United States to be in Berlin, adding that two B-29 bomber squadrons were being sent to Germany and that Bevin had agreed to accept the two proffered bomber groups. Characteristically, he asked Douglas to find out whether Bevin had explored the probable effect of this action on British public opinion, because implications to be drawn from sending the planes to England and their effect on the Russians had to be measured against what might appear as a provocative act to U.S. allies.[19]

Bevin had arranged for a special group of ministers, known as the Berlin Committee of the Cabinet, to be set up to keep abreast of developments in Germany; this group, along with Attlee and Bevin, had approved acceptance of the B-29s, and on July 13 asked the United States for dispatch of the bombers. Two days later, in Washington, the National Security Council proposed that this action be authorized. Marshall and Forrestal reported that they believed this decision would emphasize to the American people the seriousness with which the government saw the problem and would give the Air Force experience in this type of operations; the planes should be sent now, because a delay might occasion a deterioration in the situation, which might force the British to reverse their decision.

The President was in a "chipper" mood. The day before, he had been nominated as the presidential candidate by the Democratic Convention and had made a fighting speech, saying that he had independently come to the same decision about the bombers as his advisers. The sixty B-29s arrived in England on July 17. None of them was capable of carrying the atomic bomb, a fact of which the Soviets may or may not have been aware. Only a few bombers at that time had been converted for carrying the atomic bomb, and none of these was sent to Britain.

On July 19, Marshall and Forrestal met again with the President to discuss Berlin. The Secretary of State thought that the United States had the option of staying in Berlin or seeing the failure of their European policy. So far, their policy had been successful. The

Soviets had suffered a recent reversal in Finland, and Marshal Tito's show of independence in Yugoslavia worried the Russians. The less confident Forrestal pointed out that, in case of Soviet aggression, the United States had a reserve of only two and one-third divisions, only one of which could be committed with any speed. A buildup in Army forces could not come until next year. Marshall replied that they were better off than in 1940 and could encourage France and Britain by making token shipments of weapons. The President decided that they would remain in Berlin until they exhausted diplomatic means to get a solution.

Marshall's diplomatic efforts with the Russians had started on July 6 with a message reminding the Soviet Ambassador that, when the United States withdrew in the late spring of 1945 from areas assigned to the Soviet Union in Germany, freedom of access to Berlin had been understood. The right of access for the United States was the same as for the Soviet Union. He added:

> The United States categorically asserts that it is in occupation of its sector of Berlin with free access thereto as a matter of established right deriving from the defeat and surrender of Germany and confirmed by formal agreements among the principal Allies. It further declares that it will not be induced by threats, pressures or other actions to abandon these rights. It is hoped that the Soviet Government entertains no doubts whatever on this point.[20]

The Secretary added that the three Western powers were responsible for the well-being of some 2 million Germans in their sectors of Berlin and it was intolerable that any nation place their welfare in jeopardy by a blockade of Berlin. The Western powers had indicated their willingness to negotiate any differences concerning the governing of Berlin. "It is, however," Marshall concluded, "a prerequisite that the lines of communication and the movement of persons and goods between the United Kingdom, the United States and the French sectors in Berlin and the Western zones shall have been fully restored."

Having asserted the right of access, Marshall asked what the United States should do if the Soviets rejected this claim. He informed Ambassador Douglas that in this case, we should say that we are willing to negotiate all issues and, failing that, refer the matter to the International Court of Justice. But he insisted that "we should not negotiate under direct duress."[21]

From Berlin, Clay wrote that he was pleased by the firm stand. He was not certain that the Soviets would negotiate. Though he was convinced that they did not want war, they knew that the Allies did not want war either. Therefore, they would continue to apply pressure.[22]

Again Clay argued that the Russian "bluff" be called by sending a convoy of trucks to Berlin. If this were done, the difficulties would cease. Unless the Soviets had a fixed plan for war, there would be no hostilities. Murphy agreed, saying that a military convoy would run no greater danger of war than the decision to stay in Berlin. Marshall and Lovett stood on their initial opposition to a measure that placed peace at the mercy of a chance shot.

The Soviets' reply came on July 14. They held that the right of access to Berlin had depended on the continuance of quadripartite rule there. Now this accord had been violated by Western efforts to establish a West German government, which changed the situation: the Soviet government had allowed access to Vienna and Berlin, which they had captured, only because of quadripartite control.

As a practical measure, the Soviets argued that Berlin's position in the center of the Russian zone made it impossible for them to allow introduction into the city of currency that had no validity in the Soviet zone. Any negotiations about access would have to deal with other problems involving Germany.[23]

Increasingly nervous over the crisis, London asked for positive reassurances from Washington. Marshall promptly announced that at a weekend conference of the President and his advisers, a determination had been made to stay in Berlin. In addition, the Secretary proposed that the three Western powers approach Marshal Stalin and emphasize the extremely serious view they took of the Berlin situation. They did not want war and assumed the same was true of the Soviet Union, but warning should be firm that "coercion, irrespective of its motivation, obviously can lead to war if the Government applying such methods continues to pursue them to the end." After a brief delay to decide on the best tactics, the British and French agreed on this approach. Another short delay ensued because of a political crisis in France, brought on by a series of strikes. Robert Schuman, who had become Prime Minister the previous November, resigned and entered the new Cabinet as Foreign Minister.[24]

At this point, Clay and Murphy were called to Washington for consultation. In a meeting with the President, Secretaries Marshall and Forrestal, the service secretaries, and the Joint Chiefs of Staff on July 21, Clay said he was sure that the military convoy he had urged could have gotten through earlier and that even now it might still succeed. He thought they could stay in Berlin without risk of war if he had more planes. His request for large cargo planes, 160 C-54s, which could carry ten tons per trip as compared to the two and a half tons now being carried by the C-47s, was granted. Truman assured him that American policy would remain firm.[25]

Marshall sent Bohlen back to Berlin with Clay to meet with Ambassador Smith from Moscow and discuss the next step in negotiations. Smith and Bohlen then flew to London for meetings with Bevin and his advisers on July 26. Two days earlier, Bevin had told Douglas, "The abandonment of Berlin would mean the loss of Western Europe." He still hesitated about approaching Stalin but was persuaded to follow the American lead.[26]

On July 30, at staggered intervals, the American, British, and French ambassadors presented identical *aide-mémoires* to Soviet Deputy Foreign Minister V. A. Zorin, asking for interviews with Molotov and Stalin. Zorin said the situation had not changed and there was no need for further talks. Smith, who had predicted to Washington that the Soviets would not negotiate and would probably try to force the Americans out of Berlin, saw no advantage in meekness. He reminded Zorin that Stalin had told him earlier that he would see him at any time. The present situation was the gravest that Smith had seen since coming to Moscow, and his government believed that an informal exchange of views would "improve prospects of a solution."[27]

Whether Smith's blunt statements were effective or whether the Soviet leaders decided a good time for talking had arrived, Molotov received the Ambassador the next day, asking for a more specific statement of views. Two days later, Marshal Stalin invited the three ambassadors for an interview in which Smith did most of the talking. Astonished by the change in the Russian attitude, Smith cabled Marshall, who had insisted on this direct approach:

> Stalin and Molotov were undoubtedly anxious for a settlement. Doubt if I have ever seen Molotov so cordial and if one did not know real Soviet objectives in Germany would have been completely deceived by their attitude as both literally dripping with sweet reasonableness and desire not to embarrass.

To Western requests for an end to the blockade and an agreement on currency, Stalin reiterated earlier statements by his subordinates that these matters waited on the suspension of the implementation of a West German government. Smith countered that it was the two unofficial conditions of blockade and currency that were causing trouble. He implied that the Western Allies were under no pressure of time, since they could continue the air lift indefinitely, but there were dangers of collisions, recurring incidents, and increased tensions.

Stalin blandly insisted that he had never considered ousting the Western powers from Berlin. "He had always been confident that after such skirmishing they could return in the end to a basis for agreement." When Smith said no agreements could be made under duress, the Russian leader revealed what Smith had long suspected: "There would have been no restrictions if it had not been for the London decisions [to establish a West German government]. The Soviet Government was not seeking conflicts but trying to find a solution."

After examining numerous questions at issue, Stalin suggested another meeting for the following day. This was not well received, and he suddenly asked if they would like to settle the matter that evening. He could meet the American Ambassador to propose that there be "simultaneous introduction" in Berlin of the Soviet-zone ostmark in place of the Western currency, and a lifting of travel restrictions. He would not demand the postponement of the establishment of a West German government but wanted it recorded as the "insistent wish" of the Soviet Union. The Western ambassadors agreed to inform their governments at once and try to have a reply by the following day.

In his separate note to Washington, Smith suggested that it might be helpful if it were possible to suspend any part of the implementation of the London decisions on the West German government. As long as there were negotiations, physical pressure was unlikely. He added that Stalin and Molotov must be told bluntly that the West was not going to accept a Communist Germany or a central government that could be seized by a Communist coup d'état such as the one in Czechoslovakia. "If they can be made to realize this one fact their eagerness for reparations may induce them to be less aggressive on the political front."

Marshall replied that the United States could not accept the arrangements unconditionally and that agreements on the Soviet ostmark for the whole of Berlin required some form of quadripartite control. He was willing to be flexible, but there must be general agreement on the main point. The Ambassador, with recurring pessimism, felt that Stalin was following what Smith termed a typical Russian practice of taking a circuitous direction when a direct approach met resistance. He feared that if restrictions were raised and a West German government was established, the Soviets would again clamp down and would form their government in Berlin. On seeing this report, General Clay agreed. From London, Douglas concluded that, under Stalin's analysis, the Western powers would be allowed to stay in Berlin only if they canceled the London decisions.[28]

In early August, Bohlen summarized the Western dilemma for Marshall. Stalin's strong statement about suspending proposals for a West German government indicated what the main Soviet demand would be in any future Four Power meeting. He thought that certain groups in the United States and France would support a suspension of the West German government until later. However, if this action were taken as a result of a Soviet demand, it would have an adverse effect on the Germans and would be violently opposed by Clay and Murphy. In case plans for a West German government were suspended and the hoped-for resumption of Four Power talks still proved illusory, it would be difficult, if not impossible, to go back to the establishment of a West German government.[29]

Marshall had sensed the nature of the dilemma earlier in the year, when he told the President that a Four Power security arrangement seemed unlikely. Months earlier, Clay and Robertson had decided that Four Power agreement on economic accords was doubtful and decided on Bizonia control, which, at best, they hoped to expand to a trizonal system. Clay had thought that there was some hope that the Soviets would agree on one currency for the whole of Germany, but now the country had two. The March and April arrangements for a West German government had come after the Russians had made it clear that the type of federal government preferred by Britain and the United States was not acceptable. What Bohlen was now talking about was what Marshall had found to be true at Moscow in the spring of 1947 and again at London later in the same year: agreement with the Soviets required that the full reparations they believed due them from Germany be paid and that the presence of the Western Allies in Germany be reduced if not totally withdrawn.

Ernest Bevin had been a staunch supporter of the U.S. position on most issues, although he continued to argue that some part of the reparations demanded by the Soviets from the Western zone at the expense of the Germans be conceded. The United States talked about some accommodation, but the developments of the previous six months in Central Europe, the heated presidential campaign in the United States, and Western resentment over the Berlin blockade gave no basis for serious negotiation.

To Marshall and others in Washington, the best hope was to stand firm until the Soviets realized that the West could sustain the Berliners through the winter. Smith had said that as long as the Russians talked there would be no fighting, and there was a feeling that the Soviets would see the danger of a prolonged confrontation in the air corridors over Berlin, unless they were truly bent on war. Standing firm reassured the British and French to some extent and encouraged the smaller nations of Europe, and it kept Germans in the Western zones and in sectors of Berlin from despair, but there was no leverage for successful negotiation. Stepping up air deliveries and continuing to talk seemed the best course. Marshall remained set on access to Berlin, on currency reform, on the proposed West German government, and on keeping the door open for further talks.

When Stalin had talked with the Western diplomats, he had not actually made suspension of West German government plans a condition of settlement of the blockade; on August 6, however, Molotov closed this illusive gap by making the suspension the main condition for ending the blockade. Smith described Molotov's maneuver as a "typical Soviet tactic of trying to sell the same horse twice."[30] Stalin had problems with his satellite powers, and it was as worthwhile to him as to the Westerners to keep talking. The long winter ahead might bring weaknesses in Western determination, so he was willing to allow the negotiations to proceed.

Marshall's stand was all that Smith and Clay could have wished. Praising Ambassador Smith for his handling of the talks, the Secretary said there must be no weakening of the position of the Western powers. Smith should remind Molotov squarely that the Western Allies were in Berlin by right and intended to remain there; that they could accept no currency arrangements that gave Soviet officials economic control of the Western sectors, and that the Western powers could not accept the suspension of governmental proposals for the Western zone as a precondition for negotiations.[31]

Smith made Marshall's points clear in his second meeting with Molotov. At the third session, on August 12, Molotov's attitude was somewhat less friendly, although he reacted mildly to the virtual rejection of his proposed counterdraft. Smith commented to Marshall, "He was handed a rather bitter pill and, if he did not swallow it, at least he did not spit it out."[32]

Hopes for an agreement on a statement about negotiations faded on the 16th as hours of discussion went on over phrasing. The Americans decided that the Russians preferred to drag out negotiations because of the approaching meeting of the United Nations

General Assembly, possible ill-effects of bad weather on the air lift, and likely worsening of the economic situation in the Western sectors of Berlin. Smith suggested to Marshall that it was time to seek another audience with Stalin.³³

Marshall agreed. He suggested a firm statement of the Western position and added that if Stalin remained adamant he should be reminded again of Western rights in Berlin, of the danger of the situation to international peace and security, and of the fact that threats to peace would force the Western powers to bring the situation to the attention of the United Nations.³⁴

The French were becoming increasingly fearful that the United States would take unilateral action in Berlin that would draw France into war. When the French Ambassador sought reassurance, Bohlen told him that no action had been decided on and none would be taken without consultation with the British and French governments.³⁵

These and other indications of growing uneasiness in Britain and France led the United States to fear that their allies would go too far in concessions in order to reduce the possibility of war. To bolster European resolve, Marshall declared that he saw no signs of weakening in the United States. "From all reports, the country is more unified in its determination not to weaken in the face of the pressure of an illegal blockade than on any other issue we can recall in time of peace."³⁶

Before the Westerners could ask Molotov for another meeting, they received a surprise. On August 27, the Russian Foreign Minister, who had stubbornly insisted that agreements be reached in Moscow, proposed that issues be settled back in Berlin by the military governors.³⁷

The situation in that city had greatly changed since the last meeting there, some two months earlier. Planes from the Western zones moved regularly through the air corridor to Tempelhof Airport, where cargoes were soon unloaded so the planes could fly back for new supplies. Winter had not yet imposed its massive fuel requirements and the air transport was able, along with supplies seeping through from the East, to meet the minimal needs of the city. Sokolovsky, presiding at the Allied Control Council Meeting, was "mildly provocative with an evident desire to indicate mastery of the situation." The atmosphere continued to be "strained" the next day.³⁸ The feeling grew that any hope for adoption of an agreement on Berlin would be dashed.

On September 4, Sokolovsky caused great concern at the State Department and the Pentagon by announcing that within a short time the Soviet Air Force would begin maneuvers that would extend into the air corridors and over the city of Berlin. He convinced no one when he explained that these were normal air exercises. Clay noted that the corridors had not been used in earlier maneuvers and that the Soviets were aware that they were now being used for the flying in of supplies.[39]

Disturbed by Sokolovsky's truculence, Marshall asked that another appeal be made to Stalin to keep his earlier promises. He proposed that as soon as possible after September 7, the date set for a report on the situation by the military governors, the three ambassadors in Moscow should seek an interview with Molotov to declare that a breach of a definite understanding had been made by the Soviets.[40]

Uncomfortable with an American move toward a showdown, Bevin (physically exhausted and ready to leave for a week of rest in Cornwall), urged that the report by the military governors be made as scheduled on September 7 and that no walkout from the meetings be staged. He was not sure that the Russians wanted a break. He believed that the Allies should continue to insist on a lifting of restrictions but not take a rigid position on the Soviet inspection of trains going to Berlin.[41]

Murphy was reporting a totally different view. Discerning no Russian disposition to reach an agreement, he believed that language would be added to the proposed agreement that the United States could not accept. Marshall insisted that the Western Allies get back to the subject of their fundamental rights. The source of the current troubles was the Soviet conclusion that the Western Allies had lost their legal rights in Berlin. "The time has come therefore to recognize that all the troubles stem from this . . . and we are convinced that we must now insist that the Sovs [sic] recognize these rights." Marshall's words were a rehearsal for an appeal to the United Nations, rather than a position for negotiation.[42]

The Secretary sent copies of this message to Douglas and to Smith. Smith apparently concluded that he and his fellow diplomats in Moscow were being chided for not taking a tougher line. In a typical Smith reply, he said that if the statement meant what it said, there was no need for the rest of the cable, since the Russians would reply that they did not recognize our juridical rights. It was preferable to contest Soviet efforts to terminate our rights in Berlin and their refusal to honor Stalin's commitments.[43] Any settlement would be on the basis of a compromise unless the Soviets agreed to resume quadripartite authority. He thought the Western powers had to face the question whether they could cope with the present situation indefinitely or what concessions they were prepared to make if they could not. "I do not ask to know what this decision is, but it would certainly help my digestion if I knew that it had been taken."

Marshall held to his position. He declared that Sokolovsky's actions and recent "Soviet-inspired demonstrations" against the city assembly in Berlin made it plain that the Russians intended to nullify Allied rights there. Therefore, the Allies had not only a right but also an obligation "to make our position perfectly clear at this stage." The Soviets must refrain from violating Western rights or face an appeal by the Western powers to the United Nations.[44]

The Secretary of State realized, however, that the British and the French were reluctant to go so far. Douglas had spoken recently of Bevin's petulance and his statement that he had gone along with the earlier approach to Stalin only with misgivings. Whereas Marshall believed that the Soviets should be made to realize that the Westerners were willing to break off relations over the Berlin crisis, the British and French seemed to want to dodge the issues and permit the Russians to draw out discussions as they saw fit. Perturbed, Marshall discussed with Senator Vandenberg, Secretary of Army Royall, and Under Secretary of the Army Draper whether Western unity on the Berlin question was paramount or whether the three powers should make their separate approaches to Moscow. They concluded that Western unity was the main thing, and therefore Marshall was willing to go along with the British and the French as long as it was understood that there were limits to American patience.

Bedell Smith agreed that three-power unity was an overriding requirement for the presentation. They should let Stalin realize that they were fully aware that the disorders in Berlin could not continue without Soviet military support. Later that day, Marshall cabled Smith to join with the French and British ambassadors in asking Stalin to direct Sokolovsky to continue the discussions in Berlin.[45]

Molotov met the three ambassadors on the evening of September 14 to announce that Stalin was on vacation and that "his treatment" would not permit interruption. He termed the paper they had presented as one-sided and proposed that they instruct the military governors to make their report. Then he would need time to study the results. Groaning over the manufactured delays, Smith also knew that if the Allies lost patience, the Soviets would blame them for breaking off negotiations.[46]

In Smith's view, the Soviets were maneuvering to get complete control of all Berlin while leaving the impression that the city was still under quadripartite management. Their present purpose was to establish an advantageous position for the next phase. Stalin might gain points if the Western powers brought the stalemate before the United Nations. Although the West might be able to get a favorable vote, the likely abstentions by Near and Far Eastern blocs, Scandinavia, many Latin American countries, and India and Pakistan could blunt the effect of any U.N. condemnation of Soviet action. Two days later, Smith forwarded the official Russian reply to the Western protest, noting that it signified more delay. There the matter rested until the meeting of the U.N. General Assembly in Paris later in the month.[47]

Despite the general feeling of frustration in Washington, the White House, Pentagon, and State Department all showed remarkable restraint. On September 10, however, Forrestal told Marshall that, in view of the tense situation, he felt there should be a resolution as to whether we would use the atomic bomb in time of war. The Secretary suggested that Forrestal take it up with the President. On the 13th, at the White House, after the Defense Secretary had repeated the briefing on the Berlin crisis he had given the week before to Marshall, the question arose whether the bomb would be used in an emergency. Truman said that he prayed he would not have to make such a decision, but that if it became necessary they should have no doubt about his decision.[48]

That the bomb would be used if necessary was the topic of discussion on the following evening when Philip Graham, publisher of the *Washington Post,* invited the publishers of nineteen other major newspapers to his home to hear Marshall, Forrestal, Bradley, Lovett, and Bohlen discuss the Berlin crisis. The unanimous agreement of all present was that the American people would expect the bomb to be used. Although no wish for war was expressed, a number of publishers thought that the opinion of the country was in advance of Washington and that there was a groundswell of feeling against the Russian actions. Marshall later quoted to Forrestal the statement by John Foster Dulles "that the American people would crucify you if you did not use the bomb. . . ."[49]

XIX

North Atlantic Treaty

MARSHALL was greatly interested in the words Bevin had spoken to him on December 17, 1947, as to some form of future cooperation, but he wanted clarification. He asked a member of the delegation, John Hickerson, director of the Office of European Affairs, to get more details from Bevin's assistants.[1] Hickerson thus entered into the background of negotiations of the North Atlantic Treaty, in which formulation he and his chief of the Division of Western European Affairs, Theodore C. Achilles, played major roles.

At the Foreign Office, Hickerson dealt with Gladwyn Jebb. Jebb had served with the Special Operations Executive during the war and later, as a representative of the Foreign Office, helped establish the United Nations. He was now acting as a deputy to Bevin, working on plans to strengthen Western Europe against aggression. He told Hickerson that the Foreign Secretary set great store by the Treaty of Dunkirk, signed in March 1947, to protect the Western powers against German aggression. He was thinking now of a collective defense arrangement between Britain, France, and the Benelux countries (formed a few months later by the Treaty of Brussels) to which he hoped to add the United States and Canada.[2]

In mid-January 1948, Ambassador Inverchapel forwarded to Marshall the summary of a paper prepared by Bevin pointing out that the Soviet government had shaped a solid political and economic bloc, which made it difficult to hold the line against further Soviet nibbling and encroachment. With the aid of the United States and Canada, he wanted to form a Western democratic system that would include Britain, France, the Low Countries, Scandinavia, Greece, Italy, and possibly Portugal. In time, Germany and Spain should be added.[3]

George Kennan was also in favor of this and suggested that the United States receive the idea as warmly as the British Foreign Secretary had welcomed the Marshall Plan proposal. Kennan felt that a political, economic, and spiritual union should precede a military one. Since Germany would ultimately have to be brought into any effective Western union, it made no sense to organize against that country. The initiative, he believed, must come from Europe, but if a union were considered, Bevin should not worry about the U.S. relationship. If the union developed and functioned well, an American relationship, even to the military guarantees, would logically flow from it.[4]

Hickerson thought Bevin's concept magnificent but felt something was still lacking in the proposal. Suggesting to Marshall that the idea of extending the Treaty of Dunkirk to other European countries was not sufficient, he urged that the United States propose a formula like that used in the Inter-American Treaty on Regional Assistance approved at Rio de Janeiro on September 1, 1947, which Secretary Marshall had signed there. For such a pact to be effective, he thought the United States must be a member. The Rio treaty had provided that an armed attack on any of the signatories would be considered an attack on all. It was understood that, under Article 51 of the United Nations Charter, they could exercise their right of collective self-defense until the Security Council had taken the necessary steps to maintain international peace and security. No power would be required to use armed forces without its own consent.[5]

Concerned about the slowness with which congressional approval of Marshall Plan legislation was proceeding, and mindful of the need to put first things first, Marshall encouraged Bevin while remaining vague about the exact nature of American participation. It was a line that he and Lovett would follow in the early stage of discussions. Marshall assured Bevin that the United States applauded his initiative and would do everything it properly could to bring his project to fruition.[6]

Eagerly grasping at any sign of progress, the British Ambassador called Hickerson at the State Department the following day. Hickerson repeated what he had written to Marshall, that the Treaty of Dunkirk approach erred in strengthening the West against Germany, when what was needed was a strong defense against Soviet encroachment. There was no debate on this point, for Bevin's initial approach to Marshall was definitely aimed at halting Soviet advances in the West. The British were quite aware that only fear of Soviet expansion in Europe would prompt the United States to enter a defensive alliance. Thinking out loud for the benefit of the British Ambassador, Hickerson said that if some of the smaller nations felt that the United States must be a member of a proposed defensive organization, the United States would be inclined to consider it, but that any such arrangement must be within the United Nations Charter and at European initiative.[7]

Although Bevin failed to get the outright guarantee he had sought from Marshall, he unveiled his plan to the House of Commons on January 22. Four days later, the British Ambassador suggested to Under Secretary of State Lovett that the United States and Britain conclude a defensive agreement between themselves that would reinforce the plan for Western Europe. He asked that the conversations be held on this proposal before mid-February, when Britain could begin talks with France. Knowing that Marshall did not wish to be hurried on the matter, Lovett reminded the Ambassador that Marshall's interest in Bevin's project did not involve a commitment. American action must await study by the National Security Council, the President, and congressional leaders, and all this could not be done by mid-February. At this time, Marshall was speaking to various interest groups across the country to rally support in Congress for the approval of the European Recovery Program, while Vandenberg was having to cope with the opposition of twenty senators from his own party who seemed bent on reviving the isolationism of the 1920s. Neither wanted at this moment to stir up additional debate about further U.S. commitments in Europe.[8]

Ambassador Inverchapel explained that his government could not on its own supply members of a defense organization with arms. He had been encouraged by Marshall's early reactions to hope they might have useful discussions. Reflecting Marshall's caution, Lovett said that he thought Europe should take the initiative and that it was unwise for the United States to intrude into the proposal before the idea had been developed in Europe.

Bevin was getting much the same reaction from some smaller European countries as those reported by U.S. diplomatic representatives in Europe. Belgian Prime Minister Paul-Henri Spaak had said early in January that nothing would come of extending the Dunkirk formula unless the United States was involved. Bevin decided to push harder. He feared delay and dreaded even more the development of a vicious circle. Without the backing of the United States, there could be no effective union. But, apparently, without a union he could not win American support. In summoning European support for the European Recovery Program, he had been able to march boldly on the basis of the Harvard speech. But for the collective defense idea he did not have such assurance. When Inverchapel mentioned these points to Lovett and Hickerson, the Under Secretary patiently recapitulated the danger of slowing the European Recovery Program. Bevin wanted them to pour concrete before they had the blueprints. Marshall endorsed the general idea of a Western union but insisted, as he had concerning the Marshall Plan, that initiative must come from Europe.

Meanwhile, other Western European countries suffered spasms of alarm. In mid-February, the Norwegian Defense Minister, Jens C. Hauge, anxiously watching Soviet pressure on neighboring states, asked the U.S. naval and air attachés in Oslo what aid his country could expect in case of war. Though the attachés could make no answer, they reported to their superiors that Norway was looking to the West for help, taking a different tack from the careful neutralism of Sweden. On February 19, the Benelux countries advised the British and French that an extension of the Treaty of Dunkirk was not enough. They preferred a regional organization of Western Europe under the U.N. Charter.

The French Foreign Minister assured the Belgian Ambassador that France was ready to sign such a pact, provided the United States was associated with it. Secretary Marshall welcomed the proposals of the Benelux countries but repeated that they should not ask the United States to be associated with it until it was clear what all the European countries concerned were prepared to do. He considered the Four Power Pact that he had once favored as virtually dead, but would seek some means to protect Britain, France, and the Benelux countries from German attack.[9]

Cheered by these reactions, Bevin sought to smoke out the United States by dangling signs of European initiative. He suggested a private meeting between representatives of the United States, Britain, and France on ways of preventing the encroachments of dictatorships. Bidault followed Britain's lead in calling for three-power consultation. They must prevent neighbors of the Soviet Union from suffering the fate of Czechoslovakia.[10]

Hickerson, the advocate of immediate action in the State Department, warned Marshall that if the United States did not show support for the Western European states, the Soviet Union might grow bolder and more smaller states be intimidated; the United States should make its position clear. He urged Marshall to consult the National Security Council and members of Congress on steps to stop Soviet expansion. They should consider the nature and cost of U.S. military commitments to Western Europe, how to make

clear that further aggression against free countries in Western
Europe would be treated as a threat to American security, the
possibility of American participation in a North Atlantic regional
defense arrangement might be considered, and that Bevin and
Bidault be told that the United States was willing to talk with them
and perhaps others. Hickerson was saying that Europe's earnest
desire for talks was the evidence of initiative that Marshall wanted.
With this memorandum, Hickerson, supported by his subordinate
Theodore Achilles, became the leading State Department proponent of what was to become the North Atlantic pact.[11]

European pleas became more urgent in March as the Soviet
government put strong pressure on Finland to make a treaty of
mutual defense, which the Finns struggled desperately to avoid.
The Norwegians feared they might be next in line for such a pact.
In a special meeting on March 11, Norwegian Cabinet leaders cast
aside possible dependence on a league of Scandinavian neutrals
and said they would not accept a treaty such as the Soviets were
demanding of Finland. If necessary, they were prepared to go it
alone.[12]

The growing anxiety and pressure following Russia's extension
of control over Czechoslovakia made it increasingly evident that
the United States must speed up some form of assistance to the
Western European states. As Norway proclaimed her defiance,
Marshall was asking the U.S. Ambassador in Italy what could be
done to strengthen that country in the face of Communist expansion. Would inclusion of Italy in a Western regional union be of
help?[13]

From London came warning that quick action was necessary to
"prevent the collapse of the whole Scandinavian system." Bevin
had once thought that the area could be aided by adherence to the
Western-union system, but he now believed that a regional Atlantic
Approaches pact of mutual assistance under Article 51 of the U.N.
Charter, which would include the United States and Canada, was
essential. The Foreign Minister was now spelling out in some detail
what he had said along general lines to Marshall in late December.
Great urgency marked the lines of the *aide-mémoire* presented on
March 11.[14]

Marshall acted swiftly. After the next day's Cabinet meeting, he
told President Truman of the situation and got his approval for a
message to Britain and France. Marshall suggested that they go
ahead with conversations about the Western-union arrangement
and indicate that as soon as possible they would discuss further
requirements.[15]

To the Norwegians he expressed the hope that they would resist added Soviet demands and, "in absolute confidence," revealed that he was talking with the British about their situation. On the same day, he was encouraged by Denmark's assurance that it would resist Soviet pressures. However, the Danish Foreign Minister added that joining a Western union would not in itself stop the Russians. That would require a prompt and clear American declaration of support. He thought that Denmark might have to seek a military alliance with the United States but hoped that this would not be necessary before the European Recovery Program went into effect, "so as to avoid the implication that ERP had military strings attached to it."[16]

Although the earlier proposed pact was already insufficient for Western Europe's security, the growing tension spurred approval of it. On March 17, "A Treaty of Economic, Social, and Cultural Collaboration and Collective Self-Defense" between Great Britain, France, Belgium, the Netherlands, and Luxembourg was signed in Brussels, to take effect August 26, 1948.

To bolster the confidence of the signers, President Truman gave encouraging signals to Western Europe in his message to Congress on March 17. Observing that the Brussels treaty was then in the process of being approved, he declared that it

> deserves our full support. I am confident that the United States will, by appropriate means, extend to the free nations the support which the situation requires. I am sure that the determination of the free countries of Europe to protect themselves will be matched by an equal determination on our part to help them do so.[17]

The signers of the Brussels pact avidly searched the wording of Marshall's message and the stronger promise of Truman's speech. Showing how willing they were to engage in talks, they asked for additional details.[18]

Before arranging for general discussions, the United States, Britain, and Canada decided to hold secret talks at the ambassadorial level in Washington between March 22 and April 1. To bar any possible leak, the French were not included. However, since one of the British delegation was Donald MacLean, who later fled to the Soviet Union to escape arrest as a spy for Russia, Moscow must have been fully informed of the discussions.

On the morning after the meeting began, the State Department's Policy Planning Staff handed Marshall a report that was less positive than Hickerson's proposal. The staff urged that the United States not become a member of the Brussels pact although it should offer armed support. To a degree, the report followed Bevin's initial suggestion in concluding that Denmark, Norway, Sweden, and Iceland should be added immediately, and perhaps Portugal later. They should also explore the inclusion of Eire, Switzerland, Spain, and Austria. At length, as the most powerful country in the Atlantic community, the United States might find it advisable to be an associate or a full member.[19]

The proposals were important because they suggested that American assurances to the Western union should involve a commitment "to consider armed attack against them to constitute armed attack against the United States, to be dealt with by the United States in accordance with Article 51 of the U.N. Charter." Assurances would also be provided to the other free nations of Europe and the Middle East if they defended themselves with every means at hand.

A concept similar to the ultimate treaty emerged at the third meeting of the delegates. The drafting committee, made up of Gladwyn Jebb, of Great Britain, Theodore Achilles, of the United States, and Lester Pearson, of Canada, suggested a security pact for the North Atlantic area and the extension of the Brussels pact to other European countries. The United States would be a member of the security arrangement.[20]

The conference ended on April 1 with the sixth meeting. Reflecting the views of Hickerson and Achilles rather than those of Kennan and Bohlen, the recommended course of action was for the United States to contact members of the Brussels pact to discuss plans for a North Atlantic agreement. This would be followed by approaches to Norway, Denmark, Sweden, Iceland, and Italy (if the elections had been held by that time).[21]

Encouraged by reports of the meeting, Bevin urged the State Department to act quickly and decisively to give confidence to Western European countries: "The construction of a North Atlantic defense system would put heart into the whole of Western Europe and would encourage them in their resistance to the infiltration tactics which they have had to face hitherto." Brusquely, Bevin declared that a presidential statement was not enough. Recalling the days when England stood alone after the fall of France, he said grimly that he did not want Britain to be left waiting a second time "in a state of uncertainty." If that happened again, he doubted that the English would be able to weather another such test. There must be a treaty involving the United States, Canada, the United Kingdom, and the Western European countries.[22]

Bevin's bold statement provoked a tart draft reply from the State

Department: "We consider such a statement highly unfortunate and are confident it does not reflect his true feelings." Fortunately, the draft was reported to Marshall at Bogotá. His response was compassionate and understanding. He told the State Department drafters that their "proposed reply appears too much like a brush-off [to] a nation in evident dread of a great calamity. Can't we do a bit better and buck them up a little?"[23]

The proposed reply was intended to urge patience and not to deny hope. As he notified Marshall, Under Secretary Lovett at this point was striving to pave the way for congressional backing of some form of American guarantee to the Western Europeans. Both he and Marshall were convinced that it would be hopeless to try to proceed without senatorial help. In later years, Kennan was to disapprove of the degree to which Marshall and Lovett sought this aid. Although he admitted that Senator Vandenberg's support was essential for the adoption of the European Recovery Program, he felt that the State Department assumed greater vision on Vandenberg's part than he possessed and "took the form of catering to Senatorial opinion in instances where one might better have attempted to educate the protagonists to a more enlightened and effective view."[24]

Neither Marshall nor Lovett sought to play senatorial politics, but they were realistic about the difficulties of getting a Truman proposal through a Republican-controlled Congress without the support of the powerful Chairman of the Senate Foreign Relations Committee. Knowing that Marshall had found it helpful during World War II to take leaders of both parties into his confidence, Lovett, when Marshall was at conferences outside the United States, discussed every important step of the negotiations with the Senator from Michigan.

Vandenberg was dubious about getting congressional support for new and additional guarantees to Europe. He and others feared that the Europeans might be inclined to fold their arms and let the United States handle the task of defense, or that they might be encouraged to take provocative stands in their foreign policy. He doubted that the United States should be asked to go to war because of the action of countries abroad; the United States should not surrender the option of being able to decide when it should act.

The senator wanted an opportunity to see the proposed agreement before accepting extension to the North Atlantic region of Rio-treaty language (which he had favored at the Rio Conference). He cited problems he had faced in the Senate, where sixteen senators, many of them in his party, were agitating for a resolution "to overhaul the U.N. veto and other passages" of the Charter. He had been able to get one such resolution withdrawn, but others were in the works. The Foreign Relations Committee was looking for ways of making the United Nations more effective in maintaining peace. While not in favor of a formal pact, Vandenberg thought it would be helpful for the President to take note of the efforts of Western European countries to strengthen their defenses.[25]

On April 12, Bevin notified Marshall that the Brussels-pact countries had met in Paris and had agreed to establish a Consultative Council and begin military talks. He believed it imperative for the United States to begin conversations in Washington with representatives of the group. Quite apart from Bevin's initiative, and with no official status, Winston Churchill was telling the U.S. Ambassador in London that Washington should make its stand clear to the Soviet Union. As soon as the Soviets produced their atom bomb, Churchill believed there would be war. Now was the time to demand Russian withdrawal from Germany. If they interfered with rail traffic to Berlin, the Allies could hold up Soviet ship movement through the Suez and Panama canals. Ambassador Douglas disagreed with these particular measures but emphasized that the Western powers should stop the Russians by making a real show of resolution. He passed along the former Prime Minister's suggestions, not wanting or expecting Marshall to act on them, but to show that the old man was still full of fight.[26]

While some members of the House and the Senate discussed ways of strengthening the United Nations, the State Department worked with Vandenberg on a statement to encourage the Brussels-pact countries. Though the Senator agreed to propose a Senate resolution to this effect, he did not want it named for him. He said he expected to have Democratic support but was not certain about twenty-one senators of his own party.[27]

Mr. Lovett brought Marshall (still in Bogotá) up to date on April 26. Vandenberg's committee would report a resolution favoring regional agreements, and the President would invite the United Kingdom, Canada, France, the Scandinavian and the Benelux countries, Eire, Italy, and Portugal to conclude regional agreements in the North Atlantic area. This would be based on Article 51 and developed along the lines of the Rio declaration. There might also be a presidential statement on Greece, Turkey, or Iran, to be preceded by discussions with the Brussels-treaty signatories.[28]

On the eve of his return to Washington, Marshall approved the procedures outlined but said he was inclined to agree with General

Matthew Ridgway, a member of the U.S. delegation to Bogotá, that no public statement should be made about the United States' engaging in military talks since this might reduce public support for the proposal and also increase the possibility of confrontation. Marshall said that he and Norman Armour, Assistant Secretary of State for Political Affairs, believed Greece, Turkey, and Iran should not be included in a statement at that time: regional arrangements were difficult to justify in their area and there was danger of dispersing American military forces too widely. The United States was already doing a great deal for Greece and Turkey, "and I see no compelling reason for being pressured into dangerous efforts, concurrently with our Atlantic discussions."[29]

Three days after he came back from Bogotá, Marshall met with Lovett, Vandenberg, and John Foster Dulles to discuss the resolution. Vandenberg proposed amendments to the draft and warned that Kenneth Wherry, Republican political whip, and some of his supporters might try to add an amendment on Palestine. Vandenberg asked Lovett if he would talk with Senator Walter George to see if he was still against what he called a "military ERP."[30]

Vandenberg opposed encouraging European powers to draw up a military shopping list. He also feared that they were including too many countries in Europe in a so-called regional pact. Marshall, Lovett, and Dulles agreed that the United States should not issue a general invitation but felt that the five Brussels-pact countries should ask to be put in touch with sources of supply and assistance by their association with the Western Hemisphere. Vandenberg also preferred "limited and natural" regional agreements and an understanding that United States assistance would not be automatic on the basis of action by third parties.

The Michigan Senator ended by suggesting that the State Department request a resolution by the Senate Foreign Relations Committee. After that was passed, the State Department would arrange for the signers of the Brussels treaty to ask the United States for consultation. The President would then indicate that the United States "was prepared to accept an invitation to consider association on the basis of self-help and mutual aid among the European participants with such regional arrangements as affect its national security."

The four men agreed that the Brussels-pact countries should invite Canada and Greenland (Denmark), Iceland, Norway, and, perhaps, Portugal. They added that it would be a mistake to include Italy, because that would violate the regional concept. Inclusion of Greece, Turkey, and Iran was deemed unacceptable.

George Kennan, who had serious doubts about some phases of the proposed arrangement, had been away from Washington during much of the recent conversations. He had been on a fact-finding trip to the Far East during the latter part of February, all of March, and the first half of April. Ill when he returned to the United States, he had gone directly to his farm in Pennsylvania and was unable to return to his desk until near the end of April.

Two days after coming back to work, Kennan voiced his doubts about the proposals to Marshall and Lovett. He believed that Bevin and Bidault were less worried about the American stand in case of attack than about the lack of agreement on what steps could be taken to save members of the pact "from the dual catastrophes of Russian invasion and subsequent military liberation." Statements by some U.S. military officials that the Soviets were capable of overrunning the Middle East and Western Europe had added to their fears. They wanted not so much an alliance "as realistic staff talks to see what can be done about their defense." The proposed resolution was all right, but it would be well, before going into the rest of the program, to check with other Europeans whose participation might be desired. Meanwhile, he believed that U.S. military leaders might try to convince the Europeans that the United States did not accept complete defeatism with respect to Western Europe and would be willing to consider ways of impeding a Soviet advance.[31]

Kennan soon saw that Hickerson and Achilles had made a strong impression on Marshall and Lovett and were well along with the draft wanted by Vandenberg. On May 7, Kennan forwarded the draft to Lovett and Marshall, who approved it and sent it to the President; Truman agreed with its concepts, and the text was turned over to Senator Vandenberg.

Before the draft resolution was considered, Marshall had appeared before the House Foreign Affairs Committee to testify on proposed House resolutions on strengthening the Charter of the United Nations. His observations were highly pertinent to the discussion on regional treaties.

He recalled that, in creating the United Nations, the major powers had assumed that (1) they would work out effective settlements, (2) critical postwar problems could be quickly eliminated, and (3) the wartime cooperation of the great powers would continue after the conflict ended. The United Nations had been set up to keep the peace and not to make it; the peacemaking function had been assigned to the victors. Because the victors had not acted, the

United Nations had to proceed in a different way from what had been originally planned.[32]

The hopes of the peoples of the world, Marshall felt, had been shaken by recent Soviet actions, which arose from Soviet "misconceptions" concerning world civilization and the possibilities of developing a working relationship between the Soviet Union and other nations. A basic task before the United Nations and the United States was to dispel some of these misconceptions and indicate a view of what was possible between the Soviet Union and the world at large.

The first step toward an effective United Nations was to ensure the freedom and independence of its members. This condition required a healthy economic and political life and a "genuine sense of security." The United States wanted to cooperate with European countries in self-help and mutual aid. It was trying to determine a minimum military-establishment level "to restore the balance of power relationships required for international security."

Marshall outlined specific measures that the United States had supported and would support to strengthen the structure of the United Nations. But the chief problems were not of structure but of fulfillment of commitments already made. It would not help to revise the United Nations in such a way that some nations would be unwilling to join. Such changes would literally destroy the organization. "It is not changes in the form of international intercourse which we now require. It is to changes of *substance* that we must look for an improvement of the world situation. . . ."

Hearings, mostly in executive session, began on the Vandenberg resolution nearly a week later. On May 12 and 19, Lovett was the only witness. As the Chairman of the committee that had put forth the resolution, Vandenberg assisted Lovett in explaining the background. Although there were some questions in the minds of committee members on the degree of commitment made by the resolution, and some changes were made in its language, the resolution as worked out by Vandenberg and the State Department was reported out of committee by a 13–0 vote on May 19 and approved by the Senate on June 13.[33]

The close working of Marshall and Lovett, and of Hickerson and Achilles with Vandenberg and other members of the committee, had paid off. It was handled so that all members of the committee could have their say. When the session was over, those who voted for the resolution had a share in the statement and felt committed to it.

The resolution reaffirmed the policy of the United States to achieve international peace and security through the United Nations. It was the sense of the Senate that the veto should be removed from all questions involving the peaceful settlement of international disputes and the admission of new members. It particularly stressed the "association of the United States, by constitutional process, with such regional and other collective arrangements as are based on continuous and effective self-help and mutual aid, and as affect the national security."

At Bevin's request, the British Ambassador saw Marshall the day after the vote, to urge discussions of further action by Britain, France, the United States, and Canada. Marshall asked for a short delay to see if the House of Representatives would act on a proposed resolution similar to that passed by the Senate. If they adjourned without acting, he was willing to proceed on the basis of the Vandenberg resolution alone. Thinking of current developments in Germany, he emphasized the timing as all-important. Several developments were building pressure, he said, listing the resolution, the ERP, the recent Air Force appropriations increase, and recent speeches directed at the Soviet Union. For the moment, conversations should be exploratory.[34]

On June 23, after the House had adjourned without voting on the resolution, Marshall alerted the governments of Britain, France, Canada, Belgium, and the Netherlands that the United States was ready to begin exploratory talks along the lines of the Vandenberg resolution. Nothing final was to be taken up, and he did not consider it necessary to have special military representatives or Foreign Office representatives.[35]

Before the talks took place, the National Security Council outlined the U.S. position on the Western union, proposing that procedures used in drawing up the European Recovery Program be followed and that the European countries concerned should determine what they were able to do for themselves and then ask for supplementary aid. The United States should be willing to consider association with the Brussels-treaty countries and, if possible, Canada. But no commitment would be made without full bipartisan support, and nothing would be done requiring permission of Congress before that body reconvened in January 1949.[36]

Mr. Lovett took the chair as the discussions opened July 6 in Washington. The draft outlined over the following days was close to the final text presented to the Senate.[37] He realized that as they were talking the presidential campaign was gaining momentum. At the start of the negotiations, Dewey had been nominated by the

Republicans, and Vandenberg was his firm advocate. There were strong assumptions that the terms of a proposed North Atlantic treaty would have to be put through a Republican Congress, which the anticipated Dewey sweep would make even more Republican.

Lovett worked cautiously, for he knew Marshall would have not tried to go beyond what he believed Congress would approve. He opened the first meeting with the warning to the Europeans that nothing would be gained by pushing the administration and Congress too fast.

At the second meeting, Lovett asked that the delegates examine the factors making for a feeling of international insecurity, the nature of the threat, and what they considered to be the present attitude of the Soviet Union. Sir Oliver Franks, who had succeeded Lord Inverchapel on June 3 as British Ambassador in Washington, saw an immediate threat of Soviet expansion on the eastern side of the Atlantic. But he believed that determination on the part of the North Atlantic community "would minimize the risk of overt aggression." Lovett seconded the need for firmness, explaining that in recent years the United States had sought peace through meekness but that "after many heartbreaks it has reversed its policy and was seeking to deter aggression by proof of determination. The only question was how its determination should be implemented." He saw the need to strengthen the powers against ideological as well as military threats and the need to help Western-union countries resist internal as well as external pressure.[38]

At the third meeting, Lovett extolled the Rio agreement as a model to be followed. There must be staff planning, they must consider methods for making the military load supportable in Europe and in the United States, and they must counter the Russian use of fear as a weapon. Though the association of the United States and Canada with the North Atlantic powers would act as a deterrent, these countries could not go to war automatically because of an incident in Europe.[39]

Since some of the cautionary statements reflected the views not only of Vandenberg but also of Kennan and Bohlen, the two State Department representatives were asked for statements. Kennan believed that the Soviets were unlikely to launch an attack at that time. At a later meeting (the fifth), Kennan said that he and Bohlen did not mean to say there was no danger of war. Their views that there was no deliberate program of aggression did not imply that aggression might not follow a situation from which it was impossible for the Soviets to withdraw. Russia was still devastated by the war and her people were weary of conflict. If the Soviets felt their position was weakened in Eastern Europe, there was a danger of military action. The question was how to encourage the Western Europeans while discouraging the Russians from aggression and, at the same time, preparing to act if necessary. Bohlen mentioned the Russian tactic of producing fear with threats to use their armed forces. He warned the Western powers against being so victimized by this fear as to embark on excessive military expenditures, which would delay the economic recovery of Europe. Lovett agreed, noting that a number of American plants now manufactured products for European recovery. Sudden shift to wartime production would damage economic plans.[40]

By the time the fifth meeting had been held, on July 9, a working group was instructed to bring together the thinking of the ambassadorial group and develop papers on (1) the general security needs of the West, (2) the geographical limits of the security arrangement, and (3) the individual needs of the countries concerned. Fifteen meetings were held by this International Working Group between July 12 and September 9.[41]

As the working group neared the end of its labors, Lovett invited the ambassadors to his house. He explained that there would be no formal minutes, although he had kept informal notes and invited completely candid comments. The Belgian Ambassador asked specifically for an American statement as to what the United States considered desirable and practical. Lovett insisted that he stood firmly on the Vandenberg resolution and emphasized that any arrangement entered must contribute to American security. He doubted if adherence to the Brussels pact would serve that purpose.

Henri Bonnet, the French Ambassador, did not find this statement satisfactory. His government was in a spell of great indecision because plans were being discussed in Europe for establishing a West German government, representatives of the Western governments were considering military plans to resist aggression, and there were suggestions of eventual German participation. All these facts seemed to invite Soviet aggression and left-wing pressure in Paris. The Ambassador insisted on immediate military aid to France. Because his country did not regard the presence of American troops in Europe as a guarantee of Europe's defense, France therefore required increased arms and equipment.[42]

Lovett regarded this prickly cavil as an attempt to gain priority for French rearmament over that of other countries, and the other representatives agreed. The Belgian and Dutch members told him they were trying to reorient Bonnet but doubted that his government had given much thought to the basic approach, "being much more fully occupied with the immediate rearmament problem in view of the nervousness which they felt arising from the tension in Europe."

During this period, Marshall discussed with Pentagon officials efforts to organize military forces in Europe. After talking with Secretaries Forrestal and Royall, and with Generals Bradley and Alfred Gruenther, he asked Truman on August 23 to approve agreed-on points before the meeting of military representatives of Western-union countries the next day in London, to select a supreme commander and staff for Western-union forces. If there were hostilities, American troops in Europe would come under his command.[43]

Marshall and his advisers at first believed that no American should be on this staff, but a place might be reserved for an American deputy. The British wanted an American supreme commander, but Marshall suggested instead that the British support a proposal that the supreme commander be chosen from among Field Marshal Lord Montgomery, Field Marshal Lord Alexander, and General Alphonse Juin. Although Marshall had not been impressed by Montgomery's ability to get along with other commanders in World War II, he thought that in the early stages of organization "a man of the forcible character of Montgomery would probably be preferable." Truman promptly approved Marshall's recommendation but warned, "We must be very careful not to allow a foreign commander to use up our men before he goes into action in toto."

Divergencies continued to develop between Hickerson and Kennan. Although Kennan modified his early opposition to a treaty, he still did not agree with Hickerson's position. At the end of August, he suggested that Lovett would have to decide between their proposals. Kennan now favored a North Atlantic agreement but wanted it confined to that geographic area. From his earlier concept of the trans-Atlantic areas as each end of a dumbbell, he had come to see them as two anchors, one in the United States and Canada and the second in Europe containing the Brussels-pact members. He was also willing to consider association with the stepping stones—Iceland, Portugal, and Denmark. Hickerson wanted more, arguing vigorously for the inclusion of Italy and possibly Greece and Turkey. For the moment, the decision was postponed.[44]

On September 10, the working group presented its recommendations to the Exploratory Group. The members proposed to submit to their governments the background of the discussions, the guidelines for such an agreement, and provisions that should be included. Hume Wrong, Canadian representative, spoke for his associates when he said that if such a pact as they had been considering had been in effect in the 1930s, there probably would have been no war, and the same thing might have been true if there had been a pact of this kind before World War I. To his mind, the greatest potential of the North Atlantic pact was the certainty it would provide about the American long-term commitment to international security.[45]

Much had been done by the interested governments to outline an acceptable agreement, but action had to wait on the reconvening of Congress. Meanwhile, something could be done to sound out possible members not yet involved. Marshall, in Paris since September 20 for the U.N. meeting, had kept in touch with these developments in Washington while watching the situation in Germany. In October, he talked with representatives of Norway and Sweden. The Norwegian Minister pointed out the problem his country would have in joining a Western pact while Sweden remained neutral. A few days later, Marshall explored that point with the Swedish Foreign Minister, Osten Unden. After Unden had impressively traced the long history of Swedish neutrality, Marshall asked where Europe would be if Wilson and Roosevelt had followed such a course in World Wars I and II. To Unden's reply that, after all, the United States was a great power, Marshall agreed and said that for that reason we could have afforded to stand alone.[46]

In one of his sharpest attacks on the Soviet Union, Marshall said that the Western powers were confronted by a state that "appeared to be utterly ruthless and devoid of all the basic decencies of modern civilization." With the Berlin situation and the Czechoslovakian coup strongly in his mind, he declared: "If this ruthless force were not opposed, it seemed to us that we were confronted by the possibility of a gradual establishment over the world of police states, and that this was abhorrent to us. . . ." Casting aside his habitual caution in an effort to convince the Swedish Minister, he said that the United States had decided that such a force "must be met by a unity of such states as were willing to accept the challenge." This unity had been a major element in the European Recovery Program. The United States had demanded that the recipients get together. For that reason it was fantastic for the Soviets to suggest that "this program was initiated by the United States for imperialistic purposes. At the time the program was started, we had not realized that military assistance might also be essential but that now we did." He outlined current measures for rearmament and his hope they could also re-create a sound economic system in "a unified western Europe."

Five days later, Marshall approved a suggestion of Lovett's favoring American acceptance of an invitation to participate in a Western Union Chiefs of Staff Committee. He believed the decision to take part should be based mainly on military considerations. Politically, the State Department desired to strengthen the morale of the Brussels-pact countries and stimulate their efforts to coordinate and enlarge their defenses.[47]

Near the end of October, the ambassadors of the Brussels-pact countries declared that their governments had agreed in Paris to negotiate a North Atlantic treaty with the United States and Canada. They proposed that negotiations be held in Washington at a date to be set by the United States.[48]

In October, the Western Union countries confirmed the appointment of Field Marshal Montgomery as Permanent Military Chairman of the Commanders-in-Chief Committee, with General Jean de Lattre de Tassigny of France as Land Force Commander and British Air Chief Marshal Sir James Robb as air commander. Left for later was the naval command. A beginning had been made, but, as the State Department's Office of Intelligence Research commented shortly afterward, the outcome of the issue rested on "the relation of the United States to the Western European Alliance."[49]

The path toward clarifying the American relationship was made simpler after Mr. Truman's surprising re-election on November 2 and the return of Congress to Democratic control. For weeks, the President had waged a grueling battle across the country, attacking the do-nothing Congress and reaching out for various issues with which to capture the American imagination. But he had managed to keep bipartisanship on foreign policy alive. On November 6, he approved the general principles concerning a North Atlantic pact that had been agreed on by the conference in Washington on September 9.

In parts of Europe, some concern was voiced about the new events and their effect on the Soviet Union, so the Secretary of State set about calming the voiced fears of Norwegian Foreign Minister Halvard Lange. Marshall thought the critical point would come when American supplies began to flow to Western Union countries. He doubted if incidents arising from the Berlin crisis or anything except a planned incident would lead to Soviet aggression. He believed that any action would be based on a deliberate decision

by the Soviet government and that such a decision might possibly
have been made already. He thought that the main deterrent up
until the present had been American possession of the atomic
bomb. Until recently,

> I thought that the Soviet leaders probably had felt that the American
> people never would permit the use of the bomb but that in the light
> of developments of recent months, including Berlin, and of develop-
> ments here [at the General Assembly meeting in Paris] I felt the
> Soviet leaders must now realize that the use of this instrument would
> be possible and hence that the deterrent influence now was perhaps
> greater than heretofore.[50]

As the time approached for setting a date for the talks on a North
Atlantic agreement, the State Department Policy Planning Staff set
forth for the Secretary of State what it thought should be considered. Apparently Marshall gave oral approval of their agenda. Although Kennan had shifted somewhat, he still proposed a cautious
approach. The conclusion of such a pact, he believed, would not
answer the main problem of Soviet efforts to dominate Europe and
probably would not force the U.S.S.R. to modify its position. The
problem was not military but political, and the political war—now
in progress—would be decisive. The danger was that preoccupa-
tion with military affairs would delay economic recovery.[51]

Kennan was thus ready to assist the Western Union countries,
though he did not want to bring in countries outside the North
Atlantic area. He warned that including most of the European
Recovery Plan members in the pact "would amount to a final mili-
tarization of the present dividing-line through Europe." United
States policy, he believed, was still aimed toward "the eventual
peaceful withdrawal of both the United States and the U.S.S.R.
from the heart of Europe, and accordingly toward the encouragement of the growth of a third force which can absorb and take over
the territory between the two." Unless the United States proposed
to give up a peaceful solution, it should not do things that tended
to fix and make unchangeable by peaceful means the existing East-
West division. These were the views that Marshall had hoped to see
realized as he had patiently sought agreement in the settling of
German problems.

Marshall would not be on hand to discuss the next step after the
Paris meeting closed: he was in the hospital in Washington when
North Atlantic treaty negotiations were resumed on December 10.
The representatives pledged to work for a treaty by February of the

following year. At Ambassador Franks's request for a draft to show his government before Christmas, the working group plowed ahead, announcing on Christmas Eve that they had agreed on "practically all the articles of a possible pact." They could not agree, however, on whether French North Africa should be included in the guarantees given to France, whether Italy should be invited to join, and whether assurances should be given to Greece, Turkey, and probably Iran. These issues remained for the new year and the new Secretary of State, Dean Acheson. As Escott Reid put it later, Acheson was present only for the last day of creation, "but that was a particularly busy day."[52]

The story of Acheson, Hickerson, and Achilles, working with Vandenberg and Connally with the special cooperation of Senate Foreign Relations Committee staff member Francis O. Wilcox, has been well told by Acheson, Escott Reid, Timothy Ireland, Allen Henrikson, and others. It was Acheson who signed for the United States in March 1949. He has made clear the great contributions of his predecessors in their work in 1948. In a gracious compliment to their bipartisan efforts, which reflected the nonpartisan stand Marshall had maintained during his term as Secretary of State, Acheson wrote, "Senator Vandenberg, the Vandenberg-Marshall-Lovett collaboration, and its product, the Vandenberg resolution, made possible the North Atlantic Treaty."[53]

XX

Marshall, the United Nations,
and Palestine

MANY of Marshall's dealings with European and World Powers required his attendence at conferences abroad. Others focused on activities at the United Nations, usually at the temporary headquarters in New York. The problems associated with the status of Palestine required his attention in the fall of 1947. During part of the time, he found it necessary, as the true head of the U.S. delegation to the United Nations, to attend the meetings in person. But during much of the time he acted through his subordinates at the State Department and through the delegates in New York appointed by the President.

The United Nations as yet had no permanent headquarters in New York City. In 1947, it was using buildings left over from the 1939–40 World's Fair at Flushing Meadow on Long Island. Most delegation members were housed in New York hotels, with the elegant Waldorf Astoria a favorite site. When Marshall found that he had been given a suite there, he told an assistant to move him to a less expensive hotel near Pennsylvania Station. Many of the delegates staying at the Waldorf, he explained, would come to him to request loans for their countries, and it might help him keep the price down if they saw him living more simply than they were.

Former Republican Senator Warren H. Austin of Vermont had been appointed by the President to head the delegation, with Ambassador Herschel Johnson as deputy. Other delegates appointed to U.N. special committees included Eleanor Roosevelt, John Foster Dulles, Major General Matthew B. Ridgway, Philip Jessup, and Major General John Hilldring. From time to time, substitutions were made and heads of State Department divisions were summoned to attend debates on questions of special interest to them. One such was Dean Rusk, whose title of Special Assistant for Political Affairs was later changed to Assistant Secretary for the United Nations.

From Washington, Marshall normally dealt with Austin through Under Secretary Lovett. On a number of important matters, he gave direct instructions or went to New York to seek agreement among delegation members. Truman handled most U.N. matters through the Secretary of State, but since Austin was his personal representative at the U.N., the President also felt free to call directly on him or his delegation members.

The President usually consulted directly with Marshall or Lovett on foreign affairs or had Marshall discuss these matters in Cabinet meetings. In 1947, a National Security Council was established, in which the Secretary of State met regularly with the President, the secretaries of Defense and of the Treasury, the director of the Central Intelligence Agency, and the service secretaries. Departments or agencies could ask to have a special topic placed on the agenda, or, if the President so requested, would be asked by the council's secretary to prepare a paper for consideration. There was not at that time, as there is now, a National Security Adviser to give special advice to the President. The nearest thing to such a functionary was the counsel to the President, Clark Clifford. In matters of particular interest to Truman, Clifford saw that the President's view was made known to Cabinet members and his wishes carried out. The possibility of clashes came in 1947 and again in 1948, when Clifford managed Truman's campaign for the presidency. Although he steadily denied that political factors influenced his judgment, Clifford found, as the election approached, that political leaders who wished to get the President's ear focused on the office of the counsel, who described the situation to the President, explaining what each politician was trying to achieve and how he could influence the election.

Marshall was to find that much of the 1947 U.N. General Assembly session was concerned with the problem of Palestine. For some historians the problem of Palestine began with what was called the Balfour Declaration of 1917, a statement by British Foreign Secretary Arthur Balfour that Britain would favor a homeland for the Jews there. For others, the question went back to the Zionist Congress at Basel in 1897, when Theodor Herzl organized a meeting of Jewish leaders and called for the establishment of a Jewish state. For still others, the problem sprang from the dispersion of the Jews from Palestine by the Roman governors in the first and second centuries A.D. Only a small remnant was left to keep a Jewish presence in the land of their fathers.

Through the centuries, groups of several hundred or, occasionally, a few thousand Jews had ventured back, and were usually tolerated by Arabs controlling the area.

In the nineteenth century, Russian nationalism and the development of a distrust for foreigners led the tsarist government to restrict the freedom of Jews in Russia and often to launch violent attacks on Jewish villages. These pogroms and persecutions elsewhere in Eastern Europe led to widespread emigration. Herzl was moved to proclaim a Zionism that demanded a Jewish state. His appeal found sympathy abroad, not only among Jews but also among non-Jewish statesmen. Even before Balfour's declaration, an American Zionist, Supreme Court Justice Louis D. Brandeis, had won President Woodrow Wilson's approval of Zionist hopes.

After the end of World War I, the League of Nations gave Great Britain a special mandate over Palestine, with the understanding that the country would be made ready for independence at a suitable time. Britain's obligations to seek a homeland for the Jews and to prepare Palestine for independence conflicted with British national interests in the Near East. The period after World War I saw intense effort by British firms to get increasingly valuable oil concessions in Arab lands, which meant seeking Arab friendship. Stability in the Near and Middle East was an important safeguard for the Suez Canal. As the Palestinian Arabs, who outnumbered the Jews by more than two to one, saw the increasing flow of Jewish immigrants under the British mandate, they and their Arab brothers in neighboring states clamored for the British to restrict or stop the flow of Jews into the mandated area.[1]

The rise of Hitler and the flight of Jews from his control brought Jewish demands and pleas for the admission of larger numbers of their people to Palestine. But Arab nationalism had grown rapidly since the war, and it fed to a great extent on anti-Zionism. Arab groups attacked new Jewish settlements, and the Jews learned to retaliate. The British, trying to keep order, were attacked by both sides. Pointing out instances of the British favoring the Arabs, some militant young Jews organized small underground organizations to force concessions from the British through terrorism. Attempts of Jewish groups and sympathizers to send shiploads of Jews rendered homeless by World War II displacements were thwarted when the British blocked their landings or sent them back as illegal immigrants to the ports from which they had sailed.

The sufferings of the Jews at the hands of Hitler, the incontrovertible evidence that concentration-camp atrocities and the frightfulness of the Holocaust had not been anti-German propaganda, made the Zionist cause more popular than it had ever been, particularly in the United States. On the eve of Yom Kippur, the Day of Atonement, in 1946, President Truman called for a lifting of limits on the admission of Jews to Palestine.

All British attempts to solve the Palestinian problem by an Anglo-American inquiry and other measures of conciliation were rejected by both Arabs and Jews. In the spring of 1947, the British government announced that it would withdraw from its mandate by the summer of 1948 and hand the Palestine question over to the United Nations. If there was to be an orderly transition to any form of self-government by Arab and Jew, the United Nations would have to find it.[2]

Conveniently, the State Department's Division of Near Eastern Affairs had prepared for Secretary Byrnes a summary on U.S. policy in the Near East a week before Marshall became Secretary. Head of the Office of Near Eastern and African Affairs was a well-known expert on Soviet policy and the Middle East, Loy Henderson. He had been with the first group of Foreign Service officers to go to Moscow after Roosevelt recognized the Soviet Union, and was known as a hard-liner on the Soviet Union and a watchful opponent of its extension of influence in the Near and Middle East. He favored good relations with the Arabs and a policy of cooperation with the British, and the Arabs considered him a friend. To the Jews he was the leading State Department opponent to a Jewish state. One member of his division, Fraser Wilkins, prepared the summary of U.S. Middle East policy that Marshall would find as his introduction to the Palestine question a few days later.

Wilkins recalled that the Balfour Declaration had come as a result of the pleas of Chaim Weizmann, a prominent Zionist, to Sir Arthur Balfour to seek a Jewish homeland. Wilkins described the Palestinian Arabs' growing fears of becoming a minority in Palestine if the displaced Jewish population of Europe was admitted, and their preparations to resist Zionist plans. American support of the Zionist hopes for a Jewish state had been repeated in presidential statements, in congressional resolutions, and by the platforms of the two major political parties in 1944. U.S. backing of increased Jewish emigration to Palestine was creating friction between the United States and Britain, and between the United States and the Arab nations of the Middle East, who opposed any plan of partition for Palestine. For the United States, there existed the "strategic and economic importance of American oil, aviation, and telecommunication facilities in Palestine and neighboring countries." Above all, growing instability in Palestine invited Soviet Russia to extend its influence into that area.[3]

According to Wilkins, U.S. policy on Palestine consisted of five points: (1) Palestine should be given independence as quickly as possible, not as either an Arab or a Jewish state, but in a form that allowed for the aspirations of both groups. The United States could support a solution to divide the land into an Arab state, which might be joined to a neighboring Arab state, and a Jewish state controlling its own immigration and economic problems. While awaiting total independence, the country should be under a U.N. trusteeship. (2) There should be an immediate transfer of displaced persons from Jewish refugee camps in Europe to Palestine, accompanied by a liberalization of immigration laws in Western countries to admit some of the displaced Jews. (3) The Jewish national home in Palestine should continue to develop, through immigration and the purchase of land if necessary. (4) The Arab portions of Palestine should develop politically, economically, and culturally. (5) The agreement of the Arabs to this solution should be obtained, which would end the Palestine problem.

On the day Marshall was sworn into office as Secretary of State, Dean Acheson talked with the British Ambassador about Palestine. Declining to speak for either the President or Secretary Marshall, Acheson said he thought that partition was the solution most likely to be accepted, and urged the British not to withdraw from their mandate without suggesting a specific solution. Six days later, he added that it would be difficult for the United States to favor any solution that did not provide entry for 100,000 Jews into Palestine in the immediate future, and a reasonable rate of Jewish immigration thereafter. Meanwhile, the President planned to ask Congress to increase Jewish immigration to the United States. It was to be understood that the United States would favor no plan requiring the use of U.S. armed forces.[4]

The British soundings of State Department views just as Marshall was settling in arose from a period of agony in Britain. Attlee and Bevin had to face Britain's increasing inability to meet imperial demands on its resources. As Bevin hunted for any plan on which Arabs and Jews would agree in Palestine, the Prime Minister struggled with decisions on India and on aid to Greece and Turkey. In early February, the U.S. Embassy in London informed Marshall that Bevin had concluded that partition was impossible to apply, and spoke of a trusteeship proposal. Marshall had asked earlier for Acheson's recommendations on these proposals and on Jewish immigration. In turn, Acheson sought Henderson's advice. Henderson suggested that a general reply be given to the question on plans and that the United States again ask for an increase in the number of Jews to be admitted to Palestine.[5]

Within a week, Bevin announced that the Palestine question would go to the General Assembly. On February 20, Attlee declared that Britain would transfer the government of India to the Indians by June 1948; on the following day, he said that the British would have to end their financial and military support to Greece and Turkey on March 30.

Although Bevin had asked that the United States assume the burden of aid to Greece and Turkey on February 21, he was sufficiently stung by the British failure in Arab-Jewish negotiations to charge, in the House of Commons on February 25, that U.S. intervention had upset his earlier efforts, referring to Truman's October 4, 1946, pledge to support Jewish emigration to Palestine. Bevin added that when he had complained to Secretary Byrnes, the American had said that President Truman had no other choice, since there were local elections coming up in New York and Governor Dewey would make the promise if the President did not. Bevin grumbled that he could not carry out his duties if his actions were subject to American election pressures. The next day, Truman issued an angry statement that politics had nothing to do with his recommendation at the time of Yom Kippur. Rather, he had reaffirmed a position taken in 1945 and conveyed to Attlee at that time. Feelings were ruffled on both sides, but within less than a month the President proclaimed the Truman Doctrine, which included American assumption of the British burden in Turkey and Greece, and a hard-line stand against the Soviets, which Clifford was later to proclaim as the strongest presidential policy of the first term. In preparing the background to the Truman Doctrine, Acheson, interestingly, relied greatly on Loy Henderson, later to be attacked by the White House as the leader of the pro-Arab faction in the State Department.[6]

In mid-February, Bevin asked for a special session of the General Assembly to prepare recommendations on the Palestine question for the next regular session of the United Nations, in September. The special session began on April 28. On May 16, the United States proposed to the session the appointment of a committee to study the problem, made up of neutral nations: Australia, Canada, Czechoslovakia, Guatemala, India, Iran, the Netherlands, Peru, Sweden, Uruguay, and Yugoslavia. The committee was empowered to seek testimony on a broad scale on which to base recommendations for Palestine, and the General Assembly appealed to all factions in Palestine to refrain from hostile acts while the study was being made.[7]

Shortly after formation of the committee, Ambassador Austin suggested that the United States consider its own stand and perhaps make its views known in advance. Personally, he favored an independent Palestinian state, neither Jewish nor Arab. Authorization of immigration would be based on the absorptive power of the country. A period of five to ten years of preparation for independence would be needed, during which Palestine would be under a U.N. trusteeship and the United Nations would give economic and financial assistance.[8]

In forwarding Austin's ideas to Marshall, Acheson added, "Our views [Henderson's and Acheson's] which have been discussed with Senator Austin, are reflected in this letter." Marshall initialed the memorandum without comment. He must have been aware that this plan had been presented in the earlier British-American reports, known as the Morrison-Grady proposal of 1946, which the United States had refused to consider, and was rejected by the Arabs, who wanted immediate Palestinian independence, and strongly opposed by Jewish organizations preferring partition and an independent Jewish state. Britain's earlier support of a lengthy trusteeship system had caused them to be accused of trying to prolong their control of Palestine.

Meanwhile, Jewish agencies were seeking from Henderson and Acheson a definite statement of the U.S. position, American backing for an increase of immigration during the waiting period, and financial aid. They were pleased that the Russian delegation had wanted a quick end to the mandate and that Russian views were not entirely pro-Arab. Americans at the United Nations had decided that the Soviets were concealing their pro-Arab bias until they had a chance to make a flashy, dramatic show of support for the Islamic countries.[9]

On June 5, President Truman asked citizens and residents of the United States, during the period of activity by the United Nations Special Committee on Palestine, to refrain from words or acts that would further inflame the passions of the inhabitants of Palestine or promote violence there. A week later, Marshall sent a sweeping statement to twenty major U.S. diplomatic and consular posts, warning them that the United States had refrained from advocating a particular plan for Palestine and that mention of an "American plan" should be discouraged. In all discussions it should be underscored that the United States had put no plan forward, and had no plan to suggest at present.

To Ambassador Austin he explained that, after careful consideration, the State Department had concluded that no solution existed that would not be opposed in some quarters, and that it was possible that any attempt to impose a solution would require a degree of force. It was, therefore, necessary to review possible solutions from the standpoint of what could be defended before the world, now and in the future.[10]

Three days later, Rabbi Abba Hillel Silver, President of the Zionist Organization of America, appealed to Marshall to make known the government's views on the Palestinian situation. If, as he understood, the United States considered partition the proper solution, the committee should be so informed so as to avoid turmoil that might be caused by the final report. Marshall stood by the position that he and the President had advanced and would say only that they were studying the situation but were not ready to make a statement. Silver explained that in September he would preside at a meeting of Zionists in New York and wanted to be able to tell them what was the American position. Marshall asked Silver to feel free to make new suggestions, but insisted that he himself could not make a statement at the time.[11]

Another prickly issue surfaced near the end of June, when Bevin begged Marshall to bar the promotion by Americans of illegal departures of Palestine-bound immigrants, particularly from European ports. Bevin specifically asked that a strict watch be kept on members of various charitable organizations. Much of the funds encouraging illegal immigration, he noted, came from the United States.

During July, despite U.N. pleas for cessation of violence in Palestine, it increased—between Jews and Arabs, and by terrorists of both sides against British troops trying to keep order. Weizmann and David Ben-Gurion harshly condemned the hanging of two British sergeants by Jewish terrorists, but when the British reacted by killing five Jews and arresting a number of Jewish leaders in Palestine, the moderate Zionists dropped their antiterrorist strictures.[12]

Tension continued to mount toward the end of August when a small Chesapeake Bay ferry furnished by American groups entered a port in southern France and picked up some 4,500 Jewish refugees and sailed for Palestine. The British had already turned back a number of ships similarly loaded and had sent them temporarily to camps on the island of Cyprus. Trying to reduce the flow of what they called illegal immigration, British warships met the ferry, known as the *Exodus-1947*, off the coast of Palestine and forced the ship, with its passengers, to return to a French port, saying they had run out of space on Cyprus. There, most of the refugees refused to leave the ship but demanded to be taken back to their homeland. After several weeks, the French ordered the ship to leave the port and the British directed it to a port in their occupied zone of northern Germany. There the passengers were removed by force and placed in camps in Germany. When President Truman asked the State Department about the situation in August, Under Secretary Lovett replied that the Department had already expressed concern about sending Jewish refugees to Germany. On the same day, Marshall instructed the U.S. Ambassador in London to warn the British of the great shock this action would create. He agreed that illegal immigration was being aided by U.S. citizens, but repeated that the proposed action would cause great bitterness against the British in the United States and aggravate the situation. Truman agreed with this exchange. Lovett, who earlier had preferred to spark a warning, now felt that a more formal protest should be made. The British insisted that they had no other place to take so many refugees.[13]

While this solution to the refugee problem was being studied, the U.N. Special Committee on Palestine made its report. A majority report, recommended by Canada, Czechoslovakia, Guatemala, the Netherlands, Peru, Sweden, and Uruguay, proposed the partition of Palestine into a Jewish and an Arab state, which were to become independent after a two-year transitional period beginning September 1, 1947. The British government was to administer the interim government under U.N. supervision and to admit 150,000 Jews. India, Iran, and Yugoslavia had a minority plan favoring a federal state that would become independent in not less than three years. Until then, it would be under an authority designed by the U.N. Australia abstained.[14]

On September 12, Secretary General Trygve Lie recommended that an *ad hoc* committee made up of a representative of each country in the General Assembly be set up to consider the proposal of the Special Committee on Palestine. The *ad hoc* committee met on September 25, and its chairman, Herbert Evatt of Australia, asked that the Arab Higher Committee and the Jewish Agency send representatives to its meetings.[15]

The meeting of the General Assembly, which began its second year in September 1947, was the first in which Marshall had participated. Aware of the critical importance of a Palestine settlement, he made a great effort to take part in all the early meetings dealing with that subject. Mrs. Roosevelt, who had known his work during the war and had asked him to take charge of the funeral and burial arrangements for her husband, later spoke eloquently of the outstanding way in which he worked with the U. S. delegation to the United Nations. Speaking of him in later years, she declared:

He was a magnificent presiding officer. He had an extraordinary quality of patience. He would listen to everybody and ask for everybody's point of view, and if a question it was difficult to decide was coming up, he would frequently hold delegation meetings, including the people from the State Department, and ask each one of us around individually to state what we thought, before he went to meet the people on the point that was coming up, so that I think he did the very best job that I have seen done as a leader of a delegation. As the Secretary of State he was always the leader, when he was there, of the delegation in the General Assembly. He was a wonderfully good chief, and always wanted to hear what you had to report at the end of whatever job you were doing.

I could not speak of him too highly in a position which I had always had a feeling would be difficult, because I don't happen to think that military men are particularly fitted for civilian jobs of that kind. But as far as a military man could shed his militarism, General Marshall did in the period that he was Secretary, and in the way that I saw him, which was purely as the leader of the U.S. delegation in the General Assembly, I have always had the greatest admiration and the assurance that there was no greater patriot or truer servant of his country than General Marshall.[16]

His approach to the U. S. delegation on September 15 illustrated Mrs. Roosevelt's point about letting every person present have his say. He explained that as a delegation, they were faced with a dilemma. Should they take a strong position in favor of the majority report at the meeting of the General Assembly on September 17? Such action would bring a violent reaction from the Arab states; failure to favor it would bring accusations of State Department "pussyfooting." When he mentioned the danger of driving the Arabs to seek a rapprochement with the Soviet Union, Mrs. Roosevelt, ardent proponent of a Jewish state, asked if it were certain that the Russians would oppose partition. She believed that the Arabs feared the Soviets more than they did the United States. She was answered by Loy Henderson, who felt strongly that partition could be imposed on the Arabs only by force, and that they would rally to the Soviet Union if it promised support. General Hilldring replied that the Russians had already made a stand in favor of a federalized Palestine. He thought that the United States should support the plan for partition and then be willing to amend it. Mrs. Roosevelt insisted that the big issue was that the United States should help the U.N. by supporting the majority report.[17]

Marshall praised the quality of this report, which was better than he had anticipated. However, it was not enough to favor the report. It was necessary to be prepared to enforce it. Henderson reiterated that force would be needed, but he doubted that the larger nations would agree to such action. He believed the majority report had been based on expediency rather than principle, and those who submitted it did not expect to have to carry it out.

Ambassador Austin was pessimistic about making partition work. He did not see how a small state could be carved out of such a small area. Such a state "would have to defend itself with bayonets forever, until extinguished in blood. The Arabs would never be willing to have such a small state so near to their heart." He agreed with General Marshall that if they were going to favor the majority report they must be prepared to use force. The Secretary had made a strong statement the day before to the American Association for the United Nations. They should make a strong statement on Wednesday, September 17, so that it would be clear to the Arabs that they could not hope to change the position of the U.S. delegation.

John Foster Dulles, who had made no statement, was asked for his views. He said that he did not feel confident enough of them to give an opinion at the moment, "although he would speak, if necessary, with great reservations." Marshall ended the meeting by promising to send a copy of the statement he would make, before the afternoon meeting of the delegation.

Marshall's final pronouncement partly met the desire to favor the majority plan but without unequivocally endorsing it. In attempting to give voice to both groups in the U.S. delegation, Marshall avoided finality. He praised the U.N. Special Committee on Palestine for the great progress it had made in reaching a unanimous decision on eleven of the recommendations relating to Palestine. He recognized that neither party to the controversy would be satisfied with the final recommendations for partition. As for the United States, it gave great weight "not only to the recommendations which have met with the unanimous approval of the Special Committee, but also to those which have been approved by the majority of the Committee."[18]

Arab reactions were immediate and intense. Representatives of Iraq, Syria, Lebanon, Egypt, and Saudi Arabia declared that Marshall's statement had committed the United States to the majority report. Prince Faisal of Saudi Arabia, speaking for all Arabs, said that the United States had embarked on a dangerous course for the United States and the Arab world.[19]

Henderson went as far as he dared in trying to change the Secretary's mind. At the end of a statement expressing strong disapproval, Henderson said that he and his staff would loyally attempt to carry out Marshall's decision "in a manner which will minimize as far as possible the damage to our relations and interests in the Near and Middle East." His memorandum was trenchant in its declaration that he and nearly everyone in the State Department who had worked with the question favored a different approach. Henderson believed that U.S. approval of partition would add fuel to nationalist uprisings in France's African colonies, would interfere with economic cooperation in the Near East, would lead the Arabs to conclude that we were their worst enemy and to lean toward the Soviet Union, and would weaken efforts of moderate Arabs to restrain Arab terrorists. The British would not be able to get bases they needed, and we would not get the communication facilities we were seeking. U.S. business would find the Arabs increasingly uncooperative.[20]

If the United States pressed hard for partition, it would be pressed equally hard to implement the plan for partition; the problem would increase and the country would be bitterly attacked by both Jews and Arabs. Plans for partition had been considered before World War II and dismissed as unworkable. The Anglo-American inquiry immediately after the war had reached the same conclusion. Participation was not in the best interests of the United States and not in accord with the principles of the United Nations and American concepts of government. This country had no obligation to the Jews to set up a Jewish national state: the Balfour Declaration promised a Jewish national home but not a Jewish national state. There would be no workable solution until both Jews and Arabs agreed to make it work. Any imposed solution would continue the bloodshed and damage the larger countries and the United Nations.

The United States should not be too active, Henderson warned. It should help others work out plans and try to persuade both sides to go along with the one most likely to be accepted. Perhaps a trusteeship for a number of years would permit the slow adjustment of Jews and Arabs and a gradual working out of disagreements. Perhaps in time a plebiscite could be held to determine the issue. Any temporary solution should probably provide for the immediate immigration of 100,000 Jews to Palestine.

On September 23, Marshall, Ambassador Herschel Johnson, General Hilldring, General Ridgway, George Wadsworth, newly appointed Ambassador to Iraq, and Paul Alling (adviser to the delegation) met at lunch with representatives of the chief Arab states. The Arabs were vociferous in their disappointment over the Secretary's support for partition. Marshall patiently explained that in its dealings with partition in various parts of the world, the United States faced the problem of dealing with majority and minority votes. He believed that it owed to the United Nations consideration of the majority report by the appointed committee. General Hilldring and Ambassador Johnson broke in, however, to say that Marshall had not committed the United States to any part of the report.[21]

After a meeting of the U.S. delegation the following morning, Marshall talked with Mrs. Roosevelt, Dean Rusk, Charles Bohlen, alternate delegate Charles Fahy, and General Hilldring to explain the procedure he meant to follow in the U.N. debate on Palestine. The United States would make no opening statement. After general discussion of the special committee's report, during which the United States would try to get a full expression of views by the Jewish Agency and the Arab Higher Committee, he would express the view of the United States. This view would take into consideration the historical commitments of the United States, the majority report of the special committee, and the views expressed in the debate. The U.S. position should embrace the majority report with such amendments as might be considered wise to make it workable. It should also add any useful points brought out in general discussion. It must include the provision for partition and should insist on large-scale immigration. If the U.S. proposal did not get the vote of two-thirds of the General Assembly members, or if they learned that it could not hope to get two-thirds, the United States delegation should consider either forcing a vote to show the absence of two-thirds support or proposing an alternate solution that might get a two-thirds vote.[22]

The day after this meeting, the Arab Higher Committee called for a general strike in Palestine as a protest against the majority report. The Arabs demanded the immediate termination of the mandate, the establishment of an Arab democratic state, and the withdrawal of the British. On the same day, representatives of two Arab states told Ambassador Wadsworth that they had been approached by the Soviets with the suggestion that the Russians would support the Arab position on Palestine if the Arabs would support the membership of the Ukraine on the Security Council. A Polish delegate had also mentioned this idea. The Arabs had not responded, but if the United States was not going to support the Arab position, they must deal with the Soviet Union. All this at the time when Secretary Marshall was meeting with the U.S. delegation to decide that the United States was still not prepared to make a statement, because, though the United States supported the majority plan in principle, it would want to amend the proposal in regard to boundaries and economic plans. If two-thirds of the United Nations General Assembly members supported the majority plan, the United States would be willing to help enforce it but not to use organized military units. He added that the United States should make no effort to persuade members to adopt the majority plan. He was considering a public statement requesting Congress to pass legislation for increased immigration of displaced persons.[23]

For the next few days, the State Department worked on a statement to make to the General Assembly. The President accepted the language but wanted it made clear that the United States would contribute to financial and economic aid of Palestine only as a part of the United Nations contribution, that the United States was not going to pick up the British responsibility for law and order, that American contributions to that responsibility would be only a part of the United Nations effort. Lovett, who had talked with Truman, thought that the President would feel better if it were understood that any contribution to a constabulary would be a part of a United Nations effort.[24]

Ambassador Johnson announced the U.S. position to the *ad hoc* committee on October 11: the United States supported the unanimous provisions of the special committee and the proposal for partition and increased immigration.

Also on the 11th, the British began to explore the situation with the Americans. Ambassador Inverchapel asked Lovett whether the United States had fully considered the effectiveness of a voluntary constabulary to handle problems in Palestine. He also asked about the viability of a Jewish state from a defense standpoint and of an Arab state from an economic one. Lovett assured him that both aspects had been considered.[25]

A sort of byplay developed between the American and British representatives. The United States did not want the British to pull out of Palestine too soon and leave the United States holding a large part of the bag. The State Department's Robert McClintock was soon reporting to Lovett that the British and some of the Commonwealth members were increasingly speaking of "the American plan, partition," which the United States did not want attributed to them. The Americans favored partition, yes, but, not assumption of the British task of preserving order in Palestine.

Several newspapers suggested that the United States, though supposedly supporting partition, was not actually prepared to back it strongly. One member of the State Department observed that Marshall did support partition, but that if the plan could not win the two-thirds vote, the United States would adopt another course. To zealous backers of partition, such a position was defeatist or anti-Zionist or both.

On October 13, to the astonishment of most of the General Assembly, the Russians announced their support of partition. An Arab representative declared that henceforth the Arab states would follow their own interests.

After much discussion, the U.S. delegates agreed on October 23 that every attempt should be made to shorten the period of transition in Palestine so that the two independent states could be set up on July 1, 1948, with the aid of a U.N. commission. They also wanted certain adjustments in the proposed boundaries, to give certain mountainous areas to the Jews and the southern Negev (an area in southern Palestine) to the Arabs.

Both Arab and Jewish agencies grew restive during this period of American internal discussion. King Ibn Saud of Saudi Arabia warned President Truman on October 26 that U.S. support of partition was an unfriendly act to the Arabs and a deathblow to U.S. interests in Arab countries. The establishment of a Jewish state would swiftly lead to the shedding of blood and the end of that state. "The Arabs will isolate such a state from the world and lay siege to it until it dies by famine."[26]

As the General Assembly vote on the recommendations approached, it became evident that the U.S. delegation was much closer to acceptance of partition than was the Near East Division of the State Department. Working-level members of the Near East Division and U.S. delegation members tried to achieve some agreement in late October and early November. Henderson and his staff charged that some pro-Jewish delegates were going all-out for partition while ignoring strong British disagreement, and were urging quick decisions that could be put into effect only if the United States took on most of the responsibility for enforcing a settlement. Into this situation, at the close of October, the British interjected a strenuous bid to stop illegal immigration into Palestine from the

Black Sea area. The British particularly protested against private American groups' running loads of immigrants southward by using U.S. military vehicles still marked with U.S. Army signs and dressing operators in U.S. Army uniforms.[27]

The position of the Soviet Union in the United Nations raised other questions. Instead of opposing partition, as many had assumed, the Soviets seemed at one with the United States. But they also wanted an immediate British withdrawal from the mandate, which the United States saw as resulting in Russian-calculated disorder in Palestine and calls for action by the U.N. Security Council, thus bringing the Soviet Union into the Middle East. (One adviser to the U.S. delegation wondered whether the Russians wanted partition only to ensure chaos in Palestine.)

A point sharply debated before the vote concerned the disposition of the Negev. The Jewish Agency insisted this area must be Jewish, but the Near East Division of the State Department felt the area should go to the Arabs, because, as members of the division pointed out, the area was overwhelmingly Arab in population and historically had been so. On November 12, Secretary Marshall said the decision to include the Negev in the Arab state had been made by the State Department "by full delegation under the chairmanship of the Secretary."[28]

On November 18, Ambassador Johnson and General Hilldring said that most of the changes desired by the United States had been accepted in subcommittee, except the one concerning the Negev. They noted that the Jewish Agency was willing to assign part of the area to the Arabs, and believed it was best not to take the matter further at that time, since only the Arabs were likely to support the American position. The United States would be blamed should there be a breakdown in negotiations. Lovett was acting for Marshall, who was at the London Conference of the Council of Foreign Ministers, and he felt that the message of November 12 represented the State Department's considered view and that Johnson and Hilldring should support that position. If the *ad hoc* committee balked at approval, they should then vote for whatever proposal won a majority vote, indicating that the United States had deferred to that position.[29]

An episode occurred on the 19th that in some aspects presaged a confusion that was to emerge the following spring. After Marshall's instructions of November 12 and Lovett's repetition of them on the 18th, Ambassador Johnson was prepared to vote in the *ad hoc* committee according to the department's instructions. In the afternoon, President Truman, who had seen Weizmann that morn-

ing, called Hilldring to ask how things were going. When Hilldring
said that he was not happy with his instructions, Truman cautioned
that nothing should be done to upset the applecart: he agreed with
Weizmann's views and wanted the United States to go along with
the majority recommendations. Hilldring replied that because of
the differences between the President's instructions and those of
the State Department, he and Johnson would make no statement
that day but would issue one later.[30]

Lovett called the President in the late afternoon and asked about
the conversation with Hilldring. The President said that he had not
intended to change the department's instructions but did not want
the United States to be in a useless minority. Lovett sent this statement to members of the delegation.

The *ad hoc* committee voted to award the Negev to the Jewish
state, leading Loy Henderson to repeat all his previous warnings to
Lovett. He said that reactions from an Arab friend, formerly Prime
Minister of Iraq, indicated grave problems in the Middle East, and
the vote had not been in the interests of the United States. Ambassador Johnson had been wrong in suggesting that the Security
Council could handle any disorder by using military force. It would
be a serious error to introduce U.S. forces into Palestine, and worse
was "the fact that Soviet troops under our plan would be introduced into the heart of the Middle East. . . ."[31]

Lovett went to the White House on the morning of the 21st to
ascertain the President's attitude with regard to the United States'
accepting a place on a commission to implement any U.N. plan for
partitioning Palestine. Truman was decidedly reluctant to have the
United States be a member of such a commission and would accept
only if the Soviet Union were placed on it. Should U.S. forces be
required, they would go only as a part of a U.N. force. He added
that when the General Assembly met to vote on the majority report
of the *ad hoc* committee, he wanted the U.S. delegation not to use
pressure on other delegations to vote for the report, but to observe
scrupulously his commitment to the Arab states to refrain from
pressure. The President emphasized that he did not want Secretary
Marshall to be embarrassed in his dealings with Bevin in the current Council of Foreign Ministers in London by U.S. delegation
remarks on the noncooperation of the British.[32]

The U.N. Special Committee on Palestine voted on the *ad hoc*
committee's report on November 25, accepting the majority vote
for partition by a vote of 25–13, with seventeen abstentions and two
absences. On the 29th, the General Assembly voted 33–13, with ten
abstentions and one absent, to accept the report in favor of parti-

tion. Election of Bolivia, Czechoslovakia, Denmark, Panama, and the Philippines as members of the U.N. commission to deal with the plan for partition followed.[33]

In London on the evening before the first vote, Marshall and Ambassador Douglas met with Bevin and A. V. Alexander to plan British-American strategy in dealing with German problems at the forthcoming Council of Foreign Ministers. An angry Bevin snorted over Ambassador Johnson's U.N. statement that the British had been uncooperative about Palestine. The unanimous reaction in Britain, he trumpeted, was against the Jews in Palestine. This emotion, he declared, stemmed from the killing of the two British sergeants, which could never be forgiven. The anti-Jewish feeling in Britain was the greatest in 200 years. He insisted that Britain could not be involved in a partition that might require military action against the Arabs. He believed that trained Communists were among the Jews seeking illegal entry into Palestine, but Douglas questioned the accuracy of this statement. Aware of the need for Bevin's support in battles with Molotov during the coming sessions, Marshall tried his version of tact. He said that he understood the British anger at pressure from American Jews, but the situation in Palestine must be settled without delay, and he hoped that the British would not make a settlement impossible.[34]

Bevin's agitation was matched by that of the countries that had opposed partition. Angry accusations by Arab countries and their supporters were that American pressure was responsible for many countries' abstention from voting, in an effort to obtain a majority. A Philippine statement that members of Congress had threatened to withhold financial assistance for those who did not favor partition brought indignant denials from Lovett. He repeated Truman's and Marshall's strictures against such pressures. Accounts by Jewish advocates of partition reveal no government pressure but proudly point to effective Jewish Agency propaganda and personal appeals.[35]

At the end of the London Conference, in which Bevin had strongly supported Marshall, the British Foreign Secretary was still fuming over the vote for partition and repeated to Marshall Arab accusations that after the Secretary of State had left Washington for London, enormous U.S. pressure had been brought on Latin American delegates to vote for partition. Marshall said that he had opposed any kind of pressure, even to the extent of declining to give Latin American delegates any suggestions, and he had given members of the U.S. delegation firm instructions on that subject. He had the most complete confidence in General Hilldring, who was handling the matter in the special-committee vote, and he was sure he would "handle it with clean hands."[36]

Lovett felt it necessary to issue to King Farouk of Egypt a firm denial of improper American activity for partition. After reviewing statements by responsible officials, congressional resolutions, and party platforms for the past thirty years, the United States felt that it had to support partition. American public opinion had been stirred by the mistreatment of Jews in Europe and by the desire of surviving Jews to return to their ancient homeland. The United States had refrained from trying to influence other countries. Aware of Arab fears that the Jews would seek to use the area given them in Palestine as a base for further expansion in the Near East, the United States was prepared to oppose that type of aggression in the General Assembly. The United States was eager to have Arab friendship and interested in all measures to bring prosperity to the Near East. "It is the conviction of the United States Government that acquiescence on the part of the Arab states in the UNGA on Palestine, difficult though such acquiescence may be, would remove Palestine as a disturbing influence in international affairs."[37]

But no one in the State Department was genuinely hopeful. At the end of the year, the U.S. Consul General in Jerusalem cabled Marshall: ". . . terror is prevalent and normal life (i.e., normal life for Palestine) is disappearing. It is, however, compared with what may be expected in the future, a period of relative peace and restraint."

Not long before the end of the year, the Secretary of the Army, reflecting on new responsibilities for the armed forces that partition might bring, asked the National Security Council to examine the question. The Policy Planning Staff, in turn, analyzed the situation from the standpoint of the State Department.

Considering American interests without regard to a Jewish national state, the Planning Staff held that Palestine was vital to the control of the eastern Mediterranean and the Suez Canal, and it was an outlet for Middle East oil, which was essential to United States security. In view of the danger of Soviet infiltration, political, economic, and social equilibrium must be maintained.[38]

The planners noted that the General Assembly had recently approved a partition plan to go into effect when Britain gave up its mandate on August 1, 1948. A five-member U.N. Commission for Palestine was to take over mandatory responsibilities and arrange for provisional governments in the two new states. Although the Jewish Agency had agreed to partition, it was uncertain whether leftist Jews had agreed to it, and the Arabs were united in opposition to it.

The report noted that the United States had voted for partition on the assumption that the majority of the United Nations was in favor of this solution, even if it meant imposing the plan on Palestine. But all indications were that the Arabs would support neither partition nor an economic union of the two states in Palestine. Violence was increasing. If appeals were made to the Security Council to establish law and order in Palestine, who would send the troops to do it—the United States? And if it were a United Nations force, the Soviets would be part of it, introducing Soviet forces into the Palestine area.

In recent weeks, the United States had imposed an embargo on the shipment of arms and equipment to either Arabs or Jews. The lifting of this embargo could cause greater bloodshed.

Adverse possibilities for the United States in the Near East were the cancellation of agreements for air bases, the cessation of pipeline concessions, and the general, drastic worsening of trade relations. American military forces would have no access to air, military, and naval bases developed in the area by the British. Loss of or failure to benefit from increased oil production in the Middle East would badly damage the success of the Marshall Plan. Therefore, the Policy Planning Staff recommended that the United States "take no further initiative in implementing or aiding partition." It should not favor the dispatch of armed forces of any power into Palestine to implement partition, and it should maintain the embargo on arms shipments to Palestine or neighboring countries. The United States must be willing to work out a solution, such as a federal state or a trusteeship, which could be maintained without armed forces.

Dean Rusk, who had just become Director of the Office of United Nations Affairs, questioned whether events had changed the situation since the General Assembly vote of late November, and whether steps had been taken to see that the partition plan could work. What were the alternatives if it failed? He was acerbic about Britain's failure to carry out its mandatory responsibilities, suggesting that perhaps Britain should be charged with working out a solution between Arabs and Jews.[39]

As head of the Policy Planning Staff, Kennan replied that he had been asked to discuss U.S. national interests as they were affected by Palestine, not to suggest a solution. He disagreed with Rusk's strictures on the British, who had tried to have a study made earlier,

only to have it turned down by the Jewish Agency as pro-Arab.
Although responsibility for the current situation belonged to every
country that had studied the situation during the last thirty years,
the main burden lay on "Jewish leaders and organizations who have
pushed so persistently for the pursuit of objectives which could
scarcely fail to lead to violent results."[40]

Gloomily, Kennan concluded that the United States had already
accepted intolerable commitments from which it should remove
itself as rapidly as possible. It had to recognize that the situation
in Palestine defied solution at that time. "At the same time, we
should not attempt to be our brother's keeper or to offer moral
advice to other powers when we are unable to bear our own full
share of responsibility for the consequences."

Loy Henderson went beyond Kennan in pessimism. He had predicted the problem. The vote for partition was based on a belief
that Arabs and Jews could work together on the partition plan, but
the plan was impossible for either, and April brought greater unrest. The situation was not like that in Greece, when the United
States had helped the Greek government to survive despite efforts
by three Communist nations to overturn it. The majority of Palestine's inhabitants were opposed to partition and wanted to establish an Arab state. The United States should work with Great
Britain to stabilize the Middle East.[41]

Marshall and Lovett read these evidences of rampant pessimism
with concern, but stayed on the set course for the moment. Though
they did not discuss the matter with the President, they felt that
they knew his current opinions from a report on his conversation
with George Wadsworth, newly appointed Ambassador to Iraq,
before Wadsworth left for his new post. In talking of his concern
for the Near East, the President said that "he had kept in close
touch. Lovett knew the situation well; so did General Marshall. He
himself saw alike with the State Department."

Wadsworth felt that it was important to get on with economic
projects such as the Tigris-Euphrates oil development. Truman
agreed, mentioning that, though warriors of the past, such as Tam-
erlane, had destroyed civilizations, for the first time in history the
conqueror was going to reconstruct the conquered. Wadsworth
said that the Arabs wanted to submit to the World Court for an
advisory opinion the constitutional question of whether the Security Council had the power to impose partition on Palestine. The
President interrupted to say that this question must be settled here
and at the Lake Success meeting, "and he repeated that, having
kept in touch with Mr. Lovett and General Marshall, he felt that he

could go along with what the State Department might recommend."[42]

Evidence of State Department weakening on partition was reported by Rusk to Lovett on February 11. Ralph Bunche of the U.N. staff had warned Austin the previous day that if the United States gave up on partition it would mean a deathblow to the prestige of the United Nations. Rusk said that the U.N. Commission on Palestine had indicated that partition was unworkable without force. He warned that war might begin in Palestine, the Arabs against the Jewish state and U.N. representatives, or war by the U.N. against the Arabs in Palestine and against the Arab states. He reminded Lovett that the U.N. Charter authorized the United Nations to resist aggression and to keep the peace, but it did not authorize force to compel a political settlement: "The purpose of the United Nations is to keep peace, not to make war."

The next day, the Policy Planning Staff submitted to the department a working paper listing three alternatives: (1) partition even if force was necessary; (2) passiveness; and (3) a look at alternatives such as the creation of a federal state with Jewish and Arab areas, or a U.N. trusteeship for a specified period.[43]

A few days earlier, Mrs. Roosevelt had asked Marshall whether signs of U.S. weakening on partition were real. She wanted to know if the U.S. ban on shipping arms to the Jews should not be lifted, so that any police force in Palestine could be equipped with modern arms.[44]

Marshall explained to her in mid-February that the State Department was trying to formulate a peacekeeping policy, which was difficult to do because of terrorism by both Arabs and Jews in Palestine. He believed that lifting the embargo on arms would add to the violence, and that the suspension should be maintained while they were seeking a solution.

The first special report of the U.N. Commission on Palestine, on February 16, detailed strong efforts by Arabs inside and outside Palestine to prevent partition. Sporadic Jewish terrorism heightened the general discord, although the Jewish community in Palestine favored the report. Britain increased the confusion by speeding efforts to end its mandatory responsibility and to evacuate its troops. The Commission on Palestine sought the aid of the Security Council in carrying out its tasks, requesting armed assistance to keep order between the date of the report and the termination of the British mandate. To prevent bloodshed, the commission asked that a non-Palestinian force be organized to assist moderate Arab and Jewish elements in preserving order.

This report forced the issue of whether the partition resolution would be enforced or another alternative considered. Rumors that U.S. armed forces might have to enforce partition in Palestine stirred the Pentagon. Major General Alfred Gruenther of the Joint Chiefs of Staff had already reported to Secretary Forrestal that current strategic planning had been significantly altered by the possibility of sending forces to the Middle East. On February 19, Gruenther met with Truman and State and Defense Department representatives to suggest that U.S. participation in Palestine would require 89,000 to 120,000 men.[45]

President Truman was thus aware, before he left for a short vacation in the Caribbean, of the growing fear that partition without force was unworkable and that there was support in the General Assembly for reconsidering the November resolution. Just before the President left, Marshall told him that Lovett was at work on a statement for Austin to make in the Security Council, the text of which would be sent for presidential approval.

Truman assured him that they could "ignore all political factors" in whatever position they chose as right. For the benefit of U.S. diplomatic missions in the Middle East, Marshall dispatched on February 19 a statement released by the White House press secretary stressing that restraint in dealing with the Palestine situation was important to world peace.[46]

On February 21, the State Department sent to the President the working draft of the paper that Austin would present to the Security Council on the following Tuesday. The statement would call the council's attention to recommendations of the General Assembly, to the contents of the current report by the Commission on Palestine, and to the current report on security in Palestine. The council should "attempt to carry out the requests of the General Assembly with respect to the partition plan, short of the use of its enforcement powers to impose the plan upon the Mandatory Power or the people of Palestine." The council should use every effort to obtain a peaceful settlement on the basis of a plan acceptable to Jews and Arabs. If a situation developed that threatened international peace, the council should use its full powers under the United Nations Charter.[47]

Along with the draft, steps to be followed if partition was not accepted were listed for the President's special consideration. In such a case, the matter should be referred to a special session of the General Assembly. The State Department would consider it evident that the people of Palestine were not ready for self-government, "that some form of United Nations trusteeship for an additional period of time will be necessary." In view of the time needed to take further action, it might be necessary for the Security Council to ask Great Britain to continue its mandatory role for a time.

Despite the extreme care exercised to keep these discussions quiet, rumors reached the Jewish Agency, which brought them at once to Lovett. Moshe Shertok and Eliahu Epstein of the agency talked with him and a member of the Near East Division on February 21. Shertok declared that the Palestine government under British control was not impartial in its handling of Arab outrages; the only hope for peace was partition. Lovett, declining to argue these points, asked what appeals had been made to the Palestine government and what efforts had been made to seek an understanding with the Arabs. The following day, Shertok elaborated on these points at length, and on the 22nd he flatly stated that partition represented the extreme limit to which the Jews were prepared to go, for it required them to relinquish claims to areas they regarded as part of their national home. Jews were alarmed by rumors of a reopening of the situation, which meant to them that violence was being rewarded in the Middle East. The Jewish Agency would regard with the greatest anxiety any attempt to prolong the British mandate past May 15. Such action would court disaster. The basis of a permanent peace in Palestine required the establishment of a provisional government, the preparation of a properly armed Jewish-state militia, and the presence of an international force adequate in composition and size.[48]

The final draft of what Austin was to say at approximately 10:30 A.M. the next day was sent to the President on February 23. The covering letter emphasized that the statement did not mark a retreat, that if it seemed to mark a recession this was due to a lack of understanding of the Security Council's authority to impose recommendations by force. Late that evening, Marshall's message to Austin was that the President had approved the whole statement. A public announcement was to be made later by the President saying that the U.S. position had been carefully considered and was accurately presented by Austin.[49]

On the 24th, Austin spoke before the Security Council. He reviewed the actions concerning Palestine taken in the United Nations since 1947. The General Assembly had recommended partition and had set up the Commission on Palestine, and had asked the Security Council to take steps to approve these actions. The assembly had also asked the council to consider whether, during the transitional stage, the disorders in Palestine constituted a threat to international peace. He reminded the council that it had

power and responsibility to maintain order and enforce peace or
repel aggression from outside, but not to use force to impose
partition. It was desirable that the council appoint a committee
made up of its permanent members to investigate the situation and
determine what were the threats to international peace. They
should arrange talks with the Commission on Palestine, with Great
Britain, and with the parties chiefly concerned about implementation of the resolution. They should call on governments and people
of areas in and around Palestine to prevent or reduce threats to
peace by disorders in the area.[50]

Meanwhile, George Kennan and his staff were working on a
report to Marshall reviewing the situation. Their report pointed
out that the United States had decided that the security of the
Middle East was vital to national security, but that the country
should not take over or duplicate British facilities in that area,
which meant supporting the British strategic position there. The
United States was being pressured to maintain or even expand a
Jewish state in Palestine—a move against American security interests—although concessions might have to be made because of past
commitments or domestic pressures. If the United States knew
what it was doing and acted carefully, it might avoid catastrophe,
but if it accepted responsibility for sending U.S. forces into Palestine or recruiting volunteer forces or using troops from smaller
nations that might include Russian satellites, then the whole structure of policy for the Middle East and the Mediterranean would
have to be changed.[51]

The United States had a chance to prevent the Middle East from
falling under Russian influence, but to maintain the Jewish state
against the hostility of the Arabs of the area was to become involved
in a policy not in accord with American national interests, undertaken because of past commitments of dubious wisdom or because
of attachment to the United Nations. Unless there was a radical
reversal of policy, the United States would end up responsible for
protecting the Jewish population against the declared hostility of
the Arabs, or of sharing that responsibility with the Soviets and
installing them as one of the military powers of the area. "In either
case, the clarity and efficiency of a sound national policy for that
area will be shattered."

Kennan was stating a position widely held in the Pentagon by
various service chiefs, and in Foggy Bottom by State Department
officials. At the moment, the United States position was to proceed
along the lines of Austin's speech. Austin presented a resolution on
February 25 outlining the proposals of November 29 and asking for

Security Council action. Amendments were suggested, proposing that no attempt be made to carry out partition until an investigation had been made of the possible effect of that action on peace in the Middle East. While these amendments were being considered, Lovett indicated to a staff member that the Security Council would decide that nothing constructive could be done about partition and might call another meeting of the General Assembly to reconsider the question. The council might find sufficient threat to international peace to warrant sending a U.N. force there to negotiate a settlement. In that case, it should be clear that the U.N. force was on hand to keep peace, not to enforce partition.[52]

Marshall, at a February 26 press conference, declined to answer questions on the problems being discussed in New York, for he did not want any conflict between his position and that of Austin. He said that any statement must come from New York. Off the record, he declared (and this word was sent to Austin):

> I will tell you this—that so far as I am concerned and the State Department is concerned, but particularly so far as I am concerned, that in this highly emotional period of extreme bitterness and violent attacks, my intention is to see that nothing is done by the State Department in guidance for the action of its delegates to the United Nations, in response to either military threat or political threats, one or the other, nothing whatever. My intention is to see that the action of the U.S. Government is to be on a plane of integrity that will bear inspection and a common review and that there will be no bending to a military threat or any political threat so long as I am Secretary of State.[53]

The Central Intelligence Agency had also been preparing a report for more than a week, which had been agreed to by the intelligence agencies of the State, Army, Navy, and Air Force departments. This report of February 28 concluded that the partition of Palestine and the economic accord of the proposed Arab and Jewish states could not be implemented. Reactions had already been violent, and the Arabs were training troops to resist. The British were unwilling to participate in implementing any recommendation not acceptable to both sides, and they proposed to end the mandate on May 15 and leave the situation to the U.N. Commission on Palestine, which would be unable to carry out its instructions. The CIA fell back, as had the Policy Planning Staff, on the possibility of a reconsideration of the November action.[54]

Thinking over the various developments abroad and reports

from the Policy Planning Staff, the Central Intelligence Agency, and the United Nations, Marshall took to the March 5 Cabinet meeting a statement indicating that Austin had introduced a resolution in the Security Council on February 24 that called for the council's first provision for implementing partition. On February 27, the Belgian delegation had proposed that this provision be deleted from the resolution. Austin had made it clear to the council on March 2 that the vote on this measure was a vote for or against partition by peaceful means. Marshall explained that it could be that the Belgian vote might be carried by seven affirmative votes that afternoon, but that it was "almost absolutely certain" that the U.S. proposal would not get enough affirmative votes to pass. As a result, the council would set up a subcommittee to see what chance partition had, short of force. Efforts at conciliation would probably prove fruitless, and the council would then have to decide whether to attempt to carry out partition. "Without endeavoring to prophesy, the future trend seems to be that the Council will find itself unable to proceed with partition and will refer the Palestine problem to an immediate special session of the General Assembly for fresh consideration."[55] If the President read this statement, he must have been informed that partition was in danger.

Meanwhile, Clark Clifford, the President's special counsel, was studying the Palestine problem. He had gone with the President to the Caribbean and had handled messages dealing with instructions to Austin at the United Nations. On returning to Washington, he tackled the problem of bolstering Truman's image for the autumn presidential campaign.

The hesitations in the United Nations over the partition of Palestine and the likelihood of dropping partition caught Clifford's attention, and he wrote a memorandum on what should be done about Palestine to counter the views that had been set forth by the Policy Planning Staff and the Near East Division of the State Department, the intelligence offices of the Navy, Army, and Air Force, and the Central Intelligence Agency.[56]

Clifford declared that the United Nations had proposed partition in the first place and should not fail to back it in every possible way. During discussions by the five great powers, the United States should bring constant pressure on the Arab states to accept partition. He believed that not enough pressure had been applied and that there had actually been acts of appeasement. After a ten-day period for discussion, the United States should brand the Arab states as aggressors and declare that Arab actions constituted a threat to peace. The Security Council should bar the British mandatory from any action to obstruct or delay the work of the Commission on Palestine. The United States should cease its embargo on arms shipments to Palestine, which would increase the ability of the Jewish militia and Haganah, the Jewish defense organization, to defend themselves. The United States should withdraw its instructions for invalidating the passports of its citizens serving in the Palestine militia created by the United Nations, and should cooperate fully in the formation of an international security force in Palestine, with no troops furnished by great powers, but only by small states. (If Russia insisted on sending volunteers, they should be limited to a tenth of the total force.)

Whether or not the paper reached the President in this form, its essence was sent to him in a memorandum by Clifford on March 8. Aware that the President had insisted in earlier discussions that the U.S. representatives to the United Nations should not be influenced by political considerations, Clifford began by stating that the Palestine problem must not be considered in the light of how it affected Arabs, Jews, or the United Nations, but only in view of what was best for the United States. The coming election should not color the decision. "I know only too well," he wrote to Truman, "that you would not hesitate to follow a course of action that makes certain the defeat of the Democratic Party if you thought such action was best for America. What I say is, therefore, completely uninfluenced by election considerations." He reviewed United States policy since World War I to show the President's favoring of partition was in conformance with that policy. "It was a high-minded, statesman-like adoption of *the one* course that may avoid military involvement." In addition, partition was the only course in Palestine that would strengthen the United States' position in regard to the Soviet Union.[57]

He pointed out that the United Nations was dividing into factions and failing to use its peacekeeping power. The American people felt that their government was contributing to the disintegration of the United Nations.

"Nothing had contributed so much to this feeling as Senator Austin's recent statement. In large part, it seemed to be the sophistries of a lawyer attempting to tell what we *could not do* to support the United Nations—in direct contradiction to your numerous statements that we mean to do everything possible *to support* the United Nations."

From the standpoint of our own selfish interests, he continued, we must support the U. N.'s previous actions on Palestine. Continued chaos in Palestine would invite Russian intervention. Clifford added that we need not fear that the Arabs will refuse to sell us oil. They have no other choice. If anything had been omitted which would kill partition, he did not know it. First, the British mandatory had done everything possible to prevent action by the Palestine Commission. Second, the United States had placed an embargo on arms to Palestine while the British continued to sell arms to the Arabs under contract obligations. Third, the State Department had made no effort to conceal its dislike for partition, and fourth, "the United States appears in the ridiculous role of trembling before threats of a few nomadic desert tribes."

In forwarding instructions to Austin on March 5 on how to proceed in the afternoon voting, Marshall had included permission given by the President in February from the Caribbean, when Truman had insisted on partition and then, if that proved impossible to achieve, a consideration of trusteeship. Marshall emphasized that there must be a clearcut vote on partition. Austin should first ask for a vote on the Belgian amendment to delete the partition proposal, which had been brought up on the afternoon of the 5th and defeated. Then the partition requests of the General Assembly, supported by the United States, were put forward. Five nations— the United States, the Soviet Union, France, Belgium, and the Ukraine—voted for partition and economic accord in Palestine. The president of the council announced that recommendations for partition had failed to get the required seven votes for passage.

At first the United States wanted to bring up the trusteeship at this point, but decided to ask that the five permanent members of the Security Council—the United States, the Soviet Union, the United Kingdom, France, and China—consult with the interested parties—the Jewish Agency, Arab Higher Committee, the mandatory power, and the U.N. Commission on Palestine—to determine whether partition could be established by peaceful means. Ten days were allowed for this process. If the report was not favorable, Austin was to propose the calling of a special session of the General Assembly to consider a plan for a trusteeship until partition could be worked out. Marshall reminded Austin of the short time remaining before the British surrendered the mandate.

On March 6, with the President back in his office, Lovett sent to the White House the instructions given Austin the day before. Soon the President asked Lovett to come over, acknowledging receipt of the documents and promising to read them. Two days later, Marshall and Lovett discussed with him the Marshall Plan and partition of Palestine. Partition had failed of passage in the United Nations, and the permanent members of the Security Council were trying to see whether the conciliatory machinery of the council could find a way to make partition work.

No minutes of the meeting between the President, Marshall, and Lovett have been found, but Lovett dictated from Florida a week or so later a memo to Charles Bohlen on his recollection of the discussion: "The President said that we were to go through and attempt to get approval of implementation of the G[eneral] A[ssembly] resolution, but if we did not get it we could take the alternative step. *That was perfectly clear.* He said it to General Marshall and me." After lunch, Lovett said that he told McClintock (a State liaison officer on Palestine) that the President had agreed that this step be taken after the United States had been licked on partition: *"There is absolutely no question but what the President approved it."* In conclusion, Lovett added, *"There was a definite clearance there.* I stress it because Clifford told me the President said he did not know anything about it."[58]

The vote on partition had been taken at the United Nations on March 5. Yet, a few days later, the President said there was still to be a vote on partition. Although Marshall's statement at the March 5 Cabinet meeting made it clear that the U.N. vote on partition would be taken that afternoon, and that he doubted partition would be approved, Truman may have been confused because Marshall's instructions to Austin before the vote had stressed the vote on partition first.

The five permanent members of the Security Council now had to determine whether they could find agreement among the most interested parties. Problems developed almost at once when Andrei Gromyko refused to take part in formal consultations, but agreed to individual consultations. On March 9, Lovett instructed Austin to ask other council members to consult about ways of bringing partition and economic accord. As an interested party, the British found it difficult to take part in consultations but would answer questions; then Gromyko agreed to sit in on discussions with Jewish and Arab committees.[59]

Rabbi Silver and Moshe Shertok of the Jewish Agency definitely favored partition and thought it could be achieved peacefully. Later, a member of the Arab Higher Committee met with the permanent members but agreed only to forward their questions to other members of his delegation. The committee's previous, adamant refusal to consider partition still stood.

With the United Kingdom (because it was the mandatory power) and the Soviet Union (to create discord, the Americans thought) out of consultations, the other permanent members of the Security

Council—China, France, and the United States—gave their conclusions. Tsian Tingfu asked if they could not agree that peaceful implementation of partition was out of the question. André Parodi of France said that the Arabs were bound to conclude that the United Nations was not very interested in partition and, therefore, would not be inclined to favor it; he wondered, however, if the U.N. should not try to get a truce. Austin said they must try for a peaceful settlement and that was why the United States was sticking to the partition plan, if it could be done peacefully. During this time, Marshall was receiving reports from various American embassies in Arab countries to the effect that the Palestine situation "grows daily more fraught with danger to international peace."[60]

The issue now before the Security Council, Marshall declared, was whether the "Big Five" consultations had or had not produced some area of agreement that might make partition possible without bloodshed. "Since statements Austin had gathered from the interested parties clearly revealed that no party to the Palestine problem believed that partition can be carried out except by use of force it would seem that the necessary conclusions can be rapidly drawn." In this case, Austin should make the statements authorized by the President so that the council might proceed to consideration of Palestine security divorced from the political issue of partition and economic accord. In view of the rapidly approaching end of the British mandate, Marshall concluded, "The time factor is imperative and Council must act without delay."[61]

While Marshall was setting in motion action that would lead Austin to call for a special session of the General Assembly and temporary trusteeship, developments in the White House set in motion a collision between the President and the State Department. Since mid-February, the fear of Jewish leaders that American support for partition was waning had been leading them to propose another meeting between Truman and Chaim Weizmann, for whom the President evinced affection and respect. Weizmann had recently left New York for London en route to Palestine. He was persuaded to return to the United States while other Zionists asked Eddie Jacobson of Kansas City, old friend and one-time business partner of Truman, to set up a presidential interview with Weizmann. Angry about the intense pressure and the Zionists' charges that he had not acted vigorously enough in favor of a Jewish national state, however, the President declared he would see no more Zionist representatives. He wrote Jacobson from Florida that Weizmann could tell him nothing about Palestine that he did not already know.

On March 13, after Truman had returned from his vacation, Jacobson turned up at the White House without an appointment. He was admitted with the admonition not to bring up the subject of Palestine. According to his account, he made an impassioned plea to his old friend, who yielded at last and agreed to see Weizmann.

On the evening of March 18, Weizmann was brought privately to the White House for a conference. No minutes have been found, but apparently the Jewish leader believed that he had been promised that the United States stood firm on partition and would lift the embargo against arms shipments to Palestine.[62]

The past three weeks had been filled with disquieting developments in Central Europe. A pro-Communist government had been imposed on Czechoslovakia, and from Berlin, General Lucius Clay warned of ominous changes in Soviet attitudes. Discussions about the course to be adopted for Germany had been marked by incidents that would lead to the Berlin blockade in a few weeks. On March 17, the President appeared before Congress to ask for the adoption of Universal Military Training and a return to Selective Service. Perhaps preoccupied with other matters, he did not tell Marshall or Lovett about what he had promised Weizmann. Both men were then away from Washington—Marshall on a West Coast speaking tour in behalf of Marshall Plan appropriations, and Lovett on vacation in Florida until March 27.

Truman knew of the instructions that Marshall had issued to Austin on March 5 and had approved these instructions and the language of the specific statements that Austin was to make. Marshall had set no exact date for Austin's speech, but it was plain that it would probably come within ten days after the consultations by members of the U.N. permanent committee had begun. Throughout the instructions was a stress on the prevention of chaos in Palestine by creating some authority that could fill the vacuum of British withdrawal on May 15. That withdrawal was actually already in progress, and the Commission on Palestine complained that it was getting little cooperation from the mandatory forces.

Carrying out Marshall's instructions on March 19, Austin declared that the council had before it clear evidence that the Jews and Arabs of Palestine, plus the mandatory, could not agree to implement the General Assembly's plan of peaceful partition. The withdrawal of the mandatory power from Palestine on May 15 would bring chaos and heavy loss of life. Under the Charter, the council had a specific duty to take steps to bring peace in Palestine. To do this and to allow time for the interested parties to reach agreement, he proposed a temporary trusteeship under the Trusteeship Council of the United Nations, which would be without prejudice as to the rights, claims, or position of parties concerned, or as to the character of the eventual political settlement, which we hoped could be achieved without long delay. Pending that meeting, the Security Council should instruct the Commission on Palestine to suspend its activities to implement the partition plan.[63]

In his authoritative biography of Truman, Robert Donovan describes the violent reaction of proponents of partition:

> Jews flooded the White House with angry letters and telegrams. In some places Jewish war veterans paraded. Worshippers gathering in synagogues around the country Saturday, March 20, were overwhelmed by a sense of misfortune. As Weizmann was to say, it appeared that independence had been granted in the fall only to be withdrawn in the spring. Representative Cellar called Austin's speech an "underhanded turnabout." It was apparent, the *New York Times* said in an editorial, that the White House was "utterly at sea."[64]

Embarrassed by this uproar just after his meeting with Weizmann, Truman penned a hot statement on his desk calendar, saying that the State Department had pulled the rug from under his policy. He noted that while he was in the Caribbean he had approved the speech and the policy, but he charged that the State Department had reversed his policy. The third and fourth levels of the State Department had brought about the reversal while Marshall was in California and Lovett in Florida.[65]

He instructed Clark Clifford to ask Marshall to make a statement to the press. In Los Angeles, Marshall declared that the course of action followed by Austin "appeared to me after careful consideration, to be the wisest course to follow. I recommended it to the President, and he approved my recommendation."[66]

Marshall talked with Truman on March 25. He subsequently told Charles Bohlen that Truman had said he was upset because he was not aware of when Austin was going to make the statement. "He had agreed to the statement but said if he had known when it was going to be made he could have taken certain measures to have avoided the political blast of the press."[67]

Shortly afterward, Marshall testified at length before an executive session of the Senate Foreign Relations Committee concerning the change in policy. In this secret session, he emphasized the fear of getting the Soviet Union involved in any enforcement of partition. Once Soviet forces came in, the strategic situation would alter, with possible damage to the European Recovery Program.[68]

On March 25, Truman approved Austin's speech by issuing a statement drafted by Clifford, Bohlen, and Rusk that specified that the temporary trusteeship was necessary to avoid chaos when the mandate ended. Meanwhile, there must be a temporary truce; he was asking Austin to propose this to the Security Council.[69]

The truce effort stirred up heated debate among Truman's advisers. The President told the press that he would not have proposed a truce if he did not think it had a chance of working. Clifford and David Niles, White House aides who dealt with minority problems, declared that, instead of a truce, the President should lift the arms embargo and extend military aid to the Jews. Marshall, arguing that a truce had a good chance of being accepted, won Truman's approval. The Secretary discussed the idea with Moshe Shertok and thought he saw a willingness to accept a truce under certain conditions. A few days later, Shertok told the Security Council that a truce would be welcome if accompanied by the evacuation of foreign forces, and further forays of armed forces into Palestine were stopped. Perhaps he did not expect these conditions to be met, however, because he later denied that he had agreed to support a truce.[70]

On March 27, under instructions from the President, Austin presented a draft resolution for a truce, written by Clifford. The Security Council agreed to its terms on April 1, shortly after Marshall had gone to Bogotá for the Inter-American Conference.

By the time Marshall returned to the United States on April 24, the Security Council had asked groups in Palestine and nations bordering Palestine to try to establish a truce. On the 23rd, the Security Council had approved a truce team consisting of delegates from Belgium, France, and the United States to make the arrangements.

The day after Lovett reported to Marshall progress in truce talks, Marshall mentioned this information in an off-the-record press conference. Dean Rusk had opposed such a briefing, because he feared that, if details of the conference got out, truce negotiations would be upset. But since other advisers assured the Secretary that there could be no problem, he told reporters that thirteen of the fourteen points in dispute had been accepted by both sides. Rusk's fears proved true, however: Marshall found that his off-the-record briefing went into print at once, and Moshe Shertok immediately denied that he had accepted several of the points.[71]

Rusk told the President at the end of April that Jewish leaders were divided on the truce. Moderates such as Shertok supported it, but Silver, an "extremist," was creating most of the opposition. Rusk added that both Arabs and Jews hinted that the United States might push the parties into agreement. Truman asked Rusk to tell the Secretary that he was ready to take any measures Marshall thought necessary to get a truce.

May 15, the end of the mandate, was approaching with what seemed terrifying speed to the State and Defense departments, which would have to take responsibility for keeping peace in Palestine after that date. They were equally nervous that the Soviet Union might try to move forces into the area. The Jews were bent on occupying as much as possible of their allotted area before the mandate ended. King Abdullah of Trans-Jordan wanted to send armed forces into the area given to the Arabs, but Marshall, seeing how easily warfare might ensue from this action, asked Prime Minister Attlee and Foreign Secretary Bevin to restrain Abdullah, to which they agreed.[71]

Militant Arab groups were determined to destroy Jewish settlements, and Jewish leaders were equally determined to hold what they had been allotted and to have a provincial government ready to go into effect the moment the mandate ended. Thus, whereas the United States hoped to establish a truce that would avoid widespread disorder, the two principal parties were set on courses that would lead to warfare.

Marshall was especially eager to avoid the development of a situation that would require American intervention. There were growing signs of Soviet truculence in Germany that had led him two weeks earlier at Bogotá to explain to the Latin American countries that American commitments in Germany and Turkey made impossible the assumption of additional responsibilities. The editors of *Foreign Relations* report that there is no record in the State Department of the conversation, except a brief outline which the Secretary of State summarized at the White House meeting on May 12. An account published in Hebrew text later by Shertok, is paraphrased by Abba Eban in his autobiography and by Howard Sachar in his *History of Israel.* They essentially agree that Marshall warned Shertok of being misled by initial military successes. It was important not to be guided by military advisers. He spoke of Chiang Kai-shek's initial easy victories in China and his later failures. Marshall said that if the Jews gambled to continue fighting and lost, they should not come to the United States for help. Shertok's account, as reported in Sachar, quotes Marshall as saying, "However, if it turns out you are right and you will establish the Jewish state, I'll be happy. But you are undertaking a grave responsibility." Sachar adds: "In fact, Shertok took the warning seriously. With Goldmann's support, he told his Zionist supporters in New York that Marshall's words at least deserved much thought."[72]

By the first week of May, a number of gloomy and vocal State Department experts were predicting that the Jews were determined to establish a Jewish state when the mandate ended, even if it meant armed conflict. Clifford and Niles reached the same conclusions in the White House. On May 6, they beseeched the President to approve the new state of Israel in advance of its proclamation and to announce that it would be recognized at the moment of its establishment. Clifford drafted a statement for the President to issue.

When Truman saw the statement on May 12, his reaction was favorable but he said he wanted to talk with Marshall before issuing it. The result was a White House meeting later that day between the President, Marshall, Lovett, Robert McClintock, and Fraser Wilkins of the State Department, and Clifford, Niles, and Matt Connolly of the White House staff.

Lovett described for them the meeting he and Marshall had held with Shertok. Then Truman called on Clifford, who argued that, to establish his position among the Jews, the President should drop truce efforts and declare that he intended to recognize the new state of Israel as soon as it was proclaimed. Mr. Lovett cautioned that such a declaration would damage the U.S. position in the United Nations, where an American resolution for a truce was still being considered. He pointed out that they should first know the nature of the state of Israel and its boundaries. A move such as Clifford proposed would, he thought, be so politically transparent as to defeat its purpose.[73]

As Marshall listened to the discussion, he saw honesty in Lovett's charge that Clifford's was a political approach—recognition of a new state because there were enough Jews in the United States to make recognition a good ploy in an American election. He said it would damage the presidential office. Perhaps Clifford's manner upset the Secretary, because he retorted in what Clifford supposedly termed "a righteous God-damned Baptist tone" that this matter was not to be settled on the basis of politics and that if domestic politics were not involved Clifford would not be at the conference. He went on to say that if the President were to take the political advice given by Clifford "and if in the election I was to vote, I would vote against the President." He suggested that they take another look after May 16. Truman, quickly seeing that the meeting was getting out of hand, said that he was inclined to agree with Marshall but they should sleep on the matter.

Jewish leaders were soon aware of the substance of the May 12 meeting at the White House, and fresh pressures were applied to Truman. Chaim Weizmann wrote an eloquent appeal on May 13 that moved the President. The next day, he called Clifford and told him to arrange for recognition that afternoon.[74]

Clifford sent Truman's message to Under Secretary Lovett and asked that the State Department prepare the announcement, but Lovett wanted it delayed until there was a chance to get "adequate details." Clifford was sure that they would have the details, "but timing of the recognition was of the greatest possible importance to the President from the domestic point of view."

Recognizing the futility of argument, Lovett begged for time to inform Austin and friends of the United States in the United Nations, especially since the Palestine question was being debated that afternoon in New York. Clifford promised that he would try to tell Lovett the exact time of the announcement.

Clifford had already informed Eliahu Epstein of the Jewish Agency concerning White House intentions, and Epstein signaled Shertok that the State Department would give immediate recognition if there were a prompt request. Later, Epstein said that he had acted on his own in making this request. The statement was prepared by the State Department and at 5:40 P.M. Clifford told Lovett that the announcement would be made at 6:00. Lovett barely had time to inform Austin, but there was no time at all to inform others of the U.S. delegation.

The statement said that the United States accorded *de facto* recognition to the provisional government of the new state of Israel as soon as it established itself. Nothing could have been more fantastic to the U.S. delegation to the United Nations than the way the announcement was handled. A U.S. delegate, Francis Sayre, speaking at the time of the announcement, was asked if it were true and could only say that he had no information. Philip Jessup got his information from a news ticker and confirmed the story. Some strong U.S. supporters in the United Nations were furious. Dean Rusk later said that a staff member had to sit on the lap of a Cuban delegate to keep the Cuban from going to the podium to withdraw Cuba from the United Nations.[75]

Both Warren Austin and strongly pro-Israel Eleanor Roosevelt wrote Marshall that the United States had been damaged in the United Nations because of the way the situation had been handled. Austin lamented, "Nobody trusts us any more." Mrs. Roosevelt quoted several delegates as having "stated quite frankly that they don't see how they could ever follow the United States' lead because the United States changed so often without any consultation." Austin felt that one could expect the Arabs to be angry but that a number of other nations felt they had been double-crossed.[76]

Three days later, Marshall, who had been away from Washington speaking for ERP legislation, saw the President and told him about the effect the handling of the affair had on the delegation. Describing this conversation to Lovett, Marshall said that Truman had been ignorant of what had happened at the Security Council "and treated it somewhat as a joke as I had done but I think we both probably thought it was a hell of a mess." In a less jocular vein, Marshall continued, he felt that the United States had hit an all-time low in the United Nations and "had better be careful what it did in the future or we will give an final kick to the UN."

Dean Rusk heard afterward that several of Marshall's friends had urged him to resign. Marshall supposedly replied that one did not resign because the President, who had a constitutional right to make a decision, had made one.

While the problem of Germany and Soviet intentions agonized European governments, Israel's emergence threatened to play an important part in the U.S. presidential campaign. From May on, settlement of boundaries kept increasing in troublesomeness. In announcing their *de facto* independence, Jewish leaders had claimed boundaries specified in the U.N. resolution of November 1947. Since that time, both Jewish and Arab forces had attempted to extend control over territories claimed by each. By June, Arabs held most of the Negev, and the Jews had western Galilee. Late in June, Count Folke Bernadotte of Sweden, charged by the U.N. with finding an acceptable solution to the problem, suggested that each side keep what it then held, with Jerusalem going to the Arabs but with autonomy provided there for the Jews, and with protection for all the holy places. The State Department found this proposal a good basis for negotiations.

Palestine engaged the attention of platform builders at the two major American political conventions. In June, the Republican Convention promised full recognition of Israel with boundaries suggested by the 1947 U.N. resolution. Three weeks later, the Democrats made a similar pledge, adding that they would consider only such modifications as were acceptable to Israel. State Department officials continued to believe that Bernadotte's proposal might be more conducive to peace.

In August, as a guide to the U.S. special representative to Israel, a statement accepting the tenor of the Bernadotte proposal was approved in the handwriting of Truman and Marshall. It was sent to Tel Aviv in early September.

Bernadotte's plan, submitted on September 16, contained many of the suggestions made earlier in draft form. One major change was that Jerusalem would be under U.N. control rather than belonging to the Arabs, as in the earlier suggestion, which had aroused Jewish fury against the Swedish diplomat. On September 17, Bernadotte was assassinated in Israel by Jewish terrorists. Shertok was horrified and disavowed the murder.

The State Department had gone to great care to get Truman's approval in advance, but trouble spewed forth when Marshall announced from Paris:

> My Government is of the opinion that the conclusions [Bernadotte's] are sound and strongly urges the parties and the General Assembly to accept them in their entirety as the best possible basis for bringing peace to a disturbed land.[77]

The elections were too close and too uncertain for the administration's comfort, and the White House was increasingly vulnerable to New York pressures. At times during this frantic period, White House policy on Israel was based on rumors fed to the President to the effect that Governor Dewey was ready to outpromise him to the Zionists. To determined campaign advisers, State Department deliberation on overall U.S. interests was irrelevant, a bother, and politically disloyal.

No one, of course, could blame the Jewish leaders for doing their utmost to fulfill the ancient, ardent dream of Jews for a homeland, having endured century upon century of wandering and persecution, culminating in the unimaginable horror of the Holocaust. The State Department question was whether immediate full satisfaction of Jewish aims should be forced on the Arabs at the expense of enormous problems for U.S. foreign policy. Possibly some members of the State Department *were* anti-Jewish or fixated on Arab oil or on Soviet expansion in Europe, but it was more than erroneous, it was wrong to depict every person in the department who suggested caution or further delay for negotiation as lacking in loyalty to Truman or as anti-Jewish, or both. From a national point of view, there was no mandate to carry out precisely the maximum demands of Zionist groups, and no basis for condemning Marshall and Lovett because they believed a compromise approach, advocated by some of their advisers, might have points of merit. At times, because of the necessity emphasized by White House advisers of winning the fall election, the White House became in effect the foreign office of the state of Israel.

Truman's friend Eddie Jacobson was called by Chaim Weizmann to ask that Truman repudiate Marshall's statement. Rabbi Silver's organization declared that the State Department had written the Bernadotte plan, and Moshe Shertok told Marshall on October 5 that Israel wanted both the Negev *and* western Galilee. From the presidential train in Oklahoma, where the President was fighting a campaign for his political life, Clifford suggested to Truman that the Secretary of State was changing White House policy without checking with him. Not recognizing that Marshall's statement in Paris was the same one that Marshall and Lovett had discussed with him, Truman signed Clifford's message to Marshall, which said that the U.S. government had backed the U.N. resolution for partition and the Democratic Party platform had done the same, so he would have to reaffirm the early position.

There was too little face-to-face discussion. Marshall's fiery outburst with Truman and Clifford in May had left the President wary of discussing Israel with him. In mid-August, Truman had sent word to Lovett that there were certain matters he wanted to discuss with the Under Secretary, but not with the Secretary, "because of political implications." When nomination of a special representative to the new state of Israel came up, the State Department submitted several names. James G. MacDonald, Clifford's candidate, was selected while Marshall was in Walter Reed Hospital for a checkup. Clifford telephoned Lovett to say that the President had decided to appoint MacDonald. He added that the appointment should be made at once and there should be no arguments. When Lovett told Marshall what had taken place during his absence, Marshall drafted a letter of protest to the President; Lovett thought he should not send this, because Marshall knew the activities were due to the machinations of the campaign manager and not to the President. Marshall accepted Lovett's advice, and Lovett told Clifford of Marshall's distaste for the type of procedure that had been used.

In September, Clifford pushed the President hard to get the State Department in line. He drafted a message instructing the Secretary to issue *de jure* recognition of Israel, to arrange for a loan to Israel, and to support Israel for U.N. membership.

His tough approach continued as Truman fought gamely in what was considered by a majority of the U.S. press to be a hopeless presidential campaign. Near the end of September, when Rabbi Stephen Wise protested Marshall's Paris statement on the Bernadotte plan, Clifford called Lovett from the Tulsa railroad yards, where the Presidential train was stationed, to ask why a telegram disavowing Marshall's statement should not be sent within three hours. Lovett responded by citing the statement of the boundary question that had been approved by the President and demonstrated that the White House had several days' advance notice of the Marshall announcement. Confronted with this evidence, Clifford decided that the President should not send the message but should instead tell Rabbi Wise that "it seems to me that the Bernadotte Plan offered a basis for continuing efforts to secure a just settlement."[78]

To get the boundaries they wanted and believed absolutely necessary for the security of their new state, Jewish leaders kept up pressure on the White House. They demanded in telegrams and paid advertisements that the Democrats uphold their party platform. Representatives in close congressional districts, party leaders in New York and Chicago, the Democratic national chairman, campaign fundraisers—all were reminded of the importance of the Jewish vote. From the White House advisers came curt instructions to the State Department that nothing be done to create trouble for the President in the closing days of the campaign. Marshall, in Paris for the meeting of the General Assembly, was embarrassed to have to evade discussion of the Palestine question. The White House message of October 29 emphasized even more the presidential advisers' distrust of the State Department delegation in Paris, declaring that the President wanted to be advised of any U.S. statement on issues before it was made. Assuming that Clifford had written the message, Marshall directed Lovett to ask Truman about it personally. Lovett replied that Clifford had sent the message because of a press report that the Russians had proposed a postponement of a debate on Palestine but the United States had opposed the motion. He wanted to know why.[79] On the following day, the President directed that the delegates avoid taking a position on Palestine until after November 3.

As if he had just learned of the matter and wanted to set things right, the President now sent the Secretary a long expression of his appreciation for Marshall's efforts in Paris. Lovett was not hopeful. He thought restrictions on the U.S. delegation were likely to continue for a little longer, "until the silly season terminates." Next day he added:

I am sure you agree that our past experience with formally approved positions and instructions which are subsequently and suddenly altered or revoked is increasingly dangerous and intolerable. I can imagine what you have been through in Paris. It has been absolute hell here. . . .[80]

The "silly season" had been hard on the delegation. After the election, Mrs. Roosevelt expressed the views of many of her colleagues: although she had strongly supported the Israelis' claims and aspirations, she was disturbed by White House actions. She wrote Marshall after the election, "Some time there will have to be a clarification of our position and I think it should be done after those who hold different views have expressed themselves in the same meeting with the President."

Marshall never held the President responsible for the treatment he had received from White House advisers. His message of congratulation to Truman on his election, and his statements of appreciation when he resigned after his operation, were completely sincere. In 1949, Truman arranged for Marshall to head the American Red Cross; in 1950, he appointed him Secretary of Defense. It is significant that Marshall took the jobs, and that letters between the two continued to reflect mutual admiration. As for Clifford, Marshall never mentioned him thereafter.

The "silly season" was over when a fighting President won an incredible victory. Despite the time and stress spent by his campaign manager on the issue of Israel, the Democrats had failed to win New York: Henry Wallace had carried enough prospective pro-Israel voters to give the state to Dewey. Nationally, the big issue had been the economy. Dewey believed that a shift in the farm vote in the last two weeks, because of a fall in farm prices, had cost him the victory.

Marshall returned home for hospitalization, leaving John Foster Dulles as acting head of the delegation. Aware that both Dewey and Truman had favored Israel's cause, Dulles pressed for resolutions in behalf of Israel. The United States and Great Britain then had pending before the Political Committee of the General Assembly what was known as the "Conciliation Resolution," which, in essence, proposed to accept Israel as an existing nation and to set up a United Nations committee to help work out its problems with its neighbors. Dulles, feeling that the British had injected a pro-Arab tinge into the proposal, set to work to make it more balanced, and asked Ambassador Douglas in London to help him. The amended resolution passed the Political Committee by 26–21 on December 4, 1948. This action still had to be ratified in the General Assembly by a two-thirds majority. With the aid of other U.S. delegates, among whom Mrs. Roosevelt and Benjamin Cohen were the most active pro-Israel proponents, he managed to persuade some pro-Arab representatives to release their votes. Despite monolithic opposition by the Arabs, the resolution, which did not mention the Bernadotte boundaries, passed 35–15 on December 11.[81]

Before the session ended, the U.S. delegation proposed the admission of Israel as a member of the United Nations. Although the United States and the Soviet Union joined with three other countries in favor of admission, the abstention of France and Canada prevented approval. In the following spring, there was a sufficient majority in the Security Council, and on May 11, 1949, the General Assembly approved membership for Israel by a vote of 35–11.

Strengthening Latin American Ties

S O much of Marshall's time as Secretary of State was taken up
with problems of Europe, the Middle East, and the Far East
that his efforts to reinforce United States ties with Latin America
and protect areas south of the border against totalitarian aggression are often overlooked. During much of the period, there was
little that the United States could do to help the countries to the
south economically, but at two conferences, in Rio de Janeiro in
1947 and in Bogotá in 1948, Marshall tried his best.

Brazil was the only South American country Marshall had visited
officially before he became Chief of Staff. Not long after Roosevelt
had nominated him, in the spring of 1939, to succeed Malin Craig
as head of the Army, the Chief of Staff of the Brazilian Army invited
Craig to make an official visit to Brazil. Craig, feeling that Marshall
would gain insights and contacts in Brazil valuable for his next four
years, sent him instead. His visit was highly successful and laid the
basis for cooperation with this southern neighbor throughout the
war.

In the first two years of the war, as the Axis powers moved easily
into Western Europe and North Africa, Allied fears heightened
over a German push to Dakar, a port uncomfortably close to South
America, perhaps to be followed by German claims on the New
World colonies of occupied France and the Netherlands. General
Marshall and Admiral Harold Stark had moved at once to
strengthen defenses in the Caribbean and encourage military
preparations throughout the entire Western Hemisphere.

The Havana Conference of 1940 pointed toward Latin American
military cooperation, resulting in the Inter-American Defense
Board in 1942 to build up defense of the Americas. In the next year,
there was a move toward standardization of weapons and distribu-

tion of U.S. funds for defense. Many Latin American countries declared war on the Axis but let that action constitute their main effort in the war. The important exception was Brazil, whose Expeditionary Force performed well in Italy and whose Navy helped patrol the South Atlantic. Unhappily, Argentina had long been a jealous rival of the United States in international conclaves and remained antagonistic. The rise to power of General Juan Perón, first as head of the armed forces behind the government and, soon after the war, as President, integrated the various strands of Argentine *anti-yanquismo* into solid opposition to almost any aspect of U.S. policy. Argentina was regarded as so favorable to the Axis that it was not invited by the other Latin American states to a meeting in Mexico City early in 1945 to draw up the Act of Chapultepec, pledging collective action along with the United States against aggression from inside and outside the Western Hemisphere. To avoid being excluded from the San Francisco meeting later in the spring for the purpose of drawing up a United Nations Charter, Argentina declared war against the Axis and signed the Act of Chapultepec.

Relations between Argentina and the United States did not improve during the early postwar period. General Perón adroitly used the disapproval and opposition of U.S. Ambassador Spruille Braden to gain votes and win the presidency. When Braden was brought back to Washington to become Assistant Secretary for Latin American Affairs, he soon clashed with his successor as Ambassador to Argentina, George Messersmith, accusing Messersmith of being too favorable toward Perón. This contretemps was brought to Marshall's attention by Acheson in January 1947 as one of the first problems the new Secretary of State must settle. Marshall agreed with Acheson that both men should be relieved of their assignments. To balance the continuing coldness between Washington and Buenos Aires, the United States favored stronger ties with Brazil.[1]

In the flush of victory after the war, with great stockpiles of military equipment on hand, the U.S. armed services proposed enlarged programs of military aid to Latin America, with the intent, said critics, of preventing Britain's competition in influence on Latin American military policy. The State Department became concerned over the Pentagon's tendency to ship arms southward, and some in the department feared that the country's military leaders were encouraging dictatorial regimes in Latin America. Secretary Byrnes insisted that the Soviet danger to Western Europe was greater than any kind of threat to Latin America.[2]

When Marshall became head of the State Department, there was some speculation that he might change Byrnes's policy. In his closing days as Army Chief of Staff, he had suggested that Latin American countries adopt standard models of arms and equipment, so they could use material furnished by the United States and Western Allies. When he became Secretary of State, he suspended decision until he could get a clearer estimate of the situation.

By 1947, the mood of the country had changed. A demand for cuts in military spending was so strong in Congress that military leaders grew apprehensive as the stockpile of military supplies diminished. The State Department increased its warnings about political instability accompanying military regimes in Latin America and repeatedly called attention to the great costs of military subsidies.

On his return from the Moscow Conference in the spring of 1947, Marshall at first considered increased military aid for Latin America, but after June of that year, the huge demands of the proposed European Recovery Program threatened to interfere. By the time of the Rio Conference, military planners were saying that aid must go to countries that could contribute most in case of war with the Soviet Union. When the Latin American countries appealed intensely for economic assistance, the United States discouraged that possibility. As Charles Pach has recently written of the period 1947–48, "Often an impetus to intervention, Cold War thinking actually restrained, albeit temporarily, U.S. military assistance to Latin America."[3]

The main business of the Rio Conference had been foreshadowed in March 1945, when the American republics met in Mexico City and passed a resolution urging certain safeguards against future aggression. In the Act of Chapultepec they had resolved that an act of aggression against any Latin American state would be regarded as an act against all the republics but allowed each country to decide on the type of action it would take. The resolution provided for a future *ad hoc* conference to put the resolution into permanent treaty form.

It was to carry out this last provision that the Brazilian government in the summer of 1947 issued an invitation to foreign ministers of the Latin American republics and the United States for a meeting in Rio by fall. In view of the rumors that elaborate military arrangements would be discussed, Marshall at once instructed the chiefs of U.S. missions to Latin America that the only purpose of the *ad hoc* meeting was to convert the temporary Act of Chapultepec into a permanent treaty and that it was "to be deemed political rather than military in establishing terms of inter-American solidarity for the maintenance of peace and security."[4]

The host country, which had helped the Allies so effectively in the war, eagerly expected economic aid. U.S. Ambassador William Pawley had worked painstakingly to keep the Brazilians cooperative, and the United States sent an unusually strong delegation to the conference, which was to be followed by a state visit by President and Mrs. Truman and their daughter, Margaret.[5] Following the Byrnes custom of taking along prominent members of Congress who had a hand in foreign affairs, Marshall had in his party Senator Vandenberg (Chairman of the Senate Foreign Relations Committee), Senator Connolly (ranking Democrat on the committee), Representative Sol Bloom (ranking minority member of the House Foreign Affairs Committee), and former Senator Warren R. Austin, now U.S. Ambassador to the United Nations. The Secretary was accompanied by Mrs. Marshall, and his party also included the wives of Vandenberg, Connolly, and Austin, thus strengthening personal ties with these important officials.

Instead of meeting in Rio de Janeiro, the Brazilian government had arranged for working sessions to be at Petrópolis, a mountain resort twenty-seven miles from Rio. Many wealthy Brazilians had second homes there, which they made available, complete with servants, for the delegates.

Meetings which began August 15, were held in the salmon-pink casino of a large hotel, the Quitandinha. Beautiful hotel, beautiful scenery—but the prices for food and drinks brought loudly publicized complaints by delegates. At this time, a drink of whiskey cost 25–50¢ in the United States. A glass of Scotch cost $2.50 at the Quithandinha. An Ecuadorian delegate insisted that it cost him $64 a day to live and an extra amount to breathe. Representative Bloom remarked that though the coffee was free, cream cost 40¢ cents— "an outrage!" He added, "When I am gypped, I want to be gypped by experts and not by robbers."[6]

In Moscow, Marshall had been criticized for not mingling more with other delegations, so he now made a point of calling on all the missions. To aid in his interviews, Pawley had assigned to him Major Vernon "Dick" Walters, an accomplished linguist, who was Assistant Military Attaché to Brazil. Walters later recalled that on the morning of his first visit to Marshall, he appeared at breakfast in civilian dress, including a necktie of aggressive yellow. Gazing fixedly at the tie, Marshall wanted to know if he planned to wear it while he interpreted. Walters hurriedly assured him that he would change. Marshall said that would be wise, for he wanted his listeners to hear his words rather than stare at Walters's tie.[7]

All the delegates received Marshall enthusiastically; many baldly and immediately stated their need for economic help. Though he cautiously admitted the importance of that issue, he reminded them that this conference had been called to deal with threats of aggression, and they must concentrate on that. Some of his hearers sensed that he meant protection from outside aggression and insisted there should also be protection from aggression by one American state against another. Marshall replied that the first point to settle was protection from outsiders helping one American country against another; such a move would certainly be considered an act of aggression.[8]

Marshall made his main address to the conference on August 20. He had the unpalatable task of telling the delegations that the United States, even now discussing economic aid to Europe (and for that very reason), was unable to give such assistance to them. His friendliness and candor with the foreign ministers and his description of Europe's desperate economic predicament, with stress on Latin American benefits from economic recovery in Europe, prevented outspoken hostile disappointment. After his speech, the delegates adopted a Mexican resolution postponing economic questions until next year's meeting in Bogotá.[9]

Innate Latin courtesy reduced the appearance of unpleasantly contentious issues, but on August 29, Argentina insisted on a resolution of nonrecognition of any European colonies or possessions in Latin America, and "reaffirmed its sovereignty over the Falkland Islands." Senator Vandenberg, a member of the committee dealing with these matters, declared that the Argentinians could issue any unilateral statement they wanted to make, but that it would not "touch or involve or change any sovereignty in the regional zone here defined." When Guatemala and Mexico raised the question of Belize, Chile her claims on Antarctica, and Honduras her boundary problems with Nicaragua, Vandenberg repeated his observation and asked that it be made a part of the record.[10]

Marshall's openness with the delegates was rewarded toward the end of the conference, when final agreement was reached on the treaty against aggression. He was, however, unable to limit debate to political issues. Foreign Minister Jaime Torres Bodet of Mexico called for economic assistance so that Latin American countries could arm themselves for effective opposition to aggression.

The United States, knowing that nearly $800 million in Lend-

Lease and special loans had been approved for Latin America since 1942, was not going to be rushed. The political agreement must come first, and consideration of economic matters would have to wait till the following year. President Truman stressed this point in his closing speech on September 2. South America had its productive powers and many untapped resources. He begged them to help Europe where possible. He emphasized his awareness of their economic problems and, without offering a Marshall Plan for Latin America, declared his interest in a long-range scheme for economic development.[11]

On the same day, in a green-walled room of the Itamarati Palace, Marshall affixed an oversized, very inky signature to the Treaty of Rio. After representatives of all the nations had signed, the conference was officially closed by President Truman, who had flown in with his family on Sunday, August 31, in the new presidential DC-6, *Independence.* After a tumultuous welcome, the President and his family had dined at the Embassy with the Pawleys and the Marshalls before driving to Petrópolis for the conference finale. The President stayed on in Rio after some delegations had departed, to help celebrate the 125th anniversary of Brazilian independence, then returned to the United States on the battleship *Missouri.* [12]

Marshall and his party came back to the United States on the Truman plane. In contrast to the Moscow stalemate, he had grounds for being satisfied with the results at Rio. Senator Vandenberg announced on his return that the trip had been 100 percent successful. Giving credit to Marshall, but even more to Ambassador Pawley, *Time* called this the most successful hemispheric conference in years. Yet it had been a close-run affair, and only a great deal of personal diplomacy had prevented displays of anger over the lack of a Latin-American Marshall Plan.[13]

The delegates heard with equanimity that the Soviets were unhappy with the results of the Rio Conference. From Moscow, Ambassador Smith reported that published Russian accounts portrayed sinister forces at work at Rio. The meeting had merely ratified United States proposals, the State Department had carried on frenzied activity before the conference, and the United States press waged an unrestrained war of nerves. Hemispheric solidarity meant nothing more than subordination of Latin American interests to Wall Street. Differences between the United States and Argentina were exaggerated, and all problems arose from the determination of the United States to dominate Latin America. The military nature of the conference was apparent, as was the fact that all of Latin America was at the service of United States capital.[14]

There were grounds for Soviet concern. The agreement that "an armed attack by any state against an American state" should be considered "an attack against all American states" strengthened the United States against possible outside intervention in the Western Hemisphere. Set within the framework of the United Nations, the statement could be an effective formula for hemispheric defense. Before the coming year's meeting at Bogotá, the United States would proffer the Rio pact as the basis for a regional agreement to repel aggression in the North Atlantic area.

Colombia, chosen by the American republics in 1938 to be host to the Ninth International Conference of the American States in 1948, reminded the other American republics of this fact before the Rio meetings, and suggested January 1948 as a possible date. Before the end of 1947, a possible conflict with a conference in Havana led to postponement of the Bogotá Conference until spring.

As early as November 1947, when Marshall was in London, Robert Lovett, intent that Marshall should repeat his Rio success, alerted U.S. mission chiefs in Latin America as to goals to be achieved and the line the United States expected to follow at Bogotá. By mid-February 1948, Willard Thorp, Assistant Secretary for Economic Affairs, was reviewing a proposal for economic assistance to Latin America drawn up by his advisers. The Latin American countries were avidly interested in United States economic assistance, which they believed had been promised at Rio. They wanted financial aid, provision of capital equipment and supplies, and technical assistance. Large sums of money had been made available since 1942, but loans had been mostly uncoordinated and lacked the public impact of a unified program.[15]

Anticipating Latin American protests and disappointment, Thorp's advisers suggested that early in the meeting Secretary Marshall speak of past aid given and stress the U.S. desire to be of further assistance. He should propose that the Latin American Economic and Social Council of the United Nations undertake, with the cooperation of the countries involved, a program "for the development of the hemisphere based upon the economic production of each country." Marshall should insist on a friendlier attitude by Latin American countries toward financial investment by private enterprise. The entire program "should be closely linked to this country's military needs and to cooperation of Latin America in that field."

Early in March, the date of the meeting was set for the end of that month. Marshall notified the U.S. delegates to the Bogotá Conference that the three main points to be accomplished were: (1) reorganization of the Pan-American Union; (2) a plan for economic cooperation; and (3) a treaty for pacific settlement of disputes.[16]

The Secretary emphasized the importance of the second item. The Latin Americans "keenly felt that in our plans to help meet the needs of other parts of the world we have given little thought to them." This had led to a coolness which could result in a "serious and rapid decline in our relations with the countries of Latin America."

Among the agenda items to be considered were proposals for a Declaration of Rights and Duties of States, a proposal to eliminate *de facto* recognition of new governments, and a resolution for the termination of all colonies in Latin America. Since a Declaration of Human Rights was then being considered by the United Nations, Marshall suggested that the conference refer to a Latin American Juridical Council for study a general list of principles proposed for consideration. He explained United States policy in regard to *de facto* governments, noting that recognition of them did not imply approval of the policies of such governments. As to colonies, he said that the United States would avoid taking any stand that would affect the position of either party concerning European possessions. Inasmuch as overseas powers were concerned, the United Nations seemed a better place to discuss these issues.

Not long before the meeting, warnings of possible trouble in Bogotá were circulated in Washington. The U.S. Ambassador to Colombia, William Beaulac, sent word of rumors that "Communists and left wing liberals would endeavor to sabotage the Inter-American Conference in order to embarrass the Colombian Government and create difficulties among American republics." Two attacks by egg-throwing crowds against the Colombian Foreign Minister and an attack on a presidential car containing the Ecuadorian Minister had soon followed. The recent replacement of Colombia's coalition government, containing members of the Liberal Party, with a completely conservative government should have clearly indicated the probability of trouble. When various intelligence agencies were later criticized for failure to warn of possible danger, they said that Marshall had been informed but made little of the problem. No arrangements were made for special guards, or even arms for the delegates.[17]

After leaving Washington on the morning of March 29, Marshall arrived early the next afternoon at Bogotá, where he was met by the President and Prime Minister of Colombia and the "usual milling Latin American mob pushing and squeezing and shoving to get close to the Secretary." After a reception by an honor guard, a military escort took him and his immediate party to the Puyana family home. The party included: President of the U.S. Export-Import Bank William McChesney Martin, Secretary of Commerce Averell Harriman, Assistant Secretary of State Norman Armour, General Carter, Major Vernon Walters, and Sergeant George.[18]

At first the meetings of the conference were held in the Capitolo, the federal building near the center of the city. Marshall established a routine of driving each morning to a nearby building where the United States delegation had been given offices, then walking the few blocks to the conference. Often he was recognized and greeted cordially by people passing in the street.

The first plenary session of the conference opened on March 31. The next day, Marshall followed his formal statement with extemporaneous remarks noting that many of the early addresses seemed aimed at the United States. He reminded the delegates of the increasing world responsibilities of his country and the additional cost of armed forces. He recalled that, during the recent war, he had been pressured to disperse United States resources but had held to the basic aim, and that the result had been a splendid victory. He asked that the various states keep the problem in mind and permit the United States to advance cautiously. As if suddenly aware of the great mural of Simón Bolívar, Liberator of South America, that dominated the meeting hall, he spoke of the high regard in the United States for this hero and recalled that the U.S. Army leader in the battle for Okinawa in wartime Pacific fighting bore the name of Simon Bolivar Buckner. This "spontaneous" gesture had actually been carefully planned, and Marshall had practiced with his interpreter the correct pronunciation of the Liberator's name. In his anxiety to excise Marshall's North American twang, Walters laid the ground for his own confusion. After the Secretary had successfully rendered the proper Spanish accent, Walters began translating Marshall's words into Spanish, and to his horror, and the great merriment of the Latin Americans, heard himself enunciating the Liberator's name as spoken north of the border: "Sigh-mun BOLL-er-ver."[19]

Marshall took pains to visit with all the delegations. Drawing on the usual good will of Brazil, he garnered strong expressions of support from the Brazilian Ambassador to Colombia, João Neves de Fontoura. The Ambassador emphasized his country's desire to develop its potential petroleum industry. Marshall welcomed this suggestion, noting the Western Hemisphere's increasing need for oil and the hazards of depending on Middle Eastern resources in an emergency, while pointing out that the United States would be unable, out of its own oil resources, to aid Latin America in a crisis.[20]

Brazil's raising of this issue had been anticipated and even hoped for by the State Department. On the eve of leaving for Bogotá, Marshall had notified the heads of nine U.S. missions in Latin American countries that the United States did not want to initiate discussions on how to increase petroleum production, but would be prepared to discuss the issue if it came up. This topic had been left off the agenda, because the United States did not want the conference proceedings drawn out by requests from various delegations. The United States preferred the use of private enterprise to develop oil resources, but that would require safeguards in each country "against excessive national action." Marshall was likely influenced in this message by a February meeting of the Inter-American Defense Board, which had noted the great increase in the domestic demand for petroleum products in the Western Hemisphere. Demands of any future conflict would possibly require oil production beyond current capabilities. The Latin American countries were encouraged to develop oil production with the aid of private sources.

Marshall's position on the economic aid program was bolstered on April 6 by a speech by his World War II colleague John J. McCloy of the World Bank, who declared that his bank was prepared to aid Latin American countries. Two days later, William McChesney Martin warned that the World Bank was not an agency of any American government and that it might not be able to handle all requests. This problem was recognized by President Truman, who had asked Congress to expand the lending authority of the U.S. Export-Import Bank by $500 million, which would enable the bank to help finance economic development in other American republics.[21]

In explaining this aid to the delegates, Martin reiterated that the bank's loans were not intended to compete with private banks. He added that since 1940 over $900 million had been authorized by the United States for Latin American countries, of which only $466 million had been loaned, and of this nearly half had been repaid.[22]

At the conclusion of the morning session on April 9, Marshall returned to his house for lunch to find *Life* photographers swarming over the place, snapping shots and slightly delaying the meal. While they were eating, the telephone rang and the U.S. Embassy reported that Jorge Gaitan, leader of the Liberal Party, considered a rabble-rouser by the party in power, had been assassinated on a downtown street. A mob quickly formed. The murderer had been caught and beaten to death and his body then dragged to the vicinity of the presidential palace and strung up on a streetlamp. Major Walters, familiar with Latin American politics, said this meant revolution. As he spoke, shots could be heard in the streets.[23]

A State Department report later explained that everything had been set for an explosion. After the shaky coalition of Conservatives and Liberals had been replaced by an all-Conservative Cabinet, extremists among the Liberals joined Communist protests against the government, with the customary diatribes against Yankee imperialism. There were reports of intent to disrupt the conference as a means of discrediting the government. Radical student leaders from nearby states were said to be active, allegedly among them young Fidel Castro from Cuba. The assassination of a leading government opponent proved so useful to radical leaders that some observers believed the murder was carefully staged. A State Department report later in 1948 concluded that, though radical elements made effective use of Gaitan's death, the murderer was a mentally disturbed person who had acted alone. The report cited obvious divisions between various radical factions as to how to exploit the situation as evidence of a lack of planning.

Antigovernment groups seized radio stations in Bogotá and called for attacks on the government and various individuals. Street addresses were broadcast, indicating where American delegates could be found. Mobs invaded the Capitolo and burned many papers. Attacks were also made on the office building housing the U.S. Embassy. The Colombian Army, presumed loyal, was away on maneuvers, and the President had to rely on ill-equipped and often ill-trained reserves.

The members of the group at the Puyana house considered themselves under siege. A poll of those present revealed that the only weapon among them was the pistol in the possession of Marshall's orderly, Sergeant George. Marshall later took considerable amusement in writing friends that George had bravely defended them until reinforcements arrived. The police in the area seemed of little help; those stationed near the residence tried to find shelter there. After a time, General Carter called the Ministry of War and was told that a detachment of troops would be sent to protect the building.

Calls to the U.S. Embassy determined that some Americans and members of other delegations had taken refuge in a nearby National Guard barracks. Although Marshall was urged to go upstairs or to a safer part of the house in case of gunfire, he insisted on sitting near a window where he could check on developments while reading a western. He was thus occupied when he saw the War Ministry's military contingent approach the house. He watched the lieutenant in command deploy his entire force in front of the residence. Calling to Walters, the Secretary asked him to bring in the young officer. With Walters interpreting, he outlined for the lieutenant some lessons on outpost duty that he had practiced in the Philippines forty-five years earlier.

He suggested that a small guard should be posted at front and back and the remainder of the troops hidden in the garage, where they could stay under shelter, ready to be dispatched to any point of danger. Later, Carter, talking to Lovett in Washington, said that Marshall was enjoying being a soldier again.

There was no further hostile activity near the house, and as the evening grew late, members of the delegation went to bed. Harriman continued to listen to the radio, with Walters on hand to translate. Much later, they heard an announcer's agitated voice say that the Army was murdering the people and make a plea for assistance by friends of the rebellion. Soon a different voice indicated that the Army was now in control and demanded that civilians clear the streets.

In a downtown hotel, one member of the United States delegation, General Matthew B. Ridgway, had spent a sleepless night as the mob invaded the ground floor of his hotel. Without weapons, the airborne commander of World War II looked about for means to defend himself and his recent bride. He wrenched a leg from a table and determined to fight off intruders with it. Fortunately, he later explained, the man at the hotel desk directed his unruly guests to the liquor supply in the basement. When morning came, Ridgway made his way to the U.S. Embassy and called Marshall to ask for orders. The Secretary told him about the Americans and members of other delegations holed up in the National Guard Battalion barracks, and directed him to get them to safer quarters. In the afternoon, with the help of Walters's military assistants from four other delegations and with a Colombian tank and truck, the former airborne commander made his way to the barracks and brought out the refugees.

Early on the 10th, Marshall telephoned Lovett in Washington, and he in turn relayed the situation to President Truman. Truman at once instructed James Rowley, head of the Secret Service at the White House, to proceed to Bogotá and report to the Secretary of State. Lovett asked Marshall when the delegates planned to leave.

Marshall said they were going to stay if possible, but, in order to reduce housing and feeding problems, he was asking for two planes from the Panama Canal Zone to evacuate dependents from the troubled city.

Meanwhile, Marshall found that the disruption of the uprising had left many delegates and Embassy staff members without food. The Secretary called on the U.S. Army Command in the Canal Zone to send food for dependents and 4,000 raincoats for Colombian troops being brought in from warmer areas of the country to serve in chilly Bogotá. President Truman quickly approved the request.

Although members of several delegations asked that the conference be adjourned to another site, sentiment grew in favor of the United States' determination to stay. To the surprise of the Secretary of State, the Argentine representative, whose country had always been the first to oppose bitterly any sign of intervention in Latin America by the United States, suggested that U.S. Army paratroopers land in the Colombian capital. Marshall brushed aside the idea.

Meeting at the house occupied by the head of the Honduran contingent, who was then acting as president of the conference, the delegates voted to keep the meeting in Bogotá. Work had already begun to clean up the Capitolo for continued use, and U.S. Secretary of the Treasury John Snyder announced that $15 million were earmarked for a loan to patch up damages in the Colombian capital.

While repairs were under way, the delegates met in a school building in the chief residential section of the city. The President of Colombia announced the formation of a new coalition government containing members of the Liberal Party. A new Foreign Minister, Zuleta Angel, represented Colombia during the remainder of the meetings.

A sequel to the Marshall request for babyfood and raincoats was a tale that grew in the telling concerning the final settling of financial accounts. In later years, Lovett liked to relate that the Army finally totaled up the cost of its aid in the Bogotá incident and presented the bill to Secretary of State Marshall. In the quiet and comfort of the State Department, he examined the bill and decided it was not properly a charge against State but was a matter for the American Red Cross. So back the bill went to the Army, and at length officials sent it to the Red Cross. By then, Marshall was head of that agency. Once again he mulled over the charges and decided this time that they really should be settled by the Department of Defense. Then, declared Lovett with a perceptible twinkle, by the time the bill reached the Pentagon, new Secretary of Defense Marshall concluded that the papers were so tattered and worn that the bill would have to be paid by his new headquarters.[24]

For a week after the meetings resumed in Bogotá, doubts grew in Washington and in some Latin American capitals as to the wisdom of continuing the sessions. Lovett telephoned Marshall that in Congress and the U.S. press there was a growing demand for a quick end to the conference. Nervousness over signs of Communist and revolutionary activity in Central and South American countries engendered the opinion that leaders in Bogotá should hurry back to their own countries to calm their restless citizens and steady any governmental quavers.[25]

Marshall could hardly have been unaware of the pervasive uneasiness. He told delegates on April 12 that Yugoslavian newspapers had been reporting that a revolt had been well prepared to sabotage the conference and the European Recovery Program, and to influence the approaching Italian elections.

Utterly calm, Marshall assured Lovett that his continued presence in Bogotá had lessened the seeming importance of the uprising and had done far more to quell fears of Communist threats among the other delegates than could be achieved by the sudden closing of the conference. Various delegates had asked if he could stay until the end of the week. He had not promised this, although he firmly intended to stay if it proved necessary, but he also hoped to exert pressure for prompt action in the conference by threatening to leave early. The Secretary added that the State Department could help by killing rumors of differences that had developed among delegates. A recent report on such matters had given him great trouble. "Please put the brake firmly on such statements," he requested.[26]

The steering committee of the conference announced on April 22 that all meetings except its own would be resumed at the Capitolo and that April 30 would be closing day. On the 22nd, Marshall turned back an Argentine effort demanding an end to colonization and occupation of territory in Latin America by foreign powers. He explained that a resolution to this effect, backed by Argentina, Chile, and Guatemala, assumed that the conference was a court of law. If such were true, all parties to the quarrel would have to be heard. Marshall proposed that disputes be settled by peaceful means under procedure provided by the Charter of the United Nations. His proposal was accepted.[27]

Chile, Brazil, and Peru next joined the United States in advocating a strong resolution against international Communism. Mexico,

Venezuela, and Guatemala then proposed that the conference condemn all forms of totalitarianism. A resolution to that effect was passed unanimously the next day.

Feeling that final agreement was now virtually assured, Marshall announced on April 26 that he had to return home, where other serious problems awaited him. Therefore he was not present to sign the final agreement, which followed the main outline of the summary circulated by Marshall before the meeting. The Pan-American Union was to be replaced by the Organization of American States, which would be established as a regional organization within the United Nations framework. The new council, replacing the old governing board, would not have the power of the Security Council of the United Nations. Argentina had succeeded in ensuring that future decisions would be made by the twenty-one different republics. There was to be a Joint Military Staff Committee, an arrangement for compulsory arbitration of disputes, and an Economic and Social Council. The coordination of many social and economic matters would be under a secretary general.

Many problems remained to be ironed out, but Marshall had lessened Latin America's festering sense of neglect by its huge neighbor, he had made stronger the denunciation of Communism in the Western Hemisphere, and he had opened the way to greater economic support for that area. Events in Bogotá had helped rather than hurt the United States, since the conviction that the Communists had at least had a hand in the uprising had aided the passage of antitotalitarian resolutions.

Concern with Greece,
1947-48

T H E plea of Greece for the United States to take over the assistance that Britain was ending in the spring of 1947 came in the first weeks of Marshall's tour as Secretary of State and led to the Truman Doctrine and the beginnings of aid to Greece and Turkey. Marshall approved of the action, but his involvement in the mission to Moscow, the political and economic problems in Western Europe that resulted in the Harvard speech, and subsequent efforts to develop the Marshall Plan prevented him from deep personal involvement with the Greek program until late in 1947. Acheson took a leading role in the early developments. George McGhee, a young associate of Under Secretary Will Clayton, became Coordinator of Aid to Greece; he and other American military and diplomatic representatives were busy making plans to assume the British responsibilities in Greece and Turkey by the end of 1947. It was the Queen of Greece, Frederika, in London for the wedding of Princess Elizabeth and Prince Philip, who invited Marshall's closer attention to Greek problems in the fall of 1947.

Born in 1917, daughter of the Duke of Brunswick of Germany, Frederika was the granddaughter of Kaiser Wilhelm II of Germany and a great-great-grandaughter of Queen Victoria. Although born in Germany, she had most of her schooling in England. She was a favorite of her Kaiser grandfather, especially in his exile, and her affection for him led to a dependence on grandfather figures which lasted most of her life. She was married in 1938 to Prince Paul of Greece, but in three years she, her husband, and his older brother, the King, had to flee from invading German forces.[1]

Some of their period of exile was spent in South Africa, where they were guests of Prime Minister Jan Smuts. The attractive Princess-in-exile found another grandfather in Smuts, and talked philosophy and politics for hours with this elder statesman whose career stretched back to World War I. She and Paul returned to Greece after the war, where he became King on the death of his brother in April 1947. Later that year Queen Frederika was in London for the wedding of Princess Elizabeth and Prince Philip. While there, she sought the advice of Winston Churchill on how to get aid for her country. He suggested that she take advantage of the meeting of the Council of Foreign Ministers to make the acquaintance of Secretary Marshall and present her pleas for Greece directly to him. When she demurred that she would not know how to talk with such a great soldier, Churchill suggested that she talk to Marshall as one soldier to another.

With Churchill's help, an appointment was made for Marshall to meet the thirty-year-old Queen at her apartment at Claridge's. In her memoirs, she later recalled that Marshall had been startled to find one so young talking intelligently about political and military affairs, and happily concluded that she had opened an important channel for appeals for American assistance. Encouraged by her husband, Frederika began a correspondence with Marshall and other American figures of prominence that she was to continue until after the deposition of her son, Constantine. Her always handwritten letters to Marshall were sporadic, and usually long and chatty, but not too frequent. They probably gave Marshall little information that he did not have from State Department resources. He did not have to convert Truman to her cause: the President was firmly committed to Greek aid. (Marshall carefully sent copies of all correspondence with Frederika to the State Department. When he was no longer at State, he kept Acheson informed as to the letters he received from Frederika. During the Eisenhower Administration, he reminded her that he had no influence with Secretary Dulles and that any intervention by him would be of no avail. Frederika, thus advised, began a correspondence with President Eisenhower and later, after Marshall's death, with President Kennedy. Hearing of the space program, she asked the young President to let her go as an astronaut on one of the early flights.)

Marshall was aware of the serious situation in Greece without Queen Frederika's personal intervention with him in London or her subsequent letters. Some of the problems were of American making. Trying to gain favor with the Republican Congress, President Truman had appointed as head of the Mission to Aid Greece Dwight P. Griswold, former Republican governor of Nebraska. Griswold was soon at odds with Ambassador to Greece Lincoln

MacVeagh, a career diplomat who had been sent to that country in
1933 by Franklin Roosevelt. Against MacVeagh's advice, Griswold
tried to use pressure to resolve a confused situation in the Greek
Cabinet. He wanted Themistocles Sophoulis, leader of the Pop-
ulist Party, and Constantine Tsaldaris, Liberal Party leader, to
form a coalition government in which the former would be Prime
Minister and the latter Deputy Prime Minister and Foreign Minister. MacVeagh appealed to Washington for a clearcut definition of
authority, and the chief of the Near East desk, Loy Henderson,
came out to investigate. He favored MacVeagh's views, and a directive came from Washington specifying that matters of a political
nature must be handled by the Ambassador.[2]

In the resultant infighting, while Marshall was in London, in-
sinuations were floated that the House of Representatives was
going to name a subcommittee headed by a Republican representative from Nebraska to investigate the MacVeagh-Griswold situation
and, should Griswold's powers be limited, he would return home
to run for President. Meanwhile, MacVeagh's wife died and his own
health deteriorated. He was forced to undergo a serious operation,
and his long absence while recovering made possible a peaceful
interlude. Later in the spring of 1948, MacVeagh was named Ambassador to Portugal and given a presidential citation praising his
service in Greece, a gesture Marshall had suggested to Truman.
Griswold also came back to the United States in August of that year.
The new Ambassador to Greece, Henry Grady, was resolutely prepared to maintain his primacy in case of new threats.

All that was in the future. At the time when Marshall talked with
Frederika in London, the MacVeagh-Griswold feud was flourish-
ing, and the Greek Cabinet was in disagreement. Senior Greek
commanders loyal to the government were divided as to what
should be done, as everywhere the government forces suffered
from disrupted communications, terrible weather, and great
hunger.

Thus, at the beginning of 1948, the Greek problem, supposedly
settled by the Truman Doctrine, was demanding fresh attention at
a time when the Soviets were preparing to cause trouble in Berlin.
Some of these troubles had been foreseen and discussed in depth
from October 16 to November 7, 1947, in what became known as
the Pentagon Talks between British and American diplomatic and
military representatives, headed by British Ambassador Inverchapel and Under Secretary of State Lovett.

The talks ended with a memorandum to the President in late
November to the effect that the security of the Middle East and the

eastern Mediterranean was essential to the security of the United States, which should be prepared to use its power to maintain this security within the confines of the United Nations Charter.[3]

These suggestions were included in a report to the National Security Council by its Executive Secretary, Admiral Sidney W. Souers, who indicated that the staff had drawn on the views of the State Department, the CIA, and the various service branches. Summing up Greek weakness as the product of its deplorable economic situation, political division, selfishness and corruption in government, lack of effective military leadership, absence of aggressive spirit, and political interference in military matters, the planners outlined a strong course of action for the United States. They repeated that the defeat of Soviet efforts to destroy the political independence of Greece was essential to the security of the Middle East and the Mediterranean. Therefore the United States should be prepared to use political, economic, and, if necessary, military power to prevent Greece from falling under Soviet domination, as long as it seemed that the legally constituted government was determined to resist Communist aggression. The United States should be prepared to send armed forces to Greece in a manner not contravening the spirit of the United Nations Charter, if such action was clearly necessary to protect the country from Soviet aggression. The President should make the situation clear to members of Congress and ask for necessary backing in men, materiel, and equipment. This recommendation had to be keyed to other problems in the Middle East. The planners warned that, if the United States became involved in any military action in Palestine, these measures would have to be reconsidered.[4] Two days later, the Joint Chiefs of Staff added that any deployment of military force to put these recommendations into effect would make at least partial mobilization necessary.[5]

Marshall was especially impressed by a statement in the recommendations that a strong personality was needed to represent the United States government in Greece, who would be responsible for all U.S. activities there. While not prepared to place all diplomatic and military matters under one head, he had in mind the individual he wanted to pull together the military parts of the job—to advise on training and organizing the Greek military forces. Though he was prepared to keep there the present military head, Major General Walter G. Livesey, in charge of logistical matters, he wanted to give another star to Major General James A. Van Fleet, "one of the aggressive fighting corps commanders in Europe," for the larger job. He had no trouble getting concurrence from the Army

Chief of Staff: Dwight Eisenhower had been a classmate of Van
Fleet and had watched him land in the first wave on D-Day as one
of the regimental commanders of the 4th Division; later transform
an ineffective division into a fighting unit; and then take over one
of the corps at a difficult time. Supposedly because of a mixup of
Van Fleet with another officer who had a similar name and a drinking problem, Marshall had opposed the promotion at first, but once
he learned of his mistake, Van Fleet rose rapidly.

In 1984, at the age of ninety-two, Van Fleet, still a solid block of
a man, recalled the summons he received in Germany in early 1948
to return to Washington to talk with Secretary Marshall. Van Fleet
said, "If I wrote my memoirs, I would open it with that scene at the
State Department. If a movie were made of it, I would want it to
begin with General Marshall's instructions to me. He said, 'Van
Fleet, I want you to go to Greece and give them the will to win.' "
Marshall did not talk of sending armed forces, but of leadership and
economic aid.

Marshall wrote to Queen Frederika:

> This action was taken to give the Greek Government, and particu-
> larly the Greek Army, the benefit of the advice of probably the most
> aggressive and hard driving corps commander developed by U.S.
> during the war . . . and yet with all that he is of a very modest and
> retiring type. I think he can be of great help to the campaign against
> the guerrilla forces. I would appreciate your considering this per-
> sonal note to you as a confidential matter, particularly as I am hope-
> ful that, behind the scenes, your personal interest in Van Fleet may
> be helpful.[6]

In her reply of April 5, the Queen said that Van Fleet had made
an excellent impression. She added, however, that Greece needed
a Greek commander in chief, and pressed for the appointment of
General Papagos. She concluded: "To know you fills me with confidence. This is also one reason why I have written as openly as I have
done, knowing that you will consider all I have said as purely
personal and unofficial."

A revised report was made to the National Security Council on
February 12. This recalled that the President had promised to
recommend the extension of Greek aid past the expiration date of
June 30, 1948. The British had also agreed to suspend the withdrawal of their troops from Greece. The report noted that current
aid was not sufficient to permit the Greek government to withstand

Communist pressure. Among alternative courses were various military actions, such as (1) sending a token force to Greece, (2) employing available U.S. forces in the area to prevent a Communist takeover in Greece, (3) strengthening U.S. armed forces in the Mediterranean outside Greece, (4) partially mobilizing U.S. forces as an indication of America's determination to resist Communist expansion into Greece. The report had not endorsed Loy Henderson's strong recommendation that the United States promptly announce that it would send armed forces with the consent of the Greek government to prevent Greece from falling under Communist domination: the Policy Planning Staff, supported by Marshall, opposed this view as too drastic.[7]

Meanwhile, European Recovery legislation was progressing in Congress, so that Marshall was able to assure the U.S. Mission for Aid to Greece that interim aid would be available prior to the passage of the complete appropriations. In hearings before a congressional committee on March 17, Marshall was asked what effect a vote for the Communists in the forthcoming Italian elections would have on aid to Greece and Turkey. Marshall refused to believe that Italy would vote completely Communist in the April elections and thus cut off ERP assistance. In any case, the United States should not allow Italian elections to affect the aid to Greece and Turkey.[8]

Marshall also made it clear to the Senate Foreign Relations Committee, as he had to State Department planners, that although he might be willing later to consider troops for Greece, he did not want to send troops or bombers to that country and have to withdraw them ignominiously in the face of greater Communist forces. He recalled the pressures he had had to resist in World War II to avoid scattering U.S. forces around the world. He had been obliged to apply force where it would do the most good, however strong were the pleas for action elsewhere. Henderson noted to Greek diplomats that Major General A. M. Harper, deputy commander of the U.S. Army Group in Greece, was personally opposed to sending any U.S. troops to Greece. American forces sent to Greece or to the eastern Mediterranean would be caught in mousetrap operations, although Henderson did not rule out later assistance to stop blatant aggression.[9]

Fortunately, by the end of May the situation in Greece was better. The United States had extended economic aid for one year, and the Greek offensive spirit had revived as military assistance from Soviet satellites to Greek rebel forces declined. There was even some

indication that Moscow's support of Greek Communists was waning. A growing rift between Moscow and Tito of Yugoslavia threatened Yugoslav support of the Greek guerrillas. To send American
troops to Greece would be unsound unless Congress was prepared
to back any reasonable effort to aid Greece; unless intelligence
revealed that such action would not precipitate Soviet operations;
and unless we neither intended nor were forced to act militarily
elsewhere. This new draft of NSC 5 was adopted June 2, subject
to a State Department amendment noting that there would be
considerable adverse reaction worldwide to U.S. movements in
Greece unless these were in accordance with the U.N. Charter.
Thus amended, the new draft was approved by the President on
June 21.[10]

In his survey of fighting in Greece during 1941–49, historian C.
M. Woodhouse describes vividly the mixture of "defeatism and
complacency" that characterized American relations with Greece at
the beginning of 1948. The Greeks seemed inclined to shrug and
let the Americans manage Greek military affairs. Such was the situation when General Van Fleet arrived early in February 1948. Van
Fleet soon saw which Greek commanders had risen by competence
and which owed their success to politics. He was able to bring back
able men to key posts, but found it impossible to deal with those
of less ability but stronger political backing. Van Fleet could observe and give advice but he had no authority to command. Fighting in the early spring brought a few victories but fleeing guerrillas
could escape into Albania and reappear at will. From mid-June to
August 21, an offensive sought to destroy guerrilla strongholds in
the Grammos area. The fighting was fiery, and both sides suffered
heavy casualties. Even after the guerrillas were forced back into
Albania, they, like others before them, reappeared farther north.
By the time their threat to capture former holdings had been ended
in October, it was evident that the National Army could make no
additional effort in 1948.[11]

During the confused period of the Grammos offensive, Marshall
received a report from the U.S. Chargé in Athens that was less
important for what it said than for the way it was handled. A member of the Soviet Embassy staff approached the Chargé and said
that the Soviet Union was prepared to discuss problems in the
north of Greece and elsewhere. Although Marshall was very dubious about the offer, he decided it should not be flatly rejected: "any
eventual hope of solving outstanding difficulties must encourage
exchange of views." He suggested to the Chargé that the Russian

be advised to go through normal channels. He also suggested that the Chargé inform British representatives of the approach and ask whether they approved his reply.[12]

After further reflection and consultation, Marshall reminded the Chargé of possible reasons for the "peace" initiative. If the position of the Communist guerrillas continued to deteriorate, they might be seeking a political rather than a military solution. Such an approach might well appeal to many Greeks. He also suggested that the Soviets were counting on a shift in world opinion. As a result of Communist propaganda, uninformed reporting, and current Greek policies, many non-Communists outside Greece thought that the Greek government was only slightly better than the Communists. "In the U.S. a growing and not insignificant proportion of opinion sincerely questions whether U.S. can continue support of the Greek Government without compromising American ideals."[13]

To clarify his last statement, the Secretary said that the United States approved the Greek government's demand for unconditional surrender by the guerrillas, but was concerned with the government's ruthless policy toward captured and surrendered guerrillas. A more moderate policy might induce more surrenders and prevent the growth of bitterness among the friends and relatives of those captured. He urged that court-martial sentences be re-examined to reduce executions to a minimum and "as first step toward eventual halt in cycle of killing in Greece." He recognized that the Greek government did not want to be considered guilty of weakness, but it should consider avoiding capital punishment except for the chief guerrilla leaders and those responsible for heinous crimes. Simple political expediency demanded a reduction in executions for the moment. As to persons condemned for actions begun before and after the revolt of 1944, he suggested that only those guilty of the most bloody crimes be executed and that executions be postponed for several months. He asked for the number of current executions, a statement of government policy, and the advice of the Embassy on methods of approach to the Greek government along those lines.[14]

Marshall had already made plans to see the situation in Greece for himself during the course of the Paris Conference. In June 1948, Queen Frederika had written Marshall in Washington that she and her husband hoped that he would visit Greece, and he soon replied that he planned to get away from the fall General Assembly meeting in Paris for a short stay in her country. Not long after Marshall's arrival in Paris in September, Constantine Tsaldaris, head of the Greek delegation to the United Nations, complained to him about a recommended reduction of the Greek Army by 15,000 in the coming month. He wanted Marshall to ask General Van Fleet and Ambassador Henry Grady to come to Paris to discuss the implications of such a reduction. Marshall confided that he planned to go to Greece instead.

During a short mid-October break in the General Assembly meetings, the Marshalls and personal staff departed for Athens and Rome. The King and Queen of Greece interrupted their Greek-island cruise to welcome the Marshall party to the capital. In Athens, Marshall covered a great deal of ground very swiftly. In addition to the royal couple, he talked with members of the Greek Cabinet, General Van Fleet, Ambassador Grady, the British Ambassador, and the British military commander.[15]

Marshall found morale very low in the U.S. mission, particularly among the military, and in the Greek Cabinet. The Greek Army had never been fully trained, officers were over-age in grade, men tired and dispirited because, despite generally successful recent efforts, numerous guerrilla groups had been permitted to withdraw into Albania and Yugoslavia and then reappear on their flanks. The men could not visit their families, for whose safety they feared, and they faced the prospect of no better conditions, just holding their own, during the approaching winter. Ambassador Grady recommended an increase in the Army, and the British commander proposed an increase from eight to fifteen divisions, though apologizing for advocating something for which the British could not pay. Van Fleet said he would be satisfied with the existing Army if it could be better trained. All agreed that with another two divisions they could have exterminated earlier the guerrillas who were now giving them such trouble.

The minimum requirement, Marshall believed, was an increase of 15,000 men to improve and refresh the current Army. In making this suggestion, the Secretary was aware of the U.S. Army's hesitancy about asking for greater appropriations. He told Lovett that he personally was embarrassed, because he was engaging in military recommendations, which were not really proper for the Secretary of State. "However, like a lot of other people, I am only human, and I merely refer to this so you can make the best of it in connection with the Army authorities." On his return to Paris, Marshall told Bevin that he did not consider the Greek situation hopeless provided proper measures were taken in time.

Marshall never forgot Frederika, and in the years to come she wrote the General occasionally, describing problems in Greece and asking advice. On a trip to Washington before Marshall's death, she took a plane to Pinehurst to see the Marshalls and to introduce Constantine, the Crown Prince of Greece, and Sophie, who would later become Queen of Spain. She followed carefully reports on his health in the last, declining years as if in or out of office he stood for aid to Greece.

XXIII

Berlin Crisis: Part II, or Meeting in Paris, 1948

WHEN Marshall left Washington on September 19, 1948, for the third meeting of the United Nations General Assembly, in Paris, he was aware that the German question loomed above a crowded agenda. Ambassador Jefferson Caffrey had asked the Secretary and Mrs. Marshall and a small personal staff to be his guests. They arrived at the U.S. Embassy, on Avenue Gabriel near the Place de la Concorde, on September 20. Bohlen and his wife stayed nearby. Major Vernon Walters, assigned to Averell Harriman as interpreter and aide, was attached to Marshall for the duration of the conference. Also on hand were the regular members of the U.N. delegation—Austin, Dulles, Mrs. Roosevelt, Jessup.

Because of Marshall's kidney problem, a young doctor, Lieutenant Harry Pfifer, was assigned to accompany him on all trips, but ministered to ailments of other delegation members more than to any of Marshall's. Despite the security problems in Bogotá, Marshall had no personal guard. When Marshall had gone to Princeton for his first address as Secretary of State, in February 1947, both he and President Dodds of Princeton had noticed that a silent, unknown man lingered nearby. When Dodds asked Marshall if the man were a member of his party, Marshall investigated and found that the man had been sent by the State Department as a guard. Back in Washington, the Secretary asked General Carter, his personal assistant, if he were responsible. Carter denied having anything to do with the matter, but Marshall retorted, "Have this stopped. I had rather be murdered than embarrassed to death."[1]

After the scare at Bogotá, Carter had brushed up on his pistol shooting and now carried a weapon. During Marshall's residence at the Embassy, security measures for the Ambassador were sufficient. However, the assassination of Count Folke Bernadotte in

Israel during the course of the conference in Paris, and threats by terrorist groups that Marshall was next on the list, caused great anxiety for his staff whenever he was outside Paris. One evening, when the Marshalls spent the night at a hotel in Reims, members of his staff, unknown to Marshall, took turns standing guard outside his door.[2]

Marshall arrived in Paris at ten o'clock on the morning of September 20 and by noon was discussing Berlin with Ambassador Douglas and Bohlen. That evening he conferred at the French Foreign Office across the Seine, on the Quai d'Orsay, with new French Foreign Minister Robert Schuman, Bevin, and members of their staffs, on the response they should make to the Soviets for their unsatisfactory reply to an earlier message from the Allies.[3] Despite Soviet obstructionism, Marshall's words were sanguine:

> In every field the Russians are retreating. From now on Berlin is the only foothold they have against us. Everywhere else, and particularly in Germany, they are losing ground. We have put Western Germany on its feet and we are engaged in bringing about its recovery in such a way that we can really say that we are on the road to victory. The attitude of the Russians in Berlin and the manner in which they will continue their attack, will be a real indication of their intentions toward us.[4]

He was willing to join the British and French in another approach to Moscow, provided it was "concise and unequivocal." At Bevin's request, he agreed to strike out of the note to the Soviets any mention of a recourse to the U.N. should the reply be unsatisfactory. However, he asked that they accept this action as the next step if the Russians returned an unfavorable reply.[5]

Declaring the Soviet reply of September 18 unsatisfactory, the three powers on the 22nd declined to accept any restrictions in Berlin and the Western zones. In a long rehash of past positions, the Soviets retorted that they had acted in accordance with the August directive to the military governors and declared that a settlement depended on the Western powers. The Russians released their reply to the press at once.

Marshall, Bevin, and Schuman promptly met and agreed to submit the dispute to the Security Council of the United Nations. Marshall proposed to retaliate for the Soviet propaganda ploy by releasing the Allied statement to the press right away, but Bevin asked that they wait until the message had had time to reach Moscow. When Marshall wanted to know the reason for giving the

Soviets more time to prepare their response, Bevin and Schuman agreed to instant publicity.

The Allied statement was also a rehash of old arguments. It concluded: "The issue is that the Soviet Government has clearly shown . . . that it is attempting by illegal and coercive measures, in disregard of its obligations, to secure political objectives to which it is not entitled and which it could not achieve by peaceful means." The Western nations therefore were submitting the dispute to the United Nations "as a threat to international peace and security." They reserved to themselves full right to take such measures as were necessary to maintain their positions in Berlin.[6]

In Berlin, Paris, London, and Washington, the decision was praised for presenting a firm front to Allied opponents. Yet, behind the scenes, studies went on as to what might be done to resolve the problems with the Russians. At the State Department, where Bedell Smith had come on a brief visit, the Policy Planning Staff worked on a paper for the National Security Council. Often regarded as tough and unshakable, Smith seemed uncertain and full of doubts. He regretted that the Allies had ever gone to Berlin. The former capital of all Germany had become a political symbol only because they had made it so. This was water over the dam, but he hoped that the United Nations would give the Western Allies an opportunity to get out. Although he did not think that the Russians were deliberately choosing to face war, there was always the possibility of miscalculation. As Secretary Marshall had said earlier, Smith believed that time was on the side of the West in terms of current relative strength vis-à-vis the Soviet Union. The Russian recovery from the war was going slowly. On the basis of intuition, he doubted that the Russians had the A bomb, or at least would not have such bombs in quantity for five years. As a soldier, he would prefer to fight the Soviets five years hence than now.[7]

A far tougher line was proposed to Marshall by Foy Kohler, who was standing in for Smith in Moscow. In addition to strengthening the airlift and strongly supporting the municipal government of Berlin, he spoke of silencing or taking over Soviet-controlled Radio Berlin and, in case the Russians arrested non-Communist municipal leaders, he proposed that Communist Party hostages be taken in the Western zone, at once.[8]

A calmer view prevailed in Washington. Lovett warned against taking any provocative step until the Berlin issue was clarified in the United Nations. The Policy Planning Staff also urged caution. In an October 1 report, its members favored continuance of the air lift, but not belligerence. If there were incidents in Berlin, the military governors should protest. If an American plane were shot down, they should demand an explanation and say that the United States would have to take defensive measures. If the Soviets accepted responsibility for the action, this should be fully reported to Washington. If there were repeated incidents involving loss of planes, an immediate report to Washington should be made by the military governor, discussing defensive measures to be taken and requesting instructions on putting them into effect. "The U.S. Commander in Berlin should assume that there exists a grave risk of imminent war."[9]

General Clay certainly had understandings with Pentagon officials concerning stronger measures than these, and there were members of the State Department who agreed with them. Remarkably, as the presidential campaign went into its final weeks, tough talk on Berlin was minimized. Then, suddenly, as Marshall tried to get the British and French to agree on common policy, the pressures of the coming election intervened. The President called the State Department on October 5 to say that he was going to send Chief Justice Fred Vinson to Moscow to explain to Stalin the strength of America's desire for peace. Two of Truman's speechwriters, David Noyes and Albert Z. Carr, had suggested this action to strengthen the President's peace image; on October 3, Truman had persuaded the Chief Justice to make the trip, then instructed his writers to prepare a speech announcing the plan.[10]

Years later, Lovett recalled that a copy of Truman's proposed message to Moscow was sent to him from the code room. He hastily phoned the President and asked to see him at once. He said that for the first time ever he told the driver of the official car to turn on the red light and siren and race for the White House. He was immediately received by the President and announced that what Truman was proposing was impossible. When the President demanded an explanation, Lovett graphically pointed out that such action would result in the President's losing his Secretary of State and the efforts of the U.S. delegation to settle the Berlin crisis. Truman at once canceled the trip.

Lovett called Marshall in Paris to tell him that the Vinson mission was canceled. News of the mission had sent Marshall and Carter to the Embassy's Communications Center, where Carter was beginning a draft reply. Carter recalled that his proposed opening sentence began, "Never in the history of diplomatic bungling," and Marshall was chiding him that such words addressed to the President would never do. At any rate, once the Vinson mission was canceled, Marshall decided that, with some three weeks yet to go before the election, he should have a talk with the President. He apologized to Truman for not keeping him filled in on the progress of negotiations and proposed flying to Washington for a weekend conference.[11]

Truman promptly made the presidential plane available, and Marshall, Sergeant George, and Lieutenant Pfifer made the weekend trip to Washington. Even though the Vinson mission had been canceled before Marshall returned to the States, rumors sprang up that the Secretary of State had flown home to resign. When radio broadcaster Fulton Lewis, Jr., repeated the rumor on his news broadcast, Marshall categorically denied it, but Lewis insisted that as an old hand he was accustomed to diplomatic prevarication.

No proposed resignation was discussed at the meeting between Marshall, Lovett, and Truman on October 9, and it is unlikely that Marshall asked an abeyance of any other special missions in the days before the election. It seems certain that he made plain that he would leave the Cabinet shortly after the election. If the President lost the election, Marshall's job would be terminated in any case. If Truman won, the Secretary did not want to face four more years in the office and deemed it best to let a new man start in January 1949. Marshall also discussed other problems under consideration in Paris.

The day after seeing the President, Marshall met at the Pentagon with Forrestal, the service Chiefs of Staff, and Generals Joseph McNarney and Alfred Gruenther. The services were heavily involved in drawing up a military budget, faced with fitting their requirements under a low budgetary ceiling set by the President. Forrestal wanted a statement from Marshall on the importance of a stronger military force to a strong foreign policy, but Marshall declined to be drawn. Gruenther, who reported the discussion, concluded that Marshall was sympathetic to the Chiefs of Staff but not concerned about the effect of the budget ceiling on foreign relations.[12] This may have indicated that he did not want to raise more problems for the President in the closing days of the campaign or, more likely, that he expected not to have responsibility for foreign relations after a few more weeks.

A pleasant vignette of the three-day trip came while Marshall was sitting in his State Department office chatting with Bedell Smith, who was then briefly in Washington. The nurse caring for the young son of the Bohlens while they were in Paris brought the little boy to Marshall's office so that the Secretary could take back a first-hand report on the youngster. Marshall called a photographer, who took a picture of young Bohlen in Smith's lap. Bohlen recounted this story in his memoirs as characteristic of many gracious acts that Marshall performed for his associates and subordinates.[13]

Shortly after returning to Paris, Marshall took advantage of a break in the sessions to visit Rome and Athens. Meanwhile, noninvolved countries in the Security Council—Argentina, Belgium, Canada, China, Colombia, and Syria—offered a resolution on October 22 to settle the crisis. The United States, Great Britain, and France agreed, but the Soviet Union vetoed the motion.[14]

The Western nations decided to leave it on the Security Council agenda while seeking other approaches to the problem. On November 13, U.N. Secretary General Trygve Lie and the current president of the General Assembly, Herbert Evatt of Australia, asked the disputants to resolve their differences. Marshall reviewed American efforts to find a solution within the United Nations and said that the United States was willing to resume negotiations when the Soviet blockade was lifted.[15]

Shortly before this action at the U.N., the U.S. presidential election had been settled by the surprising victory of President Truman. Two photographs made as the results came in by radio to the American delegation in Paris show Marshall, Austin, and Dulles listening to the returns. In the first photograph, the faces of the Republicans, Dulles and Austin, show definite elation, while Marshall looks thoughtful. In the second photograph, Marshall is still looking thoughtful but Dulles and Austin are now definitely aware that Dulles will not be the next Secretary of State.

The election settled one thing for Marshall. For a number of months he had again looked forward to retirement. In July he wrote Stimson of his coming retirement "in early winter." Katherine, he added, had been counting the days "until I can with honor leave the Government Service and settle down to a normal life with her at Pinehurst and Leesburg." In early September, replying to a note from a sometime tennis partner, the actor Walter Huston, he spoke of his coming trip to Paris as "the end of my run because my agreement was only to stay to the end of the year." Now that the Democrats were again in control of both houses of Congress, Marshall's nonpartisan status would no longer be needed to help get measures through a Republican Congress. In the midst of a job he had never wanted and at the end of a trying campaign, there was now no reason that he could not have the kidney operation he had postponed since June.

Near Thanksgiving, Marshall decided that the business of the General Assembly was nearly finished and he could return for the operation and be out of the hospital by Christmas. It seemed that the session would soon adjourn, but if it did not, Marshall left the impression he would return to Paris. The question was whom he should leave in charge in his absence. Former Senator Austin, Ambassador to the United Nations, was unwell, and Marshall had already decided he was ineffective in any case. The Secretary preferred Philip Jessup, whom he considered the ablest of the delegation, but Jessup was a junior member. Dulles was thoroughly familiar with their activities. During the campaign, he had been given great freedom to move about Europe and also to consult with Dewey, and in the closing days of the campaign both Marshall and Dulles had assumed Dulles would be the next Secretary of State. Marshall had said to him shortly before the election that they should provide some continuity in the period before the new administration began.

President Truman did not care to have an adviser of his former opponent heading the delegation, and wanted Jessup appointed. When Marshall persisted in asking for Dulles, the President came around. Marshall subsequently described his discussion with Dulles:

> I told him that I wanted to recommend him . . . but that I had to have certain assurances. I asked his complete agreement that he would support the President; take it on the chin if anything is difficult—as I have. Never use the situation here politically. Don't be a Democrat or a Republican: You represent the President. He said, "I will have to consult my own view." . . . I said, recommend what you feel to the President, but you represent him. . . . Without that promise I will not recommend. He said, "In that case, I promise." I said, If you break faith in a political way, I will advertise you on every damn radio in the country, and I am in a position to do it. I allowed six hours to elapse and then said he had been chosen by the President. His face was a study while I was telling him all this.[16]

On being named head of the U.S. delegation, Dulles asked for clear instructions on the German issue. He had been embarrassed recently by an article in the Paris *Herald-Tribune* saying he was at odds with Clay and the State Department on U.S. policy on Germany. Dulles outlined his ideas on what he thought he should do and then asked Marshall for comments.

In one of his last statements on the German question as Secretary of State, Marshall laid out the course he wanted Dulles to follow. He declared that: (1) the United States would not be forced out of Berlin; (2) the United States wanted to solve the Berlin situation by ending the blockade; (3) the United States would not negotiate under duress; (4) the United States would accept the Soviet ostmark for Berlin if there were a proper Four Power supervision of currency; (5) recent Soviet actions made currency problems harder to work out, and the coming municipal elections in Berlin threatened to split the city further; and (7) they must, with the aid of neutrals, work out the means to prevent the Russians from disregarding the rights of the Western powers.[17] "We will not be traded out of Berlin," he insisted. Marshall noted that in submitting the Berlin matter to the Security Council, the United States took the risk of accepting a situation that was not wholly perfect, but this could be done with certain safeguards of the U.S. position.[18]

Marshall's resolute views on Berlin were apparently not known to all members of the State Department, where discussions continued about postponing elections in Berlin to avoid splitting the city. These discussions stirred Ambassador Murphy to strong protest. He pointed out that the city was already split and that the postponement of elections would only confuse the Germans and delight the Russians. He said that he had not called Clay's attention to his message, because the very mention of election postponement would elicit "explosive reactions." Marshall made it clear that there was no intention of canceling the elections.[19]

The elections were held as scheduled in the Western sectors of the city. Despite the efforts of Communist-dominated organizations to stage a boycott of the elections, over 86 percent of the eligible electorate voted against pro-Soviet candidates. Spurred by such an outpouring, the three Western military governors met at the Allied Kommandatura building on December 21, for the first time since June 16. They invited their Russian colleague to return, nine months after he had walked out, thus indicating that they intended to continue meetings.[20]

The peace Marshall had wanted for Berlin had not yet come. The air lift was still in progress, and a bitter winter remained to imperil the efforts of the Allies. But the will of the West Berliners was firm and confident, and there were signs that the air lift could continue. Marshall could be content to leave office at this point. Though the battle was not won, it still went forward. In much of the early effort, Marshall had had no great part. Clay had ordered the first stages of the air lift and gained the backing of the Pentagon, the State Department, and the White House. The Germans themselves had helped by managing to survive and produce with what the air lift brought. Marshall had worked to keep unity among the Allies, had urged a firm stance while showing willingness to use the machinery of the United Nations. He had opposed provocative stands and was willing to negotiate basic legal issues once the blockade was lifted. His feeling that he had a role to perform had held him in Paris beyond medical prudence.

He was out of office and recuperating when spring came. As he gained strength, Germany's strength was also increasing. The steady drone of the planes, the increasing deliveries of coal and food, sustained hope, and European feeling solidified against the Soviets. At last Stalin sensed that his plan had failed. A reporter's questions about what it would take to break the deadlock led him to give a signal, which the Allies took up almost at once. The atmosphere changed and plans were set in motion to lift the blockade and to return in part to a more open city. Trouble was not at an end and there would be other deep crises, but this one had passed.

XXIV

Change of Pace

MARSHALL returned from Paris near the end of November. On December 7, he underwent surgery at Walter Reed Hospital for the removal of his right kidney. Contrary to some accounts, there had been no deterioration of his health while he was at the General Assembly meeting. Doctors had told him in June that he had a cyst on his kidney which should be removed, but they agreed that he could finish important business awaiting him at the United Nations in New York and in Paris. In addition to a heavy schedule, he spent his October break visiting a number of U.S. battle memorials in France and made trips to Greece and Italy. With the election of President Truman out of the way, he wanted his retirement from the State Department to coincide with the President's inauguration in January. He decided to have his operation before the end of the year.

His first days back in Washington were spent tying up loose ends. Then, without fanfare, he checked into the hospital. Colonel Clifford Kimbrough, who had examined him earlier in the summer, performed the operation. The cyst, removed with the kidney, was benign, but there were painful aftereffects, and recuperation dragged slowly for the Secretary. He had longed to get to Pinehurst before Christmas, but the hospital would not release him until near the end of the year.[1]

The announcement of the successful operation set off a round of messages from old friends, accompanied by queries as to his future plans. Mrs. Marshall had to divide attendance at the hospital with the duties of hostess to Madame Chiang Kai-shek at Leesburg during this time. Madame had written earlier that she planned to visit the United States and had been invited to stay with the Marshalls. Always somewhat uneasy about Mrs. Marshall's health, the Secre-

tary grumbled to close friends that it was hard on her to have to
check on how he was feeling every day while her hands were full
entertaining her guest.

As mentioned earlier, Mrs. Marshall and Madame Chiang had
become close friends during the summer and fall of 1946, when the
Chiangs had lent her a cottage in the hills at Kuling, next door to
their own summer place, to escape the terrible heat of Nanking. In
after years, Madame made at least one other visit to Leesburg and,
after the General's death, invited Mrs. Marshall to visit in her apartment when Madame came to Washington.

The Chinese "first lady" had kept up a correspondence with
General Marshall for several months concerning problems in China
and wished to cheer him up while he was in the hospital. Mrs.
Marshall had been in the midst of writing her book, *Together,* when
she went to China in 1946. She may have discussed it with Madame,
or, more likely, the Generalissimo's wife saw a copy of the book at
Leesburg while visiting there. In the book Mrs. Marshall had mentioned that her favorite tribute to the General was made by one of
his childhood friends, Mary Kate O'Bryon, who had said in 1939
that Uniontown's welcome to the new Chief of Staff was really "for
'Flicker,' the snub-nosed, freckle-faced red-head who was a natural-
born leader of boydom in the 90's." Madame Chiang Kai-shek
seized on the nickname and used it again and again in her saluta-
tions to the patient and in other letters afterward. In mock appeal
to "General Flicker," she complained of slave labor at Leesburg.[2]

When Marshall was finally able to go to Pinehurst, near the end
of the year, he complained of the soreness left by his surgery and
did not seem to progress toward full recovery. President Truman
decided that the General needed warmth and sunshine and arranged for the Marshalls to go to the naval base in Puerto Rico,
where Admiral Daniel Barbey made elegant guest quarters available for their use.

Puerto Rican days were followed by an invitation from Leonard
Nicholson, Marshall's V.M.I. roommate and owner of the New Orleans *Times-Picayune,* for the Marshalls to spend Mardi Gras in New
Orleans. Mardi Gras evolved into a period of lazy rest in the Nicholson guesthouse some miles from New Orleans. As spring approached, the General showed greater animation, although he
avoided a number of speeches and committee memberships that
were offered to him.

Truman reluctantly accepted his resignation as Secretary of State
and, as Marshall wished, set the date to coincide with the presidential inauguration. The President did not need Marshall's advice on

the man to succeed him. He had learned Dean Acheson's worth in the years Acheson served as deputy to Byrnes and to Marshall.

The new Secretary was one of Marshall's most eloquent admirers, and he allowed himself to write with far more than usual personal feeling in a letter to Marshall setting forth the qualities he had learned from him. Marshall would remember it months later, when he sat in Truman's Cabinet with Acheson.

By the summer of 1949, the President was mulling over means of bringing Marshall back into public service as head of the American Red Cross. There were signs that Basil O'Connor, head of the American Red Cross since 1944, might soon retire. Why not, thought the President, give Marshall that job? It would associate him again with public affairs in a way that carried fewer burdens than had his previous appointments.

Truman observers have tended to emphasize that the President was seeking a sinecure for Marshall, an imposing title with little work. Actually, Truman knew that a situation was festering in the American Red Cross that Marshall's prestige and peace-seeking character might save from bursting into bitter disagreement.

It has also been suggested that the President wanted to ensure the General a better income, but that had already been done when Congress passed legislation making permanent the five-star rank held by nine generals and admirals, and establishing that those holding this rank should be considered as continuing on active duty and draw full salaries and benefits. Truman himself had proposed that they be given adequate office space in a government building and each be allowed an aide, a secretary, and an orderly. The various service secretaries were to arrange air transportation where possible.

Basil O'Connor had been named by President Roosevelt to succeed Norman Davis as Chairman of the Red Cross when Davis died in 1944. O'Connor was very hardworking but had managed to offend and alienate some of the older Red Cross leaders. Many of the disagreements had been smothered during the war, when the Red Cross had given outstanding service to servicemen, refugees, prisoners of war, and others desolated throughout the world.

Part of the trouble came from the apparent domination of the organization in the late thirties by wealthy and socially prominent Eastern-establishment figures on the Red Cross board of governors. Active heads of chapters in other cities and regions complained that they had no voice in operations. Volunteer workers, a highly important part of the Red Cross's activities, charged that they were not used or involved in decisions. These charges and complaints boiled down to the bitter feeling that a very few people ran the organization.[3]

In 1946, the Red Cross made a decision to create a special committee headed by E. Roland Harriman, Averell Harriman's brother, a partner in Brown Brothers, Harriman, and manager of the North Atlantic region of the Red Cross during the war. He and his committee members undertook to meet some of the chief complaints of others in the organization, and their proposed changes were approved by Congress and President Truman in the spring of 1947. The President of the United States was to appoint the President, and the board of governors was enlarged and rearranged to give far more representation to the chapters.[4] Chairman O'Connor now became President.

Despite O'Connor's efforts to stop controversy, sharp criticism persisted. By 1948, it was evident that the organization needed a leader of great stature who had not been associated with the infighting, and who could respond to the claims of all factions without prejudice. O'Connor made it plain that he was ready to step down.

Truman naturally thought of Marshall. His appeals for the European Recovery Program were of the exact kind needed by the American Red Cross. During the war he had sought public support for Red Cross drives, and his war's-end reports praised the organization's service to the men of the armed forces and their families. His 1948 speeches for ERP showed his effectiveness in convincing the same types of people that the Red Cross needed. Few were aware of another factor that made him so desirable as O'Connor's successor. As Pershing's aide in France after World War I and later in the United States, he came into contact with many Eastern-establishment figures, whose influence was still needed by the Red Cross. He was perhaps the one person who could bridge the gap between the factions.

O'Connor told Truman that he would like to give up his post by October 1, 1949. In late September, the President announced that Marshall had agreed to accept the position.

Marshall's various appointments always brought a profusion of congratulations from many quarters, but his files show greater unanimity on the wisdom of this selection than any of the others. The letters reflect the esteem in which he was held by many admirers, who seemed to welcome the chance to keep him longer in the public eye, rather than let him drop into the obscurity of retirement. Almost the first message came from his former personal secretary at the State Department, Mildred Asbjornson, speaking for herself and other secretaries there who had worked for him. She expressed their hopes that his new responsibilities would not "seriously curtail or limit his tomato growing, Japanese beetle warfare and other agricultural pursuits at Leesburg." Omar Bradley, now Chairman of the Joint Chiefs of Staff, said simply, "Once again you have accepted a selfless task for the nation." "It is characteristic that you should give still further of your time and energies to the nation and to humanity," wrote J. Lawton Collins, now Army Chief of Staff. General William Draper, Jr., back in New York after Army service, noted that he had just been approached by the Red Cross to head the coming funds drive in Manhattan and the Bronx when he heard that Marshall was to be the new head: "I was happy to accept and again become one of your junior lieutenants." Robert Cutler, who had served in the War Department and been a regional Red Cross leader who disagreed with O'Connor, offered his services to Marshall, "whom I consider the wisest leader I have ever served."

Favorable reaction from the military was not unexpected, but the outpouring of support from both older and younger leaders showed how wise Truman's choice had been. Mrs. Henry P. Davison, wife of the Morgan partner who headed the Red Cross in World War I, regretted that her age would prevent her from serving with him. Mrs. Dwight F. Davis, former head of the Women's Division of the Red Cross, who had resigned because of disagreements with O'Connor, also welcomed the appointment.[5]

Secretary of Labor Maurice Tobin saw "a poetic rightness in the fact that a man who won his greatness as a soldier and diplomat is now taking over the world's chief enterprise of mercy." Lord Woolton, head of British Red Cross, echoed the same feeling: "The fact that you, after your great services to the world in other fields, have come to join us will indeed enhance our power immeasurably." Equally pleasing to Marshall were letters from members of struggling local chapters who wrote that his acceptance of the appointment gave their workers an immediate lift. T. J. Watson of IBM spoke for a number of businessmen whose support was essential to the Red Cross when he wrote, "No one in the world is as well qualified as you to head up this worthwhile organization."

The only obvious regrets came from Marshall's very close friends who felt he should be taking the retirement to which he was entitled. Ambassador James Bruce, who served in Argentina, 1947–49, recalled that, several years before, Marshall had told him that he had promised Mrs. Marshall to take a year's rest. "A few days later, I picked up the paper and you were on your way to China." Another friend, who thought the General had served the country long enough, lamented, "It seems that your dream of spending the rest of your life in the country with Mrs. Marshall is no nearer fulfillment than it was last year." Stanton Griffis, who had served as ambassador to Poland and Egypt while Marshall was Secretary of State, was of two minds about the appointment: "It tremendously increases my pride in the Red Cross. . . . And, as for you, well, you are a glutton for punishment. Take my advice and protect yourself in the clutches." To help the General stand the strain of his new job, Griffis said that a few years back he had obtained a large amount of bourbon of rare vintage, and he was sending along a few bottles.

That a man of Marshall's caliber was willing to accept this duty gave an extra touch of importance to an important cause, and made people more willing to join in the work. Marshall could have let this fact alone be his contribution, but he did not want a sinecure; he wanted to work his passage. Nearly sixty-nine, weakened by an operation, he set about his new assignment as though he had never before served his country.

Many of the flood of letters he had received suggested what he should do as head of the Red Cross, changes to make, courses to establish: (1) give new drive to the organization; (2) win back the disaffected; (3) avoid controversy with local fund drives and regional organizations; 4) promote the Blood Bank; (5) strengthen the volunteer program. There were fewer suggestions as to how to accomplish these important goals.

As Army Chief of Staff, Marshall had been almost constantly on the road—visiting field units, assessing training, looking for new leaders, checking into pockets of discontent, encouraging all laborers in the vineyard. In this new job, he had much to build on other than his tremendous reputation. All his travels throughout the country, whether as Chief of Staff or to win Marshall Plan support, had given him contacts that were invaluable—with leaders of civic organizations, farm groups, business groups, religious establishments. They would listen to him.

He set out to eliminate friction, to fire the workers with enthusiasm, to smooth out dissension. In the early months of the year he spent as head of the Red Cross, he was on the road constantly. In the last months, the coming of the Korean War gave added emphasis to the Blood Bank program, and to morale-building services concerned with the troops and their families, thus gaining added support for overall programs.

The number of personal trips he made surprised even him.

These differed from the wartime visits to drill fields, maneuvers, and camps. During the war, he had avoided parades, inspections, official reviews, preferring to slip into a camp, talk with troops, then go away; some officers had criticized him because he did not make more of a splash. He became somewhat more of a public-relations man in working for the European Recovery Program, having to use the press and radio, to create photographic opportunities, to build morale by having himself photographed with local people. He had not changed his views, but had been forced to admit the value of publicity, and had accepted patiently the task of standing still for just one more shot.

Some of his friends laughingly said he sounded like a barnstorming candidate as he told them of the staggering list of places he must visit, dinners where he had to make an appearance and speak a few words, and meetings he had to attend. Near the end of 1949, he wrote Queen Frederika of Greece, who had asked about his new job, that although he was at Pinehurst for the winter, he would be traveling constantly on Red Cross business from January 15 until March 7, some 20,000 miles. Since taking over in October, he had covered 9,000 miles. In fact, he said, he would be increasingly busy until he took a few days off for rest in August.[6] The coming of the Korean War in June would increase the duties of the Red Cross, and July brought even greater responsibilities: it was then that he became aware that he might soon be asked to shoulder still greater burdens.

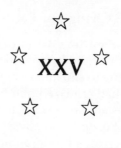

XXV

Back to Duty

GENERAL and Mrs. Marshall were vacationing at Huron Mountain resort in Michigan in August 1950 when he was called to the telephone at a country store nearby. It was the usual rural scene with local citizens sitting around and peering covertly at the elderly visitor as he came to take his phone call from Washington. They had been told, of course, that the U.S. President was on the phone, waiting to speak to the former Secretary of State. Aware that he could be overheard, Marshall was laconic and brief. The onlookers heard little more than "Yes, Mr. President," for Truman only asked that Marshall drop in to see him when he was next in Washington. The phone call opened the way for Marshall's third recall to active duty since his retirement as Chief of Staff five years previously.

The General could not have been surprised that Truman was about to ask him to succeed Louis Johnson as Secretary of Defense, because he had known before the beginning of the Korean War in late June that friction was great between Johnson and Dean Acheson, and Truman preferred the latter. Acheson had talked with Marshall shortly after the conflict began, and then Marshall was called to the Pentagon for a briefing. General Ridgway thought this briefing not sufficient and gave him another. On July 4, Truman and his daughter, Margaret, drove out to Leesburg, ostensibly for a pleasant visit. Truman later wrote that he had decided by late June to remove Johnson from the Cabinet, but he obviously wanted to see how familiar Marshall was with the immediate international situation and whether he was still a strong man on whom the President could rely in the swiftly developing crisis in Korea.[1]

Louis Johnson, the tall, bald Secretary of Defense, had long been a cyclonic presence on the American scene. He was a partner in a prestigious West Virginia law firm with offices in Washington. National commander of the American Legion in 1932–33, he had used his position to gain national political standing. He was brought into the administration by Roosevelt in June 1937 as Assistant Secretary of War, and became a counterweight to Harry Woodring, the isolationist Secretary of War. Marshall had found himself embarrassed by the fights between the two men when he was Deputy Chief of Staff. Johnson thought he had a promise of Woodring's place, but Roosevelt had decided instead to name the Republican Henry L. Stimson. As a leading fund raiser for Truman in 1948, Johnson asked for and got the post of Secretary of Defense which Forrestal had held since the position was created in 1947. In congratulating Johnson on his new position, Marshall wrote him that he would do well to avoid playing politics. Johnson had not taken the advice. He picked Stephen Early, Roosevelt's press secretary, as his deputy, and it was widely believed that this was a first step in his campaign for the presidency. It was his tendency to quarrel with members of the Cabinet, and particularly with Acheson, that angered Truman. In September 1950, the President wrote:

> Louis began to show an inordinate egotistical desire to run the whole government. He offended every member of the cabinet. We never had a cabinet meeting that he did not show plainly that he knew more about the problems of the Treasury, Commerce, Labor, Agriculture than did the Secretaries of those departments. He played no favorites; all of them were included. He disliked Cap Krug —a kindly person who finally left under pressure; he disliked Chapman, Krug's successor. He never missed an opportunity to say mean things about my personal staff.
>
> Then he tried to use the White House press men for blowing himself up and everyone else down, particularly the Secretary of State. He had conferences with enemy Senators of mine—Wherry, McCarthy, Brewster, Taft, Hickenlooper—and made terrible statements to them. After doing a good job on implementing the unification plan which I'd drawn up after World War II, on the advice of every field commander, army, navy, and air, he almost wrecked the whole thing. He misrepresented the facts to every committee before which he appeared. All this was carefully reported to me factually by men who were present—I have no spy system.[2]

The Korean War brought blame for Johnson's "crippling" defense cuts, which followed the President's budget-cutting promises of 1948. Later, Truman was accused of making the Defense Secre-

tary a scapegoat for his own sins, but even before the war he had
decided that Johnson would have to go, and the war simplified the
solution to an enlarging internal fight.

Marshall went to see Truman on September 6, after returning to
Leesburg from Michigan. Truman told him that he had to get rid
of Johnson and asked if Marshall would "act as Secretary of Defense through the crisis if I could get Congressional approval."
Marshall warned, "I want you to think about the fact that my appointment may reflect upon you and your Administration. They are
still charging me with the downfall of Chiang's government in
China. I want to help, not hurt you." Moved by this candor, Truman wrote his wife, "Can you think of anyone else saying that? I
can't and he's of the *great.*"[3]

Marshall set no conditions except that he would stay only for six
months to a year. He did request that Robert Lovett, long-time
colleague and friend, be named Deputy Secretary of Defense, and
he seems to have supposed that Lovett would succeed him when
he retired.

On September 7, the President was recounting to Mrs. Truman
the details of his talk with Marshall and said that he would have to
break the bad news to Louis Johnson, hoping that Johnson would,
because of the attacks on him, resign and let Marshall take the post.
"If he doesn't, I shall simply fire him as I did Wallace and Morgen-
thau." In his September 14 diary entry, he said that he had determined on September 1 (a Friday) that Johnson must go, but
decided to wait until Monday and then postponed telling him for
another week (which would be the 12th). Before the 12th came, an
article in *The New York Times* stated that Johnson was to be dismissed. Johnson called Truman on the 11th to ask what it all meant,
and Truman told him he would have to resign. The President then
asked Deputy Secretary of Defense Early to prepare a letter of
resignation for his chief. Johnson attended the Cabinet meeting on
September 12 and followed Truman into his office to ask that he
not be fired, while handing the President an unsigned letter of
resignation. Truman told him that he must sign it and later revealed to Mrs. Truman that the Secretary was weeping as he did so.
The President at once telephoned General Marshall and then arranged for a press release.[4]

Johnson's carefully drafted letter indicated that various difficulties and pressures had created great controversies and divisions in
Washington, and that since much criticism was aimed at him, he
proposed to resign. As instructed, he recommended that Truman
choose General Marshall, who could pull the country together.[5]

The prospect of Marshall's appointment won strong support in the Cabinet and in Congress, where most Democratic members approved the change, though many Republicans suggested taking a second look. Arthur Krock in *The New York Times* saw the appointment as solving several problems for the White House. The country had lost confidence in the administration and in the Department of Defense. The public saw Marshall as "eminently qualified to correct past errors and prevent the commission of new ones." Marshall would halt the war between Defense and State and stop the interservice battling. Although some critics thought Marshall was vulnerable on China, the Republicans would not dare go too far on that tack, "lest the country turn on them in anger and disgust."[6]

The *Times*, in its editorial comment on the nomination, suggested that Truman was probably more to blame for defense problems than Johnson. The Secretary would be succeeded "by a man of great force, immense experience, and keen foresight, to whom no aura of politics attaches and in whom the people place unbounded confidence." The *Washington Post* made many of the same points. Marshall was a military man with a civilian mind, "a truly authentic American in his respect for and devotion to our American system of government." The *Post* felt this was of the greatest importance. The country seemed to be moving toward a garrison state, a situation in which "the military is under constant temptation to take advantage of its power. But it is fortunate that in these circumstances there is a Marshall to fall back upon."[7]

Walter Lippmann found it interesting and fortunate that the appointment came at the time of the Inchon victory in Korea, and also when plans were afoot to use German forces in Western European defense. Marshall was "the soldier who understood that the revolution in Asia cannot be dealt with by American military intervention. He is the soldier who understood that European society must be made worth defending."[8]

The *Chicago Tribune* sounded the sour note that would become a battle cry for the most reactionary opponents of the administration. Its editorial blared that Johnson had been thrown out to save Acheson. Acheson had brought in Marshall, who had betrayed China to Stalin's agents, thus making Korea indefensible. The paper reiterated its old charges of Marshall's conspiracy with Roosevelt to withhold information from officers at Pearl Harbor, the disarming of Chiang Kai-shek, and the failure of the Marshall Plan. It was vintage Colonel McCormick, and the attack continued —as Marshall had warned Truman it would.[9] The *Tribune*'s cartoonist first showed Marshall as a simpleton lackey of a villainous British-type Acheson, later depicting him as a senile clown cutting out paper dolls.

In the Senate hearings that followed, Democrats and most Republican members of the Senate Committee on the Armed Forces asked for a quick confirmation. Senators Cain of Washington and Knowland of California paid tribute to Marshall's war contributions, but wondered about the wisdom of permitting a soldier to head the Department of Defense.

Had the nomination been a simple matter of a vote in the Senate, Marshall might have escaped some of the worst abuse. Even then it could not have approached the unamimous confirmation that a Republican-controlled Senate gave him in 1947 as Secretary of State. Because the Democrats' President had been elected in 1948 and the Democrats had recaptured Congress, partisanship was back in style.

The chief objection (and a valid one) was that a military man should not be Secretary of Defense. This point had been raised in the debate on the unification bill in 1947. The National Security Act passed that year provided that "a person who has within ten years been on active duty as a commissioned officer in a regular component of the armed services shall not be eligible for appointment as Secretary of Defense."

After these questions had been aired, the Chairman mentioned that a list of questions had been submitted by Senator William Jenner of Indiana, not a member of the committee. One of the right-wing Republican senators who had launched several attacks against the administration, Jenner was within two years of another senatorial election campaign, and the Marshall nomination offered an opportunity for partisan advantage. Senator Leverett Saltonstall of Massachusetts argued that some of the questions should be discussed only in executive session, but Senator Lyndon Johnson said that since they had been asked in open session, they should be answered there. Though some of Jenner's questions were straightforward requests for information, most of them were loaded.[10]

Marshall sat at one end of a table and Jenner at the other. Marshall gazed impassively at the Senator, only occasionally chuckling in recognition that Jenner was trying to make a political point rather than seeking information.

Why did he permit the signing of Lend-Lease agreements "which gave the Russians priority at the expense of 'the American fighting forces?' " Marshall replied that he had signed no such agreement, but that the aid had been made by the government to help in the fight against the Nazis. Why did he secure the appointment of Alger Hiss as executive secretary of the American Secretariat at Dumbarton Oaks? Marshall replied (correctly) that he did not recall having anything to do with that arrangement. Why did he accept a commission to force Chiang Kai-shek to take Communist China and its armies into the National Government of China? Marshall replied that the query begged the question.

"Why did you join in the suppression of the Wedemeyer Report on China?" was expected to give the General trouble. In his clipped, crisp voice, Marshall declared, "I did not join in the suppression of the report. I personally suppressed it." He continued:

> I sent General Wedemeyer over there as a last resort to find out what we might do and when his report came back, it involved a trusteeship for Manchuria with the Russians also being involved. Chiang Kai-shek had said flatly he would resign before accepting any relationship in which the British or Russians had a part. In addition the report had come at the time when the United States and Britain were dealing with the Greek question in the U.N. and they didn't want to bring up the idea of trusteeship.

In a low, hard tone of conviction, he went on, "Besides that, this was a report from a man I sent to find out something for me and not for a public speech, but it became, frankly, I guess, a political issue at the time."

Why did he not protest policies at Tehran, Yalta, and Potsdam that handed half the world to Stalin on a silver platter? Marshall reminded the interrogator that he had not attended political meetings at those conferences, and that the Joint Chiefs were represented by Admiral Leahy.

Did he favor turning over U.S. sovereignty to a superstate and making American armed forces a permanent foreign legion? The General snorted with a short laugh: "That pretty well covers the waterfront. No, I am not in favor of that."

"Will you assure the American people unequivocally that as Secretary of Defense you will not be dominated by or carry out the policies of the Secretary of State Dean Acheson, who will not turn his back on Alger Hiss?" As though he had been asked, "When did you stop beating your wife?," Marshall said, "I will not answer that question."

In the last go-round, Jenner asked where Marshall had been the night before Pearl Harbor. Marshall said he was fairly sure that he had been at home but he could not be positive. He repeated, as he had in earlier interrogations, "that Mr. Roosevelt had nothing whatsoever to do with where I was that evening and never discussed it with me afterward, and it had no relationship to his actions at all."

The committee went into executive session and ended by approving the nomination 10–2, with Knowland and Cain voting the noes.[11]

The debate on amending the National Security Act came in the two houses of Congress on September 15. In the House of Representatives, debate was limited and the chief excitement was provided by Representative Dewey Short of Missouri, sometime teacher and preacher, devoted to conviviality, the Bible, Shakespeare, and stump oratory, when he brought cheering Republicans to their feet by calling Marshall "a catspaw and a pawn" who had been called back "to bail out desperate men who are in a hole." He proposed that Representative Carl Vinson's name be substituted for that of Marshall, and Representative James Fulton was ready to make such a motion when Vinson, long-time Chairman of the Naval Affairs Committee and now Chairman of the House Armed Services Committee, stopped it. The House also tried to make the initial amendment acceptable to those who feared that the door was open to military domination by adding an amendment to the proposed legislation stipulating that the exemption was to apply only to Marshall. This was sent on to the Senate, where it was accepted.

Since the vote came late in a congressional election year, many representatives were missing. Twenty-seven Republicans, including Javits, Keating, John Lodge, Van Zandt, and Richard Nixon, voted with 193 Democrats to pass the amendment 220–105 (the 105 consisting of a hundred Republicans and five Democrats).[12]

In the Senate, Harry F. Byrd, Sr., led the fight for the amendment in the absence of Senator Millard Tydings. Terming Marshall one of the greatest and ablest leaders available in one of history's severest crises, he lauded the General's devotion to duty, which made him willing to accept one more burden. He stressed Marshall's lack of personal ambition and said that ten years earlier Marshall had persuaded him to stop the publication of an article the Virginia Senator had written calling for Marshall's election as President.

Most of the opponents of the measure voiced opposition to a military man's heading the Defense Department, but several strongly criticized the administration's foreign policy. Senator Taft, already regarded as the leading candidate for the Republican presidential nomination in 1952, said he felt that, if he voted for Marshall, he would be approving a policy favorable to Communism in the Far East, which had dominated the Far East Division of the State

Department, and would be approving Acheson's policy in China, Formosa, and Korea. Senator Knowland and several other critics of Acheson repeated this theme, but it remained for Senator Jenner, who had failed to draw blood with his earlier questions, to create the big scene. William S. White, correspondent for *The New York Times,* described the speech: "As Senator Jenner delivered his speech, at times in shouts and half-screams, the entire Senate, on the Republican as well as the Democratic side, sat with stony faces." Jenner said that the Democratic Party had been captured from the inside and used to hasten the destruction of the country. Those responsible would go into history as America's greatest criminals in peace and war. This was a desperate administration trying to cover up "its bloody tracks of treason." The appointment of George Marshall was an attempt of the administration "to swallow up the treachery of the past in the new treachery they are planning for the future."[13]

In the most memorable words that he would ever speak, Jenner thundered:

> General Marshall is not only willing, he is eager to play the role of a front man for traitors.
>
> The truth is this is no new role for him, for General George C. Marshall is a living lie.

Senator Lucas tried to protest but was waved aside and drowned out as Jenner continued his diatribe—a dress rehearsal of the longer attack that Joseph McCarthy would unleash a year later. Jenner attacked Roosevelt, Truman, Marshall, and Acheson for Pearl Harbor, sell-outs to Russia, betrayal of China, a disastrous Marshall Plan. They were now depending on the Marshall appointment to save them, but it would not work.

"Unless he, himself, were desperate, he could not possibly agree to continue as an errand boy, a front man, a stooge, or a conspirator for this Administration's crazy assortment of collectivist cutthroat crackpots and Communist fellow-travelling appeasers." It was tragic, he concluded, that Marshall was not enough of a patriot to tell the truth, "instead of joining hands once more with this criminal crowd of traitors and Communist appeasers, who, under the continuing influence and direction of Mr. Truman and Mr. Acheson, are still selling America down the river."

The Senate was accustomed to vehement charges and loose rhetoric, but Jenner had gone beyond the pale. When he had finished, Leverett Saltonstall, tall, graying Republican from Massachusetts,

former Governor of his state, whose long, square-jawed face might
have descended from Richard Saltonstall, who had come to America in 1620, struggled to his feet. He was ill but had come to support
a man for whom he had long held great respect.

Pale and stunned by Jenner's invective, he declared in shocked,
halting tones:

> I wish I had the words and the voice to express how strongly I
> disagree with many of the statements which have just been made.
> . . . If there is any man whose public life has been above censure
> . . . it is George C. Marshall. . . .
> I wish I had the vocabulary to answer the statement that General
> Marshall's life is a lie, because if ever there was a life spent in the
> interest of our country, a life that is not a lie, it is the life of George
> C. Marshall.[14]

When told of this attack in the Senate, Marshall said, "Jenner?
Jenner? I do not believe I know the man."

The virulence of Jenner's speech surprised many Republicans
who opposed changing the National Security Act. The party leaders
—Cain, Knowland, Mundt, Malone, Ferguson, and Taft—carefully
dissociated themselves from the highly personal attack, while warning against the Far Eastern policies of Secretary Acheson. Taft
made the final speech on the Republican side, praising Marshall as
a general but expressing fear about amending the National Security
Act. Senator Virgil Chapman of Kentucky, mindful that Eisenhower
was being pushed as a candidate for the Republican nomination
against Taft, asked the Ohio Senator whether the same bar against
a general for Secretary of Defense would apply if a general were a
presidential candidate. Cautiously, Taft said that it did not necessarily apply, but an argument could be made against having a general as such a candidate. "As a rule—with the great exception of
General Washington—that has not been a particular political success." After that neat answer, which some Democrats felt disposed
of both Eisenhower and MacArthur, Vice President Barkley called
for the vote.

Fifteen Republicans—Darby, Dworshak, Hendrikson, Ives,
Morse, Mundt, Saltonstall, Schoeppel, Smith of Maine, Thye,
Tobey, Wiley, and Williams—voted with forty-two Democrats to
approve the nomination 57–11. Shortly after confirmation, Mar-
shall was sworn in at the Pentagon by legal counsel Felix Larkin.
He was back in familiar surroundings.[15]

Several newspaper columnists who had been following the debate speculated as to Marshall's reasons for undertaking the job, and Taft had wondered why a man who had lost a kidney would assume the office in an election year, when much of the abuse would be directed at him.

In *The New York Times Magazine,* William S. White, conservative Texan and long-time member of the *Times* staff, wrote perceptively on September 24 about the General, posing rhetorical questions and answers as to why Marshall had agreed to leave the peace and quiet of Leesburg for the old hurly-burly. He mentioned "sense of duty." But he believed, and on this he is persuasive, that Marshall could not close his eyes to the problems that had broken over Johnson. He had spent forty-five years as a professional soldier. He did not consider himself a great Secretary of State. "What he does have reason to know quite well is that in military matters there are few, if any, who can teach him the rubrics. This new job, as Secretary of Defense, he must have said to himself, I can do."

The harshness of the campaign and the rough days ahead might be matters to dread for Mrs. Marshall but not for him, White thought. "The General is a man of toughness and of a realism so profound that the fact of the deep hostility to him held by many isolationists is treated in his mind exactly as the fact that there are a certain number of miles, some of them on narrow, uneven roads, between here and Leesburg."

Marshall, he noted, was one of the least politically partisan of men. He was no more an admirer of parts of the New Deal than was the chairman of the Republican National Committee. Marshall held to the theory that every man and country should work his or its passage.

He was not a saber rattler: "There is in him far less confidence in purely military strength than there is in many a professor or editorial writer." He did not try to grab power. He would not forget who was President of the United States or omit any courtesy, and he would not forget who was Secretary of State.

Now he comes back, the man who lives in high memory, the man who had finished and done. It will be a terrible chore to a man of 69, whose life has been spent for thirty years in enterprises that did not sleep. Will it kill the General, as so many are so poignantly afraid? Perhaps it will, perhaps not. In any case he is not one of those to whom a legendary infantry commander once called: "Come on you b———s, do you want to live forever?"[16]

In November, after the attacks made on his nomination for Secretary of Defense, Marshall showed his disdain for political expediency by requesting President Truman to present the name of Mrs. Anna M. Rosenberg of New York for the post of Assistant Secretary of Defense for Manpower. A more cautious man would have thought twice about the nomination, given the current climate of opinion. Marshall's recommendation was a New Dealer, a Jew, an Easterner, and a woman; proposed for a top job in a man's world —getting more troops for the armed forces.

In the late fall of 1950, one of Marshall's problems was the lack of an adequate reservoir of manpower to meet the demands of Korea and of commitments in Europe, while maintaining a sufficient reserve at home. He had long been conscious of the recurring problem that faced the armed services in peacetime: how to maintain sufficient manpower for defense without a continuing draft or without a professional army.

Before the end of World War II, he had called to Washington his old friend and adviser, John McAulay Palmer, long-time advocate of a citizen army, to work out plans for the postwar period. Ensconced in a special office in the Library of Congress, Palmer produced a detailed plan. Marshall had included it in his final report to the Secretary of War under the name "Universal Military Training," and had pressed for this legislation before going to China and while he was Secretary of State. However, Congress had not been favorable, and the armed forces were tentative about it. The coming of the Korean War made desperately necessary large increases in the armed forces and the scraping up of every reserve that could be found. He knew that manpower was one of the first problems he must tackle.[17]

Mrs. Rosenberg's name had come to his attention several times during the war and again in recent weeks. Born in Hungary in 1901, she had been brought to New York as a child and acquired American citizenship through her father's naturalization. By the 1920s she was working in the field of industrial and labor relations. As head of a public-relations firm, she had such diverse clients as R. H. Macy, Lazard Freres, *Encyclopedia Britannica,* and Nelson Rockefeller. In the early days of the New Deal, she served on a number of regional boards dealing with the National Recovery Administration, Defense, Health and Welfare Services, the War Manpower Commission, and the Office of the Coordinator of Inter-American Affairs (she had recommended Nelson Rockefeller to President Roosevelt for that position). President Roosevelt in 1944 and President Truman in 1945 had sent her to Europe to study the Army's manpower problems. There she won the friendship of Generals Eisenhower and Walter Bedell Smith. On the basis of her work in Europe, Eisenhower later helped get her the Medal of Freedom and the Medal of Merit.[18]

From 1942 to 1945, she was a member of the President's Labor Advisory Board, and, from 1944 to 1947, a member of the Advisory Board of the Office of War Mobilization and Reconversion. Successive Governors Herbert Lehman and Thomas Dewey of New York had in turn put her on the New York War Council. She was a member of the Manpower Consulting Committee of the Army and Navy Munitions Board, and consultant to Stuart Symington in his capacity as Chairman of the National Security Resources Board. From Marshall's standpoint, her most important qualification was that she was a member of the Advisory Board on Universal Military Training and had helped prepare the Compton Report backing the proposal.

In late October 1950, Marshall called her to Washington to discuss his problem. He told her that the man who had just left his office had turned him down because he had promised to take his wife on a trip. "I told him that there is a Mrs. Marshall and I promised her three times I would come home. And I haven't been able to do it." Mrs. Rosenberg said she couldn't imagine how anyone could refuse him. "There was a twinkle in his eye, but he didn't say anything."[19]

Two days later, he offered her the job. Meanwhile, he had asked their mutual friend Bernard Baruch to help convince her to accept. She later asked him why he had not offered the position when she was right in his office. He said that he had had to get his courage up, but had thought after what she said that she would take it. Lest there be any doubt in her mind as to what she was plunging into, he told her that the people trying to get at him would attack her. She agreed to take the job, but suggested there be no announcement until after the coming election, so the appointment would not be used against the administration.

However, rumors began to appear, so on the morning of the election, Marshall recommended the appointment to President Truman, who announced the recess appointment as of November 15. Immediate reaction was favorable, though there were areas of the Pentagon expressing a few doubts and it became evident that some of Mrs. Rosenberg's future colleagues failed to share Marshall's enthusiasm.

There was nothing anonymous in her appearance, but her striking looks came from vividness rather than beauty. Her tiny frame was always stylishly clad, and her vivacity kept her many bracelets jangling. Her high heels beat a rapid staccato on the floors of Pentagon corridors, and she spoke clearly and distinctly with a minimum of gobbledygook. Those meeting her for the first time felt that here was a personage. Old-hand newsmen liked and respected her.

Marshall was anxious to get a hurried confirmation so she could give full attention to her duties. He furnished Senator Millard Tydings, Chairman of the Armed Services Committee, with full details about her qualifications and a statement that he alone was responsible for her selection. Fulton Lewis, Jr., the popular radio newscaster who was ever looking for subversion, went on the air with a warning against her after digging through files of the House Un-American Committee. The Armed Services Committee favored her candidacy but decided to hear her response to accusations of left-wing leanings. On November 29, she appeared before the committee, to reveal that she had answered all charges earlier before the House committee and been cleared. Vigorously denying that she was now or ever had been a Communist or belonged to a Communist front organization, she pointed out that the House committee had discovered that another Anna Rosenberg was involved. When Senator Saltonstall declared that he had checked with some members of the House committee and they agreed with her statements, and that General Marshall had recommended her and had said her services were vital to the war effort, the nine members of the committee present—Tydings, Harry Byrd, Sr., Lyndon Johnson, Virgil Chapman, Lester Hunt, Styles Bridges, Chan Gurney, Leverett Saltonstall, and Harry P. Cain—voted unanimously in her favor.

Everything seemed set, but the "lunatic fringe," as Marshall called the extremists, was hard at work. Millard Tydings had been defeated in Maryland for reelection to the Senate in a vicious campaign in which his enemies had circulated a faked photograph, cut and pasted and rephotographed to show him in friendly conversation with the former head of the Communist Party in the United States. Richard Russell of Georgia replaced him as Chairman of the Armed Services Committee. Since the Georgian had not been present for the November hearing, opponents of the confirmation decided to bring their case to him. Representative Ed Lee Gossett of Texas, accompanied by Benjamin A. Freedman of New York, a right-wing activist, appeared with what they declared to be positive information that Anna Rosenberg was a Communist.

Freedman told Russell that Dr. J. B. Matthews, a staff member of the committee, had informed him that FBI files on Mrs. Rosenberg would show that she belonged to pro-Communist organizations and was unfit to work in the Defense Department. He said that Ralph de Sola of New York, a reformed Communist, had been a member of the John Reed Club in New York in the 1930s and was ready to testify that he had seen Anna Rosenberg on several occasions there, and that he recognized the photograph of the woman of that name now being considered for the Pentagon position. He added that Mrs. Rosenberg, a member of the New York educational system, had placed his (de Sola's) wife in the system so that she could bring in more Communists. He identified a member of the John Reed Club who had told him that Mrs. Rosenberg was an important member of the Communist Party but had warned him not to reveal her affiliation since the party intended to use her to get inside the government apparatus. He added that in a later position she had passed on the qualifications of a number of Harry Hopkins' staff, two of whom were anarchists.

This was steamy stuff, but Russell was unwilling to reopen the hearings unless a signed charge was made against her. Freedman obliged. Informed that a charge had been signed, Fulton Lewis, Jr., sent his reporter, Kenneth Nellor, to New York to get a statement from de Sola. He was accompanied by Donald Surine, an investigator on the staff of Senator Joseph McCarthy. Freedman had told Surine that he would have to get a letter from Gerald L. K. Smith, a professional anti-left agitator, before either he (Freedman) or de Sola would talk. Smith gave Nellor and Surine a letter for Freedman in which he congratulated the self-styled "excommunicated Jew" on his great fight to keep "the Zionist Jew Anna Rosenberg from becoming the dictator of the Pentagon." He urged Freedman to aid the two investigators helping them in the fight. He particularly wanted them to assist Fulton Lewis, Jr., who "is doing a magnificent job in the Rosenberg matter." Smith urged that the letter be destroyed, but it turned up in Drew Pearson's column.[20]

At a reconvened hearing, with Senator Russell in the chair, J. B. Matthews denied much of what Freedman had said about him, citing an abject letter of apology from Freedman. Freedman promptly declared that he was apologizing for releasing Matthews's statements without permission, but not for their substance. His testimony was not straightforward, and Nellor and Surine denounced him for saying that they had told witnesses that they were from the Senate Armed Forces Committee.

De Sola's performance was also a disaster. As he was being sharply questioned by committee members, his stories began to fall apart. The man who had supposedly identified Rosenberg several times at the John Reed Club denied the story, and de Sola's wife repudiated statements attributed to her.

The hearings became a circus when Marjorie Shearon, fired from the Senate Committee on Labor and Public Welfare when Republicans were in power, read into the proceedings a list of individuals favoring some form of national insurance that had been signed by Mrs. Rosenberg and 250 other well-known Americans. She said that many of them had been cited for radical activities, among others Senator Murray of Montana and Senator Wayne Morse of Oregon, the latter being a member of the committee. It came out finally that she had at one time favored a particular national insurance plan that Mrs. Rosenberg had opposed.

A number of hearing supporters began to grow wary. Surine had brought Freedman and de Sola to McCarthy's office, but later he declared that it was only to leave their coats and that Senator McCarthy never saw them. McCarthy went to great lengths to deny any association with anti-Semitism and ultimately voted for the Rosenberg confirmation. Fulton Lewis, Jr., who had done so much to stir up the whole affair, toned down his accusations and spoke ill of Freedman. Freedman then lit into the "smearbund" that had repudiated him, and Gerald L. K. Smith reacted with fury when Lewis was critical of him, fuming that when "the Jewish campaign to whitewash the Rosenberg woman" was organized, Lewis was found to be involved up to his neck. "The Jews had put pressure on him and Lewis had proved that he feared the Jews more than he hated Communism."

Meanwhile Mrs. Rosenberg's friends were sending a deluge of letters and telegrams which ultimately went into the committee's file. Former Secretary of State Byrnes, Generals Eisenhower and Bedell Smith (then head of the C.I.A.), Bernard Baruch, and a multitude of others wrote in support and praise of her. Eleanor Roosevelt asked earnestly of Mrs. Rosenberg what she could do to help.[21]

Mrs. Rosenberg made clear to Marshall a point she did not have to make to Mrs. Roosevelt: that the attacks on her had been based not so much on a serious belief that she was a Communist as on the fact that she had been an active backer of New Deal social legislation. Numerous letters sent in by doctors objecting to her appointment to the Defense Department were evidently due to her support of some form of national health insurance.

Aware of the emotional pressure under which Mrs. Rosenberg was laboring, Marshall made strenuous efforts to present her side of the case to the senators. The Defense Department counsel, Felix

Larkin, made available all wanted records. Marshall asked for the F.B.I. files on Mrs. Rosenberg and, after reviewing them, requested that the President release them for study by representatives of the committee. Senators Byrd, Hunt, and Cain were selected to read the files. When Russell took up the duties of Chairman, Marshall suggested that he be added to the list, but Russell declined unless the whole committee could read the files. Ultimately, the committee was satisfied by assurances from the three and from Marshall that there was nothing to substantiate the charges.

The F.B.I. had been helpful in settling the affair. An Anna Rosenberg was found in California who had belonged to the John Reed Club of New York, but had left the group when she moved to California, before de Sola said he had met her at the club. Feeling that J. Edgar Hoover had made a special effort to help, Marshall called to thank him, and then wrote a letter praising him to Truman and sent a copy to the F.B.I. director. The latter responded genially, adding, "Quite frankly, I regarded our efforts in this case as part of the routine operations of the F.B.I. . . ."[22]

Despite the favorable attitude of the committee, Marshall feared that Russell might allow the hearings to drag on to the end of the year. He was uneasy about the reaction of public opinion, because hostile witnesses could air charges before they came before the committee, while the favorable letters would not be revealed until the final report was made. In what was for him an unusual action, he rang up Baruch on December 10, urging action to get an immediate committee report. He wanted Baruch to come to Washington to talk with Russell, or call friends of Russell in Atlanta or Savannah who might help. "Can you now, by telephone, bring such immediate action and heavy pressure to bear?"[23]

Whether or not Baruch intervened, the hearings continued until December 14. On that day, the committee determined there was no basis for the allegations against Mrs. Rosenberg and unanimously proposed that she be confirmed. William Knowland, Estes Kefauver, Wayne Morse, and Richard Russell joined those who had previously voted for her. Harry Byrd was appointed to handle the nomination on the floor.

Marshall watched the result closely. Mrs. Rosenberg later recalled that he kept coming into her office on the day of the Senate vote to see if she had heard anything. He finally said he would be having a meeting in his office with the Joint Chiefs of Staff before they were to go to the White House, and he asked that she break into the meeting if she heard the results before they left.

"When I got word, I rushed in. He and the Joint Chiefs had their coats on. I was choked up. He said when I told him I was confirmed: 'That's good. Go home and get a facial; you look like hell.' The Joint Chiefs looked shocked that General Marshall would know anything about a facial."[24]

It was Marshall's nature to arrange his priorities so that he could devote his full strength and time to the main problems. He liked to develop a staff that understood what he wanted and that, with a minimum of instruction, would produce what he wanted. He could raise a standard, could make clear the direction in which the armed services were to proceed, and interject suggestions and support where needed to back younger subordinates who would do the day-by-day work. President Truman wanted a man who would restore confidence in the Department of Defense. It was for his strength of character as much as for his administrative leadership that he was called again to duty in 1950.

One of the calculated assets of Marshall's return to public service was the return of Robert A. Lovett into government service. Marshall had known the Wall Street banker since 1940, had worked closely with him in the War Department during the war and at the State Department, where Lovett had been his Under Secretary for most of his term there. He prized Lovett's brilliance, his tendency to go straight to the heart of matters, his great sense of humor, his aversion to the limelight, and his ability to work well with a wide collection of military, political, and business leaders here and abroad. Lovett's banking ties to Europe had long made him familiar with European problems and thinking on defense and foreign policy. His wider experience in military and foreign-policy matters had made him sensitive to events currently affecting the national interests of the United States. Lovett would keep many of the matters of detail off his superior's desk. Most important to Marshall was that Lovett thought as he did, and when he was out of the country Lovett could act on a matter as if they had just discussed it face to face. If Lovett considered that a Marshall proposal was wrong, he felt easy about suggesting another course of action.

Lovett, the Joint Chiefs of Staff, and the service secretaries knew Marshall's ideas on international security and national defense. His character, his known distaste for intrigue, his demand for simplicity of plans and organization, his fierce insistence on clear channels of command, his belief in responsibility and loyalty up and down, all contributed to a bracing atmosphere and set a high standard for governmental operations. His secure position in the affections of many Americans, his standing among allies abroad, and his reputa-

tion for requiring steady accomplishment of himself and his colleagues cut through the inertia of bureaucratic unconcern.

A return to a smooth working relationship between the Departments of State and Defense was the best result of Marshall's appointment and may have been the President's main objective in
making the appointment, because he knew that Marshall and Acheson had been an effective team in the past. Marshall had corre-
sponded with the State Department through Acheson while on his
mission to China. Acheson had served as his Under Secretary of
State in the transitional months when he was first named to State,
and had run the department at home while Marshall was at the
Moscow Conference. Acheson, in turn, knew thoroughly the ideas
and methods of Marshall. He had been impressed by Marshall's
frequent admonition "Don't fight the problem," and his ability to
leave emotion outside the conference room. "I reserve my personal
feelings for Mrs. Marshall," he was recorded as saying by Acheson.

Perhaps by design, but just as likely from instinctive courtesy,
Marshall eased tensions between the two most prestigious departments of the government. He arranged regular conferences between himself and Acheson and between their staffs. He knew life
on both sides of the river, having directed the building of the
Pentagon as well as the original part of the building occupied by
the State Department.

Marshall did not find it necessary to stand on ceremony. Emphasizing that by protocol the State Department outranked the Department of Defense, he insisted that the younger Acheson walk ahead
of him in line. When Acheson tried to refuse, Marshall settled the
question by seizing Acheson's arm and pushing him into first place.
At the first conference between the secretaries and their staffs,
Marshall carefully placed himself on the civilian side of the table,
across from the admirals and generals. These were more than
passages of courtesy; they were signals that defense and foreign
policy were parts of a whole once more.

Marshall knew that critics of the administration held Acheson
responsible for every woe affecting American foreign policy, that
paranoid circles regarded him as a malignant growth, that some
members of both parties believed that Truman had sacrificed Johnson to save Acheson's skin, and that Marshall was being brought in
to save his policies. Marshall did not have to be directed to stop the
bickering between departments. He never believed that a war could
be won by conflict at home. In the early days of the war, Admiral
King had been kept waiting for an appointment with Marshall for

so long that he had stormed out of the General's anteroom in a rage. The General went to him to apologize. They could not wage war together, explained the General persuasively, unless they agreed not to let personal differences divide them.

Acheson knew that Marshall was incapable of undermining him, and he was grateful for the strength he would draw from the association. He gladly came to the Pentagon for meetings with Marshall and sent his representatives to meet with Marshall's staff. Aware of Marshall's long seniority in government and his standing in Truman's eyes, the Secretary of State was prepared to defer to the General. The result was the most successful collaboration in the history of the two departments.

A successful Secretary of Defense has to depend on the Joint Chiefs of Staff. It was necessary to keep them working together and to keep interservice battles to a minimum. Marshall knew the problem well, because he himself had for six years been one of the powerful service barons, voracious for his share of men and weapons for the growing Army and Army Air Force. Roosevelt had given him direct responsibility for the task of training troops, for selecting and testing officers and for planning and conducting operations. For these matters he could go directly to the President, without going through the Secretary of War. He had managed to work closely with Stimson and to keep the Secretary informed and involved while gaining his complete support at the White House. Since unification, many of the Chiefs felt constrained by the Secretary of Defense. Although the service secretaries had tended to fade into the background on operational matters, there had been unfavorable reactions to civilian assistants in the office of the Secretary of Defense who reduced the role of the military chiefs.

In this minefield, Marshall had the advantage of already knowing all of those with whom he would work. General Omar Bradley, Chairman of the Joint Chiefs of Staff, had been one of the great commanders of World War II, and Marshall had been intimately involved with his career. Since serving as an instructor in the Infantry School at Fort Benning in the late 1920s, Bradley had been recognized as a Marshall protégé. He was one of the "Marshall men" with whom the General kept in touch between wars. Bradley's was early a starred name on the list Marshall kept of future Army leaders.

Bradley was Marshall's model of a field commander. Calm, utterly without flamboyance, patient, capable of hard decisions without screaming and cursing, cooperative, successful in molding winning armies, Bradley would have been Marshall's choice for

Chairman of the Joint Chiefs of Staff had he not already been in the job. He had long been a favorite general of fellow Missourian Harry Truman, and it was the President who had wanted him as Chairman of the Joint Chiefs and who had proposed that he be awarded his fifth star. All this gave extra clout to a position that was not so fully developed as it would later be.

Although Bradley was on a close personal basis with Marshall, sometimes as hunting companion, he had never lost his awe of his chief. It was never "the Old Man" or "Marshall," but always "General Marshall." Although he was aware of the new Defense Secretary's instructions that officers were to enter his office immediately when they had key matters to discuss, Bradley always stopped at the door to ask the assistant, "Is it all right for me to go in?" In conference, he would venture a different opinion if he thought he had more facts, but he worked closely and easily with his long-time superior.[25]

Bradley's successor as Chief of Staff, J. Lawton Collins, was another long-time Marshall favorite. They had been at Benning together, and Marshall had called on Collins to plan the reorganization of Army divisions. Marshall was also a friend of Collins's older brother, Major General James L. Collins, former aide to Pershing and a member of his staff during World War I, but his admiration for the younger brother was based on the latter's dazzling performance of duties in World War II. Marshall had wanted him for division command in the early Pacific fighting and suggested to MacArthur that Collins would make a fine corps leader. When MacArthur pronounced him too young for such responsibility, Marshall called him to Eisenhower's attention and Collins was given one of the two corps that landed in Normandy, seizing Cherbourg and heading forces in the Saint Lo breakout. His exploits as one of the top corps commanders in World War II won him the nickname of "Lightnin' Joe" and put him in line to succeed Bradley as Chief of Staff, and he was there when Marshall came to the Defense desk.[26]

Marshall did not know General Hoyt Vandenberg, Chief of Staff of the Air Force, so intimately as he did Bradley and Collins, but he knew a great deal about his background. Nephew of Senator Arthur Vandenberg, Hoyt Vandenberg first came to Marshall's attention as Operations and Training officer of the Army Air Forces in Washington when the United States entered the war. He served in North Africa and Europe before heading the Ninth Air Force in the United Kingdom. After the war, he was in quick succession director of intelligence for the War Department, then, while Marshall was Secretary of State, head of Central Intelligence (predecessor of the Central Intelligence Agency) and subsequently Vice Chief of Air Staff and then Chief of the Air Force, holding this position throughout Marshall's time as Secretary of Defense.

Commentators speaking or writing about Marshall's familial relations with most of the Joint Chiefs nearly always excepted Admiral Forrest Sherman as being the only one he did not really know. Actually, Marshall considered Sherman a member of the "young Navy" who was personally friendly to him. He knew of his outstanding performance as Nimitz's Deputy Chief of Plans in the Pacific. While in the Pacific, Sherman had written Marshall to ask about the care of his horse, left behind in the Fort Myer stables. The General told him that all was well with the horse, and that as long as Sherman continued his fine performance he need have no worries.

It could be said that Marshall was on even stronger ground with Congress than he had been as Secretary of State. True, Senator Vandenberg was dying and he did not have the same relationship with Taft, Knowland, Wherry, and Bridges, who were among the anti-administration faction in the Senate. But the Democrats were in control. He had worked with Vice President Barkley during the war years on such ticklish matters as the development of the atomic bomb, and he had good working relations with Walter George, chairman of the Senate Foreign Relations Committee. Floor Leader Lucas had been a friend in the early 1930s in Chicago. In the House, Speaker Rayburn had worked with him both during the war and at the State Department. He was friendly with the majority leader, McCormack, and could depend for support on Vinson, Chairman of the Armed Services Committee.

Marshall would need all the help he could get. At this most difficult time for the armed forces, the Army's most highly valued general would use a battlefield in the Far East to flaunt his own convictions against those of his superiors in the Pentagon, the State Department, and the White House.

Korea Blazes

THE new Secretary of Defense was no stranger to the early background of the Korean problem. As Chief of Staff in the closing days of World War II, he had participated in crucial decisions regarding that country. During this period, the 38th Parallel was drawn between North and South Korea, and a forerunner of the U.S. Military Advisory Group for South Korea was set up. During the year that Marshall spent in China, the United States increased its commitment to that area.

After receiving the Japanese surrender of South Korea, the United States had intended to end its occupation and pave the way for the establishment of a unified government. Washington hoped that its example would encourage the Soviet Union to withdraw its troops from North Korea.

Japan had annexed Korea in 1910 and had proceeded ruthlessly to impose autocratic rule throughout the peninsula, so that Korea presented the Allies with the difficult problem of restoring a long-dispossessed government. Committees for Korean independence had developed outside the country during World War I. In 1919, Dr. Syngman Rhee, prominent in the independence movement, announced at Shanghai the formation of a provisional government for Korea, and began a propaganda campaign in the Far East and the United States. Six years later, the Soviet Union encouraged the establishment of a Communist independence movement for Korea. The United States, Great Britain, and the Soviet Union included Korean independence in their declaration at the Tehran Conference in 1943; "a free and independent Korea" was henceforth listed among Allied war aims.

Although Korea was not specifically included at Yalta among the countries to be freed from Japan's control, the United States obtained informal Soviet agreement at Yalta, and again in May 1945, to a four-power trusteeship for Korea.[1]

At Potsdam, General Marshall reminded President Truman that the Joint Chiefs of Staff needed guidance on the handling of Korean claims. He also discussed with the Russian Chief of Staff, General Alexei Antonov, the proposed Soviet course of action in Korea at the end of the war. Antonov, in turn, asked whether the United States would be operating against the shores of Korea in coordination with a Russian land offensive, and was told that plans for Korea waited on the ending of Japanese control. Marshall feared that attempts to land in Korea before the invasion of Japan would be subject to kamikaze attacks, but he thought that Korea could be controlled from the airfields in Kyushu, once they were taken over from the Japanese.[2]

The Soviet Union's declaration of war on Japan on August 9 hastened the dispatch of a U.S. directive to MacArthur for taking the Japanese surrender. Aware that the Russians were poised to move into Korea, Secretary of State Byrnes proposed that the U.S. commanders accept the surrender of Japanese forces as far north as possible. Assistant Secretary of War John J. McCloy, responsible for military occupation and civil affairs, asked Colonel Charles H. Bonesteel and Colonel Dean Rusk (who had spent much of the war with Stilwell), of the War Department staff, to draw a proposed northern line for the area of Korea that the United States would occupy. The 38th Parallel was selected because it included Seoul, the capital, and seemed to be as far north as the U.S. forces could be expected to reach. Rusk was surprised when the line was accepted by the Russians.[3]

Russian troops were already moving into Manchuria and Korea when Truman approved the directive drawn up by the Joint Chiefs and sent it on to London and then Moscow. On getting Allied concurrence, he forwarded it to the Commander in Chief, Far East. MacArthur named Lieutenant General John R. Hodge, commander of the XXIV Corps, to take the surrender. He instructed him to occupy Seoul, make friendly contact with the Soviet forces, and avoid incidents.[4]

Hodge ran into difficulties when Syngman Rhee and Kim Koo, leader of the provisional government, returned to Korea in the fall. Not only did Rhee sharply disagree with Communist groups that had become active in South Korea, but he also became critical and resentful of Hodge. The American General had been told to make a gradual shift from U.S. occupation control to self-government.

Rhee's demands that he speed up the process led Hodge to ask Washington for authority to overrule Rhee.

Marshall, beset with occupation problems in Germany and in Japan, directed MacArthur to seek a single administration for the whole of Korea but realized that it might be a year before a four-power trusteeship could take over affairs in the country. The Far Eastern commander recalled that efforts to cooperate with the Soviet government had so far met with little success.[5]

State Department officials had begun to doubt the wisdom of trusteeship for Korea, and the idea was anathema to Koreans, for it promised another period of foreign occupation. In November, the U.S. political adviser in that country suggested to Secretary Byrnes that the concept be dropped. Byrnes said that, if the Soviet Union would accept unification and independence for Korea, trusteeship might not be needed.[6]

As Marshall was leaving on his mission to China, an announcement of four-power discussion of a trusteeship led to riots in South Korea, which had to be put down by American troops. Even while occupied by problems on mainland China, Marshall knew of continuing difficulties between the United States and the Soviet Union over the Korean situation. From the beginning, the Russians had blocked off North Korea from the rest of the country. American proposals in January and February 1946 to integrate North and South Korea were met by Soviet insistence on keeping the two zones but coordinating the control. Soviet newspapers attacked the United States for trying to impose a trusteeship.[7]

By February, a Communist regime had been established in the North led by a Korean who had served in the Soviet Army under the name Kim Il Sung. With a compliant government in control, the Soviets withdrew all but 10,000 troops from Korea by mid-year 1946. By fall, the United States had reduced its troops in the South, but was disturbed by reports that the Soviets were training a large North Korean force that would be capable of defeating South Korea.

MacArthur was still seeking a Korean settlement during the late winter of 1946. As Secretary of State Marshall prepared for the Moscow Conference in early March 1947, his advisers suggested that he raise the question of Korean independence. While he was away, representatives of State, War, and Navy discussed the future role of the United States in Korea. Secretary of War Patterson, aware of the rapid reduction of U.S. military forces, favored withdrawal. Secretary of Navy Forrestal agreed, saying that Korea's importance to American policy had been exaggerated. It remained for Acheson, sitting in for the Secretary of State, to remind them that Marshall wanted to go slow on withdrawal because of the damage to U.S. prestige in the Far East. In later talks, Patterson and Acheson held to their earlier stands while Forrestal accepted Marshall's warning of a Communist takeover of the whole country if all American forces were suddenly pulled out.[8]

Already bitterly at odds with the United States over events in Germany, Molotov accused the American presence in Korea of causing the breakdown of talks there. However, he said that the Russians were ready to resume talks at Seoul in late May. Marshall insisted that all interested groups be admitted to discussions before the Joint Commission on Korea and their right to freedom of expression be guaranteed. The United States agreed to a provisional democratic government, local government by free elections, and economic development of the country. Molotov finally agreed to these American amendments to Soviet proposals.[9]

During a May 7 meeting of State, Army, and Navy representatives, Marshall disagreed with Patterson's reiteration that U.S. forces should be withdrawn from Korea because of its lack of strategic importance. His experiences in China, with the Russians in Manchuria, and more recently with the Soviets in Germany increased his awareness of the North Korean threat to the South. Dubious about the effectiveness of the training and reorganization of the South Korean constabulary, he suggested that there be a one-year program of rehabilitation and that the State Department take over nonmilitary features of the occupation. A provisional government for South Korea could be set up after a suitable election law was provided.[10]

In late July, overestimating his power, Syngman Rhee assailed Koreans who cooperated with the Joint Commission, attacked any suggestion of a trusteeship, urged that negotiations with the Soviets stop, and asked that the Korean problem be submitted to the United Nations. The State Department suggested that the United Nations plan elections for Korea with U.N. observers present. If the Soviet Union opposed this action, State proposed that the whole matter be referred to the United Nations.[11]

In early August, State, War, and Navy representatives proposed to reduce the military commitment to Korea "as soon as possible without abandoning Korea to Soviet domination." They wanted to fix a deadline for the Joint Commission report, failing which the U.S. would submit its own report to the powers that had signed the agreement for the establishment of a unified, democratic Korea. If these powers failed to act on the report, the United States would then submit the matter to the United Nations. Secretary of State Marshall approved this proposal.[12]

Marshall complained to Molotov on August 11 about the Joint Commission's lack of action. Denying any delays, the Soviet Foreign Minister accused American authorities with the persecution of Koreans who supported Moscow. On August 26, concluding that the Joint Commission would never be permitted to act, Acting Secretary of State Lovett asked that the proposals be submitted to the four powers that had signed the Korean agreement. Molotov replied that there was no hope of Russian acceptance of four-power action.[13]

The pattern of action was all too familiar to Marshall. In mid-September, the State Department asked the Joint Chiefs of Staff to state the extent of military interest in Korea. State's Policy Planning Staff had already assumed that Korea was not militarily essential to the United States and that "our policy should be to cut our losses and get out of there as gracefully but promptly as possible," much the idea that Patterson had set forth earlier. To some degree it was the view of General Hodge. Forrestal replied for the Joint Chiefs near the end of the month. From the standpoint of military security, "the United States has little strategic interest in maintaining the present troops and bases in Korea." In case of war, Korea would be a liability. Any American offensive northward would bypass Korea, air action would neutralize it at less cost than ground action, the 45,000 troops in Korea could be used more effectively elsewhere, and troops left there might be forced to withdraw later with a loss of prestige.[14]

Meanwhile, the United States was readying action in the United Nations. Explaining the American position to the General Assembly, Marshall said that China and Britain had agreed with the United States in its efforts to get a provisional government for Korea, but the Soviet Union had opposed these proposals. Further attempts at bilateral negotiation would only delay the establishment of an independent state. Molotov's reply on October 10, proposing simultaneous U.S. and Soviet withdrawal of military forces by the end of 1948, was met by an American request that the U.N. set elections not later than March 31, 1948. The assembly accepted the U.S. substitute resolution, and established a U.N. Commission for Korea.[15]

Near the end of the year, American officials began to plan for future withdrawal. The Department of the Army directed MacArthur and Hodge to make preparatory arrangements, and Eisenhower, then Chief of Staff, asked Marshall to retain Hodge until the end of the occupation. General Saltzman, Assistant Secretary of State for Occupied Areas, added that a sudden relief of Hodge would be regarded as a victory by Syngman Rhee and his followers. Marshall agreed, unless serious delays made changes in deadlines.[16]

The Soviet Union denied the new U.N. commission access to North Korea. The interim committee of the General Assembly then directed the commission to hold an election in South Korea. Assuming that a government would emerge by summer, the State Department advised that the United States stay flexible on the date for withdrawal: time was needed to prepare South Korean defenses and to train a South Korean security force.[17]

Marshall wondered if the poorly trained and scantily armed 25,000 constabulary of South Korea could be shaped to resist North Korea's forces by the time the United States withdrew from Korea. Remembering the organization of the Philippine Scouts from the days of his first military experiences, he asked whether South Korean soldiers could be put into American units until they were properly trained.[18]

The National Security Council on April 2, 1948, delineated the existing American options in Korea: (1) abandoning the South Koreans (not considered feasible); (2) supporting the South Koreans by training troops and providing other assistance; (3) withdrawing troops there by the end of the year; and (4) continuing cooperation with the United Nations. The council emphasized that the United States should avoid getting so involved "that any action taken by any faction in Korea . . . could be considered a *casus belli* by the U.S." The council also held that further negotiation with the Soviet Union on the unification and independence of Korea should not be written off.[19]

The U.N.-sponsored elections took place in South Korea on May 10. Two days later, at his press conference, Marshall declared "the fact that some 90 per cent of the registered voters cast their ballots, despite the lawless efforts of a communist-dominated minority to prevent or sabotage the election, is a clear revelation that the Korean people are determined to form their own government by democratic means."[20]

In mid-August, the first Korean-controlled government since 1910 was established at Seoul, with Syngman Rhee as head. He was delighted to have General MacArthur declaim:

In this hour as the forces of righteousness advance, the triumph is dulled by one of the greatest tragedies of contemporary history. An artificial barrier has divided your land. This barrier must and shall be torn down. Nothing shall prevent the ultimate unity of your people as free men of a free nation.[21]

His words struck a gallant and very popular note, but they did not exactly indicate the cautious approach that the Joint Chiefs of Staff and the State Department recommended. When speaking later of MacArthur's October visit to Korea, Rhee declared that the General had privately assured him that he would protect Korea "as I would protect the United States or California against aggression."[22] This was a remarkable statement, because MacArthur no longer had principal responsibility for Korean independence.

North Korea held no elections. A body called the "Supreme People's Assembly" of North Korea ratified a constitution and proclaimed a People's Democratic Republic with Kim Il Sung as Prime Minister in early September 1948. The Soviet Union recognized this new government, followed by Poland, Mongolia, Czechoslovakia, Rumania, and Yugoslavia. Moscow announced that it would begin to withdraw its troops in mid-October and complete the process by the end of the year.

At the end of December 1948, Moscow announced that all its troops had been withdrawn. The United States increased its evacuation of troops and, near the end of June 1949, brought out its last regular units, leaving behind a small Military Advisory Group.[23]

But there was no real peace. A summary of that period later stated:

The withdrawal of the respective occupation troops left the two hostile Korean regimes facing one another, each claiming to be the only legitimate government, each augmenting its armed forces, and each eager to settle the question by force of arms.[24]

The Advisory Group had grown out of an early-1948 statement by the Joint Strategic Survey Committee that a strong South Korean constabulary might be able to deter North Korean aggression. General MacArthur had advised against building a South Korean army and favored increasing the constabulary to 50,000 men. Near the end of 1948, at Syngman Rhee's request, the Far Eastern commander made available members of his own headquarters, some 472 officers and men, to become the U.S. Military Advisory Group to the Republic of Korea under Brigadier General William J. Rob-

erts. MacArthur was to be responsible for logistical support to the
waterline and for the evacuation of American citizens in case of
emergency.[25]

MacArthur took a cautious stand. He favored a South Korean
force large enough to maintain internal security but organized in
such a way as to make clear that it offered no danger to North
Korea. Arms were provided for a 50,000-man "constabulary
force." In September 1948, apparently using MacArthur's argument, Marshall recommended the program to the Department of
the Army.

Marshall left the State Department in January 1949 and did not
deal with Korean matters again until September 1950. During this
intervening period, the Koreans benefited from arms and equipment left behind by the U.S. troops. In August 1949, at President
Rhee's request for additional support, Truman recommended such
aid to Congress. Yet, although a military assistance agreement was
signed in January 1950, little was made available before the opening of hostilities in June.

The Soviets had been reported to be busy equipping North Korean ground troops and making air support available. In March
1950, the U.S. Advisory Group commander estimated that the
South Korean ground force was stronger than that of the North but
that North Korean air forces could tip the scales. Testifying before
a congressional committee in early June 1950, U.S. Ambassador
John J. Muccio warned that Soviet aid would give the North Koreans victory in an armed confrontation.

Tension between the two Koreas increased as summer approached. In May, the United Nations held elections for a new
National Assembly. The North Korean government attacked the
election and demanded the establishment of an all-Korean legislative body to draw up a new constitution and organize a national
government. Its continued assault on the leaders of the South
Korean government as traitors and its demands that the U.N. commission leave made peace seem increasingly unlikely. Observers
charged the North Koreans with offensive action along the 38th
Parallel and soon afterward warned of guerrilla activities south of
the line. On June 25, 1950, Washington time, North Korean forces
invaded South Korea.[26]

Korea had been substantially written off as unessential to American interests before the attack, and no one in the United States had
definitely foreseen an incident at that time. Inasmuch as North
Korea's capabilities were regarded as limited, American intelli-

gence agencies suggested that trouble was likely to come to Indo-china before it did in Korea.

Marshall, naturally, had little intimate day-by-day knowledge of the situation. Red Cross business was taking up much of his time. Delegates to a national Red Cross meeting were gathering in Detroit at the time of the attack. On June 25, the General attended the Red Cross board of governors' meeting there, and spoke at the morning session the next day.

President Truman was at his home in Independence when the attack came. Acheson called him at once and got his consent to request a meeting of the United Nations Security Council for the following day. Truman flew east to talk with his advisers at Blair House, and the Security Council met in New York without representation from the Soviet Union. The Soviets were boycotting the Council because it refused to recognize the Chinese Communist regime as entitled to the permanent seat allotted to China in the Council.

The Council voted nine ayes to one abstaining for an American resolution requesting an end to the hostilities in Korea and the restoration of the *status quo*. It also asked for U.N. aid to carry the resolution into effect. Even before Truman arrived in Washington, the Joint Chiefs gave MacArthur operational control over U.S. military forces in Korea and directed him to be prepared to send U.S. forces to Korea if the United Nations asked for such aid.

On June 27, the Security Council called for an end to the fighting and asked United Nations members to give the aid necessary "to repel the armed attack and to restore international peace and security in the area." Truman had already authorized U.S. air and naval forces to support South Korean forces south of the 38th Parallel. It was clear that the United States, if necessary, was prepared to act alone, but the President preferred to act in concert with the U.N. Although at times the collaboration was to be irksome, it helped to avoid direct confrontation with the Soviet Union and rallied a considerable part of world opinion against the Soviet abetting of North Korean aggression.

Turning down a proposed directive by MacArthur that could imply action against the Russians, the Joint Chiefs of Staff permitted him to hit military targets in North Korea but warned against striking areas near Manchuria or Soviet territory. He was reminded that there was no commitment to fight the Soviet Union. Even if Red forces crossed into Korea, U.S. troops were to take no action to aggravate the situation.

After a quick visit to Korea, MacArthur informed Washington that current lines could be held and lost ground retaken if U.S. ground forces could be committed. He wanted to send in a regimental combat team at once and build up two divisions in Japan to be available against a counterattack. Truman at once authorized him to use all ground forces then available in the Far East.

More than a show of force was needed to help the South Koreans. Despite the landing of American troops, the South Koreans were pushed back, revealing the weakness in training and organization that Marshall and others had feared. Within two weeks of his optimistic report, MacArthur called for four or four and a half U.S. divisions, with some supporting airborne and armored troops. Two days later, he had to increase his estimates.

Forces in Okinawa and Hawaii were instructed to aid MacArthur, and reserve units in the United States were alerted. The slender American resources were soon strained to the limit. The United States had to build a reserve, because any further call on regular forces left nothing to send to Europe in case of trouble. MacArthur would later accuse the United States of not trying to win, but military limitations of the country meant that armed assistance to Korea had to be measured against U.S. commitments to NATO, a factor that he and his adherents in the United States did not like to accept.

Asked to restrain the North Koreans, the Soviet Union flatly declared that South Korea had been the aggressor. At this point, an Anglo-French resolution was passed by the U.N. Security Council with seven affirmative votes against four abstentions (the Soviet Union still refused to be present) to give the United States command of forces supplied by United Nations members for the support of South Korea. President Truman was appointed executive for the Council, and troops supplied by United Nations countries were to be led by an American commander. With the recommendation of the Joint Chiefs of Staff, General MacArthur got that assignment; Syngman Rhee then transferred South Korean forces to MacArthur's command. His new U.N. command was established in Tokyo one month after the invasion of South Korea. He made periodic reports to the Joint Chiefs, who forwarded them through the Secretary of Defense to the Secretary of State, who, after informing President Truman, passed the reports to the U.N. Security Council.

Although command of forces in the field was exercised as if the troops were all American, two elements of possible conflict appeared. First of all, the State Department and the recently established Defense Department were brought into the command channel in a way that had not existed in World War II. Lack of agreement between the secretaries of the two departments could cause a breakdown in operations. Accustomed to dealing directly with the Joint Chief of Staff in World War II, MacArthur found that he was responsible to the secretaries of State and Defense as well as to the Joint Chiefs of Staff, and he was required to heed the views of the United Nations.

The contributing nations acted only under American pressure, since their main anxiety concerned possible Soviet offenses in Europe. They were reluctant to weaken their resistance to Soviet expansion in Europe. European efforts to curb the aggressive policies of the United Nations commander came through the Secretary of State, who was viewed with increased suspicion by MacArthur and his supporters in Congress. The complicated system of command and responsibility was certain to create frustration and violent resentment, and when it involved a temperament such as MacArthur's, it created angry trumpet calls about planned opposition and conspiracy.

Limiting the capabilities of the United Nations command were the United States' global commitments and the steady deterioration of the armed forces since World War II. In 1950 and 1951, Washington constantly had to face the question whether a more aggressive policy in the Far East might destroy the defensive alliance so carefully developed in Western Europe. For MacArthur, the answer was as simple as it had been in the Pacific during World War II: the chief enemy was in the Far East, and as commander there he must have everything he needed to win and the authority to wage his fight as he saw fit.[27]

The Allied forces were extremely weak compared with those of World War II, but the British placed naval units at the disposal of the U.N. commander before the end of June. Australia, New Zealand, and Canada soon offered naval and air units as well. The Chinese Nationalists eagerly offered to join the fray from Formosa, but fear that such an ally might bring in another enemy—the Chinese Communists—led to a refusal with thanks for the offer.

These token efforts were otherwise gratefully received, but as the situation darkened in Korea, more help was expected. British Ambassador Franks quickly briefed Prime Minister Clement Attlee on the danger in the situation. By 1950, the degree of economic recovery in Britain had made her once more the greatest world power after the United States and the Soviet Union. Britain and the United States were again dealing as a partnership, but the reality of that

partnership was soon to be tested. Franks noticed a prickly growth
of questions about and criticisms of Britain's role in the Korean
crisis: Americans had a tendency to assume, in those cases where
the British had been slow to support the United States, that ultimate cooperation came only from American pressure. Therefore,
Franks insisted to Attlee that, if the British planned to add token
ground forces to the naval units already provided, they must add
them quickly.[28]

Intent on keeping the Anglo-American partnership intact, Foreign Secretary Bevin hastened to follow Franks's advice. Other
offers from other countries followed. By September, when Marshall
became Secretary of Defense, eleven countries were giving aid to
the U.N. effort in Korea.[29]

The United States, as Franks had made clear, had acted quickly
against a Communist threat. But it had decided to do so within the
framework of the United Nations, and a large section of the country
regarded its action as a defense of the United Nations, which would
have broken up if this aggression had not been challenged. The
Americans, the Ambassador added, were proud to assume the
lion's share of the defense, but they wanted the support of other
members, as a clear indication of the U.N. character of the operations and as a test of the faith of other U.N. members. Washington
was caught up in the emotional drive of a country at war. Although
this feeling had not yet spread to the rest of the United States, it
would as soon as the President called for an increase in the armed
forces and set priorities and controls on industry. This American
mood was something that must be taken into consideration by the
British government in evaluating its contribution.[30]

Franks's prediction of a call by Truman for more troops and
supplies became a reality. In early July, the ground-force ceiling
was raised by 50,000 to 680,000. By the end of July, it had increased
to 834,000. A month later, it was raised to 1 million. To get this
number, the Army had to cease being a volunteer force and use the
authority it had been given under the Selective Service Extension
Act of 1948, which it had hitherto scarcely used. On July 25, a call
was made for a draft of 50,000 to be inducted in September, and
on September 12, Truman reluctantly called up four National
Guard divisions and two National Guard regimental combat
teams.[31]

These early, frantic attempts to raise troops displayed the nation's unpreparedness and fueled attacks against Secretary of Defense Louis Johnson. The early belief that the few U.S. forces in the
Far East would be sufficient to reinforce South Korean troops

evaporated when some of the South Korean divisions disintegrated. General Walton H. Walker, World War II corps commander in Europe, now commander of the Eighth Army, which was made up of U.S. and Korean soldiers, pulled back and formed what he called the Pusan perimeter, near the South Korean port of that name. It was an area that could be reinforced and supplied and would afford an escape route should that prove necessary as the North Koreans advanced southward. He declared that the Eighth Army would not surrender.

With Walker dug in, MacArthur began to see some hope. As the North Koreans moved southward, their supply lines were open to air and sea attack. Having made good use of amphibious attack in the Southwest Pacific, MacArthur began to muse on a landing at Inchon, on the Korean western coast, southwest of Seoul. He tried out his idea on General Collins and General Vandenberg when they visited him in mid-July. Collins raised some questions of feasibility, but the two men left without giving a definite reply. To every high-ranking visitor from Washington that summer—among them Averell Harriman, General Matthew Ridgway, General Lauris Norstad—MacArthur urged the need for some action before the Chinese Communists and the Russians could further strengthen the North Koreans. He did not always mention Inchon: those who heard of his idea for a landing there did not seem to think it a suitable place.

The U.N. commander told the Joint Chiefs that he would launch an attack in mid-September, and in late August he set plans specifically for a landing at Inchon at that time. Although he met skepticism on all sides, he held out stubbornly for Inchon in the face of doubts from senior officers of the Marines (who would have to make the landing), the Navy, and the Air Force. Even when General Collins and Admiral Sherman flew out to discuss alternative plans, and General Lemuel Shepherd of the Fleet Marine Force expressed grave doubts, MacArthur held out for Inchon and Inchon only.[32]

Near the end of August, the Joint Chiefs approved a landing but asked for a substitute plan for a landing at Kunsan, far south of Inchon. As if to make it clear that they were still in charge, they reminded MacArthur that they would want full details and plans for any future operations. On August 30, MacArthur issued directives for the Inchon attack. One week before the September 15 landings, the Joint Chiefs of Staff agreed to his plan, sending nearly all the Marine reserves from the Atlantic and trying to bring the 7th U.S. Infantry Division up to strength.

The landings were a tremendous success. Following heavy air

and naval bombardment, the Marines went ashore and by evening had more than one-third of the port. From his ship headquarters, MacArthur praised the forces under his command and announced that the North Koreans were retreating toward Seoul with heavy losses.

It was a great vindication for MacArthur's plan and his willingness to take risks, and many who had opposed his idea forgot that they had done so in admiration of his success. Later, he would decide that nearly everyone had been against him and that he had triumphed despite their opposition. Actually, Washington had expressed proper concern and urged the consideration of alternatives, but had finally endorsed his plan and then done everything possible to strengthen his hand.

MacArthur's victory contained serious portents for his future. Just as Hitler had won some of his early gambles over the doubts of his military advisers and came to hold their advice in contempt, so MacArthur now tended to dismiss Washington-voiced reservations about any of his plans. Never given to underrating the soundness of his own judgment, MacArthur allowed his self-confidence to soar after his Inchon victory. He became certain of his destiny, and his conviction hardened that he had to depend, in the last analysis, on his own genius.

XXVII

Marshall and Korea

G E N E R A L Walker used the Inchon landings to break out of the Pusan area, aided by the severance of North Korean supply lines, which forced withdrawal of the North Korean troops on September 23. Elements of the 1st Cavalry Division drove northwestward and three days later linked up with the 7th Division at Osan, south of Seoul. The enemy was now on the run.

MacArthur's September moves had been decided and virtually completed before Marshall was confirmed as Secretary of Defense, but he arrived in time for an important presidential directive permitting MacArthur to cross the 38th Parallel.[1]

Military commanders feel they must be free to continue in hot pursuit of a fleeing enemy; only extremely serious factors would bar such a tactic. The Joint Chiefs of Staff understood the political reasons for holding to boundaries, but they also favored the doctrine of hot pursuit. In this instance, they reasoned that, since the United Nations had directed the forces under MacArthur to restore peace and unity to Korea, there was a legal basis for crossing the 38th Parallel. But there was also the serious intimation that such an action might provoke the Chinese Communists or the Soviet Union into intervention in the Korean conflict.

The Joint Chiefs of Staff had told Secretary Johnson before the Inchon landing that MacArthur's first objective should be to destroy the North Korean forces. This would require fighting south and north of the 38th Parallel, with the attendant risk of spreading the conflict, but they saw a possible way out of the dilemma: let the South Koreans cross the border.

As an overall objective, the Joint Chiefs wanted to complete the occupation of South Korea and then remove the United Nations forces as soon as possible. They wanted President Rhee to return

to his liberated capital and call for a general election to establish
a unified government for Korea. In a meeting on September 7, the
National Security Council incorporated the JCS views into agreed
policy recommendations for the President. Truman approved the
NSC recommendations two days later. But a week later, the directives had not been issued by Secretary Johnson: on the 12th, he
submitted his resignation, to take effect a week later.[2]

Thus it was Marshall who received the Joint Chiefs' proposal on
September 25. Dealing only with the military aspects of the operation, the Joint Chiefs reminded the new Secretary of Defense that
other officials were also concerned and should be consulted.[3] General Charles Bolté, Army Chief of Operations (G-3), urged immediate action, since MacArthur was approaching the 38th Parallel. The
State Department quickly approved, adding instructions for a return of the Korean government to Seoul, and the President sent out
the directive on September 27.[4]

The U.N. commander was told that his task was to destroy the
forces of North Korea and that he could conduct operations north
of the 38th Parallel to do this. But definite limits were set on the
conditions under which such operations could proceed: (1) if there
had been prior entry into North Korea by Chinese Communist or
Soviet forces; (2) if there had been an announcement of the entry
of such forces into North Korea; or (3) if there was a threat by such
forces to counter a move of the U.N. forces northward. Under no
circumstances was MacArthur to cross the Korean border at points
of junction with Communist China or the Soviet Union. In addition, no non-Korean forces were to be used along these borders.
Air and naval actions against Manchurian or Soviet territory in
support of MacArthur's military operations were distinctly banned.

If major Chinese Communist forces were employed south of the
38th Parallel, MacArthur was to go on the defensive, act passively,
and notify Washington. He was not to discontinue air and naval
actions north of the 38th Parallel in Korea merely because Chinese
or Soviet forces were found there, but if they announced a plan to
occupy North Korea and warned MacArthur against attacking, he
was to report to Washington.[5]

If major Chinese Communist forces were employed south of the
38th Parallel, he was to continue action as long as there seemed to
be a reasonable prospect of success against them. If only small
forces were encountered, he should continue his operations.

In case of the occupation of North Korea by U.N. forces, South
Korean forces should be used to disarm the enemy and to perform
the main task of countering guerrilla warfare. He was to aid in the

restoration of the Republic of Korea at Seoul, but must remember that sovereignty over the whole of Korea still had to be decided by the United Nations.

Washington officials could have gone no further to ensure against a chance clash with the Chinese Communists or the Soviet Union. Every possible effort was made to keep the operation under the aegis of the United Nations. But these conditions seemed timid strictures to a commander flushed with victory.

Marshall shared the views of MacArthur and the Joint Chiefs of Staff about a commander's need to follow up a victory. When General Walker announced that he would stop on the 38th Parallel to regroup, while waiting for the U.N. to approve pursuit, Marshall radioed MacArthur that a statement to this effect might embarrass U.N. members who might prefer not to take a vote on the issue at the time. Marshall made unequivocal the Pentagon's viewpoint by saying, "We want you to feel unhampered tactically and strategically to proceed north of the 38th Parallel."[6] The Far Eastern commander made the most of this encouragement, later arguing that it freed him from the restrictions of the directive. Actually, he had merely been assured that Walker did not have to stop and regroup while waiting for further rulings. MacArthur enthusiastically responded that until the enemy capitulated, "I regard all of Korea open for our military operations."[7]

On September 28, MacArthur informed the Joint Chiefs that he planned to send the Eighth Army north during the last half of October to capture the North Korean capital of Pyongyong and to launch an amphibious attack on the eastern coast of Korea at Wonsan, the chief port. He sought to allay the Joint Chiefs' fears by declaring that there was no indication of entry into North Korea by major Chinese Communist or Soviet forces. Most of his assumptions concerning the success of the landings were correct, but his views as to enemy intentions would lead to serious trouble.[8]

MacArthur scoffed when he heard of Chou En-lai's remark to K. M. Pannikar, Indian Ambassador in Peking, that China would send troops into North Korea if MacArthur's force drove into that area, and pronounced the threat as all bluff: if Chou meant business, he would not have broadcast his intentions.

Despite his assurance, MacArthur soon afterward reported Chinese forces moving toward the North Korean border. On October 9, the Joint Chiefs of Staff notified him that if major Chinese forces invaded North Korea, he should have his troops continue fighting as long as there was a reasonable chance of success. But he was not to attack Chinese Communist territory without authorization from

Washington.[9] Their constant caution was born of the fact that this
was still a United Nations operation, and there was the innate fear
that MacArthur might be tempted to move on his own.

MacArthur was optimistic and reassuring with Truman at their
Western Pacific meeting on October 15. Believing that MacArthur
had been out of direct touch with Washington for too long, and
aware that such a conference might have a favorable influence on
congressional races a few weeks later, the President decided that he
should see the commander personally. He arranged for a meeting
at Wake Island, with General Bradley representing the Joint Chiefs
of Staff, Secretary of the Army Frank Pace, Assistant Secretary of
State Rusk, Ambassador Philip Jessup, and presidential adviser
Averell Harriman. Since no detailed preparations were made,
Secretaries Acheson and Marshall decided not to attend, and the
conference did not come to grips with existing major problems.
MacArthur said the situation in Korea was under control and that
resistance would halt by Thanksgiving. In fact, he thought that the
Eighth Army might be withdrawn by Christmas. Hard put for rein-
forcements for Europe, Bradley asked if he could get a division
from Korea for Europe and was promised one by January.[10]

MacArthur seemed supremely confident. He expressed little
worry about the Chinese Communists. Though the Chinese had
large forces along the Yalu, he doubted they would cross the border because of their lack of air power. The magic of the victor of
Inchon was still potent.

Superficially, there seemed to be reason for confidence. South
Korean troops had moved steadily northward, capturing Wonsan
on October 11. To the west, General Walker's troops took Pyongyong, the North Korean capital, on October 19. On October 24,
MacArthur ordered all-out action by Walker and removed restrictions on the use of non-Koreans. Since the Joint Chiefs had not
changed their earlier instruction, they questioned his action. He
replied that his directive had been only temporary, that Marshall's
message of September 30 had lifted any bar to his action, and that
he had covered the subject at Wake Island.[11] Washington failed to
call his hand.

His optimism had built grandiose hopes in Washington. The
Department of the Army began to talk of redeploying two divisions
from Korea to other parts of the world. Fears concerning other
danger spots led Secretary Marshall to order the Army strength
ceiling lifted to 1,263,000 for fiscal year 1951. It was not assumed
that the men would be needed for Korea. The Army actually proposed a reduction of U.N. forces in Korea requiring American

logistical support. At the urging of the Joint Chiefs, Marshall discussed the reduction of those forces with Acheson in early November. Even as early as October 22, General Walker had suggested that ammunition arriving in Korea be diverted to Japan. Staff headquarters in Japan asked permission to send back to the United States several ships carrying ammunition and bombs.[12]

The Chinese Communists had begun to move before MacArthur reassured Truman at Wake Island. Approximately 100,000 Chinese troops had crossed the border; by the end of October, Chinese military units had their first clash with South Korean and American forces. Because MacArthur's troops were driving northward, the incidents were not taken seriously. But not only were South Korean forces in the Eighth Army badly mauled (General Walker reported on November 1 that ROK II Corps had ceased to exist as an effective fighting force), but a regiment of the U.S. 1st Cavalry Division was surrounded and one of its battalions destroyed. Indeed, the Eighth Army was sufficiently challenged for Walker to stop his advance to regroup disorganized units.[13]

A somber MacArthur asked for reinforcements on November 7. Two days earlier, after hearing reports of the losses inflicted by the Chinese on the Eighth Army, MacArthur directed his air forces to destroy the Korean ends of all international bridges along the Yalu in northeastern Korea, to slow the flood of Chinese troops moving southward. General George Stratemeyer, the air chief, repeated the order to the Pentagon for information. Lovett checked with the State Department and found it would be necessary to consult with the British. Informed of these developments, Secretary Marshall ruled that, unless the Chinese were threatening the security of all MacArthur's forces, the bombing was unwise.[14] From his home in Independence, the President ordered the bombing postponed and asked for an explanation. This message was passed on to MacArthur by the Joint Chiefs in the form of a directive banning the bombing of targets within five miles of the Manchurian border.[15]

MacArthur replied with some disdain that the bombings were "within the scope of the rules of war and the resolutions and directions which I have received from the United Nations," and predicted dire results for his troops if he were limited in action. Acting as though Truman knew nothing of his proposals, he declared he could not take responsibility for results without Truman's "personal and direct understanding of the situation."[16] He asked that the ban be rescinded at once.

Truman was impressed enough to allow Stratemeyer to go ahead with the bombing of the bridges, but he warned MacArthur against enlarging the conflict, and especially forbade him to hit north of the Yalu. The uneasy Joint Chiefs of Staff now asked for notices of impending attacks.[17]

Though MacArthur's bombers began attacks on the Korean ends of the international bridges on November 8, airmen bitterly complained that enemy fighters could attack them from north of the Yalu, then dart immediately back to where the Allied planes were forbidden to follow. The French, upset by even the restricted Allied bombing, proposed a resolution to reassure the Chinese Communists. Sympathetic to the plight of the fliers, Marshall told Acheson that it should be spelled out to United Nations member countries that "a sanctuary for attacking Chinese aircraft is not 'explicitly or implicitly affirmed by any United Nations action.' "[18]

In an effort to prevent a wider spread in the fighting, six members of the United Nations, including the United States, Great Britain, and France, presented a resolution to the Security Council on November 10 asking that the Chinese withdraw from Korea and assuring them that the United Nations would not violate the northern frontier. The Soviet Union vetoed the resolution.[19]

As enemy fighters continued to attack from north of the Yalu, the Joint Chiefs asked Marshall if U.N. planes could not pursue the enemy beyond the border. Marshall accepted their proposal, later indicating that both Truman and Acheson did so too, but felt they must first notify U.N. allies before so acting. When these allies expressed fear of provoking Soviet action, the United States dropped the proposal.[20]

As the Chinese continued their buildup south of the Yalu, the Pentagon wondered whether MacArthur's mission should not be re-examined. He protested that it was feasible to continue his drive to destroy Chinese forces and get complete control of Korea. Reminded that British approval was necessary before enlarging the conflict, MacArthur was furious. He spoke bitingly of the British "Munich mentality" and complained that any concession to the Chinese Communists would destroy American prestige in Asia. A halt by United Nations forces south of the Yalu would repeat the British appeasement of China that had lost the respect of Asia.[21]

Behind his bitter words lay a long-time dislike of the British and a scarcely concealed contempt for officials in Washington. His anger blinded him to the mockery the Chinese had made of his assurance to Truman that the Chinese and the Russians had written off North Korea. He was convinced that, if left to his own methods, he could defeat both the North Koreans and the Chinese Communists without arousing the Soviet Union, never reflecting that he had been equally confident of defeating the North Koreans without arousing the Chinese Communists. Careful reflection would have reminded him that there was no grand military reserve in the United States, that he had recently promised Bradley a division from Korea for Europe, and that he needed the small forces provided by Britain and other U.N. members to maintain (what the Soviets called a pretense) a United Nations effort. As long as he fought as commander of the United Nations forces, he might suffer inconveniences and frustration but he gained some advantage in world opinion from the continued support of the neutrals, a backing Washington sought in a time of global tension. The U.N. cover, however illusory, confronted the Chinese Communists and the Soviet Union with a challenge of opinion outside the United States.

The dangerous international situation was examined by the National Security Council on November 9. Its members reached a consensus that MacArthur's military directives would not be changed but that the United States should assure Europe that it did not intend to allow its commitments in Korea to interfere with previous pledges to European security. Any final decision on Korea must be made in common with the United Nations.

While the debate continued on bombings, MacArthur prepared for ground-force action. Believing that the limited U.N. air action had isolated the battle area, stopped enemy troop reinforcements, and slowed down movement of their supplies, MacArthur set Walker's offensive for November 24. He announced that the Eighth Army was ready to complete "the compression and close the vise." On that hopeful note, Walker opened his offensive.[22]

Although MacArthur did not seem unduly worried about Chinese activity, the other nations in the U.N. continued to be fearful. The State Department investigated means of establishing a buffer zone, which might reduce the possibility of general war. Marshall suggested that it would be wise for the United States to advance a solution before our Allies began to make demands. To formal suggestions sent to him for comment, the Far Eastern commander replied that failing to advance would merely bring on the perils of appeasement without furnishing a solution.[23]

MacArthur had his warning, but there was enough ambiguity in his instructions that he believed himself free to act as he wished. On November 24, Walker attacked as planned, and very soon the prospect of sending troops back to Japan by Christmas disappeared. In the darkness on the 25th, in bitter cold, the Chinese struck with such force against Walker's right and center that a Korean corps was scattered and an American corps in the center was thrown back.

On the 27th, Walker reported a Chinese attack in strength against him. Major General Edward M. Almond's X Corps was hit at the same time, and the supply lines of his Marine unit were cut the following day. Without enough troops to deal with the new situation, and faced with considerations that lay outside his sphere, MacArthur passed from the offensive to the defensive.[24]

On November 28, MacArthur reported to the Joint Chiefs that the Allies now faced a totally different war. With his current strength he was unable to meet the changed situation. He found "an entire[ly] new picture which broadens the potentialities to world embracing considerations beyond the sphere of decision by the Theater Commander. This command has done everything humanly possible within its capabilities but is now faced with conditions beyond its control and strength. . . ." The Allies now "must find their solution within the councils of the United Nations and chancellories of the world."[25]

This open request for sympathy from home met with a favorable response. At a meeting of the National Security Council on the 28th, when Vice President Barkley recalled the Far Eastern commander's assurance that the troops would be out of Korea by Christmas, Bradley said that current developments had completely surprised MacArthur, and Truman declared they could not allow the commander to lose face before the enemy. Secretary Marshall, having already insisted that "it would not help to interfere in MacArthur's operations on the spot" (a view that he, Bradley, and other generals held consistently), now said they must regard MacArthur's optimistic statement as an embarrassment that "we must get around in some manner." He added that the failed offensive "was necessary to find out what the Communists were up to. Now we know." There was no "we told you so" attitude toward MacArthur's troubles on the part of Marshall and other U.S. officials. Rather, they hunted for ways to help him.[26]

But Washington still opposed unilateral action. Marshall agreed with the views of the three armed-forces secretaries that: (1) they must act through the United Nations; (2) they must avoid a separate conflict; and (3) they must not attempt to hold the Soviets responsible now. To become involved in a general war with China "would be to fall into a carefully laid Russian trap." They should, therefore, not go into Chinese Communist territory or use Chiang Kai-shek's

Nationalist forces, as MacArthur was again advising. Marshall
stressed the recommendation to work through the United Nations
and to maintain the Allied image in Korea.[27]

To MacArthur's recommendation that the Chinese Nationalists
be used in the fight, the Joint Chiefs of Staff replied in a message
that drew on drafts by Marshall and Acheson:

> It [your proposal] involves world-wide consequences. We shall
> have to consider the possibility that it would disrupt the united
> position of the nations associated with us in the United Nations, and
> leave us isolated. . . . It might extend hostilities to Formosa and
> other areas. Incidentally, our position of leadership in the Far East
> is being most seriously compromised in the United Nations. The
> utmost care will be necessary to avoid the disruption of the essential
> Allied line-up in the organization.[28]

At the same time, the President evinced to Marshall his desire to
keep closer tabs on developments by asking that all JCS instructions to MacArthur be sent through Secretary Marshall to the President.

The Communist attack at the end of the month intensified Allied
concern. In London, the Australian Resident Minister called on Sir
William Strang, Permanent Under Secretary for Foreign Affairs, to
ask whether MacArthur was suffering from faulty intelligence or
from a deliberate effort to get the U.N. forces embroiled with the
Communist Chinese. Strang said that he thought the recent offensive had been unwise from both the military and political viewpoints. Acheson and Rusk had recently been at pains to indicate
that the State Department would listen to U.N. views. The White
House and the Pentagon seemed to have a steady policy. They had
tended to feel that the theater commander must be given "a pretty
free hand" within the limits of his directive, but wherever political
matters were concerned, other nations must be consulted. At the
moment, the British government was suggesting that the time was
ripe to discuss a demilitarized zone.[29]

On November 30, wishing to calm the public about the Korean
situation, President Truman upset members of the United Nations
even more. He began his news conference well, assuring reporters
that the United States would continue to work with the United
Nations to halt aggression in Korea, and promising aid to American
allies against possible threats elsewhere. He repeated assurances to
the Chinese Communists that the United States and the United
Nations had no aggressive intentions against China. In conclusion,

he added that MacArthur had done a good job and had not exceeded his authority.[30]

During the question period, Truman said that the United States would take whatever action was needed to meet the military situation. Asked, "Will that include the atomic bomb?," the President replied, "That includes every weapon we have." When the reporter persisted in trying to pin him down, the President grew cautious, but left an element of disquiet when he said: "There has always been active consideration of its use. I don't want to see it used. It is a terrible weapon, and it should not be used on innocent men, women, and children who have nothing whatever to do with this military aggression. That happens when it is used."

A White House spokesman immediately recognized the misunderstandings possible and issued a clarification to the effect that, although the possible use of any weapon was implicit in possession of that weapon, use of the atomic bomb had to be authorized by the President, "and no such authorization has been given." The language used in the press conference did not "represent any change in the situation." This statement may have allayed apprehension at home, but there were flutterings abroad, where serious questions arose as to MacArthur's intentions in Korea.[31]

On December 1, a full-dress discussion of the situation, necessary because of what Acheson called "the virtual state of panic which seemed to exist among our friends in New York," was held in the Pentagon. The secretaries of State and of Defense, the service secretaries, the Joint Chiefs of Staff, the head of the CIA, and representatives from other departments and agencies were present.

Acheson said that friendly powers in the United Nations were complaining of a lack of U.S. leadership and blaming many of the present problems on MacArthur. It was necessary to regain unity.[32]

Marshall asked General Bradley to show Acheson the most recent Joint Chiefs message to MacArthur. They had instructed the Far Eastern commander to withdraw Almond's X Corps from its exposed position and to try to coordinate forces on the coasts so that they could not be outflanked. Marshall had inserted a statement that the region northeast of the waist of Korea (the area bordering on the U.S.S.R.) was to be avoided except in case of military considerations relating to the security of the command.

The Joint Chiefs wanted to set a line that could be held and to avoid actions that might bring in the Soviet Union. They disagreed on the military value of Korea. General Collins declared that it was not worth a nickel as long as the Russians held Vladivostok and positions on the other side of Korea. Bedell Smith, director of the CIA, wartime Chief of Staff for Eisenhower, and former Ambassador to the Soviet Union, said, "We should get out of Korea although we do not solve the problem by getting out." Smith thought that the Russians probably did not want war now but would be willing to have it if they could "bog us down in Asia." As he saw the situation, "They could bleed us to death in Asia while defeating the armament effort in Europe." Admiral Sherman and other conferees believed that Korea was worth holding. Deputy Secretary of Defense Lovett summarized the consensus when he said that Korea was not decisive for the United States, that though the loss of Korea might jeopardize Japan and result in its eventual loss, it was Western Europe that was America's main concern, and the United States would accept the loss of Korea rather than any loss in Europe. It was best to hold in Korea to get better political results. We might withdraw if the Chinese did also, although this might mean abandoning Korea.

Further discussion led to the idea that perhaps there should be a cease-fire, but not just yet. Secretary Marshall stated that acceptance of a cease-fire would represent a "great weakness on our part."

To MacArthur, agonizing over the situation in Korea, Washington officials were indecisive and timorous. He did not sense that their discussions showed sympathy with his plight, a realistic attitude about the U.S. global position, and an effort to end "near panic" among American supporters in the United Nations. Washington knew well what was at stake and wanted to inspect all probabilities before making a decisive move. General Collins flew to Tokyo and Korea for another look around before the full discussion of the situation and its implications with Prime Minister Attlee, who had asked for a conference with the President and his advisers.

The military view on December 1 was pessimistic, and the CIA statement of possible Soviet intentions did not lighten the atmosphere. Much of it followed the reasoning that Bedell Smith had outlined on the 1st. While uncertain of Soviet intentions to force a war with the United States in the Far East, the seniors among the American military recognized that the onset of a war between the United States and Communist China would: (1) divert U.S. and U.N. efforts to an indecisive theater; (2) create dissension between the United States and its allies; (3) disrupt the coherence achieved by the U.N. in its original response to Communist aggression in Korea; (4) obstruct plans for the defense of Western Europe; and (5) speed Communist gains in Korea and Southeast Asia.[33]

Truman met with Acheson, Marshall, and Bradley on December
2 to discuss the possible submission to the General Assembly of a
resolution that had previously been sent to the Security Council but
defeated by a Russian veto, asking that the Chinese Communists
refrain from intervention in Korea. Both Truman and Marshall saw
this as a waste of time. They agreed that it might be worthwhile to
approach the Soviet Union or the Chinese Communists for a cease-
fire, directly or through an intermediary, or to make this attempt
through a resolution in the United Nations. Marshall and Acheson
thought that the Communists might ask a very high price. Marshall
added that the United States was in a dilemma as to how it could
save its troops and its national honor. He believed that we could
not in "all good conscience" abandon the South Koreans.[34]

There was agreement on the need to build up defense forces and
to place orders for greatly increased amounts of equipment and
weapons. On the previous day, Truman had asked for additional
appropriation for the Defense Department of $16.8 billion, nearly
$2 billion more than the original request for the year, and a supple-
ment of more than $1 billion for the Atomic Energy Committee;
therefore, no request for additional appropriations was suggested
for the moment.[35]

In recent discussions, some officials had suggested the censor-
ship of public statements by the military concerning the precarious
situation in Korea. Though Marshall thought that idea would be
difficult to carry out, he may have felt differently on reading MacArthur's interviews with *The New York Times* and *U.S. News & World
Report*. In the first interview, MacArthur denied that he had received any suggestion that he stop his advance short of the international boundary; in the second, published on December 8, he
criticized the limitations on his operations as being without precedent in military history. He followed the interviews with a wire to
President Truman that was censorious of the policies of Washington authorities.[36]

MacArthur had already made it clear to the Joint Chiefs of Staff
that they lacked comprehension of his situation. With the slender
forces available to him and with the power of the Chinese forces
before him, he complained, he could not establish a line across the
waist of Korea. Unless ground reinforcements "of the greatest
magnitude are promptly supplied," the command would be forced
to keep diminishing strength, engaging in a series of withdrawals
into beachhead positions, thus placing him completely on the defensive.[37]

At the meeting on December 3, the situation looked a little less hopeless. There was a greater inclination to question the evacuation of Korea. Admiral Sherman opposed a cease-fire and suggested they tell the Chinese Communists that if they continued their actions they would find themselves at war with the United States. Marshall asked about the situation in Indochina and the French attitude regarding the Korean situation. Acheson said that the French were weak and shellshocked and anxious for a deal that "would give an illusion of reality." Rusk thought they would try to make an arrangement with Ho Chi Minh and then withdraw. They would waffle on the Korean situation unless there was a solid United Nations front. To get that front, the United States must stand firm. "We could solidify the U.N. with us standing on the 38th Parallel. If the Chinese cross the Parallel it would solidify our U.N. support." Aware of growing Allied dissatisfaction with the U.S. handling of the Korean military situation, Marshall observed that "the attitude described in the U.N. was illogical, amounting almost to bad faith, but that one had to recognize that such situations do arise in international relations." He recalled critical reactions in the press at the time of the Battle of the Bulge. "We must accept the U.N. procedure and try to improve [it] but not expect perfection."[38]

On the morning of December 4, Acheson talked with members of his staff, as he had on the previous day, about the gravity of the situation. Rusk argued they they should put up the best fight possible in Korea. George Kennan emphasized the need to retain a position there. When Rusk urged, and Acheson agreed, that something should be done to strengthen the military's will to resist while not allowing them to bomb Manchuria, Under Secretary of State James Webb suggested that Acheson get in touch with Secretary Marshall. Acheson at once phoned Marshall to say that he felt they should try to hold on rather than talk of withdrawing or of adopting a policy of bombing or blockading China. Marshall agreed with two of Acheson's provisos: that they first see whether MacArthur could withdraw X Corps from the eastern coast of Korea, and that they not dig themselves into a hole without an exit. Acheson then sent Kennan and Rusk for further discussions with Marshall. Kennan mentioned the political implications of a decision to withdraw, pointing that they should be borne in mind by the military authorities. Lovett entered the meeting at this time to report that he and Admiral Sherman had just returned from Capitol Hill and the reaction there now was that going into Korea had been a mistake and that we should pull out as quickly as possible. Acheson recorded: "General Marshall was not impressed. This sort of fluctuation in

Congressional opinion was not new to him. The present mood might not last for long."[39]

Prime Minister Attlee and his party opened discussions with Truman at the White House on December 4. Beneath the customary politeness, the opening exchanges evinced some strain. Attlee delicately made the point that many members of the United Nations were not at one with the United States as to actions enlarging the war with China. Any such development would be a victory for the Soviet Union's position. He discussed the possible Chinese Communist price for a cease-fire: recognition of the Communist regime in China, settlement of the Formosa question, and settlement in Korea. He did not know how much they would ask, but he was certain that the Western powers should not get so involved in the East as to open Europe to attack. "The West is, after all, the vital part in our line against communism. We cannot take action that will weaken it. We must strengthen our hand in the West as much as possible."[40]

Marshall and Acheson met Attlee's arguments for negotiations with Communist China by mentioning the effect on Japan and the Philippines of any concessions to the Chinese, and by expressing their doubts that concessions would have any effect on China's allegiance to Moscow. In response to Attlee's suggestion that the Chinese Communists were not Soviet satellites, Marshall recalled an earlier meeting with Chou En-lai in which the Chinese leader had insisted that his people were Marxian Communists and that he resented their being called agrarian reformers. Marshall stressed that the Chinese Communists made not the slightest attempt to conceal their Moscow affiliations. They regarded the Russians as coreligionists, and their troops were thoroughly indoctrinated. The President said that he depended on Marshall's views, though he granted that the Chinese Communists also had nationalist emotions. "The Russians cannot dominate them forever, but that is a long-range view and does not help us just now." Later that evening, Acheson met with some of the British delegation and insisted that allies should not expect the United States to give way in the Far East and then act vigorously in Europe in support of the same Allies who had urged concessions in the Far East.

In the second meeting, the tone was still formally polite and the views unchanged. Attlee, almost certainly voicing the opinions of other U.N. countries, mentioned Britain's support for the United States but wondered about other U.N. members and their attitude toward a widening of the conflict. He considered it unwise to make the Chinese Communists feel that they were left with the Soviets as their only friends. Acheson took the lead in the discussion, but on the question of seating the Chinese Communists in the U.N., he later said he wished "to provoke" Marshall to speak. When the British mentioned Formosa, Marshall intervened to point out that if U.N. forces should fail in Korea and the Chinese Communists had a great triumph, "we are greatly weakened if Formosa goes to them. As a military matter only, with Japan to the north and the Philippines and Indonesia to the south, the problem which would confront us would be the driving of a wedge in among those island defenses. They could make it awkward for us and we could be greatly weakened." General Bradley interjected, "We may fail in Korea, but if so, we must draw the line on Formosa." Marshall agreed. "We would be taking a step to liquidate our position in the Pacific if we surrendered it. It is hard enough, anyway, to settle the Japanese question. From the military point of view it was very dangerous to give up Formosa. There were other dangers in Indochina, Malaya, and Hong Kong, but if we split the island chain that would really be serious."[41]

Attlee conceded that these were sound military points about Formosa but said that keeping Chiang Kai-shek in control there was not in accord with the Declaration of Cairo, which stated that the island belonged to China. Acheson replied that in Cairo the Allies had been talking about a different China, not one supplied with Soviet planes and pilots. A member of the British delegation said they had to settle the matter of the Chinese seat in the U.N., but it might be possible to separate the safeguarding of Formosa from recognition of the government, since Chiang Kai-shek was a provocation.

Acheson then asked Marshall to speak to this statement. Marshall declared that it would be difficult to find a replacement for Chiang. Although "his followers and party were corrupt," Marshall believed that the Generalissimo was personally free of dishonesty. Attlee suggested that a U.N. commission might be set up on the island to hold it until the Chinese Communists behaved. When Secretary of the Treasury John Snyder pointed out that this would depend on whether Chiang cooperated, the Prime Minister inquired "whether he would not have to do what he was told." The President quickly suggested that they adjourn until the next day.

On December 5, thirteen members of the United Nations—Afghanistan, Burma, Egypt, India, Indonesia, Iran, Iraq, Lebanon, Pakistan, the Philippines, Saudi Arabia, Syria, and Yemen—appealed to the North Koreans and Chinese Communists to declare they would not cross the 38th Parallel. Such a declaration would allow time to consider steps to resolve the conflict in Korea and prevent another world war.[42]

At a dinner at the British Embassy on December 6, referring to the conference of the previous day concerning Western Europe, Acheson bluntly stated that there was a feeling in the United States that the British were not doing all they could for their own defense effort. He thought that, if the President and General Marshall could be convinced they *were*, it would do much to dampen the distrust in our country.[43]

Attlee countered by raising the "difficult and delicate question" of General MacArthur's command in Korea. Europe had the feeling that the participating countries had little to say in what was being done. General Bradley and Secretary Marshall replied that MacArthur was doing what he had been told to do by the U.N. in regard to holding Korea and arranging for elections. Marshall pointed out that the British had been consulted, mentioning such matters as the handling of "hot pursuit" and the bombing of Manchuria. When the British proposed a committee to handle the war, Bradley objected that a committee could not fight a war. If others did not agree with what was being done, they should say so and would be given assistance in withdrawing from the conflict. If they stayed, they had to accept the responsibilities that had been assigned to the United Nations command. The President summarized the American view when he said they should stay in Korea and fight. If they had support from others, fine. But they would stay on anyway.

Marshall was absent at the beginning of the meeting on December 7 but came in time to declare that, if there were reasonable steps to avoid a war with Communist China, the United States would take them, in the interests of avoiding a global war. But it was almost impossible to negotiate with the Chinese Communists. As to Formosa, our military men had said that it was not of great military importance to us but would become so in the hands of an enemy. The United States would be in an almost intolerable position if it sacrificed prestige in the Pacific and abandoned its specific commitment to Korea. Though he had no solution, Marshall thought that a little time would be useful.[44]

Sir Oliver Franks, British Ambassador, now sought to smooth over differences, observing that they were fewer than they may have seemed. Personally, he thought that the British delegation had been strongly moved by U.S. military views on Formosa. They were not asking the United States to give up Formosa or to talk about a precise time for beginning negotiations. When it came to letting the Chinese Communists into the U.N., however, he believed it was a question of looking at facts rather than acting on the basis of a nation's dislike for Communist Chinese.

The final meeting with the British Prime Minister came on Friday, December 8, at the White House. Attlee and Truman had reached agreement on the atomic bomb, and Acheson and members of the British entourage had ironed out other matters. General Collins returned from Tokyo to announce encouraging news from Korea. He thought that the Eighth Army could retire in an orderly way to Pusan, and that the X Corps could be evacuated from the Hamhung area to join the Eighth Army there.[45]

The final communiqué of the Washington meeting was carefully drawn. Attlee could report to the British and to friends in the United Nations that he had not approved some items the Americans advanced; the Americans could insist that they had safeguarded their position. The British could be pleased by the American agreement that NATO should be developed and strengthened and that a Supreme Commander in Europe would soon be appointed. The United States indicated that it was willing to negotiate some points of agreement if the Chinese Communists and North Koreans halted their advance. The United Kingdom had recognized the People's Republic of China and considered that its representatives should hold the seat reserved for China in the United Nations. As to Formosa, both Chinese governments held that the Cairo Declaration was valid. The United States wanted the issue settled by peaceful means and in a way that would safeguard the interests of the people of Formosa and the security and peace of the Pacific, and believed that consideration of the question by the United Nations would contribute to that end.

As for the atomic bomb, the President stated that he hoped world conditions would never call for its use. He proposed to keep the Prime Minister at all times informed of developments that might bring about a change in the situation.

On December 8, MacArthur ordered General Almond's X Corps withdrawn to the area of Pusan. In a large-scale evacuation by sea designed to preserve equipment and weapons as well as manpower, 105,000 U.N. troops, 100,000 Korean civilians, 17,000 vehicles, and more than a third of a million tons of supplies were successfully moved south.[46]

Three weeks later, the Joint Chiefs of Staff sent MacArthur a new directive, which Marshall thought necessary in order to consolidate the various instructions that had gone out in recent weeks. This directive assumed that the enemy was capable of forcing the U.N. troops out of Korea but believed that such action could be made very costly to the aggressors, adding that Korea was not the place to fight a major war. The directive stated that the United States was not prepared to commit its "remaining available ground forces to action against Chinese Communist forces in Korea in face of the increased threat of general war." On the other hand, resistance to enemy attack "would be of great importance to our national interest if this could be accomplished without incurring serious losses. . . ." MacArthur was now directed to fall back to more defensible positions, as he had proposed earlier in the month. Far from a heroic statement, it was an attempt to find room to maneuver politically. MacArthur, on invitation, gave his comments the following day.[47]

He paid little attention to the bar against extending the war, but spoke of his earlier views as to attacking mainland China. His reply may have been written before he received the JCS message. Otherwise, his recommendations seemed designed to be contrary to everything that U.S. representatives had discussed with the British. MacArthur recommended:

(1) Blockade the coast of China; (2) destroy through naval gunfire and air bombardment China's industrial capacity to wage war; (3) secure reinforcements from the Nationalist garrison on Formosa to strengthen our position in Korea if we decide to continue the fight for that peninsula; and (4) release existing restrictions upon the Formosan garrison for diversionary action (possibly leading to counter-invasion) against vulnerable areas of the Chinese mainland. . . .

He saw no reason to worry about expanding the war to mainland China, since the Chinese were now fully committed and the possibility of Soviet intervention would not be affected by any action that the United States took against China. He may have been unaware of a Soviet agreement providing for Soviet aid in case of attack. He could not hope to have U.N. support for this venture, nor could it have the moral support of a U.N. action against aggression against South Korea. It would undo everything leaders in Washington had attempted to gain from the meeting with the British and from recent activity in the United Nations. MacArthur confirmed the fears of many U.N. members by declaring that Korea's defense needs were more immediate than those of Europe.

The directive of the Joint Chiefs was sent just after significant changes in the Far Eastern command had taken place. Two days before Christmas, General Walker was killed in a jeep accident.

When the possibility of his death in action had been discussed a short time before by MacArthur and Collins, the former had said that in that case he wanted General Matthew Ridgway as Walker's replacement. Ridgway, Deputy Chief of Staff for Operations and Administration for the Army, fully familiar with MacArthur's problems, was approved at once by Marshall and Truman; he reached Tokyo on the evening of Christmas Day. No appointment could have been more acceptable to Marshall. Since Ridgway's service under him in Tientsin in the 1920s, Marshall had watched and aided the career of the new Eighth Army commander. He had noted Ridgway's advancement with pride and had helped him develop his airborne units. Others in the Pentagon shared Marshall's enthusiasm. As an airborne-division commander, Ridgway had been part of Bradley's D-Day forces and part of General Collins's VII Corps in the Normandy fighting. His reputation was that of an officer with charisma and brilliant leadership, who knew the problems of the Department of the Army and of the troops in Korea. His loyalty to Washington was complete, a quality soon to be treasured.[48]

General Ridgway found MacArthur ready to turn over the Eighth Army to him. It was up to him to advance or to withdraw. He decided to stay. Many of his officers had succumbed to defensive thinking, and he worked to turn this situation around.

Immediately he was tested by the enemy. Perhaps believing that the Americans would be celebrating on New Year's Eve, the Chinese chose that day to strike along a wide front. Ridgway deliberately pulled his troops back to a more easily defended line north of the Han River near Seoul. Two days later, he was forced to give up the Korean capital and withdraw south of the river. On the 4th, he fell back to a new line.

This situation made matters no easier for MacArthur, for Washington still demanded caution. As early as September 1949, it was known that the Soviets had tested an atomic bomb. Washington was also aware that the Russians had signed a security treaty with the Chinese Communists, which became public in February 1951. The JCS instruction of January 9, in reply to MacArthur's recommendations to expand the war, was largely to "wait and see" and had little resemblance to the more positive talk before the end of the year. Blockade required U.N. approval. Naval and air attacks on China must wait on Chinese attacks outside Korea. MacArthur was to fall back on successive positions, inflicting the greatest possible casualties on the enemy while keeping in mind the safety of his own troops and the protection of Japan. If he found it necessary to evacuate troops to avoid losses in men and materiel, the action was approved.[49]

MacArthur, fearing the ease with which he could be made a scapegoat, replied that the decision was not up to him and asked Washington to declare whether he was or was not to withdraw. Under current restrictions, his position in Korea was untenable. But if political considerations required it, he could hold until his force was destroyed.

The Far Eastern commander nettled Marshall by remarking that the morale of his men would "become a serious threat to their battle efficiency unless the political basis upon which they are asked to trade life for time is clearly delineated."[50] Deciding that these words expressed MacArthur's ideas rather than those of his men, the Secretary remarked to Dean Rusk that when a general complained about the morale of his troops, it was time to look into his own morale.

Meanwhile, the Joint Chiefs recommended to Secretary Marshall that they make an attempt to stabilize the situation in Korea, and, if that proved impossible, then to withdraw. There should be no further ground augmentation, but two National Guard divisions might be sent to Japan. If a position could be established or if they were forced to evacuate, then a naval blockade of China should be put into effect, and air reconnaissance of the Chinese coastal areas and Manchuria should be permitted. Although Chinese Nationalist troops should not be used in Korea, restrictions on their actions elsewhere should be removed. The memorandum was forwarded, at Marshall's request, to the National Security Council for discussion.[51]

The President sought to ease MacArthur's frustrations on January 13 by stressing the value of a successful defense in Korea. U.S. action should be concerned with consolidating the great majority of U.N. members on our side. Pending a major buildup of U.S. strength, "we must act with great prudence in so far as extending the area of hostilities is concerned." It would be good to take other courses of action, but steps that "might in themselves be fully justified and which might lend some assistance to the campaign in Korea would not be beneficial if they thereby involved Japan or Western Europe in large-scale hostilities. . . ." Truman noted that if we did have to withdraw, it should be evident that this course had been forced upon us by military necessity and that we would not accept it until aggression was ended. Making it clear that he was accepting the responsibility MacArthur had refused, the President said that, in making a final decision about Korea, "I shall have to give constant thought to the main threat from the Soviet Union and to the need for a rapid expansion of our armed forces to meet this great danger. . . . The entire nation," he concluded his message to MacArthur, "is grateful for your splendid leadership. . . ."[52]

Arriving in Tokyo to discuss the situation, Generals Collins and Vandenberg tried to clarify Washington's course of action. MacArthur read the President's message to them and said it removed all doubts as to his mission and responsibility. He interpreted it as a directive to remain in Korea indefinitely. Before returning to the United States, Collins announced that U.S. troops were going to stay and fight. He was optimistic about the situation in Korea. The Eighth Army was improving under Ridgway's leadership. The Chinese had not tried to push south of the Han River and were suffering from supply problems and lowered morale. Ridgway was now "prepared to punish severely any mass attack." He believed that they could stay from two to three months.[53]

Several months later, during the Senate hearings on his relief, MacArthur claimed that the Joint Chiefs, in their memorandum of January 12, had agreed with his own views on expanding the war with China, but that they had been overruled by "higher authority." In actuality, General Marshall had forwarded their memorandum, as soon as he received it, to the National Security Council for consideration at its next scheduled meeting on January 17. Moreover, as subsequent testimony revealed, the original impetus for the memorandum had been the alarming military situation in late 1950, when recommendations were needed for the contingency that U.N. units might be forced out of Korea—a situation that had considerably altered by January 12. Although the Chiefs did agree with MacArthur that, in view of the massive Chinese intervention, certain restrictions on actions against Communist China should be lifted, they at the same time strongly disagreed with his view that the danger of Soviet intervention should be discounted. Their memorandum stressed that everything possible should be done to "delay a general war with Russia until we have achieved the requisite degree of military and industrial mobilization." Whereas MacArthur favored an immediate U.S. naval blockade of China, the Joint Chiefs felt strongly that such action should await due preparation, and come after U.N. forces had been forced to evacuate or had established a defense line. Even then, they felt, implementation should depend "upon circumstances then obtaining." Admiral Sherman, who wrote the initial draft of the JCS memorandum, testified later that he had never favored a unilateral U.S. blockade but felt it should be a joint U.N. effort. As to bombing the mainland of China, the January 12 memorandum reiterated that this should be undertaken only "at such time as the Chinese Communists attack any of our forces outside of Korea."[54]

All these questions were considered and debated at length in the National Security Council and its subcommittees during January and February, as General Marshall later testified. General Collins's optimistic report in mid-January on the changed military picture in Korea relieved much of the pressure in Washington for hasty decisions on either withdrawing U.N. forces or expanding the war. As Marshall put it:

> Thereafter, the situation of our forces in Korea continued to improve and during the latter half of January the enemy forces remained on the defensive. Throughout February and March our forces maintained the initiative against the enemy. . . . As the result of this change in the military situation from that which prevailed during the early part of January, it became unnecessary to put into effect all of the courses of action outlined in the Joint Chiefs' memorandum of January 12. . . . None of these proposed courses of action were vetoed or disapproved by me or by any higher authority. Action with respect to most of them was considered inadvisable in view of the radical change in the situation which originally had given rise to them. . . .[55]

Relief of MacArthur

AS the Allies' situation improved in Korea, Marshall and Acheson worked in the United Nations for a cease-fire. Their efforts came to nothing, however, when the Chinese Communists set the price—a seat in the United Nations and withdrawal of U.S. protection of Formosa. Not long after this failed attempt, the United States won support for a General Assembly resolution naming the People's Republic of China as the aggressor and asking that United Nations objectives in Korea be achieved by peaceful means. Most of the Soviet bloc voted against the resolution, and some neighboring countries abstained.

Not wanting to remain on the defensive, General Ridgway began probing areas south of the Han River in late January. He favored sending troops to the river but doubted if they could retake Seoul. On February 5, he directed Almond to attack the enemy's center and drive the Chinese back across the Han in the west. Although this objective was accomplished, the Chinese immediately, on the night of February 13–14, in the see-saw fashion of recent weeks, thrust at the center of Ridgway's forces, opening a drive that continued until logistical problems forced them to pull back. Ridgway counterattacked on February 21 and by the end of the month had reached his objectives.[1]

At the first sign of a favorable change in the situation south of the 38th Parallel, MacArthur responded to an appeal from his Air Force commander and asked the Joint Chiefs to lift their restrictions on bombing the port of Rashin, near the Soviet border, to reduce the flow of supplies to the enemy. Alarmed, Secretary Acheson warned Marshall of the danger of provoking a major military incident with the Soviet Union for a target whose bombing was not worth the risk. After careful study, the Joint Chiefs agreed that the target was not so vital as MacArthur believed, and turned down his request. Marshall recommended that the President approve their decision.

Mindful of MacArthur's determination to punish the enemy, Acheson fretted in late February, as Ridgway's troops approached the 38th Parallel. He asked Marshall to revise MacArthur's directive, limiting his authority to cross the line. The Joint Chiefs of Staff opposed this suggestion, feeling that the Far Eastern commander should be able to move far enough across the Parallel to prevent the enemy from concentrating his forces just north of the line. The secretaries of Army and Air and Acting Secretary of the Navy Kimball favored a halt at the line.[2]

Mulling over these contradictory opinions, Marshall recalled his military experience and decided against sending Acheson's memorandum to the President. He believed that freedom to maneuver was essential to MacArthur and that it was too early to make a final ruling about crossing the 38th Parallel. He sent the various viewpoints to Averell Harriman and told him to use his judgment in briefing the President.[3]

Ridgway again attacked from his center on March 7, and within a week the enemy began to withdraw. March 18 saw Seoul once more under U.N. control. It seemed that the enemy might pull back of the 38th Parallel.

MacArthur had been told in January that he should try to hold or make small advances in Korea to provide a suitable basis for opening cease-fire negotiations. The recent gains seemed to provide that opportunity. The Joint Chiefs notified him on March 20 that the State Department was preparing a presidential announcement to indicate that the clearance of aggressors from South Korea would make negotiations timely. There was a feeling in U.N. circles that diplomatic negotiations should precede any crossing of the 38th Parallel. The State Department asked what freedom of action MacArthur would need during the new few weeks of diplomatic soundings to provide security for U.N. forces and maintain contact with the enemy.[4]

MacArthur replied the next day that, in view of the restrictions already placed upon him, present directives were adequate, but he hoped no further limits would be imposed.[5]

The situation was obviously delicate; a wise decision would have been to leave the matter with the diplomats. But, in a public statement on March 24, MacArthur spoke of recent successes and boasted that, despite the restrictions on U.N. forces, China had been unable to conquer South Korea. He then raised questions that might well have waited.

> The enemy therefore must by now be painfully aware that a decision of the United Nations to depart from its tolerant effort to contain the war to the area of Korea, through an expansion of our military operations to his coastal areas and interior bases doom Red China to the risk of imminent military collapse.

The fundamental problems were political and must find their solutions in the political sphere. But in the area of his authority as a military commander, he was ready to confer in the field, with the enemy commander in chief, at any time.[6]

General Marshall subsequently told a joint congressional committee of the unhappy developments caused by this statement.

> At the time the foregoing statement was issued, the clearance of the proposed Presidential declaration with the other thirteen nations having forces in Korea had very nearly been completed. In view of the serious impact of General MacArthur's statement on the negotiations with these nations, it became necessary to abandon the effort, thus losing whatever chance there may have been at the time to negotiate a settlement of the Korean conflict.[7]

The British Foreign Office at once instructed Ambassador Franks to leave no doubt in the State Department that the British government was strongly opposed to allowing U.N. forces to advance north of the 38th Parallel. The British Chiefs of Staff felt that such an action would make the Chinese unwilling to negotiate and was militarily unsound. From New York, where he headed the British delegation to the United Nations, Sir Gladwyn Jebb dismissed MacArthur's statements. He assumed that the Truman Administration did not accept his views, but said that unless they disavowed him, they would be misunderstood. Of MacArthur's bombing proposals, he declared that if MacArthur believed that the U.N. General Assembly was going to authorize extension of the war beyond the confines of Korea, "he must be conscious only of public opinion in the Philippines, some of the banana nations, and the lunatic fringe of the Republican Party."[8]

Writing in *The New York Times,* the paper's military analyst, Hanson Baldwin, praised MacArthur's great service in the past but added that in a democracy there was a fine line as to what a military

leader could say about political matters; MacArthur had not followed too fine a line. He enumerated MacArthur's military mistakes
in Korea and his intelligence failures. His "granitic self-confidence
was such that he had long since outlived his usefulness." Baldwin
concluded that so great was MacArthur's power with many elements of the U.S. population that he was not likely to be removed
until a treaty had been concluded with Japan or the Korean business settled.[9]

Truman later denounced MacArthur's statement as an ultimatum to the enemy, and thought of recalling him. Instead, he summoned Acheson, Rusk, and Lovett (acting for Marshall) to discuss
a suitable reply. They reviewed various earlier warnings about public statements by government agencies and officials and, in particular, noted that the directive of December 6 specified that such
statements must be cleared in advance. The message that went to
MacArthur was surprisingly mild. The General was reminded of the
December directive. If the enemy requested an armistice, he was
directed to refer the matter to the Joint Chiefs of Staff.

MacArthur said later that he assumed that as a military commander he had the right to talk with the leader of opposing forces. At
the moment, he informed Ridgway that he proposed to continue
operations north of the 38th Parallel but not beyond the point that
logistical support would allow. Ridgway gathered that small forces
could cross the line if the opportunity arose.[10]

The new British Foreign Secretary, Herbert Morrison, who had
replaced a seriously ailing Bevin (he died shortly after MacArthur
was relieved, on April 14) at the end of March, proposed that all
countries with forces in the United Nations command restate their
desire for a unified and independent Korea, their willingness to
withdraw all foreign troops, and their readiness to reach these ends
by nonmilitary means. On behalf of the U.N. command, President
Truman would announce the support of these views. Then the
Chinese Communists and the Soviet Union would be asked for
suggestions as to the best way to put these measures into effect.[11]

Before this proposal reached Korea, General Ridgway suggested
moving far enough north of the 38th Parallel to destroy enemy
forces and supplies. MacArthur approved the move without referring to Washington. By March 30, the Eighth Army had cleared
most of the enemy from the area south of the line. Three days later,
Ridgway discussed with MacArthur the possibility of moving to line
Kansas, a phase line beginning some twenty miles north of Seoul
and running eastward to the coast about twenty-five miles north of
the 38th Parallel. Two days afterward, MacArthur informed the

Joint Chiefs that Ridgway was making this move and that, when it was completed, he would proceed to line *Wyoming*, which screened line *Kansas* in the west, to seize an area where enemy forces and supplies were concentrated. After these actions, Ridgway would keep contact with the enemy by sending out large patrols but did not plan any major advances.

By April 9, two U.S. corps and one South Korean corps were on line *Kansas* and two other corps were approaching their objectives. MacArthur had warned that the enemy might launch a counterattack after April 1, and Ridgway was preparing an orderly withdrawal to a better position.

In the strained atmosphere existing between MacArthur's Tokyo headquarters and Washington officials, and with U.N. supporters of the Korean effort clamorous for a cease-fire, MacArthur's plans were seen as a challenge to all Washington authority. President Truman continued to think of recalling the General. Marshall later said that the major factor in MacArthur's relief was his message of March 24; Truman waited to study the situation more carefully and to be certain of his ground.

MacArthur had lighted a fuse that would accelerate the explosion in what he called an "amiable acknowledgement" of a letter from Joseph Martin, Republican leader of the House, who had asked the General to comment on a recent speech in which Martin had proposed releasing Chiang Kai-shek to attack the Chinese mainland. MacArthur wrote that this was a logical move and criticized the U.N.'s current emphasis on Europe instead of Asia, adding that "there was no substitute for victory."[12] He evidently did not recall that Senator Vandenberg's efforts in 1943–44 to get the Republican presidential nomination for the General had been shattered when MacArthur wrote two letters to a Nebraska congressman who criticized the Administration and urged that MacArthur be nominated to save the country; the congressman had given the letters to the press.

Martin released his letter from MacArthur on April 5. The next day, Truman sought advice from Marshall, Acheson, Harriman, and Bradley. Harriman said that MacArthur should have been dismissed two years earlier. Everyone present later recalled that Marshall urged caution, pointing to problems that might arise concerning military appropriations in Congress. Bradley said that he joined Marshall in warning against overly hasty action to relieve the General, and also wanted to consult General Collins, who was away, before making a final decision. Secretary Acheson was also cautious and delayed matters until Bradley had a chance to meet with the Joint Chiefs over the weekend. As for Truman, he wrote later that his mind was made up but that he wanted to consult his advisers.[13]

He asked the four to discuss the matter further and meet again with him on Saturday morning. That afternoon, according to Acheson, Marshall suggested that they bring MacArthur back for discussion. With his customary acumen, Acheson advised against this action, noting that it would provide MacArthur with a dramatic opportunity to make an appeal to Congress and the country. Marshall dropped the idea, but he wanted to limit the size of the explosion. He and Bradley continued to search for an alternative to immediate relief. They thought perhaps Marshall should write a personal letter to MacArthur pointing out the serious implications of his actions.[14]

When the same four met again with President Truman on Saturday, April 7, they all recommended postponement of a decision until after the weekend, to give the President time to consult other government officials. Later that afternoon, Truman talked to Vice President Barkley, who was in the hospital, Speaker Sam Rayburn, Chief Justice Vinson, and others. Barkley admitted that he was somewhat embarrassed: "Personally I had long admired him [MacArthur] and felt a sort of family connection, as my youngest daughter is married to his nephew and namesake. General MacArthur . . . had attended their wedding in my home in Washington." When Truman asked Barkley for his views, he said, after learning from the military that there was no chance of a compromise, that there was the choice of relieving the General or allowing him to remain in defiance of his Commander in Chief—and that meant that he must be relieved. Chief Justice Vinson advised caution: the authority of the President was at stake and constitutional questions were involved.[15]

On Sunday afternoon, General Bradley conferred with Collins, Sherman, and Vandenberg, and later all four met with Secretary Marshall, who asked each of them individually to state his opinion on the matter. They all agreed that, from a military point of view, the General should be relieved. Next morning Bradley, Marshall, Harriman, and Acheson joined the President. After Bradley presented the views of the Joint Chiefs, Marshall recalled that "With the unanimous concurrence of all those present, the President at that time took his decision to relieve General MacArthur."[16]

All political and military leaders consulted by the President concurred in his decision. Truman then asked Bradley to prepare a message relieving MacArthur and a statement explaining the action. Since the United Nations was involved, he suggested that Bradley also bring Acheson into the process. Bradley, in turn, asked General Collins, who was the agent for the Joint Chiefs in direct dealings with MacArthur, to write the messages. These were drawn up in the normal manner. The first message was a terse statement, in accordance with Army practice, that MacArthur was relieved. There was an accompanying statement for the public indicating that this was because MacArthur had been "unable to give his wholehearted support to the policies of the United States Government and of the United Nations." Added was a gracious reminder that relief should not be allowed to conceal the debt of gratitude owed him "for the distinguished and exceptional service which he has rendered his country in posts of great responsibility. . . ."[17]

Once the decision was made, Truman discussed with his advisers the best way to break the news to MacArthur. Since Secretary of the Army Frank Pace was in Korea en route to Tokyo, Marshall suggested, and the President agreed, that he should notify the General personally.[18] New developments interfered, however. Walter Trohan, chief of the *Chicago Tribune* bureau in Washington, later recorded that he was responsible for the change in plans. Having received a "tip" from Tokyo, and noticing great activity at the White House and hurried visits by General Bradley and the others, he notified his paper that MacArthur was about to be relieved. As Trohan put it, "If we hadn't pushed he [Truman] would have done it in a more orderly fashion."[19]

When Truman received word of the expected premature publication of the news, he decided that he could wait no longer and called a special press conference after midnight to announce the relief. There had been a power failure in the relay station in Korea, so Pace failed to get the message. The result was that Mrs. MacArthur heard the news flash on the radio and told the General. Even those Americans who did not blame the President for throwing out a national hero thought the way he did it was boorish and ungracious. As Schnabel and Watson said, "As it turned out, this commendable effort to avoid embarrassing General MacArthur went astray, resulting in considerable embarrassment to the Administration and increased public sympathy for General MacArthur. . . ."

Truman's message relieving MacArthur instructed him to turn over his command to General Ridgway. The Joint Chiefs, not knowing whether Ridgway might want to continue in command of troops in Korea, notified him that General James Van Fleet was available to him to be used as he thought best. Ridgway at once placed Van

Fleet in charge of the Eighth Army. Van Fleet always believed that Marshall was responsible for his selection. Marshall had liked his record as division and corps commander in Europe, where he served under Bradley and Collins, and had backed him for a position in Greece.[20]

European satisfaction over MacArthur's relief was apparent. From Paris, the British Ambassador radioed the Foreign Office that the French Foreign Minister had referred to the relief "in terms of heart-felt appreciation." It would now be possible to get a new approach to the problem of Korea. The Foreign Office asked Franks to tell Acheson that he had the full support and understanding of London. In Parliament, where discussions on Korea were going on, leaders of both parties stressed the critical importance of restraint in the Far East, while praising MacArthur's great leadership during the war.

MacArthur left Tokyo at once for the United States, where he received an almost hysterical welcome. The tremendous ovations were more than honor and respect for a hero of three wars; they also fed on the violent opposition to Truman and his administration felt by many. Secretary of Defense Marshall took the lead in arranging the military welcome, as he had for Eisenhower, Bradley, Patton, and others after World War II. He saw to it that transportation was available to bring to Washington former members of MacArthur's staff. At the ceremony in MacArthur's honor on April 19 at the Washington Monument, Marshall was one of the first to greet him.

As in a later time, when Washington and the nation sought to relieve frustrations over the seizure of hostages in Tehran, in welcoming MacArthur many Americans tried to purge their disappointments and anger over the humiliations inflicted on their forces by the North Koreans and the Chinese Communists, backed by the Soviet Union. Reaction against Truman and his chief advisers was bitter. Acheson, long under fire, was violently excoriated; nor was Marshall spared. A few old Army friends turned against him, and some graduates of the Virginia Military Institute who had later served with MacArthur strongly condemned him.

Political opponents of the administration quickly took advantage of the reaction. Senator Taft, announced contender for the Republican presidential nomination in 1952, was quite willing to have MacArthur in his corner, probably because he saw in him a counterfoil to the candidacy of General Eisenhower, whose selection by Truman as Commander, Supreme Headquarters, Allied Powers in Europe, made him a possible presidential contender on either ticket. MacArthur's proclamation that there was no substitute for victory, his suggestion that the leadership in Washington was indecisive, the hint that Washington was soft on Communism, were themes Taft was keen to stress. But as MacArthur moved about the country, receiving the cheers of adoring crowds, Taft must have feared that the Old Soldier, instead of fading away, might become a serious rival for the Republican nomination.

If Taft had such fears, they soon proved groundless, for the worship of MacArthur began to ebb. In a special election in Kentucky, the Republican candidate for the U.S. House of Representatives lost when he tried to make the removal of MacArthur the main issue of his campaign. An important reason for this shift in sentiment was that the country's most respected military leaders supported the power of the Commander in Chief. Whatever their views on his political programs, they could see that Truman had the constitutional power and the duty to dismiss a commander at odds with presidential policy. Leaders of both parties were unequivocal on this principle. Marshall and his colleagues had agreed with the decision and would uphold the President. To a man, the Joint Chiefs of Staff had proved their courage and leadership in World War II. It became clear that Eisenhower in Europe, and Ridgway and Van Fleet in the Far East—old Marshall men—approved the action that had been taken. There had been no real likelihood that the returning proconsul would try to dislodge the governing powers of Washington. It was said that MacArthur had been away from the United States so long that he had lost touch with America, and that his period of almost absolute power in Japan had given him autocratic tendencies, but there was never any doubt that he remembered American dedication to the principle of civilian control. Although he never ceased to insist that he was right in his plans and recommendations and that Truman and those around him lost the victory that could have been gained, he accepted civilian rule. He must have realized that he personally had never permitted any subordinate the freedom to question his authority. He had not believed that Truman would challenge him, but once that happened, he respected the position if not the man who gave the order.

General Van Fleet assumed command of the Eighth Army on April 14. Ridgway let him prepare for an advance, but warned that the enemy was capable of launching a counterattack, and advised him not to overextend his lines. On April 22, the Chinese struck. The collapse of a South Korean division was followed by a pullback, in accordance with plan. In the face of heavy pressure, Van Fleet had established a defense line just north of Seoul by the end of the month.[21]

Ridgway let Washington know that the forces under his command would not act in any way to broaden the conflict. A line was drawn beyond which troops could not go without his permission. He drummed into his subordinates that the current conflict carried a threat of World War III. Washington and the American people wanted to avoid war, but with honor. Every commander was directed to bear that responsibility in mind.

Washington had drawn up new directives for Ridgway, which were approved by the President even as Ridgway's staff prepared a draft directive that he wanted officials in Washington to consider.[22]

Facing the U.N. forces in Korea was a formidable enemy force of half a million Chinese and a North Korean army of some 200,000. The U.N. had 270,000 U.S. and Allied troops and approximately 235,000 South Korean troops. In Manchuria, the Chinese had around 750,000 men. Van Fleet still spoke of new advances, but evidence of an enemy buildup made it necessary to drop such plans.[23]

On May 16, the Chinese opened a main attack in the east. Noting that in the west the Chinese force was small, Ridgway ordered Van Fleet to attack in that area on the 19th. He caught the enemy overextended and drove the Chinese back in confusion. At the end of May, he announced that the enemy had lost heavily in men and materiel—a major defeat. He decided the time ripe for negotiations.

Marshall, Acheson, and the Joint Chiefs of Staff had discussed an armistice as early as March 19, but decided the time was unsuitable. On April 5, the Joint Chiefs notified Marshall that the Korean problem could not be decided by military action alone. They made four recommendations: (1) continue the present military policy until a political objective could be found, without changing the U.S. position regarding the Soviet Union, Formosa, and seating Communist Chinese in the U.N.; (2) develop South Korean units to take over the U.N. fighting; (3) prepare for naval and air attacks against the mainland of China; and (4) determine the views of U.N. supporters towards the U.S. if its forces attacked the Chinese mainland. The proposals under (3) were to be considered if the U.N. forces evacuated Korea or if the Chinese Communists threatened action outside Korea.

On May 17, President Truman approved a statement of policy outlined by the National Security Council, asking for an attempt to stabilize the Korean situation, which it agreed could not be done by military action alone. The government would seek a suitable armistice through the United Nations. But until this was done, current military activity should be continued. Blockades, operations against the Chinese mainland, and "exploitation" of Chinese Nationalists would be considered.

The most efficient way to use South Korean units was a difficult problem. Marshall's interest was caught by a proposal to put U.S. officers at the head of ten new Korean divisions, but Ridgway did not favor the ten divisions Rhee wanted, and felt that the American officers were more needed in U.S. units. By the end of May, the Joint Chiefs believed that dependable South Korean forces could be developed to replace U.N. troops. Rhee, fearing a weakening of U.S. support for South Korean aspirations, declared that if the Americans would equip his troops, the United States could withdraw. Alarmed American leaders warned the Korean President of the damage his statement could cause. If the Chinese Communists believed that they would have to fight only South Korean forces, they would never be willing to negotiate a cease-fire.

One June 1, Ridgway sent to Washington his proposals for an amended directive in which he would be asked to inflict a maximum number of casualties on the Chinese to create conditions favorable to a settlement. To simplify his problems, the Joint Chiefs, after discussions with Truman, Marshall, and Acheson, won approval for Ridgway to operate north of the 38th Parallel; on June 10, the President authorized him to undertake such tactical operations as might be necessary to carry out his mission. Truman was willing to trust Ridgway with discretionary authority, which had been more carefully hedged in the case of MacArthur.[24]

A break in the stalemate appeared imminent on June 23, when the Soviet representative to the U.N. Security Council announced that the Soviet Union would favor negotiations for a cease-fire. On June 29, Washington instructed Ridgway to broadcast a message to the Chinese Communist commander in Korea suggesting that if he wanted a cease-fire the U.N. forces would name a representative to negotiate, and suggested a Danish hospital ship in Kaesong as a meeting place. On July 1, the North Korean army and the Chinese "volunteers" in Korea offered to meet in the Kaesong area, rather than on the Danish ship. Ridgway accepted the change and said that he was prepared to start negotiations on July 10. Thus the path was opened for a cease-fire, but the making of peace was many months and another administration away.

As the likelihood of a cease-fire increased, Marshall made a brief trip to Tokyo and Korea to assess the situation himself. Only five or six people knew of his trip before he slipped away from Washington on June 5, 1951. After a short stop in Tokyo, Marshall, with Ridgway and his public relations officer, Colonel James T. Quirk, set off for Korea. Colonel Quirk recalled that they visited I Corps in the worst flying weather he had experienced. General Ridgway said that he thought they had better call off the rest of the trip and go back by jeep. Marshall asked the General whether he would turn back if he were alone. Ridgway said, 'No,' and the Secretary said 'Let's go!' "The pilots shuddered, as did we, and off we went into squalls, rain, and wind, bouncing all over the sky in [the] light plane. I always ride with the phones on and the pilots were swearing and sweating it out but agreed that if the Old Man could do it so could they. It was so dangerous it was silly but Generals are like that. They think they always have to be braver than anyone else and they get away with it." It was to be Marshall's last view of an active battle front.[25]

Back in Tokyo, Marshall held another press conference, trying to set at rest the rumor that he had brought a new directive for Ridgway. At lunch one day, Quirk recalled that Marshall told Ridgway that conditions were worse in Korea than anyone back in the United States, himself included, could appreciate. He added, according to Quirk, that he knew Chou En-lai pretty well and thought that when he went home he would recommend to the president that they tell Chou that unless there was an end to the fighting, "we are going to give them a taste of the atom."[26]

Marshall was back in Washington on June 12, a week after he left, and just in time to catch the full force of a bitter attack by Senator Joseph McCarthy. Defeats in Korea and the removal of MacArthur in the spring had aroused ancient hostilities against Marshall. In his life of Senator McCarthy, Thomas Reeves wrote that the Senator had been "particularly aggravated by the General's defense of Acheson, Lattimore, Jessup, and Anna Rosenberg." In April of 1950, McCarthy had called Marshall "completely unfit," "completely incompetent," and declared that as Secretary of State Marshall had "boned up" on China by reading the works of Owen Lattimore. Reeves says, "That December he demanded the General's dismissal from the Truman cabinet. McCarthy's wrath was greatly intensified by Marshall's support of the decision to remove MacArthur."[27]

Perhaps the Senator decided to bore in on Marshall as a target because of special honors paid the General on May 15, 1951, by the state of Virginia and the Virginia Military Institute. On New Market

Day, fifty years after Marshall had completed his courses at the Institute, he was invited back there for the dedication of the sally port to a new portion of the barracks. To the arches named for George Washington and Stonewall Jackson, there was now added the "Marshall Arch." At a special meal honoring his class, Marshall recalled some of his memories of those years in the past. He had been teased unmercifully and hazed because of his Pennsylvania twang, he reminded them, but he was the only Yankee V.M.I. cadet to have an arch named after him.

A different reception awaited him on the Senate floor on June 14. McCarthy had been given by Forrest A. Davis, former editorial writer for the *Cincinnati Enquirer,* the manuscript of an diatribe against Marshall he had just finished writing. McCarthy made some alterations in the manuscript and later implied that he had written the whole paper with some help from his researchers. Reporters who heard him read his attack in the Senate had a strong impression that he was seeing some of the material for the first time.[28]

McCarthy had given notice of his performance. The galleries were packed but almost no Senators were on the floor, and most of them fled as he read. His speech, published as *America's Retreat from Victory: The Story of George Catlett Marshall,* ran to nearly 60,000 words. It was sent to daily newspapers throughout the country and to the schools of Wisconsin.

Tiring after nearly three hours of reading, McCarthy began to skip pages and concluded by placing the full text into the *Congressional Record. Time* reported that only two senators remained and the galleries were now half empty. The magazine commented: "In familiar fashion, McCarthy twisted quotes, drew unwarranted conclusions from the facts he did get right, accused Marshall of having made common cause with Stalin since 1943."

Davis was a skilled writer. He listed books by friends and colleagues of Marshall—Churchill, Sherwood, Mark Clark, James Byrnes, Admiral Leahy. He, or members of McCarthy's staff, lifted statements out of context, added comments in quotations that were not in the original, omitted qualifying sentences, included rhetorical speculations by unnamed Democrats as to why Marshall went wrong, and cited as fact unproved charges made from various hearings. The State Department later compiled the actual complete statements from the various sources cited, which lauded the man their hacked-off sections had been spliced together to condemn.

In *McCarthy and His Enemies,* William Buckley and L. Brent Bozell conceded that although the senator later denied that he had accused Marshall of treason, it "was not unreasonable to conclude that McCarthy was accusing Marshall of anything less than pro-Communism." Although McCarthy had stopped short of uttering "treason," he had declared that Marshall's career was "steeped in falsehood and that when his story is fully told it would be of a conspiracy so black that its principals shall be forever deserving of the maledictions of all honest men . . ." Buckley and Bozell declared that the Senator had followed an unusual sort of reasoning by which he assumed that if some action of Marshall's had helped the Communists, "Marshall wished it to be so." As to whether the attack had been harmful to Marshall, the authors asserted:

> Marshall's loyalty was not doubted in any reasonable quarters. On the other hand Marshall no longer rides as high as he once did in the esteem of his countrymen . . . To the extent that McCarthy, through his careful analysis of Marshall's record, has contributed to cutting Marshall down to size, he has performed a valuable service . . ."[29]

The attacks may have reaffirmed Marshall's intent to step down from a position that he had agreed to hold for only six months to a year. In Eisenhower's diary the November 6, 1950, entry reads: "Marshall, the best public servant of the lot, obviously wants to quit." Certainly the last months of his Secretaryship had not encouraged him to stay. He had restored confidence in the armed forces, had ended open warfare between Foggy Bottom and the Pentagon, had increased the size of the services, had helped the President over a possible crisis over the MacArthur firing. Lovett was assuming more and more of the workload. Why not leave the frenetic pace of Washington for the quiet of Leesburg and Pinehurst?

XXIX

Retirement

MARSHALL'S last day as Secretary of Defense began quietly. At a staff meeting that September morning, he casually remarked, "At eleven o'clock I cease to be Secretary of Defense." He explained that originally he planned to serve only six months but that President Truman had asked him to continue until the last day of June 1951, then asked him to stay until September 1. There was always a new crisis and no good time to go. Off the record, Marshall said he was resigning for personal reasons, in particular because he was worried about Mrs. Marshall's health.[1]

He noted that he had just completed fifty years of government service, which included a year with the Red Cross, during which he traveled 35,000 miles. The past year had been marked by remarkable cooperation with Congress, something he felt that we easily lose sight of. He praised the press in the Pentagon—his relations with newspeople had been fine. He paid special tribute to the outstanding Defense Department staff—the most efficient group, its work marked by integrity, competence, and genuine loyalty—that he had ever seen in time of peace. He had been very fortunate to have Lovett. There was no one in the United States with Lovett's understanding of and competence for the job.

In conclusion, Marshall said that he could not take credit for what had been done. He had pushed a few things. Now he proposed to sit down and reflect and see what others were going to do.

Mrs. Rosenberg insisted that he review a group of servicewomen before he left. Otherwise, he and Lovett, who succeeded him, saw the occasion as a simple changing of the guard. They had worked together and thought so alike that Marshall's departure was regarded merely as a drive home to Leesburg. Lovett would now sign himself Secretary rather than Under Secretary, and continue to work exactly as before. General Carter remained on Lovett's staff, and Marshall asked Colonel George to work part time for the new Secretary.

Before World War II, Marshall would have reverted to his permanent rank, major general, when he retired, and have been entitled to a pension based on his Army service. But in 1948 President Truman had recommended that Congress make permanent the rank of five-star officers—Leahy, Marshall, King, MacArthur, Nimitz, Eisenhower, Arnold, Halsey, and Bradley were to be retained on active duty with full pay and all benefits of a five-star general or admiral. Truman added that each man should have a government office, an aide, a secretary, and an orderly. The law establishing five-star rank provided that the order of priority set forth in December 1944, with the temporary five-star position, would continue. Admiral Leahy was the ranking five-star officer in the Navy, and Marshall held the same rank in the Army, a priority each kept until his death.[2]

Unlike most retiring officers, Marshall did not have to find a new home. He still had the house at Leesburg, Dodona Manor, bought by Mrs. Marshall in 1942, and the cottage at Pinehurst, which she had purchased during the closing months of the war. Within two weeks after he returned from the China Mission in January 1947, Marshall wrote friends that he was working as a "common laborer" at Leesburg under the strict supervision of his wife, cleaning out gutters, among other things—persiflage revealing his pleasure in such long-deferred domestic activities. He returned from Moscow in April of that year in time to put in a vegetable garden. While he was in Walter Reed Hospital after his operation at the end of 1948, Madame Chiang Kai-shek was a house guest at Dodona Manor and wrote him from there that she was doing coolie labor to help cultivate the garden. In the spring, when Marshall was recuperating and the garden prospering, he wrote Madame that he was sorry not to be able to send her some of the fruits of her labor.[3]

Both the General and Mrs. Marshall liked to relate that when he came home to Leesburg after his operation, some of their neighbors asked Mrs. Marshall what they could give him for a welcome-home gift. She replied that the only thing she could think of that he would really appreciate was a load or two of manure for the garden. It was duly delivered.[4]

This story always prompted the General to recall that while he was Secretary of State someone told him that a way to improve the soil of his garden was to imitate early American Indian cultivators by placing a fishhead under each seed or slip planted. Marshall's inquiries resulted in the Friday delivery of baskets of fishheads that he put in the back of his car in the State Department garage, forgetting momentarily that he would not be home over the weekend. By Monday there was considerable dismay among those parking in the vicinity of his car. Later the Italian Government sent Marshall a beautifully decorated peasant cart filled with pungent cheeses. The cart, for some reason, remained so long in the State Department reception area that it became necessary to remove the contents. "Between fishheads and strong cheeses," Marshall like to say, "I'm afraid we were in bad odor at the State Department."

After saying this, he always stopped the laughter to add that the story had a sequel. He took the fishheads to Leesburg and planted them according to instructions. That night, the Marshalls heard an extraordinary amount of cat yowlings and of course the next morning revealed that the stray cats of Leesburg had dug up and presumably consumed every fishhead, leaving his seeds and seedlings wilting in the sun.

Leesburg and Pinehurst responded well to the Marshalls. They went regularly to the Espicopal Church and some of his jackets and suits turned up for sale at church bazaars. They went to local festivals and clubs. One year Senator Harry Byrd, Sr. succeeded in getting Marshall to crown the Apple Queen at fall festivities near Byrd's farm.

At Pinehurst, lacking gardening opportunities during the winter months, Marshall became an interested spectator at golf tournaments, riding in a golf cart to follow the players. He developed friendships with visitors who came during the cold months. One acquaintance was John Marquand. Some people who read his *Melville Goodwin U.S.A.* were sure that the writer had incorporated Marshall's characteristics. Also nearby was the cottage of Mr. and Mrs. Ernest Ives. Mrs. Ives was the sister of Adlai Stevenson, whom Marshall had met when Stevenson worked for Navy Secretary Frank Knox during the war, and knew later when Stevenson was Governor of Illinois. Stevenson often stopped to see the Marshalls when he visited the Iveses.

Marshall's presence at meetings of the Pinehurst Rotary Club had a disconcerting effect on guest speakers who were to talk on military affairs or foreign policy. Theodore Ropp, professor of military history at Duke University, well remembers speaking there on World War II strategy, with the U.S. Army Chief of Staff during World War II listening intently directly in front of him. Ropp was greatly relieved when the General congratulated him warmly on his handling of the topic.[5]

At Pinehurst the Marshalls were visited by old friends going to or returning from Southern vacation areas, and, in turn, they were invited to vacation homes. Margaret Emerson, who had a home in the Poconos sitting amidst its guest houses like a mother hen with baby chickens (the place had been once owned by J. P. Morgan), was sometimes hostess to the Marshalls. The Marshalls urged Erskine Wood, the General's old fishing friend from Portland, Oregon, to join them there shortly after his wife died. Wood liked to tell, as an example of Marshall tact and thoughtfulness, that on his first morning with them he had gone for a walk without straightening up his room. When he came back, he found that the General had made his bed.

On a coastal fishing trip, Marshall found a fishing partner in Corty, young grandson of a retired political scientist. Corty later sent him letters, decorated with pictures of fish and real fishhooks. Marshall's delighted reply to Corty's first letter called forth more examples of the boy's drawings.[6]

In 1951 President Truman offered to reappoint Marshall to the American Red Cross position, but the General declined. He did accept the nonpaying chairmanship of the American Battle Monuments Commission that had once been held by his old chief, General Pershing. He also accepted the nonpaying position of Chairman of the V.M.I. Foundation, fundraiser for his alma mater. But Marshall did not go on boards of corporations. Early in 1950, his old friend Edward Stettinius had persuaded him to become a director of Pan American Airways, headed by Stettinius's brother-in-law, Juan Trippe. Marshall received a director's fee for attending one or two board meetings but he resigned when he was appointed Secretary of Defense.

Marshall was also careful about investing, undoubtedly due to an embarrassing experience that occurred not long after he retired as Chief of Staff. Louis Marx, the toy manufacturer, decided to establish a small cosmetics company and invited several friends to make small investments. Like many self-made men, Marx sought the friendship of prominent people, and when the General became Chief of Staff, Marx sent toys to the Marshalls at Christmas to be distributed to children on the post. He expanded this practice to include Generals Eisenhower, Bradley, and Bedell Smith, and they were all offered an opportunity to buy stock in his cosmetics company. Soon after Marshall went on the China Mission, Marx asked him through his secretary for $100 for stock, which she sent out of his account. Marshall was happily surprised at the end of the year to receive a dividend. The company flourished, amply repaying investors, but Marx found that this sideline was robbing him of time for toy manufacturing. He dropped the project, compensating stockholders several times over for their stock. The transaction later caught the attention of Westbrook Pegler, radically conservative newspaper columnist, noted for vigorous attacks on labor unions, President and Mrs. Roosevelt, and members of the Roosevelt administration. Pegler trumpeted that the military investors, at least Eisenhower and Bedell Smith, had been favored by Marx because for a short time after the liberation of Paris, the U.S. Army had controlled the opening of American businesses there, and Marx had been permitted to do business in Paris. Pegler wrote the generals, demanding explanations. Marshall replied in detail, indicating the nature of his investment and denying any *quid pro quo* in the transaction. Pegler announced that he was satisfied that Marshall had come clean, and demanded that the others do the same. After this episode, Marshall was wary of any investments that might be considered as a conflict of interest.[7]

Marshall firmly declined to write his memoirs. Rumors continued for some years that he refused a million dollars for his autobiography. He supposedly told one publisher that he had not spent his life serving the government in order to sell his life story to the *Saturday Evening Post.* A representative of a large agency seeking book and newspaper rights related that he was authorized to offer the General "a six or seven figure price," but Marshall said when the agent approached him, "I know why you have come. I am not writing my memoirs." He told some publishers that if he wrote his memoirs he would have to tell all the truth and that would hurt too many people. It was Marshall's conviction that books written by important commanders could stir controversies damaging to the Army. This conviction grew out of Marshall's own experience after World War I after he had submitted a manuscript on his experience in the war to a publisher and was told that at the moment there was no interest in books concerning that conflict. He left the manuscript with the publisher and it remained there until he became Chief of Staff years later. The publisher then proposed publication, but Marshall declined and asked that the manuscript be returned to him to be destroyed. Marshall never meant to imply that he was hiding secrets. Several years later, a copy of the manuscript that he had given his stepdaughter in 1939 was published. The contents of his memoirs of World War I prove that he was oversensitive about causing controversy. The book was an excellent summary of the problems of planning and training in the early days of the AEF and was incapable of giving offense.

In 1946, Mrs. Marshall wrote an account of her life as an Army wife from her marriage to Marshall in 1930 until their return to Leesburg from Fort Myer in late November 1945. She had not been lured by offers from large publishing houses, but by the suggestion of her brother, Tristam Tupper (magazine and motion picture script writer), who had founded a small publishing house, Tupper and Love, at the end of World War II. Mrs. Marshall's book was one of their first publications. She had kept a scrapbook of newspaper clippings and radio broadcasts, which she used as background material, and gave a lively account of her own experiences and of a very human Marshall. The book was adopted by a major book club and provided her with a comfortable financial nest egg.[8]

After the fall of 1952, the Marshalls settled down to the enjoyment of a simple life. Each year they stayed in Leesburg from May until their annual checkup at Walter Reed Hospital and then went to Pinehurst for the winter.

Marshall was to find it difficult to avoid notice in the 1952 fall Presidential campaign between Eisenhower and Adlai Stevenson. Initially, Marshall must have thought that his only participation would be his congratulatory note to Eisenhower when he won the nomination in June 1952. Thanking Marshall for his "fine note," Eisenhower wrote that if he, when working with the General on war plans in 1942, had suggested that he would be leading his party in a fight for the Presidency ten years later, Marshall would have had him locked up as a dangerous character. He thought that Marshall must have had similar thoughts when he was called back to duty in late November 1945. Eisenhower felt he was performing a useful service. "But the whole atmosphere is so different from that to which soldiers of long service become accustomed that I sometimes find it difficult to adjust myself. Since you are well aware of this through your own experience, I will not belabor the point."[9]

As the campaign got under way in the fall, Marshall had letters from Eisenhower backers wanting to know why he was not actively backing his old protégé. His usual reply was that he never voted, sometimes adding the old wheeze that his father was a Democrat, his mother a Republican, and he was an Episcopalian.

The anti-Marshall tirades of Senator Joseph McCarthy continued, even though the response from Leesburg was silence. In his avidity to attack the Truman Administration and get himself reelected, McCarthy harped continually on Marshall's anti-Americanism.

Many of Eisenhower's friends were sure that Eisenhower would eventually disavow McCarthy's increasingly blatant attacks, and in the fall of 1952, when he prepared to campaign in Wisconsin, Eisenhower decided to make a strong defense of his former chief. Emmet Hughes, a *Time-Life* writer on loan to write speeches, was asked by Eisenhower if this part of the campaign could be made an occasion for paying tribute to Marshall "right in McCarthy's back yard." Hughes gladly drafted praise of Marshall's selflessness and patriotism, noting that charges of disloyalty were "a sobering lesson in the way freedom should *not* defend itself."[10]

Someone leaked to Governor Koehler of Wisconsin what Eisenhower planned to say. The Governor, Senator McCarthy, and the Republican National Committeeman from Wisconsin, flew to Peoria, which Eisenhower's campaign had reached, to talk with the candidate. Koehler argued that an Eisenhower rebuke to McCarthy on his home grounds would damage the whole Republican Party and adversely affect the Republican majority in Wisconsin. Sherman Adams, one of Eisenhower's chief political advisers, also insited that the offending paragraphs be removed. They were deleted. McCarthy sat on the platform with Eisenhower and escaped unscathed. The damage was done, and it was Eisenhower who suffered, although Wisconsin went Republican and he won the election. He wrote former Minnesota Governor Harold Stassen that he did not see how he could campaign if he went against Koehler's wishes. Eisenhower later wrote that he would never have withdrawn his statement if he had known that his attitude toward Marshall would be so distorted.

Marshall never made any public comment about the whole affair. When he heard that his former chief, Harry Woodring, one time Secretary of War, had attacked him, Marshall shook his head and said, "Poor fellow. They used him. They took him to McCarthy's office and got him to sign a statement."[11]

It was becoming—had become—more and more a part of Marshall's nature, this man who had found it hard to control his temper half of his life, to wish that people would behave well but to see calmly that they often did not. He was resigned but not bitter. It was Mrs. Marshall who was hurt and angry on his behalf. Gradually, over the years, she, too, mellowed. In her nineties, she said to Marshall's biographer, "Don't attack President Eisenhower about the McCarthy thing; he did everything in the world to make it up to George and me."

President Truman was outraged over Eisenhower's failure to defend Marshall in Wisconsin. Truman's accusations of Eisen-

hower's ingratitude to the man who had made him became a fierce
drumbeat against Eisenhower for the rest of the 1952 campaign
and, indeed, for the rest of his life.

When the Marshall Library was dedicated in Lexington, Virginia,
in May 1964, Eisenhower was one of the speakers. He paid a glow-
ing tribute to Marshall that was enthusiastically received. Later
Eisenhower expressed to Marshall's biographer his surprise at the
crowd's reaction, because he had been a little ashamed that his
speech was not better. The author replied that people were pleased
to see how high Marshall stood in his estimation. Eisenhower replied, "But everybody knows that!"

"No, sir, not everybody."

After a second's pause, he countered, "Oh, that damned Wisconsin thing. You know about that. It was a political matter."[12]

After Eisenhower's victory over Stevenson, Marshall wrote out in
longhand on November 7 to the new President:

> Congratulations on your triumph seem rather futile in view of the
> immensity of your victory.
>
> I pray for you in the tremendous years you are facing. I pray
> especially for you in the choice of those to be near you. That choice,
> more than anything else, will determine the problems of the years
> and the record in history. Make them measure up to your standards.
>
> I hope the severity of the campaign did not wear you down seri-
> ously, or Mrs. Eisenhower. I thought she did a wonderful job for
> you.

Eisenhower replied:

> Nothing has touched me as much as your letter of congratulations.
> I know that the months ahead will be difficult ones—I am counting
> heavily upon the help of the finest and most dedicated men and
> women in our country.
>
> I agree with you that Mamie was a wonderful help in the cam-
> paign. Both of us have bounced back with surprising vigor—and at
> this moment we are trying to catch up on rest and relaxation.
>
> Mamie joins me in best wishes and warm regard.
>
> > Affectionately,
> > Eisenhower.[13]

Marshall also had a kind word for the defeated candidate. To
Adlai Stevenson, he wrote:

I send you my sympathy in the results of the campaign.

You fought a great fight. In my opinion your political speeches reached a new high in statesmanship. You deserved far better of the electorate and you will be recognized increasingly as a truly great American. [Marshall to Stevenson, 7 Nov 52.]

When time came for the inauguration, Eisenhower invited the Marshalls to the swearing in and to sit in the reviewing stand at the White House for the parade. These were not new experiences for Marshall, for as Pershing's senior aide, he undoubtedly attended Harding's inaugural ceremonies for which Pershing was the marshal. In Washington on business in 1933, Marshall saw the Roosevelt inauguration. In 1941 he led the parade as marshal, and in 1945 he attended the brief swearing-in at the White House. Marshall had resigned as Secretary of Defense the day after Truman was sworn in as President in 1949, and this inauguration of 1953 would be the last one he would attend.

At the Capitol rotunda, Marshall missed seeing President and Mrs. Truman in the crowd, but mentioned meeting Margaret in a warm letter of farewell he wrote the outgoing President. Truman replied:

I don't remember when I have received a letter that I appreciated more than I did yours of January twenty-fourth. Margaret told me she had seen you in the Capitol Rotunda. I must have passed you without seeing you—it was unintentional. Margaret had quite a time high-hatting Mrs. Truman and me because she had a chance to speak to you.

He concluded: "One of the things that I appreciate more than anything else that has happened to me is the fact that I have you for a friend."[14]

Truman was hurt and angry that men who had served under him, such as Lewis Douglas and William Pawley, supported Eisenhower in 1952, but he never felt that Marshall had been coopted by the new masters of the White House. Eisenhower grew ever more cordial to the Marshalls, but some of the new President's advisers made clear that Marshall was not exempt from their criticisms of the Roosevelt and Truman administrations. Of those who had formerly been close to him, Marshall mentioned only his former Army legislative liaison officer with Congress, General Wilton Persons, who was unusually jubilant about clearing out of the White House circles those persons associated with Roosevelt and Truman. Marshall contrasted his actions with those of Bryce Harlow, who had also served him in dealings with Congress, who became a White House insider but had no feud with former administrations. Of the new cabinet, Marshall knew Dulles best. They had worked together, but he expected and wanted no favors from the State Department, nor from anyone in the Government. As Marshall wrote Queen Frederika later when she wanted him to intercede for Greece with the State Department, he had no entrée there and any attempt to intervene would do more harm than good.

During his mission to China, Marshall had been given a small office in the Pentagon for his papers, over which one of his former secretaries, Mrs. Sally Chamberlin, presided. After he left the Secretaryship of Defense, Marshall was assigned a suite one floor below that of the Army Chief of Staff, near the Mall entrance, where his important papers were kept and a secretary and an aide handled his mail. Both by personal inclination for privacy and a desire not to appear to be attempting to influence military policy, Marshall seldom came to the office. He notified the Chief of Staff that visiting generals could feel free to use the space and he suggested that his aide, Colonel George, should work part time for the Secretary of Defense. Not until three years before his death did Marshall take back control of the office to assign it to his biographer who worked there in his files. Until Marshall's death, his office dealt with a heavy correspondence, much of it from veterans who felt they knew at least one general to whom they could appeal. Much of the correspondence was passed on by his staff to other Pentagon offices for action. He continued to write many personal letters, usually drafting them in longhand at Leesburg or Pinehurst and sending them to his Pentagon secretary for typing.

Whatever the administration, Marshall felt at home in the Pentagon until he died. Every Chief of Staff after he returned in November 1945 until the time of his death was a man who had served closely with him, with the single exception of General Lemnitzer, who was chief when Marshall died. Lemnitzer had served under Eisenhower and in great operations in North Africa and Italy, of which Marshall was cognizant and appreciative. Eisenhower, Bradley, Collins, Ridgway, and Taylor had all been Marshall men.

President Eisenhower always kept the Marshalls in mind for state dinners at the White House, particularly when foreign visitors came. In 1953, when Elizabeth II of England succeeded her father, George VI, Eisenhower appointed a distinguished commission, headed by Marshall and including Chief Justice Warren and Gen-

eral Bradley, to represent the United States at the London ceremonies. Marshall had met the young Princess during World War II,
had been in London at the time of her marriage, and had seen her
in Washington when she visited the city with her husband. When
George VI died, Marshall wrote her a letter of condolence, and
received a handwritten reply from the new Queen:

Dear General Marshall:
  I was deeply touched by your kind letter of sympathy, and I do
want to thank you with all my heart for your thought in writing.
  I know that the King very much enjoyed meeting you, and I
remember so well when you came here during the war.
  It seems impossible to believe that he has left us—he was so full
of ideas, of plans for the future, but we shall try to carry on as he
would wish.
  With again my thanks to you and Mrs. Marshall for thinking of us
at this time of great sorrows.
  I am, yours very sincerely,

                                                        Elizabeth R.[15]

Accompanied by Colonel George, the Marshalls sailed on the
United States and came back on the *America*. His first ocean voyage
to England in forty-three years possibly brought to his mind the
trip there he and Lily, his first wife, had made in 1910, when he was
a first lieutenant. His 1917 and 1919 voyages were to France. This
second trip to England by ship came after Marshall had flown to the
United Kingdom several times as Chief of Staff and Secretary of
State, and dealt with the British as Secretary of Defense, and it
marked the shape and development of his career over that intervening period.
  Although Eisenhower had sent Marshall on the journey, it was
Truman to whom Marshall wrote the best description we have of
the trip. The former President had asked Marshall to send him a
letter about the ceremonies, and Marshall obliged with an un-
characteristically detailed letter, noting that while some of the de-
scriptions might be boring to Truman, they should interest Mrs.
Truman.[16]
  The Marshalls were put up in Grosvenor House with a room
overlooking Hyde Park and the parade route. On the day of the
Coronation, Mrs. Marshall and many other special guests not invited to Westminster Abbey stationed themselves near Lancaster
House, which served as headquarters for many of the guests, where
they watched the beginnings of the procession to the Abbey. After

the Queen had passed, Mrs. Marshall went into Lancaster House for tea and then General Sir Leslie Hollis, Marshall's military aide for the day, arranged for her to go back to the hotel from which she saw the parade after the Coronation. For Marshall, inside Westminster Abbey, it was an occasion that he found unique in his long life. He had seen Presidents inaugurated; now, seated with the chief dignitaries near the altar, for the first time he witnessed the crowning of a Queen.

As Prime Minister Churchill passed the General on the way to the altar, he paused. "He dignified me in the Abbey by turning out of the procession to shake hands with me after he had reached the dais." Unmentioned by Marshall, but related afterward by Bradley and others of the American delegation, was that Alanbrooke and Montgomery followed Churchill's example. He also made no reference to an incident which General Bradley related. As Marshall passed up the aisle to his seat near the altar, the audience stood up. Puzzled, Marshall looked around to see what dignitary had come in, and it was he. No British account of the ceremony mentions this occurrence.

Of the entertainment that followed, he described to the Trumans with almost boyish pleasure those things that impressed him.

> I received a very gracious and warm welcome on all occasions and was particularly favored in the seating at the great banquets—Buckingham Palace and Lancaster House. Only one member of the delegation—myself—was invited to these affairs. The banquet at Buckingham Palace was the most brilliant gathering I had ever seen. The Queen's party of about thirty was seated at an oval table in the center of the hall, surrounded by tables of twelve. I was included at her table with the Princess Alice as my partner, and was, I think, the only commoner so honored. I sat between the Princess and the Queen Mother, and two chairs removed from the Queen.[17]

Later in the letter, Marshall noted that Churchill "got hold of me when we had left the ladies" at the dinner, "and had me sit with him for quite a long time and had me participate with him in the drinks they put on a small table alongside him." Before that, the Duke of Edinburgh and the Duke of Gloucester had talked to Marshall for about twenty minutes.

Other highlights of the six-day official trip were a lunch at an annex of the Abbey, where he sat at Lord Salisbury's table and had as his partner the daughter of Leopold of Belgium, who was "very

attractive looking and had a head on her like Frederika in Athens."
On his left was "the Emperor-King of the Himalayas—that is a
pretty big one for you to swallow out in Missouri." The Lancaster
House banquet was also brilliant and he sat at the table presided
over by Lady Churchill with the Duke of Edinburgh and the Duchess of Devonshire, the Queen's Lady-in-Waiting.

Marshall described some of the other social affairs, noting that
Truman should tell Margaret that his Secret Service man, an ex-
professor at Oxford in search of higher pay, was the same man who
had been assigned to Margaret when she visited the United Kingdom. He thought that Truman might be interested that he had
spoken at the English-speaking Union along with Halifax and Alanbrooke, and at a dinner in his honor at the House of Lords given
by the Progress Trust, consisting of eight lords and fifteen members of the House of Commons. Marshall talked for forty minutes,
avoiding foreign policy, but mentioning differences between the
Americans and the British because of varying national problems
and makeup of population. Marshall was startled by the question
period in which queries were posed by every member present, each
one asking about the Suez Canal.

He and Mrs. Marshall sat with Churchill in the Steward's box at
the Derby, which he termed "quite an occasion." A private luncheon that Churchill gave for the Marshalls and the Salisburys was
mentioned without details. Marshall wrote more about a luncheon
given by the Duke and Duchess of Gloucester. The Duchess was a
sister of Lady Mary Burghley, described by Marshall as "my best
friend over here." Far more details were given about a visit out of
London to the home of Sir John Dill's military aide early in the war,
Sir Reginald MacDonald-Buchanan, whose wife Marshall thought
"was sole heir to the Guinness Stout business." "They had a beautiful place about two hundred miles out of London. I think their
family has had nine Derby winners and most of the portraits were
of horses."

Marshall was struck, he wrote Truman, by the heavy pressures on
the Prime Minister.

> The strain he underwent during the Coronation bears [beggars?]
> description, because all of the colonials were meeting with him on
> service matters, and all of the visiting royalties and the prime minis-
> ters were seeking interviews with him on a variety of subjects. He
> mentioned matters in the Far East, but made no reference whatever
> to the Middle East, a very pointed omission.

The Marshalls returned from England full of contentment, but in September they both had severe colds, which in his case hung on to become influenza. At the end of October "through heavy persuasion [Katherine] literally forced me into coming up to Walter Reed," he wrote Truman. The projected hospitalization coincided with a White House invitation to attend a state dinner for King Paul and Queen Frederika of Greece, and when Marshall explained why he would not be able to attend the dinner, Eisenhower at once arranged for his naval aide to send a two-engine plane to Pinehurst to bring the Marshalls to the army hospital. Before they left came the announcement from the Nobel Prize Committee that Marshall would be given its Prize for Peace on December 10.

President Eisenhower congratulated Marshall on the Prize while expressing disappointment that the General would miss the dinner. At times, Eisenhower added, he found it difficult to understand why some people were picked for awards, but "this time I thoroughly approve." Secretary of State Acheson sent ecstatic congratulations: "All of us in your former command—and I hope and believe, all people—are proud and happy. The award was right and proper and just. I hope that it has brought you and Mrs. Marshall some of the joy it has brought us."[18]

Truman, one of those who had proposed Marshall for the Peace Prize, was almost beside himself in his delight, some of which he expressed in an evening interview with Edward R. Murrow, which Marshall saw. He wrote the former President: "I watched it with considerable interest and, as you can well imagine, was deeply appreciative of the honor which you paid me. As usual, you were most generous and kind and, while the years pass into oblivion, I will never forget your unstinting support. . . ." About the Prize itself he added:

> While the award is individual in nature, it is, in effect, a tribute to the American people for their unselfish devotion to the welfare of free people everywhere. I hope you will share this distinction with me because it was through your guidance and leadership that the European Recovery Plan was made possible.[19]

Marshall wrote Madame Chiang Kai-shek of the bouts with flu that had prevented him and his wife from attending the state dinner honoring the first visit of Queen Frederika to the United States, but they had seen her after all, for she had made a quick flight from New York to visit them at Walter Reed. "She is a very beautiful and most interesting woman and you might consider her 'working' royalty,

as she certainly devotes all of her time and energy to her people."
Recalling that Madame had come to see him at Walter Reed Hospital when he was recovering from his kidney operation in December 1948, he said that the thought had just struck him that "whenever I receive women of this stature, I am a patient in the hospital."[20]

When thanking the President for sending the plane and for his congratulations, Marshall said that he knew little about the ceremonies (he assumed the Peace Prize would be given in Stockholm along with the other Nobel awards, instead of at Oslo), but he hoped to go by ship by a southern route to avoid bad weather. "You have been most gracious in your thoughts of me and I am grateful. I hope you will give Mrs. Eisenhower our warmest regards."[21]

Mrs. Marshall was strongly opposed to Marshall's making the trip because she feared for his health, and she did not feel up to going herself. When his doctors thought that a voyage by the southern route to Europe might provide beneficial sunshine and relaxation, the General decided to take the new Italian liner, the *Andrea Doria,* from New York to Naples. He thought his health would improve and he would have time on shipboard to write his speech. His hopes proved incorrect. As he later wrote Truman:

> I had a most difficult time with the Oslo business. I left Water Reed and started on the trip. The ocean voyage was cold and damp which didn't help matters. It was an eight day affair and I planned to prepare my Oslo so-called lecture enroute. I found it utterly impossible to concentrate and I landed in Naples without a line. I flew up to Gruenther's [General Alfred Gruenther had succeeded Eisenhower as SHAPE commander outside Paris] and there, in bed, the next morning I managed to dictate for an hour and a quarter, rather in desperation as my time was running out.[22]

He still needed more help. Gruenther and some of his staff officers made suggestions and Colonel Andrew Goodpaster (soon to go to the White House as special assistant to the President and ultimately to become commander of SHAPE), got down on the floor in Marshall's bedroom and put the various sections of the dictated bits together.[23]

From Paris, Marshall flew to Oslo the day before the award. On the afternoon of December 10 at a hall in the city, the King of Norway and other dignitaries gathered to witness presentation of the awards for 1952 and 1953. Dr. Albert Schweitzer, the great missionary doctor in Africa, received the first award, which was accepted on his behalf by the French Ambassador to Norway. Then

C. J. Hambro, prominent member of the Nobel Peace Prize Committee, spoke at length of Marshall's record as a soldier and of his postwar achievements. He paid special tribute to his efforts to reconstruct Europe and rehabilitate the economies of countries through the European Recovery Plan. He emphasized that this first Nobel Peace Prize to go to a professional soldier was not given for military deeds but for his work in the cause of peace. Marshall was called forward to receive his prize.

As the General stood on the platform, three young men in the balcony rushed forward and began dropping handbills that accused Marshall of military crimes, all the while screaming, "Murderer! Murderer!" Marshall looked up calmly, and the King and his party rose to their feet, followed by the entire audience, to give the General a thunderous ovation. Members of the air crew that had flown Marshall to Oslo were sitting near the demonstrators. As no guards were near, the crew members seized the young men and rushed them out of the balcony where they were handed over to guards who had appeared.[24]

Later at the formal dinner, Marshall in white tie and tails gave his address. He had anticipated opposition to a soldier receiving a prize for peace and his address contained an answer to the demonstrators:

> There has been considerable comment over the awarding of a Nobel Peace Prize to a soldier. I am afraid this does not seem quite so remarkable to me as it quite evidently appears to others. . . . The cost of war is constantly spread before me, written neatly in many ledgers whose columns are gravestones. I am greatly moved to find some means or method of avoiding another calamity of war.

Marshall did not suggest any immediate abandonment of arms. In the present world, the maintenance of peace seemed to require military power and Allied cohesion. "But the maintenance of large armies for an indefinite period is not practical or a promising basis for policy." Returning to a theme he had announced in his first important speech as Chief of Staff in 1939, at the American Historical Association, Marshall declared the necessity of better education in the field of history. All too often history had been used to show a highly colored national point of view. "Maybe in this case it can find a way of facing facts and discounting the distorted records of the past."

He spoke of the great role of democracy and of the tremendous moral strength of the gospel of freedom and self-respect for the individual, but he insisted, as he had in arguments for the Marshall Plan, "that these democratic principles do not flourish on empty stomachs, and that people turn to false promises of dictators because they are hopeless for anything that promises something better than the miserable existence they endure." In the end, material things are not enough. "The most important thing for the world today in my opinion is a spiritual regeneration which would establish a feeling of good faith among men generally."[25]

Marshall was never particularly proud of this speech—carpentered together hastily by a sick man with the last minute help of a few friends—but considering the circumstances of its construction, it had the force of sharp, personal conviction.

The trip certainly did not aid the General's health. The day after he made his speech he flew to Frankfurt where General Thomas Handy, Commanding General of the European Command and Marshall's former deputy, took him home with him to Heidelberg and kept Marshall there until he flew to the States a few days later. At the end of February 1954, in explaining his delay in answering Truman's request for a memorandum on the China Mission that he wanted to use in his memoirs, Marshall said that he had stayed in bed the whole time in Europe except for the two days in Oslo. On his return to Pinehurst, he had again gone to bed and stayed there until mid-February. He hoped soon to be able to concentrate on the material he had promised.[26]

The long siege of flu and/or penumonia marked the beginning of deterioration of his health. Minor problems became more common and he came more often to Walter Reed Hospital for treatment. President Eisenhower always arranged for him to have the Chief Executive's suite. Late in 1954, the President wrote that of all Americans he had known personally, "I think General Marshall possessed more of the qualities of greatness than any other."[26A]

The year 1956 marked the beginning of a biographical project, favored by the President, which was to occupy a considerable part of Marshall's time from September 1956 until the following spring. The project had been long urged by alumni of V.M.I. and by former members of his staff and was part of an earlier effort by his alma mater to have a special collection honoring him at the V.M.I. Museum. After the war ended, the Superintendent of the school asked General Marshall to contribute items for their collection, rich in artifacts of "Stonewall Jackson," other leaders of the Civil War, and graduates who had made their reputations in conflicts since. Mrs. Marshall suggested that V.M.I. send a truck.

At the end of 1952, when President Truman was nearing the end of his Presidency and considering a presidential library based on the Roosevelt model, he suggested to his press secretary, Joseph Short, a V.M.I. graduate, that his school should build a Marshall Library. Short talked to the Acting Superintendent of V.M.I., General William Stokes, and he and several prominent V.M.I. graduates came to the White House for a meeting. They were assured that President Truman would issue a directive for government departments to make available copies of papers pertinent to General Marshall's career for the library. This group, and the President of neighboring Washington and Lee University, quickly formed the George C. Marshall Research Foundation to collect the General's papers and artifacts and to plan a library and museum.[27]

Lacking money, the Foundation could do little to develop the project until early in 1956, when they received backing from John D. Rockefeller, Jr. The philanthropist greatly admired General Marshall, as did his sons, Nelson and David. Concerned that Marshall might not have adequate finances for his old age, Rockefeller made confidential inquiries through Kenneth Chorley, director of Colonial Williamsburg, who reported that the permanent five-star rank arrangement took care of the General's personal financial needs, but that V.M.I. was searching for funds for a Marshall Library. Rockefeller got in touch with John C. Hagan, an investment banker of Richmond, who was President of the Marshall Foundation, and asked how much Hagan needed for the project. Hagan estimated that $100,000 would be required and was told, "You must need more than that," and got a personal check from Rockefeller for $150,000.

Marshall had finally convinced his friends that he would not write his memoirs or even any short article of reminiscence. When he was seventy-five, several of the officers who had been close to him, Frank McCarthy, George, and Carter, urged him to give interviews to a potential biographer. In 1956 he finally agreed to take part in such a program, making clear that he wanted someone who would not ask questions that could be easily found in his papers, that the historian not be of his choosing, and that no money resulting from a biography should go to himself or to his family. Because he had no money to endow a library, royalties from a book based on interviews and his private papers were to go to the research program.

Interviews with the historian selected by the Marshall Foundation began at Leesburg in the fall of 1956 and continued at Pinehurst and, rarely, at the Pentagon. It was evident that Marshall was becoming very frail. He began to experience difficulty in walking. At Leesburg he set interviews for the afternoon, because his bedroom was on the second floor and he did not want to go up and down stairs during the day. But his memory was good and he enjoyed recalling the past, especially his boyhood. He joked that he had heard Mrs. Marshall saying that she had to take him for a walk in the garden as though he were an invalid. In the spring of 1957 he complained of being unable to recall details and proposed that interviews be postponed until he came back to Leesburg for the summer. But, even then, he found reasons for delays, and except for short questions involving single responses, the interviews were not resumed.

In August 1958 the General was at Walter Reed for removal of a small cyst on his eye and some dental work. As usual, President Eisenhower sent flowers to add cheer to his room. Marshall told the President that he had been in the hospital for nearly a week and that all had gone well and he expected to leave soon. Then he fell and broke a rib. After a little more time there, he began rapid improvement, his appetite improved, and he gained eight pounds. He wrote the President:

> I am comfortably situated in your fine suite and, again, you have my deepest thanks for this gracious gesture on your part. As usual, I am receiving the best attention, which of course is typical of Heaton [General Leonard Heaton, head of the hospital] and his people.[28]

Marshall wrote as though he were completely well, but the medical authorities were less certain. When he returned to Pinehurst a few weeks later, they arranged for the hospital at nearby Fort Bragg to furnish medical corpsmen around the clock to sit outside his door when he was in his bedroom.

The Marshalls had a quiet Christmas. Early in the new year, the medical corpsman heard sounds of the General strangling and hurriedly entered the room to find that Marshall had suffered a stroke and swallowed his tongue. Giving first aid while the ambulance was coming, the corpsman soon had the General in the Fort Bragg hospital. The stroke was crippling, but Marshall improved enough to be taken to Walter Reed Hospital in the spring. He recovered sufficiently to sit in a wheelchair and receive visitors and could occasionally talk to old friends during the summer. But when the City of Aachen sent him its Charlemagne Prize to be awarded in a special ceremony, he sat quietly but did not understand what was happening. When Secretary of the Army Wilbur Brucker invited him to receive one of the first flags with up-to-date campaign streamers, Marshall was unable to attend and Colonel George received it for him. A series of brain spasms then made him dependent on tubes to carry food and oxygen. Mrs. Marshall was either in his room or staying in a special cottage nearby, during the whole period.[29]

When Marshall came for his long stay in Walter Reed, Secretary of State Dulles was there with cancer that had returned. Dulles was aware that he had the Presidential Suite, where Marshall usually stayed, and tried to give it to Marshall, but the General declined. Several weeks later Eisenhower brought Winston Churchill for a farewell visit to Dulles. Then they looked in on Marshall. Although he would outlive Dulles he seemed in a far worse condition. He did not know the man with whom he had argued for many hours over global strategy nor the protégé whose rise he had favored. Churchill wiped tears from his eyes.

Get-well cards and personal messages poured in. Many Marshall detractors softened, but some kept up a litany of hate: "Old man, before you die, tell the true story of Pearl Harbor"; or "Explain your conspiracy with the Communists." Such messages were put with other nasty items gathered over the years. Had Marshall seen them in possession of his faculties, they would not have bothered him.

In addition to members of Marshall's family and his aide, who saw him frequently, General Eisenhower's personal physician, Major General Howard Snyder (who had been Marshall's Inspector General for Medical Services), made a daily check on Marshall's condition at Eisenhower's request. His old friend, Major General Morrison Stayer, who had watched over his health years before at Fort Benning, came down from Carlisle to check on him and finally said, "I can't come any more. He is paying the price of a strong physical constitution." The brain spasms had taken away his sight, his hearing, and his speech, but with the aid of machines he stayed alive.

For several months, while he was still conscious, the visitors brought back the past. To General Herron, of Leavenworth days, Marshall told a Christmas story of pre–World War I years, lively and sentimental. General Bull, with Marshall at Benning, at the Pentagon, then with Ike in Europe, talked about old times and Marshall asked about Forrest Harding, a former battalion commander under him in China in the 1920s and then with them at Infantry School.

Many of the old colleagues kept in touch by telephone even if they could not come by. One day, when he no longer recognized anyone, a visitor who went back to Lily's day, his goddaughter, Rose Page Wilson, came hoping for a farewell word and left crushed. Queen Frederika wrote Colonel George for information and was given no hope.

Finally, in the early evening of October 16, 1959, the General died quietly. Preparations for his funeral were already under way.

It was Marshall himself who had drawn up the broad outlines of a state funeral for an Army "great" when, in 1937, Pershing seemed to be dying in Tucson. General Malin Craig, knowing Marshall's closeness to Pershing, ordered him from Vancouver Barracks to draw up funeral plans. Pershing somehow found out about them and that a train had been sent for his body. Swearing that he would be up to serve as the best man at the wedding of his son, Pershing lived until 1948. When Marshall became Chief of Staff in 1939, he ordered additions to the funeral plans but classified them secret. When Pershing died in the summer of 1948, Marshall, as Secretary of State, was one of the chief mourners in the long procession. The General lay in state in the Capitol, there were many marching troops behind the caisson, and planes flew overhead. Despite a heavy downpour on a sweltering day, twenty top Army generals, led by Eisenhower and Bradley, marched behind the casket, completely soaked in the steaming heat, from the Capitol to Arlington Cemetery. The heat almost caused the collapse of General Charles Gates Dawes, old friend of both Pershing and Marshall.[30]

Nothing about a state funeral was to Marshall's taste. On his way to Oslo in late 1953, aware of his pneumonia, he talked with his aide of funeral plans for himself. "I don't want a state funeral," he insisted. Colonel George replied that if he died during the Eisenhower administration he would certainly get the most elaborate funeral possible unless he left definite orders to the contrary. Finally, in 1956, the General wrote out the instructions he had given orally in 1953.[31]

Marshall forbade a funeral in the National Cathedral and ruled out lying in state in the Capitol Rotunda, as had been done for Pershing and would be done for MacArthur. He did not want invitation lists made up for special guests, he wanted no funeral eulogy, interment was to be private, and there was to be no long list of honorary pallbearers. He specified that a short list was to include Sergeant Powder, his chief wartime orderly, and his postwar orderly, Sergeant William Heffner. His postwar aide, C. J. George, and his onetime Secretary General Staff, Frank McCarthy, were on the list, and Robert Lovett, "if it is convenient," and Bedell Smith, "if he is in town." Ambassador James Bruce was added, and the rest of the list was left to Mrs. Marshall and the Office of the Chief of Staff. Mrs. Marshall added a friend from their Chicago days, William Spencer, a Leesburg neighbor, Colonel Fletcher, and a friend from Pinehurst, and Admiral Stark and General Bradley. The Chief of Staff, General Lemnitzer, completed the list. The military canon of the National Cathedral, Luther Miller, who had been Marshall's chaplain in Tientsin in the 1920s and his Chief of Chaplains at the end of the war, and who would say final prayers over Eisenhower ten years later, was in charge of the service.

Mrs. Marshall altered the arrangements slightly to have the unopened coffin rest overnight in Bethlehem Chapel of the National Cathedral, and a large crowd of visitors went through the line to pay respects. Cadets from V.M.I. joined representatives of all the services in the guard of honor.

On October 20, a radiant fall day, the coffin was brought by motor hearse from the Cathedral to Fort Myer Chapel, where the General had asked that the brief service be held. He was also obeyed in that there was no procession, but sensibly, a list was drawn up by Mrs. Marshall of members of his personal staff and others whom she and the Chief of Staff's Office knew would want to attend the service. These people were sent telegrams giving the time of the funeral. Some former colleagues, such as Lucius Clay and Robert Murphy, called to ask if they would be seated if they came and were added to the list. It included Marshall's longtime Pentagon barber, Joseph Abbate, better known as Joe Abbott. In 1956, Abbott turned up at Leesburg to show Marshall his new wife and to chide the General over an old grudge. Marshall had been photographed at the Potsdam Conference having his hair cut by a soldier of the Berlin garrison. Marshall had never seen this soldier before, but the photograph appeared in newspapers around the world. "And now he is in the barber magazine," declared the aggrieved Abbott, reminding the General that he had cut his hair for years and was never photographed with him. Marshall later got the Pope to bless a special parchment and brought it back to Joe, who forgave him to the extent that his son was named George Marshall Abbott.[32]

Before the drive to the Chapel, as the pallbearers gathered in Marshall's Pentagon office, Sergeant Wing, the Chinese orderly who had gone with Marshall to China and Moscow, came to the office and asked if he could once more be at the General's side.

Colonel George asked Marshall's biographer if he would see that Wing had a place, and the two were seated just behind the Achesons.

Shortly before the family entered the Chapel, former President Truman and his military aide, Harry Vaughan, and President Eisenhower with his aide, Robert Schulz, came in and sat side by side in the same pew at the front, across from the pews reserved for Mrs. Marshall, her daughter and family, and Allen's widow and young son.[33]

The service was brief and simple as Marshall had enjoined. Knowing that Marshall wanted no eulogy, Canon Miller's only allusion to the General he had served over the years was in the prayer, "take Thy servant George." Once the abbreviated Episcopal service was over, the casket was placed on a caisson, and the honor guard, the family, the pallbearers, and the honorary pallbearers moved from the Chapel to the grave, down the hill from the Tomb of the Unknown Soldier, where Lily and her mother had long ago been buried. In the sunlit afternoon those remaining in the Chapel heard the sharp volleys of gunfire by the honor guard followed by the slow, silver sound of taps.[34]

Five days after the twenty-ninth anniversary of his second marriage, and a little more than two months before his seventy-ninth birthday, George Marshall had completed his tour of duty.

EPILOGUE

AT Marshall's firm direction, Chaplain Luther Miller gave no eulogy at the funeral of a man he had long admired. The simple service met Marshall's sense of fitness and order. In time, many who knew him and had worked with him gave voice to their admiration. Dean Acheson, his Under Secretary of State at a critical time in history and later a fellow Cabinet member, was eloquent about the immensity of Marshall's integrity and evoked Plato to do justice to his virtue, character, honor. John J. McCloy thought that of all the men he knew, Marshall came closest to touching the mantle of greatness. Robert Lovett, more a brother than the General's natural brother, offered to serve him in any capacity. These men, and many of their contemporaries, on whom Marshall had left his thumbprint, always took pride in remembering their association with him.

The citation accompanying Harvard's honorary degree in 1947 called him "a soldier and statesman whose ability and character brook only one comparison in the history of the nation." The reference, of course, was to Washington, whose hand at moments of crisis helped steady a nation and who had said: "Let us raise a standard to which the wise and honest can repair." A man not easy to approach, a man of firm religious belief who considered one's devotions private and divorced from politics, a man capable of tumultuous outbursts of temper who strove to control his anger, a man constrained to duty and service to the state.

"Presence" is the strand running through all tributes to Marshall. Robert A. Lovett, who observed him over a long period of time, said in this connection, "You were aware of the fact that he was there whether he opened his mouth or not, and that had an impact on any group of people wherever it was . . ." The General's hard-won serenity came not from egotism, but from a certainty born of self-knowledge, self-discipline, and the sure grasp of his profession. He became at peace with himself because he had done the best he could in whatever he had put his hand to. This inner peace increased his aloofness to a degree; certainly it made him indifferent to the calumniations of detractors.

His lack of concern with his reputation was evident in his early deprecation of his father's studies of family history, and the family's collateral kinship to the great Chief Justice John Marshall, whose father's brother was the General's great-great-grandfather. The family went back at least to the early 1700's in Virginia and to the later part of that century in Kentucky. Marshall was well-anchored in the pre-revolutionary history of the country. His father's place of business was in western Pennsylvania, where young George Washington had gone in the mid 1700's. Washington's Fort Necessity was just outside the city of Marshall's birth, Braddock's gravesite provided a picnic ground, and a favorite fishing ground was the Jumonville Glen where Washington had his first skirmish with the French. When he went to the Virginia Military Institute, where a brother and cousins had preceded him, he was fully conscious that the Marshalls were a part of Virginia's history.

Commissioned in the Army in 1902, young Lieutenant Marshall arrived in the Philippines at the close of the Insurrection that had followed the Spanish-American War. As a second lieutenant, he saw service at a time when the United States was tentatively stepping into a global role. He would serve with the A.E.F. in France, and he would lead the U.S. Army and Air Forces in 1939–45 as his country emerged from the Allied defeat of the Axis as one of the superpowers of the world.

He served six rough years as Chief of Staff and was nearly sixty-five when, after one week of retirement, he accepted a thankless position involving a hopeless task, which many of his friends believed the President should never have asked of him.

He undertook the China Mission for the same reason he served as Secretary of State when he returned to Washington, then accepted a tour of duty as head of the American Red Cross, and finally, served as Secretary of Defense after the beginning of the Korean War. The President asked him to do so. At last, in 1951, he was permitted to retire.

Such a record could hardly have been predicted for the gawky youngster of sixteen who came to the Virginia Military Institute in 1897. The first year his grades were barely average, but by his last year, he was in the upper third of his class. As a cadet officer, in the military field that he was already considering for a career, he excelled from the beginning. First Corporal at the end of his first year, First Sergeant at the end of the second, and First Captain in his last year.

When he went to the School of the Line at Fort Leavenworth in 1906, he was still a second lieutenant in a course intended for captains. Many of his class had served in the Spanish-American War or in the Philippine Insurrection, but Marshall placed first, by sheer hard work. At the end of his second year, his standing led to his selection for the next two years as instructor for the courses he had just completed.

The careful ordering of his life became all-important to him, after he suffered two near breakdowns from overwork and inability to cast off the burdens of the day. As Chief of Staff he determined to reduce pressure by demanding brevity in papers, conciseness in briefings, and a vigorous, responsible staff. Men presenting plans for his consideration were expected to understand them and to be prepared to offer solid recommendations when they finished.

To those with whom he worked, Marshall offered complete loyalty, both in support of his superiors and of those under his command. He early determined to follow the lead of each of the Presidents he served, to work as a team member with him and his staff. This loyalty required frank language to the man in the White House and ruled out covert appeals to Congress or leaks to the press. His commanders got his backing almost before they knew that they needed it. When he decided that MacArthur must be shifted from the Philippines to Australia early in the war, he quickly cut off any suggestion that the Pacific commander was trying to avoid capture by making clear that he was leaving at the President's direct order, by recommending the award of the Medal of Honor, and by asking the Prime Minister of Australia to announce that he had invited MacArthur to head the Allied forces in that country. When Eisenhower was hard pressed in the Ardennes, Marshall told him that the Pentagon staff had been given orders to leave him free to concentrate on his battle. When an attempt was made to put Montgomery in charge of the ground battle, the Chief of Staff's New Year message to Eisenhower was, "You are doing a fine job and go on and give them hell."

He could be ruthless to all who tried to escape assignments that they considered unimportant or unlikely to advance their careers. He was merciless to commanders who could not work with other services or other nationalities. He was occasionally criticized for quick judgments on men he suspected of putting personal advancement ahead of the task at hand.

To Congress and the public, he was completely open, admitting mistakes, accepting responsibility, explaining what America must do to put its house in order. During the war, with Secretary of War Henry L. Stimson solidly behind him, he resisted pressures by individual congressmen for appointments and favors. When a state's congressional delegation was trying to keep at the head of a division a commander he thought unfit, arguing that this officer was a constituent, Marshall asked whose constituents were the 12,000 to 15,000 soldiers who might suffer from that officer's mistakes.

Since he had nothing to hide, he did not flinch at Congressional investigations. To staff members who wanted to hold back on revelations to a Senate committee, he argued, "it must be assumed that members of Congress are as patriotic as we are . . . I do not believe that we should adopt an attitude of official nervousness." He believed that it was his duty to make clear what was needed to prepare for American security and for victory. When asked early in the war whether he was not seeking more than he needed, he replied: "That was the first time I knew of in American history that American troops in the field had too much of anything and that I [would be] very, very happy [if] I was responsible." Said Speaker of the House Sam Rayburn, "He has the presence of a great man. He doesn't dissemble . . . Marshall was simple, able, and candid. He would tell the truth even if it hurt his cause. Congress always respected him. They would give him things they would give to no one else."

In choosing commanders, Marshall used no single criterion. Eisenhower and Bradley conformed to his personal model, quietly efficient, non-showy, working with a minimum of noise and friction. Yet he tolerated, was even fond of, the colorful and the profane, such as Patton and Stilwell. Violent language and outrageous conduct were less important than an officer's will to fight. He asked President Roosevelt to bring MacArthur out of retirement and give him the Far East Command several months before Pearl Harbor. But, innately, for the long pull, he liked the quiet men, who did their jobs with little fanfare and a minimum of display.

He had little patience with those who could not work as a team, and who insisted that their unit or their theater must have more than others. He applied the scornful term "localitis" to commanders who were so blind to the needs of other fronts that they could not see the broad view required for victory. He ridiculed the commanders so impressed by the perquisites of their position that on reaching a new post they changed the location of a flagpole or flowerbeds. He barred military attachés from accepting favors from heads of countries getting military assistance from the United States. And he leaned backward with members of his own family in the military to the point that Mrs. Marshall remarked that kinship with him seemed to result in a special penalty.

During the war he told his Secretary, General Staff, that if the latter scheduled him to receive a decoration, or an honorary degree, or to have a book written about him, he would transfer him out of Washington. He waived the first prohibition twice, when the President insisted that he accept awards, but explained his feeling about personal honors clearly: "I thought for me to be receiving any decorations while our men were in the jungles of New Guinea, or the islands of the Pacific especially, or anywhere else there was heavy fighting . . . would not appear at all well."

He was an austere man, but he did have a quiet sense of humor and a passion for simple justice. Some of the grimness attributed to him is countered by his recollection of an incident near the end of his first tour in the Philippines, when he and ten or fifteen friends were having dinner on the second floor of a Manila hotel. The room was large, with a great curtain-festooned bay window. Someone proposed that they improvise an operetta using the window area with its curtains as a stage. They scurried about making preparations until a military policeman knocked on the door to complain that somebody in the room was dropping furniture out the window and onto people in the street. Years later, Marshall recalled, when he was Assistant Commandant at Fort Benning, the culprit of the Manila occasion, now a stern member of the Inspector General's Office, came to investigate the semi-outrageous conduct of two young officers. Marshall suggested a moderation of punishment. The zealous officer retorted, "I hope you don't condone that kind of conduct." Said Marshall, "At least they didn't drop chairs out of the window." "You know," he recalled with a chuckle, "they got off rather light."

In addition to the care of any good commander for the equipping and training of his troops, Marshall gave special thought to the individual. He was concerned that civilian soldiers be taught why they were fighting, and insisted that each unit prepare regular lectures on this subject. When he found that many such talks were poor, he arranged for Frank Capra to produce a series of movies on *Why We Fight*.

He reacted strongly to efforts by some elements of the press and some politicians who encouraged soldiers to protest the extension of the Selective Service Act in 1941. Despite his conviction that the Army must be a thinking army, he believed there was a point at which such agitation must halt. To the House Military Affairs Committee he said that he could not allow recruits to engage in politics. "We must treat them as soldiers; we cannot have a political club and call it an Army . . . Without discipline an Army is not only impotent but it is a menace to the state."

He would not coddle troops; neither would he kill their spirit. "Theirs not to reason why—theirs but to do or die" did not fit a citizen army as he saw it. He believed in a discipline based on respect rather than fear, "on the effect of good example given by officers, on the intelligent comprehension by all ranks of why an order has to be and why it must be carried out; on a sense of duty, an *esprit de corps.*"

He never allowed himself to become too busy to forget the war's cost in lives. He later recalled, "I was very careful to send Mr. Roosevelt every few days a statement of our casualties, and it was done in a rather effective way, graphically and in colors, so it would be quite clear to him when he had only a moment or two to consider, because I tried to keep before him all the time the casualty results because you get hardened to these things and you have to be very careful to keep them always in the forefront of your mind."

In his address to the first graduating class of officer candidates at the Infantry School at Fort Benning early in the war, General Marshall explained the problems of commanding American troops. Characteristics of individual initiative and independence of thought, which make them potentially the best soldiers in the world, could become possible sources of weakness without good leadership. The American soldier's unusual intelligence could become "explosive or positively destructive . . . under adverse conditions, unless the leadership is wise and determined, and unless the leader commands the complete respect of his men."

He emphasized alertness and initiative as essential qualities in both junior and senior officers. "Passive inactivity because you have not been given specific instructions to do this or do that is a serious deficiency," he said. After listing the various responsibilities of the new officers, he concluded: "Remember this: the truly great leader overcomes all difficulties, and campaigns and battles are nothing but a long series of difficulties to be overcome. The lack of equipment, the lack of food, the lack of this or that are only excuses; the real leader displays his qualities in his triumph over adversity, however great it may be."

As Army Chief of Staff, Marshall fully accepted civilian control of the armed services. Although he well understood the relationship of the defense establishment to the execution of foreign policy, he stayed out of politics. After his death, Mrs. Rosenberg was asked whether she felt that the General was basically conservative or liberal, Republican or Democrat, in his thinking. "He didn't care about those things," she said, "he was for what he felt was right." He disapproved of the entrance of military men into politics, and in his two Cabinet posts he refrained from partisan activity. Throughout his adult life he declined to vote. When he came to Washington to be sworn in as Secretary of State, his first act was to announce to the press that there was no way in which he could be induced to run for office. His policy paid high dividends at a time when the Republican Party controlled both houses of Congress while the President was a Democrat. By working closely with Republican leaders, particularly Senator Arthur Vandenberg, he was able to get firm backing on Capitol Hill.

In the making of military strategy, he played a prominent part, attending all the great conferences with President Roosevelt and Prime Minister Churchill. Committed to a Europe First strategy before Pearl Harbor, he continued that view despite pressure to shift to the Pacific. He led the fight in the Combined Chiefs of Staff conferences for a direct cross channel attack in Europe, rather than a slower peripheral or Mediterranean strategy.

More than any Chief of Staff, he was always conscious of the global battle and made every effort to aid the Allies—British, Chinese, and Russian—while keeping American forces at full fighting strength.

In foreign policy, Marshall believed that firmness required military strength. He warned constantly against slapping an opponent in the face while one was virtually disarmed. He deplored the use of harsh rhetoric, insisting that one must permit one's enemies room to maneuver. Although totally opposed to Communism, he was the last important American leader to conclude that the Soviets preferred prolonging world chaos to making peace.

He returned from the Moscow Conference convinced that the United States must take the lead in helping Europe recover from the chaos left by the war. He believed that Europe should take the lead by listing its assets, then asking the United States for the economic aid it needed, and he believed sincerely in inviting *all* European countries to come into a recovery program on a constructive basis.

When his second attempt to get a German treaty failed in London in 1947, he listened sympathetically to Bevin's ideas about the need for formation of some type of Western alliance, and was convinced that any such group should work within the framework of the United Nations. His efforts and those of Lovett in 1948 were to bear fruit early in his successor's tour as Secretary of State.

In his year as Secretary of Defense, he worked to rebuild the armed forces, and supported President Truman's intent to work closely with the United Nations in Korea and to limit any expansion of the conflict in the Far East. Throughout his last months in office, he worked to make the unification of the armed forces succeed and to press for a system of Universal Military Training, insisting that this was the best protection against any form of military control.

In their recent book, *Thinking in Time*, Richard Neustadt and Ernest May single out Marshall for high praise because of his ability to see what from the past should be carried into the future. His opposition to furnishing American forces to settle the China problem is seen as Marshall's awareness of entanglement from which withdrawal would be difficult. This wariness led him to favor limiting any expansion of the Korean War.

George Kennan enumerated, in his memoirs, some of the qualities that he saw in Marshall: "his unshakable integrity, his consistent courtesy and gentlemanliness of conduct; his ironclad sense of duty; his imperturbability—the imperturbability of a good conscience—in the face of harassments, pressures and criticisms; his deliberateness and conscientiousness of decision; his serene readiness—once a decision had been made—to abide by its consequences, whatever they might be; his indifference to the whims and moods of public opinion." Many of these were old-fashioned characteristics then; they may seem even more archaic now. But they helped make Marshall a world leader, and they might still stand in good stead to leaders in a new era.

Douglas Freeman, biographer of two Virginians, Washington and Lee, once remarked that when Marshall's friends asked themselves what were Marshall's most noble qualities, they turned almost at once to Jefferson's tribute to Washington: "His integrity was most pure, his justice the most inflexible I have ever known, no motives of interest or consanguinity, of friendship or hatred, being able to bias his decisions." "Succeeding generations," Winston Churchill insisted, "must not be allowed to forget his achievements and his example."

Appendix

WASHINGTON BIRTHDAY REMARKS AT PRINCETON UNIVERSITY FEBRUARY 22, 1947

I had an engagement with your distinguished President to attend this ceremony exactly one year ago. Instead I celebrated Washington's birthday in China. Now, a year later, I am glad that it is at last possible for me to keep my engagement.

I do not wish at this time to engage in a discussion of specific international questions. But I would like to talk to you about the homefront as it relates to international affairs, and about your personal interests as American citizens.

As you all must recognize, we are living today in a most difficult period. The war years were critical, at times alarmingly so. But I think that the present period is in many respects even more critical. The problems are different but no less vital to the national security than those during the days of active fighting. But the more serious aspect is the fact that we no longer display that intensity, that unity of purpose with which we concentrated upon the war task and achieveed the victory.

Now that an immediate peril is not plainly visible, there is a natural tendency to relax and to return to business as usual, politics as usual, pleasure as usual. Many of our people have become indifferent to what I might term the long-time dangers to the nation's security. It is natural and necessary, that there should be a relaxation of wartime tensions. But I feel that we are seriously failing in our attitude toward the international problems whose solution will largely determine our future. The public appears generally in the attitude of a spectator—interested, yes, but, whose serious thinking is directed to local, immediate matters. Spectators of life are not those who will retain their liberties nor are they likely to contribute to their country's security.

There are many who deplore, but few who are willing to act, to act directly or to influence political action. Action depends upon conviction, and conviction in turn depends upon understanding—a general understanding both of the past history of man on this globe and an understanding that action is a basic necessity of man's nature. Justice Holmes said, "Man is born to act. To act is to affirm the worth of an end, and to affirm the worth of an end is to create an ideal." So I say to you as earnestly as I can that the attitude of the spectator is the culminating frustration of man's nature.

We have had a cessation of hostilities, but we have no genuine peace. Here at home we are in a state of transition between a war and peace economy. In Europe and Asia fear and famine still prevail. Power relationships are in a state of flux. Order has yet to be brought out of confusion. Peace has yet to be secured. And how this is accomplished will depend very much upon the American people.

Most of the other countries of the world find themselves exhausted economically, financially and physically. If the world is to get on its feet, if the productive facilities of the world are to be restored, if democratic processes in many countries are to resume their functioning, a strong lead and definite assistance from the United States will be necessary.

What are we going to do about it? That is the critical problem with regard to which I have a heavy responsibility.

We do not lack for knowledge of what to do for our future security. The lessons of history provide plain guidance. But, can we tear our thoughts sufficiently away from the personal and local problems of the moment to see the world picture and our relation to it in proper perspective? We should think now in long terms of years rather than in terms of months and their immediate political issues.

Twenty-five years ago the people of this country, and of the world for that matter, had the opportunity to make vital decisions regarding their future welfare. I think we must agree that the negative course of action followed by the United States after the First World War did not achieve order or security, and that it had a direct bearing upon the recent war and its endless tragedies.

There were people in those days who understood the lessons of history, who knew well what should be done in order to minimize the danger of another world disaster, but their combined voice was a feeble one and their proposals were ignored. Now this, in my opinion, is where you come into the picture.

In order to take a full part in the life which is before you, I think you must in effect relive the past so that you may turn to the present with deep convictions and an understanding of what manner of country this is for which men for many generations have laid down their lives. Therefore, a deep understanding of history is necessary—not merely recent history which concerns itself with the trivia surrounding conspicuous men and events, but an understanding of that history which records the main currents of the past activities of men and which leads to an understanding of what has created and what has destroyed great civilizations. You should have an understanding of what course of action has created power and security and of the mistakes which have undermined the power and security of many nations, and above all, a clear understanding of the institutions upon which human liberty and individual freedom have depended, and the struggles to gain and maintain them.

It has been said that one should be interested in the past only as a guide to the future. I do not fully concur with this. One usually emerges from an intimate understanding of the past with its lessons and its wisdom, with convictions which put fire in the soul. I doubt seriously whether a man can think with full wisdom and with deep convictions regarding certain of the basic international issues today who has not at least reviewed in his mind the period of the Peloponnesian War and the Fall of Athens.

I am therefore greatly concerned that the young men and women of this country, men like yourselves and the students in every university, college and high school in the United States, shall acquire a genuine understanding of lessons of history as they relate to governments and the characteristics of nations and peoples, and as to the causes of the wars which have destroyed so much of human life and progress. You should fully understand the special position that the United States now occupies in the world, geographically, financially, militarily, and scientifically, and the implications involved. The development of a sense of responsibility for world order and security, the development of a sense of overwhelming importance of this country's acts, and failures to act, in relation to world order and security—these, in my opinion, are great musts for your generation.

It is rather bromidic to say that there is little new in the world or that the world is a very small place. But I think we seldom realize our own ignorance of what has happened in the past except by way of a chronological sequence of events with the related dates. There have been wars and revolutions; there have been republics, kingdoms and empires; there has been tribal rule and various experiments in government, till it would seem that there is small possibility of any new departure. But the important thing is to understand the true significance, the lessons of these historic events and periods.

There is another consideration in connection with the course to be followed by the young people of this country today to which I attach great importance. And that is that young men and women should take an active part as workers in one of the political parties so that they will get the feel of government, so that they will become intimately aware of the influence of political organization upon the government of the hometown, of the state, and the nation. We have had two wonderful examples of this course in the lives of Theodore and Franklin D. Roosevelt—members of opposing political parties, great Americans who rendered magnificent services to their country. You can do no better in starting your active life as citizens than by emulating their example.

Address of Secretary of State George C. Marshall at Harvard University, June 5, 1947.

President Dr. Conant, Members of the Board of Overseers, Ladies and Gentlemen: I am profoundly grateful and touched by the great distinction and honor, a great compliment, accorded me by the authorities of Harvard this morning. I am overwhelmed as a matter of fact and I am rather fearful of my inability to maintain such a high rating as you have been generous enough to accord to me. In these historic and lovely surroundings, this perfect day and this very wonderful assembly, it is a tremendously impressive thing to an individual in my position. But to speak more seriously:

I need not tell you that the world situation is very serious. That must be apparent to all intelligent people. I think one difficulty is that the problem is one of such enormous complexity that the very mass of facts presented to the public by press and radio make it exceedingly difficult for the man in the street to reach a clear appraisement of the situation. Furthermore, the people of this country are distant from the troubled areas of the earth and it is hard for them to comprehend the plight and consequent reactions of the long-suffering peoples of Europe and the effect of those reactions on their governments in connections with our efforts to promote peace in the world.

In considering the requirements for the rehabilitation of Europe, the physical loss of life, the visible destructions of cities, factories, mines and railroads was correctly estimated, but it has become obvious during recent months that this visible destruction was probably less serious than the dislocation of the entire fabric of European economy. For the past ten years conditions have been highly abnormal. The feverish preparation for war and the more feverish maintenance of the war effort engulfed all aspects of national economies. Machinery has fallen into disrepair or is entirely obsolete. Under the arbitrary and destructive Nazi rule, virtually every possible enterprise was geared into the German war machine. Long-standing commercial ties, private institutions, banks, insurance companies and shipping companies disappeared, through loss of capital, absorption through nationalization or by simple destruction. In many countries, confidence in the local currency has been severely shaken. The breakdown of the business structure of Europe during the war was complete. Recovery has been seriously retarded by the fact that two years after the close of hostilities a peace settlement with Germany and Austria has not been agreed upon. But even given a more prompt solution of these difficult problems, the rehabilitation of the economic structure of Europe quite evidently will require a much longer time and greater effort than had been foreseen.

There is a phase of this matter which is both interesting and serious. The farmer has always produced the foodstuffs to exchange with the city dweller for the other necessities of life. This division of labor is the basis of modern civilization. At the present time it is threatened with breakdown. The town and city industries are not producing adequate goods to exchange with the food-producing farmer. Raw materials and fuel are in short supply. Machinery, as I have said, is lacking or worn out. The farmer or the peasant cannot find the goods for sale which he desires to purchase. So the sale of his farm produce for money which he cannot use seems to him an unprofitable transaction. He, therefore, has withdrawn many fields from crop cultivation and is using them for grazing. He feeds more grain to stock and finds for himself and his family an ample supply of food, however short he may be on clothing and the other ordinary gadgets of civilization. Meanwhile people in the cities are short of food and fuel and in some places approaching starvation limits. So the governments are forced to use their foreign money and credits to procure these necessities abroad. This process exhausts funds which are urgently needed for reconstruction. Thus a very serious situation is rapidly developing which bodes no good for the world. The modern system of the division of labor upon which the exchange of products is based is in danger of breaking down.

The truth of the matter is that Europe's requirements for the next three or four years of foreign food and other essential products—principally from America—are so much greater than her present ability to pay that she must have substantial additional help, or face economic, social and political deterioration of a very grave character.

The remedy seems to lie in breaking the vicious circle and restoring the confidence of the people of Europe and the economic future of their own countries and of Europe as a whole. The manufacturer and the farmer throughout wide areas must be able and willing to exchange their products for currencies the continuing value of which is not open to question.

Aside from the demoralizing effect on the world at large and the possibilities of disturbances arising as a result of the desperation of the people concerned, the consequences to the economy of the United States should be apparent to all. It is logical that the United States should do whatever it is able to do to assist in the return of normal economic health in the world, without which there can be no political stability and no assured peace. Our policy is directed not against any country or doctrine but against hunger, poverty, desperation and chaos. Its purpose should be the revival of a working economy in the world so as to permit the emergence of political and social conditions in which free institutions can exist. Such assistance, I am convinced, must not be on a piecemeal basis as various crises develop. Any assistance that this Government may render in the future should provide a cure rather than a mere palliative. Any government that is willing to assist in the task of recovery will find full cooperation, I am sure, on the part of the United States Government. Any government which maneuvers to block the recovery of other countries cannot expect help from us. *(Applause)* Furthermore, governments, political parties or groups which seek to perpetuate human misery in order to profit therefrom politically or otherwise will encounter the opposition of the United States. *(Applause)*

It is already evident that, before the United States Government can proceed much further in its efforts to alleviate the situation and help start the European world on its way to recovery, there must be some agreement among the countries of Europe as to the requirements of the situation and the part those countries themselves will take in order to give proper effect to whatever action might be undertaken by this Government. It would be neither fitting nor efficacious for our Government to undertake to draw up unilaterally a program designed to place Europe on its feet economically. This is the business of the Europeans. The initiative, I think, must come from Europe. The role of this country should consist of friendly aid in the drafting of a European program and of later support of such a program so far as it may be practical for us to do so. The program should be a joint one, agreed to by a number, if not all European nations.

An essential part of any successful action on the part of the United States is an understanding on the part of the people of America of the character of the problem and the remedies to be applied. Political passion and prejudice should have no part. With foresight, and a willingness on the part of our people to face up to the vast responsibilities which history has clearly placed upon our country, the difficulties I have outlined can and will be overcome. I am sorry that on each occasion I have said something publicly in regard to our international situation, I have been forced by the necessities of the case to enter into rather technical discussions. But to my mind it is of vast importance that our people reach some general understanding of what the complications really are rather than react from a passion or a prejudice or an emotion of the moment. As I said more formally a moment ago, we are remote from the scene of these troubles. It is virtually impossible at this distance merely by reading or listening or even seeing photographs and motion pictures to grasp at all the real significance of the situation. Yet the whole world's future hangs on a proper judgment, it hangs, I think, to a large extent on the realization of the American people of just what are the very dominant factors, what are the reactions of the people, what are the justifications of those reactions, what are the sufferings, what is needed, what can best be done, what must be done. Thank you very much.

Acknowledgments

Grants for Research

Grants for the employment of research assistants, copying and typing, and travel for the preparation of this volume have come from the German Marshall Fund, the National Endowment for the Humanities, and the Mary W. Harriman Foundation. I drew on interviews and library materials collected for the George C. Marshall Research Library, supported by the work resulting from earlier grants by John D. Rockefeller, Jr., Mrs. John D. Rockefeller, Jr., the Rockefeller Brothers Fund, John Lee Pratt, Mrs. Oveta Culp Hobby, the Scaife Fund, the Old Dominion Fund, and the Ford Foundation.

General Marshall agreed to be interviewed and gave his papers to the George C. Marshall Research Foundation with the condition that no monetary returns from a book or books based on his materials would go to him or his family but would be used for the research program of the Marshall Foundation. In accordance, the trustees of the Foundation, in employing me to collect his papers and to write his authorized biography, asked that I waive the right to any royalties from the biography except royalties that I might receive for any work on Marshall privately written after I had completed the authorized biography. During the years I was with the Marshall Foundation, my salary was paid from grants. During the ten and one-half years that I was Director of the Dwight D. Eisenhower Institute for Historical Research, the National Museum of American History, Smithsonian Institution, I was permitted to work on this volume as part of my duties. Research assistants and typists, the cost of copying hundreds of thousands of documents from the National Archives and other sources for the George C. Marshall Research Library, and separate office space were paid for by nongovernmental sources. Much of the research and writing was done on my own time and I have received no payment for my services in revising the manuscript since my retirement. My wife has typed the final drafts of the manuscript as a gift to the Marshall Foundation and I have paid the expenses for a private office for more than two years.

All materials copied or obtained for my use in writing this book belong to the George C. Marshall Research Library, Lexington, Virginia, and will be available to scholars. A large part of the copying and annotating more than one and one-half million pages of records has been done over thirty years by a staff under my supervision. These materials make up a large part of the research holdings of the Marshall Library.

The Marshall Foundation

The Marshall Foundation, which holds title to the personal papers and artifacts donated by General and Mrs. Marshall and friends, and the papers and books

529

collected by the Foundation, was founded in Lexington, Virginia, in 1953 under the presidency of Mr. John C. Hagan. Shortly thereafter, an advisory board headed by Robert A. Lovett was formed to give advice to the trustees under Mr. Hagan. I was employed by the Foundation first as Director of the George C. Marshall Research Center, and later as Director of the George C. Marshall Library and the Executive Director of the Marshall Foundation. In 1959, General Omar N. Bradley became President of the Marshall Foundation. Mr. Lovett became Chairman of the Marshall Foundation, a title which he held until 1985, a year before his death. In 1969, Lieutenant General Marshall S. Carter succeeded General Bradley as President. In the fall of 1974, Ambassador Fred L. Hadsel succeeded me as Director of the Library. In the summer of 1985, Ross R. Millhiser became Chairman of the Foundation and Ambassador Gordon Beyer was selected to fill the combined position of President of the Foundation and Director of the Library. Most of this volume was written and submitted to the publisher during the tenure of General Carter and Ambassador Hadsel, but I have had the full support of Mr. Millhiser and Ambassador Beyer during the final revising. Royster Lyle, Jr., and Gerald L. Nay served as deputy directors under Ambassador Hadsel.

Howard C. Petersen, Forrest C. Pogue, Benjamin H. Powell, Jr., 2nd Lieut. David E. Quantock, George P. Ramsey, Jr., W. Thomas Rice, Gen. Matthew B. Ridgway, Lynda Johnson Robb, Mary G. Roebling, William P. Rogers, Dean Rusk, Maj. Gen. Charles E. Saltzman, William J. Schieffelin III, Isadore M. Scott, Lt. Gen. Brent Scowcroft, Lt. Gen. George R. E. Shell, James R. Shepley, William E. Simon, Lt. Gen. DeWitt C. Smith, Jr., Elmer B. Staats, Wallace Stettinius, George A. Stinson, Capt. Kathryn Stone, Capt. Steven W. Swann, Gen. Maxwell D. Taylor, Gen. James A. Van Fleet, Cyrus R. Vance, Gen. Sam S. Walker, Thomas J. Watson, Jr., Langbourne M. Williams, John D. Wilson, Morton M. Winston.

Inasmuch as I left the Marshall Library in the summer of 1974 to go to the Smithsonian Institution, I have not had day-by-day contact with the Lexington staff. Therefore, I wish to thank through Fred Hadsel and now Gordon Beyer the members of their staffs. However, I wish to thank those who worked for me there over part or all of an eighteen-year period and have been there during part or all of the writing of this volume. These members include Royster Lyle, Jr., my assistants, Mrs. Boyd Stuart, Mrs. Bryan Tolley, Hughey Johnson, Jorge Piercey, and Ted Camper. Marguerite Old, and the late Mrs. Henry A. Wise, who as a volunteer, indexed articles for me and made summaries of *Congressional Record* debates pertaining to the European Recovery Program. I have received assistance on the book from Archivist Anthony Crawford and his successor, John Jacob. In his search for documents for the Marshall Papers project, Larry Bland has brought important material to my attention. During the period that she worked as librarian at the Marshall Library, Mrs. Barbara Vandegrift conducted a valuable interview with BBC correspondent Leonard Miall, and got an article by Miall pertaining to his broadcast of the Marshall Plan speech.

In the Arlington Marshall project, centered in my office here, where research on the book and writing were coordinated, Mrs. Dorothy Dean typed the final draft of Volume II, all of the drafts of Volume III, and all of the early drafts of Volume IV. She also kept track of my books and papers. Working in that office and in the National Archives were my research associates, Sidney W. Lowery, an expert on Eastern Europe, and James S. Nanney, an expert on Russian history.

While working on research materials for my use, they also helped find and select a much larger body of material for the Marshall Library. Lowery, who worked for me some seven years, found and brought together material on such topics as the recognition of Israel, Universal Military Training, the battle for the European Recovery Program, negotiations for the North Atlantic Treaty, Marshall and Greece, and the like. When I found it necessary to reduce my coverage of the Mission to China by almost half, Lowery helped with the difficult task of making the footnotes agree with the new text. He also found original documents to correlate with my chapters on the Korean War, based on secondary sources. Nanney, working for a shorter time, focused mainly on matters involving Germany and negotiations with the Soviets. He made available to me his paper on U.S. military aid to China in the period covered by this volume. He translated a number of Russian speeches and articles for my use. He also gathered material on such topics as the Bogotá riots and Marshall and Intelligence. Both associates worked briefly in files at the Marshall Library and at the U.S. Military History Institute, and found books for me in the Pentagon Library, the Martin Luther King, Jr., Library in Washington, and the Aurora Hills branch of the Arlington Library. Lowery completed a research project I began at the Hoover Institution Library and reviewed a number of interviews that I had borrowed from the Truman Library as well as checking taped-recorded reels of interviews from the Dulles Collection at Princeton University.

Smithsonian Institution

I wish to express my gratitude to the Secretary of the Smithsonian during almost all of my stay there, S. Dillon Ripley; to the Directors and acting directors of the National Museum of History and Technology (later of American History); to Daniel Boorstin, who persuaded me to go there; Silvio Bedini, who signed the contract; and Directors Brooke Hindle, Otto Mayr, and Roger Kennedy, under whom I worked. I am grateful to them and to my executive assistant at the Eisenhower Institute, James S. Hutchins, and to Mrs. Barbara Lane my secretary. I also profited from the advice and information offered by curators of that period, Philip K. Lundeberg, Harold Langley, Donald Kloster, Craddock Goins. At the Woodrow Wilson International Center, where I was an adjunct Fellow for three years, I was often invited to seminars and lectures on international relations by the director, James Billington, and head of the National Security Institute, Sam Wells, Jr.

National Archives

Members of my archival and research staff worked in the Federal Record Center in Alexandria until the Army collections were moved to the National Archives, where they were located during the writing of this book. I wish to thank directors James Bertram Rhoads, head of the Archives during much of the period, Robert Warner, and Frank Burke, acting director in recent months. Research on this volume was assisted by Robert Wolfe, Edward Reese, William C. Cunliffe, Terry Hammett, and Milton Gustafson.

Libraries

The single most helpful library outside of the Marshall Library was the Harry S. Truman Library headed by Benedict O. Zobrist. My contacts began there before the Library was finished, when I talked with President Truman at his office in the Federal Reserve Building, Kansas City, and with Philip Lagferquist and James Fuchs at the incompleted Library, and then continued with the late Director, Philip Brooks. I drew heavily on help in the research files on Dennis Bilger. Others who aided me were Elizabeth Shafly, Harry Clark, Warren Ohrvall, George Curtis, John Curry. They have cheerfully aided me during many visits there and have made material available by mail.

The Franklin D. Roosevelt Library and the Dwight D. Eisenhower Library yielded fewer materials for my purposes, but William Emerson and John Wickman and their staffs have fully cooperated. At Carlisle Barracks, the U. S. Army Research Institute has helped me in many ways. Richard Sommers, Archivist, and the staff were particularly helpful. I received assistance over a long period at the Special Collections Library at Yale University in regard to the Henry L. Stimson Diary and his papers. At Princeton University, I was well received in the John Foster Dulles Collection.

Other libraries, where I have worked for shorter periods of time, but have always received a splendid reception, are the New York Historical Society, the Maryland Historical Society, and the Hoover Institution. Locally, I used some of the manuscript collections at the Library of Congress, the Dr. Martin Luther King, Jr., Library, Washington, the Aurora Hills branch of the Arlington County Library, and the Smithsonian Library branch in the National Museum of American History, which borrowed many volumes for me. I am particularly grateful to the late Louis Starr and Elizabeth Mason of the Columbia University Library's Oral History Collection.

I owe special thanks to the staff of the Public Record Office, Kew, where I did research during five visits over a period of years. I especially appreciate the effort they took to show me the mysteries of computers and the care they took with my orders for copies of documents.

I have drawn on the resources of the Pentagon Library during the years I worked in the Pentagon on other historical projects and throughout the years of the Marshall project. The director during most of my research on this volume was Mrs. Mary L. Shaffer. During much of that time my wife, Christine, who was a member of the staff, served as messenger to bring books for my use.

Government Historical Offices

The Marshall project has benefited enormously from the good wishes and cooperation of the various historical sections of the armed forces. During the writing of this volume, I have had the advice and assistance of Dr. Alfred Goldberg, Defense Department Historian. I read the manuscript of Stephen Reardon's history of the Defense Department in its early development and then Doris Condit's early work on the Defense Department under Marshall and Lovett. In both cases, I was one of a rather large panel, made up of historians and former officials, who read the draft chapters and discussed the actual story of the period. In the Historical Office of the Joint Chiefs of Staff, I have been aided by various historians: Dr. Robert J. Watson, Vernon Davis, Helen Bailey, Kenneth Condit, Walter Poole, James Schnabel, and others.

With a close personal connection with the Historical Section (now the Center of Military History) of the Department of The Army that extends directly back to 1944, I have known personally most of the historians of that organization and have served on the advisory committees of the Center and of its U.S. Army Military History Institute. While writing this volume, I worked closely with the Chief of Military History, Brigadier General James L. Collins, Jr., with the Chief Historians, Maurice Matloff and David Trask, with deputies Robert W. Coakley and Charles B. MacDonald and librarian Hanna Zeidlik. I especially wish to thank the Archivist of the U.S. Army Military History Institute, Carlisle Barracks, Pennsylvania, Richard Sommers.

I have also worked closely with the Office of Naval History and the Office of Air Force History and served on their advisory boards. In the Navy Department, I worked with Vice Admiral Edwin Hooper and Rear Admiral John Kane, and with Senior Historian Dean Allard. In the Air Force, I worked with Stanley Falk, who for a time held the positions of Director of the Office and of Chief Historian, Major General John Huston, Director, and Richard Kohn, who holds both jobs.

On Marine Corps activities, I received help from the Director of the Marine Corps Historical Center, Edwin H. Simmons, and members of his staff, Henry I.

Shaw, Jr., and Benis M. Frank. From Richard A. Baker, Director, Senate Historical Office, and his deputy, Donald A. Ritchie, I received material on Senate Hearings and committee staff activities.

Official Records

As the footnotes indicate, I have drawn heavily on the State Department's Foreign Relations volumes. I found many of the original papers in Marshall's own files, and I directed the copying of thousands of pages more. In those cases where the papers were later published in official volumes, I have keyed footnotes to those sources.

Assistance on Interviews in Taiwan

In 1977, I traveled to Taiwan and the United Kingdom, France, Germany, Holland, Norway, Denmark, and Italy with a grant from the National Endowment for the Humanities. Original arrangements were made in Taipei by James Huskey, an American student then doing research in Taiwan. Later Dr. Chin-tung Liang of St. John's University alerted Chang Chun, senior adviser to the Government of Taiwan. During my stay, the Government furnished me with the services of an interpreter and guide, Johnny Sand, a car and driver, and arranged for a special luncheon and dinner as well as paying the hotel bill. As a result, the money in the original grant was sufficient to pay for my interviews in western Europe.

To my publisher, I am indebted for patience and understanding during the lengthy period when I was carrying out other major responsibilities while trying to write this biography. Alan Williams and Daniel Frank won my friendship while working on this last volume. The writing was started under the editorship of Alan Williams, who gave occasional encouragement and advice. When I turned in the first draft, he had just left for another position. Daniel Frank and I have worked well together. Dan proposed the rearrangement of some chapters, the pruning of others, the dropping of sections not pertinent to this volume, and the brightening of some dull passages. I have profited greatly from his advice.

Above all, I am eternally indebted to my wife, Christine, who shared the frustrations of a harassed author who alienated old friends and associates by repeatedly refusing invitations. She managed to endure bouts of rudeness and bad temper when she made suggestions for bettering the book. For careful typing of the final version of this book, for catching errors, for numerous good suggestions, and for restoring my sense of humor and proportion, I express my fondest thanks.

With this volume, I complete a project begun more than thirty years ago in the summer of 1956 to collect Marshall's papers, interview him and several hundred associates, and write four volumes on his life and times. If I count a year I spent in 1943–44 as assistant to the historian of Second Army, a year as a combat historian, Europe, 1944–45, nearly seven years as an Army historian in Paris and Frankfurt and the War Department, I can add an extra ten years to my work in Marshall's papers. However the years are counted, the acquaintanceship with the General has enriched my life.

Forrest C. Pogue
Arlington, Virginia

Selected Bibliography

Acheson, Dean. *Sketches from Life of Men I Have Known.* New York: Harper, 1961.
———. *Present at the Creation: My Years in the State Department.* New York: W. W. Norton, 1969.
———. *Morning and Noon.* Boston: Little, Brown, 1965.
———. *The Korean War.* New York: W. W. Norton, 1971.
Alphand, Hervé. *L'etonnement d'être. Journal, 1939–1973.* Paris: Fayard, 1973.
Alvarez, David J. *Bureaucracy and Cold War Diplomacy: The United States and Turkey, 1943–1946.* Thessaloniki: Institute for Balkan Studies, 1980.
Alperovitz, Gar. *Atomic Diplomacy: Hiroshima and Potsdam.* New York: Vintage, 1965.
Ambrose, Stephen E. *Eisenhower: Soldier, General of the Army, President-Elect, 1890–1952.* New York: Simon and Schuster, 1983.
———. *Eisenhower: President and Elder Statesman, 1952–69.* New York: Simon and Schuster, 1984.
———. *Rise to Globalism: American Foreign Policy Since 1938.* New York: Viking Penguin, 1976.
Appleman, Roy E. *South to the Naktong, North to the Yalu.* Washington: Department of the Army, 1961.
Arkes, Hadley. *Bureaucracy, the Marshall Plan, and the National Interest.* Princeton: Princeton University, 1972.
Arnold, G. L. *The Pattern of World Conflict.* New York: Dial, 1955.
Attlee, Clement. *Twilight of Empire. Memoirs of Prime Minister Clement Attlee.* New York: A. S. Barnes, 1962.
Azcarate, Pablo de. *Mission in Palestine, 1948–1952.* Washington: Middle East Institute, 1966.
Backer, John H. *Priming the German Economy, American Occupational Policies, 1945–1948.* Durham: Duke University, 1971.
———. *The Decision to Divide Germany, American Foreign Policy in Transition.* Durham: Duke University, 1978.
———. *Winds of History; the German Years of Lucius DuBignon Clay.* New York: Van Nostrand Reinhold Company, 1983.
Bader, William B. *Austria Between East and West, 1945–1955.* Stanford, Ca.: Stanford University, 1966.
Balfour, Michael. *Four-Power Control in Germany, 1945–46.* London: Oxford University, 1956.
Ball, Mary M. *NATO and the European Union Movement.* New York: Praeger, 1959.
Barkley, Alben W. *That Reminds Me.* Garden City, N.Y.: Doubleday, 1954.
Barnet, Richard J. and Marcus G. Raskin. *After 20 Years: Alternatives to the Cold War in Europe.* New York: Random House, 1965.
Barnett, A. Doak. *China on the Eve of Communist Takeover.* New York: Praeger, 1963.

535

Barrett, David D. *Dixie Mission: The United States Army Observer Group in Yenan, 1944.* Berkeley: Center for Chinese Studies, University of California, 1970.

Bayley, Edwin R. *Joe McCarthy and the Press.* New York: Pantheon Books, 1981.

Beal, John R. *Marshall in China.* Garden City, N.Y.: Doubleday, 1970.

Beer, Francis A. *Integration and Disintegration in NATO.* Columbus: Ohio State University, 1969.

Beloff, Max. *The United States and the Unity of Europe.* Washington: Brookings Institution, 1963.

Bernstein, Barton J. and Allen J. Matusow. *The Truman Administration: A Documentary History.* New York: Harper and Row, 1966.

Bernstein, Barton J., ed. *Politics and Policies of the Truman Administration.* Chicago: Quadrangle, 1970.

——. *The Atomic Bomb, the Critical Issues.* Boston: Little, Brown, 1976.

——. "Roosevelt, Truman and the Atomic Bomb; A Reinterpretation." *Pol. Sci. Quarterly,* V. 90, no. 1. Spring 1975, 23–69.

Beugel, Ernst Hans van der. *From Marshall Aid to Atlantic Partnership: European Integration as a Concern of American Foreign Policy.* New York: Elsevier, 1966.

Bloomfield, Lincoln Palmer. *The United Nations and U.S. Foreign Policy: A New Look at the National Interest.* Rev. ed. Boston: Little, Brown, 1967.

Blumenson, Martin. *Mark Clark; the Last of the Great World War II Commanders.* New York: Congdon and Weed, 1984.

Bohlen, Charles E. *The Transformation of American Foreign Policy.* New York: W. W. Norton, 1969.

——. *Witness to History, 1929–1969.* New York: W. W. Norton, 1973.

Boorman, Howard L. and Richard C. Howard, eds. *Biographical Dictionary of Republican China.* 4 v. New York: Columbia University, 1967–1971.

Bradley, Omar N. and Clay Blair. *A General's Life.* New York: Simon and Schuster, 1983.

Brandt, Conrad with Benjamin Schwartz and John K. Fairbank. *A Documentary History of Chinese Communism.* Cambridge: Harvard University, 1968.

Browder, Robert P. and Thomas G. Smith. *Independent, a Biography of Lewis W. Douglas.* New York: Alfred Knopf, 1986.

Buchan, Alastair Francis and Philip Windsor. *Arms and Stability in Europe.* New York: Praeger, 1963.

Buckley, William F., Jr. and L. Brent Bozell. *McCarthy and His Enemies.* Chicago: Regnery, 1954.

Buhite, Russell D. *Patrick J. Hurley and American Foreign Policy.* Ithaca, N.Y.: Cornell University, 1973.

Bullock, Alan. *Ernest Bevin, Foreign Secretary, 1945–1951.* New York: W. W. Norton, 1983.

Bundy, McGeorge. *The Pattern of Responsibility.* Boston: Houghton Mifflin, 1952.

Burnham, James. *Containment of Liberalism? An Inquiry into the Aims of United States Foreign Policy.* New York: Day, 1953.

Burns, Richard Dean, comp. *Harry S. Truman: A Bibliography of His Times and Presidency,* compiled for the Harry S. Truman Library Institute. Wilmington, Del.: Scholarly Resources, Inc., 1984.

Burrows, Sir Bernard and Christopher Irwin. *The Security of Western Europe: Towards a Common Defense Policy.* London: Charles Knight, 1972.

Byrnes, James F. *Speaking Frankly.* New York: Harper, 1947.

——. *All in One Lifetime.* New York: Harper, 1958.

Cagle, Malcolm W. and Frank A. Manson. *The Sea War in Korea.* Annapolis: U.S. Naval Institute, 1957.

Campbell, John K. and Philip Sherrard. *Modern Greece.* New York: Praeger, 1968.

Caraley, Demetrios. *The Politics of Military Unification: A Study of Conflict and the Policy Process.* New York: Columbia University, 1966.

Caute, David. *The Great Fear: the Anti-Communist Purge Under Truman and Eisenhower.* New York: Simon and Schuster, 1978.

Chan, F. Gilbert, ed. *China at the Crossroads: Nationalists and Communists, 1927–1949.* Boulder, Colo.: Westview, 1980.

Chang, Carsun. *The Third Force in China.* New York: Bookman, 1952.

Chassin, Lionel Max. *The Communist Conquest of China.* Cambridge, Mass.: Harvard University, 1965.

Ch'en, Jerome. *Mao and the Chinese Revolution.* London: Oxford University, 1967.

Chiang-Kai-shek. *Soviet Russia in China.* New York: Farrar, Strauss and Cudahy, 1957.

Clay, Lucius D. *Decision in Germany.* Garden City, N.Y.: Doubleday, 1950.

Cleveland, Harlan. *NATO: The Transatlantic Bargain.* New York: Harper and Row, 1970.

Cline, Ray S. *Secrets, Spies and Scholars; the Essential CIA.* Washington: Acropolis Books, 1976.

Clogg, Richard. *A Short History of Modern Greece.* Cambridge, Mass.: Cambridge University, 1979.

Clubb, O. Edmund. *Twentieth Century China.* New York: Columbia University, 1964.
——. *China and Russia, The "Great Game."* New York: Columbia University, 1971.

Cohen, Warren I. *America's Response to China: An Interpretative History of Sino-American Relations.* New York: John Wiley, 1971.
——. *Dean Rusk.* Totowa, N.J.: Cooper Square, 1980.
——. *New Features in American-East Asia Relations; Essays Presented to Dorothy Borg.* New York: Columbia University, 1983.

Collier, Basil. *The War in the Far East, 1941–1945: A Military History.* New York: Morrow, 1969.

Collier, Richard. *Bridge Across the Sky, The Berlin Blockade and Airlift: 1948–1949.* New York: McGraw Hill, 1978.

Collins, J. Lawton. *Lightning Joe, an Autobiography.* Baton Rouge, La.: Louisiana State University, 1979.
——. *War In Peacetime. The History and Lessons of Korea.* Boston: Houghton Mifflin, 1969.

Condit, Kenneth W. *The Joint Chiefs of Staff and National Policy, 1947–1949.* V. II, parts 1 and 2. Washington: JCS, 1976.

Cook, Fred J. *The Nightmare Decade: the Life and Times of Senator Joe McCarthy.* New York: Random House, 1971.

Cox, Midshipman 1stcl Samuel J. "U.S. Naval Strategy and Foreign Policy in China, 1945–50." (Trident Scholar Project Report 105). U. S. Naval Academy, Annapolis, 1980.

Crosby, Donald F. *God, Church, and Flag; Senator Joseph R. McCarthy and the Catholic Church, 1950–1957.* Chapel Hill: University of North Carolina, 1978.

Crossman, Richard H. S. *A Nation Reborn: The Israel of Weizmann, Bevin, and Ben Gurion.* London: Hamish Hamilton, 1960.

Crozier, Brian. *The Man Who Lost China.* New York: Scribner's, 1976.

Cummings, Bruce. *The Origins of the Korean War; Liberation and the Emergence of Separate Regimes, 1945–47.* Princeton: Princeton University, 1981.

Curry, George. *James F. Byrnes.* New York: Cooper Square Publishers, 1965.

Daniels, Jonathan. *The Man of Independence.* New York: J. B. Lippincott, 1950.

Davies, John Paton, Jr. *Dragon by the Tail.* New York: W. W. Norton, 1972.

Davis, Vincent. *Postwar Defense Policy and the U. S. Navy, 1942–46.* Chapel Hill: University of North Carolina, 1966.

Davison, Walter F. *The Berlin Blockade: A Study in Cold War Politics.* Princeton: Princeton University, 1958.

De Santis, Hugh. *The Diplomacy of Silence: The American Foreign Service, the Soviet Union, and the Cold War, 1933–1947.* Chicago: University of Chicago, 1981.

Donovan, Robert J. *Conflict and Crisis: The Presidency of Harry S. Truman, 1945–1948.* New York: W. W. Norton, 1977.

——. *Tumultuous Years; the Presidency of Harry S. Truman, 1949–1953.* New York: W. W. Norton, 1982.

Dulles, Eleanor L. *One Germany or Two: The Struggle at the Heart of Europe.* Stanford: Hoover Institution, 1970.

Dulles, Foster R. *American Policy Toward Communist China, 1949–1969.* New York: Thomas Crowell, 1972.

——. *The American Red Cross. A History.* New York: Harper, 1950.

——. *China and America: The Story of Their Relations Since 1784.* Princeton: Princeton University, 1946.

Dulles, John F. *War or Peace.* New York: Macmillan, 1950.

Ebban, Abba. *My People: The Story of the Jews.* New York: Behrman House and Random House, 1968.

——. *An Autobiography.* New York: Random House, 1977.

Eden, Anthony. *The Memoirs of Anthony Eden: Full Circle.* Boston: Houghton Mifflin, 1960.

——. *The Reckoning.* Boston: Houghton Mifflin, 1965.

Etzold, Thomas H. and John Lewis Gaddis (eds.) *Containment: Documents on American Policy and Strategy, 1945–1950.* New York: Columbia University, 1978.

Fairbank, John K. *Chinabound; a Fifty Year Memoir.* New York: Harper and Row, 1982.

——. *The United States and China.* Cambridge, Mass.: Harvard University, 1948.

Fearey, Robert A. *The Occupation of Japan: Second Phase, 1948–50.* New York: Macmillan, 1950.

Feis, Herbert. *The China Tangle.* Princeton: Princeton University, 1953.

——. *The Atomic Bomb and the End of World War II.* Princeton: Princeton University, 1966.

——. *The Birth of Israel: The Tousled Diplomatic Bed.* New York: W. W. Norton, 1969.

——. *From Trust to Terror.* New York: W. W. Norton, 1970.

Ferrell, Robert H., *George C. Marshall, 1947–1949.* V. XV. New York: Cooper Square, 1966.

——. *Off the Record, The Private Papers of Harry S. Truman.* New York: Harper and Row, 1980.

——. *The Eisenhower Diaries.* New York: W. W. Norton, 1981.

Field, James A., Jr. *History of United States Naval Operations, Korea.* Washington: U.S. Naval History Division, 1962.

Fitzgerald, Charles P. *The Birth of Communist China.* Rev. and enl. ed. New York: Praeger, 1966.

Forrestal, James. *The Forrestal Diaries.* Edited by Walter Millis. New York: Viking, 1951.

Frederica, Queen of the Hellenes. *A Measure of Understanding.* New York: Viking, 1971.

Freeland, Richard M. *The Truman Doctrine and the Origins of McCarthyism.* New York: Alfred A. Knopf, 1975.

Futrell, Robert F. *United States Air Forces in Korea, 1950–1953.* New York: Duell, Sloan and Pearce, 1961.

Gaddis, John L. *The United States and the Origins of the Cold War, 1941–1947.* New York: Columbia University, 1972.

——. *Strategies of Containment; a Critical Appraisal of Postwar American National Security Policy.* New York: Oxford University, 1982.

Ganin, Zvi. *Truman, American Jewry, and Israel, 1945–1948.* New York: Holmes and Meier, 1979.

Gardner, Lloyd O. *Architects of Illusion, Men and Ideas in American Foreign Policy, 1941–1949.* Chicago: Quadrangle, 1970.

Gellman, Barton. *Contending with Kennan; Toward a Philosophy of American Power.* New York: Praeger, 1984.

Gerson, Louis L. *John Foster Dulles, 1953–1959.* V. XVII. New York: Cooper Square, 1968.

Gimbel, John. *The American Occupation of Germany: Politics and the Military, 1945–1949.* Stanford: Stanford University, 1968.

——. *The Origins of the Marshall Plan.* Stanford: Stanford University, 1976.

Gladwyn, Lord. *Memoirs of Lord Gladwyn.* New York: Weybright and Tilly, 1972.

Gittings, John. *The Role of the Chinese Army.* London: Oxford University, 1967.

Glubb, Sir John Bagot. *A Soldier with the Arabs.* New York: Harper, 1957.

Goldmann, Nahum. *Autobiography.* New York: Holt, Rinehart and Winston, 1969.

Gottlieb, Manuel. *The German Peace Settlement and the Berlin Crisis.* New York: Paine-Whitman, 1960.

Goulden, Joseph C. *Korea. The Untold Story of the War.* New York: Times Books, 1982.

Groves, Leslie R. *Now It Can Be Told.* New York: Harper, 1962.

Gugeler, Russell A. *Combat Cations in Korea.* Washington: Department of the Army, 1970.

Guillermaz, Jacques. *A History of the Chinese Communist Party, 1921–1949.* New York: Random House, 1972.

Hadley, Arthur T. *The Straw Giant. Triumph and Failure: American Armed Forces.* New York: Random House, 1986

Halle, Louis J. *The Cold War as History.* New York: Harper and Row, 1967.

Hallstein, Walter. *Europe in the Making.* New York: W. W. Norton, 1972.

Hamby, Alonzo L. *Beyond the New Deal: Harry S. Truman and American Liberalism.* New York: Columbia University, 1973.

Hammond, Thomas T., ed. *Witnesses to the Origins of the Cold War.* Seattle, Washington: University of Washington, 1982.

Harriman, W. Averell *Peace with Russia?* New York: Simon and Schuster, 1959.

——. *America and Russia in a Changing World; a Half Century of Personal Observation.* Garden City, N.Y.: Doubleday, 1971.

—— and Elie Abel. *Special Envoy to Churchill and Stalin, 1941–1946.* New York: Random House, 1975.

Harris, Seymour B. *The European Recovery Program.* Cambridge, Mass.: Harvard University, 1948.

Haynes, Richard F. *The Awesome Power: Harry S. Truman as Commander in Chief.* Baton Rouge, La.: Louisiana State University, 1973.

Head, William P. *America's China Sojourn: American Foreign Policy and Its Effect on*

Sino-American Relationships, 1942–1948. Lanham, Md.: University Press of America, 1983.

Hechler, Ken. *Working with Truman; a Personal Memoir of the White House Years.* New York: Putnam's, 1982.

Heller, Francis H., ed. *The Korean War; a 25-Year Perspective.* (Papers of a Harry S. Truman Institute Conference in 1975). Lawrence, Kan.: Regents Press of Kansas, 1977.

Herken, Gregg. *The Atomic Bomb in the Cold War, 1945–1950.* New York: Alfred A. Knopf, 1980.

Hermes, Walter G. *Truce Tent and Fighting Front.* Washington: Department of the Army, 1966.

Higgins, Trumbull. *Korea and the Fall of MacArthur, A Precis in Limited War.* New York: Oxford University, 1960.

Hinton, Harold C. *China's Turbulent Quest.* Rev. ed. Bloomington, Ind.: Indiana University, 1972.

Holley, I. B., Jr. *General John M. Palmer, Citizen Soldiers, and the Army of a Democracy.* Westport, Conn.: Greenwood, 1982.

Ho, Ping-ti and Tang Tsou, eds. *China's Crisis, China's Heritage and the Communist Political System.* 2v. Chicago: University of Chicago, 1968.

Hsiung, S. I. *The Life of Chiang Kai-shek.* London: Peter Davies, 1948.

Huntington, Samuel P. *The Soldier and The State. The Theory and Politics of Civil-Military Relations.* Cambridge: Harvard University, 1957.

Hurewitz, J. C. *The Struggle for Palestine.* New York: W. W. Norton, 1950.

——. *Diplomacy in the Near and Middle East: A Documentary Record.* 2 v. Princeton, N.J.: Van Nostrand, 1956.

Ireland, Timothy P. *Creating the Entangling Alliance; the Origins of the North Atlantic Treaty Organization.* Westport, Conn.: Greenwood, 1981.

Iriye, Akira. *Power and Culture: The Japanese-American War, 1941–1945.* Cambridge, Mass.: Harvard University, 1981.

Isaacson, Walter and Evan Thomas. *The Wise Men. Six Friends and the World They Made. Acheson, Bohlen, Harriman, Kennan, Lovett, McCloy.* New York: Simon and Schuster, 1986.

Ismay, Lord. *NATO: The First Five Years, 1949–1954.* Paris: North Atlantic Treaty Organization, 1954.

James, D. Clayton. *The Years of MacArthur, 1941–1945.* v.II. Boston: Houghton Mifflin, 1975.

——. *The Years of MacArthur: Triumph and Disaster, 1945–1964.* v. III. Boston: Houghton Mifflin, 1985.

Jessup, Philip C. *The Birth of Nations.* New York: Columbia University, 1974.

Jones, Joseph M. *The Fifteen Weeks.* New York: Viking, 1955.

Jones, Vincent C. *Manhattan: The Army and the Atomic Bomb.* Washington: GPO, 1985.

Kahn, E. J., Jr. *Harvard: Through Change and Through Storm.* New York: W. W. Norton, 1969.

——. *The China Hands.* New York: Viking, 1972.

Kaplan, Lawrence S. *A Community of Interests: NATO and the Military Assistance Program, 1948–1951.* Washington: USGPO, 1980.

——. *The United States and NATO; the Formative Years.* Lexington, Ky.: University Press of Kentucky, 1984.

Kennan, George F. *American Diplomacy, 1900–1950.* New York: Mentor, 1950.

——. *On Dealing with the Communist World.* New York: Harper and Row, 1964.

——. *Memoirs* (1925–1950). Boston: Little, Brown, 1967.

Kirk, George. *The Middle East, 1945–1950.* London: Oxford University, 1954.

Knorr, Klaus Eugen, ed. *NATO and American Security.* Princeton: Princeton University, 1959.

Koen, Ross Y. *The China Lobby in American Politics.* New York: Macmillan, 1960.

Kolko, Gabriel. *The Politics of War: The World and United States Foreign Policy, 1943–1945.* New York: Random House, 1969.

—— and Joyce Kolko. *The Limits of Power: The World and United States Foreign Policy, 1945–1954.* New York: Harper and Row, 1972.

Korbel, Josef. *The Communist Subversion of Czechoslovakia, 1938–1948.* Princeton: Princeton University, 1959.

Kousoulas, Dimitrios G. *Revolution and Defeat, The Story of the Greek Communist Party.* New York: Oxford University, 1965.

Kubek, Anthony. *How the Far East Was Lost, American Policy and the Creation of Communist China.* Chicago: Regnery, 1963.

Kublick, Bruce. *American Policy and the Division of Germany, The Clash with Russia over Reparations.* Ithaca, N.Y.: Cornell University, 1972.

Kuniholm, Bruce R. *The Origins of the Cold War in the Near East.* Princeton: Princeton University, 1980.

Kurzman, Dan. *Genesis 1948: The First Israeli-Arab War.* Cleveland, Ohio: World, 1970.

La Feber, Walter. *America, Russia, and the Cold War, 1945–1975.* 3rd ed. New York: John Wiley, 1976.

Leonhard, Wolfgang. *Child of the Revolution.* Chicago: Regnery, 1958.

Liang, Chin-tung. *General Stilwell in China, 1942–1944: The Full Story.* New York: St. John's University, 1972.

Lichterman, Martin. "To Yalu and Back," in *American Civil-Military Decisions.* Edited by Harold Stein. New York: The Twentieth Century Fund, 1963.

Lie, Trygve. *In the Cause of Peace.* New York: Macmillan, 1954.

Lilienthal, Alfred. *What Price Israel?* Chicago: Regnery, 1953.

——. *The Zionist Connection.* New York: Dodd, Mead, 1978.

Lilienthal, David E. 5 v. *Journals.* New York: Harper and Row, 1965.

Lippmann, Walter. *The Cold War: A Study in U.S. Foreign Policy.* New York: Harper and Row, 1972.

Litvinoff, Barnet. *Weizmann, Last of the Patriarchs.* New York: Putnam's, 1976.

Liu, F. F. *A Military History of Modern China, 1924–1949.* Princeton: Princeton University, 1956.

Louis, William R. and Robert W. Stookey, eds. *The End of the Palestine Mandate.* Austin, Texas: University of Texas, 1986.

Lukacs, John A. *A History of the Cold War.* Garden City, N.Y.: Doubleday, 1961.

MacArthur, Douglas. *Reminiscences.* New York: McGraw-Hill, 1964.

Maddox, Robert J. *The New Left and the Origins of the Cold War.* Princeton: Princeton University, 1973.

Manchester, William. *American Caesar: Douglas MacArthur, 1880–1964.* Boston: Little, Brown, 1978.

Mandelbaum, Michael. *The Nuclear Revolution: International Politics Before and After Hiroshima.* New York: Cambridge University, 1981.

Martin, John B. *Adlai Stevenson of Illinois.* Garden City, N.Y.: Doubleday, 1976.

——. *Adlai Stevenson and the World.* Garden City, N.Y.: Doubleday, 1977.

Masiny, Vojtech. *Russia's Road to the Cold War.* New York: Columbia University, 1979.

Matthews, Kenneth. *Memories of a Mountain War: Greece, 1944–1949*. London: Longman, 1972.

May, Gary. *China Scapegoat: The Diplomatic Ordeal of John Carter Vincent*. Washington: New Republic, 1979.

Mazuzan, George T. *Warren R. Austin at the U.N., 1946–1953*. Kent, Ohio: Kent State University, 1977.

McCagg, William O., Jr. *Stalin Embattled, 1943–1948*. Detroit: Wayne State University, 1978.

McCarthy, Joseph R. *America's Retreat from Victory: The Story of George Catlett Marshall*. New York: Devin-Adair, 1951.

McCloy, John J. *The Atlantic Alliance, Its Origin and Its Future*. New York: Columbia University, 1969.

McDonald, James G. *My Mission in Israel*. New York: Simon and Schuster, 1951.

McLellan, David S. *Dean Acheson, the State Department Years*. New York: Dodd, Mead, 1976.

McNeill, William H. *America, Britain, and Russia: Their Cooperation and Conflict, 1941–1946*. London: Oxford University, 1953.

———. *The Greek Dilemma: War and Aftermath*. London: Gollancz, 1947.

Mee, Charles L., Jr. *The Marshall Plan; the Launching of the Pax Americana*. New York: Simon and Schuster, 1984.

Meir, Golda. *My Life*. New York: Putnam's, 1975.

Melby, John F. *The Mandate of Heaven (China 1945–1949)*. Toronto: University of Toronto, 1968.

Messer, Robert L. *The End of an Alliance: James F. Byrnes, Roosevelt, Truman, and the Origins of the Cold War*. Chapel Hill: University of North Carolina, 1982.

Middleton, Drew. *The Atlantic Community: A Study in Unity and Disunity*. New York: McKay, 1965.

Miles, Milton E. *A Different Kind of War*. Garden City, N.Y.: Doubleday, 1967.

Miller, Merle. *Plain Speaking: An Oral Biography of Harry S. Truman*. New York: Barkley-Putnam, 1973.

Millis, Walter, with Harvey G. Mansfield and Harold Stein. *Arms and the State: Civil-Military Elements in National Policy*. New York: The Twentieth Century Fund, 1958.

Milward, Alan S. *The Reconstruction of Western Europe, 1945–51*. London: Methuen, 1984.

Monroe, Elizabeth. *Britain's Moment in the Middle East, 1914–1956*. London: Chatto and Windus, 1963.

Mosley, Leonard. *Marshall, Hero for Our Times*. New York: Hearst Books, 1983.

Murphy, Robert. *Diplomat Among Warriors*. Garden City, N.Y.: Doubleday, 1964.

Nettl, J. Peter. *The Eastern Zone and Soviet Policy in Germany, 1945–1950*. London: Oxford University, 1951.

Ninkovich, Frank A. *The Diplomacy of Ideas: U.S. Foreign Policy and Cultural Relations, 1938–1950*. New York: Cambridge University, 1981.

North, Robert C. *Moscow and the Chinese Communists*. Stanford: Stanford University, 1963.

O'Ballance, Edgar. *The Greek Civil War, 1944–1949*. New York: Praeger, 1966.

O'Sullivan, John and Alam M. Meckler. *The Draft and Its Enemies; a Documentary History*. Urbana: University of Illinois Press, 1974.

Paige, Glenn D. *The Korean Decision: June 24–30, 1950*. New York: Free, 1968.

Palmer, John M. *America in Arms, The Experience of the United States with Military Organization*. New Haven, Conn.: Yale University, 1941.

Paterson, Thomas G., ed. *Cold War Critics*. Chicago: Quadrangle, 1971.

———. *Soviet-American Confrontation: Postwar Reconstruction and the Origins of the Cold War*. Baltimore: Johns Hopkins University, 1973.

———, ed. *Containment and the Cold War: American Foreign Policy Since 1945*. Reading, Mass.: Addison-Wesley, 1973.

Perry, John Curtis. *Beneath the Eagle's Wings, Americans in Occupied Japan*. New York: Dodd Mead, 1981.

Phillips, Cabell. *The Truman Presidency*. New York: Macmillan, 1966.

Poole, Walter S. *The Joint Chiefs of Staff and National Policy, 1950–1952*. V. IV. Washington: JCS, 1979.

Price, Harry B. *The Marshall Plan and Its Meaning*. Ithaca, N.Y.: Cornell University, 1955.

Pruessen, Roland W. *John Foster Dulles; the Road to Power*. New York: The Free Press, 1982.

Purifoy, Lewis McCarroll. *Harry Truman's China Policy: McCarthyism and the Diplomacy of Hysteria, 1947–1951*. New York: New Viewpoints, 1976.

Ransom, Harry Howe. *The Intelligence Establishment*. Cambridge: Harvard University, 1970.

Reardon-Anderson, James. *Yenan and the Great Powers; the Origins of Chinese Communist Foreign Policy, 1944–46*. New York: Columbia University, 1980.

Rees, David. *Korea: The Limited War*. New York: St. Martin's, 1964.

Reid, Escott. *Time of Fear and Hope; the Making of the North Atlantic Treaty, 1947–1949*. Toronto: McClelland and Stewart, 1977.

Rezun, Miron. *The Soviet Union and Iran: Soviet Policy in Iran from the Beginnings of the Pahlavi Dynasty Until the Soviet Invasion in 1941*. Leiden: Sijthoff/Geneva: Institut Universitaire de Hautes Etudes Internationales, 1981.

Richardson, James L. *Germany and the Atlantic Alliance: The Interaction of Strategy and Politics*. Cambridge, Mass.: Harvard University, 1966.

Ridgway, Matthew B. *The Korean War*. Garden City, N.Y.: Doubleday, 1967.

———. *Soldier, The Memoirs of Matthew B. Ridgway*, New York: Harper, 1956.

Romanus, Charles F. and Riley Sunderland. *Stilwell's Command Problems*. Washington: Department of the Army, 1956.

———. *Time Runs Out in CBI*. Washington: Department of the Army, 1959.

Rose, Lisle A. *Dubious Victory, the United States and the End of World War II*. Kent, Ohio: Kent State University, 1973.

Rovere, Richard H. and Arthur M. Schlesinger, Jr. *The General and the President and the Future of American Foreign Policy*. New York: Farrar, Straus, 1951.

———. *Senator Joe McCarthy*. New York: Harcourt, Brace, Jovanovich, 1959.

Royal Institute of International Affairs. *Atlantic Alliance: NATO's Role in the Free World*. New York: Royal Institute of International Affairs, 1952.

Sachar, Howard M. *Europe Leaves the Middle East, 1936–1954*. New York: Knopf, 1972.

———. *A History of Israel from the rise of Zionism to our Time*. New York: Knopf, 1979.

Schaller, Michael. *The U.S. Crusade in China, 1938–1945*. New York: Columbia University, 1979.

Schmitt, Hans A. *The Path of European Union; from the Marshall Plan to the Common Market*. Baton Rouge, La.: Louisiana State University, 1962.

———, ed. *U.S. Occupation in Europe After World War II*. (Papers given at Conference at the George C. Marshall Research Library, 1976.) Lawrence, Kan.: Regents Press of Kansas, 1978.

Schnabel, James F. *Policy and Direction: The First Year.* Washington: Department of the Army, 1972.

——. *The Story of the Joint Chiefs of Staff; the Joint Chiefs of Staff and National Policy, 1945–1947.* vol. I. Washington: Historical Department, Joint Chiefs of Staff, 1979.

Schnabel, James F. and Robert J. Watson, *The Korean War.* Washington: JCS, 1978.

Schoenberger, Walter S. *Decision of Destiny.* Athens: Ohio University, 1969.

Schratz, Paul, ed. *Evaluation of the American Military Establishment Since World War II.* Lexington, Va.: Marshall Foundation, 1978.

Schwarz, Jordan A. *The Speculator; Bernard M. Baruch in Washington, 1917–1965.* Chapel Hill: University of North Carolina Press, 1981.

Sebald, William J. and Russell Brines. *With MacArthur in Japan: A Personal History of the Occupation.* New York: W. W. Norton, 1965.

Service, John S. *Lost Chance in China, the World War II Despatches of John S. Service,* edited by Joseph W. Esherick. New York: Random House, 1974.

——. *The Amerasia Papers: Some Problems in the History of U.S.-China Relations.* No. 7. Berkeley: Center for Chinese Studies, University of California, 1971.

Sherry, Michael S. *Preparing for the Next War.* New Haven, Conn.: Yale University, 1977.

Sherwin, Martin J. *A World Destroyed: The Atomic Bomb and the Grand Alliance.* New York: Knopf, 1975.

Shlain, Avi. *The United States and the Berlin Blockade, 1945–1949; a Study in Crisis Decision-Making.* Berkeley: University of California, 1983.

Shulman, Marshall D. *Stalin's Foreign Policy Reappraised.* Cambridge, Mass.: Harvard University, 1963.

Smith, Gaddis. *Dean Acheson, 1949–1953.* V. XVI. New York: Cooper Square, 1972.

Smith, Jean E. *The Defense of Berlin.* Baltimore: Johns Hopkins, 1963.

——, ed. *The Papers of General Lucius D. Clay.* 2 v. Bloomington, Ind.: Indiana University, 1974.

Smith, Robert R. *Triumph in the Philippines.* Washington: Department of the Army, 1963.

Smith, Walter B. *My Three Years in Moscow.* Philadelphia, Pa.: Lippincott, 1950.

Snell, John L. *The War-time Origins of the East-West Dilemma over Germany.* New Orleans, La.: Hauser, 1959.

Snetsinger, John. *Truman, the Jewish Vote, and the Creation of Israel.* Stanford, Calif.: Hoover Institution, 1974.

Spanier, John W. *The Truman-MacArthur Controversy and the Korean War.* Cambridge, Mass.: Belknap, 1959.

Spector, Ronald H. *Eagle Against the Sun; the American War with Japan.,* New York: Macmillan, 1985.

Stavrianos, L. S. *Greece: American Dilemma and Opportunity.* Chicago, 1952.

Steel, Ronald. *Walter Lippmann and the American Century.* Boston: Little, Brown, 1980.

Steele, A. T. *The American People and China.* New York: McGraw-Hill, 1966.

Stuart, John L. *Fifty Years in China.* New York: Random House, 1954.

Stueck, William W., Jr. *The Road to Confrontation, American Policy toward China and Korea, 1947–1950.* Chapel Hill: University of North Carolina, 1981.

——. *The Wedemeyer Mission; American Politics and Foreign Policy During the Cold War.* Athens, Ga.: University of Georgia, 1984.

Sykes, Christopher. *Crossroads to Israel, 1917–1948.* Bloomington, Ind.: Indiana University, 1965.

Theoharis, Athan. *Seeds of Repression, Harry S. Truman and the Origins of McCarthyism.* Chicago: Quadrangle, 1971.

Thornton, Richard C. *China: The Struggle for Power, 1917–1972.* Bloomington, Ind.: Indiana University, 1973.

Tong, Hollington K. *Chiang Kai-shek, Soldier and Statesman.* 2 v. London: Hurst and Blackett, 1937.

Truman, Harry S. *Memoirs, Years of Trial and Hope.* V. 2. New York: Doubleday, 1956.

Truman, Margaret. *Harry S. Truman.* New York: Morrow, 1973.

Tsou, Tang. *America's Failure in China, 1941–50.* 2 v. Chicago: University of Chicago, 1963.

———, ed. *China in Crisis.* 2 v. Chicago: University of Chicago, 1968.

Tuchman, Barbara W. *Stilwell and the American Experience in China, 1911–45.* New York: Macmillan, 1971.

———. *Notes from China.* New York: Collier Books, 1972.

U.S. Marine Operations in Korea, 1950–1953. I–V. Washington: Hqs. USMC, 1972.

U.S. Office of the Secretary of Defense. *The Department of Defense, 1944.* Washington: GPO, 1978.

U. S. State Department. *U. S. Relations with China, 1944–49.* (Called the China White Paper.) Washington: GPO, 1949.

Vandenberg, Arthur H., Jr., ed. *The Private Papers of Senator Vandenberg.* Boston: Houghton Mifflin, 1952.

Varg, Paul A. *The Closing of the Door, Sino-American Relations, 1936–1946.* Ann Arbor, Mich.: Michigan State University, 1973.

Walker, Richard L. and George Curry. *E. R. Stettinius, Jr., 1944–1945, and James F. Byrnes, 1945–1947.* V. XIV. New York: Cooper Square, 1965.

Walters, Vernon A. *Silent Missions.* Garden City, N.Y.: Doubleday, 1978.

Warburg, James P. *Put Yourself in Marshall's Place.* New York: Simon and Schuster, 1948.

Ward, Barbara. *Policy for the West.* New York: W. W. Norton, 1951.

———. *The West at Bay.* New York: W. W. Norton, 1951.

Ward, Patricia D. *The Threat of Peace; James F. Byrnes and the Council of Foreign Ministers, 1945–1946.* Kent, Ohio: Kent State University, 1979.

Wedemeyer, Albert C. *Wedemeyer Reports!* New York: Holt, 1958.

Weigley, Russell F. *The American Way of War, A History of United States Military Strategy and Policy.* New York: Macmillan, 1973.

Weiler, Lawrence D. and Anne P. Simons. *The United States and the United Nations.* New York: Manhattan, 1967.

Weizmann, Chaim. *Trial and Error, The Autobiography of Chaim Weizmann.* New York: Harper, 1949.

———. *The Letters and Papers of Chaim Weizmann.* London: Oxford University, 1968.

Weizmann, Vera. *The Impossible Takes Longer, The Memoirs of Vera Weizmann as told to David Tutsey.* New York: Harper and Row, 1967.

West, Philip. *Yenching University and Sino-Western Relations, 1916–1942.* Cambridge, Mass.: Harvard University, 1976.

Wexler, Imanuel. *The Marshall Plan Revisited; the European Recovery Program in Economic Perspective.* Westport, Conn.: Greenwood, 1983.

Wheeler-Bennett, Sir John and Anthony Nicholls. *The Semblance of Peace: The Political Settlement after the Second World War.* New York: St. Martin's, 1972.

White, Theodore H., ed. *The Stilwell Papers.* New York: Sloane, 1948.

White, Theodore. *Fire in the Ashes, Europe in Mid-Century.* New York: Sloane, 1953.

White, Theodore H. and Annalee Jacoby. *Thunder Out of China.* New York: Sloane, 1946, 1961.

Whiting, Alan S. *China Crosses the Yalu: The Decision to Enter the Korean War.* New York: Macmillan, 1960.

Whitnah, Donald and Edgar L. Erickson. *The American Occupation of Austria. Planning and Early Years.* Westport, Conn.: Greenwood, 1984.

Whitney, Courtney. *MacArthur: His Rendezvous with History.* New York: Knopf, 1956.

Williams, Francis. *Ernest Bevin, Portrait of a Great Englishman.* London: Hutchinson, 1952.

Williams, William A. *The Tragedy of American Diplomacy.* New York: Dell, 1972.

Willoughby, Charles A. and John Chamberlain. *MacArthur 1941–1951.* New York: McGraw-Hill Book, 1954.

Wilson, Evan M. *Decision on Palestine, How the U.S. Came to Recognize Israel.* Stanford, Calif.: Hoover Institution, 1979.

Wise, Henry A. *Drawing Out the Man; the V.M.I. Story.* Charlottesville: University of Virginia, 1978.

Woodhouse, Christopher M. *Apple of Discord: A Survey of Recent Greek Politics in their International Setting.* London: 1948.

——. *A Short History of Modern Greece.* New York: Praeger, 1968.

——. *The Struggle for Greece, 1941–1949.* London: Hart-Davis, MacGibbon, 1976.

Xydis, Stephen G. *Greece and the Great Powers, 1944–1947: Prelude to the "Truman Doctrine."* Thessaloniki: Institute for Balkan Studies, 1963.

Yergin, Daniel. *Shattered Peace: The Origins of the Cold War and the National Security State.* Boston: Houghton Mifflin, 1977.

Zotos, Stephanos. *Greece: The Struggle for Freedom.* New York: Crowell, 1967.

INTERVIEWS BY FORREST C. POGUE

The following people granted me interviews pertinent to this volume: Dean Acheson, Washington; Hervé Alphand, Paris; Lord Attlee, House of Lords, London; Lord Avon, (Anthony Eden), Pewsey, U.K.; Col. David Barrett, Pentagon; Sir John Balfour, London; Charles E. Bohlen, U.S. Embassy, Paris; Gen. Omar N. Bradley, Pentagon; General Harold R. Bull, Pentagon; Harvey Bundy, Boston; James F. Byrnes, Greenville, South Carolina; Henry Byroade, Arlington, Virginia; Admiral Robert B. Carney, Washington; Lieutenant General Marshall S. Carter, Colorado Springs, Washington, Lexington, Virginia; Chen Li-fu, Taipei; General Mark Clark, The Citadel, South Carolina; Will L. Clayton, Houston; Gen. J. Lawton Collins, Washington; Lewis Douglas, New York; Gen. Ira Eaker, Washington; Dwight D. Eisenhower, Pentagon and Gettysburg; George Elsey, Train to New York; Lord (Sir Oliver) Franks, Oxford, U.K.; Col. C. J. George, Pentagon, Lexington; Lt. Gen. Alvan C. Gillem, Atlanta; Gen. Andrew J. Goodpaster, Washington; Frank Graham, United Nations, New York; Lt. Gen. Leslie Groves, Washington; Gen. Thomas T. Handy, Washington; E. Roland Harriman (with George Elsey), New York; W. Averell Harriman, Independence, Missiouri, Georgetown, Washington; William Heffner, Washington; Lt. Gen. C. D. Herron, Washington; Richard Hickey, Washington; Oveta Culp Hobby, Houston; Anna Rosenberg Hoffman, New York; Paul G. Hoffman, United Nations, New York; Gen. John E. Hull, Pentagon; Carlisle Humelsine, Williamsburg, Virginia, Washington; Lord Ismay, London and Broadway, England, New York; Philip Jessup, New York; Louis Johnson, Washington; George Kennan, Princeton; W. John Kenney, (with Adm. Carney), Washington; Fl. Adm. William Leahy, White House offices; Brig. Gen. George A. Lincoln, Colorado, New York; Senator Henry Cabot Lodge, Washington; Robert A. Lovett,

New York; Gen. Douglas MacArthur, New York; George C. Marshall, Pentagon, Leesburg and Pinehurst; Katherine Tupper Marshall, Leesburg and Pinehurst, Virginia; Frank McCarthy, Richmond, Pentagon, Lexington, Virginia; Canon Luther Miller, Washington Cathedral; Montgomery Viscount of Alamein, Surrey, England; Earl, Mountbatten of Burma, Earl. London; Frank Pace, New York; Ambassador William Pawley, Miami and Washington; Speaker Sam Rayburn, Bonham, Texas; Sir Frank Roberts, London; Walter Robertson, Richmond, Virginia; Lord Roll, London; Eleanor Roosevelt, New York; Dean Rusk, New York; Gen. Matthew B. Ridgway, Pittsburgh; James Shepley, Washington and New York; Lord Sherfeld (Sir Roger Makins), London; Gen. Walter B. Smith, Washington; Maj. Gen. Howard Snyder, Washington; Gen. Carl Spaatz, Washington; Brig. Gen. Morrison Stayer, Carlisle, Pennsylvania; John Steelman, Washington; Adlai E. Stevenson, Chicago; Dirk Stikker, The Hague; Mrs. Joseph W. Stilwell, Carmel, California; Gen. Maxwell Taylor, Pentagon; Lt. Gen. Thomas Timberman, Washington; Harry S. Truman, Kansas City and Independence, Missouri; Gen. George V. Underwood, (with Marshall S. Carter), Colorado Springs; Ernst H. Van den Beugel, The Hague; Gen. James Van Fleet, Lexington, Virginia; Wang Shih-chieh, Taipei; Lt. Gen. Vernon Walters, Washington; Gen. Albert C. Wedemeyer, Poolesville, Maryland; Madge Pendleton White, Washington; Richard Wing, Pentagon; Col. and Mrs. J. J. Winn, Leesburg, Virginia; Gotz Wold, Oslo; Tyler Wood, Lexington, Virginia; George Yeh, Taipei; Yu Ta-wei, Taipei.

INTERVIEWS IN HARRY S. TRUMAN LIBRARY, INDEPENDENCE, MISSOURI

Theodore Achilles, George Elsey, Loy Henderson, John Hickerson, Philip Sprouse, Walter Trohan.

INTERVIEWS AT PRINCETON UNIVERSITY, JOHN FOSTER DULLES COLLECTION

Lucius D. Clay, Abba Eban, John Hickerson.

INTERVIEWS AT COLUMBIA UNIVERSITY, ORAL HISTORY COLLECTION

Lucius D. Clay, Will L. Clayton.

INTERVIEWS AT THE U. S. ARMY INSTITUTE, CARLISLE BARRACKS, PENNSYLVANIA

General Matthew B. ridgway, General Lucius D. Clay.

CONFERENCE GROUP ON GERMANY (INTERVIEWS BY GEORGE REMOSER AND ROBERT WOLFE WITH SOME AID FROM JAMES S. NANNEY)

Lucius D. Clay, James Riddleberger.

Notes

PROLOGUE: RESPONSE TO DUTY

1. Citation for Oak Leaf Cluster to Distinguished Service Medal for Gen. of the Army George C. Marshall, read at ceremony, Pentagon, 26Nov45, in appendix of Katherine T. Marshall, *Together,* 290–91.
2. Remarks by Gen. Marshall at Pentagon ceremony, 26Nov45, ML.
3. Ibid.
4. Accounts have been given of this episode in Pres. Truman's *Memoirs,* II, 85–86; in int. by author 20Oct59 with Sergeant Richard Wing, who took the call and summoned the General; in int. by author 20Jun69 with Marshall's driver, Marjorie Payne Lunger. I have followed the account given by Katherine T. Marshall, *Together,* 282.

I: FINAL BATTLES

1. I have drawn general details on the last months of the war in the Pacific from my ints. with Gen. Marshall; Robert Smith, *Return to the Philippines;* Samuel E. Morison, *Leyte, The Liberation of the Philippines,* and *Victory in the Pacific;* D. Clayton James, *The Years of MacArthur,* II; Thomas Buell, *Master of Sea Power.* For the development of the atomic bomb, I have drawn on my ints. with Marshall and with Gen. Leslie Groves. For general details, I have relied heavily on Richard G. Hewlett and Oscar E. Anderson, Jr., *The New World,* I. Other ints. include those with Gen. Thomas T. Handy, Harvey Bundy, Speaker Sam Rayburn. Stimson's *Diary* was of great value. The Army's official volume, Vincent C. Jones, *Manhattan: The Army and the Atomic Bomb,* came out after my manuscript for this book had been submitted. Its account of the Army's organization is detailed. The index, like mine, fails to give any idea of the number of times Marshall is mentioned in the book. For the immediate background, see Forrest C. Pogue, *George C. Marshall: Organizer of Victory,* ch. XXII.
2. JCS directive to MacArthur, Nimitz, Stilwell, 3Oct44, WARX 40782, ML.
3. Samuel E. Morison, *Leyte,* 338.
4. Ibid.
5. Hanson Baldwin, *Battles Lost and Won,* ch. II.
6. *Report of the Chief of Staff of the U S Army to Secretary of War, 1943–45,* 84–86.
7. JCS mtg. with Pres., 18Jun45.
8. Stimson *Diary,* 10May45.
9. Hewlett and Anderson, *New World;* Stimson *Diary,* 9Oct44.
10. Hewlett and Anderson, *New World,* 46, 51.
11. Hewlett and Anderson, *New World,* 73.
12. Int. by author with Marshall, 11Feb57; personal information on Groves from ints. by author with Lt. Gen. Leslie R. Groves, 7, 10May70. In Mar42 Marshall directed Brig. Gen. William D. Styer, Deputy Chief of Staff of the new Army Service Forces, to keep in contact with the atomic project. For details of the Manhattan Project and its various chiefs, see Jones, *Manhattan: The Army and the Atomic Bomb.* On Groves's appointment, see the following papers from GCM Files, ML: Bush to Bundy, n.d. (17Sep42 on envelope); Harrison and Bundy File no. 7, WDS/TYR memo 5May42, ASF

CG's file folder *Styer Corres.*, Corres. Box 64; Marshall to Bundy, 12Feb42.

13. Int. by author with Gen. Groves, 7, 10May70; int. by author with Marshall, 11Feb57.

14. Groves, *Now It Can Be Told*, 185–91. According to Buell in his life of King, the Chief of Naval Operations was not told of the atomic bomb until 1943.

15. Groves, *Now It Can Be Told*, 190–98.

16. Stimson *Diary*, 14,15,18Feb45; int. by author with Marshall, 11Feb57.

17. Int. by author with Speaker Sam Rayburn, 6Nov57. See also Bush to Bundy, 24Feb44, with note "Mtg 18 Feb 44 by K ['Katie'] M [Nichols]" in Harrison and Bundy File, no. 7, ML.

18. Int. by author with Marshall, 11Feb57.

19. Int. by author with Rayburn, 6Nov57.

20. Gen. Groves recalled that Truman accepted the reply with good grace. Groves, *Now It Can Be Told*, 365. For the moment, Truman left the Secretary boiling. He wrote in his diary, 13Mar44, "Truman is a nuisance and pretty untrustworthy man. He talks smoothly but acts meanly." Although Stimson never deleted the comment, his later judgments were most generous.

21. Stimson *Diary*, 26Feb45.

22. Ibid.

23. Marshall does not give the date, but he returned from Yalta about the time mentioned. Though he does not name the representative, his description checks with Stimson's; int. by author with Marshall, 11Feb57. Rep. George Mahon, a member of the committee, in the 1970s told the author that he did not recall the incident and that it was not characteristic of Marshall.

24. Groves, *Now It Can Be Told*, 365.

25. Cordell Hull, *Memoirs*, 309; John Wheeler–Bennett and Anthony Nichols, *The Semblance of Peace*.

26. William D. Leahy, *I Was There*, 263–65; Hewlett and Anderson, *New World*, 327.

27. Groves to Marshall, 30Dec44, ML.; Groves, *Now It Can Be Told*, 157:
"The most straightforward proposal for the bomb's design utilized the gun-assembly method to bring a critical mass of fissionable material together. In this method one subcritical mass of fissionable material was fired as a projectile into a second subcritical mass of fissionable material, the target, producing momentarily a supercritical mass which would explode. This principle was employed in the design of the Thin Man bomb that was dropped on Hiroshima."
"Another method was proposed that utilized the effects of implosion, by directing the blast of conventional high explosives inward toward a quantity of fissionable material. The force of this blast litterally squeezed the material together until it reached a critical mass and detonated. This principle was used in the Fat Man bomb which was delivered against Nagasaki."

28. Harry S. Truman, *Harry S. Truman Memoirs*, I, 10, says that just after the first Cabinet meeting after he had been sworn in as Pres., Secretary Stimson stayed behind to inform him briefly of the atomic bomb. Truman mentioned that as a senator he had asked Stimson earlier about certain mysterious building projects and had been told they were top-secret. Truman states flatly, "I did not learn anything whatever as to what that secret was until the Secretary spoke to me after the first Cabinet meeting."

29. Stimson *Diary*, 1,2,3,4May45.

30. Memo of mtg., Stimson, Marshall, and McCloy, 29May45, init. JJMcC, ML. Speaking of this and other discussions during the period when Marshall was asked to make a recommendation, McCloy says that he was struck by Marshall's resistance to making a final decision. As the fortieth anniversary of the dropping of the bomb neared in 1985, McCloy wrote several memoranda about his recollections. In three telephone conversations with the author, he quoted Marshall as saying, "Don't ask *me* to make the decision." Marshall also said that there were more than military matters concerned: there were possible effects with "primordial considerations." At

the same time, minutes of these meetings indicate that on purely military grounds, Marshall favored using the bomb to shorten the war.

31. Ibid. David Lilienthal, *Journals*, II, 196, tells of Marshall's mention of this conversation in 1947. At the same time he spoke of plans that had been considered if the home islands had to be invaded. Assuming there would be enough bombs, he envisaged the use of several in front of invading units. Supposedly, such ideas were informal plans mulled over by a very few people in the Pentagon, because MacArthur and Nimitz were working on actual invasion plans before they knew of the atomic bomb and before there were more than two available. The bombs had not been tested. Marshall told the author about these ideas in his int. of 11Feb57.
32. Stimson *Diary*, 31May45.
33. JCS mtg. with Pres., 18June45.
34. Stimson *Diary*, 4Jun45; Hewlett and Anderson, *New World*, 165.
35. Int. by author with Marshall, 11Feb57, ML.
36. The Combined Policy Comm. included Stimson and Bush for the United States, Field Marshal Wilson for the British, and Clarence Howe for Canada. Also sitting in were British Amb. Lord Halifax, British scientific adviser Sir James Chadwick, Counselor of the British Embassy Roger Makins, Harrison, Bundy, and Groves. Stimson *Diary*, 4Jul45.
37. Much of the Pres.'s activity was chronicled in the Ship's Log, 6Jul–7Aug45, of the *Augusta*, printed in FRUS 1945, *Conference at Berlin (Potsdam Conference)*, II, 4–28. Leahy, *I Was There*, 286–88. See also Arnold, *Global Mission;* Stimson *Diary*, 15Jul45. Marshall flight plan in Air Travel (GMC), 1939–45, ML.
38. Stimson *Diary*, 16,17Jul45.
39. Ibid., 21,22Jul45.
40. Ibid., 23Jul45.
41. Ibid., 24Jul45; Truman *Memoirs*, II, 420–21, includes text of directive.
42. Hewlett and Anderson, *New World*, 395–97.
43. Truman *Memoirs*, 420–21. In this

book published in 1955, Truman takes full responsibility for the decision. He says that with the directive of 24Jul45 to Spaatz, the first use of an atomic bomb on a military target had been set in motion. No formal reply was received, but Radio Tokyo said that the Japanese would continue to fight. "The bomb was scheduled to be dropped after August 3 unless Japan surrendered before that day." It seems clear that the directive to Spaatz mentioned above was in motion. No indication has been found to show that another directive was given by the President. Yet on 12Jan53, he wrote an editor of the Army Air Forces official history that he had sent a directive from mid-ocean to drop the bomb. (See copy of letter to James L. Cate in W. F. Craven and J. L. Cate, *The Army Air Forces in World War II*, V, between 712 and 713.) Truman seems to have confused his issuance of approval of a revised presidential announcement to be issued after the bomb was dropped which Stimson sent him on 30Jul, asking for approval by 1Aug. The Pres. went aboard the *Augusta* on 2Aug, when the countdown process was almost in its final stages and only a positive order to withhold the bomb or a surrender by the Japanese would have halted the progression. His unconscious confusion would apparently account for his failure to repeat the statement in the book. Craven and Cate handled it by publishing his letter. Vincent Jones, in *The Army and the Atomic Bomb*, 533–34, reprints a summary of the letter without noting Hewlett and Anderson's caveat that no evidence of a message from mid-ocean had been found.
44. Stimson *Diary*, 28Jul45.
45. Ibid., 30Jul45. Stimson to Truman, 30Jul45, FRUS 1945, *Berlin Conference (Potsdam)*, 1574.
46. Hewlett and Anderson, *New World*, 397–406, give a valuable summary of final phases of operations against Hiroshima and Nagasaki.
47. Stimson *Diary*, 10Aug45.
48. Int. by author with Marshall, 11Feb57.

II: NOT BY STILL WATERS

1. MacArthur to Marshall, 22Nov45; Marshall to MacArthur, 27Nov45, Marshall Personal File, ML.
2. Stimson to Marshall, 8May45; Stimson reconstruction of comments for Marshall, Marshall Person File, ML.
3. Stimson to Truman, 18Sep45, in Stimson *Diary* for that date, 18Sep45. Statement in Stimson and Bundy, *On Active Service*, 663–64.
4. Stimson *Diary*, 10Sep45.
5. Gen. Walter Bedell Smith to Marshall, 3Dec45, Marshall Personal File, ML.
6. Isaac Newell to Marshall, Marshall Personal File, ML.
7. Katherine T. Marshall to Frank McCarthy, 30Dec45, Marshall Personal File, ML.

III: TOO MANY HATS — TOO MANY HATES

1. For background, see Charles Romanus and Riley Sunderland. *Stilwell's Mission to China;* Romanus and Sunderland, *Stilwell's Command Problems;* Pogue, *George C. Marshall: Education of a General,* ch. XIV; Pogue, *George C. Marshall: Ordeal and Hope,* ch. XVI; Pogue, *George C. Marshall: Organizer of Victory,* ch. XXII.
2. Int. by author with Marshall, 29Oct56. Author's notes.
3. Int. by author with Marshall, 21Nov56.
4. Int. by author with Marshall, 29Oct56.
5. Int. by author with Marshall, 21Nov56.
6. Int. by author with Marshall, 29Oct56.
7. Int. by author with Marshall, 21Nov56.
8. Marshall to Pres., 15Feb44, with attached letter, Alsop to Soong, 12Jul43, ML.
9. Marshall to Stilwell, WAR 59012, 1Jul44.
10. Stilwell to Marshall, CHC 1241, 3Jul44.
11. JCS for Pres., 4July44.
12. Roosevelt to Generalissimo, WAR SVC 6080, 6Jul44, Stilwell Papers, Oklahoma File.
13. Marshall to Stilwell, 7Jul44, CM-OUT 62514.
14. CKS to Roosevelt, 8Jul44, OPD Exec 9, Item 20.
15. Roosevelt to CKS, 13Jul (received 15Jul)44, #25, Stilwell Files.
16. CKS to Roosevelt, 23Jul44, forwarded by Hopkins to Marshall, 16Aug44, OPD Exec 10, Item 6.
17. Stimson *Diary*, 27Jul and 3Aug44.
18. Marshall to Stilwell, 4Aug44, CM-OUT 75342 OPD Exec 20, Item 60, Case 6. Hurley was later to say that in late July Marshall and Stimson had asked him about Chennault as a possible commander in China. Even for the purpose of sounding out Hurley's views, it seems remarkable that they would have made a suggestion that they would never for a moment have entertained. Hurley added that they seemed pleased when he said he was not in favor of such an appointment.
19. Proposed draft with changes, Roosevelt to CKS, sent 21Aug44, OPD Exec 10, Item 61.
20. Marshall to Stilwell, CM-OUT 25105, 4Sep44, OPD Msg. File.
21. Chennault, *Way of a Fighter*, 316–17; see also 210.
22. *Stilwell Papers*, 321–22, 317.
23. John Davies to Hopkins, 30Aug44, in Hopkins to Roosevelt, 8Sep44.
24. Hurley to President, RAD CFB 22983, 23Sep44, OPD 201, Stilwell, Item 6, ML.
25. Stilwell to Marshall, CFB 22638, CM-N14238, 15Sep44. See also Stilwell to Marshall, 12Sep44, CFD 22467, Stilwell Papers, Oklahoma File.
26. Later used against Stilwell was his diary entry: ". . . if the G-mo controls distribution I am sunk. The Reds will get nothing. Only the G-mo's hench-

men will be supplied and my troops (the Yoke Force) will suck the hind tit." *Stilwell Papers*, 331; see also Romanus and Sunderland, *Stilwell's Command Problems*, 439.

27. Chennault, *Way of a Fighter*, 320–21.
28. Pres. to Generalissimo, 16Sep44, in Gen. Handy Memo for Sec. War, enc. text of message, which was sent 18Sep from Washington, OPD Exec 10, Item 59. Text also in FRUS 1944, 257–58.
29. Roosevelt to Chiang Kai-shek (enc. msg. from WD to Stilwell), WH 68, filed in Washington 16Sep44, delivered 0945, 19Sep44. Roosevelt to Marshall, 3May44, OPD Exec 10, Item 57. General Marshall wrote to Stilwell on 7May: "The President is forwarding Gauss (American Ambassador to China) message . . . indicates that he desires if possible be delivered in person with a complete Chinese translation. . . ." He added that all msgs. were to relate to the War Dept. the time of delivery. Marshall to Stilwell, 7May44, CM-OUT 33493, OPD Msg. File. This practice grew from reports that members of the Generalissimo's household did not deliver unpleasant msgs.
30. Hurley testimony, *Hearings on the Military Situation in the Far East*, IV, 2866.
31. *Stilwell Papers*, 333.
32. Ibid., 333–34.
33. Hurley to Pres., RAD CFB, 22988, 23Sep44, OPD 201, Stilwell, Item 5.
34. Leahy to Marshall, 25Sep44, enc. Hurley to Pres., 23Sep44, CFB 22988, OPD Exec 10, Item 61, China File.
35. Hurley to Pres., 13Oct44, *Far Eastern Hearings*, IV, 2879. According to Romanus and Sunderland in *Stilwell's Command Problems*, 541, "the Operations Division missed every warning hint and presented the whole course of events to Handy and Marshall in bright, affirmative tones." The brief of the msg. was prepared on 25Sep44.
36. Stilwell to Marshall, CFB 22995, 22Sep44, Stilwell Papers, Oklahoma File.
37. Memo, Stilwell for Hurley, 23Sep44, Item 31, Bk. 1, Hurley Papers.
38. Hurley statement in *Far Eastern Hear-

ings*, IV, 2875–76. See Cmdr. J. V. Smith, naval aide to the Pres., to Col. Frank McCarthy for Gen. Marshall, 27Sep44, enc. Hurley to Pres., CFB 232212, containing the *aide-mémoire*, 25Sep44, OPD Exec 10, Item 60.
39. Stilwell to Marshall, CFB 23443, 29Sep44, Stilwell Papers, Oklahoma File; *Stilwell Papers*, 337.
40. Hurley to Roosevelt, RAD CFB 23864, 6Oct44, Hurley Papers, Stilwell to Marshall, CFB 23685, 7Oct44, Stilwell to Marshall, CFB 24034, 9Oct44, all in Stilwell Personal File. See Sherwood, *Roosevelt and Hopkins*, 804–5, on Soong's undated cable to Hopkins; and Romanus and Sunderland, *Stilwell's Command Problems*, 457 and no. 39, for the text of Soong's message and their view that Sherwood was probably mistaken in suggesting that spring rather than Sep44 was the time of Soong's initial request. Hopkins denied the statement attributed to him in Hopkins to Hurley, WH 79, 7Oct44. When stories of Kung's purported action were announced in New Delhi on 31Oct, Kung declared that the accounts were "highly misleading and unfounded." *New York Herald-Tribune*, 1Nov44.
41. *Stilwell Papers*, 339; Stimson *Diary*, 3Oct44. See *Forrestal Diaries*, 5Oct44, p.12, on the two messages prepared by Marshall's directive and the Pres.'s calmer view.
42. Leahy for Hull, 5Oct44; forwarding draft, Roosevelt to Hurley for Generalissimo, 5Oct44; see also Marshall memo to JCS, 28Sep44; both in OPD Exec 20, Item 60. Stimson *Diary*, 5Oct44; *Stilwell Papers*, 7Oct44; Hopkins to Roosevelt, 9Oct44, Hopkins Papers, Bk. 1.
43. Soong to Hurley, 9Oct44, Hurley Papers; Hurley to President, 11Oct44, OPD Exec 20, Item 60.
44. Stilwell to Marshall, CFB 24101, 10Oct44, Stilwell Papers.
45. McCarthy to Handy, 18Oct44, inc. Pres. for Generalissimo, OPD Exec 10, Item 60.
46. Chennault, *Way of a Fighter*, 310–18; Joseph and Stewart Alsop, "Importance of Stilwell's Ouster to Chinese

Unity Is Traced," *New York Herald Tribune,* 14Jan46; Ronald Lewin, *Slim,* 141–42; Slim, *Defeat into Victory,* 215, 319.

47. *Biennial Report of the Chief of Staff of the*

United States Army, 59–60. For the story of Stilwell's return and subsequent assignments, see Pogue, *George C. Marshall: Organizer of Victory,* 478–79.

IV: PROBLEMS MULTIPLY
IN CHINA

1. Wedemeyer to Marshall, 6Nov44, Wedemeyer Files, Box 1, Folders 1, 2, Index 6, Strategy Radios, ML.

2. Wedemeyer to Marshall, 4Dec44, Wedemeyer Files, Box 1, Folders 1, 2, Index 6, Strategy Radios, ML.

3. Wedemeyer to Marshall, 10Dec44, GCM Peronal File, Pentagon Classified, ML.

4. Ibid., enc. copies of Wedemeyer's exchange of letter with Chennault.

5. Wedemeyer to Marshall for JCS, 22Jan45, CFB X 31783, Wedemeyer Files, Box 1, Folders 1, 2, Index 6, Strategy Files, ML.

6. Wedemeyer to Marshall, 8Sep45, GCM Personal File, Pentagon Classified, ML.

7. JCS to CG, U.S. Forces, China Theater, 24Oct44, FRUS 1944, VI, 178–80, JCS to Wedemeyer, 10Aug45, FRUS 1945, VII, 527–28.

8. War Dept. Memo, 1Nov45, Consul in Tientsin to Sec. State, 1Nov45, Marshall to Wedemeyer, 3Nov45; Robertson to Sec. State, 4Nov45, FRUS 1945, VII, 600–602.

9. Wedemeyer to Marshall, 27Oct45, GCM Personal File, Pentagon Classified, ML.

10. Wedemeyer to Marshall, 5Nov45, re mtg. of secs. State, War, and Navy, 6Nov45, FRUS 1945, VII, 603–7.

11. OPD to Wedemeyer, 9Nov45, JCS to Wedemeyer, 9Nov45, FRUS 1945, VII, 610–11.

12. Wedemeyer to Marshall, 9Nov45, FRUS 1945, VII, 611–13.

13. Wedemeyer to Marshall, 14Nov45, FRUS 1945, VII, 627–28.

14. Vincent to Sec. State, 12Nov45, FRUS 1945, VII, 614–17.

15. Telephone conv., General Embick to General Hull, 10Nov45, ABC 336 China, Sec 1-B (75), ML.

16. Sen. Byrnes from Conf 26Nov56, in

Dept. of State *Bull.* 2Dec45, 882–83. James F. Byrnes, *Once in a Lifetime,* 328–29.

17. Hurley to Truman, 26Nov45, FRUS 1945, VII, 722–26; see White House amendment, 27Nov45; Marshall appointment, ibid., 726; for Truman's version, see Truman, *Years of Trial and Hope,* 86; see also Acheson, *Present at the Creation,* 134–35.

18. Hull to Wedemeyer, 30Nov45, with other drafts, CM-OUT 86183, OPD 336TS, 30Nov45, ML.

19. Wedemeyer to Eisenhower, 20Nov45, FRUS 1945, VII, 650–60.

20. Wedemeyer to Eisenhower, 23Nov45, FRUS 1945, VII, 662–65.

21. Patterson and Forrestal to Sec. State, 26Nov45, FRUS 1945, VII, 670–72.

22. Ibid., 676–77.

23. Mtg. of Secs., FRUS 1945, VII, 684–85.

24. Memo, Marshall to Leahy, 30Nov45, FRUS 1945, VII, 747–48.

25. Ibid.

26. Memo prepared in State Dept., 8Dec45, Hull to Marshall, 8Dec45, FRUS 1945, VII, 754–59.

27. Marshall to Leahy, 30Nov45, FRUS 1945, VII, 746–48.

28. Sec. State to WD, 9Dec45, incl. excerpt from his testimony, FRUS 1945, VII, 760–61.

29. Ibid.

30. Marshall, memo of conv., mtg. of Marshall with Pres., Sec. State, and Leahy at 3:30 P.M., 11Dec45, FRUS 1945, VII, 767–79.

31. Ibid.

32. Int. with James R. Shepley, 15Jul57; int. with Gen. John E. Hull, 8,22Aug57.

33. Memo of conv. by Marshall, notes on mtg. with Pres. and Under Sec. State, 14Dec45, FRUS 1945, VII, 770. James Shepley later said that Truman told Marshall, "If you don't like this, write

your own." Int. with James R. Shepley, 15Jul57.

34. Truman to Marshall, 15Dec45, FRUS 1945, VII, 770–73.
35. Ibid.
36. Acheson, *Present at the Creation*, 144.
37. Ltr., Davis to author, 14Mar75.
38. Memo on conf. in Gen. Hull's office,

15Dec45, OPD 336 TS, Case 228 (only), Item 32.
39. Ltr., Davis, 14Mar75, ML.
40. Ibid.
41. Ibid.
42. Int. by author with Byroade, 22Jul69.
43. Ibid.

V : CHINA PASSAGE

1. Shepley, memo to Marshall, 19Dec45, FRUS 1945, VII, 774–77.
2. Ibid.
3. *Wedemeyer Reports!*, 363; int. by author with Gen. Wedemeyer, 1Feb58.
4. Int. with Robertson, 6Sep62.
5. Ibid.
6. Mins. kept by Wedemeyer, 21Dec met. in Nanking, FRUS 1945, VII, 794–99.
7. Ibid.
8. Ibid.
9. Ibid.
10. Marshall's residence there was at 28 Niu Kuo Tao, with his office on the first floor and his staff on the second. I have depended on Chief Warrant Officer Richard Hickey's letter of 21Apr81 for much of this description.
11. Notes on conf. between Marshall and Chou En-lai, 23Dec45, FRUS 1945, VII, 800–804.
12. Notes on conf. between Marshall and Soong, 24Dec45, Chungking, FRUS 1945, VII, 804–13. See n. 15 below for more on Carsun Chang.
13. Ibid.
14. Notes by Marshall on conf. with Pres. and Mme. Chiang Kai-shek after Christmas dinner, 26Dec45.
15. Marshall to Truman, 30Dec45, FRUS 1945, VII, 825–26. In all of these talks, Marshall looked for a leader of a third party who would bring non-Kuomintang and non-Communists together into an effective organization. His candidate for a time was Chang Chia-sen, known to Westerners as Carsun Chang. Once a leader of a movement for parliamentary democracy in China, he was arrested and went abroad to avoid trouble from 1929 to 1932. On his return to China, he organized another party, which was outlawed by the Kuomintang. Surfacing again in 1934 as the National Socialist Party, it favored a more aggressive policy against Japan. After the Japanese attack of 1937, Carsun Chang urged unity with the Kuomintang, and he was invited to join the National Defense Advisory Council and, in 1938, to be a member of the Peoples' Political Council. Although the government shut down an institute that advocated his principles, it favored his efforts to bring minority groups together in the Chinese Democratic League to oppose the Japanese. In 1945 he was invited to be a member of the Chinese delegation to the U.N. Conf. in San Francisco. In 1946 he attended the Political Consultative Conf. in Chungking as a representative of the Democratic League. Although Marshall was impressed by Carsun Chang, he ultimately decided Chang could not hold minority groups together to forge a third force for China.
16. Shepley to Marshall, 30Dec45, FRUS 1945, 827–28.
17. Memos of convs. between Byrnes and Soviet leaders, 15–23Dec45, FRUS 1945, 835–39, 840–50.
18. Marshall to Truman, 1Jan46, FRUS 1946, IX, 1–2.
19. Notes on Marshall conv. with Chou En-lai, 3Jan46, FRUS 1946, IX, 11–17.
20. Notes on Marshall conv. with Chou En-lai, 5Jan46, FRUS 1946, IX, 20–25.
21. *Biographical Dictionary of Republican China*, II, 206–11.
22. Ibid., III, 395–97, on Wang Shih-chieh.
23. Marshall statement on Wang, ML.
24. *Biographical Dictionary of Republican China*, II, 206–11.

25. Ibid., 391–405.
26. Wedemeyer to Marshall, 7Jan46, FRUS 1946, IX, 39–40.
27. Robertson to Marshall, 7Jan46, FRUS 1946, IX, 41–42.
28. Notes on first five mtgs. of Comm. of Three, 7–9Jan46, FRUS 1946, IX, 43–116; for Marshall's description of the dispute over Jehol and Chahar, see his official report on his mission to China, pt. 1, 19–21, ML.
29. Kennan to Sec. State, 10Jan46, FRUS 1946, IX, 116–19; repeated to U.S. Emb. in Chungking.
30. Mins. of mtg. of Comm. of Three, 10Jan46, FRUS 1946, IX, 127.
31. Marshall to Truman, 10Jan46, FRUS 1946, IX, 129–30.
32. See memo by Philip Sprouse to State Dept., 8Jan46, sent by Walter Robertson, 11Jan46, FRUS 1946, IX, 132–33, 234–45.
33. Marshall to Truman, 24Jan46, FRUS 1946, IX, 143–43.
34. Ibid., 143.
35. Marshall to Truman, 31Jan46, FRUS 1946, IX, 149; Barbara Tuchman, "If Mao Had Come to Washington: An Essay in Alternatives," *Foreign Affairs*, Oct72. For Mao's earlier views on cooperation with the United States, see John Service's int. with Mao, 23Aug44, *Lost Chance in China*, 295–307.
36. Smyth to Sec. State, 15Feb46, FRUS 1946, IX, 154–55, 156–57.
37. Marshall to Wedemeyer, Wedemeyer to Marshall, 13Jan46, FRUS 1946, IX, 177 ff.
38. Memo of mtg., Marshall and Gen. Chang Chih-chung, 23Jan46, notes by Col. Caughey, FRUS 1946, IX, 194–96.
39. Ibid., 196.
40. Marshall mtg. between Gen. Chang Chih-chung, 31Jan46, FRUS 1946, IX, 201–2.
41. Mins. of mtg., Marshall between Chou En-lai, 1Feb46, FRUS 1946, IX, 203.
42. Marshall to Truman, 4Feb46, FRUS 1946, IX, 207–8.
43. Mins. of mtg., Marshall between Gen. Chang Chih-Chung, 5Feb66, FRUS 1946, IX, 209–11.
44. Mins. of informal mtg. mil. subcomm., 11Feb46, FRUS 1946, IX, 211–15.
45. Mins. of mtg. between Marshall and Chang Chih-chung, 12Feb46, FRUS 1946, IX, 220–22.
46. Mins. of mtg. of Military Subcomm. between GCM, Chang Chih-chung, and Chou En-lai, 15Feb46, FRUS 1946, IX, 224–35.
47. Mins. of mtg. of Military Subcomm., 16Feb46, FRUS 1946, IX, 235–47.
48. Ibid.
49. Mins. of mtg. of Military Subcomm. between GCM, Chang, and Chou, 18Feb46, FRUS 1946, IX, 248–58.
50. Ibid.
51. Mins. of mtg. between Marshall and Chou, 18Feb46, FRUS 1946, 258–59.
52. Marshall to Truman, 19Feb46, FRUS 1946, IX, 260–62.
53. Ibid.
54. Mins. of mtg. between Marshall and Chang Chih-chung, 20Feb46, FRUS 1946, IX, 262–63.
55. Mins. of mtg. between Marshall and Chou, 21Feb46, FRUS 1946, IX, 262–64, 265–77.
56. Mins. of Mtg. of Military Subcommittee, 22Feb46, FRUS 1946, IX, 278–89.
57. Mins. of signing of military agreement, 25Feb46, FRUS 1946, IX, 291–95.
58. Ibid.
59. Melby, *Mandate of Heaven*, 95.

VI: SEEKING A CEASE-FIRE

1. Chou En-lai to Marshall, 13Jan46, FRUS 1946, IX, 342. Chang Chun to Chou En-lai, 13Jan46, FRUS 1946, IX, 342–43, 343–45.
2. Mins. of mtg. between Marshall and Chang Chun, 14Jan46, Mins. of mtg. between Marshall and Chou En-lai, 24Jan46, FRUS 1946, IX, 345–49.
3. Byroade to Marshall, 21Jan46, FRUS 1946, IX, 369–70.
4. Marshall to Truman, 9Feb46, FRUS 1946, IX, 426–29.
5. Ibid.
6. Truman to Marshall, 13Feb46, FRUS 1946, IX, 434–35.

7. Smyth to Sec. State, 23Feb46, FRUS 1946, IX, 439–41.

8. Mins. of mtg. between Marshall and Chou En-lai, 25Feb46, FRUS 1946, IX, 441–42.

9. Marshall to McCarthy, 22Feb46, McCarthy File, ML.

10. Marshall to Truman, 27Feb46, FRUS 1946, IX, 445–46; Marshall to Robertson, 21Feb46, ML, said he expected to end his work in China by August.

11. Melby, *Mandate of Heaven*, 96.

12. Marshall comments at Exec. Hq., 28Feb46, FRUS 1946, IX, 463–64.

13. Marshall comments, 1Mar46, FRUS 1946, IX, 467.

14. Marshall comments during mtg. at Tsinan, 2Mar46, FRUS 1946, IX, 472–73.

15. Trip to Taiyuan, 3Mar46, FRUS 1946, IX, 493–97.

16. I am indebted to James Reardon-Anderson's *Yenan and the Great Powers*, part of which I was shown in its pre-publication stage, for a perceptive analysis of the various shifts in Soviet and Chinese Communist positions.

17. Terrill, *Mao Tse-tung*, 183.

18. *Time*, 18Mar46.

19. Mtg. between Marshall and Mao Tse-tung, 4Mar46, FRUS 1946, IX, 501–2, 510; Terrill, *Mao*, 183. Terrill added that Mao did not meet an American official again until three wars and four Presidents later.

20. Marshall to Truman, 6Mar46, FRUS 1946, IX, 510–11; Truman to Marshall, 7Mar46, FRUS 1946, IX, 511.

21. Shepley to Marshall, 7Mar46, FRUS 1946, IX, 511–12.

22. Ludden memo to Marshall, 9Mar46, FRUS 1946, IX, 513–16. Ludden was one of the old China hands later accused of pro-Communist leanings, seriously compromising his career in the Foreign Service.

23. Mtg. of Comm. of Three, 11Mar46, FRUS 1946, IX, 543–53.

24. Memo by Marshall of statement by Chiang Kai-shek, 10Mar46, FRUS 1946, IX, 528–29.

25. Chou En-lai to Marshall, 10Mar46, FRUS 1946, IX, 529–35.

26. Mins. of Chou En-lai int. with Marshall, 11Mar46, FRUS 1946, IX, 535–38.

27. CKS to Truman, 11Mar46, FRUS 1946, IX, 540.

28. Wedemeyer to Eisenhower (from Nanking), 11Mar46, WDCSA 091, China, 1946 (15Mar46), ML.

29. Marshall Memo to Truman, 18Mar46, containing text of communication from Chiang Kai-shek to Marshall, State Dept. File DC/R 121.893/3-1946, with handwritten note to Sec. Byrnes from Marshall suggesting that he show it to Acheson.

VII: DISASTROUS INTERLUDE

1. *Time*, 25Mar46.

2. Marshall press conf., 16Mar46, *China White Paper*, 141–43.

3. Col. L. J. Lincoln, Asiatic Sec., Theater Group, to Gen. H. A. Craig, 15Mar46, OPD 319.1TS, 15Mar46, ML.

4. Int. by author with Admiral C. M. Cooke, Nov60.

5. Mins. of mtg. of Military Subcomm., 17Mar46, FRUS 1946, IX, 566–76.

6. Marshall to Gillem, 18Mar46, FRUS 1946, IX, 576.

7. Ibid.

8. Marshall to Gillem, 21Mar46, FRUS 1946, IX, 590–91.

9. Gillem to Byroade, 22Mar46, Caughey to Gillem, 23Mar46, Gillem to Marshall, 25Mar46, Gillem to Marshall, 27Mar46, FRUS 1946, IX, 593–96, 600–605.

10. Marshall to Gillem, 6Apr46, FRUS 1946, IX, 737–38.

11. Int. by author with Lt. Gen. A. C. Gillem, Sr., 22Jun62.

12. Wedemeyer (in Shanghai), Shanghai 82583, ML.

13. Wedemeyer to Hurley, 31Mar46, Hurley Papers, cited in Russell Buhite, *Hurley*, 318.

14. Madame Chiang Kai-shek to Marshall, 2Apr46, ML.

15. Marshall to Joan Bright, 4May46, ML. The description of the place is from telephone conv., letters, and ints. by author with Richard G. Hickey, ML.

16. Marshall to Bryden, 14Apr46; John Robinson Beal, *Marshall in China*, 147.

17. Marshall to Stettinius, 9Aug46, ML.

18. Beal, *Marshall in China*, 142–48.

19. Memo of Marshall conv. with Yu Ta-wei, 22Apr46, FRUS 1946, IX, 788–90.

20. Mins. of mtgs. between Marshall and Chou En-lai, 23,27,29Apr46; mins. of mtg. between Marshall and Gen Hsu Yung-chang, 23Apr46, FRUS 1946, IX, 790–805.

21. Melby, *Mandate of Heaven*, 114; mins. of mtg. between Marshall and Chou En-lai, Marshall and Gen Hsu Yung-chang, 4May46, FRUS 1946, IX, 650–53, 813–14.

22. Wedemeyer to Marshall, 4May46, GCM China Mission File, ML.

23. Melby, *Mandate of Heaven*, 117; Marshall to Truman, 6May46, mins. of mtg. between Marshall and Gen Yu Ta-wei, 8May46, FRUS 1946, IX, 818, 820–22.

24. Eisenhower letter to Marshall, 28May46, State Dept. RG 59, Mission to China Folder, "Report to the President"; Eisenhower to Marshall, 4Jun46, RAD, Eisenhower Papers; Acheson, *Present at the Creation*, 192–93; Truman *Memoirs*, v. 1, *Years of Decision*, 553. Marshall explained all this in a memo for the record dated 12Feb48, GCM Personal File, Pentagon Classified, ML.

25. Mins. of conf. between Marshall and Chiang Kai-shek, 12May46, FRUS 1946, IX, 840–41.

26. Marshall, *Report on His Mission to China*, 143–44.

27. Ibid., 138–39; mins. of conf. between Marshall and Chou En-lai, 21May46, FRUS 1946, IX, 878–79.

28. Chiang Kai-shek, *Soviet Russia in China*, 160; Tang Tsou, *America's Failure in China, 1941–50*, 420.

29. Marshall to Truman, 22May46, mins. of mtg. with Chou En-lai, 23May46, FRUS 1946, IX, 881–90.

30. Mins. of mtg. with Chou En-lai, 30May46; Marshall to Chiang Kai-shek, 31May45, FRUS 1946, IX, 925–26; for a summary of Marshall's exchange of messages with the Generalissimo during the former's absence from Nanking, see Marshall *Report*, 145–51.

31. Mins. of mtg. between Marshall and Chou En-lai, 3Jun46, FRUS 1946, IX, 950–73.

32. Marshall memo to Chou En-lai, 4Jun46, Marshall to Truman, 5Jun46, FRUS 1946, IX, 976–79; Melby, *Mandate of Heaven*, 129.

33. Mins. of conf. between Marshall and Chou En-lai, 10Jun46, Marshall to Carter, 10Jun46, FRUS 1946, IX, 1008–21. West Pointer Col. Marshall S. Carter had been selected by Acheson to succeed Col. Davis as liaison between the Pentagon and State and Marshall. Carter had served part of the war in OPD and later with Gen. Wedemeyer's headquarters in China.

34. Memo by Second Sec. of Emb. Melby, 13Jun46, FRUS 1946, IX, 1045–46.

35. Memo of conv. by Second Sec. of Emb., 14Jun46, FRUS 1946, IX, 1046–47.

36. Marshall to Truman, 17Jun45, FRUS 1946, IX, 1099–1101.

37. Smyth to Sec. State, 21Jun46, FRUS 1946, IX, 1123, 1272.

38. Mins. of mtg. of Comm. of Three, 24Jun46, FRUS 1946, IX, 1169–88.

39. Marshall to Truman, 29Jun46, FRUS 1946, IX, 1262.

40. Mins. of mtg. between Marshall and Gen Yu Ta-wei, 20June46, FRUS 1946, IX, 1105–6; Beal, *Marshall in China*, 97.

41. Notes of mtg. between Marshall and Chiang Kai-shek, Nanking, 30Jun46, FRUS 1946, IX, 1263–65; int. by author with Marshall, 29Oct56, ML.

42. Beal, *Marshall in China*, 109–110.

VIII: PICKING UP THE PIECES

1. Gen. Wedemeyer says that Hurley suggested the appointment in Sep45 and that he asked Marshall about it.

2. Marshall to Eisenhower for Byrnes, 11May46, Marshall to Wedemeyer, 1Jun46, FRUS 1946, IX, 833, 927; Wedemeyer to Marshall, 29May46, Marshall China Mission File, ML.

3. Eisenhower to Marshall, 2Jul1946, FRUS 1946, IX, 1277; Wedemeyer to Handy, 15Jul45, WDCSA 091, Marshall China Mission File, ML;

Wedemeyer, *Wedemeyer Reports!*, 369–70; ints. by author with Wedemeyer and Acheson, ML.

4. For details on Stuart's life, see his *Fifty Years in China*, chs. I, II.
5. Philip West, *Yenching University and Sino-Western Relations, 1915–52*, ch. II.
6. Stuart, *Fifty Years in China*, 164–65.
7. *Time*, 27May46, 50 ff.
8. Stuart, *Fifty Years in China*, 165–6; Stuart to Sec. State, 21July46, FRUS 1946, IX, 1388–93, 1394–95.
9. Marshall to Truman, 22Jul46, FRUS 1946, IX, 1394–95.
10. Mins. of int., Marshall with Chiang Kai-shek, 8Aug46, FRUS 1946, IX, 1468–71; Marshall, *Report*, 230 ff.
11. Con. Gen. Tientsin to Sec. State, 30Jul46, FRUS 1946, IX, 1418; Report by Col. M. F. Davis 8Oct46, FRUS 1946 X, 320–30.
12. Mins. of mtg. of Marshall and Chou En-lai, record of conf. at Emb., 6Aug46, FRUS 1946, IX, 1443–60; Marshall *Report*, 227.
13. Mins. of mtg. of Marshall and Chou En-lai, 15Aug46, Stuart to Sec. State, FRUS 1946, X, 8–20, 46–48.
14. Notes on conv. between Marshall and Chiang Kai-shek, 16Aug46; Marshall to Truman, 16Aug46, FRUS 1946, X, 51–53, 59–90.
15. Mins. of mtg. of Marshall with Yu Ta-wei, 30Aug46, FRUS 1946, X, 109–10; Marshall *Report*, 271.
16. Marshall to Carter, 22Jul46, Carter to Marshall, 23Jul46, Marshall to Carter, 24Jul46, FRUS 1946, X, 753–55.
17. Marshall *Report*, 476; Marshall to Carter, 26Jul46, FRUS 1946, X, 755. For the reaction in the Pentagon, where objections were raised that the measures would interfere with the program of military aid to China, see memo of Col. T. N. Dupuy to Gen. Lincoln, 20Aug46, P & O China Aid Program, 45–49, Box 3 (Tab 6), ML.
18. Caughey to Gillem, 27Sep46, FRUS 1946, X, 761; see also Carter memo to Gen. Hodes, 4Oct46, SDCSA 091 China 1946, ML; Marshall *Report*, 476.
19. Beal, *Marshall in China*, 175–6.
20. Mins. of mtgs. between Marshall and Chou En-lai, 5Sep46, 6Sep46, FRUS 1946, X, 132–40, 153–58.

21. Marshall to Truman, 6Sep46, FRUS 1946, X, 160–62.
22. Stuart to Sec. State, 17Sep46, FRUS 1946, X, 195.
23. Memo by Chou En-lai to Marshall, 15Sep46, FRUS 1946, X, 189–94.
24. Marshall to Truman, 23Sep46, FRUS 1946, X, 217–19; Truman to Marshall, 26Sep46, FRUS 1946, X, 217–19, 225.
25. Stuart to Sec. State, 27Sep46, FRUS 1946, X, 231–37.
26. Mins. of mtg. between Marshall and Communist reps., 29Sep46, FRUS 1946, X, 243–56.
27. Memo by Chou En-lai to Marshall, 30Sep46, FRUS 1946, X, 258–59.
28. Notes on mtg. of Marshall and Stuart, 1Oct46, FRUS 1946, X, 260–62. Approximately at this time, Marshall made the arms embargo explicit by his order to Gillem.
29. Marshall to Chiang Kai-shek, 1Oct46, FRUS 1946, X, 267–68. See the excellent summary in Marshall to Acheson, 2Oct46, FRUS 1946, 271–74.
30. Stuart to Sec. State, 3Oct46.
31. Marshall's notes of mtg. with Chiang Kai-shek, 4Oct46, Marshall to Truman, 5Oct46, FRUS 1946, X, 287–92. [The paragraphs covered by these messages overlap. Some statements are repeated in slightly different form.]
32. Marshall to Truman, 5Oct46, FRUS 1946, X, 291.
33. Marshall to Carter, 6Oct46, FRUS 1946, X, 289–99.
34. Stuart to Sec State, 7Oct46, FRUS 1946, X, 308–10.
35. Mtg. between Marshall and Stuart, 8Oct46, Mins of Mtg between Marshall and Communist reps, 8Oct46, FRUS 1946, X, 311–12, 314–19.
36. Int. by author with Gen. Gillem, 11Jun62.
37. Mtg. between Marshall and Chou En-lai, 9Oct46, FRUS 1946, 332–42.
38. Int. by author with Gillem, 11Jun62.
39. Stuart to Sec State, 9Oct46, FRUS 1946, 332–41; Stuart, *Fifty Years in China*, 170.
40. Marshall's redraft of statement for Chiang Kai-shek, FRUS 1946, X, 375–76.
41. Mtg between Marshall and Stuart, 16Oct46, FRUS 1946, X, 375–76.
42. Marshall to Truman, 17Oct46, FRUS 1946, X, 381–84.

43. Marshall Rpt, 388, 447; Mtg. between Marshall and National generals, 24Oct46, FRUS 1946, X, 414–17.
44. Marshall to Truman, 26Oct46, FRUS 1946, X, 435–37.
45. Mtg. between Marshall and Stuart, 29Oct46, FRUS 1946, X, 449; Marshall Rpt., 414–15.
46. Melby, *Mandate of Heaven,* 161.
47. Marshall to Truman, 8Nov46, FRUS 1946, X, 490–91.
48. Mtg. between Marshall and Chou En-lai, 10Nov46, FRUS 1946, X, 490–91.
49. Mtg. of Comm. of Three, 11Nov46, FRUS 1946, X, 511–20; Marshall Rpt. 334–37.
50. Mtg. between Marshall and Chou En-lai, 12Nov36, FRUS 1946, X, 524–34;
Stuart to Sec State, 16Nov46, Marshall to Truman, 16Nov46, FRUS 1946, X, 543, 547–48.
51. Carter to Marshall, 17Nov46, FRUS 1946, X, 548–49.
52. Melby, *Mandate of Heaven,* 172.
53. Beal, *Marshall in China,* 313; Marshall to Truman, 1Dec46, FRUS 1946, X, 575–78.
54. Marshall to Truman, 23Nov46, FRUS 1946, X, 558–59.
55. Melby, *Mandate of Heaven,* 173.
56. Beal, *Marshall in China,* 313; Marshall to Truman, 1Dec46, FRUS 1946, X, 575–78.
57. Carter to Marshall, 3Dec46, FRUS 1946, X, 583.
58. Mtg. between Marshall and Stuart, 5Dec46, FRUS 1946, X, 591–94.

IX: END OF THE MISSION

1. Mins. of mtg. between Marshall and Dr. Wei Tao-ming, 4Dec46, FRUS 1946, 602–5.
2. Acheson's msg., sent Marshall by Carter, 6Dec46, FRUS 1946, X, 593–94.
3. Beal, *Marshall in China,* 313. Mrs. Marshall flew to Guam in plane assigned to General Marshall.
4. Ibid., p. 313; int. by author with Maj. Gen. George V. Underwood, 21Oct70.
5. Stuart to Sec. State, 27Dec46, Marshall to Truman, 26Dec46, FRUS 1946, X, 665–66, 661–65.
6. Beal, *Marshall in China,* 345.
7. Ibid.
8. Carter to Marshall, 3Jan47, Marshall to Carter, 4Jan47, FRUS 1947, X, 680–81.
9. Marshall notes on mtg. with Generalissimo, 6Jan47, FRUS 1946, X, 684–85.
10. Marshall notes on mtg. with Wang Shih-chieh, 7Jan47, mtg. between Marshall and T. V. Soong, 7Jan57, FRUS 1946, X, 688, 689–91.
11. Stuart, *Fifty Years in China,* 177–78.
12. Personal statement by Marshall, 7Jan47, U.S. State Dept., *China* (called White Paper), 686–89.

X: IN A CIVILIAN SETTING

1. *Washington Star* and *Washington Post,* 22Jan47.
2. Note of James Shepley to Col. Marshall S. Carter, 21Jan47.
3. Marshall statement, quoted in *Washington Star,* 22Jan47.
4. James Reston column, *New York Times,* 22Jan47; David Lawrence column, 22Jan47.
5. Acheson, *Present at the Creation,* 213–14, notes that the move of the State Dept. from its old site to the building erected at the request of Sec. Stimson and Gen. Marshall in 1941 was one of the first items he discussed with Mar-
shall after he was sworn in. Marshall gave necessary directions and preparations for the move, which began while he was in Moscow. In explaining to his new enlisted assistant, Sgt. C. J. George, just why he was taking his soon-to-be-discharged orderly, Sgt. Wing, to Moscow instead of the new member of his staff, he said he would want George in Washington to look after his interests during arrangements for the move. (Sgt. George had entered the Army out of high school in the period before the war and had been commissioned during the war,

advancing to major. He left the Army after the war, but changed his mind and returned to duty as a sergeant. Assigned to the Pentagon motor pool, he was temporarily assigned as Marshall's driver when the new Secretary arrived. After several weeks he was assigned to permanent duty with Marshall, first as driver, then as an assistant who became an aide, a part-time secretary, and a sometime speech writer. The Korean War restored his commissioned rank. He remained with Marshall at the State Dept., the Red Cross, and the Defense Dept., and was military aide throughout Marshall's retirement. His replacement as orderly-driver was Sgt. William Heffner, who remained in the job until Marshall's death.)

6. Dean Acheson, *Morning and Noon,* gives the main details of his early career.

7. Acheson, *Present at the Creation,* 141.

8. Int. by author with Dean Acheson, 20Oct57.

9. Acheson, *Present at the Creation,* 189–90.

10. Int. by author with Robert A. Lovett, 28Aug77.

11. Acheson, *Present at the Creation,* 151.

12. State Dept. Study, "A Program of Management Reform for the Department of State," cited in Marshall Library News Letter, v. 11, no. 2, Winter 71.

13. George Kennan, *Memoirs, 1925–50,* 187.

14. Kennan, *Memoirs,* 294. For Kennan's shift of emphasis, see John L. Gaddis, *Strategies of Containment,* ch. 2.

15. Amb. Walter B. Smith to Sec. State, 7Jan47, FRUS 1947, II, 139–42.

16. Marshall speech at *New York Herald-Tribune* Forum, 20Oct45, cited in Michael Sherry, *Preparing for the Next War,* 218.

17. Many of the incidents are summarized in *Eisenhower Papers, Chief of Staff Years,* III, 753, n 1. See an article on the problem by R. Altin Lee, "Army Mutiny of 1946," *Journal of American History,* 1953, v. 3, 555–71. (I personally watched demonstrations in Frankfurt against the U.S. headquarters building.)

18. Marshall directive cited in Sherry, *Preparing for the Next War,* 193, Fn. 6.

19. Marshall, *Report to the Secretary of War, 1943–45,* 118.

20. Sec War (Patterson to State Dep. Hilldring) enc. War Dept. Staff paper 26Feb47, FRUS 1947, II, 277–81.

21. Patterson to Marshall 18Feb47, Marshall to Patterson 28Feb47, FRUS 1947, II, 170–71, 185.

XI: THE TRUMAN DOCTRINE

A convenient summary of factors that bore directly on the Truman Doctrine can be found in Bruce Kuniholm, *The Origins of the Cold War in the Near East.*

1. File of corres. between Marshall and Acting Pres. Frank D. Fackenthal, 21Feb47, convocation, furnished by Virginia Xanthos of University staff, ML.

2. Loy Henderson, in an int. filed at the Truman Library, said that Marshall was away because of his practice of leaving his office early each Friday to go to his home in Leesburg. His appointment books (in ML) show otherwise.

   Quite possibly the Greek and Turkish situations had been discussed before the morning of February 21. U.S. Ambassador to Greece Lincoln MacVeagh had previously warned of an approaching crisis. Paul Porter of the economic mission to Greece and Mark Ethridge, chief of the U.N. mission to Greece, had made similar suggestions of impending trouble. But the messages of February 21 that Acheson received and summarized for Marshall were not discussed with him then at the State Department, because the itinerary for his trip shows that he was picked up by car at his quarters at 7:30 A.M. and taken to Union Station, where he joined General Eisenhower in his special coach.

   Sgt. C. J. George's memo for Gen. Marshall, 20Feb47, ML. See *Eisenhower Papers,* v. VIII, 1535, n. 2.

3. Text of speech in Marshall Speech File, ML. Appen, 525–28.

4. Ibid. Walter Wanger, the film producer, in congratulating Marshall on the speech, said that he should give a more comprehensive talk later along the same lines. Marshall replied that he planned to do so after his return from the Soviet Union. While this should not be overstressed, it is clear that he was thinking of the need to alert the United States to its responsibilities.

5. Memo of director of the Office of the Near East Div. to Sec. State, 24Feb47, memo of conv. between Marshall and Inverchapel by Loy Henderson, 24Feb47, memo titled "Under Secretary of State to Secretary concerning visit, 24Feb47," FRUS 1947, V, 42–45. A notation says the last memo was prepared for Marshall to sign for the Pres. and pertained to Marshall rather than to the Under Secretary. See Acheson, *Present at the Creation*, 218–19.

6. Mins. of Spec. Comm., 24Feb47, FRUS 1947, V, 45–47.

7. Jones, *Fifteen Weeks*, 139; Acheson, *Present at the Creation*, 219.

8. This and the following paragraphs are based on a Sec. State statement (undated but attached to note of 27Feb47, to Pres.), which Marshall noted he made to congressmen that morning, FRUS 1947, V, 60–62.

9. Truman *Memoirs*, 126; Vandenberg, *Vandenberg Papers*, 318–19. Jones, *Fifteen Weeks*, 139–42; Acheson, *Present at the Creation*, 219. Ms. Lynn Eden, former Smithsonian Fellow at the Eisenhower Institute, at my request checked the Vandenberg papers at the University of Michigan. She found no diary entries concerning this period, but two copies of the Marshall statement. The younger Vandenberg clearly drew on this source, leaving no indication that Acheson had spoken. He actually quotes Marshall saying the choice was between acting with energy or losing by default. On that point, says the editor, he struck a responsive note with Vandenberg.

10. Robert Donovan, *Conflict and Crisis*, 282–86; Jones, *Fifteen Weeks*, 153–60. The Joseph Jones and Clark Clifford papers at the Truman Library contain various drafts of the speech.

11. Charles Bohlen, *Witness to History*, 261.

12. Donovan, *Conflict and Crisis*, 281–83.

13. Acheson, *Present at the Creation*, 221.

XII: MEETING AT MOSCOW

Besides the official records, I have drawn heavily on Col. Marshall S. Carter's letters to his wife. Important books are: Walter Bedell Smith, *My Three Years in Moscow;* Lucius Clay, *Decision in Germany;* John Backer, *Winds of History;* Alan Bullock, *Ernest Bevin, Foreign Secretary;* Charles Bohlen, *Witness to History;* John Gimbel, *The Origins of the Marshall Plan.*

1. *Time*, 10Mar47. Col. Marshall S. Carter, conscious of the historical importance of the trip, decided to combine personal letters to his wife with comments on the trip. Copies of the letters to his wife and parents for this trip, and later ones written when he accompanied Marshall to Rio de Janeiro and Bogotá, are in ML.

2. Benjamin Cohen, one of the early New Dealers, had joined with Thomas Corcoran in writing some of the early Roosevelt measures. As counselor to the State Dept. under James Byrnes, he had become involved in early postwar German policy. He wrote some of the key briefing papers for Marshall before his trip to Moscow. H. Freeman Matthews had served for the State Dept. in European assignments during World War II and was highly regarded as an expert on such matters.

Sec. Byrnes, recognizing the importance of Senate approval of treaties, took the Chairman of the Senate Foreign Relations Committee, Republican Arthur H. Vandenberg, and the ranking Democratic minority member, Tom Connally, with him to the U.N. mtg. in London in 1946. Marshall saw the value of this support. He saw to it that Vandenberg and Connally were with him at the conf. in Rio de Janeiro in 1947.

3. Ronald K. Pruessen, *John Foster Dulles,*

338; Eleanor Lansing Dulles, *Chances of a Lifetime*, 220–21.

4. Bohlen, *Witness to History*, 1–240.
5. Notes on Marshall mtgs. with Prime Min. Paul Ramadier and Pres. Vincent Auriol, 6Mar47, FRUS 1947, II, 190–95. Acting For. Min. Pierre-Henri Teitgen sat in with Auriol at the conf.
6. Carter to Mrs. Carter, 6Mar47, Carter Papers, ML.
7. See ref. to this mtg. with Senate For. Rels. Comm. in an earlier chapter. Probably it should be placed here, along with a statement about the lengthy briefings given by Cohen, Riddleberger, Bohlen, Thorp, and others. It may have been an injection of Byrnes's so-called moderate philosophy, noted earlier, or a philosophy colored by Kennan's views, a touch of Forrestal, and parts of Acheson, Henderson, and others. Although Marshall was pounded with various studies reflecting the growing fear and antagonism toward the Soviets, it would seem difficult to inject a hard line into him in little more than a month. The anti-Soviet remarks seen in his speeches after his return from Moscow depend more on his reactions to Stalin and Molotov at the Moscow Conf. than on any material he got from the briefings. Clifford, later to accuse Marshall of being a prisoner of the State Dept., was in accord with those in State who took a hard line on the Russians.
8. Lucius Clay, *Decision in Germany*, 147. Clay says the group arrived on the 8th, but see summary of telegram from Paris to State on 7Mar, saying that Marshall arrived shortly after noon in Paris on 6Mar, and left next day at 2:00 P.M. for Germany. He spent two nights in Germany. FRUS 1947, II, 190; Walter Bedell Smith, *My Three Years in Moscow*, 215–16.
9. Smith, *Three Years*, 213–14; Carter to Mrs. Carter, 14Mar47, Carter Papers; *Life*, Mar47, had an article and photos of Spaso House.
10. Int. by author with Carter, April 18, 1980.
11. Ibid.
12. Clay, *Decision in Germany*, 147.
13. Pruessen, *John Foster Dulles*, 345.
14. Carter to Mrs. Carter, 20Mar47, Carter Papers, ML.
15. Carter to Mrs. Carter, 21Mar47, 9Apr47.
16. Alan Bullock, *Ernest Bevin, Foreign Secretary*, 848–56. See also the delightful ch. on Bevin in Dean Acheson, *Sketches from Life.*
17. Georges Bidault, *Resistance: The Political Autobiography of Georges Bidault.*
18. Mins. of mtg. of Marshall, Bidault, and others, 13Mar47, FRUS 1947, II, 246–49.
19. Marshall to President and Acheson, 13Mar47, FRUS 1947, II, 249–51. At Moscow, Marshall continued the practice he had begun in China of sending almost nightly summaries of the days' discussions. Most of those from China were written by Marshall personally. At Moscow he wrote the first msg., then, since Carter was also attending the sessions, asked him to write them. Carter, in turn, assigned most of the task to Bromley Smith, a member of the State Dept. staff who had accompanied them to Moscow. The author has used these summaries, signed by Marshall, as if they were actually written by him, since they summarize what he said and heard.
20. Smith, *My Three Years in Moscow*, 214–20: Marshall to Truman, 14Mar45, FRUS 1947, II, 251–52.
21. Marshall to Pres., 17Mar47, FRUS 1947, II, 256–57.
22. U.S. Delegation Mins. CFM, 18 Mar47, 260–61; Clay, *Decision in Germany*, 151, has a slightly different version.
23. Marshall to Acting Sec. State, 19Mar47, FRUS 1947, II, 263.
24. Marshall to Acting Sec. State, 20Mar47, FRUS 1947, II, 265.
25. Memo of conv., Marshall with Bevin, 22Mar47, FRUS 1947, II, 272–75.
26. Marshall to Actg Sec State 26Mar47, FRUS 1947, II, 292.
27. Gimbel, *Origins of the Marshall Plan*, 186–89.
28. Sec State to Acting Sec State, 2Apr47, FRUS 1947, II, 304–06.
29. Sec State to Acting Sec State, 8Apr47, FRUS 1947, II, 313–15.
30. Memo of conv., Marshall and Bevin, 8Apr47, FRUS 1947, II, 315–17.

31. Sec. State to Acting Sec. State, 10Apr47, FRUS 1947, II, 323–25.
32. Sec. State to Acting Sec. State, 15Apr47, FRUS 1947, II, 334–36.
33. A description of the discussion between Stalin and Marshall is in a memo that Bohlen says he prepared, in *Witness to History*, 263. Memo of Conv. Marshall, Bevin et al), 15Apr47, FRUS 1947, II, 337–44.
34. Marshall to Acting Sec. State, 16Apr47, FRUS 1947, II, 347.
35. Marshall to Acting Sec. State, 22Apr47, FRUS 1947, II, 376.
36. Marshall to Acting Sec. State, 23Apr47, FRUS 1947, II, 375–76.
37. Marshall to Acting Sec. State, 25Apr47, FRUS 1947, II, 388–90.
38. Smith, *My Three Years in Moscow*, 227–29.
39. John Backer, *The Decision to Divide Germany*, 45.
40. Marshall to Acting Sec. State, 19Apr47, about his talk with Bevin the day before, FRUS 1947, II, 357–58. See also Bullock, *Ernest Bevin, Foreign Secretary*, 390–91. Bevin wanted to discuss bizonal proposals with Marshall, Clay, and Robertson in Berlin, but since he could not fly because of his health, he suggested that Marshall arrange for a brief conf. with Clay and Robertson at Templehof before the Secretary took off for the United States.
41. Marshall memo on conv. with Bidault, 20Apr47, FRUS 1947, II, 367–70.
42. Bidault, *Resistance*, 114.
43. Robert Murphy, *Diplomat Among Warriors*, 342.
44. Int. by author with Marshall, 14Nov56.
45. Bohlen, *Witness to History*, 263.

XIII: THE HARVARD SPEECH

1. Int. with Lt. Gen. Marshall S. Carter, 11Nov60; int. with Bohlen (Paris), 7Jun67.
2. Text of speech as delivered to the press, 28Apr47, ML.
3. Eisenhower to Clay, 18Mar47, copy of letter in Eisenhower files given to me by Stephen Ambrose.
4. Acheson to Sec. War, 5Mar47, memo by Gen. Hilldring, 17Mar47, Sheppard of Bur. of Budget to Dir. of Budget, 7Apr47, C. Tyler Wood to Acheson, 17Apr47; rpt. of SWNCC, 21Apr47, FRUS 1947, III, 204, 220.
5. Fn to above report indicating the final report was submitted 3Oct47. FRUS 1947, III, 219.

   One survey was prompted by a request from the Bureau of the Budget for the setting of priorities. A preliminary report on various programs already in train was made by Tyler Wood, special assistant to Assistant Secretary for Economic Affairs Willard Thorp. Among other things, it noted the study being made of other possible requirements which soon must be considered. Thorp, Wood, and other members of the State Department concerned with economic affairs, were soon at work on special studies on economic aid. Wood, a former broker, began a series of luncheons with colleagues that provided material for later consideration.
6. Acheson, *Present at the Creation*, 228–30. Truman quote is on 228.
7. Ibid., 236.
8. For background, see int. by author with Marshall, 19Nov56; int. by author with George Kennan, Princeton, 17Feb59. See also the memo Kennan had prepared before that on the Policy Planning Staff; the copy given the author is in ML; see Kennan, *Memoirs*, 313. For details on the founding of the Policy Planning Staff, see FRUS 1947, III, 220, n. 2. Ronald Steel, *Walter Lippmann and the American Century*, 440–42. Neither Acheson nor Kennan mentions Lippmann in this connection, although Joseph Jones says he used an article by Lippmann in writing the Delta Speech.
9. Views expressed in the Policy Planning Staff on 15May were reported by Kennan the next day. See Kennan memo, 16May47, and Kennan to Acheson, 23May47, FRUS 1947, III, 220–23, 223–30.
10. Int. by author with Marshall, 19Nov56; int. with Kennan, 17Feb59;

Kennan, *Memoirs*, 330–35.

11. Memo by Under Sec. Will L. Clayton, 27May47, FRUS 1947, III, 230–32.
12. Acheson to Sec. State, 28May47, FRUS 1947, III, 232–33.
13. See file of corres. with Dr. James B. Conant on this degree, in 1945, 1946, 1947, and Laird Bell Correspondence in Harvard Speech File, ML.
14. Int. by author with Marshall, 19Nov56.
15. Memo, Marshall to Gen. Carter, 30May47, ML.
16. Int. by author with Bohlen, 31May67, at U.S. Emb. in Paris, ML.
17. The basic facts about the ceremonies are in a detailed article in *Harvard Alumni Bulletin*, 14Jun47, v. 49, no. 17, 714. See also *New York Times*, 6Jun47. E. J. Kahn, Jr., *Harvard: Through Change and Through Storm*, ch. XXIII, has interesting details on commencements and alumni meetings at Harvard. He incorrectly says that Marshall and MacArthur were offered open-ended degrees—Come and get them when you can. He says all others were proposed by a committee of fellows in December and then approved by the corporation and overseers in January. Prof. Robert Blackburn, present at the speech, got additional material from Harvard for me.
18. Text of reading copy initialed by Marshall, at Marshall Museum display, ML.
19. *New York Times*, 6Jun47.
20. Int. by author with Sir John Balfour, 25Nov77.
21. Balfour to Butler, 29May47, enc. 23May statement on talk with Acheson on 22May, For. Off. Files, British Pub. Rec. Off., Kew (copy in ML).
22. Int. by Barbara Vandegrift with Leonard Miall at ML, 19Sep77. Miall had published earlier accounts, which he gave the ML. Much of the material given to the author by Balfour and to Mrs. Vandegrift by Miall may also be found in John Wheeler-Bennett and Anthony Nicholls, *The Semblance of Peace*, 568–71. In a few cases, pertaining to authorship of the Harvard speech and the surmise about some of Marshall's actions, their book is in error.
23. Nevile Butler to Balfour, 10Jun47, Pub. Rec. Off., Kew, AN 1976. 17/45.

XIV: PRELIMINARIES FOR ERP

1. Marshall to Emb. in France (similar to text repeated to other missions), 12Jun47, FRUS 1947, III, 249–51.
2. *New York Times*, 7Jun47.
3. This and the following paragraph are based on Inverchapel to Sec. State, 14Jun47, Gallman to Sec. State, 16Jun47, FRUS 1947, III, 253–55. See also Bullock, *Ernest Bevin, Foreign Secretary*, 404–9.
4. Caffery to Sec. State, 18Jun47, FRUS 1947, III, 259–60.
5. Memo of conv., Sec. State with Henri Bonnet and H. Freeman Matthews, 13Jun37, FRUS 1947, III, 251–53.
6. Memo of conv. with Polish Amb. by Benjamin Cohen, n.d., FRUS 1947, III, 260–61.
7. Smith to Marshall, 26Jun47, FRUS 1947, III, 294–95.
8. Caffery to Sec. State, 19Jun47, FRUS 1947, III, 262.
9. Pres. to press, 22Jun47, proposals for study by Policy Planning Staff, 19Jun47, FRUS 1947, III, 264–66. (gives names of Harriman Committee)
10. Clayton memo on mtg. with British Cabinet members and Amb. Douglas, 24Jun47, FRUS 1947, III, 268–76.
11. Memo on mtg. of Clayton with British Cabinet members, 25Jun47, FRUS 1947, III, 280–81.
12. Memo on mtg. of Clayton with British Cabinet members, 26Jun47, FRUS 1947, III, 288–89.
13. Caffery to Sec. State, 28Jun47 (re 27Jun mtg.), Caffery to Sec. State, 28Jun47, Caffery to Sec. State, 29Jun47, FRUS 1947, III, 298–301.
14. Caffery to Sec. State, 1Jul47, FRUS 1947, III, 302.
15. Caffery to Marshall, 29Jun47, FRUS 1947, III, 301.
16. Caffery to Sec. State, 1Jul47, FRUS 1947, III, 303–4.
17. Douglas to Sec. State, 3Jul47, FRUS 1947, III, 306.

18. Marshall to Emb. in France, 3Jul47, FRUS 1947, III, 308.
19. Caffery to Sec. State, 3Jul47, FRUS 1947, III, 308–9.
20. Ibid.
21. Marshall to Clayton, 3Jul47, FRUS 1947, III, 309–10.
22. Douglas to Sec. State, 4Jul47, FRUS 1947, III, 310–12.
23. Ibid.
24. Caffery to Sec. State, 4Jul47, FRUS 1947, III, 312–13.
25. Steinhardt to Marshall, 7Jul47, FRUS 1947, III, 313–14.
26. Steinhardt to Sec. State, 10Jul47, FRUS 1947, III, 319–20.
27. Griffis to Sec. State, 1089, 10Jul47, Griffis to Marshall, 1092, 10Jul47, FRUS 1947, III, 320–22.
28. Smith to Sec. State, 11Jul47, FRUS 1947, III, 327.
29. This and the following paragraphs are derived from Policy Planning Staff memo, GFK notes for Marshall, 21Jul47, FRUS 1947, III, 335–37.
30. Memo on Paris discussions, 8Aug47, FRUS 1947, III, 345–50.
31. Lovett and Wood to Clayton, 11Aug47, FRUS 1947, III, 350–51.
32. Caffery for Clayton to Lovett, 12Aug47, Lovett to Caffery, 14Aug47, FRUS 1947, III, 356–60.
33. Memo by Policy Planning Staff, PPS-6, 14Aug47, FRUS 1947, III, 360–63.
34. Lovett to Douglas, 20Aug47, Douglas to Lovett, 21Aug47, Clayton and Caffery to State Dept., 20Aug47, FRUS 1947, III, 367–69, 364–67.
35. Lovett to Marshall, 24Aug47, with n. (p. 375) containing Marshall's reply, 24Aug47, FRUS 1947, III, 372–75.
36. Lovett to Caffery, 24Aug47, Clayton to Lovett, 25Aug47, FRUS 1947, III, 376–79.
37. This and the following paragraphs are derived from memo by Kennan on ERP, 4Sep47, initialed by Marshall, FRUS 1947, III, 397–405.

38. Acting Sec. State for Marshall to Truman, 6Sep47, with n. that statement was to be released 10Sep47, FRUS 1947, III, 410–11.
39. Douglas to Marshall, 9Sep47, Caffery et al. to Marshall, 11Sep47, FRUS 1947, III, 420, 421–23.
40. Statements by Lovett and Truman on 24, 25Sep47, State Dept. *Bulletin,* 4Oct47.
41. I have followed the extremely useful summary of the report given in Harry B. Price's *The Marshall Plan and Its Meaning;* U.S. Dept. of State, Comm. of Econ. Cooperation, "General Report," I, 27; Ernest H. van den Beugel, *From Marshall Aid to Atlantic Partnership,* 86–88. Van den Beugel was a member of the coordinating group.
42. Informal *aide-mémoire* by Franks to Lovett, 22Oct47, FRUS 1947, III, 446–80.
43. CEEC Washington delegation to State Dept., 27Oct47, FRUS 1947, III, 452–56.
44. Van den Beugel, *Marshall Aid to Atlantic Partnership,* 92–93.
45. Ibid., 93.
46. Record of mtg. between members of Advisory Steering Comm. and the CEEC delegation, 4Nov47, which contains ref. to informal *aide-mémoire,* Lovett to Franks, 3Nov47, FRUS 1947, III, 461–70.
47. Van den Beugel, *Marshall Aid to Atlantic Partnership,* 94–97.
48. Memo., 20Sep47, FRUS 1947, III, 472. The memo was apparently prepared by the Advisory Steering Comm. for the use of the President.
49. Lovett to Truman, 13Oct47, FRUS 1947, III, 478–81. Marshall was at the U.N. session in New York.
50. Lovett to Marshall, 4Dec47, FRUS 1947, III, 482–84.
51. Donovan, *Conflict and Crisis,* 287, quoting Clark Clifford.

XV: THE FIGHT FOR ERP

1. *Time,* 3Jan44.
2. Ibid, 5Jan48. David Lilienthal, *Journals,* II, 275, says that he was told near the end of 1947 that Henry Luce wanted *him* to be voted "Man of the Year." After Marshall's selection for that title, a *Time* editor told Lilienthal that Luce had made an "impassioned" speech for his candidacy but a secret vote of all the editors ruled otherwise.

3. Because of Marshall's dependence on this group in his personal efforts to sell the European Recovery Program, it is useful to cite the following statement from the history of the Plan sponsored by the Economic Cooperation Administration on the Marshall Plan, and written by Harry B. Price:

"Extensive groundwork was also being laid, concurrently, by the executive agencies of the government, under the general direction of Under Secretary of State Robert A. Lovett. Part of this consisted in support given to the Harriman, Nourse and Krug Committees. Part was in further converting the Marshall Plan from a general conception into a specific program that could be presented to Congress.

"Participants in this intensive effort, to name but a few, included Willard Thorp, C. Tyler Wood, Paul Nitze who provided much of the intellectual and organizing drive, Lincoln Gordon, C. H. Bonesteel III, Charles Kindleberger, Ernest Gross, and Ambassador Douglas, who was called back repeatedly from London to give political guidance and to conduct key consultations with members of Congress." (Price, *Marshall Plan and Its Meaning*, p. 45–46)
4. Int. by author with Marshall, 19Nov56.
5. *New York Times*, 9Jan48.
6. Vandenberg to Douglas,
7. Senate For. Rels. Comm., *Hearings on European Recovery Program*, 8Jan48.
8. House of Reps. Comm. on For. Affs, *Hearings on the European Recovery Program*, 12Jan48.
9. Hadley Arkes, *Bureaucracy, the Marshall Plan, and the National Interest*, 346–49, analyzes congressional thinking on the administrator issue.
10. Int. by author with Marshall, 20Nov56.
11. Marshall speech before Pittsburgh Chamber of Commerce, 13Jan48, in Marshall Speech File, ML.
12. Marshall speech before National Cotton Council, Atlanta, 22Jan48, in Marshall Speech File, ML.
13. *Time*, 26Jan48.
14. Marshall speech by telephone from Knoxville, to National Farm Institute, Des Moines, 13Feb48, Marshall Speech File, ML; int. by author with Marshall, 20Nov48.
15. *Washington Post*, 11Feb48, article in *New York Times*, 11Feb48, memo by C. J. George to Marshall, 13Feb48, *Time*, 29Feb48, ML.
16. *Time*, 22Mar48; Marshall address to Federal Council of Churches, National Cathedral, Washington, 11Mar48, in Marshall Speech file, ML. For more complete details on the Czech Crisis, see 361–62.
17. Donovan, *Conflict and Crisis*, 380.
18. Marshall address at University of California, Berkeley, 19Mar48, Marshall Speech File, ML.
19. Marshall address at University of California, Los Angeles, 20Nov48, Marshall Speech File.
20. *The Private Papers of Senator Vandenberg*, 388–93.
21. *Time*, 24Mar48.
22. Marshall speech to General Federation of Women's Clubs, 28May48, Portland, Ore., Marshall Speech File, ML.
23. Int. by author with Marshall, 20Nov56.
24. *Private Papers of Senator Vandenberg*, 396–98.
25. Ibid., 394.
26. Acheson, *Present at the Creation*, 241–42.
27. *Time*, 12Apr48.
28. Int. by author with Paul Gray Hoffman, 19, Oct. 1960.

XVI: AMERICAN DIVISION OVER CHINA

1. John Carter Vincent to Marshall, 7Feb47; Memo by Vincent to Marshall, 7Feb47, FRUS 1947, VII, 789–93, 793–94.
2. Mtg. of Marshall with Secretaries Patterson and Forrestal, 12Feb47, FRUS 1947, VII, 795–97.
3. Marshall to Vincent, 27Feb47, FRUS 1947, VII, 803–04.
4. Stuart to Marshall, 12Mar47; Stuart to

Marshall, 19Mar47, FRUS 1947, VII, 58–60, 63–67; Marshall to Stuart, 16Mar47, FRUS 1947, VII, 68.

5. Stuart to Marshall, 21Mar47, FRUS 1947, VII, 73–81.

6. Stuart to Marshall, 22Mar47; Stuart to Marshall, 23Mar47, FRUS 1947, VII, 80–81, 82–83.

7. Stuart to Marshall, 29Mar47; Stuart to Marshall, 4Apr47, FRUS 1947, VII, 91–95.

8. Stuart to Marshall, 21Mar47; Ringwalt to Vincent, 2Apr47, FRUS 1947, VII, 811–13, 813–14.

9. Timberman to Butterworth, 22Apr47; Memo by Vincent giving Marshall directions for transfer of arms and ammo, 26May47, FRUS 1947, VII, 821–822, 825–26.

10. Stuart to Marshall, 26Mar47; Stuart to Marshall, 12Apr47, FRUS 1947, VII, 87–88, 96–97.

11. Stuart to Marshall, 8May47, FRUS 1947, VII, 114–17.

12. Stuart to Marshall, 20May47; Stuart to Marshall, 21May47; Stuart to Marshall, 21May47, FRUS 1947, VII, 131–33, 135–38.

13. Stuart to Marshall, 4Jun47; Stuart to Marshall, 4Jun47, FRUS 1947, VII, 160, 161–62.

14. Vincent to Marshall, 5Jun47; Vincent to Marshall, 6Jun47, FRUS 1947, VII, 165–66, 169.

15. Memo by JCS to SWNCC, 9Jun47, FRUS 1947, VII, 838–48.

16. Memo by Dir. Off. of Far Eastern Aff. (Vincent) to Marshall, 20Jun47, FRUS 1947, VII, 849–50.

17. Mtg. of Marshall, Patterson, and Forrestal, 26Jun47; Memo by Vincent, 27Jun47; Memo by Under Sec. Acheson, 27Jun47, FRUS 1947, VII, 849, 850–52, 853–54, 855.

18. Marshall to Stuart, 3Jul47, FRUS 1947, VII, 213.

19. William Stueck's *The Wedemeyer Mission* appeared after I had written this chapter. It gives an exellent summary of the problems involved with the Mission. Marshall's explanation of the background of the Mission is given in his memo to Acheson, 2Jul47, FRUS 1947, VII, 634–35.

20. Memo Wedemeyer to Marshall, 2Jul47, FRUS 1947, VII, 636–38.

21 Final Directive to Wedemeyer by Truman, 9Jul47, FRUS 1947, VII, 640–41.

22 Stuart to Marshall, 16Jul47; Marshall to Stuart, 16Jul47, FRUS 1947, VII, 650–51.

23. Ludden to Wedemeyer, 23Jul47; FRUS 1947, VII, 656–60.

24. Wedemeyer to Marshall, 29Jul47, FRUS 1947, VII, 682–86.

25. Wedemeyer to Marshall, 8Aug47, FRUS 1947, VII, 712–15.

26. Wedemeyer to Marshall, 17Aug47, FRUS 1947, VII, 725–26.

27. Wedemeyer's remarks, 23Aug47, are in State Dept., *US Relations With China*, (White Paper), 758–62. Wedemeyer, *Wedemeyer Reports!*, 387–95, discusses what he intended to do in his later report.

28. Wedemeyer to Marshall, 7Sep47; Wedemeyer to Marshall, 8Sep47, FRUS 1947, VII, 769–70, 770–71.

29. Butterworth to Marshall, 26Sep47; Humelsine to Lovett, 28Sep47, FRUS 1947, VII, 778, 779.

30. Wedemeyer, Ret., 19Sep47; State Dept., *US Relations With China* (White Paper), 764–814.

31. State Dept., *US Relations With China* (White Paper), 380–84.

32. See FRUS 1948, VII, 492–620.

XVII: THE GERMAN PROBLEM

Robert P. Browder and Thomas G. Smith, *Independent, a Biography of Lewis W. Douglas*, ch. 21, is valuable for this chapter.

1. Hickerson ints. at Truman Library and at Princeton in Dulles collection.

2. Joseph M. Dodge to Sec. State, 4Nov47, FRUS 1947, II, 673–75.

3. Text of speech by Sec. Marshall to Council of For. Rels. and Chamber of Commerce, Chicago, Palmer House, 18Nov47, Marshall Speech Book, ML.

4. Marshall to State, Pres., Lovett, and others, 25Nov47, U.S. Delegation to State, Pres., and others, 26Nov47, FRUS 1947, II, 731–33, 733–34.

5. Clay, *Decision in Germany*, 344–45.
6. Memo of conv. between Marshall and Bidault, 28Nov47, FRUS 1947, II, 737–39.
7. U.S. Delegation to Truman and others, 28Nov47, FRUS 1947, II, 736–37.
8. U.S. Delegation to Truman and others, 4Dec47, FRUS 1947, II, 742–44.
9. U.S. Delegation to Truman and others, 5Dec47, FRUS 1947, II, 747–48.
10. Ibid., 748–50.
11. Marshall to Lovett, 6Dec47, on 4Dec47 conv. with Bevin and others.
12. Marshall to Truman, Lovett, and others, 8Dec47, FRUS 1947, II, 756–58.
13. Lovett to Marshall, enc. Truman message, 11Dec47, FRUS 1947, II, 764.
14. Marshall to Truman and others, 12Dec47, Marshall to Lovett, 13Dec47, FRUS 1947, II, 766–70; State Dept. *Bulletin*, 28Dec47; Clay, *Decision in Germany*, 348. Slightly different paraphrase in FRUS, 767.
15. Marshall to Truman and others, 15Dec47, FRUS 1947, II, 770–72.
16. Ibid.
17. British memo of conv. between Marshall and Bevin, n.d., FRUS 1947, II, 815–22.
18. Memo by Amb. Murphy of conv. between Marshall, Bevin, and others, 18Dec47, FRUS 1947, II, 827–29; memo by Frank Roberts of conv. between Marshall, Bevin, and others, 18Dec47, ibid., 822–29.
19. Marshall to Inverchapel, 8Jan48, FRUS 1948, II, 24–26. N. 1 on p. 24 includes a summary of recommendations by the British Cabinet transmitted by Inverchapel.
20. For messages dealing with this early period, see FRUS 1948, II, 1–25. For Bidault's complaint, see Caffery to Marshall, 10Jan48, FRUS 1948, II, 20–21, n. 2 on p. 21.
21. Associate Chief of the Div. of Western Eur. Affs. (W. Wallner), 16Jan48, FRUS 1948, II, 27–28.
22. Memo by Marshall on conv. with Amb. Bonnet, 20Jan48, FRUS 1948, II, 37–38.
23. Chief, Div. of Western Eur. Aff. (Achilles), to French For. Min., 13Feb48, Sec. State to Pres., 11Feb48, FRUS 1948, II, 60, 63–64.
24. Sec. State to U.S. Emb. France, 19Feb48, Sec. State to U.S. Embs., 20Feb48, FRUS 1948, II, 70–73.
25. List of full delegation, ed. note, memo by Benelux countries (Belgium, Netherlands, Luxembourg), 28Feb48, FRUS 1948, II, 85–87, 91, 103–4.
26. Douglas to Sec. State, 25Feb48, FRUS 1948, II, 89–90.
27. Douglas to State Dept., 3Mar48, Douglas to State Dept., 4Mar48, FRUS 1948, II, 120, 128–30.
28. Douglas to Lovett, 6Mar48, FRUS 1948, II, 138–39.
29. Communiqué of London Conf., 6Mar48, FRUS 1948, II, 141–44.
30. Ibid., 143.
31. Murphy to Sec. State, 30Mar48, Murphy to Sec. State, 1Apr48, FRUS 1948, II, 154–56, 158–60.
32. Murphy to State Dept., 8Apr48, FRUS 1948, II, 169–70; Clay, *Decision in Germany*, 397–98.
33. Douglas to Marshall, 27Apr48, Sec. State and Lovell to Douglas, 28Apr48, FRUS 1948, II, 205–7.
34. Douglas to Marshall, 12May48, FRUS 1948, II, 235–37.
35. Royall to Marshall, 18May48, Lovett for Marshall to Royall, 25May48, FRUS 1948, II, 251–53.
36. Douglas to Sec. State, 1May48, FRUS 1948, II, 214–15.
37. Douglas to Sec. State, 21May48, FRUS 1948, II, 208–9.
38. Caffery to Sec. State, 24May48, Caffery to Sec. State, 25May48, FRUS 1948, II, 273–74, 281.
39. Caffery to Sec. State, 2Jun48, FRUS 1948, II, 317–18.
40. Marshall to U.S. Emb. in Paris, 7Jun48, Sec. State to U.S. Emb. in Paris, 7Jun48, FRUS 1948, II, 320.
41. Amb. Kirk to Sec. State, 9Jun48, Caffery to Sec. State, 9Jun48, ed. statement, FRUS 1948, II, 320.
42. Caffery to Sec. State, 10Jun48, FRUS 1948, II, 319–20.
43. Caffery to Marshall, 10Jun48, FRUS 1948, II, 327–28.
44. Douglas to Sec. State, 17Jun48, FRUS 1948, II, 331–35.
45. Caffery to Sec. State, 17Jun48, ed. note containing announcement of Amb. Bonnet on Assembly action, FRUS 1948, II, 335–37.

XVIII: THE BERLIN CRISIS

In chs. XVII and XXI, both on the Berlin crisis, I have drawn on Lucius D. Clay, *Decision in Germany;* Walter Bedell Smith, *My Three Years in Moscow;* John Backer, *Winds of History: The German Years of Lucius DuBignon Clay;* Alan Bullock, *Ernest Bevin, Foreign Secretary;* Thomas Paterson, *Soviet American Confrontation;* Daniel Yergin, *Shattered Peace.*

1. Kennan, *Memoirs, 1925–50,* 403; report by the Policy Planning Staff, 6Nov47, FRUS 1947, II, 771–77. *Forrestal Diaries,* entry of 7Nov47, 340–42. Truman asked for a copy of the paper.
2. Strang to Bevin, Feb48, For. Off. Files, PRO, copies in ML.
3. Clay to Chamberlin, 5Mar47, in *The Papers of General Lucius D. Clay,* Jean Edward Smith, ed. II, 568–69.
4. Mil. Gov. to For. Off., 3Mar48, 70480, FO 371, PRO, ML.
5. For this and the next two paragraphs, see Donovan, *Conflict and Crisis,* and papers of Clark Clifford and George Elsey in the Truman Library, copies in ML.
6. Murphy to Sec. State, 20Mar48, FRUS 1948, II, 883–84; Clay, *Decision in Germany,* 355–57.
7. Murphy to Saltzman at State Dept., 1Apr48, FRUS 1948, II, 886–89. See also the messages in *The Papers of Lucius D. Clay,* II, 597–618.
8. Lovett to Marshall, 2Apr48, FRUS 1948, II, 889–90.
9. Douglas to Marshall, 28Apr48, FRUS 1948, II, 899–900; see nn. on the statement by Lovett and Marshall.
10. Clay, *Decision in Germany,* 365–66.
11. For a helpful summary of the air lift, see Richard Collier, *Bridge Across the Sky: The Berlin Blockade and Airlift.*
12. Murphy to U.S. Emb., Paris, 4Jul48, FRUS 1948, II, 948–50; Clay, *Decision in Germany,* 367; Clay to Draper, 25Jun48, in *Clay Papers,* II, 696–97.
13. Dr. Evan L. Lewis, in a letter to the author, 16Sep85, says that he was a resident at Walter Reed Hospital when Marshall was examined. His description of the infection is like that given in the diagnosis in Marshall's medical file (in ML). Lewis was impressed by Marshall's belief that the Berlin crisis was so serious that he was prepared to risk his life to wait until after the U.N. General Assembly meeting in the fall.
14. Forrestal, *Diaries,* 451–52.
15. Ibid., 452–54.
16. Policy Planning Staff Memo, 23Jun48,
17. John L. Gaddis, *Strategies of Containment,* 56–75.
18. Marshall statement of 30Jun48, State Dept. *Bulletin,* v. 19, Jul48, 54.
19. Forrestal, *Diaries,* 455–56. Entries in these pages are for July 2, 9, and 15 and cover topics discussed in this and the next three paragraphs. See also Harry R. Borowski, *A Hollow Threat,* Chs. VI and VII.
20. Marshall to Soviet Amb., Washington, 6Jul48, FRUS 1948, II, 950–53.
21. Marshall to U.S. Amb., London, 9Jul48, FRUS 1948, II, 954–56.
22. Clay to Dept. of Army, 10Jul48, FRUS 1948, II, 956–58.
23. Soviet Amb. to Sec. State, 14Jul48, FRUS 1948, II, 960–64.
24. Lovett memo of conv., 15Jul48, Marshall to Douglas, 20Jul48, Marshall to Douglas, 21Jul48, teletype conv., Douglas to Sec. State, 22Jul48, FRUS 1948, II, 975–76, 977–82, 982–83.
25. N. to teletype, 22Jul48, FRUS 1948, II, 977; Truman, *Memoirs,* II, 124–26; Clay, *Decision in Germany,* 368.
26. Record of teletype conv., 26Jul48, Smith to Sec. State, 30Jul48, FRUS 1948, II, 993–96; Smith, *My Three Years in Moscow,* 240.
27. Smith to Sec. State, 3Aug48, Smith to Sec. State, 3Aug48, FRUS 1948, II, 999–1007; The first msg. was drafted by Ambs. of US, Br. & Fr. to the State Dept. The second after Smith sent a message written by the three ambs., he dispatched it with his private comments to Marshall and Lovett.
28. Smith to Sec. State, 4Aug48, Clay to Dept. of Army, 4Aug48, FRUS 1948, II, 1010–13; Page 1013 gives the gist of Douglas's comments (not printed in the vol.).
29. Bohlen to Marshall and others, 4Aug48, FRUS 1948, II, 1024–27, 1035–38.

30. Smith to Sec. State, 6Aug48, FRUS 1948, II, 1018–21.
31. Marshall to Smith, 7Aug48, FRUS 1948, II, 1021–23.
32. Smith to Sec. State, 9Aug48, 12Aug48, FRUS 1948, II, 1024–27, 1035–38.
33. Smith to Sec. State, 2:00 A.M., 17Aug48, after mtg. on 16Aug, FRUS 1948, II, 1042–47.
34. Sec. State to Smith, 17Aug, FRUS 1948, II, 1053–56.
35. Bohlen memo, 21Aug48, FRUS 1948, II, 1058–60.
36. See exchange of msgs. between Washington and Moscow, 24–26Aug48, FRUS 1948, II, 1072–85.
37. Murphy to Marshall, 31Aug48, 1Sep48, FRUS 1948, II, 1099–1103.
38. Murphy to Marshall, 1Sep48, FRUS 1948, II, 1100-03. Bohlen memo, 2Sep48, FRUS 1948, II, 1108–9.
39. Murphy to Sec. State, 2240, 4Sep48, FRUS 1948, II, 1118–22.
40. Marshall to Douglas, 5Sep48, FRUS 1948, II, 1122–24.
41. Douglas to Sec. State, 5Sep48, Douglas to Sec. State, 6Sep48, FRUS 1948, II, 1126–31.
42. Murphy to Sec. State, 7,8Sep48, Marshall to Smith, citing telecon msg. to Douglas, 8Sep48, FRUS 1948, II, 1132–40, 1140–42.
43. Smith to Sec. State, 9Sep48, FRUS 1948, II, 1142–44.
44. Marshall to Smith, 1092, 10Sep48, Marshall to Murphy, 1610, 11Sep48, FRUS 1948, II, 1145–49.
45. Smith to Marshall, 1950, 12Sep48, Marshall to Smith, 1100, 12Sep48, aide-mémoire, 1101, 12Sep48, Marshall to Smith, 12Sep48, FRUS 1948, II, 1150–56.
46. Smith to Marshall, 1976, 14Sep48, FRUS 1948, II, 1157–60.
47. Smith to Sec. State, 16Sep48, Smith to Sec. State, 2034, 18Sep48, FRUS 1948, II, 1160–62, 1166–79.
48. Forrestal Diaries, 487.
49. Ibid., 487–89.

XIX: NORTH ATLANTIC TREATY

I have found particularly helpful: Alan Bullock, *Ernest Bevin, Foreign Secretary;* Timothy Ireland, *Creation of the Entangling Alliance;* Escott Reid, *Time of Fear and Hope: The Making of the North Atlantic Treaty, 1947–49;* Gear Lundestad, *America, Scandinavia, and the Cold War, 1945–48; The Private Papers of Senator Vandenberg;* Lord Gladwyn, *Memoirs of Lord Gladwyn.*

1. Int. by Richard McKinzie with John Hickerson, 10Nov72, Truman Library Oral History Collection. Hickerson says it was the first time he ever heard of the ideas that led to the North Atlantic Treaty Organization. This is contrary to the view that the plan was hatched over lunch between Marshall and Bevin at Bevin's quarters. It also helps demolish the notion that Marshall and Dulles worked on the project on the voyage home from the London Conf.: Marshall flew back while Dulles returned by ship. See Herbert Feis, *From Trust to Terror*, n. 3 on 286.
2. Hickerson int., 10Nov72. See also Lord Gladwyn, *Memoirs of Lord Gladwyn,*
3. Brit. Amb. to U.S. Sec. State, 13Jan48, FRUS 1948, III, 3–6.
4. Kennan to Marshall, 20Jan48, FRUS 1948, III, 7–8.
5. Hickerson to Marshall, 19Jan48, FRUS 1948, III, 6–7.
6. Sec. State to Brit. Amb., 20Jan48, FRUS 1948, III, 8–9.
7. Memo of conv. between Inverchapel, Hickerson, and others, 21Jan48, FRUS 1948, III, 9–12.
8. Conv. between Inverchapel and Lovett, 27Jan48, Inverchapel to Lovett, 28Jan48, Conv. between Inverchapel and Lovett, 7Feb48, FRUS 1948, III, 12–22.
9. Amer. Amb. to Norway (Bay) to Sec. State, 19Feb48, Caffery to Sec. State, 19Feb48, FRUS 1948, III, 24–26.
10. Douglas to Marshall, 26Feb48, Marshall to Caffery, 27Feb48, Sec. State to Douglas, 4Mar48, FRUS 1948, III, 32–34, 38.
11. Hickerson to Sec. State, 4Mar48, FRUS 1948, III, 40–42. Apparently perplexed by Marshall's slowness in pushing the North Atlantic idea, Hickerson concluded that Marshall did not

like Bevin and therefore was slow to act. Several persons checked with this author to see if I had such evidence. Indications are that Marshall got along well with Bevin. Lovett, Lord Franks, and Sir Frank Roberts (private secretary to Bevin) all denied any basis for such a belief. They emphasized that there was no evidence that Marshall ever allowed his personal feelings about people to interfere with his working with them. Some said that Marshall was nettled that Bevin gave him extremely short notice on the Greek-Turkish crisis. Possibly Hickerson caused Acheson to say that Marshall was displeased with Bevin at the London meeting, because of Bevin's promise to make a motion and failure to do so. Evidently Marshall and Lovett proceeded slowly because Vandenberg warned that they should not bring too many new issues before Congress when they had not yet completed all details on the appropriations for ERP.

12. Amb. in Norway (Bay) to Sec. State, 11Mar48, FRUS 1948, III, 42–44.

13. Sec. State to U.S. Amb. Italy, 11Mar48, FRUS 1948, III, 45–46.

14. Brit. *aide-mémoire* to Sec. State, 11Mar48, FRUS 1948, III, 46–48.

15. Marshall to Brit. Amb., 12Mar48, Marshall to Pres. Truman, 12Mar48, FRUS 1948, III, 48, 50.

16. Sec. State to U.S. Amb., Norway, 12Mar48, Amb. Denmark to Sec. State, 12Mar48, FRUS 1948, III, 51.

17. Extracts, Truman msg. to Congress, 17Mar48, FRUS 1948, III, 54–55.

18. Bidault and Bevin to Sec. State, 17Mar48, FRUS 1948, III, 46–48.

19. Rpt. of Policy Planning Staff, 23Mar48, FRUS 1948, III, 54–56; Timothy P. Ireland, *Creating the Entangling Alliance: The Origins of the North Atlantic Treaty Organization*, 82–83; Kennan, *Memoirs*, 404–9.

20. Mins. of third mtg., Pentagon, 24Mar48, FRUS 1948, III, 66–67.

21. Mins. of final mtg., Pentagon, 1Apr48, FRUS 1948, III, 71–78.

22. Bevin to Brit. Emb. for Lovett, 9Apr48, FRUS 1948, III, 79–80.

23. Draft copy of reply, State Dept. to Bevin, Marshall to State Dept., 840.-

02/4-1848, State Dept. Files. Natl. Archives, copy in ML.

24. Kennan, *Memoirs*, 404–5.

25. Conv. between Vandenberg and Lovett, 11Apr48, FRUS 1948, III, 82–84.

26. Bevin and Bidault to Sec. State, 17Apr48, Douglas to Lovett, 17Apr48, FRUS 1948, III, 90–91.

27. Conv. between Vandenberg and Lovett, 18Apr48, FRUS 1948, III, 91–96.

28. Lovett to Marshall, 20Apr48, FRUS 1948, III, 96–97.

29. Marshall to Lovett, 23Apr48, FRUS 1948, III, 103.

30. Conv. between Marshall, Vandenberg, Dulles, and Lovett, 27Apr48, FRUS 1948, III, 104–8.

31. Kennan to Lovett, 29Apr48, FRUS 1948, III, 108–9.

32. U.S. State Dept. press release, 5May48, text of statement of Sec. Marshall before House For. Aff. Comm., FRUS 1948, III, 111–12.

33. See Hearings in Exec. Sess. before the Comm. on For. Rels., U.S. Senate, on Senate Res. 209. A detailed and persuasive account of the importance of Senator Vandenberg in the framing of U.S. foreign policy in this period is given in Daryl J. Hudson, "Vandenberg Reconsidered: Senate Resolution 239 and American Foreign Policy," *Diplomatic History*, v. I, no. 1, Winter 1977, 47–63.

34. Memo of conv. between Marshall and Brit. Amb., 14June48, FRUS 1948, III, 136–37.

35. Marshall to French Amb., 23Jun48, FRUS 1948, III, 139.

36. Rpt. by Nat. Security Council, 28Jun48, FRUS 1948, III, 140–41.

37. Escott Reid, *Time of Fear and Hope: The Making of the North Atlantic Treaty, 1947–49*, 62–63.

38. Mins. of second mtg. of exploratory talks, 6Jul48, FRUS 1948, III, 152–53.

39. Mins. of third mtg., 7Jul48, FRUS 1948, III, 155–60.

40. Mins. of fifth mtg., 9Jul48, FRUS 1948, III, 169–83.

41. Ed. note in FRUS 1948, III, 182.

42. Mins. of conv. between Lovett and European diplomat, 20Aug48, FRUS 1948, III, 214–21.

43. Marshall to Truman, 23Aug48, FRUS 1948, III, 221–22.

44. Kennan to Lovett, 31Aug48, FRUS 1948, III, 225.
45. Mins. of mtg., 10Sep48, FRUS 1948, III, 249–50.
46. Mins. of conv. between Marshall and Swedish For. Min., 14Oct48, FRUS 1948, III, 264–66.
47. Lovett to Marshall, 19Oct48, FRUS 1948, III, 260–67.
48. Western Union Countries to Dept. State, 29Oct48, FRUS 1948, III, 270.
49. Rpt. by Off. of Intellig. Research, 17Nov48, FRUS 1948, III, 273–77.
50. Marshall memo on conv. with For. Min. Lange, 20Nov48, FRUS 1948, III, 279–81.
51. Policy Planning Staff paper, 23Nov38, FRUS 1948, III, 283–88. In his opposition to including other than North Atlantic powers in the treaty, Kennan challenged John Hickerson's views. Both Hickerson and Achilles feared the adverse effect of Kennan and Bohlen on Congress. In an int. filed with the Dulles Oral History Collection, Theodore Achilles said that he and Hickerson felt that Bohlen, as counselor to the State Dept., would harm the prospects for NATO legislation in Congress, and that they persuaded Lovett to help get Bohlen transferred elsewhere. Lovett assured the author that this was not true. The author then wrote Achilles that it would be most unusual for Lovett to act behind Marshall's back in regard to an adviser on whom Marshall heavily depended. The record shows that Bohlen remained as counselor until after Marshall left office and that Acheson took Bohlen with him on trips to the Hill to confer with the Senate For. Rel. Committee. Bohlen was rewarded with the post of Min. to France, where part of his duties were concerned with NATO. His successor as counselor was George Kennan. Achilles replied good-humoredly that this incident probably showed that one shouldn't depend on the memories of old men. Later articles by Achilles made no mention of any adverse influence by Bohlen.
52. Reid, *Time of Fear and Hope*, 63.
53. Acheson, *Present at the Creation*, 266.

XX: MARSHALL, THE UNITED NATIONS, AND PALESTINE

1. For the historical record of Palestine, see Howard M. Sachar, *A History of Israel*.
2. Ibid., 279.
3. Fraser Wilkins memo, 14Jan47, FRUS 1947, V, 1004–5.
4. Memo of conv. Inverchapel and Acheson, 21Jan47, FRUS 1947, V, 1008–11.
5. Bevin to Marshall, 7Feb47, FRUS 1947, V, 1033–35.
6. Exec. Secretariat to Marshall, 25Feb47, 1056–57; Truman statement, 26Feb47, FRUS 1947, V, 1057–58; Bullock, *Ernest Bevin, Foreign Secretary*.
7. Memo, Marshall to Truman, 16May47, FRUS 1947, V, 1083–86.
8. Austin to Marshall, 22May47, FRUS 1947, V, 1086–90.
9. Conv. Shertok and Epstein of the Jewish Agency with Acheson, 29May47, FRUS 1947, V, 1094–96.
10. Ed. note, 6Jun47, Marshall to diplomatic and consular offices, 13Jun47, FRUS 1947, V, 1101–3.
11. Mins. of conv. between Silver and Sec. State, 10Jun47, FRUS 1947, V, 1105–7.
12. Bevin to Marshall, 27Jun47, FRUS 1947, V, 1112–13.
13. Memo on Cabinet mtg., 22Aug47, Lovett to U.S. Emb. London, 22Aug47, Douglas to Sec. State, 26Aug47, FRUS 1947, V, 1138–40, 1140–42.
14. Ed. note on U.N. Spec. Comm. on Palestine, FRUS 1947, V, 1143.
15. Ed. note on *ad hoc* comm., FRUS 1947, V, 1146.
16. Int. by author with Mrs. Roosevelt. 17Mar58.
17. Extracts from mins. of sixth mtg. of U.S. delegation to second Sess. Gen. Assembly, 15Sep47, FRUS 1947, V, 1146–47.
18. Marshall statement to Gen. Assembly, 17Sep47, FRUS 1947, V, 1151.
19. Ed. note on protests, FRUS 1947, V, 1158–59.

20. Henderson to Marshall, 22Sep47, FRUS 1947, V, 1153–58.

21. Memo of luncheon given by Marshall for Arab diplomats, 23Sep47, FRUS 1947, V, 1159–62.

22. Memo by Gen. Hilldring, 24Sep47, V, 1169.

23. Memo of conv. between Amb. Wadsworth and Arab delegates, by Samuel Kopper, 30Oct47, FRUS 1947, V, 2272–76.

24. Memo, Gen. Hilldring to Sec. State, 9Oct47, FRUS 1947, V, 1177–78.

25. Memo of conv. between Brit. Amb. and Lovett, 15Oct47, FRUS 1947, V, 1181–83.

26. Ibn Saud msg. to Truman, 30Oct47, FRUS 1947, V, 1212.

27. Brit Emb. to State Dept., 31Oct47, FRUS 1947, V, 1227–38.

28. Sec. State to Austin, 12Nov47, FRUS 1947, V, 1255–56.

29. Austin, for Johnson and Hilldring, to Lovett, 18Nov47, Lovett to Austin, 19Nov47, FRUS 1947, V, 1266–68, 1269–70.

30. N. to memo by McClintock, 19Nov47, FRUS 1947, V, 1271–72.

31. Henderson to Lovett, 29Nov47, FRUS 1947, V, 1281–83.

32. Lovett to Johnson and Hilldring, 24Nov47, FRUS 1947, V, 1283–84.

33. Austin to Sec. State, 25Nov47, Austin to Sec. State, 29Nov47, FRUS 1947, V, 1287.

34. Bullock, *Ernest Bevin, Foreign Secretary*, 477; Marshall to Lovett, 25Nov47, FRUS 1947, V, 1287–88.

35. Lovett to Truman, 10Dec47, FRUS 1947, V, 1306–7.

36. Marshall to Lovett, 17Dec47, FRUS 1947, V, 1312–13.

37. Lovett to U.S. Emb. Egypt, 20Dec47, FRUS 1947, V, 1319.

38. Policy Planning Staff to Marshall, 19Jan48, FRUS 1948, V, 347–54.

39. Rusk to Lovett, 26Jan48, FRUS 1948, V, 556–62.

40. Kennan comments on Rusk memo, 29Jan48, FRUS 1948, V, 574–90.

41. Henderson to Lovett and Rusk, 6Feb48, FRUS 1948, V, 600–603.

42. Memo, George Wadsworth to Henderson, 4Feb48, FRUS 1948, V, 592–99.

43. Memo, Policy Planning Staff (sgd. George Butler), 11Feb48, FRUS 1948, V, 619–25.

44. Marshall to Mrs. Roosevelt (with summary of two notes from her to him), 16Feb48, FRUS 1948, V, 624.

45. Ed. note, FRUS 1948, V, 632–33.

46. Marshall to Lovett, 19Feb44, Marshall to U.S. Emb. Iraq, 19Feb48, FRUS 1948, V, 653–54.

47. Paper prepared by State Dept. for Pres., n. 1 showing in detail when the msg. was sent and rec'd on Pres.'s ship, 21Feb48, FRUS 1948, V, 637.

48. Memo of conv. between Lovett and Shertok, 21Feb48, FRUS 1948, V, 648–49.

49. State Dept. to Pres., 23Feb48 (incl. statement for release), FRUS 1948, V, 648–49.

50. George T. Mazuzan, *Warren R. Austin at the U.N., 1946–53*, 109–11; extracts from speech, FRUS 1948, V, 651–54.

51. Policy Planning Staff Rpt., 24Feb48, FRUS 1948, V, 655–57.

52. Statement by Austin at U.N., 25Feb48, FRUS 1948, V, 657–58.

53. Marshall press statement of 26 Feb in Marshall to Austin, 27Feb48, FRUS 1948, V, 665–66.

54. Rpt. by CIA, 28Feb48, FRUS 1948, V, 666–75.

55. Memo, Sec. State to Pres. and Cabinet, 5Mar48, FRUS 1948, V, 678–79.

56. Memo, Spec. Counsel Clark Clifford to Pres., 6Mar48, FRUS 1948, V, 687–89.

57. Memo, Clifford to Truman, 8Mar48, FRUS 1948, V, 690ff.

58. Humelsine to Marshall, 22Mar48, FRUS 1948, V, 149–50.

59. Austin to Sec. State, 15Mar48, FRUS 1948, V, 725–28.

60. Austin to Marshall, 17Mar48, FRUS 1948, V, 732–37.

61. Marshall to Austin, 16Mar48, FRUS 1948, V, 728–29.

62. For an account of Weizmann's visit, see Barnet Litvinov, *Weizmann*, 253–54; Truman, *Memoirs*, II, 161.

63. Statement, Austin to Security Council, 19Mar48, FRUS 1948, V, 342–44.

64. Donovan, *Conflicts and Crisis*, 375.

65. Ed. note, FRUS 1948, V, 743–46; Donovan, *Conflicts and Crisis*, 376.

66. Ed. note, FRUS 1948, V, 748–49.

67. Marshall note to Bohlen, 22Mar48, FRUS 1948, V, 750.
68. U.S. Senate, Exec. Sess.,
69. Marshall to U.S. Emb. Egypt, 25Mar48, FRUS 1948, V, 759–60.
70. Conv. between Marshall, Lovett, Shertok, et al., 26Mar48, FRUS 1948, V, 761–64.
71. Shertok to Marshall, 29Apr48, FRUS 1948, V, 874–76.
72. Conv. between Lovett and Inverchapel, 25Apr48, Douglas to Sec. State, 29Apr48, FRUS 1948, V, 868–69, 876–77; Sachar, *Israel,* 310.
73. Memo of conv. between Pres. and advisers, kept by McClintock and sgd. by

Marshall, 12May48, FRUS 1948, V, 972–73.
74. Memo by Lovett on conv. with Clifford, 17May48, FRUS 1948, V, 1006.
75. Ed. note, FRUS 1948, V, 993.
76. Austin to Marshall, 19May48, FRUS 1948, V, 1013–15.
77. Marshall to diplomatic missions, 21Sep48, FRUS 1948, V, 1415–16.
78. Memo by Lovett for files, 30Sep48, FRUS 1948, V, 1437–38.
79. Lovett to Marshall, 29Oct48, FRUS 1948, V, 1527.
80. Lovett to Marshall, 30Oct48, FRUS 1948, V, 1584.
81. Ed. note, FRUS 1948, V, 1661–62.

XXI: STRENGTHENING LATIN AMERICAN TIES

1. Acheson, *Present at the Creation,* 188–90.
2. Charles J. Pach, Jr., "The Commitment of U.S. Military Aid to Latin America, 1944–49," *Diplomatic History,* Summer 1982, vol. 6, no. 3, 225–27; see also Roger R. Trask, "The Impact of the Cold War on United States–Latin American Relations, 1945–1949," *Diplomatic History,* Summer 1977, vI, no. 3, 271–84. An excellent summary of Brazilian-U.S. relations in this period may be found in Frank D. McCann, "Brazil, The United States and World War II," *Diplomatic History,* Winter 1979, v. III, no. 1, 59–76.
3. Pach, "Committment of U.S. Military Aid," 226.
4. Marshall to diplomatic missions, 3Jul47, FRUS 1947, VIII, 9.
5. For detailed coverage of problems with Brazil for the period 1945–60, see Stanley B. Hilton, "The United States, Brazil, and the Cold War, 1945–1960: End of the Special Relationship," *Journal of American History,* December 1981, v. 68, no. 3, 599–624.
6. *Time,* 25Aug47.
7. Vernon Walters, *Silent Missions,* gives the outline of his career and the story of his service at the Rio Conference. See also int. by author with Carter, Walters, and George, 22Oct59.
8. Memo of conv. between Marshall and

Goes de Monteiro, 21Aug47, filed 22Aug47, FRUS 1947, VIII, 54–55.
9. Marshall to Acting Sec. State, 21Aug47, FRUS 1947, VIII, 52.
10. Marshall to Acting Sec. State, 29Aug47, FRUS 1947, VIII, 75.
11. Memo on Truman speech of 2Sep47, FRUS 1947, VIII, 78.
12. Walters, *Silent Missions,* 146; Margaret Truman, *Harry S. Truman,* 408–11.
13. *Time,* 15Sep47; *Private Papers of Senator Vandenberg,* including Mrs. Vandenberg's tribute to the Marshalls, 360–71.
14. Smith to Sec. State, 17Sep47, FRUS 1947, VIII, 85–86.
15. Ness memo to Thorp, 19Feb48, FRUS 1948, IX, 2–9.
16. Marshall to U.S. diplomatic representatives to Latin Amer. republics, 9Mar48, FRUS 1948, IX, 11–16.
17. Amb. William Beaulac to Sec. State, 22Mar48, FRUS 1948, IX, 22–23.
18. Gen. Carter to his wife, 30Mar48.
19. Int. by author with Carter, Walters, and George, 22Oct59; M/Sgt C. J. George was Marshall's orderly and assistant. Sec. State to Acting Sec. State, 1Apr48, FRUS 1948, IX, 28.
20. Memo of Marshall conv. with Neves by Amb. Pawley, 2Apr48, FRUS 1948, IX, 26–28.
21. Martin Speech, 4, 9Apr48, FRUS 1948, IX, 36–39.
22. Ibid., 38.

23. For details of the uprising, I have drawn on a composite picture given in Walters, *Secret Missions,* 150–69; Ridgway, *Soldier,* 178; int. by author with Carter, Walters, and George, 22Oct59. I have also drawn on a paper by my research associate Dr. James Nanney on "The CIA and the Bogotazo." ML has copies of a few letters from Mrs. William Pawley relating to the problems in Bogotá, and William McChesney Martin has given me some of his recollections of the episode. Rpts. by William Beau-

lac, in FRUS 1948, VIII, 39–41, give pertinent details.

24. The author has heard Lovett tell this version of the story in private conversations and speeches. Gen. Carter says that Pres. Truman authorized payment when he authorized shipment.

25. Lovett to Marshall, 19Apr48, FRUS 1948, IX, 49.

26. Marshall to Lovett, 20Apr48, FRUS 1948, IX, 53.

27. Amb. Beaulac to Acting Sec. State, 22Apr48, FRUS 1948, IX, 54–55.

XXII: CONCERN WITH GREECE, 1947–48

1. The early paragraphs of this chapter are based on Queen Frederika's *A Measure of Understanding,* (1971) which draws heavily on her correspondence with Gen. Marshall in the years from 1947 until the onset of his last illness in 1959. After his death, she asked the Marshall Foundation to return the handwritten correspondence.

2. Based on a political summary by John O. Iatrides, ed. of *Ambassador MacVeagh's Reports, 1933–1947,* 714–33.

3. Remarks by Acting Sec. Lovett, Lovett to Truman, 24Nov48, FRUS 1948, V, 614–24.

4. Rpt. to Nat. Security Council, 6Jan48, Leahy to Forrestal, 8Jan48, FRUS 1948, IV, 2–7, 8–9.

5. Int. by author with Gen. James Van Fleet, 15Apr86.

6. These letters are published in Queen Frederika's *A Measure of Understanding,* Ch. 9. See Sec. State to Mission for Aid to Greece, 26Jan48, FRUS 1948, IV, 36–38; int. by author with Gen.

James Van Fleet, Lexington, Va., 15Apr84, ML.

7. Rpt. by NSC to Pres., 12Feb48, Henderson memo of 16Feb48, FRUS 1948, IV, 37–41, 48.

8. Sec. State to Greek Mission for Aid to Greece, 12Mar48, Sec. State to Vandenberg, 18Mar48, FRUS 1948, IV, 60, 61–62.

9. Henderson to U.S. Chargé in Greece, 25Mar48, FRUS 1948, IV, 64–65.

10. Rpt. to NSC, 25Mar48, FRUS 1948, IV, 73–95, 100.

11. C.M. Woodhouse, *The Struggle for Peace, 1941–49,* 236–37.

12. Ibid., 239–45.

13. Marshall to Chargé in Athens, 21Jul48, Sec. State to Chargé in Athens, 2Aug48, FRUS 1948, IV, 115–16, 117–18.

14. Marshall to U.S. Emb. Athens, 6Aug48, FRUS 1948, IV, 118–20.

15. Memo of conv. with Grady by Sec. State, 18Oct48; Sec. State to Lovett, 20Oct48, FRUS 1948, IV, 161–62, 162–64.

XXIII: BERLIN CRISIS: PART II, OR MEETING IN PARIS, 1948

1. Int. by author with Marshall S. Carter, C. J. George, and Vernon Walters, 21Oct59.

2. Ibid.; Vernon Walters, *Secret Missions,* 181.

3. Mins. of mtg. of Marshall with for. mins. of Britain and France, Paris, 20Sep48, FRUS 1948, II, 1173–76.

4. Mins. of mtg. of Marshall with for.

mins. of Britain and France, Paris, 21Sep48, FRUS 1948, II, 1177–80.

5. Lovett to the Soviet Amb. Washington, 22Sep48, Soviet Amb. to Lovett, 25Sep48, FRUS 1948, II, 1180–84.

6. Mins. of agreement between Marshall, Bevin, and Schuman, Paris, 26Sep48, FRUS 1948, 1184–87.

7. Mins. of Policy Planning Staff (Amb.

Smith present), 28Sep48, FRUS 1948, II, 1194–97.

8. U.S. Chargé, Moscow, to Washington, 30Sep48, FRUS 1948, II, 1197–98.

9. Acting Sec. State to Bohlen, Paris, 20Oct48, rpt. of Policy Planning Staff, 1Oct48, FRUS 1948, II, 1198–1200.

10. Int. by author with Robert A. Lovett, New York City, 28Aug73. Cf. Donovan, *Conflict and Crisis*, 423–25. Donovan says Truman asked Lovett to arrange a broadcast to announce the Vinson mission and then called Marshall in Paris. Int. by author with Marshall S. Carter, 21Oct59, Washington, gives gist of Marshall & Truman transatlantic conv. See also Kenneth Hechler, *Working with Truman*, 98–99.

11. Int. by author with Marshall S. Carter, Washington, 21Oct59.

12. James F. Forrestal, *Forrestal Diaries*, 500–502.

13. Bohlen, *Witness to History*, 270.

14. Ed. note, FRUS 1948, II, 1233–34.

15. Ed. note, FRUS 1948, II, 1241–52.

16. Statement to author by Marshall in 1957.

17. Dulles to Sec. State, 24Nov48, FRUS 1948, II, 1262–66.

18. Marshall to Emb. in France, 25Nov48, FRUS 1948, II, 1266–68.

19. Murphy to Sec. State, 2816, 26Nov48, Marshall to Bohlen and Jessup, 602, FRUS 1948, II, 1268–70, 1272.

20. Ed. note, 1276, and Murphy to Sec State, 2950, 21Dec48, FRUS 1948, II, 1281–82.

X X I V : C H A N G E   O F   P A C E

1. Diagnosis of Marshall's condition is contained in Marshall's medical record for December 1948, copy in personal file, ML.

2. Mme Chiang Kai-shek undated report (shortly after operation in December) to Gen. Flicker.

3. Foster Rhea Dulles, *The American Red Cross*, 531–38.

4. Ibid., 536.

5. The letters mentioned in nn. 6 and 7 are from a large file covering a short period after Marshall's appointment was announced. Letters are in alphabetic order.

6. Marshall to Queen Frederika, 23Dec-49.

X X V :   B A C K   T O   D U T Y

I have drawn heavily in this chapter on interviews with Gen. Marshall, former Pres. Truman, Dean Acheson, Louis Johnson, Col. C. J. George, and Robert A. Lovett. Especially helpful was Robert H. Ferrell, ed., *Off the Record: The Private Papers of Harry S. Truman*. At the time I was writing this and the following chs. on Marshall in the Dept. of Def., I read the initial draft of Steven L. Rearden, *The Formative Years, 1947–50*, the first volume in the history of the office of Sec. Defense. I am indebted to it for special insights into the Defense Department. I have also read the unpublished volume in the same series, by Doris M. Condit on the dept. during the Marshall and Lovett years.

1. Truman to Mrs. Truman, 7Sep50, in *Off the Record*, 189–90, gives the background of the appointment. Margaret Truman in *Harry S. Truman*, 404, has an account of visiting the Marshalls at Leesburg.

2. Truman to Mrs. Truman, 7Sep50, Diary entry, 14Sep50, *Off the Record*, 189–90, 193. The two entries are slightly confusing about the date of the meeting, but Marshall's appointments calendar shows that he met the Pres. on 6Sep.

3. Truman to Mrs. Truman, *Off the Record*, 189.

4. Truman Diary, 14Sep50, 192–94.

5. Johnson to Truman, 12Sep50, Sec. Def. files, ML.

6. *New York Times*, 17Sep50.

7. *Washington Post*, 14Sep50.

8. Lawrence and Lippman columns in *New York Herald-Tribune*, 19Sep50.

9. *Chicago Tribune*, 14Sep50.

10. The questions to Marshall and his answers are all from hearings before the Comm. on Armed Services, U.S. Sen-

ate, 81st Cong., 2nd sess., "On the Nomination of General of the Army George C. Marshall to Be Secretary of Defense," Sec. Def. Files, ML; Marx Leva Memo to Lovett, 23Oct50, Sec. Def. Files (SC 040 OS), ML. 81st Cong., 2nd sess., House, rpt. 3094, authorizing appointment of Gen. of the Army George C. Marshall as Sec. Def., Sec. Def. Files, ML.

11. *New York Times*, 16Sep50. Approving were Byrd, Russell, Chapman, Johnson, Kefauver, Hunt, Gurney, Saltonstall, and Morse.
12. *New York Times*, 16Sep50.
13. *Cong. Record*, U.S. Senate, 15Sep50.
14. *New York Times*, 16Sep50, describes Saltonstall's reaction.
15. *New York Times*, 21Sep50.
16. William S. White, "Again for Marshall, It Is 'Duty'," *New York Times Magazine*, 24Sep50.
17. I. B. Holley, Jr., *General John M. Palmer: Citizen Soldier and the Army of Democracy*, ch. 51.
18. The folder on Mrs. Rosenberg in the Marshall Personal File, ML, gives a complete biographical background.
19. Int. by author with Mrs. Anna Rosenberg, New York City, 10Dec57.
20. Quotations on the testimony and associated materials are from the Harry F. Byrd report, "Nomination of Mrs.

Anna Rosenberg," 19Dec50, 81st Cong., 2d sess., ML.
21. Rosenberg to Mrs. Roosevelt, 12Dec50, Marshall Personal File, ML.
22. Marshall to Truman, 18Dec50, J. Edgar Hoover to Marshall, 19Dec50, Marshall Personal File, ML.
23. Notes by Marshall Carter for Marshall on a telephone call to Bernard Baruch, 11Dec50, Marshall Personal File, ML.
24. Int. by author with Mrs. Rosenberg, 10Dec57. She gave a slightly different version at a dinner over which the author presided in honor of Marshall's hundredth birthday.
25. Marshall's earlier relationship with Bradley is described in Pogue, *Organizer of Victory*, 183.
26. Collins said of Marshall: "He had great character, wonderful intelligence, and stimulated everyone under him with a spirit of progressiveness and not being content with things as they were but investigating and inquiring into new ways of doing things. . . . I think he sacrificed his own desires to come back and serve his country as Secretary of State and as Secretary of Defense, thereby setting an example for the future to follow. . . ." Int. by author with Gen. J. Lawton Collins, 23Jan58.

XXVI: KOREA BLAZES

For operational details and command problems in this ch., I have been aided at every stage by the excellent official volumes: James R. Schnabel, *Policy and Direction: The First Year*, and Roy E. Appleman, *South to the Naktong, North to the Yalu*. As a part of the ML project of adding to the Marshall Papers by copying a mass of key documents, I directed the copying of many documents cited in the notes of these two books.

1. Bruce Cumings, *The Origins of the Korean War*, chs. 1–3.
2. Trippartite Meeting, 24Jul45, FRUS 1945, *Conference at Berlin*, II, 351–52.
3. Rusk memo, FRUS 1945, VI, 1039.
4. Schnabel, *Policy and Direction*, 13–20, deals with this and the material in the following paragraph.
5. Marshall to MacArthur, 1Oct45, FRUS 1945, VI, 1067–68; MacArthur to Marshall, 4Oct45, OPD file, ML.
6. Pol. adviser to Sec. State, 20Nov45, Byrnes to Langdon, 26Nov45, FRUS 1945, VI, 1129–33, 1137–38.
7. Schnabel, *Policy and Direction*, 23–26.

8. Mins. of Comm. of Three mtg., 9Apr47, Patterson File, Comm. of Three, Box 3, Xerox 2327, ML.
9. Molotov to Marshall, 19Apr47, Marshall to Molotov, 30Apr47, FRUS 1947, VI, 632–35, 638–39.
10. Mins. of Comm. of Three mtg., 4May47, Patterson File, Box 3, Xerox 2327, ML.
11. Hilldring to Hodge, 21May47, giving Marshall's views, Hodge to MacArthur and State Dept., 27Jul47, Allison for State to *ad hoc* comm. (SWNCC), 29Jul47, FRUS 1947, VI, 647–48, 734–36.

12. Rpt. by *ad hoc* comm. on Korea, 4Aug47, Hilldring to Marshall, 6Aug47, FRUS 1947, 738–44.

13. Marshall to Molotov, 11Aug47, Molotov to Marshall, 27Aug47, Lovett to pol. adviser to Korea, 2Sep47, Molotov to Marshall, 4Sep47, FRUS 1947, VI, 748–49, 771–74, 776–81.

14. SWNCC to JCS, 15Sep47, Sec. Def. to Sec. State, 26Sep47, Policy Planning Staff to director, Off. Far Eastern Aff., 24Sep47, FRUS 1947, VI, 789, 817–18, 814.

15. Ed. note, motion by Austin, 17Sep47, FRUS 1947, VI, 792.

16. Eisenhower to Marshall, 3Dec47, Saltzman to Marshall, 4Dec47, Marshall to Eisenhower, 4Dec47, FRUS 1947, VI, 868, 869–90.

17. Interim Comm. of U.N. Gen. Assembly, 26Feb48, Butterworth to Sec. State, 48Mar48, FRUS 1948, VI, 1137–39.

18. Memo of mtg., Marshall with Butterworth and others of State Dept., 5Mar48, FRUS 1948, VI, 1139–41.

19. Rpt. by Nat. Security Council on position of U.S. with rel. to Korea, 2Apr48, FRUS 1948, VI, 1163–69.

20. Marshall press conf., 12May48, FRUS 1948, VI, 1195.

21. Royal Inst. Internat. Aff., *Summary of International Affairs, 1947–48*, 324.

22. Schnabel, *Policy and Direction*, 28.

23. Marshall to Royall, 17Sep48, Marshall to Hoffman, 17Sep48, FRUS 1948, 1323–37.

24. Royal Inst. Intnat. Aff., *Summary, 1947–48*, 327.

25. Schnabel, *Policy and Direction*, 32–35.

26. Ibid., 61–66, gives a summary of the beginning of the war.

27. For a survey of the battle as seen from Washington, see Robert J. Donovan, *Tumultuous Years*, chs. 22–26; the view from Tokyo is in D. Clayton James, *Triumph and Disaster, 1945–64*, chs. XIII–XIV; the official Army account can be found in Schnabel, *Policy and Direction*, 66–187.

28. Franks to Prime Min., 15Jul50, FO 372/84089 27910, Pub. Rec. Off.

29. Alan Bullock, *Ernest Bevin, Foreign Secretary, 1945–51*, 790–94.

30. Franks to Prime Min., 15Jun50, FO 371/84089 27910, Pub. Rec. Off.

31. Schnabel, *Policy and Direction*, 123–24, has an excellent summary of the manpower measures.

32. James, *Triumph and Disaster*, 467–85.

XXVII: MARSHALL AND KOREA

For the views of the Chief of Staff during this period, see J. Lawton Collins, *War in Peacetime*, and *Lightning Joe: An Autobiography*. See also Matthew B. Ridgway, *The Korean War*.

1. One of Marshall's first acts as Sec. Def. was to send MacArthur an expression of "personal tribute to the courageous campaign you directed in Korea and the daring and perfect strategical operation which virtually terminated the struggle...." MacArthur was suitably grateful, expressing appreciation for Marshall's "unfailing support." He said, "It brings back vividly the memories of past wars and the complete coordination and perfect unity of cooperation which has always existed in our mutual relationships and martial endeavors." Marshall to MacArthur, 30Sep50, Rad. WCL 46338, MacArthur to Marshall, 1Oct50, Rad. Z 18560, GCM Personal File, ML.

2. Memo by JCS to Sec. Def., 7Sep50, FRUS 1950, VII, 707–8; NSC 81, "Courses of Action with Respect to Korea," memo by Sec. State, "NSC Meeting, 7Sep50," NSC 81/1, "United States Courses of Action with Respect to Korea," FRUS 1950, VII, 685–93, 705–7, 712–21.

3. Schnabel, *Policy and Direction: The First Year*, 181.

4. Sec. State to Acting Sec. State, 26Sep50, Acting Sec. State to U.S. mission at U.N., 26Sep50, Marshall to Acheson, 26Sep50, Sec. Def. to Pres. 27Sep50, FRUS 1950, VII, 774–75, 781–82.

5. JCS to MacArthur, 27Sep50, Rad. JCS 92801, JCS Decimal File (CCS 383.21 Korea), ML.

6. Marshall to MacArthur, 29Sep50, FRUS 1950, VII, 826.

7. MacArthur to Marshall, 30Sep50, Rad. C 65034, JCS Decimal File

(CCS 383.21 Korea), ML.

8. MacArthur to JCS, 28Sep50, Rad. C 64805, JCS Decimal File (CCS 383.21 Korea), ML.

9. JCS to MacArthur, 9Oct50, FRUS 1950, VII, 915.

10. Substance of statements made at Wake Island Conf., 15Oct50, comp. by Gen. of the Army Omar N. Bradley from notes kept by the conferees, FRUS 1950, VII, 948–60. In a later account of the conf., Truman spoke of having rebuked MacArthur's high-handedness, but the meeting seems to have gone well.

11. Ed. note, FRUS 1950, VII, 993–94.

12. Schnabel, *Policy and Direction*, 222–30.

13. Roy E. Appleman, *South to the Naktong, North to the Yalu*, 673–81, 689–708, 765–69.

14. Memo of conv. by Sec. State with Acheson, Lovett, Rusk, 6Nov50, FRUS 1950, VII, 1055–57.

15. JCS to MacArthur, 6Nov50, and n. on following page, FRUS 1950, VII, 1057–58.

16. MacArthur to Dept. of Army, 6Nov50, Rad. C-68396, JCS Decimal File (CCS 383.21 Korea), ML.

17. JCS to MacArthur, 6Nov50, FRUS 1950, VII, 1075–77.

18. Memo, Rusk to Acheson, 7Nov50, Marshall to Acheson, 10Nov50, FRUS 1950, VII, 1077, 1126.

19. Jt. res. of Security Council, 10Nov50, FRUS 1950, VII, 1126–27.

20. Testimony of Marshall, Vandenberg, and Acheson, *MacArthur Hearings*, 320.1410, 1723, 1912.

21. JCS to MacArthur, 8Nov50, MacArthur to JCS, 9Nov50, FRUS 1950, VII, 1097–98, 1107–10.

22. James, *Triumph and Disaster*, 535.

23. Memo of conv. by Amb. Jessup re mtg. in Pentagon, 21Nov50, MacArthur to JCS, 25Nov50, FRUS 1950, 1204–8, 1222–24.

24. James, *Triumph and Disaster*, 526–27.

25. Ibid., 536.

26. Memo by Amb. Jessup on Nat. Security Council mtg. with Pres., 28Nov50, FRUS 1950, VII, 1242–49.

27. Schnabel, *Policy and Direction*, 282.

28. JCS to MacArthur, 29Nov50, FRUS 1950, VII, 1253–54.

29. Emb. U.K. to Sec. State, 28Nov50,

Sec. State to Emb. U.K., 28Nov50, State Dept. memos of conv., 29Nov50, FRUS 1950, VII, 1241, 1249–51, 1252–53, 1257–58.

30. *Public Papers of the Presidents of the United States: Harry S. Truman*, 724–28.

31. Ed. notes summarizing press conf., incl. text of White House clarification, FRUS 1950, VII, 1261–62.

32. Memo of conv. by Amb. Jessup re mtg. in JCS conf. room, Pentagon, 1Dec50, [incl. Secs. of State, Defense, Army, Navy and Air Force and JCS]. FRUS 1950, VII, 1276–82.

33. Memo by CIA, 2Dec50 (later issued as NIE-11), FRUS 1950, VII, 1308–10.

34. Res. submitted on 19Nov by six nations, incl. the U.S., asking Chinese Communists to refrain from further intervention in North Korea, but assuring that the U.N. intended to keep the frontier inviolate. Vote, on 30Nov, was 9–1, with India not participating. Ed. note, FRUS 1950, VII, 1126–27, 1268.

35. At the outset of the Korean War, the entire U.S. Army had a total of ten divisions, nine of them seriously under strength. By mid-July, total U.S. military personnel had increased from 1,463,544 to 1,730,500. Shortly after Marshall became Sec. Def., he approved the JCS request to expand forces to 2,806,735 for the remainder of the fiscal year. For the Army alone, this meant an increase of seven divisions by June 1951. Walter S. Poole, *The Joint Chiefs of Staff and National Policy*, IV, 1950–52, 38–39, 41, 45.

Truman, in Jan50, requested a military budget for fiscal 1951 of $13,-545,000,000. In April, he asked for supplemental $350 million, but Cong. had not completed action on this request before the beginning of the Korean War in June. In July and August, Truman asked for $11,643,106,000 more, which was approved in late Sep. The President's supplemental request of 1Dec brought the total requested for fiscal 1951 to $42,984,862,250. Ibid., p. 46; Kenneth W. Condit, *The Joint Chiefs of Staff and National Policy*, II, 1947–49, Ch. VIII.

36. Exchange of letters with Arthur Krock in *New York Times*, 1Dec50; *U.S. News*

& *World Report*, 8Dec50, 16–22; msg. to Hugh Baillie, *New York Times*, 2Dec50.

37. MacArthur to JCS, 3Dec50, FRUS 1950, VII, 1320–22.

38. Memo of mtg. at Pentagon of Marshall, Acheson, Joint Chiefs and staffs, 3Dec50, FRUS 1950, VII, 1323–34.

39. Memo by Lucius D. Battle on mtg. of Acheson and staff, 4Dec50, FRUS 1950, VII, 1345–47; Acheson, *Present at the Creation*, 477; see also text of Kennan note to Acheson that day, ibid., 476.

40. Mins. of first mtg. at White House of Truman, Attlee, and staffs, 4Dec50, memo re evening discussion mtg. of Acheson with British, 4Dec50, memo re mtg. of Acheson and staff, 5Dec50, memo re Acheson mtg. with Brit., 5Dec50, FRUS 1950, VII, 1361–77, 1382–86, 1390–92.

41. Mins. of second mtg. on "Williamsburg" of Truman and Attlee and staffs, 5Dec50, FRUS 1950, VII, 1392–1408, 1426.

42. State Dept. memo, 5Dec50, FRUS 1950, VII, 1408–10.

43. Memo by Lucius D. Battle on mtg. of 6Dec50, FRUS, 1950, VII, 1430–32.

44. Mins. of fifth mtg. at White House of Truman, Attlee, and staffs, 7Dec50, FRUS 1950, VII, 1449–61.

45. Mins. of sixth (last) mtg. at White House of Truman, Attlee, and staffs, 8Dec50, FRUS 1950, VII, 1468–79.

46. Schnabel, *Policy and Direction*, 305.

47. JCS to MacArthur, 29Dec50, MacArthur to JCS, 30Dec50, FRUS 1950, VII, 1625–26, 1630–33.

48. Acheson, *The Korean War*, 96–97; James, *Triumph and Disaster*, 545–46.

49. JCS to MacArthur, 9Jan51, FRUS 1951, VII, 41–43.

50. MacArthur to JCS, 10Jan51, FRUS 1951, VII, 56–57.

51. JCS memo to Sec. Def., 12Jan51, FRUS 1951, VII, 71–72.

52. Truman to MacArthur, 13Jan51, FRUS 1951, VII, 77–78.

53. Memo by Lucius Battle, 19Jan51, FRUS 1951, VII, 102–5.

54. *MacArthur Hearings*, pt. I, 13–15, 166, 324.

55. Ibid., 324.

XXVIII: RELIEF OF MACARTHUR

1. Schnabel, *Policy and Direction: The First Year*, 332–40.

2. Acheson to Marshall, 23Feb51, memo to Sec. Def. from 3 service sec., 24Feb51, JCS memo to Sec. Def., 27Feb51, Marshall to Acheson, 1Mar51, enc. JCS memo to Sec. Def., 27Feb51, FRUS 1951, VII, 189–95, 202–6.

3. Schnabel, *Policy and Direction*, 354–59.

4. JCS to MacArthur, 20Mar51, FRUS 1951, VII, 251.

5. MacArthur to JCS, 21Mar51, FRUS 1951, VII, 255–56.

6. Statement of MacArthur on Sec. State to dipl. officers, 24Mar51, FRUS 1951, VII, 265–66.

7. Statement by Sec., Marshall, 7May51, MacArthur Hearings, Part I, 344.

8. Statement by Sir Gladwyn Jebb.

9. Hanson Baldwin, *New York Times*,

10. Schnabel, *Policy and Direction*, 361–64.

11. Brit. For. Min. to Brit. Emb., Washington, n.d., FRUS 1951, VII, 280–82.

12. *MacArthur Hearings, Part I*, 340.

13. Memo by Gen. Bradley, 24Apr51, GCM Personal File, ML; Truman's notes, as dictated to Eben Ayers and George Elsey, 28Apr51, Truman Library.

14. Acheson, *Present at the Creation*, 521; Truman, *Years of Trial and Hope*, 447.

15. Alben W. Barkley, *That Reminds Me*, 213.

16. Contrary to the version in Truman's *Memoirs*, Marshall was reluctant to agree to the relief of MacArthur throughout the weekend and did not give his assent until the Monday-morning meeting with the Pres., after Bradley had presented the views of the Joint Chiefs. Bradley memo, 24Apr51; Marshall question, *MacArthur Hearings*, pt. I, 343–45; Collins, *War in Peacetime*, 283–84; Schnabel and Watson, *The Joint Chiefs of Staff and National Policy*, v. III, "The Korean War," pt. 1, 540.

17. Collins, *War in Peacetime*, 284; Acheson, *Present at the Creation*, 522; Tru-

man, *Years of Trial and Hope,* 448.

18. James, *Triumph and Disaster,* 597–98.

19. Int. by Jerry N. Hess with Walter Trohan, 7Oct70, Truman Library; Marshall statement, *MacArthur Hearings,* 343–45; Truman, *Years of Trial and Hope,* 448–49.

20. Schnabel and Watson, *The Joint Chiefs of Staff and National Policy,* v. III, pt. 1, 543–46.

21. JCS to Ridgway, 12Apr51, Rad. JCS 88374, JCS Decimal File (CCS 838.21 Korea), ML.

22. *New York Times,* 20Apr51.

23. Schnabel, *Policy and Direction,* 379–90.

24. Ibid., 392–407.

25. Excerpt of letter of Colonel James T. Quirk to his wife (n.d., but it was written around June 12, 1951.) Marshall

mentioned the trip to an old friend, Colonel Fay W. Brabson, in a letter written 12Jun51.

26. Lt. Rory T. Quirk (son of the Colonel) to author, 17Oct76. Quirk repeated the story as his father remembered it. When author asked General Ridgway about the account, the General said he did not recall Marshall's mention of the atomic bomb but that he had confidence in Quirk. He did remembered the terrible flying weather.

27. Reeves, *The Life and Times of Joe McCarthy,* 373–74.

28. *Times,* 23Jun50.

29. William F. Buckley, Jr., and Brent Bozell, *McCarthy and His Enemies,* Appen. F.

XXIX: RETIREMENT

1. Unsigned and undated notes, apparently by Marshall S. Carter, found in Marshall's Defense Department file. I have followed a rough paraphrase in the account.

2. Pogue, *George C. Marshall: Organizer of Victory,* 365, fn 44. A special file in ML, compiled by the author, has copies of the legislation. Shortly after Marshall's death the author rewrote the Marshall entry in the *Encyclopaedia Britannica.* Several years later his statement that Marshall was the highest-ranking general in the Army when he died was challenged by an Army officer in a letter to the *Britannica.* To support the entry, the author submitted copies of the legislation and pages from the *Army Register* showing Army ranks annually from 1948 until after Marshall's death. The assembled records are in this file.

3. Marshall to Mme. Chiang Kai-shek, 5Feb47; Mme. Chiang Kai-shek to Marshall, 19Dec48; Marshall to Mme. Chiang Kai-shek, 6Apr49, in Marshall Personal File, ML.

4. Ints. by author with General and Mrs. Marshall,

5. Statement of Dr. Theodore Ropp to author in 1959.

6. Letters from Samuel "Corty" Slaymaker IV to Marshall in Marshall Museum display, Lexington, Va.

7. Documents and correspondence retailing to these transactions are in the Louis Marx file, Marshall Personal files, ML. Marx had a special reason for showing gratitude to Marshall. In 1944, his wife was in the last stages of cancer. Hoping that penicillin might be helpful, he found that the armed services controlled the reserve stocks. He asked Marshall to authorize the release of a small amount to him. Marshall had received other such requests earlier and, in one case involving an old friend, had insisted that he could do nothing. When the friend's wife died, Marshall had received a bitter letter. Since then, the Army had arranged for physicians and hospitals to get small amounts of the antibiotic on the condition that they repay the loan from another source of supply. Marshall recommended this source of supply.

8. The original manuscript of *Together,* with some editorial changes by Marshall on part of the manuscript (apparently he did not see all of it in manuscript form), is in ML. Part of the correspondence regarding publication can be find in Mrs. Marshall's files there. No statement of royalties is available.

9. Eisenhower to Marshall, 1952, Marshall Personal file, ML.

10. Stephen E. Ambrose, *Eisenhower, Soldier, General of the Army, President-Elect,* 563–67.

11. Notes by author of a telephone conversation with former President Eisenhower in May 1964. Leonard Mosley used these notes in his book on Marshall but suggested that the full transcript of the conversation was in the Eisenhower Library at Abilene. There is a tape there of an interview with Eisenhower made by the author at Gettysburg in July 1962, but this tape does not concern the postwar period and can be used only with the author's permission, which has never been given. Eisenhower's phone call to the author was for the purpose of giving the Marshall Library title to his speech at the Library's dedication, so that it could collect the fee offered by the *Atlantic Monthly* for publication of the speech.

12. Not mentioned in the campaign was a purported episode that surfaced years later, concerning events that were said to have occurred as early as 1945. Eisenhower, and, indirectly, Marshall, were participants according to the story, which came out in 1973 with the publication of Merle Miller's *Plain Speaking,* a book on Harry Truman. As part of a project for a television series on Truman, Miller, a *Yank* editor in World War II and later a best-selling novelist, was sent to Independence in 1961 to interview the former President. The series was never made, but Miller had his notes and tapes. After Truman's death, Miller put much of the material in his book on Truman and published it in 1973. Although much of the material was taped, Miller freely admitted that some of the most outrageous stories had been put down later in his notes. In his introduction to the book, Miller speaks of occasions when he and Truman would adjourn to a nearby restaurant lounge and have two or three scotches or bourbons before lunch. In later speeches Miller told his audience that the most revealing information was given in pre-lunch conversations, so that it is difficult to know how much of the untaped material was intended as fact by

Truman or how accurate Miller's memory was. Some of these stories, such as the account of the President's meeting with MacArthur at Wake Island, are contrary to what others who were there have said, and different from Truman's own published account.

The question of accuracy concerns not only Eisenhower, but involves uncharacteristic behavior by Marshall that requires examination in this biography.

According to Miller, Truman told him that after the war ended in Europe, Eisenhower wrote Marshall that he was coming home to divorce Mamie so he could marry his secretary and former jeep driver, Kay Summersby. Marshall was reported to have replied that if Eisenhower came near doing such a thing, "he'd not only bust him out of the Army, he'd see to it that for the rest of his life he would not be able to draw a peaceful breath." Truman added that one of the last things he did as President was "to get the letters from his [Eisenhower's] file in the Pentagon, and I destroyed them" (Miller, *Plain Speaking,* pp. 368–69).

When asked about the tale in 1973, Harry Vaughan, Truman's military aide during the White House years, could only recall that in 1952 Truman had said that he had heard that the Taft adherents were trying to get their hands on the correspondence and that Truman had sent him to the Pentagon to pick up some papers from the office of the Chief of Staff. Vaughan admitted that he had not looked at the papers but did not believe that Truman destroyed them and suggested that he had probably sent them to Leesburg or to the Marshall Foundation. The Marshall Foundation did not exist in 1952, and any papers sent to Leesburg found their way back to Marshall's papers in his Pentagon office. Colonel George, Marshall's aide at the time, who sat in the office where Marshall's papers were stored, declared that no such correspondence was there nor had anyone asked for it. General J. Lawton Collins, Chief of

Staff at the time, asserted that his office never furnished any papers pertaining to the matter to the White House, and was positive that no member of his staff would do so without telling him. Eisenhower's files had gone with him to Columbia University when he became its president (Miller, *Plain Speaking,* pp. 367–69).

Vaughan later wondered why Truman would tell Miller of any such affair if his purpose in destroying the letters had been to protect Mrs. Eisenhower from embarrassment, since the published account had the opposite effect.

Individuals closely associated with Marshall and Eisenhower doubt the authenticity of the account as published. Neither the action nor the language was in Marshall's style. He sometimes wrote letters to generals under him pointing out actions or attitudes that needed changing, but he never threatened and his language was courteous. Moreover, Marshall knew that a general nominated by the President and confirmed by the Senate could not be "busted" by anyone without a court-martial, and that a divorce was not a basis for such action. Furthermore, it was a part of the Marshall–Eisenhower relationship that the Supreme Commander did not put a highly personal request in writing. When Eisenhower had asked the Chief of Staff to commission Mrs. Summersby in 1944, he made an oral request and the first indication of it in Marshall's files is his own directive that she be commissioned. When members of his staff said there was no precedent for commissioning an Englishwoman, Marshall replied that MacArthur had personally directed commissioning of Australian women as WAC officers in the Pacific, and that he (Marshall) had promised the commission to Eisenhower, adding that at a time when the commander was faced with many burdens in the field, he thought they should do what they could to help him. (Pogue, *George C. Marshall: Organizer of Victory,* 113, has the story of the commissioning. Leonard Mosley,

in his book on Marshall, suggests that the commissioning came as a result of activities by Colonel Florence Newsome of Marshall's staff in gratitude for entertainment she had received in Paris by Lieutenant Summersby. In a telephone conversation with the author, Colonel Newsome indignantly denied Mosley's statement, explaining that her visit to Paris was as escort officer for a group of congressmen visiting Eisenhower's headquarters, and came after Lieutenant Summersby had been commissioned. Colonel Newsome added that had she known when the commission was in the works, she would have opposed it.

At the end of the war in Europe, Eisenhower was under pressure from both Democrats and Republicans to be a Presidential candidate in 1948, and thus highly unlikely to make such a statement. The Eisenhower letter, which *can* be found in his files and in Marshall's, specifically asked Marshall if Mrs. Eisenhower could be sent to join him in Europe. Marshall was sympathetic, but with the war in the Pacific still on, and when other wives could not be sent overseas, said it was unwise.

Marshall, Eisenhower, and Truman were all dead when Miller's book appeared, so the story must rest on the record. Miller's account of Truman statement must be set against earlier taped interviews with Truman by Marshall's biographer, who was thoroughly familiar with Marshall's files, which do not allude to the Eisenhower–Summersby story nor to some of the accusations against MacArthur.

After the book appeared, Miller spoke on it at a meeting of the National Oral History Association, and was closely questioned. When asked if he had submitted his transcripts of the interviews of 1961 to Truman or his staff, Miller said, "No, they wouldn't have allowed me to use them."

13. Marshall to Eisenhower, 7Nov52; Eisenhower to Marshall, 10Nov52, Marshall Personal file, ML.
14. Truman to Marshall, 24Jan53, Marshall Personal file, ML.

15. Handwritten letter, Elizabeth II to Marshall, 28Feb1952, Marshall Personal file, ML.

16. The details are in a lengthy letter, Marshall to Truman, 8Sep53. Other details in Colonel George to Frank McCarthy, 23Jun53, and in Leslie Hollis, *Clock with Four Faces.*

17. Marshall to Truman, 4Nov53, Marshall Personal file, ML.

18. Eisenhower to Marshall, 2Nov53; Acheson to Marshall, 4 Nov 53, Marshall Personal file, ML.

19. Marshall to Truman, 2Nov53, Marshall Personal file, ML.

20. Marshall to Mme. Chiang Kai-shek, 6Nov53; Marshall Personal file, ML.

21. Marshall to Eisenhower, 2Nov53, Marshall Personal file, ML.

22. Marshall to Truman, 27Feb54, Marshall Personal file, ML.

23. Int. by author with Col. C. J. George, 18Nov80; statement of General Goodpaster to author, 8 May 1986.

24. The author attended the awards ceremony in Oslo and sat in the balcony during the demonstration. Later he picked up copies of the handbills. These, plus copies of the program, and of the Dec. 11 Oslo newspapers, are in the ML.

25. Marshall's address in Oslo, 10Dec53, Marshall speech book, ML.

26. Marshall to Truman, 27Feb54.

26A. Eisenhower to Everett E. Hazlett, 8Dec54, in *Ike's Letters to a Friend, 1941–58.* Ed. by Robert W. Griffith. Lawrence, Kansas: University Press of Kansas. Eisenhower noted that Churchill perhaps had more of the qualities of greatness than any other person he had known. Others who ranked high were Chancellor Adenauer and Henry L. Stimson. Among members of Congress he included Senator Vandenberg and Senator Walter George. Of those he had not met, he ranked John Quincy Adams, in his later years, first.

27. Details of the biographical project which the author was named to head in Aug. 54 have been taped for the Marshall Foundation. He has collected the papers connected with the founding of the Research Center and the individuals involved.

28. Marshall to Eisenhower, 14Aug58, Marshall Personal file, ML.

29. The story of the period from the first stroke to the General's death was gleaned by the author from daily verbal reports by Colonel George, who sat in the office next to where the author was working on the biography. Stories of visits by Herron, Bull, Stayer, Snyder, and others were given the author by those individuals. Powder talked with him after leaving the hospital. Rose Page Wilson tells her poignant story in *General Marshall Remembered.*

30. The author watched Pershing's funeral procession in 1948 and recalls the drenching rain and heat, the phalanx of marching generals, glimpses of Marshall and Dawes in the procession. Later, he saw the complete plans for the funeral.

31. The instructions, in Marshall's handwriting, were given to Colonel George, who later gave the author a copy. Mosley's biography relies on a statement by General Handy, who did not see the handwritten instructions.

    In Marshall's office, Colonel George began the list of those to be notified, several weeks before Marshall's death. Miss Mary Louise Spilman, Marshall's secretary, helped check the list from Marshall's personal file, and the author was asked to suggest names from several hundred associates of Marshall whom he had interviewed. A copy of the list drawn up by George, with additions in the handwriting of Mrs. Marshall, Colonel George, and the author, is in ML.

32. Mosley lacked access to the files on the funeral, and lists as present Marshall's favorite barber, Nicholas J. Totalo, so much liked by the General that he went with him to all the great conferences. Totalo, who barbered Marshall only once, was not at the funeral. Marshall's longtime barber, who was at the funeral, but never at any conferences, was civilian Joe Abbott (originally Abbate), whose chiding was related with delight by Marshall to Colonel George. Mosley apparently was misled by a photograph in the Marshall Museum, which

shows a soldier-barber, Totalo, cutting Marshall's hair at Potsdam, and concluded that Marshall had taken him there, as well as to the other great conferences. There was no Filipino orderly at the funeral, since Marshall never had an orderly of that nationality, unless during the 1913–16 period in Manila. Marshall did have an orderly named Semanko, of Ukrainian descent, but he did not attend the funeral. The orderly who did attend, American-born Richard Wing, of Chinese descent, had gone with Marshall to China in 1946 and to Paris and Moscow in 1947. As related in the text, he arrived at the Pentagon the morning of the funeral, and George made arrangements for him to attend with the author.

33. Although he writes of the instructions that Marshall gave, Mosley seems unaware that Marshall specifically ruled out a funeral in the Cathedral. Eisenhower and Truman did not crowd into its Bethlehem Chapel. Marshall's coffin had stayed there the night before the funeral, but by the General's express wish, the funeral was at the Fort Myer chapel.

34. The remaining details of the funeral are from the author's personal recollections. In greater detail, they are in the funeral file in ML.

EPILOGUE

In an effort to draw together the chief characteristics of Marshall that I have described in the previous volumes, I found the simplest solution to be the use of much of what I had to say in pages 13–20 in the Harmon Memorial Lecture which I gave on "George C, Marshall: Global Statesman" at the Airt Force Academy in 1968. The quotations there were drawn in turn from Volumes I and II of the biography and fron a draft of Volume III, which I was then writing. In a few cases I have used several paragraphs intact but have paraphrased and condensed much of the others. Where I quote his contemporaries, I have used material from my interviews with the individuals concerned. The quotation from George F. Kennan may be found in his *Memoirs (1925–50)*, pages 345–46. Marshall is discussed in Richard E. Neustadt and Ernest R. May, *Thinking in Time: The Uses of History for Decision makers*, chapter 14. The citation from Douglas Freeman's editorial is in Forrest C. Pogue, *Oranizer of Victory*, 34. Churchill's statement is in a letter John C. Hagan, Jr., President of the Marshall Foundation, cited in Harmon Lecture.

Index